Apple's Europe

An Uncommon Guide

Apple's Europe

An Uncommon Guide

R. W. Apple Jr.

Illustrations by Mark Hampton

Atheneum   *New York*
1986

Library of Congress Cataloging-in-Publication Data

Apple, R. W. (Raymond Walter), 1934–
Apple's Europe, an uncommon guide.

1. Europe—Description and travel—1971–
Guide-books. I. Title. II. Title: Europe, an uncommon
guide.
D909.A57   1986   914'.04558   85-48292
ISBN 0-689-11607-1

Published simultaneously in Canada by Collier Macmillan Canada, Inc.
Composition by Heritage Printers, Inc., Charlotte, North Carolina
Manufactured by Fairfield Graphics, Fairfield, Pennsylvania
Designed by Harry Ford
First Edition

For My Parents

WHO FIRST TOOK ME TO EUROPE

INTRODUCTION

T H I S is an enthusiast's book, a collection of essays celebrating places that I have visited, and suggesting how likeminded readers might make some of the same journeys. Like any expatriate—I have fallen into that anomalous category, I suppose, for fourteen of the last twenty-one years—I have always been bombarded with questions by visitors from home. What should I do in Amsterdam? Can you suggest a weekend trip from London? Where do you like to eat in Venice? Any ideas for something different in Spain? Those are the sorts of questions to which I hope you might find answers here, with enough practical information to smooth the way but without any thought of matching the encyclopedic coverage of the Blue Guides or Gault-Millau.

Wherever possible, I have looked for the offbeat, the out-of-the-way, the places that the locals know about but visitors often do not. It seems to me that too many Americans save their money for a big trip to Europe only to find themselves steered, by ignorant travel agents or careless tourist operators, into places that exist largely for foreigners. This book is an attempt to do something about that, starting with a few hints on what to bring along and some suggestions about places that I think will reward the visitor even when the crush is worst in high summer. It is addressed to the sophisticate, not the package tourist, but I have tried to bear in mind that nobody, least of all me, is sophisticated in all things and in all places. I have also attempted not to confuse sophistication with snobbery. To give an example of what I mean, I find nothing naïve about spending one's first morning in a new city taking a bus tour; there is no better way to get the lay of the land quickly and easily.

Inevitably, the shape of the book has been affected by my own passions and prejudices. My kind of travel centers on art and architecture, music and natural beauty, good food and good drink. I see Europe's past as the key to appreciating its present, so I try to know as much about the history of a place as I can before I go there, and to learn as much more as I can while traveling there. There is a lot here about medieval churches, country restaurants and great men, and nothing at all about ski resorts, cruises and rental villas.

I have tried, when writing about regions rather than individual places, to suggest the density of history and civilization that sets Europe apart from other continents. Drive through almost any country, keep your eyes open and you will soon discover that every 25 kilometers or so you will come across a town or city that you know something about, however vaguely—this place has a famous native son, that one a world-famous food specialty; this place produces a widely known wine, that one embodies a craft tradition; this place has a storied work of art, that one was the site of a famous battle. We all know about Leonardo da Vinci, about truffles, about Sancerre and paisley shawls and the Bayeux tapestry and the battle of Bosworth Field—but how many could place them geographically? Doing that, putting things in context, is one of the abiding joys of European travel.

Inevitably, too, because most of the pieces printed here originally appeared, in different form, in *The New York Times*, the needs of the newspaper have helped to determine the contents. There is more in the book about Britain than any other country because for most of the last decade I have lived in Britain and have been responsible primarily for writing about it. There are only two pieces about France, although I spend a great deal of time there, because colleagues based in Paris covered the subject comprehensively. I wish I had had the chance to write about the miraculous Leonardo in Cracow in Poland, which I saw at the height of the Solidarity crisis, or about my favorite villages in the

Cotswolds, or about the luminous Baroque churches in Bavaria. For one reason or another, I didn't; perhaps another time.

What I can guarantee to the properly skeptical reader is that I have seen what I have written about. I took no one else's word for the beauty of a mountain landscape or the excellence of a restaurant's cuisine. For better or for worse, this is Europe seen through a single set of eyes.

Use this book as you see fit, but please, please use it a little bit at a time. See part of Italy in one trip, another part in another; it is far too much to swallow in a single gulp. As for "grand tours" of six or seven countries, they were exhausting enough in the train-and-steamship era, when people spent two or even three months making them; in the jet age, they are worse than staying home.

For the most part, I have omitted prices, because the inflation and the fluctuations in currency rates that are baleful parts of modern travel tend to make them inaccurate almost before they are printed. Best to inquire when booking hotel rooms, and to add fifteen percent for safety to any restaurant prices quoted here or anywhere else.

My thanks are due, first, to colleagues at *The New York Times*: to A. M. Rosenthal, the executive editor, who sent me to London; to Arthur Gelb, the deputy managing editor, who encouraged me to write about travel; to Michael Leahy, the brilliant editor of the weekly travel section, a man who always assumes, like Harold Ross, that if he likes a writer and a writer likes a subject, the odds are that something good will come out of it, and who treats everyone with a gentlemanly good humor that makes working for him a privilege; to the staff of the London Bureau of the *Times*, past and present, who made reservations, checked facts and helped in a thousand other ways, especially Marion Underhill, Derek Seymour, Merida Welles and Pamela Kent; and to other willing hands in the Paris, Rome and Bonn offices.

My publisher, Alfred Knopf Jr., an old friend from the dear dead days when I reported on the world of books, proposed this venture, and Sydney Gruson, vice chairman of the New York Times Company, made it possible to use in book form material from the paper's pages.

INTRODUCTION

I owe special words of gratitude and esteem to two friends: Egon Ronay, the Hungarian-born gastronome, *bon viveur* and guidebook editor, who encouraged me to write at length about food at a time when, full of enthusiasm, I was considerably less full of confidence, and who shared all of his knowledge and ardor with me; and Mark Hampton, the gifted New York interior designer, who, with his wife, Duane, traveled with my wife and me to Egypt, Israel and Jordan a few years ago and then found time in a frantically busy schedule to do the drawings that grace this book.

Hundreds upon hundreds of people—embassy officials, tourist information bureau experts, hoteliers and restaurateurs, curators and superintendents, friends and acquaintances—provided information that led me to most of the good things in these pages. I list only the few who did most, hoping that those whose names do not appear will understand my reluctance to overdo things: in Britain, Paul and Kay Henderson, Peter Herbert, Helen O'Neill, John J. Tovey, Harry Diamond, Michael Parkinson and Nico Ladenis; in France, Jonathan Randal, Natasha Chassagne, Paul Bocuse, Jean Hugel, David Stevens and Jean-Claude Vrinat; in Italy, Franco and Raimonda Buitoni, Arrigo Cipriani, Natale Rusconi, Peter and Anne Marshall Zwack, Anna-Maria Hanke and Burton Anderson; in Hungary, Klara Fogarasy; in the Soviet Union, Boris Zakharov; in Scandinavia, Per Vassbotn and Juliana Balint.

The warmest thanks of all must be reserved for my wife, Betsey, my partner in so many of the wanderings recounted here. Ever curious about what lies around the next corner, ever full of ideas for the next journey, ever cheerful, except during my occasional bouts of wretched excess, she is the perfect traveling companion. Many of the brighter images and many of the clearer insights in this book are hers.

All of the errors, which seem inevitable in this sort of project, are mine and mine alone.

LONDON / LECHLADE, GLOUCESTERSHIRE
OCTOBER 1985

CONTENTS

xi

CONTENTS

Apple's Europe

An Uncommon Guide

CHAPTER I

In General

---

1. *Packing*

F O R more than twenty-five years now, I have been traveling for a living and for pleasure, and I have had an incurable case of wanderlust, which is still with me, for a good bit longer than that. I guess it started when I was about ten years old. My Uncle Ivan, who was something of a tosspot and therefore irresistible to a small boy growing up amid the middle-class verities of Akron, Ohio, showed me some faded photographs of his prewar trip across the Gobi Desert, and I was hooked. As simple as that.

Since then, I have meandered through all fifty states, through the Caribbean and Africa, Europe and Asia, Australia and the Middle East—more than one hundred countries all told. I have visited every country in Europe except Albania, every county in Britain, every *département* in France, every *Land* in West Germany. When I get home from one trip, I sometimes pull the guidebooks off the shelves and start to think about the next one even before I unpack my bags. And twice a year, when vacation time comes around, my wife and I travel some more.

Now I do not aspire to emulate, during these wanderings, the dashingly elegant men often pictured in fashion magazines; I couldn't manage it if I had to, as a matter of fact. I'm too thick in the middle and too short in the neck, among other things.

3

But I have to look reasonably respectable when interviewing ambassadors and foreign ministers—wouldn't do to look like a grease monkey—and I have to have a supply of comfortable, serviceable clothes for less exalted moments. The trick is to find things that pack easily, stand up to the rigors of third-world laundries and serve a variety of purposes. Unless I'm spending an unusually long period on the road—say, a month or more—I try to get all my clothes into a leather-reinforced canvas bag that slips under an airline seat. There are three reasons for that: It eliminates the probability that Air Djibouti will lose my luggage, gets me out of the airport more quickly on arrival and guarantees that I can carry everything comfortably, no matter how far I have to walk when the taxis or the porters go on strike and no matter how beastly the weather.

The key to my system, however, is The Briefcase. At the moment, it is a rather fancy Porsche job, black leather with a wooden frame, but only because my old, more plebeian model was stolen in Naples a while back, and the insurance payoff was generous. Anything that is sturdy—especially in the handle—will do; I usually look for something that measures about eighteen by fourteen by four inches. I keep it with me, packed, all the time. If I have to sprint for the airport on short notice—as I did, for example, when the Pope was shot—I can throw in a clean shirt and survive, when I get where I'm going, for a couple of days before buying what I will need. On more normal trips, it functions as a portable office.

Here is what I carry in it:

1. A miniature toilet kit, one of those given by Pan Am to first-class passengers, beefed up with a collapsible toothbrush filched from an Italian hotel, a sample bottle of after shave and miniature first-aid packets (aspirin, Merthiolate, adhesive tape, Lomotil) that I found in a Mexican drugstore.

2. A pocket calculator.

3. Checkbooks, an address book, the current Michelin guide to hotels and restaurants in major European cities, the current Pocket Flight Guide, published by Official Airlines Guides, and three of the slim guides published by Mitchell Beazley in London covering the wines, the museums and the architecture of the world. These last insure that I won't spend a weekend moping around a hotel room in Bulgaria, unaware of the delights outside.

4. A Braun travel alarm clock (Model AB310), which unfolds to reveal not only the clock face but also a world time chart. It has an alarm that gets louder the longer you try to ignore it, an infuriating but extremely utilitarian feature.

5. A Sony ICF-7600D radio, the foreign correspondent's best friend. The size of a paperback book, it will pull in long-, short- and medium-wave broadcasts, plus FM, in the most unlikely spots, enabling one to listen to the trusty, fusty BBC World Service rather than relying for a summary of the day's news on newspapers controlled by dubious governments and written in languages that one understands badly, if at all. I would rather be without a typewriter than without it.

6. A Durabeam flashlight, a versatile little item that can light one's path or, with minor adjustment, sit on a desk and illuminate a book or a map when the power fails in Ouagadougou.

7. Spare batteries for the clock, flashlight and radio.

8. A small supply of traveler's checks plus a leather pouch containing change for most of the European and Middle Eastern countries (my main areas of preoccupation at the moment). Phone calls often have to be made from airports when the currency-exchange counters are closed.

9. A Swiss Army knife. Invaluable for its corkscrew, among other things, this can also cause trouble; mine was seized and never returned, despite an elaborate charade involving two separate "receipts," by a security officer at the Venice summit meeting a few years ago.

10. Folding sunglasses.

11. A miniature leather tool kit containing pliers, a crescent wrench, screwdrivers of several types and sizes, a hammer, a drill and an awl. Made in West Germany, found in a store in Washington, useful for repairs to many of the above items, to say nothing of balky hotel plumbing and decrepit rental cars.

12. A portable pepper mill. An absurd possession, I know, but beloved all the same; it's amazing what a few turns of the machine will do for a meal prepared by the culinary sadists of the Iraqi Army.

13. A thin but comprehensive atlas. How else do you figure out the quickest route from Barcelona to Budapest in a hurry?

There is also room for a small camera or tape recorder if I think I am going to need them, but usually I don't.

The rest of my packing is based upon the notion that one should dress as informally as the circumstances allow, both for comfort and for convenience; casual clothes pack more easily than formal ones. I never, never get dressed up for plane trips. For those it is always The Uniform: trousers made out of corduroy with a few strands of elastic woven into it, which makes them not only wrinkle-resistant but also forgiving of an occasional excessive evening at the dinner table; a polo shirt for hot or temperate climates, a turtleneck for cold ones; and a jacket, sometimes a leather version from Spain, sometimes a lighter, sailcloth version from Ireland.

Always oxford-cloth boxer shorts, always black socks, always a pair of Italian loafers; the monotony gives my wife, who is far more chic than I, ample scope for mockery. Never any synthetic fabrics, because they are clammy in cold weather, sticky in hot. I like the polo shirts sold by Trimingham's in Bermuda (they are available by mail) because they are pure cotton, because they are nearly indestructible and because they have very long tails (that thick middle again). I like the dress shirts from Turnbull & Asser in London for the same reasons and also because their bright stripes cheer me up on bad days, even when I remember, as I usually do, how much they cost.

So a few of each of those items go into the under-seat bag, plus a blazer and one good medium-weight suit, usually dark blue because it will just about pass if I strike it rich and get invited to a formal dinner or an opera gala. A couple of knit ties, black and blue, because they don't show the dirt and don't crease; three or four silk pocket squares, for a bit of variety; a cotton bathrobe; a toilet kit; a quick-dry bathing suit, the one exception to the no-synthetics rule; a pair of boots for rainy or snowy or dusty days, and that about does it.

Oh, yes, one more thing: I am an inveterate accumulator of books and other impedimenta on the road, so I always slip into the bottom of the suitcase a collapsible canvas bag. The best I have ever found is made by the Finnish company Marimekko; it looks like an ordinary weekend sailor's carryall, but it has a pair of flaps tucked inside that can be pulled up and zipped shut. If the bag gets too heavy, it can be closed and checked on planes.

That set of gear has seen me happily through hundreds of

trips in the last fifteen years—trips for work or pleasure or both. Though I seldom feel especially natty, I usually feel passably well turned out, and I almost never worry about lacking something I need. Except in Naples . . .

2. *Not So Fully Booked*

ONE day early in April 1985, an American visitor to London walked into Huntsman, the Savile Row tailors, and asked to order a bespoke suit. He was told that no more orders would be taken at least until October. A few days later, another American called a three-star restaurant in rural France to reserve a table for a Saturday in July. He was told that they were fully booked.

Those kinds of experiences seem likely to become the norm in Europe; barring a catastrophic slump in the value of the dollar, six or seven million Americans will cross the Atlantic each summer. Inevitably, they will find the hotels full, the museums so crowded that they will see only the backs of other Americans' heads, transportation facilities overtaxed and the natives a bit dazed by it all.

But the invasion will be uneven; some countries will be more crowded than others, some cities within a given country will be more crowded than others, and some parts of a given city will be more crowded than others. A mob will gather around the "Mona Lisa" in the Louvre every day, but, downstairs, the magnificent collection of artifacts from Babylon and Persepolis and elsewhere in the Middle East will be deserted. So with some forethought, it should still be possible to enjoy a European summer vacation with a European flavor, and to avoid the sickening sensation of having flown three thousand miles just to join a simulated Chicago rush hour.

A first suggestion would be to stay away from the beaches, especially in August, when they are always mobbed by Europeans anyway. You will find more Lebensraum in any one of a dozen American states if you long for surf and sand. A second would be

7

to think about Eastern Europe as well as Western Europe, at least for part of your trip. Russia, Yugoslavia, Czechoslovakia and Hungary all have much to offer, especially if you do not insist on luxury accommodation.

Nowhere will the crowds be worse than in London, Paris and the much beloved Italian trio of Rome, Florence and Venice. But there are strategies for coping: in London, for example, you might skip the National Gallery and visit the inexplicably uncrowded Courtauld Institute Galleries, which have masterpieces by Manet and Gauguin and Cézanne; in Paris, it's fun to forget the two- and three-star restaurants and concentrate on the neighborhood bistros; in Venice, you can walk north from St. Mark's Square, leaving behind a million pigeons and a half-million people, and explore the smaller churches, with their Bellinis and Tintorettos, in almost perfect tranquillity.

Go to the Yorkshire Dales or the Derbyshire Peaks instead of the Lake District or the Cotswolds, to the Auvergne instead of the Loire, to Galicia instead of Andalusia, to Franconia instead of the Black Forest, to Umbria or the Marches instead of Tuscany or the Veneto.

It will take some study and planning, but the time will be well spent. To start you off, here are a dozen suggestions:

Mull

This island, reached by ferry from Oban, guards the southwest approach to Scotland—a remote and austerely beautiful outpost of peak, moor, castle and loch. In May and June, the wildflowers bloom and the nights are never inky black. A few months later, the hillsides are burnished in autumnal gold. Mull will be familiar to those who have followed David Balfour's adventures in Robert Louis Stevenson's *Kidnapped*; it is also spectacular walking country. The nearby island of Iona, where Saint Columba planted the seed of Christianity in Scotland, has a twelfth-century abbey and the graves of forty-eight Scottish kings, including Duncan, murdered by Macbeth in 1040.

Boats ply between Mull and Staffa, with its enormous black basaltic columns, rising from the sea like organ pipes, and Fingal's Cave, which was immortalized by Mendelssohn. Tiroran House at Tiroran, which rejoices in a wild lochside site beneath awesome crags, has nine pretty rooms, dependably good food and enough peace and quiet for Saint Simeon Stylites.

East Anglia

Visiting the country houses, gardens and cathedrals is one of the enduring pleasures of a trip to England, but Chatsworth, Canterbury, Sissinghurst and their like are no fit targets in summer. A trip through East Anglia, the "thumb" that sticks out into the North Sea from the east coast, is likely to be much more rewarding.

An itinerary might include Cambridge, with King's College Chapel, probably Britain's finest late-Gothic building, and the Backs, the shaded lawns along the gentle River Cam, and the splendid Fitzwilliam Museum, which has fine Egyptian and Greek collections and major paintings; the Roman museum in Colchester Castle; burly Ely Cathedral, crowned by a wonderful octagonal lantern dating from 1322; the bucolic "Constable country" around East Bergholt; the half-timbered village of Lavenham, and a pair of memorable houses—Holkham Hall, a Palladian gem, and Blickling, whose Jacobean façade is framed by massive hedges. My wife and I like Shipdham Place, a relaxed little converted rectory with hearty cooking, not far from East Dereham; another good stopping place is Le Talbooth and its hotel annex. But the best food in the region is at Weeks in out-of-the-way Glemsford, where the charming Ian and Sue Weeks—he in the kitchen, she in the dining room—show how much skill and invention four hands can muster.

The Finnish Lakes

The Finnish combination of lakes and birch trees has, for me, an almost mystical appeal; it embodies the spirit of northern Europe in the same way that the Tuscan combination of hills and cypresses embodies that of the south. There are more than sixty thousand lakes in Finland, covering nine percent of the country's territory, and most of them are in the central region.

You could make your headquarters near Hämeenlinna, at the recently renovated Rantasipi Aulanko, which lies within a national park and provides full facilities for swimming, golf, tennis, boating, riding, shooting and cycling, or at its sister hotel, the Rantasipi Laajavuori, near Jyväskylä, a town that has several buildings designed by the great Alvar Aalto. Boats, including hydrofoils and lake steamers, supplement a good road system in knitting together this paradise of cold, deep water and enigmatic green forests. Walk, ride the boats, take a sauna a day, admire the crispness of the architecture and of the products that the talented Finns design for their everyday use. Then, renewed, you might visit Savonlinna, which lies to the northeast, not far from the Soviet border, and its mighty fortress of Olavinlinna, a moated medieval bastion that is unmatched in Scandinavia. For three weeks in July, the central courtyard houses one of Europe's better small opera festivals.

Belgium

Belgium needs a good press agent. Its churches and museums are crammed with the works of native sons whom the whole world admires—Renier de Huy and Godefroid de Huy, two of the geniuses of medieval enamelwork and sculpture; Jan van Eyck and Rogier van der Weyden and Petrus Christus and Hans Memling, masters of perspective, color and detail, and finally Rubens and Van Dyck, the superstars of the seventeenth century. Its restaurants are the equal of France's, and Comme Chez Soi in Brussels is one of a half-dozen contenders for the best in Europe. Its forests are captivating—particularly the Ardennes, in the south, with its game, its hams, its deeply cut river valleys and its inns. And yet, with the exception of Bruges and Ghent, Belgium remains *terra incognita* to most American tourists; it is known to too many people as a land of bad drivers, dowdy women and dull men—the apotheosis of the bourgeois.

Spend a few days in any one of a number of good hotels in Brussels. After you have explored the Grand' Place, one of Europe's noblest squares, and the art museums, and the wealth of Art Nouveau buildings, make a series of day trips—to Antwerp, where you should see not only the Beaux-Arts Museum but also the cathedral, with two great Rubenses, and the choice collection put together by the nineteenth-century connoisseur Mayer van den Bergh; to Ghent for van Eyck and to Bruges for van Eyck and Memling and the canals; to Liège, if only to see the incredible, richly sculptured Romanesque baptismal font in the Church of St. Barthélemy. A few days in the Ardennes (try the seductive Auberge du Moulin Hideux at Noirefontaine) would provide a perfect coda.

The German Expressionists

Only in Germany can one see the work of these painters, who helped to shape the Modern Movement, in its full scope. There were two major groups of Expressionists—*Die Brücke,* or The Bridge, which included Kirchner, Heckel, Nolde and Schmidt-Rotluff, who shared a passion for pure colors and often slashing draftsmanship; and *Der Blaue Reiter,* or The Blue Knight, which included more radical, abstract and semiabstract painters such as Marc, Macke, Klee and Kandinsky.

Happily for our purposes, many of the museums with the best collections are off the beaten track, in cities better known to business people than tourists. Several are clustered in the north-western part of Germany, conveniently linked by Autobahn: the Kunsthalle in Hamburg, the Kunsthalle in Bremen, the Folk-wang Museum in Essen, the Kunsthalle in Bielefeld and the Kunstsammlung Nordrhein-Westfalen and the Kunstmuseum in Düsseldorf. Hamburg and Düsseldorf also offer superb shopping and excellent music; in Hamburg, you can choose between the Atlantic Hotel Kempinski or the Vier Jahreszeiten if you're feeling flush, or stay at the cozy, centrally located little Prem if you're not, and there are similar good choices in most of the stops on this journey. At Seebüll, north of Hamburg on the Danish border, is the outstanding small museum devoted to the works of Emil Nolde, including the *Life of Christ,* considered his masterpiece.

Along the Upper Danube

Although the waters of the river do not often display the color of which Strauss's great waltz sings, its two-hundred mile course from Passau in Germany to Vienna is enough to stir the heart of any romantic. Along the banks stand castles, church towers, vine-yards and fine Renaissance houses. The trip can be made by boat, but a leisurely motor trip is better, because it affords the chance to explore and to dawdle. You will want to visit villages such as Wesenufer, where flowers seem to spill from every balcony; crag-top ruins such as those at Struden and Sarmingstein; valleys such as the Nibelungengau, with its links to Wagnerian legend, and the Wachau, with its orchards and steeply terraced vineyards.

The highlights are two abbeys: St. Florian, with Bruckner's grave and fourteen paintings by the Danubian master Albrecht Altdorfer—by far the largest extant collection—and Melk, the finest Baroque building in Austria, built by Jakob Prandtauer on a bluff 150 feet above the river. Perhaps you will react like Patrick Leigh-Fermor, who, walking in the 1930s from London to Constantinople, as Istanbul was then known, concluded that "Melk is high noon." Almost every little town has its inn, invariably clean and colorful, where one can sample the local wine, and there are larger establishments in Linz, Krems and Dürnstein, where the antique-filled Hotel Richard Löwenherz is laid out in an old vaulted convent. Jamek, at Weissenkirchen in the Wachau, is one of the best restaurants in Austria.

Budapest

Of all the cities of Eastern Europe, I like Budapest best, even though it lacks Leningrad's art treasures and Prague's architectural splendor. I like it best because of its sense of exuberance, because of its food and above all because of its people, the witty, articulate, handsome, talented Hungarians. A relatively liberal economic policy means that it has good hotels, shops with full shelves (Herend porcelain and phonograph records are special bargains) and a central market bursting with fruits and flowers and cheese and, of course, peppers in every color of the rainbow. I usually stay at the Hilton, built around the ruins of a thirteenth-century Dominican church atop Castle Hill.

Visit the National Museum, which holds antiquities as well as Saint Stephen's Crown, a treasure of Byzantine art, which was seized by the United States in 1945 and returned in 1978; see the Fine Arts Museum, which has extensive holdings of Spanish pictures, surprisingly enough (El Greco, Goya); go to a performance at the newly restored State Opera, have dinner at the Matyas Pince, where only the best gypsy bands play. At every turn, you will be fascinated by this brave, cosmopolitan city—especially if you can persuade an English-speaking Hungarian to tell you the latest anti-Soviet jokes.

Alsace

Some of the best eating in the world is crowded into this strip of eastern France, which faces the Black Forest across the Rhine. There, too, are the peaks of the Vosges, the stunning Isenheim altarpiece of Matthias Grünewald at Colmar and the bustling city of Strasbourg, seat of the European parliament. The Auberge de l'Ill in Illhaeusern, set beneath weeping willows along a little river, is the most reasonably priced and one of the best of France's three-star restaurants, and there is no more warm-hearted host than the elfin Jean-Pierre Haeberlin. His own water-colors help to make the dining rooms so pleasant that one would enjoy spending an evening in them even if the place served no food. Crocodile at Strasbourg, Aux Armes de France at Ammer-schwihr and Schillinger at Colmar are other fine tables, but you should also sample the old-style regional cuisine—especially the *choucroute*, the more refined French version of sauerkraut—at a brasserie or a simple village bistro.

Between meals, stroll through Colmar, which is full of quirky half-timbered buildings, and see Strasbourg, which has a fine cathedral, several good museums and an old quarter called Petite France, where medieval buildings are reflected in canals. By no means miss Riquewihr, a town untouched by the wars that have ravaged this border area for centuries; it looks today much as it looked in the sixteenth century. Riquewihr lies in the heart of the Alsatian vineyards, and it is the headquarters of Hugel, per-haps the most esteemed name among Alsatian growers. Jean Hugel, whose family has been in the trade for hundreds of years, is a hearty, broad-shouldered man who speaks perfect English, and he and his co-workers are happy to show interested Ameri-cans around the cellars.

Milan

Italy's second-largest city is its economic capital; southern Italians find its people so energetic that they often call them "the Germans." But Milan is also an art city. In addition to the white, multispired Duomo, it boasts the Brera gallery, with famous works by Piero della Francesca and Raphael; the Ambrosiana gallery, with one Leonardo masterpiece and maybe two (the attribution of the second is disputed); the most celebrated of all paintings, Leonardo's *Last Supper*, once again undergoing restoration but still largely visible, and one of Europe's most inviting small museums, a kind of Milanese Frick named the Poldi Pezzoli.

The Via Monte Napoleone is one of the world's great fashion avenues, and nearby streets house the showrooms of Europe's best modern design industry—Artemide, Arteluce, Memphis, Cassina. The food is fabulous; try Gualtiero Marchesi for Italian nouvelle cuisine, or Aimo e Nadia, less well known but perhaps even better; Al Porto for fish; Alfredo Gran San Bernardo or Savini for the local classics, veal scallopine and rice with saffron. Through much of the year, La Scala presents the world's greatest orchestras, singers and recitalists. So who needs to join the sweltering hordes in Rome and Florence in summer?

Modena

There are at least two or three dozen small towns and cities in Italy that are worth an excursion; some are very well known, like Assisi and Verona, others much less so, like Todi and Volterra. One place that never seems to me to get its due is Modena, the industrial city of about 180,000 northwest of Bologna where Ferrari and Maserati cars, among other things, are produced.

Its cathedral, which has just been restored, is one of the very finest Romanesque buildings in Italy, notably especially for the sculptured decoration (bas-reliefs, doorways) executed by a twelfth-century Lombard master known as Wiligelmo. Inside, the sober brickwork is relieved by a graceful rood screen supported by Lombard lions. The local dominance of the Este family is reflected in a library containing fifteen thousand manuscripts, the most beautiful of which are on view, and a good small picture gallery.

Dr. Giorgio Fini, whose company sells millions of bottles of *aceto balsamico* (a dark, potent herb vinegar) and millions of *zamponi* (pigs' feet) each year, also operates a neat, modern hotel in Modena plus a restaurant with about two hundred regional specialties. Easy excursions can be made to Mantua (Mantegna frescoes), Parma (ham, cheese, Correggio frescoes and a baptistery with magnificent carving by Antelami, a fit rival for Wiligelmo) and Ferrara (the Este palace).

Barcelona

Where to go in Spain? The coast will be jammed, the old Moorish cities of the south ditto, Toledo even more ditto, and Madrid will be too hot. The proud and compelling Catalan capital would be my choice. I agree with James Michener when he writes, "to travel across Spain and finally to reach Barcelona is like drinking a respectable red wine and finishing with a bottle of champagne."

This is the city of Antonio Gaudi, the fiercely individualistic architect considered one of the fathers of Art Nouveau. His Sagrada Familia church, begun in 1884, is still under construction; it is open to the public, and you can also visit Güell Park and two downtown apartment buildings, the Casa Battló and the Casa Milá. Museums abound—the vast Museum of Catalonian Art on Montjuich Hill, which is filled with treasures removed from Pyrenean churches; museums devoted to the work of two famous Catalan modernists, Pablo Picasso and Joan Miró; the Mares Museum, with a renowned collection of polychrome wood sculpture, and the Cambó collection, with works by Raphael, Botticelli and Titian.

This is the place to shop for leather goods of all kinds, at prices a third of those in New York, and for elegant modern jewelry. And Barcelona offers absolutely superb food, which shows the influence of neighboring France, ranging from simple local fish dishes (try the restaurant Siete Puertas) to highly innovative cooking in lush surroundings (try Ama Lur and Jaume de Provença). Perhaps best of all is Raco d'En Binu, about twenty miles northeast at Argentona. Stay at the soothingly old-fashioned Ritz if you can.

The Peloponnesus

The peninsula west of Athens has more than its share of glorious archeological sites, it is less crowded than Athens or Delphi or the main islands, and its people are incredibly warm-hearted toward Americans, whatever the Papandreou government may be saying or doing at the moment. A year or so ago, my wife and I stopped at a rural taverna for a quick lunch and stayed for several hours, talking to local people who introduced themselves through the simple expedient of sending samples of what they were eating and drinking to our table. The landscape is, well, Arcadian—a word we take from the name of the hilly area in the central part of the Peloponnesus.

In a week's unhurried driving, you could see the ruins at Corinth; the theater at Epidaurus, probably the best preserved in Greece; the charming coastal islands of Spetsei, Poros and Hydra, all of which can be reached by ferry; Agamemnon's capital at Mycenae, excavated by the brilliant German amateur Heinrich Schliemann, starting in 1876; Sparta, evocative in name but sterile in reality; remote Mistra, with lovely apricot-orange Byzantine churches scattered across a hillside and filled with luminous frescoes; Bassae, a perfect little temple isolated on its ridge between two ravines, and Olympia, birthplace of the Games.

There are adequate hotels, and a few good ones, in such centers as Nauplia, near Mycenae, and Sparta and Olympia. But this is a circuit best made without firm plans, stopping where whim dictates, even if the accommodation may be rudimentary.

CHAPTER II

London

1. *From Spire to Spire*

PROBABLY none of the world's great churches bears the imprint of one man as clearly as St. Paul's Cathedral, London, bears that of Christopher Wren. But if that elegant Baroque masterpiece proclaims Wren's genius as a manipulator of volume and a synthesizer of contradictory details, his churches in the City of London demonstrate that he was gifted miniaturist as well.

When the Great Fire of 1666 swept through the City—the congested area where London had its beginnings and where its financial activities are concentrated to this day—it consumed not only the old St. Paul's but also most of the ninety-seven parish churches. Wren was then thirty-four years old and teaching at Oxford; through his friendship with Charles II, he was commissioned to rebuild not only the cathedral, but also no fewer than fifty-one churches.

In lesser hands, the churches might have ended up looking alike; in his, each looked distinctive. As Sir John Betjeman once commented, they had only two things in common—prominent fonts and prominent altars with carved and painted altarpieces. "Thus were emphasized," said Sir John, "the two sacraments essential to salvation, baptism and Holy Communion." But in

17

every other way, Wren's churches varied widely: some were brick
and some were stone; some had lead-sheathed steeples and some
had steeples of bare stone; some had domes and some did not;
some had one aisle, some had two and some had none. Most were
built in what came to be known as English Baroque, but a few
were frankly neo-Gothic.

Over the centuries, as more and more offices and fewer and
fewer houses came to occupy the Square Mile, as the City is
known, the churches lost their congregations. Many were sold.
Others were destroyed in the German bombing raids of 1940 and
never rebuilt. Many were drastically modified, almost always
with unfortunate results. But twenty-three Wren churches survive in their entirety, and the towers of several others can still
be seen. Even more than St. Paul's, even more than Wren's
other great buildings—the Royal Naval College at Greenwich,
the Royal Hospital in Chelsea and the east front of Hampton
Court—the City churches enable the modern visitor to explore
the chaste, beautiful world of Christopher Wren.

But the Wren churches are not the whole story. In a day's walk
through the City one can see others, each with its special appeal,
be it a magnificently carved font cover, a Norman chancel or
monuments of men long dead whose names live on in the tradition of the English-speaking peoples. Such a walk is especially
pleasant in December, when the churches are decorated for
Christmas, and their carved festoons of wood or stone are echoed
by garlands and swags of evergreens.

What follows is a modest proposal for such a walk. Each visitor can extend it, curtail it or modify it to suit himself or herself;
the more ambitious might want to do a bit of homework beforehand, for which I would recommend the appropriate pages in
The Cities of London and Westminster, the first of two volumes
that Sir Nikolaus Pevsner devotes to London in his monumental
survey *The Buildings of England* (Penguin, available in Britain
only). I have here made a purely personal choice, based on long,
fruitful hours of exploration during lunch breaks.

A good place to begin is at All Hallows-by-the-Tower, which
stands close to the Thames in the shadow of the Tower of London (you can get there easily by taking the Underground to the
Tower Hill stop). Like many of the City churches, it is an oasis
of calm amid the roaring traffic. It was from this church, spared

in the Great Fire, that Samuel Pepys gazed out upon the smoldering ruins to observe, as he recorded in his diary for September 5, 1666, "the saddest sight of desolation that I ever saw."

All Hallows dates from Saxon times, probably from the seventh century. It was saved in 1666 by Admiral Sir William Penn, who ordered his sailors to blow up the houses near the church to create a firebreak. (The Admiral's son, also named William, was baptized in the church and later went on to found Pennsylvania.) German bombers were less easily deterred, and in December 1940, they destroyed all but the crypt, a few walls and the tower; what you will see is mostly a reconstruction.

The visit is nonetheless worthwhile, largely because of the baptistery in the southwest corner, outside which stands a fine eighth-century arch, and in which stands one of the greatest works of England's master woodcarver, Grinling Gibbons. It is a limewood cover for the font, showing three cherubs prancing around a pillar of grain and flowers, with a dove on top. Notice how Gibbons gave each of the cherubs an individual personality.

Emerging from the church, take the pedestrian subway to the other side of the street, turn left and then bear right on Great Tower Street. Two blocks farther along, recross the street and walk down Idol Lane. In a moment, you will see a church tower. Stop and look at it from there; the closer views are not as good. This lofty tower which is all that remains of St. Dunstan-in-the-East, is probably Wren's best work in the Gothic style, an airy confection of four tiers whose spire is poised on flying buttresses. Trees grow where the nave of the church stood before 1940.

Now bear right (you have no choice) into St. Dunstan's Lane and, after a few steps, turn right up the street called St. Mary-at-Hill to the church of the same name. Just beyond a clock projecting from an almost plain wall, you will see a blue sign marking a passageway that leads to a courtyard and to the door of the church—one of Wren's loveliest creations, with a great Palladian window at the east end and superb woodwork of the seventeenth, eighteenth and nineteenth centuries (altarpiece, pulpit, staircase, organ case). A shallow dome rises above the center of four intersecting barrel vaults, all in pale blue, white and gold plaster that lends an air of ineffable serenity. It is in the style of Robert Adam and hence technically inappropriate, but never mind; it works. As Pevsner points out, the layout is that of many Byzantine churches, which Wren probably adapted from a church at Haarlem in the Netherlands.

Returning to the street, turn right, pausing first to look left at the tower of Wren's St. Margaret Pattens. The building in front of you as you walk down the hill is Billingsgate Market, once the home of London's fish merchants, now closed. Turn right again along Thames Street when you reach it and walk a couple of blocks to the church of St. Magnus the Martyr. This church, distinguished by a 180-foot tower with a gold weathervane, was Wren's welcome to pedestrians crossing the old London Bridge from the south, who passed under the arch in the porch. The interior, which T. S. Eliot said evoked the "inexplicable splendor of Ionian white and gold," is one of the architect's richest.

Make next for the tall monument to the north, walking up Fish Street. This is, in fact, The Monument, Wren's memorial to the Great Fire, which is 202 feet tall and stands 202 feet from the baker's shop in Pudding Lane where the blaze is said to have begun. Don't bother to climb the 311 steps; ugly office slabs now obscure the view. Instead, turn left into Monument Street, then right into King William Street, then left again (through the pedestrian subways) into Cannon Street. After two blocks, you will reach Abchurch Lane, which leads to a lovely little piazzetta next to St. Mary Abchurch, a tiny gem.

Here you can see Wren's sleight of hand at work. Squeezed into a site barely eighty feet square, the church is entirely anonymous, even drab, from the outside. But, as Pevsner says, "the interior is a surprise, for though the area is small, it is made to look very spacious indeed by giving it one big dome on eight arches." The dome cannot be seen from the street. The exquisitely detailed reredos, or altar screen, is by Gibbons; there are documents to prove it. This church, little visited, is sometimes locked; inquire at the public house nearby if need be.

Continue up the lane, turning left into King William Street (again) and following the sidewalk around to the left when you reach the big intersection ahead. The huge building before you is the Bank of England; the church on your right is St. Mary Woolnoth by Nicholas Hawksmoor, another English master of the Baroque, and is well worth a visit if you aren't pressed for time. Turn left just beyond the Mansion House, the seat of London's Lord Mayor, into Walbrook, and you should see the tower of St. Stephen Walbrook rising just ahead of you.

This church is undergoing extensive restoration and may still be closed when you get there; but it is worth checking, for here Wren designed a dome prefiguring that of St. Paul's, coffered on the inside in the style of the Pantheon in Rome, and here he demonstrated, in Betjeman's words, "how to make a plain rectangle interesting and full of vistas." It would never occur to you that the space was rectangular unless someone told you, for Wren has combined a basilical plan—an oblong with a projecting apse—with a Greek cross with a dome, filling the whole with a white forest of slender Corinthian columns that seem to lead toward infinity. For me, this is the most majestic and intellectually exciting building in the City—and that includes St. Paul's. I hope you see it.

By now it should be time for lunch. Walk straight out of the church and up a street called Bucklersbury, crossing Queen Victoria Street; when you reach Cheapside, turn left. On your left, just after crossing Queen Street, you will see St. Mary-le-Bow, our next goal, and right behind it, at 10 Bow Churchyard, the Bow Wine Vaults. Here they will give you a couple of glasses of decent Beaujolais, homemade soup, an ample slice of rare roast beef, a salad and coffee, all for about $10, which isn't bad for London these days. (If you are feeling flush, Le Poulbot, a few yards farther along Cheapside, will feed you the City's best French cooking for about $50 a head, if you order a simple wine.)

Bow church itself boasts Wren's most famous steeple, full of the gentle fantasy that this happy man loved. The church took its name from the Norman arches or bows in the crypt, so Wren embellished the architectural pun by putting stone arches at each corner of the balustrade topping the belfry. The belfry itself is the home of "Bow Bells," which are woven into the folklore of Britain. A true Cockney, it is said, is someone born within the sound of these bells; during World War II, their recorded peal was broadcast worldwide by the BBC and came to symbolize liberation to millions of people in occupied Europe. The interior, completely rebuilt since 1941, is pleasant but less interesting. I would spend most of my time here standing at the foot of the nearby statue of Captain John Smith (of whom more later), studying the tower and the eight-foot ten-inch winged copper dragon on the top.

Continue down Cheapside past Foster Lane, pausing there to enjoy the unaccustomed rear view of St. Paul's, then bear right into St. Martin-le-Grand. When you see a round building looming ahead (this is the London Museum, which should be visited on another day), turn left into Little Britain and follow it, bending first right and then left, until you stand on the edge of a great open square. On your right you will see a passageway leading beneath a thirteenth-century gate.

The gate was originally the entrance to the nave of St. Bartholomew the Great, and the courtyard you cross was the nave itself. What is left of the church is the crossing and the chancel of the great abbey church, built in 1123 and mostly destroyed by Henry VIII in 1539, but even the stump is breath-taking—the most powerful of all the City churches, in my view, and the only one largely in the Norman style brought to England by William the Conqueror. The massive round piers, the plain but sensitively scalloped capitals and the gallery above, with four arches inside each larger arch, show Norman Romanesque at its most movingly somber. The lady chapel, behind the high altar, looks effete by comparison.

Walk south now, with the square on your right and St. Bartholomew's Hospital on your left. When you reach the Holborn Viaduct, turn into St. Sepulchre, architecturally the least distinguished church, perhaps, on our tour, but a fascinating place all the same. It is the biggest church in the City, an amalgam of pre-Fire and post-Fire styles that ends up looking Victorian.

For music lovers, the point of attraction is the chapel off the north aisle, with a book of remembrance devoted to famous musicians, kneeling cushions embroidered with their names and the ashes of Sir Henry Wood, the much-loved creator of the Prom concerts. The church also contains a superb old organ played by Handel and Mendelssohn. And Americans will not want to miss, in the south aisle, the tomb of Captain John Smith, "sometime governor of Virginia and admiral of New England."

Next, cross Holborn Viaduct and walk down Old Bailey, the street that houses London's famous central criminal court, turning left at Ludgate Hill, up which the royal coaches and horses toil for royal weddings and jubilees. The façade of St. Paul's,

Wren's undoubted ecclesiastical masterpiece, towers above you. The present cathedral, the fourth or fifth to stand on the site, came to be a symbol of survival for London and the nation during the Blitz, defying even the smoke and flames of the raid of December 29, 1940, when the City and the docks were engulfed by fire. Against the pale dawn sky, serene and unmarked, the great 250-foot-high dome provided reassurance that Britain had lived to fight yet another day.

A few days before the Great Fire, Wren had visited what was then St. Paul's to see what could be done to save the decaying fabric of the thirteenth-century cathedral, with its seventeenth-century classical façade by Inigo Jones. The conflagration was devastating; after the fire, Wren wrote in his diary, "St. Paul's is now a sad ruin and that beautiful portico now rent in pieces."

What Wren put in its place—beginning on June 21, 1675, and ending thirty-three years later, when the architect, by then seventy-five years old, saw his son fit the top stone into place on the lantern—has changed relatively little over the years. An enormous structure, covering seventy-eight thousand square feet, it is dominated inside and out by the dome (by two domes, in fact; the one seen from the outside is not the one seen from the inside, there being three concentric shells).

Outside, the impression is of restraint, of a classicism that is just yielding to the Baroque. Inside, one is overwhelmed by the volume of enclosed space, by the warmth of the stone and finally, as one reaches the crossing, by the gold and mosaic work. Even here, however, the English taste for understatement is evident— St. Paul's has little in common, for example, with the exuberant encrustations of Bavarian and Austrian Baroque churches.

Walk slowly down the nave in order to sense the full splendor of the crossing and the dome. If your taste runs to fantasy, you might try to imagine what it was like for Lady Diana Spencer, as she then was, to walk those 180 feet with the world watching. You can climb, if you wish, to the Whispering Gallery, where the state trumpeters were placed for the royal wedding. Then spend some time studying the memorials to eminent Britons— the Wellington monument on the left of the nave, statues of Sir Joshua Reynolds and Dr. Johnson, among others, by the dome piers, and a tablet marking the position of Churchill's casket during his state funeral on January 30, 1965. The work of Gibbons is all around, in stone this time, a profusion of cherubs and swags and garlands.

Before leaving, descend into the crypt. I had never seen it until the morning of the royal wedding, when the reporters were let out of the church by that route. It seemed eerily appropriate, somehow, to see there the dozens of tombs, memorials and busts (tributes to Nelson and Lawrence of Arabia among them) after all the magnificence that had just unfolded overhead.

Emerging from the church, walk straight down the hill, under the railway bridge, across Ludgate Circus and into Fleet Street. Turn left at the first intersection to St. Bride, which is of interest for two reasons: its wedding-cake steeple, with four octagons stacked one atop the other, at 226 feet loftier than any other Wren creation; and the list of its one-time parishioners. You cannot fail to see the steeple on your way down Ludgate Hill.

When you enter the church—the interior has been rebuilt since World War II—consider for a moment those who have stood on this spot before you: Chaucer, Shakespeare, Milton, Pepys, Dryden, Johnson and Boswell, Burke, Pope, Wordsworth, Keats, Dickens. . . .

Since this is still the newspaper neighborhood, there are plenty of pubs in which to rest your feet and slake your thirst; the Cheshire Cheese is in a courtyard just up Fleet Street. Down New Bridge Street toward the river is the Blackfriars Underground station, where you can catch a train back to your hotel.

2. *In Churchill's Footsteps*

M A N Y visitors to Britain, especially those who have made several trips there, like to see places associated with great men of the past. Some people visit as many of Vanbrugh's or Wren's buildings as they can, some make a pilgrimage to the spots in the Lake District frequented by the Romantic poets, some seek out the settings of the main events in Henry VIII's tempestuous life.

Sir Winston Churchill has been dead for only twenty years,

and it may not occur to many people to think of the great wartime leader in the same way that they see figures from the seventeenth or eighteenth century. But since he died, on January 25, 1965, at 28 Hyde Park Gate in London, a kind of Churchill industry has sprung up in Britain, devoted to keeping his memory alive. A three-day tour makes it possible to visit a number of the places associated with the man of whom Queen Elizabeth II once said, "He had no need for distinction greater than the name of Winston Churchill."

I would suggest that one day be spent in London and two on easy day trips northwest and south of the city, preferably with a rental car, although it is possible to visit the principal sites by train.

Start in Parliament Square. There, not far from statues of Disraeli, Derby, Peel, Palmerston, Smuts and Abraham Lincoln, stands Ivor Roberts-Jones's portrayal of Churchill. Bundled up in an army greatcoat, jaw jutting in that pose of bulldog defiance, stick in hand, he looks across the street to Big Ben and the House of Commons, where he spent more than sixty years of his life. Nearby is St. Margaret's Church, Westminster, famous because Sir Walter Raleigh is buried in the chancel, but of interest to Churchill enthusiasts because it was there, in 1908, that he married Clementine Hozier. Just beyond St. Margaret's is Westminster Abbey, and in its floor, not far from the tomb of the Unknown Warrior, is a stone slab bearing the words, "Remember Winston Churchill." They put it there a few months after he died, on the twenty-fifth anniversary of the Battle of Britain.

It is in the House of Commons, however, that Churchill's spirit seems so very palpable—and not only because of Oscar Nemon's bronze of the Prime Minister, hands on hips, body thrust forward, standing in the members' lobby. Few weeks pass without some Member of Parliament quoting Churchill in debate. The chamber itself is new, built to replace the one destroyed in an air raid during World War II, but it is a replica of the old. As Prime Minister during the war, Churchill occupied the seat opposite the brown dispatch box on the front bench to the right of the Speaker. Like prime ministers before and after him, Churchill rested his notes on the box and gripped its sides as he told Parliament and the nation that he had "nothing to offer but blood, toil, tears and sweat." After he resigned as Prime

Minister, in 1955, he retreated to a corner seat in the front row below the gangway, again to the Speaker's right; although back-benchers are not assigned regular seats, Sir Winston claimed that place as his own. No one challenged his right to it.

Churchill spent the most fevered hours of the war in a place that, until recently, few Londoners and even fewer visitors knew about: the Cabinet War Rooms. But now the maze of subter-ranean rooms where the Cabinet met, in secret, during the Blitz and afterward, is open to the public from 10:00 A.M. to 5:50 P.M., daily except Mondays and holidays. The entrance is behind the Treasury, just off Parliament Square.

The cramped, austere rooms remain exactly as they were on the last day of the war—the bedrooms with their metal cots, the planning rooms with their maps of shipping lanes and bomb-ing paths covered with multicolored pins, the communications center with its seemingly chaotic jumble of archaic-looking tele-phones. The Cabinet room is a bare, low-ceilinged space, almost filled by a C-shaped table covered with black cloth made from fabric originally intended for policemen's trousers. At each place is a cheap tubular-steel chair, a blotting pad, a pencil and a name card. Anthony Eden sat here, Lord Beaverbrook there, and Clement Attlee next to the Prime Minister. The guide asks his visitors to sit around the table while he plays recordings of some of Churchill's broadcasts, and it is hard to believe that the great man is not hiding somewhere in this warren of 180 rooms.

It is equally hard to believe that some of the key decisions of the greatest war in history were taken in this unprepossessing place, which was not even bombproof and was equipped with materials scrounged from many sources, so that government pur-chase orders would not give the secret away. It was a typically English piece of muddling through; Hitler might have his lavish Führer bunker, but for Churchill a converted cellar was enough.

The British leader's impetuousness and high spirits shine through. Guides like to tell how the Prime Minister's valet used to hide his boots to keep him from rushing, childlike, out into St. James's Park to watch the air raids. And one sees the little room where he talked to President Roosevelt on a special tele-phone; its door was appropriated from a public toilet, and when Churchill entered the room, he often turned the sign on the door to "Engaged."

If there is time left over, the Imperial War Museum in Lambeth, south of the Thames, has several exhibits touching on Churchill's wartime career. (It is open every day except Good Friday, Christmas and Boxing Day—December 26.) Then, if you are driving, head for Oxford on the M40. En route, you may pass the Harrow School, which is now in London's northwestern suburbs but in Churchill's school days lay in the countryside. There he demonstrated his almost total indifference to formal education, with the important exception of the English language.

From Oxford, take the A34 toward Woodstock, which is fifty-five miles from London. Just before that village you will come to Blenheim Palace, the vast yellow mansion designed by Vanbrugh and built by a grateful nation for the Duke of Marlborough after his victory over the French at Blenheim in Bavaria in 1704. Alternately, you can take the train from Paddington Station to Oxford and then continue to Blenheim, seven miles away, by taxi. The house is open daily for conducted tours from 11:30 A.M. to 5:00 P.M., March through October.

The Churchillian purpose of the trip is to see the room where the future Prime Minister was born, in November 1874. His mother, the American Jeanette Jerome, was seven months pregnant when she insisted on attending a ball at Blenheim. When labor set in unexpectedly, she rushed into a small room whose simple brass bed was being used that evening for coats. They were hurriedly cleared away, and her son was born there within a few minutes. The event gave rise to one of Sir Winston's wisecracks. Asked how his mother had happened to be at Blenheim that night, he replied, "Although present on that occasion, I have no clear recollection of the events leading up to it."

In the room where he was born, a lock of Churchill's hair (at the age of five) is on exhibit, as are photographs, letters and documents. In adjacent rooms, large photomurals trace his career as student, soldier, war correspondent, statesman and historian; the picture is completed by recordings from his speeches, excerpts from letters and some of his paintings.

Blenheim is now owned and from time to time occupied by the eleventh Duke of Marlborough, the great-grandson of Sir Winston's uncle. But the place is interesting for many other reasons in addition to its Churchill connections. The exterior of the three-hundred-room house is one of the finest examples of English Baroque. The magnificent park, with its lake, created by the landscape architect Capability Brown, its bridge, hundreds of old oaks and victory column, was described without too much exaggeration by Churchill's father, Lord Randolph Churchill, as "the finest view in England." The ceremonial rooms of the house are almost too grand; the eye begins to rebel at the opulence of Meissen and Sèvres, Sargent and Reynolds and Van Dyck, velvet upholstery and Flemish tapestries and Persian rugs, boule furniture and ormolu clocks and even Grinling Gibbons sculpture. Still, the house remains one of the glorious treasure troves of England, and the pale, 180-foot Long Library, with the great Willis pipe organ at the end, is worth a visit in itself.

You might have lunch at the Bear, a sixteenth-century coaching inn in Woodstock, which serves good country meals for about $20, including a drink and tip. Then you should visit the tiny churchyard at Bladon, only a couple of miles away, where Churchill lies buried in the shadow of a pretty steeple. His grave, next to those of his father and mother, is marked by a massive stone with the simplest of inscriptions: "Winston Leonard Spencer Churchill 1874–1965."

On another day, take the A21, A233 and B2026 from London south into Kent, through the village of Westerham (which displays another Oscar Nemon sculpture of Churchill) to Churchill's country house at Chartwell, twenty-five miles from the center of the city. If you are traveling by train, there is service from Charing Cross Station to Sevenoaks; Chartwell is seven miles from Sevenoaks and can be reached by taxi.

Churchill bought the house and seventy-nine acres of ground in 1922. There he painted, fed his golden orf, which are like big goldfish, and dictated his books to his secretary. He built a brick wall and a cottage in the grounds with his own hands and helped to construct the ponds. Now the property of the National Trust, the house has a rose garden, a view of the Kentish countryside and the best collection of Churchilliana anywhere. Notice his regalia as a Knight of the Garter, his collection of outlandish hats, his wartime "siren suits," and the model of the floating D-day harbor at Arromanches. The house, which is open on Wednesdays, Thursdays, Saturdays and Sundays from April to mid-October, also has several pictures by this century's most famous Sunday painter. There is a son-et-lumière show in summer—a very good one.

Motorists can combine a visit to Chartwell with excursions to two other houses in the area, both near Sevenoaks—Knole, the seat of the Sackville-Wests, and Penshurst Place, which has belonged to the Sidney family since 1522. I would also suggest a stop in the charming half-timbered village of Chiddingstone, which belongs in its entirety to the National Trust. It is only a few miles from Penshurst, and it has one of my favorite pubs, the Castle, where you can have a pint of beer and a simple lunch for $5.

3. *Classic Dining . . .*

T H E last quarter-century has been hard on the grand old luxury restaurants of Europe's major cities. The Hostaria dell'Orso in Rome, Maxim's and Lasserre in Paris, Sabatini in Florence, the Sacher in Vienna, Horcher in Madrid, Mirabelle in London—all of them still exist, and a few still serve very good food, but none of them can any longer be considered a pacesetter.

One need not look far for an explanation. The old-fashioned gastronomic palaces were owned by businessmen who employed chefs to turn out classic dishes and a few unchanging specialties; most of the top tables of today are in restaurants owned by chefs who put a premium on innovation. Very often the new places are small, and some are understaffed, as the true *grand-luxe* restaurant never was and must never be; many cannot afford, in this era of high wages, the whole panoply of *commis*, waiter, captain, maître d'hôtel and sommelier. And although well appointed, they are seldom opulent in the tradition of 1960.

There are, of course, several exceptions. Taillevent in Paris, considered by many to be that city's greatest restaurant, is owned by Jean-Claude Vrinat, a brilliant front-of-the-house man, not by the chef, Claude Deligne; and the most talked-about restaurant on the Côte d'Azur, the Chantecler in the Négresco Hotel in

Nice, has been restored to its prewar glory by a hired hand, the young chef Jacques Maximin.

Egon Ronay, the British gastronome and guidebook editor, estimates that building, outfitting and staffing a truly luxurious restaurant in Mayfair or Knightsbridge in central London would cost something like three million dollars before the first meal was served. Not surprisingly, not many such places come into being these days, in the British capital or elsewhere.

Two of the best luxury restaurants in London, and a couple of others that come close to the top of the list, are to be found in hotels. Anton Mossiman of the Dorchester, a Swiss, and Michel Bourdin of the Connaught, a Frenchman, are enabled by the resources of the big corporations that own their hotels to show off their talents in sumptuous settings that they could never have afforded by themselves. For whatever reasons—a dislike for management, a preference for big kitchens, inertia—Messrs. Deligne, Mossiman, Maximin and Bourdin have chosen not to strike out on their own, at least for now.

To my mind, the truly posh establishment is best reserved for special occasions—birthdays, anniversaries, holidays, the one or two splurges of a trip. For most people, economics dictate that course; for the rest, a sense of proportion ought to. Nothing is likely to pall faster than a succession of meals in luxury restaurants, by which I mean those that provide sophisticated cooking, rich and elaborate and often organized in five or more courses; great wines; costly place settings and surroundings, including a profusion of flowers; and prompt, polished service.

It is intriguing, in this connection, to notice the habits of the proprietors of superstar restaurants in France. Last summer, in Eugénie-les-Bains, the night after having served a group of us mere mortals the same Rabelaisian feast he was cooking for the President of France, Michel Guérard asked us to join him for dinner. It could not have been simpler: no cream, no caviar, no foie gras, no lobster, no oysters. Simple foods, simply but beautifully cooked, with a seraphic chocolate mousse at the end. Likewise, on his days off, the elegant M. Vrinat likes to pop into plebeian bistros like Chez la Vieille, Adrienne Biasin's snuggery on the Rue de l'Arbre-Sec.

All of this is by way of prelude to answering a question that visitors to London often ask: Where should we go for a really gala evening, no holds barred, wear the glad rags, something to remember, cost really no object?

Only three places come instantly to mind: the Connaught, the Dorchester and Le Gavroche. At none of the three, in my view, is the food as good as at Chez Nico in Battersea or at La Tante Claire in Chelsea. But both of them, despite such ravishing dishes as the crab and sole mousseline with Sauterne sauce at the former and the rabbit with basil and tarragon and morels at the latter, would have to be classified as comfortable rather than swank. (Tante Claire will have completed a renovation by the time you read this, doubling its space and acquiring a thirties décor in which Noël Coward would have felt at home, and Chez Nico will have finished its expansion as well.)

At the Connaught, Michel Bourdin, whose grandmother ran a brasserie in Paris, has had his flirtations in recent years with nouvelle cuisine, but the backbone of the menu remains as traditional as the frock coats of the captains. Edwardian favorites to match the mellow paneling—Irish stew, steak-and-kidney pie, bread-and-butter pudding—coexist happily with elaborate dishes from the classical French repertory such as the game chartreuse. In less attentive hands, these things can quickly become routine and even drab, but not here. Mr. Bourdin has also managed to persuade the affluent patrons of his regal establishment to order some newer, lighter dishes such as his *rendezvous de pêcheur*, a marriage of the best fish that the market has to offer on any given day.

The grace of Jean-Pierre Chevallier, who manages the restaurant, the sage advice of the sommeliers (delivered in vaguely Hapsburg accents), the names of favored customers of yesteryear still clinging to dishes they favored (oysters Christian Dior, consommé Cole Porter), the elegant dress of one's fellow diners— all of these elements help create a mood of discreet richness that is unmatched in London. (16 Carlos Place W1, telephone 499-7070; MasterCard.)

Mr. Mosimann is up to something completely different in the Terrace Restaurant of the Dorchester. If the Connaught is Old Money, even when the accents at some tables owe more to Houston than to Eton, the Terrace is New. At a cost that must have run to around a million dollars, the Dorchester hired Albert Pinto to create a Chinese-modern-romantic décor with a dance floor. Mr. Mosimann has developed dishes of inspired simplicity, such as *sole gratinée à l'huile aux herbes* and *médaillons d'agneau aux fleurs de thyme*. Recently he has been experimenting with what he calls cuisine naturelle, using a minimum of sugar, butter and cream. As an example of pure finesse, it would be hard to match his perfectly poached chicken breast, served with four or five raw vegetables, cut into matchsticks and marinated in lime juice or stock.

One can also order a "menu surprise" that will bring six undisclosed courses to the table, but this can create a problem. It is necessary to leave the choice of wines to the waiter, and on two occasions, even though I had specified that I would like modest ones, I have been served punishingly expensive bottles. The same thing has happened to friends, so state your wishes firmly. Another problem here is inconsistency; the whisper in the trade is that Mr. Mosimann is peerless as a cook (and, indeed, as a teacher of other cooks), but that he has his problems in managing a brigade of the size needed to serve not only the Terrace and the excellent Dorchester Grill, which specializes in modernized English fare, but also room service and the private dining rooms. (Park Lane W1, 629-8888; closed Sunday; American Express, Diners, Visa, MasterCard.)

Le Gavroche is the showplace of the most successful chain of haute-cuisine restaurants in the world—that of the Roux brothers. Former cooks in aristocratic private houses, Albert and Michel Roux are technical geniuses; Albert, who presides at the Gavroche, starts the careers of his young apprentices by painstakingly teaching them how to fry an egg.

Michelin gives the Gavroche three stars. Although I think two would be closer to the mark—Le Gavroche is simply not as good as Girardet in Switzerland or Jamin and Troisgros in France—this is without doubt *the* London restaurant for classic French cooking and service.

Michel, the younger, taller and leaner of the brothers, runs the Waterside Inn at Bray, a fifty-five-minute drive west of London, in a lovely setting of weeping willows and oaks beside the Thames River. The Waterside also gets three Michelin stars, and a third Roux property, Le Poulbot, in the City, gets one. Two bistros—Le Gamin, near St. Paul's Cathedral, and Gavvers, on the site of the original Gavroche—complete the empire. Gavvers gets a red M, which the guide awards to restaurants serving a somewhat less elaborate but nonetheless always carefully prepared meal.

The names of the London restaurants are linked by a theme. *Gamin* and *gavroche* are French words for street urchins; *gavvers* was the Sloane Rangers' nickname for the old Gavroche, and Francis Poulbot was a French artist who specialized in depicting urchins.

In addition, the restaurants share a tendency, mildly irritating to those familiar with gastronomic French, to use women's names rather than traditional terms to describe their specialties. The Gavroche, for example, offers chicken Geneviève and tournedos Arlette, among other dishes. Albert Roux confesses that it is his doing.

"I guess I'm a little like a painter," he said in an interview. "When he fancies someone, he puts her on canvas. When someone comes to my attention, I put her into the frying pan."

Albert Roux makes very, very few mistakes in the kitchen, and the staff in the clublike dining room responds with appropriate pomp and panache. Among the dishes that linger in my memory are a salad of lobster and wild mushrooms, a woodcock of a quality equal to those served two decades ago at Lucas-Carton in Paris, a braid of red mullet and John Dory, the two fishes served with a chive sauce, and an anise-flavored soufflé Suissesse. The cheeses, sent from Boulogne by Phillipe Olivier and ripened in the restaurant's larder, are the best in the city.

Two minor grumbles: the style verges upon excessive richness, and the wine prices are truly terrifying (some bottles at more than $750). (43 Upper Brook Street W1, 408-0881; closed Saturday, Sunday, major holidays and a week at Christmas; American Express, Diners, Visa, MasterCard.)

In addition to Chez Nico (129 Queenstown Road SW8, 720-6960; Visa) and La Tante Claire (68 Royal Hospital Road SW3, 352-6045; American Express, Diners), there are a few other contenders that, for one reason or another, I have excluded from my very short list of London's best posh places. Here are brief notes on a half-dozen of them:

Bombay Brasserie (140 Gloucester Road SW7, 370-4040; American Express, Diners, Visa, MasterCard). This airy restaurant with languidly turning overhead fans and wicker chairs, owned by the Taj Hotel chain of India, proves once again that eating ethnic can be a luxurious experience. The leafy, glass-walled conservatory (ask for a table there when you reserve) is an especially evocative environment in which to savor the subtlety of the work of the chef, Sandip Chaterjee; try, for example, his sautéed crab Malabar with grated coconut, or the fish (pomfret or gray mullet) with fenugreek. The menu includes seafood in the Goan style, spicy Tandoori specialties, Parsee dishes and vegetarian items from Gujarat.

Capital Hotel (22 Basil Street SW3, 589-5171; American Express, Diners, Visa, MasterCard). David Levin, one of the most skilled of Britain's rising hoteliers, redid his dining room not long ago, discarding the Bauhaus fittings and substituting striped curtains and Louis XIV chairs. The cooking of Brian Turner remains as it was—rich and refined, with perhaps a trifle too much imagination on occasion. His *piccata* of beef with capers, a *marquise* of white chocolate and various fish dishes show a sure hand that is also evident in the steaks, especially the *côte de boeuf*, from his charcoal grill. There is an agreeable lack of stuffiness about the place, which probably has something to do with the outgoing personality of Mr. Turner, a Yorkshireman whose father ran a fish-and-chips shop.

Chelsea Room (in the Hyatt Carlton Tower Hotel, 2 Cadogan Place SW1, 235-5411; closed three days at Christmas; American Express, Diners, Visa, MasterCard). Bernard Gaume, the chef, and Jean Quero, the manager, have slowly and without fanfare built this into a restaurant of surprising quality for a chain hotel. The rather chilly room has recently been made more intimate and redecorated in pastel tones, and Mr. Gaume remains a wizard with fish (warm oysters with three sauces, turbot and lobster with cucumbers). Some of the other dishes are less brilliant, to my taste, which is why the Chelsea Room just misses my main list.

Rue St. Jacques (5 Charlotte Street W1, 637-0222; closed Saturday lunch and Sunday; American Express, Diners, Visa, MasterCard). Too small, really, to fit into the *grand-luxe* category, this newish restaurant is nonetheless an elegant setting (huge mirrors, pillow-strewn banquettes) in which to sample the cuisine of Gunther Schlender, the German chef. He has the ability to achieve depth of flavor without heaviness; witness his fabulous venison consommé and his ethereal lobster mousse flavored with old Armagnac. Vincent Calcerano, the Belgian maître d'hôtel, is a real pro.

Scott's (20 Mount Street W1, 629-5248; closed Sunday lunch and major holidays; American Express, Diners, Visa, Master-Card). Suppose you are in a festive mood, but not too hungry. Make for Scott's—not the respectable but unexciting main restaurant, but the adjacent oyster bar. A glass or two of champagne, some Colchesters or a few slices of irreproachable smoked salmon or a grilled sole (or even a couple of spoonfuls of one of the half-dozen caviars on offer, in which case double your price estimate) should solve the problem quite nicely.

Wilton's (55 Jermyn Street SW1, 629-9955; closed Saturday, Sunday, major holidays and three weeks in July and August; American Express, Diners). I know, I know: the cooking is nothing to shout from the rooftops about, especially in the more complex dishes, and the prices are ludicrously high for simple fare. But Wilton's is the last genuinely Edwardian restaurant left in London, and I love it for its Art Nouveau glass partitions (unchanged in the 1985 move from Bury Street), for its bossy waitresses in lab technicians' smocks, for its oysters and soles and baby lobsters and roasted game birds, and above all for the indomitable, near-octogenarian Mrs. Marks, who once refused to give me a bill when my meal was terminated a few minutes early—there were a few tears of Calvados left in my glass—by a small fire in the kitchen.

4. . . . and a Few Simpler Haunts

YOU ought to go to the Gay Hussar at lunch, because that's when Victor Sassie is there. Without him, the food is just as good—the most satisfying Hungarian food I've ever eaten outside Hungary. The clientele is pretty much the same, too—writers and Labour politicians, mostly, although a greater number of casual passers-by seem to drop in at dinner. But without Victor, there is no one to tell you that you're ordering the wrong things, drinking too much wine, generally lousing things up.

Victor turned seventy not long ago. He comes from Barrow-in-Furness, in the northwest of England, but he learned his trade at the feet of the great Karoly Gundel in Budapest before World War II. When it started, his was just one of dozens of "foreign" restaurants in Soho, then practically the only place in London, outside the hotels, where you found anything other than English cooking. Twenty years ago, when Soho began changing, with sex shops replacing the bistros, the Gay Hussar carried on. Now Soho is changing again, with bistros replacing the sex shops; the Gay Hussar, at 2 Greek Street, is still carrying on. It always seems exactly the same, which makes it the ideal place for people choking on change.

You will find there the kind of solicitousness that has almost vanished from restaurants. I remember the time when the president of a gastronomic society asked Victor whether he would close the place to the public one day so the group could take it over for a banquet. Most people in the trade would have replied, "Name the day," but not Victor. "Oh, I couldn't do that," he said, his lugubrious face expressing something akin to alarm. "Some of my regulars wouldn't know where to eat."

The soups are remarkable—mushroom soup, Szeged fish soup, a celery soup based on a celery-root stock—all laced with a bit of sour cream, all hearty enough to sustain a Transylvanian peasant in January. The cucumber salad (just cucumbers, sour cream and sweet paprika) is a small masterpiece. I usually order the stuffed cabbage as a main course, but the smoked goose and the roast duck and the braised calf's foot are just as good. Finish with poppyseed strudel, if you can.

Amazingly enough, two people can share a bottle of very palatable Hungarian wine and eat more than their fill (the portions are enormous) for about $45; no credit cards. There is no better value for money anywhere in central London. And you can spend a happy half hour after lunch, if the spirit moves you, browsing at Milroys, next door, which has the best selection of single-malt whiskies south of Edinburgh.

The Tate Gallery is an aesthetic feast known to millions for its Hogarths and Gainsboroughs, its unrivaled collections of Turners and Blakes and its Rothko room. But unbeknownst to most of the thousands who visit it each day, the Tate also offers, in its ground-floor restaurant, some of the most astonishing bargains in fine wines to be found in the world.

The restaurant's wine list, which is mimeographed so that it can be easily revised every month or so, lists about twenty red Bordeaux, a dozen red Burgundies of the first rank and several classic white Burgundies, as well as Champagnes, Sauternes, Rhines and Moselles.

The prices at the Tate have been called "really incredible" by Michael Broadbent, head of the wine department at Christie's, the London auction house. If you were lucky enough to know a *negociant* in Beaune and another in Bordeaux willing to sell their wines to you at wholesale, you would still pay nearly twice as much as you would at the Tate's restaurant.

A few years ago, four of us gathered at the Tate restaurant, which features seventeenth- and nineteenth-century English dishes, and consumed the following in the course of a two-and-a-half-hour lunch:

A 1966 Champagne from Bollinger, marked "récemment dé-gorgé," meaning that it had been allowed to mature several years longer than normal before the sediment was disgorged; a 1961 Château Lynch-Bages, a well regarded red Bordeaux from Pauillac, the village that produces Lafite, Latour and Mouton; a 1961 Corton Clos du Roi, a red Burgundy from the Côte d'Or, bottled by Henri Thevenot, a small, painstaking grower held in high esteem by connoisseurs; and a 1967 Château Suduiraut, a Sauternes that in good years—and 1967 was one—ranks just below Château d'Yquem.

All were superb. The Champagne seemed a bit listless as an apéritif, but demonstrated a creamy excellence with the first course. The Lynch-Bages was at a peak after twenty years, and with the cheese, the Corton was a perfect contrast to the Lynch-Bages—voluptuousness versus elegance. The Suduiraut was no anti-climax.

The bargains at the Tate are made possible by the care and skill of Thomas Machen, the young manager. He is one of those Englishmen who were weaned on good claret (the local term for red Bordeaux) and who resolved early on to make wine their lifework. A recent list included such treasures as a 1976 Leoville-Poyferre at only $20.50.

Wines are bought young at the most competitive prices from London merchants and laid down in three cellars—one for current listings, one for wines that are maturing and one for house wines. They are marked up only 40 percent, as compared with the 75 to 150 percent that most restaurateurs, confronted, unlike Mr. Machen, with high rents, must charge to cover their overheads.

As a result, the place sells forty-five thousand bottles of wine a year. The tables are booked three to four days in advance, and customers who live on the Continent often Telex for reservations.

If you have children with you, they will doubtless clamor for American food; if not, you may discover how rare is the London restaurant that is inexpensive, relaxed and good-humored, and provides interesting things to eat. The answer to both problems is Bob Payton, a hulking Chicagoan who abandoned the advertising business nine years ago, opened a tiny pizzeria on borrowed money and struck it rich. He now has several places in London, including the Chicago Pizza Pie Factory at 17 Hanover Square (no sign, so look for the red door), with deep-dish pies, U.S. beer and a blizzard of Windy City street signs and other memorabilia, and the Chicago Rib Shack at 1 Raphael Street in Knightsbridge, with ribs, barbecue sandwiches, cole slaw and an irresistible construction called an onion loaf. Both places are great fun, despite the boss's lamentable weakness for puns; he wishes you "bone appetit" at the Rib Shack, and he insisted on calling his new fish restaurant Payton Plaice.

CHAPTER III

Britain

---

1. *Rocky Solidarity*

T H E Romans came to northeast England, and after them the rapacious Danes; the Normans arrived in the years after William conquered, following the early Christian settlers from Ireland, who came by way of Iona in Scotland. But not many modern tourists tarry in the bluff Northeast, which is not quite English but not quite anything else. It is still so closely linked to Scandinavia that its main city, Newcastle-upon-Tyne (the place to which one used to be counseled never to carry coals), asked King Olav V of Norway, not Queen Elizabeth II, to open its new Civic Center in 1968.

I have been fascinated for years by this region, which most people call Northumbria. (Officially and somewhat artificially, the area is now divided into four counties—Northumberland, Durham, Cleveland and Tyne and Wear). There are few parts of Europe, I am convinced, where one can so vividly sense the rich, turbulent flux of two thousand years of history. Savage moors and gentle gardens, Roman relics a thousand miles and more from Caesar's capital, bold Norman castles and churches, hidden gems of Baroque and Palladian architecture, two of the best small museums in Britain—the variety is quite extraordinary. And the whole is unforgettably capped by Durham, in its magnificent cliff-top setting above an oxbow in the river Wear, with a rugged old castle and a cathedral that, for me, stands as the supreme masterpiece of the medieval stonemason, challenged only by Vézelay in Burgundy.

If the weather is unreliable, and it is, so is that in Bath and Edinburgh and the Cotswolds, and plenty of travelers go there. The Durham moors can be breath-taking on a winter's day, the white of the snowfields broken by the dark gray of the dry-stone walls, and the craggy cliffs along the North Sea can look almost benign in the summer sun.

Forget for but a moment the Roman years in this uncompromising countryside, and consider its role in the creation of Christian England. Less than a century after Saint Augustine arrived as a representative from Rome to cosmopolitan Canterbury, Saint Aidan came from Iona to Holy Island off the wild Northumbrian coast. He and his successors, most notably Saint Cuthbert, made of an unprepossessing rock a bright beacon of faith, which shines forever in the sumptuous Lindisfarne Gospels, housed now in the British Museum in London but illuminated on this wind-swept island that stood then on the very rim of civilization.

To get there today, you leave Route A1 near Beal for a four-and-a-half-mile drive across a narrow causeway that can be negotiated only at low tide (the permissible hours are published each day in *The Northern Echo* and other local newspapers). The most prominent landmark is the little sixteenth-century castle, converted into a house by Lutyens early in this century, which is more remarkable for its site atop a mesalike rock than for its architecture or contents. Not far away lie the evocative red sandstone ruins of the priory, founded in 1083, a stirring place, with one delicate arch still in place over the crossing, with one huge column carved with chevrons like those at Durham and with other stones so eroded by wind and rain that they resemble the wilder Art Nouveau fantasies of Gaudi.

Saint Cuthbert was first buried on Holy Island, but when the Danes descended in 875, the monks exhumed his body and began eight years of wandering in search of sanctuary. For a century, from 883 to 995, the saint found peace at Chester-le-Street, but then his bones were dug up again and taken to what is now Durham. A city grew up there around a Saxon cathedral, which was replaced by the glorious Norman church that we see today, begun in 1093.

Durham Cathedral is memorable for more than its size and for more than Saint Cuthbert's hard-won final resting place. It is renowned among architectural historians as the first cathedral ever to have a stone rib vault over the nave instead of a barrel vault or a flat wood roof. It has the richest treasury of any church in England, where many of the relics were destroyed by the vengeful Henry VIII; this houses a seventh-century pectoral cross, eighth-century manuscripts, tenth-century vestments and a twelfth-century brass door knocker which, if touched by fugitives from the law, guaranteed safety inside.

But it is the all-but-indescribable majesty of the vast nave, solemn and inspiring despite the burly cylindrical columns with their almost barbaric incised decoration and a profusion of zigzag motifs, that leaves the deepest impression. To Dr. Johnson, the nave suggested "rocky solidity and indeterminate duration." Somehow, the thrust of the vaulting and the vivacity of the arcades banishes any thought of inert heaviness. Somehow, the rhythmic Romanesque nave coexists harmoniously with the Gothic busyness of the Galilee Porch at the west end of the cathedral and the Chapel of the Nine Altars at the east end, and with such splendid details as Prior Castell's five-hundred-year-old clock and the highest bishop's throne in all of Christendom.

"There it stands," wrote Nikolaus Pevsner, "one of the most magnificent sights of England, flanked on one side by the Bishop's Castle, on the top of its steep wooded hill with its mighty tower over the crossing and the two slenderer western towers to balance its weight."

Providentially, the best lunch in the city is to be had for $7 a person in the cathedral undercroft (tart cucumber soup, quiches, fresh salads and an exemplary trifle most days). A visit to the cathedral can thus be easily combined with a look at the castle, now part of Durham University, and at the nearby Gulbenkian Museum, endowed by the legendary Levantine fixer known as "Mr. Five Percent." It has one of Europe's most notable collections of Oriental arts.

Not only Saint Cuthbert is buried at Durham; the Galilee Porch shelters the tomb of the Venerable Bede, whose history of early Christian Britain, written in the eighth century, is one of our main sources of knowledge of that epoch. Bede worked and died at Jarrow, north of Durham, on the south bank of the river Tyne, which is perhaps better known as the starting point of the great hunger marches of the Depression. St. Paul's Church, now rather incongruously surrounded by housing projects, mills and tank farms, retains the choir though not the nave that Bede knew, with a chair that may have been his, a niche for communion vessels that he almost certainly used and a tiny, circular Saxon window containing the earliest colored glass in Europe. Still farther north stands another reminder of Northumbria's Christian past, Brinkburn Priory, a beautifully restored Norman church in creamy stone, with a fine north door, in the valley of the River Coquet (whence comes, each February, the first salmon of the season, presented according to tradition to the Duke of Northumberland).

The most spectacular evidence of the Roman presence in the region—indeed, the finest Roman relic in Britain—is the ruins of Hadrian's Wall. Built to deter the ceaseless raids of the hostile Picts, it ran for seventy-three miles from Bowness on the west to Wallsend on the east, up hill and down dale, a fifteen-foot-high stone rampart punctuated here and there by turrets and forts. It was finished in about A.D. 125. In certain places, where the remains are more or less complete, you can almost see the legionnaires uneasily manning the parapets in this climate so totally different from their own. Walking is the best way to explore the wall, but you can also drive along Route B6318 from Greenhead to Chollerford, pausing at Housesteads Fort, near a crossroads with the charming name Once Brewed; at the park at Chesters and near Haltwhistle. There are interesting carved stones in the small museum at Housesteads, in the larger Museum of Antiquities at Newcastle and in the Abbey Church at Hexham, which holds the tomb of Flavinus, a Roman standard-bearer, as well as rich furnishings of other periods—a Saxon crypt, bishop's chair and chalice, and the famous Acca Cross of 740; two fifteenth-century chantries with vivid stone caricatures and a striking sixteenth-century pulpit.

For an inexpensive lunch, you might try the jolly little Milecastle Inn at Haltwhistle, which makes its own venison sausages; the General Havelock Inn at Haydon Bridge is a bit fancier and provides solid, savory English dishes like vegetable soup, leg of lamb and roast duck, along with delicious pastries.

To the south lie the underpopulated moors, covered with heather and gorse and sheep and cut by lovely valleys. From Haydon Bridge, you can follow B6295 south through Allendale, then turn east along A689 through Weardale for a mile or so before turning south again onto an unnumbered tar road leading from St. John's Chapel across a desolately beautiful fell to Langdon Beck in Teesdale. Turn east again there onto B6277, stopping for a look at High Force, the noblest waterfall in England, where the Tees plunges over a basalt cliff. The word *force* is another echo of Scandinavia; *foss* is the word for waterfall in Norwegian.

Then follow the signs to Barnard Castle, where you will come upon a vast brick pile in the style of a French château, housing the Bowes Museum. Founded by an eccentric ancestor of the present Queen Mother, the museum strikes a jarringly cosmopolitan note after the isolated stone farmhouses, the shepherds and their keen little black-and-white dogs that one encounters in the dales. Its collections of porcelain and of French furniture are noteworthy, and there are fine paintings, too (Sassetta, Goya and El Greco in particular). Owned by the County of Durham, the museum is very well maintained—better than many in London—and has an agreeably unpompous atmosphere.

Although this part of England has fewer stately homes than almost any other, three fine buildings are tucked into rural corners surprisingly close to industrial Newcastle.

One of them, Washington Old Hall, parts of which date from 1183, has a special appeal for Americans; it was the ancestral home of the family of George Washington, or Wessyngton, as the name then was. Jimmy Carter visited it when he came to Britain for a summit conference.

A few miles west (near Rowlands Gill, and well signposted) is one of the most arresting Palladian buildings in England, Gibside Chapel by James Payne, a little-known gem full of crisp classical detail, including box pews and a three-decker pulpit. The chapel is surrounded by a park landscaped by one of Northumberland's most eminent sons, Lancelot "Capability" Brown.

North of Newcastle, near the coast, is the finest secular building in the region, Seaton Delaval Hall, one of the three Baroque masterpieces of Sir John Vanbrugh. Built in 1720, Seaton Delaval Hall is much smaller than the other two, Blenheim and Castle Howard, and much of it was gutted by fire 150 years ago, but it is an immensely impressive, almost theatrical structure. The central block, with octagonal turrets at each corner and huge columns on two façades, is flanked by long wings, one of which contains the most monumental stables that any horse ever lived in; the ashlar stone partitions are worthy of a classical temple, as are the names of the horses that once occupied them: Hercules, Zephyrus . . .

Despite the latitude, gardens flourish in Northumbria. Among the notable spots are Howick Gardens, near Craster, best in the spring, with a profusion of narcissus, and two National Trust properties, Wallington House and Cragside. Wallington is famous for its rocky stream lined with alpine plants and dwarf shrubs and for its ancient fuchsias, some of them with trunks (trunks!) nine inches thick; Cragside is a much more rugged sort of place, a 940-acre tract of lakes, huge outcrops of gray limestone and towering conifers like those of the western United States. Its rhododendrons blaze with intense color in June.

Finally, there are the castles, dozens of them, the legacy of the border wars of the fourteenth century. Raby, near the Bowes Museum, and Warkworth, near Brinkburn Priory, are well worth visiting, but I prefer the redoubtable trio on or near the north coast: Alnwick (pronounced AN-ick), Bamburgh (BAM-boro) and Dunstanburgh (DUN-stan-boro).

This is Percy country, the home of one of England's greatest families, founded by one of the knights who came from Normandy with William the Conqueror. Sir Henry Percy, Shakespeare's Hotspur, was a clansman, and the current leader of the family, the Duke of Northumberland, lives in Alnwick Castle. Built in the eleventh century, restored in the nineteenth, it makes an unforgettable picture when viewed from the bridge across the Aln River. The bridge is decorated with the Percy symbol, a stiff-tailed lion. Canaletto's depiction of the same scene may be seen inside the castle.

Not far north, perched on its crag above waves of dune grass, is Bamburgh, imposing despite clumsy refurbishment, and on a headland near the village of Embleton, from which they are reached by a mile-long footpath, stand the gaunt ruins of Dunstanburgh, immortalized in one of Turner's greatest paintings.

The best way to see all of this is to rent a car, set up a base near Newcastle and make day trips. (You can also take jaunts into the Scottish border country.)

A perfect headquarters is now at hand, thanks to the recent conversion of a fine manor house near Longhorsley into the Linden Hall Hotel. It isn't cheap, but it offers impeccably and imaginatively furnished bedrooms with handsome bathrooms, a staff whose unspoiled country courtesy will delight you and total quiet at the heart of a wooded estate. The food is good, especially when the chef does not overreach himself; the smoked salmon, prepared at nearby Craster over oak fires, is the best I have ever eaten, and the oysters from Orkney are superb. There is also a pub on the property that serves simple regional dishes.

A bigger, less costly, less personal but still attractive alternative is the Gosforth Park Hotel, near Newcastle, and a good budget choice would be the George, which sits beside an old stone bridge at Chollerford, near the wall.

2. *From Buttertubs Pass to Blubberhouse Moor*

YORKSHIRE is an enormous place, and it used to be even bigger. Before the bureaucrats in London redrew the map a decade ago, splitting it into five pieces, the county covered 6,081 square miles, more than twelve percent of England. Sydney Smith, the nineteenth-century wit and divine, wrote that one Yorkshire parish was "so far out of the way that it was actually 12 miles from a lemon." Even today, North Yorkshire, the largest remaining fragment, is the biggest county in the country.

It is also one of the great British beauty spots—less well known to foreigners, perhaps, than the Lake District or the West Country or the Scottish Highlands, but just as beguiling. It could not be more different from the industrial Yorkshire to the south, from Sheffield and its blast furnaces, Doncaster and its coal mines, Leeds and its textile mills. The only things it shares with them is a name and a common passion for the county cricket

47

team. ("My father taught me the difference between fame and immortality," says Michael Parkinson, the British broadcaster. "Fame is appearing on television every week; immortality is playing for Yorkshire and wearing the white rose.")

North Yorkshire is a land of moors and dales, rude stone farmhouses crouching against the wind, with only a wisp of smoke to suggest human life; of quiet villages drawn up neatly around a green; of frowning castles and manor houses that bear witness to a scale of living so lavish that we can scarcely comprehend it. This has been one of the great stages of the drama of English history, trod by Hadrian in the second century after Christ, by the Saxon scholar Alcuin, later a key figure in the Carolingian Renaissance at Aachen, by the marauding Danes, by the brave medieval monks who built their mighty abbeys in lonely if lovely valleys, by the robust Yorkist noblemen from whom the Tudors wrested the throne of England only after thirty bloody years of the Wars of the Roses. Soothed by the pastoral calm of our day, one still hears echoes of a more strident past.

Begin in York, already a capital, as the poet Humbert Wolfe said, when London was "a nameless stew." A train from London will get you there in two hours, and a plane will get you to nearby Leeds in about one; in either case, rent a car on arrival, because many of Yorkshire's treasures lie well off the beaten track. The Minster or cathedral is, of course, York's most celebrated sight, and rightly so; the damage wrought by the fire of 1984 is rapidly being repaired. But you will get a better feeling for the antiquity of the city if you begin with a walk around at least part of the well-restored city walls, about three miles in circumference, which date largely from the fourteenth century; from a point near Monk Bar, a gatehouse where you mount the wall, you will get the best view of the great church.

It is the largest cathedral in Britain other than the much later St. Paul's in London, and it ranks with Lincoln, Canterbury and Durham as the most remarkable medieval survivals. Its vigorously sculptured west front, its more severe but equally exceptional east front, its rood screen with life-size statues of every English king from William the Conqueror to Henry VI, its graphically detailed octagonal Chapter House, with a seemingly unsupported roof, the Roman foundations exposed in its undercroft, even such odd bits as the intricate, modern (1955) astronomical clock—

each would justify a lingering visit in itself. But the glory of York Minster is its Gothic stained glass, which has no equal in Britain and few anywhere. Take a pair of binoculars, without which it is not possible fully to appreciate the great Flamboyant rose window at the west end, the grisaille (gray and white) glass of the thirteenth-century "Five Sisters" window in the north transept, and above all the immense east window, the largest sheet of medieval glazing in the world ("as big as a tennis court," all the guidebooks say).

Take time, too, for a visit to the new Jorvik Viking Center on the street named Coppergate, built over the site of important excavations, with a reconstructed Viking village and an exhibition of artifacts unearthed in the city. Then stroll down the cramped old street known as The Shambles, beyond which lies the six-hundred-year-old Merchant Adventurers' Hall, with splendid timberwork. York also has one of England's finest Palladian buildings, the Assembly Rooms on Blake Street, built by the Earl of Burlington after a grand tour on which he fell in love with the villas of the Veneto. From this and a handful of similar buildings the Palladian style spread throughout the American colonies. The Assembly Rooms are not always open; ask at the tourist office in Exhibition Square, or write ahead, if you can.

The best lunch spot I know is St. William's Restaurant, housed in a Gothic college at the east end of the Minster; two can have a quiche, a sparklingly fresh salad and a bottle of wine for $20. Now, where to stay? I strongly suggest that you pick one place and make it your headquarters, striking out on day trips until your time is exhausted or your curiosity sated. Here are five suggestions:

1. In the southern outskirts of York stands Middlethorpe Hall, a Queen Anne house in cherry-red brick that should have thirty-one rooms open by the time this appears. I first saw the place when it was still being renovated, at a cost of two million dollars; my wife and I were much taken by the elegance of the public rooms on a return visit, and whereas neither the food nor the bedrooms quite attain the same standard, Middlethorpe is clearly the best in the region.

2. At Pool-in-Wharfedale, just outside North Yorkshire because it is on the "wrong" side of the little River Wharfe, Michael Gill has added four pretty bedrooms (one, for instance, with

modern décor, one in the Indian style) to the Pool Court restaurant he has run in a late Georgian house for more than a decade. Pool Court's nouvelle cuisine is excellent if sometimes too rich, and the wine list spectacular (but be prepared to pay prices not much lower than those in the United States). The Box Tree, with two Michelin stars—excellent food but a distressingly precious ambience—is just down the road at Ilkley.

3. Farther north, in Kirkby Fleetham, in a blissfully quiet location beside a Knights Templar church dating from 1140, lies Kirkby Fleetham Hall. It is less expensive than the first two hotels and it offers outstanding wines at fair prices. It is also less stylish; furniture is rather ineptly placed and the service is disorganized, but the predominantly English cooking is first-rate, and David and Chris Grant, the owners, couldn't be nicer. A good choice, I'd say, for those who would enjoy the illusion of staying in a slightly loose-jointed private house. The maze of lanes leading to the place is baffling, so ask for their map when you write for a reservation.

4 and 5. If the budget won't quite stretch to cover any of those, you might try two slightly more modest places: the Devonshire Arms at Bolton Abbey, one of the manifold holdings of the Duke of Devonshire, and the cozy Lastingham Grange Hotel in the unspoiled village of that name, to which a reader in Chapel Hill, North Carolina (!) first directed my attention.

With a good map in front of you, you can now get down to planning your sorties into the countryside. There is no dearth of choices.

One trip should certainly take you into the rude landscapes of the western part of the county, much of which is covered by the Yorkshire Dales National Park. The high country is bleak, a special taste that I happen to share with James Herriot, the veterinarian author of *All Creatures Great and Small*. He says that "it is up there on the empty moors with the curlews crying that I have been able to find peace and tranquillity of mind." In summer you will see not only curlews but lapwings and emperor moths; in autumn you will see the red grouse and smell the heather; in winter, as ever, you will see the sheep, which, as they slogged through the breast-high snowdrifts, reminded my wife of camels crossing the sand.

The valleys are more welcoming: soft vistas of woods and water and hills, punctuated here and there by an abbey or a castle. Try Wensleydale, famous for its cheese, stopping at Bolton Castle, where Mary, Queen of Scots, was imprisoned for six months; at Aysgarth, with its sixteenth-century bridge and its waterfalls, and at West Burton, one of the perennial contenders for the most beautiful village in Britain. They are only a few miles apart. Or head for Swaledale, a lot wilder, with the ruined but still awe-inspiring Richmond Castle clinging to the cliff face above the foaming river. Or Wharfedale, with charming Bolton Abbey, whose church has been used as a place of worship since 1170, and the wonderfully named Blubberhouse Moor, and one of the better pubs in the Dales, the Black Horse at Grassington.

To get a proper picture of the area, you must cross from one dale to another, and the classic route is the steep but quite safe road across Buttertubs Pass linking Hawes in Wensleydale with Thwaite in Swaledale. The summit is only 1,726 feet up, but it feels higher.

On another day, you might visit little Ripon Cathedral, noted for its pristine Saxon crypt and for the spirited carvings on the bottoms of the seats in the choir (the English call them misericords). In the same neighborhood are Newby Hall, which was remodeled by the great Scottish architect Robert Adam, and where you will enjoy his boldly original use of color inside as much as the brightly hued gardens outside; the tree-lined streets of Harrogate, with good shopping; and Harewood House, a mile or so south of the county border but too good to miss—ceilings by Adam, park by Capability Brown, furniture by Chippendale and paintings by El Greco, Tintoretto, Turner and many, many others.

The high point of that day could be a visit to Fountains Abbey, especially if you follow the signs not to the abbey but to Studley, park your car and walk. The path leads along the little River Skell, past small temples and statuary put there entirely to enhance the view, until suddenly you round a bend and see in the distance perhaps the most romantic sight in Britain: the abbey ruins standing upon perfectly groomed lawns.

Built between 1135 and 1526 by Cistercian monks, followers of the austere rule of Saint Bernard, Fountains offers as clear a picture as we now have of how a medieval abbey worked. Take your time, and study especially the long, vaulted dormitory, the eleven-bay nave and the Chapel of Nine Altars.

A third day could happily be spent along the southern edge of the North York Moors National Park, with a detour onto the unearthly moors themselves if you wish. If you have time, you might look at Pickering and Helmsley castles, two more fascinating feudal strongholds, but by no means miss the ruins of Rievaulx Abbey, another Cistercian foundation, tucked into a deep, forgotten valley alongside a sleepy village. The ruins have a graceful choir, which is seen to good advantage from Rievaulx Terrace, laid out and adorned with neoclassical temples in the eighteenth century to satisfy the longing of that era for the picturesque. Nor, of course, will you want to miss Castle Howard, the monumental seat of one of England's grandest families, near Malton. It was there, in and around the vast Baroque pile designed by Sir John Vanbrugh with the assistance of the equally eminent Nicholas Hawksmoor, that *Brideshead Revisited* was filmed. But Castle Howard had no need of television to seal its fame; a monument to the ostentatious taste of another time, it has long been one of the most visited stately homes in England, loved not only for its epic proportions and its dramatic façades but also for its Great Hall, which soars upward for eighty feet and yet retains a domestic scale.

So astonished was Horace Walpole when he first gazed upon the house and its elaborate grounds that he wrote: "Nobody informed me that I should at one view see a palace, a town, a fortified city, temples on high places, woods worthy of being each a metropolis for the Druids, the noblest lawn in the world fenced in by half the horizon, and a mausoleum that would tempt one to be buried alive; in short, I have seen gigantic palaces before, but never a sublime one."

Try to time this swing, if you can, so that you can have dinner at the Plough Inn, a simple whitewashed pub in Fadmoor, near Rievaulx, where a talented self-taught cook named Katherine Brown provides copious meals at unbelievably low prices. It is open for dinner from Tuesday through Saturday, and you *must* book.

If you have more time, there are still other areas to be explored—the region to the east and southeast of York, for example, most of which is now technically in the county of Humberside. A few targets: Burton Agnes Hall, near Bridlington, a red-brick Elizabethan house by Robert Smythson, the greatest architect of his day, with a remarkable oak staircase; Selby Abbey, one of the best-preserved monastic churches in Britain, with many good Norman elements; and the glorious Minster at otherwise eminently forgettable Beverley, fine enough to rival many cathedrals, and especially notable for the Percy tomb (1305).

Or, if you are a Brontë fan, you could drop down into West Yorkshire to Haworth, south of Ilkley, to see the old parsonage where Charlotte (*Jane Eyre*) and Emily (*Wuthering Heights*) grew up under the affectionate and watchful care of devoted servants; nearby is the Black Bull pub, where their brother, Bramwell, went to drink and to pick fights.

The best part I cannot tell you about. The best part, for you, is the village more beautiful than West Burton, the ruined abbey more evocative than Fountains, the valley more inspiring than Swaledale that you will come upon as you wander.

3. *Bath and Beyond*

THERE is no shortage of classic excursions from London. The paths that lead to Windsor Castle and Hampton Court, to Oxford and the Cotswolds, to Cambridge and to Stratford-upon-Avon are well worn. Millions of people have made those jaunts, and most have been delighted.

But if you want to try something a bit different, and you have two days and a night at your disposal, I would suggest that you head due west from London for an outing that combines several thousand years of history with undulating countryside and a couple of charming villages. Good eating and atmospheric drinking, too.

About nine o'clock in the morning, drive past Harrods, along the Great West Road and onto the M4 motorway. Follow your nose past Heathrow Airport and across Berkshire and Wiltshire to Exit 18; there, turn south onto highway A46 and follow it into Bath. The trip should take just over two hours. (The high-speed train from London's Paddington Station reaches Bath in about an hour and a half. There are two trains an hour.)

Bath has been there, astride the Avon, clinging to the hillsides, for more than two thousand years. The Romans, who made it one of their principal colonial spas, called the place Aquae Sulis. The city's golden era came, however, in the late eighteenth century, when a succession of gifted architects gave it a Georgian splendor and order—a kind of serenity in stone—that happily survives.

"This is not the capital of a vanished empire," says Jan Morris, the writer, who used to live there, "or the seat of a discredited dynasty, like Venice or Vienna. Bath's function was never very significant. People came here first to cure their agues, then to have fun. Yet a transient flowering of fashion has left behind one of the loveliest cities in the world, ironically preserved by its loss of glory."

The place to begin is the Pump Room, built at the end of the eighteenth century to provide a comfortable place for visitors to drink the curative local waters. It no longer serves that exact function; the stuff may still be good for nerves, gout and so on, but it has also caused several bouts of illness, so the tap has been temporarily turned off.

If there on a weekday morning, sit at one of the tables in the vast room, with its Corinthian columns, and order coffee. You will find yourself surrounded by a vanishing culture of innocence: a string trio on the stage, with potted palms on the balcony above their heads, playing show tunes; a brace of elderly gentlewomen at the next table, complaining about change; and from his niche on the back wall, Beau Nash watching imperturbably.

It was Richard Nash who ordered the building of the Bath that you will see, with its classically confident façades in golden stone. A dandy and a gambler who wore a big white hat, he made Bath the favorite spa of British society. For a decade or so in the 1730s and 1740s, his "court" was more popular than the King's.

Through a Pump Room doorway and down a few steps lie the remnants of the Roman Baths, which rank with Hadrian's Wall as physical evidence of the Roman presence in Britain.

Like those who come from abroad to live in Britain in modern times, the Romans were plagued by the climate, and they found Bath's warm waters good for chest ills and rheumatism. The great lead-lined pool is still there, filled with water, and so is evidence of the engineering marvels that enabled the Roman centurions to relieve their aching legs with the ancient equivalents of our Turkish baths (hot and moist) and Finnish baths (hot and dry).

Recent digs have filled the museum with intriguing artifacts and greatly enhanced the impact of a visit to the baths. Expertly displayed within the excavated area itself are a portion of the portico of the temple of Sulis Minerva, a local deity, which includes a striking representation of a Gorgon's head; a relief of a hound carrying a stag, and a superbly wrought bronze bust of Minerva.

For lunch, you might try the Canary at 3 Queen Street, which does a good Somerset rarebit, or the Moon and Sixpence wine bar at 6A Broad Street, with a good warm-weather buffet; both are close by. Rather grander possibilities are the Hole in the Wall, perhaps Britain's best restaurant in the 1960s, now enjoying a revival under Tim and Sue Cumming, and the restaurant of the Priory Hotel, of which more later.

After lunch, explore Georgian Bath. You can do it by car, but walking is better because it provides a sense of the block-by-block rhythm of the architecture and not a blurred impression of major monuments. See the Assembly Rooms, redecorated in period style by Oliver Messel after World War II, with a comprehensive and charming costume museum, and the elegant Pulteney Bridge by Robert Adam, with shops along its sides, like the Ponte Vecchio in Florence. The bridge should be viewed from the riverside promenade.

Bath's enduring glory is the crescents, an architectural form developed there. Do not miss the Royal Crescent, one of the great set pieces in Europe, a semiellipse more than six hundred feet long, punctuated by one hundred Ionic pilasters, or the serpentine Lansdowne Crescent, melodramatically set on a hillside, or the Circus, the masterpiece of its designer, John Wood.

The Circus has three crescents, and because only three roads enter it, one always faces a façade on approaching—an arrangement that assures a vivid impression. One should walk all the way around the Circus to view the hundreds of stone ornaments, each different, above the first-floor windows, and the plaques marking the houses where Gainsborough, Pitt the Prime Minister, and Clive of India, the soldier-statesman, once lived.

Bath and its environs boast the biggest concentration of fine hotels anywhere in provincial Britain. The grandest is the Royal Crescent, installed in the center of the great colonnade, which has been restored to its full Georgian glory. The sweeping horseshoe staircase, the chandeliers, the marble fireplaces more than make up for slightly lackluster meals. The Priory, set in pretty grounds a mile outside of the city, has a traditional atmosphere and improving cooking. Farther south is a trio of star establishments—Ston Easton Park at Ston Easton, perhaps the most stunningly renovated country-house hotel in Britain, rather formal, with good English food but less satisfactory French dishes; Hunstrete House at Hunstrete, whose pretty chintzes, pastel wallpapers and fresh flowers show Thea Dupays's sure hand as a decorator; and my own favorite in the region, the Homewood Park Hotel at Hinton Charterhouse. Stephen and Penny Ross, who own it, had less to start with than the others; this is a solid Victorian house rather than a mansion. But they have fitted it out most attractively, he cooks with great panache, especially when it comes to fish and sweets, and together they give the place a relaxed warmth that my wife and I find highly congenial. You must book early for any of these places.

Next morning, head south on the A39 toward Wells. If you start by 9:30, you will have time for a quick look at Prior Park, which Nikolaus Pevsner called the most ambitious Palladian villa in England. The exterior can always be inspected, the chapel at certain hours. But do not dally; the goal is to reach the village of Chewton Mendip, seventeen miles away, by 10:30.

Just beyond the village, a road leads off to the right toward Cheddar. Take it, then turn right almost immediately into a farm lane. The small cluster of buildings ahead is a rarity—one of the very few places left that make Cheddar cheese in the traditional cylindrical shape by painstaking traditional methods.

Cheddar is made all over the world, far from its native Somerset; even there, it is made mostly in factories. The real thing is nutty, creamy and utterly unlike the soap-textured blocks sold in supermarkets. The proprietor of the farm at Chewton Mendip, Viscount Chewton, says the factories "are just preserving milk."

Every day of the year, between 10:30 and 11:30 A.M., visitors can see the genuine article being made. Jamie Chewton, the forty-five-year-old Viscount, may well show you the place himself,

56

clad for work in jeans and checked shirt. A little shop sells cheese for about $2 a pound, and it will export whole cheeses.

Ten minutes farther down the A39, and you are in Wells. It is called a city, under British law, because it has a cathedral, but it is actually a small town, huddled around its magnificent, mostly thirteenth-century masterpiece. The collection of statues on the west front, many of them sadly eroded by the weather, has been restored in the last decade, and is once again one of the finest collections of medieval sculpture in Europe.

After visiting the cathedral—note especially the unique scissors arch built to shore up the tower—and strolling in its grounds, visitors have a choice: if they can't hold off the hunger pangs for a while, they should take the B3139 and the 366 to Norton St. Philip (about fifteen miles) and the George Inn. It dates to 1223 and has a pretty courtyard, a collection of copper pots in the eaves and handsome brass beer spigots. Sandwiches, good salads and cheese, several types of beer and an honest atmosphere make for a fine lunch.

If thirst and hunger can be kept at bay, one should continue on the A39 to Glastonbury, five miles from Wells, with its ruined Romanesque abbey. Founded on the spot where, according to tradition, Joseph of Arimathea deposited the chalice from the Last Supper, the abbey was a center of eleventh-century enlightenment. It soars above the neatly clipped grass of its park and retains much of its majesty.

To reach Norton St. Philip from Glastonbury, follow the A361, the A36 and the B3110. Then, after lunch, take the A366, the A36 back into the outskirts of Bath and the A4 east to a pub called Cross Keys. Turn left onto a small road with regular signs pointing to Castle Combe. It is a delightful ride through rolling fields dotted with cattle.

Castle Combe is a jigsaw-puzzle painter's vision of an English village, and it is inevitably thronged with tourists on weekends. But go anyway. Laid out in a valley alongside a rushing stream, with slate-roofed stone cottages and picturesque shop signs, it is one of those places that charm regardless of crowds.

Castle Combe is used to a bit of hubbub. It was once a weaving center (some say the first blanket was made there), and a few years ago it was used as the set for the movie *Dr. Doolittle*. Its imposing manor house, now a hotel where you might take tea, once belonged to Sir John Fastolf, on whom Shakespeare is thought to have based Falstaff.

But perhaps you don't feel like ending your day with a dose of quaintness; don't worry, it happens to all of us. Visit instead the American Museum, the best of its kind in Europe, which is laid out in the manor house at Claverton, just before you reach the Bath suburbs on the A36. There you can wander through whole rooms from American houses of the seventeenth to the nineteenth centuries, including a Shaker room and a Pennsylvania Dutch room. There are particularly good collections of quilts and folk art, and, if you are as lucky as we were one day, you might even see Britons dressed up as Yanks and Rebs, staging a mock battle from our Civil War on the broad lawns sweeping down to the Avon.

4. Nine Hundred Years of English Building

B RADFORD-ON-AVON is one among thousands of English towns. It is known to few people—to far fewer, certainly, than Shakespeare's home, Stratford-upon-Avon, or the industrial town in Yorkshire that is also called Bradford. This Bradford lies at the western extremity of Wiltshire, just southeast of Bath, on a river that has nothing in common (except its name) with that familiar to Anne Hathaway.

But you will find Bradford-on-Avon in all the books about European architectural history, alongside such more famous places as Autun and Monreale and Aachen. The reason is simple: This provincial town of eight thousand souls is one of the treasure troves of English building, one of the rare places where the amateur can see the kinds of structures that Englishmen have chosen to erect over the last nine hundred years and more.

It is also a good place around which to build a second visit to that corner of England where Wiltshire, Somerset and Avon come together. Having seen Bath and Wells and Glastonbury, most people crave a return trip, with a few new sights thrown in for spice. You might include on your schedule a trio of fine country mansions—Longleat, the seat of the Marquess of Bath, which is probably the greatest Renaissance house in England; magnificent Wilton House, with its famous double cube room hung with Van Dycks; and Bowood House, which has a superb park by Capability Brown (especially lovely in daffodil season) and an orangery designed by Robert Adam. Also within reach are Salisbury Cathedral, whose slender spire is so well known from Constable's paintings; prehistoric Stonehenge and a similar, less-frequented but far more impressive monument called Avebury Circle; and the breath-taking gardens at Stourhead, laid out around a lake whose shore is dotted with Palladian temples. Start, however, at Bradford-on-Avon, so you don't risk missing it.

You enter the town, no matter where you are coming from, by descending toward the river and toward the seventeenth-century town bridge, which incorporates two thirteenth-century arches. It is one of the few bridges left in Europe with a chapel built into it; the chapel was later converted into a lockup.

Leave your car in the parking lot nearby, cross the footbridge, and you will soon find yourself outside the Church of St. Laurence. This is a relic of that dark and little-understood episode in English history between the departure of the Romans and the arrival of the Normans—a genuine Saxon artifact, of a quality duplicated in only two or three other places. Astonishingly, it was lost for hundreds of years, obscured by later buildings huddled around it, its original purpose unknown because of its conversion to ordinary domestic use.

It was "found" in 1856 by a local vicar of archeological bent. Today it stands revealed, a reminder, with its dark and tiny Romanesque nave, only twenty-five feet long, of the defensive posture of Christianity in the Middle Ages, of the church as sanctuary in the most literal sense. It is not a subtle building, nor a very delicate one. But its external "shadow" arcades, its round arches and its reliefs of angels are reminders of the power of relatively primitive art, here making its appeal across the nearly thirteen centuries that have passed since this stern little building was begun by Saint Aldhelm, sometime around A.D. 700.

Not far away, along the road to Frome (pronounced Froom), stands Barton Farm, with its tithe barn, perhaps the best in Britain. This is a kind of agricultural cathedral, 168 feet long, of stone with bays crossed by arches made of naturally curved pieces of oak, dating from the early fourteenth century. Here were stored the tithes, or offerings, contributed by local people to the great nunnery at Shaftesbury.

Kingston House, also known as "The Hall," is a gem of the Renaissance, built about 1600. William Dean Howells, the novelist, described it as being "full of Italian feeling in an English environment," and others have called it the small-scale counterpart of Longleat. Unhappily for visitors, Kingston House is not generally open to the public, but people in the area report that its pretty garden can usually be visited in season; they advise making inquiries locally—at the house itself or at the tourist office, or even at one of the town pubs.

But Bradford is at bottom a Georgian town, inevitably influenced by the great Palladian buildings of Bath. The town is smack in the middle of the limestone belt that runs through England from the Channel to the Humber in Yorkshire, and the stone has shaped the look of the place.

It is pleasant to stroll through the town, picking out Georgian buildings on every block; there are so many that they seem commonplace, serving as houses or offices or whatever, without any self-conscious charm or artiness. One of the outstanding examples is the Palladian wing added in 1734 to the old gabled house of the Yerburys, a family of rich clothiers. The architect was John Wood the elder, designer of Bath's Royal Crescent.

This building is named Belcombe Court, and it was a favorite of the late, much-loved English architectural historian Alec Clifton-Taylor. On a BBC broadcast not long before he died, he called it "a very proud building, wearing a great air of authority, with a big pediment rising above a strong entablature supported by smooth Ionic pilasters." Wood himself thought the pilasters the best he had ever done. To see this building and others like it is to be reminded of a robustly self-assured Britain, one where the most far-seeing of men little dreamed that the loss of the American colonies lay less than half a century in the future.

There is much more to be seen amidst the abundance of pale yellow Georgian limestone—an aqueduct dating from 1804, for example, and a wealth of Victorian industrial architecture. It is a place for wandering, and your rambles will be helped by the leaflet put out by the local Preservation Trust. You can buy a copy at the public library, at the side of the car park not far from the town bridge.

I would make my headquarters at an idiosyncratic hotel called Beechfield House, which lies at Beanacre, only about ten minutes' drive from Bradford. Peter Crawford-Rolt, the owner, also presides in the kitchen, and his menu refreshingly mingles French, English and Caribbean influences, the last reflecting his time working at island resorts. The vegetables, which come from a vast kitchen garden, are among the best on offer anywhere in Britain. Mr. Crawford-Rolt and his wife, Gillian, create something close to a house-party mood, and in good weather they stage barbecues around their swimming pool.

Lacock, an unspoiled village completely owned by the National Trust, is just up the road. For longer trips, the Crawford-Rolts will put you in touch with Shaw Classic Cars of Melksham, who provide chauffeur-driven vintage Rolls-Royces, Buicks and other vehicles.

5. *Chiffon and Rubber Boots*

JOHN Christie was an eccentric, strong-willed millionaire landowner, a former science master at Eton, who married Audrey Mildmay, a soprano who had sung with the Carl Rosa Opera Company, the rather tattered troupe then struggling to keep the operatic flame burning in England. They lived at Glyndebourne, a manor house tucked into a particularly verdant fold of the Sussex downs, a few miles from the Channel. In the twilight of empire, the grand aristocratic flourish was still alive and well in the land, and John Christie decided to add a little opera house to his country seat so that Audrey could sing there.

Almost by chance, he was able to secure as music director the German conductor Fritz Busch, who had been music director of the Staatsoper in Dresden, who had left his homeland because of the rise of Hitler and who took the job, he later confessed, because he thought the first season at Glyndebourne would also be the last. (His brother, Adolf, the great violinist, emigrated to the United States and founded, along with his son-in-law, Rudolf Serkin, the Marlboro School of Music.) With Busch as producer came Carl Ebert, another German, a protégé of Max

Reinhardt, and, a year or so later, Rudolf Bing, just beginning his journey from Austria to the Metropolitan Opera in New York.

That was in 1934, and the new company—the Glyndebourne Festival Opera—produced two operas by Mozart, *Le Nozze di Figaro* and *Così fan Tutte*. In many ways, they represented a revolution. They were sung in Italian, in a day when they were still being sung in German in Vienna and in English in London; they were full of minutely studied musical and dramatic detail, the result of painstaking rehearsal; and they made a point of carefully integrated ensemble singing rather than focusing exclusively on the stars (among whom was Miss Mildmay).

"Of course," wrote the eminent philosopher Sir Isaiah Berlin in a reminiscent essay, "Munich, Vienna, Covent Garden have served Mozart nobly, and above all Salzburg, then and now. But I wish to testify that for me, and I believe I speak for a good many of us in this country, the idea of what an opera by Mozart is and can be, was altered—indeed, transformed—by Glyndebourne and it alone."

Fifty years have passed, a global war has been fought and standards of operatic production have risen everywhere. But Glyndebourne remains (dare one say it?) unique. In the jubilee summer of 1984, *Figaro* and *Così*, Glyndebourne's all-time favorites, were once again on stage in Sussex, the ideal of an integrated company survives untarnished, and the Christie family remains, still living in the big house and still in charge of the festival, in the person of John and Audrey's son George, who turned fifty that year and whom Queen Elizabeth II knighted in homage to Glyndebourne's half-century.

There is much more to Glyndebourne than the productions themselves (and the cynics like to say that most of the wealthy patrons who go there are not really all that interested in Mozart and Rossini). Bernard Levin, the critic, calls the place "the enchanted garden." Above all, there is the sense of timeless occasion—the afternoon trip down from London on the train or by car, men in dinner jackets and women in long dresses at lunchtime, the precurtain Pimm's in the walled gardens adjacent to the theater, and especially the picnics in the broader lakeside gardens during the seventy-five-minute intermission. Carrying wicker hampers, folding chairs and tables, wine coolers and all the other paraphernalia of the quintessentially English picnic, the operagoers eat their dinner while black-and-white cows watch from the pastures around them. I have seen silver candelabra on some of those tables, and whole partridges and great slabs of beef, and, England being England, I have seen people trying to eat with a fork in one hand and an umbrella in the other. One night I even saw a woman in a chiffon evening gown and rubber boots.

But just as the tennis is good at Wimbledon and the racing good at Ascot, those other social fixtures of the English summer, the opera is good at Glyndebourne, and the people in charge never allow themselves to be lulled into thinking that they are staging a garden party. The people in charge, in addition to Sir George, are Bernard Haitink, the Dutch-born musical director; Sir Peter Hall of the National Theatre, the artistic director; and Brian Dickie, the general administrator.

"The thing that makes Glyndebourne different," Sir Peter once told me, "is that they give you time. People here care very much, they try very hard, like amateurs in the old sense of the word. We rehearse for weeks, not days, and anyone who wants to sing here must stay here—none of this jetting in and out that so destroys productions in many houses. We don't do instant opera."

Although the pay is very low (Sir Peter estimates that a singer earns a tenth as much at Glyndebourne as for a similar engagement at Salzburg, for example), the tradition of careful preparation, as well as the ambience of the place, the interweaving of professional and personal lives in a bucolic setting, lures good voices here. Many use their stay to learn new roles that they will sing later in major capitals. An example is Maria Ewing, the Detroit-born soprano who is Sir Peter's third wife; she sang Carmen here before doing the role at the Met. Miss Ewing said she found the atmosphere at Glyndebourne ideal—"serious but never heavy, relaxed but never casual, even if it seems so."

Glyndebourne started with Mozart and has stayed with him. But over the years it has added Strauss, Rossini (especially under Vittorio Gui, who succeeded Busch) and others; it broke new ground with a series of Baroque operas by Monteverdi and Cavalli, a series brought to a climax with *The Coronation of Poppea*, all conducted by Raymond Leppard. Sir Peter now plans to devote himself to Verdi, a composer more associated with the grandeur of huge stages than with the intimacy of Glyndebourne. He began in 1985 with *Falstaff*. He argues that the Italian's early and middle works were in fact written for theaters about the size of the one here, which seats 830, and says he hopes to "strip away some of the usual grandiloquence while maintaining the genuinely heroic qualities." Like many of his predecessors, he speaks feelingly of the possibilities available to a director when the audience can "see the eyes of the actors" and thus relate directly to the emotions that they portray.

Ever since it began, Glyndebourne has had a reputation for discovering young singers. Among those who sang here early in their careers, long before they gained international renown, were Elisabeth Söderström, Luciano Pavarotti, Birgit Nilsson, Joan Sutherland, Mirella Freni, Ileana Cotrubas and Janet Baker. Miss Baker started in the chorus. The tradition continues, as it must, for the festival cannot afford to pay the prices demanded by most international stars (although some still return, such as Miss Söderström and Frederica von Stade, and, in 1987, Lucia Popp). Of late, it has looked to the United States for much of its talent because, as Brian Dickie commented, "it is a tremendously fertile hunting ground, with good young singers in great profusion, far better trained than most of those one hears in France or even in Italy."

The day has long since passed when Glyndebourne was the extension of one man's wallet. John Christie personally met the entire prewar deficit of about £100,000—$140,000 at the current exchange rate but vastly more at the time. Today every performance is sold out and there is no deficit, and that has been achieved even though Glyndebourne is the only opera house in Europe that gets not a penny in government subsidies. It meets ninety-two percent of its costs from the box office, the annual program and other direct sources, including the bars. The other eight percent comes from corporate sponsorship and gifts. On the whole, says Mr. Dickie, "we are happy to depend upon our own success, because it means we can do things on our own terms, at our own pace, without having to put up with people who deign to give us two days of rehearsal time."

But it also means that ticket costs are high; an orchestra seat costs fifty-five dollars, which in British terms is a great deal of money. Glyndebourne is often attacked as the province of an elite, which it most surely is. Almost eighty-five percent of the tickets go to the 5,000 individual members and 250 corporate members of the Festival Society—there is an endless waiting list for memberships—and that means there are only about 125 for the general public for each performance.

Most of those are allocated by lot. If you would like to try your luck, write to the Glyndebourne Festival Opera, Lewes, East Sussex, sometime around the first of the year, asking them to send you the following summer's program. Then make your choice and send off a second letter. Perhaps you will succeed; I have a suspicion, never confirmed, that foreigners are sometimes given a break in the lottery. If you do win, try to book a room at the Priory Hotel, Rushlake Green, East Sussex, a lovingly restored fifteenth-century building about forty-five minutes' drive from Glyndebourne. Lavish bedrooms, a wonderful wine list and superlative picnic hampers—including crystal and bone china, of course—make it the perfect complement to the opera.

Why has Glyndebourne never been duplicated elsewhere? "I haven't the vaguest idea," replied Sir George, a self-effacing man whom every member of the company calls by his first name. "But I do think you need a family, because that keeps it from becoming too institutional." The lack of the heavy institutional hand is nicely symbolized in Sussex by the fact that there are no trash bins in the gardens; the picnickers take away every cork, every bit of aluminum foil, when they pack up to return to the opera house after the intermission.

6. *More than Grit*

FOR more than a century Glasgow was the second-largest city in the British Empire. The empire and Glasgow's days of glory are only memories now, and the typical foreign visitor to Scotland is more likely to head for Edinburgh or the Highlands, in search of the picturesque, than to tarry in the somewhat sooty precincts of Clydeside. In part, that is Glasgow's own fault; perhaps the greatest of all Victorian cities, it was so thoroughly vandalized during the late 1950s and 1960s by the urban renewers and the lumpen architects that its more desolate quarters are often used by film makers as a backdrop for pictures set in the Soviet Union or East Germany.

But the traveler who seeks to know Scotland and the Scots, and not simply to be charmed, would be well advised to set aside a couple of days for Glasgow—for the chip-on-the-shoulder vigor of its people, for the revelations of its architecture and for the unexpected richness of its cultural life. To these can now be added an extraordinary new attraction, the Burrell Collection, which was justly described by Peter Wilson, the late chairman of Sotheby's, as "one of the most remarkable assemblages of works of art ever brought together by one man" and certainly the best of its kind in Britain.

Sir William Burrell was a wealthy Glasgow shipowner with a lifelong passion for collecting. He started collecting at fifteen and grew into a kind of Scottish Hearst, some of whose castoffs he bought at bargain prices; a late twelfth-century portal from the church at Montron, near Château-Thierry, cost Hearst £4,500 and crossed the Atlantic twice before Burrell scooped it up for a mere £550. Ever the canny buyer, the Scotsman on another occasion picked up a fourteenth-century Chinese vase, now worth at least $400,000, for less than $1,000. Such bargains enabled him to compete with Morgan and Frick and Widener, even though his fortune was dwarfed by those of the Americans. By the time he died, in 1958, at the age of ninety-six, Sir William had assembled more than eight thousand treasures, which he left to the city along with a substantial endowment.

Unfortunately, his will specified a location for the projected building that proved unworkable, and the collection spent decades in storage around Glasgow. But finally, after lengthy negotiations with the trustees and enormous difficulties in raising the requisite thirty million dollars, a museum was built in Pollok Country Park, three miles from the center of the city, and it was opened by Queen Elizabeth II in 1983. Its completion, says Sir John Rothenstein, the eminent English art historian, "gives the city an honored place among the great art centers of Europe."

The building itself, designed by a little-known English architect named Barry Gasson, is a real joy. At its core are three rooms from Sir William's home, Hutton Castle, in Berwick-on-Tweed; there are also small galleries for objets d'art, and fifteen medieval and Renaissance stone doorways have been incorporated into the structure. Wrapped around all of this is a relatively open, glass-walled space devoted to ancient civilizations, to the Orient, to European paintings and to tapestries.

On two sides, the surrounding lawns and trees seem almost to invade the museum; on a third, the glass wall is used for the highly effective display of stained glass.

The stained glass (including twelfth-century fragments from Abbot Suger's great cathedral at St-Denis, the first important Gothic building) runs to seven hundred items, one of the world's finest collections, and only the Metropolitan Museum of New York has comparable holdings of Gothic tapestries (including major items from Germany, Switzerland, France and the Low Countries).

But it is the scope of the collection that sets it apart. Sir William assembled an astonishing range of masterpieces in many areas—glowing Virgins by Bellini and Memling; a gently charming *Judgment of Paris*, attributed to Domenico Veneziano, the fifteenth-century Italian painter, by whom only twelve pictures are known to have survived, but more likely by a contemporary, Pesellino, according to recent scholarship; a Rembrandt self-portrait; substantial collections of works by Degas and Manet; fine Chou Dynasty pieces and Neolithic burial urns; a magnificent twelfth-century bronze, perhaps German, showing three soldiers holding kite-shaped shields; a Babylonian terra-cotta lion's head; carpets, furniture, porcelain, pottery, jade, gold, silver and glass. Out of Sir William's legacy and other funds, the collection bought the Warwick Vase in 1979 for half a million dollars to keep it from going to the Metropolitan. It, too, can now be seen at the Pollok Country Park, a colossal marble antique, weighing more than eight tons, discovered in Rome in 1771 and so coveted over the next century that it was the first item Napoleon planned to plunder had he succeeded in conquering Britain.

Despite recurrent cash crises, the determinedly egalitarian City Council has decreed that admission to the Burrell Collection be free to all; it is open from 10:00 A.M. to 5:00 P.M. Monday to Saturday, 2:00 to 5:00 P.M. on Sundays, and closed only on Christmas and New Year's Day.

Present-day Glasgow is a hard-drinking, proletarian town, pungent in its humor, and left-wing in its politics since the 1920s. With its great industries, notably shipbuilding, in probably terminal decline, it faces appalling economic problems. Yet its indomitable people, Protestants and Catholics, orange and green, give it a yeastiness foreign to much of Britain; one Glaswegian of my acquaintance describes his fellow townspeople as "stubborn, individualistic, a little bit pushy and relentlessly straightforward."

This was the city of James Watt, the great mechanical engineer; of Adam Smith; of Alexander Fleming, discoverer and developer of penicillin; of Sir Thomas Lipton, who made a fortune selling tea and spent it in vain pursuit of the America's Cup; of Lord Reith, the creator of the BBC; and of the master builders from whose yards came the *Cutty Sark* and the *Lusitania* and the *Queen Elizabeth* 2. It was the city of the Gorbals, once famous as Europe's worst slum. But it was above all the city that epitomized the self-assurance of the Victorian age, and even now, as Jonathan Meades, an associate editor of *The Tatler*, conceded in a generally baleful piece not long ago, "it has a vestigial splendor which the cretins have not quite destroyed."

That splendor is visible in the massive, grimy building of Sir Gilbert Scott's Gothic revival University of Glasgow (1864); in the buildings around George Square, which Maurice Lindsay, the Glaswegian author and critic, calls "a primer in Victorian excess and elegance"; and in the work of Alexander "Greek" Thomson, who showed in the Caledonia Road Church and the St. Vincent Street Church, as well as in his row houses along Great Western Terrace, one of which once belonged to Burrell, just how forceful the neoclassical architecture of the second half of the nineteenth century could be. There is no better place to sense the prosperity, the solidity and the confidence verging on smugness that characterized British life just a century ago.

Even then, however, there was a revolutionary spirit stirring in Glasgow. Its greatest exemplar was Charles Rennie Mackintosh, Britain's most original twentieth-century architect and one of the principal founders of the Modern Movement. Once scorned by his native city, then forgotten, Mackintosh has become a cult figure in the last decade, and fortunately a number of his buildings, with their majestic outlines lightened by decorative detail in iron and stained glass, have survived. So has a great deal of his elegant furniture, decorated with stylized floral motifs, delicately inlaid, unbelievably "modern" in the clarity of its lines.

After a long struggle, the new Mackintosh wing of the Hunterian Art Gallery, which is part of the University of Glasgow, has been completed and is open to the public. For a time, it appeared that to pay the last installment of the construction costs, the university would have to sell part of its collection of paintings and other works by James Abbott McNeill Whistler, which is equaled only by the holdings of the Freer Gallery in Washington. Fortunately, the sale was averted at the last moment.

The Mackintosh wing has posters, stained glass and other materials designed by Mackintosh and his wife, Margaret MacDonald. It also has on display the guest bedroom suite from the house at 78 Derngate in Northampton; the architect designed Mondrianesque furniture and textiles for the house in 1916.

But the centerpiece of the wing is a reconstruction of the interior of another house, at 78 Southpark Avenue in Glasgow, where the Mackintoshes lived from 1906 to 1914. The house was used by the university as a staff residence until 1963, when it was demolished. All the furniture and fittings were removed, however, and they have now been reassembled within the new wing. It is a remarkable series of five rooms, characterized by the architect's skillful manipulation of light and space and especially his use of whites and off-whites in the drawing room. The furniture, which constitutes Mackintosh's own collection of his work between 1896 and 1906, is an equally stunning display of geometric versatility, lightened by the sparing use of botanical themes.

The studio-drawing room, for example, includes white and black armchairs, side chairs and desk chairs, and oval, circular and square tables. For its time, it is astonishing stuff, equaled only by the work of Frank Lloyd Wright in Chicago and Josef Hoffmann in Vienna.

Mackintosh's rooms demonstrate his success in living up to one of his stern maxims: There is hope in error, none in the icy perfections of the mere stylist.

The reconstruction inevitably produces odd exterior effects—

the front door, which does not open, is fifteen feet above street level—but it convincingly conveys the impression of a house. An enormous effort has been made to guarantee authenticity. People who knew the house were interviewed; paints, wallpapers and fabrics were specially produced to match old samples, and Mackintosh's detailed drawings and notes were followed to the letter.

It is surprising, considering the relatively small number of Mackintosh designs that were built, that so many structures have been preserved through the seventy years since he left Glasgow for exile in England and France. More and more of his works have become accessible to the public recently, including the following in Glasgow:

The Willow Tea Rooms, built in 1904 and restored in 1979 and 1980, have been leased to a jeweler and are open during business hours, although few of the furnishings have survived.

The Martyrs' Public School, which dates from 1895 and includes an elegant doorway, a spectacular main hall and much else that suggests what was to come, is open on weekdays from 9:30 A.M. to 12:00 and from 2:30 to 4:00.

The Scotland Street School, a massively turreted building from 1904 that is reminiscent of some of Gropius's work a decade later, is open on Wednesday afternoons, with guided tours at 2:30 P.M. and 3:00.

Mackintosh's masterpiece is the Glasgow School of Art at 167 Renfrew Street, designed in 1896, which clings castlelike to the side of a hill; it has been called the most important protomodern building in Europe. The library is a triumph of spatial organization.

Hill House in Helensburgh, twenty-three miles northwest of Glasgow, is probably Mackintosh's finest domestic building, designed for the publisher Walter Blackie. It has recently been taken over by the National Trust for Scotland. More information on this and other buildings can be had from the Charles Rennie Mackintosh Society, 870 Garscube Road, which is itself housed in the architect's Queen's Cross Church. The office is open Tuesday, Thursday and Friday afternoons (041-946-6600).

Those in search of a more earthy Glasgow will get a real sense of the style and the accent of the rambunctious Glaswegian at the Barras, a congeries of shops and stalls in the East End. Open only on Saturdays and Sundays, this is the Glasgow equivalent

of the Paris flea market, except that its traders sell everything—
antiques, food, dresses, video tapes, guitars.

If you have Scottish blood, you might call at the newly established Roots Bureau, housed in Stirling's Library, Royal Exchange
Square, where they will discuss what clan you came from, where
its ancestral territories lay and other such lore. The service is free.
You can then spend yourself silly on kilts and related gear at
specialists like Argyle House, 232 Buchanan Street, or R. G. Law-
rie, Ltd., 110 Buchanan Street.

There are four top-level hotels in Glasgow: the modern, ten-
story Albany, slightly to the southwest of the city center; the
neighboring Holiday Inn, considerably grander than its American
counterparts; the smaller Grosvenor, on the northwest side of
town, which conceals contemporary luxury behind a magnificent
classical façade; and the new Skean Dhu, which is in the center of
town.

If you prefer to stay outside town, Houston House at Uphall,
twenty miles east (and only nine miles from Edinburgh), offers
prettily furnished rooms in an old, whitewashed, step-gabled
house or in a more modern wing, with the added attractions of a
tranquil garden, one of the best wine cellars in Europe and palatable if often clumsily served food. About the same distance to
the north, at Dunblane, near Stirling, is the more elaborate
Cromlix House, with fine antique furnishings but a certain cold-
ness in atmosphere.

The best restaurant in town at the moment is Poachers on
Ruthven Lane, a cozy urban farmhouse, hung with plants; it
serves excellent fish dishes, lamb and game birds at prices that are
fairly stiff for this region. The Ubiquitous Chip at 12 Ashton
Lane is more creative (meat loaf in a suet crust, imaginatively
stuffed duck) and its wine list is outstanding (and outstandingly
good value) but the place is annoyingly inconsistent. On a less
ambitious plane, good open-faced sandwiches are found at the
Danish Food Center, 56 St. Vincent Street; and such dishes as coq
au vin or steak au poivre, correctly done, at a wine bar named
Lautrec's, 14 Woodlands Terrace.

For truly outstanding food, however, it is necessary to drive an
hour or so to the east, to the far side of Edinburgh, to two of the
most honest and enterprising restaurants in Britain. At Gullane,
east of the city, is a tiny, almost doll-size house called La Poti-

nière, no more than a five-iron shot from the Muirfield golf links. It is open for lunch Monday through Friday and for dinner only on Saturday, and you must book weeks ahead (telephone 0620-843214) but is well worth the effort to sample Hilary Brown's set meals, which always include an exquisite soup and often a faultlessly cooked chicken, and David Brown's inexpensive wines. (Only a couple of years ago, he was selling 1966 Gruaud-Larose for less than $15.)

At Peat Inn, northwest of Edinburgh, David Wilson—as warm, talented and unpretentious as the Browns—offers pâtés, delicious fish and shellfish, lamb, perfectly timed vegetables and another star-studded, judiciously priced wine list. He closes on Sunday and Monday and serves a limited menu at lunch. You can eat in either place for $35 a couple if you order simple wines, which is what you shouldn't do—you'll never find bottles like theirs in the States at such prices.

CHAPTER IV

More Britain

---

1. *Restaurant Revolution*

U NLESS you have an uncontrollable passion for kippers or steak-and-kidney pie you probably won't go to Britain to eat, but if you go for other reasons you will find that you can eat very well indeed. Slowly, ever so slowly, over the last twenty-five years, good restaurants have come into being in almost all parts of the kingdom. Brown Windsor soup, thank heavens, is an endangered species. But you must choose where you eat carefully, and you must be prepared to pay for quality.

The English have the strangest approach to the pleasures of the table of any European people. Only in Britain is a politician likely to be pilloried in the press for liking good wine and good food, as Roy Jenkins was, and only in Britain is good wine and good food so much the province of the more privileged elements. Go to Spain, a much poorer country, and you will find in the simplest of bars a delicious assortment of *tapas*, the little nibbles that accompany so well a glass or two of fino. But go to a London pub and you are in danger of finding nothing more appetizing than a Scotch egg, which consists of a hard-cooked egg rolled in sausage meat, usually served stale, to go with your pint of beer.

Bernard Levin says in his book *Enthusiasms* that his pieces about architecture or music or the theater never arouse quite the

same scorn from those who disagree with him as his pieces about food. "To take pleasure in good food and wine, and to express that pleasure," he writes, "is by some considered altogether impermissible, and even arouses the most unbridled hostility." He finds incomprehensible the view that "because eating is something we all have to do, it is somehow wrong to enjoy a universal necessity."

Eating in Britain, like most things there, has a good deal to do with class. French families of modest means save for months to eat a superb meal on a birthday or a holiday; I remember chatting in the three-star establishment of Paul Bocuse outside Lyon one night with the local postmaster and his wife, there to celebrate their wedding anniversary. Neither they nor the waiters saw anything surprising about their presence in a dining room full of richer and more cosmopolitan people from a half-dozen countries. They were accustomed, they told me, to eating in restaurants about once a week, and they went to the best bistros they could afford except for their twice- or thrice-yearly splurges. When they ate at home, I am sure, they also ate well, if simply. There are just not very many people like that in Britain, and without people like that, there is no way that good restaurants will ever be the norm, as they are in France and Italy and Belgium and to a lesser extent in Germany and Austria.

It follows that, with honorable exceptions, the British make poor waiters who know little about what they are serving and are therefore utterly incapable of guiding a client. It follows, likewise, that chefs have no status. The proprietor of the best trattoria in an Italian town is a man of some renown and not a little standing. But the British rank a gifted cook just marginally above a good garage mechanic. It follows that it is still considered somewhat bad form to praise a Mayfair hostess too enthusiastically for her food. And it follows, finally, that the British in general are bad restaurant clients, lacking a sense of adventure, afraid that they will commit a social gaffe, reluctant to return a bad dish to the kitchen or to express dissatisfaction with the service when paying the bill.

There is no gastronomic magazine of broad circulation in Britain, and the general level of food criticism is poor. The three excellent guidebooks (which are more important, if one is to find the gems among the clutter, in Britain than anywhere else in Europe) are the products of a French tire company (Michelin), of an inexhaustible Hungarian émigré with deep roots in the restaurant trade (Egon Ronay) and of a band of dedicated amateurs who report without compensation (*The Good Food Guide*).

Yet I would far rather eat at Chez Nico (either the London branch or the new country outpost near Reading) or at Le Manoir aux Quat' Saisons near Oxford than in any grand restaurant in Germany, Austria, Spain or Scandinavia, and there are only a very few in the United States in their class. The chefs of both places are foreigners, it is true, but there is an increasing supply of home-grown talent, too, including men and women like Richard Shepherd of Langan's Brasserie in London, Joyce Molyneux of the Carved Angel in Dartmouth, Marion Jones of the Croque-en-Bouche near Worcester, George Perry-Smith of the Riverside in Cornwall and Francis Coulson of Sharrow Bay in the Lake District. They could all hold their own in any country. Michel and Albert Roux, the French brothers who own Le Gavroche and the Waterside Inn, are full of praise for their young English apprentices.

Several things have conspired to bring this about, the most important of which is the radical socioeconomic change that has taken place since World War II. After the war, all but the richest members of the aristocracy found it impossible to maintain large staffs and large houses, and many began eating regularly in restaurants for the first time, creating a new clientele. Members of the new meritocracy that was encouraged by the gradual easing of class barriers also became regular clients. The availability of cheap travel to the Continent, opened up by the jet airplane and all the apparatus of mass tourism, taught people whose culinary horizons had been confined to Blackpool and Brighton to appreciate the delights of Málaga and Taormina. To this was added the contribution of two seminal figures—Elizabeth David, whose sprightly cookbooks have taught two generations of British chefs as well as household cooks how to approximate the flavors and aromas of the Mediterranean in northern Europe, and Raymond Postgate, the historian and *bon viveur* who founded *The Good Food Guide* in 1951.

As in the United States, the best restaurants in Britain are a heterogeneous lot. A few, a very few, are survivors from the old days. I think especially of the Gay Hussar, the last of the great Soho establishments. Or of the Riverside, a tiny place tucked into a romantic cove in remotest Cornwall that seems to have leapt from the pages of Daphne du Maurier, where George Perry-Smith still turns out the classics—lamb *boulangère,* salmon in pastry with ginger and currants, *St. Emilion au chocolat*—that made his reputation at the Hole in the Wall in Bath.

Many are the products, direct or indirect, of the remarkable Roux brothers, who were private cooks in France and Britain before founding their gastronomic dynasty. In addition to their own places, they have helped to finance restaurants set up by a number of their alumni, including Pierre Koffmann's quite wonderful Tante Claire, and Jean-Louis Taillebaud's very good Interlude de Tabaillau in Covent Garden (so called because that is the way Albert Roux mangled the name).

Still others are the creations of amateurs. Paul Henderson, who runs the magnificent Gidleigh Park at Chagford in Devon (with his wife, Kay, and Shaun Hill in the kitchen), used to be a management consultant, Tim Hart of Hambleton Hall in Leicestershire fled from the City, John Tovey of Miller Howe in the Lake District was an actor and David Brown of the minuscule La Potinière in Gullane, near Edinburgh, surely the best restaurant in Scotland, was an art student. One advantage of this pattern is the eclecticism that it can produce, of which a particularly happy example is Pomegranates in London's Pimlico, where Patrick Gwynne-Jones offers Turkish, Scandinavian, French, Chinese, Mexican, Argentine and Indonesian dishes that he came to love during his wanderings as a seaman.

Then there is the extraordinary Nico Ladenis, who made his mark at Chez Nico in Battersea, on the "wrong" side of the Thames but only five minutes by cab from Chelsea. It is now in the capable hands of his protegé, Philip Britten. Self-taught, Ladenis is a perfectionist proud of the fact that he succeeded without help from the Roux brothers or anyone else. Ladenis's individualism, and the simplicity of both the décor and the service at his original place, make it all the more remarkable that he won a second Michelin star; he hopes for three at his much grander establishment, also called Chez Nico, at Shinfield in Berkshire. His cooking is French, a careful personal version of nouvelle cuisine stripped of empty flourishes and characterized by great depth of flavor; his blood, however, is Greek, and his temperament passionate.

Natural allies, he and Ronay feuded for years before coming to terms, and his restaurants are no fit places for those who treasure calm, because Ladenis is as likely to charge into the dining room to debate a gastronomic point with a client as he is to explode at a sous-chef who has created a microscopically thin skin on a sauce by leaving it under the salamander two seconds too long. But they are most definitely places for those who like to eat well, because the cooking, improving every month, may soon equal the best in the country.

It is sad that many of the best small places are finding it hard to survive in times of economic stringency, staff shortages and increasingly tight government regulations controlling wages and benefits. A last-minute cancellation by a party of six can wipe out the profit margin for the day. Sad, too, that unknowing clients (including, in these days of the strong dollar, a fair number of Americans), who are more interested in telling their friends that they have visited the "in" place than in eating, can frustrate chefs and cut into profit margins by ordering meagerly. Tante Claire has suffered more than it should have from this malady.

But saddest of all, there is no sign that the current dearth of good, simple restaurants—the equivalent of France's bistros, Italy's trattorias, Spain's and Greece's fish places—will be ending soon. It is not that Britain lacks good ingredients suitable to straightforward methods of preparation. But fishermen find no market for John Dory, the same delicate fish that Venetians and Bretons devour. Few restaurants get the most out of Scottish beef or Welsh lamb, which are among the best in the world. Fewer still take the trouble to collect the wild mushrooms that abound in the woods or the crayfish that swarm in the streams. The excellence of English cheese—not just Cheddar and Stilton but Wensleydale and Double Gloucester and Blue Cheshire—is a well-kept secret. You will find more tired tournedos Rossini and paella on menus than Lancashire hot-pot and blackberry pie. A pity, especially for visitors, because no one on vacation wants to eat grandly every day (even if he or she could afford it), and foreigners would like to sample the local fare.

In a sense, the need is met by the Asian restaurants that have flourished in the last two decades, especially in London. Most are relatively inexpensive, and if you pretend that the empire lives on, as some Britons do, you could imagine that you are eating "local." Try the Indian cooking at the zippy Bombay Brasserie or the cheerful, cooperatively owned Last Days of the Raj in Covent Garden; the dim sum at Chuen Cheng Ku near Leicester Square; the whole range of Chinese dishes at the Diamond in Soho (cheap, cheerful and Cantonese), the Mao Tai in Chelsea (Hunanese and Szechuan) or, at a rather higher price, the impressive Zen near Sloane Square; and hurry, hurry, hurry to Philip Harris's utterly delightful Bahn Thai, hidden in a basement out beyond Harrods.

2. Four Favorites: Gidleigh Park, The Walnut Tree Inn, Le Manoir aux Quat' Saisons, Miller Howe

T H E fumbling amateur hotelkeeper is a recognizable English type: London businessman, tired of commuting, buys a rundown country house, puts his wife in the kitchen, hires a couple of southern European waiters, buys a few job lots of cheap wine. Inevitably, people are incautious enough to give the new place a try. Almost inevitably, they regret it.

Happily for me, my arrival in Britain coincided with the emergence of a number of places that are not like that at all, including Tim and Steffa Hart's idyllic Hambleton Hall, Peter Herbert's elegant Gravetye Manor south of London and Grete Hobbs's baronial Inverlochy Castle in Scotland.

But my favorite is a place run by a man who is not only an amateur but also an American. Gidleigh Park, nestled into a valley above the burbling River Teign, on the lowest slopes of Dartmoor in the west of England, is the creation of Paul and Kay Henderson, who met at Purdue University, came to Europe in pursuit of his career as a management consultant, and ate themselves silly in the best French restaurants they could afford whenever they had any free time. She taught herself how to cook, he scraped together the money, and in 1977 they bought a battered mock-Tudor house. I chose it for my fiftieth birthday dinner, and I did *not* regret it.

Lest you think that I have been carried away by the novelty of an English country hotel run by Americans, I cite here the verdicts of more sober judges. The Michelin guide gives Gidleigh Park a star—as far as I know, the first time an American cook has ever won one—and prints its symbol in red, a tribute to the ambience of the place. Britain's prestigious *Good Food Guide* rates it 15/20, one of the four highest scores given to country houses. And in 1982, Paul Henderson's astonishing cellar was judged the best of the year in a national competition conducted by Egon Ronay and two other lovers of fine vintages.

Gidleigh is in Devon, that loveliest of English counties, with its intensely green hills quilted by dry-stone walls. The nearest road is a mile and a half away; you reach the hotel by a narrow lane than was disgracefully potholed until very recently. ("If I sold a quarter of my wines," said Mr. Henderson in the early days, in the tones of a man discussing the dismemberment of his mother, "I suppose I could afford to fix the lane.") No other building is visible from the thirty acres of grounds. The air reminds me of that in Wyoming. There are rhododendrons in late spring, there is blazing foliage in the fall. And there is a pretty herb garden, soon to be joined by a greenhouse to assure a year-round supply of basil and tarragon. Paul Henderson, one-time Marine, is one of those relentlessly organized Americans who do things.

The Hendersons have transformed the house, built in 1928, at a cost of a million dollars. (They lost a bundle the first year, a fair amount the second, broke even the third and began making a profit only in 1981.) One is not overwhelmed with chintz and country clutter; the emphasis is on good antiques from their former house in London, comfortable armchairs and fresh flowers. In the cooler months, which, to be frank, means about eleven months of the year, there are fires in all the public rooms, and they are burning when the first guest comes down, because Mr. Henderson comes down before anyone else.

The place has twelve bedrooms, all with plumbing and lighting to meet the fussiest American standards. He talks to his guests, records their tastes and backgrounds on file cards, and fosters the gentle illusion that Gidleigh is still a private home. The bar is always open, and if no one is behind it, you take what you like and tell Paul later. The bedrooms, the library, the entry hall and the drawing room are loaded with books (on local flowers and trees, the West Country, cathedrals, wine . . .) that fit the time and place and mood.

Breakfast hours are listed, but the fact is that you can have breakfast anytime you please. It is a good introduction to the style of the dining room, because it is based on superlative products, competently cooked. The kippers are from Loch Fyne, which means they are the best. The croissants are baked in the house. The orange juice is freshly squeezed, the butter is unsalted, the eggs are never more than a day old. And the bacon, may my Middle Western forebears forgive me, is even better than those great smoky slabs that used to come out of Iowa before some evil genius discovered that lesser things were far more profitable.

At dinner, Kay Henderson and her gifted partner, Shaun Hill, do first courses like vegetable terrines and timbales, salads of quail and tiny green beans and fancy lettuces, a ragout of monk-fish and brill, a consommé with herb pasta and scallops. Among their main courses that I like are the duck breast with green peppercorns and a light cream sauce with Armagnac, superb English lamb with a gutsy wine-and-herb sauce and veal shanks with white wine sauce and a julienne of lemon. The antecedents, clearly, are Vergé and Guérard and Troisgros; but unlike other disciples, Mrs. Henderson does not feel compelled to use kiwi fruit and raspberry wine vinegar in every other dish to prove her credentials. The desserts are sinful, and the cheeses come from farms, not factories—most notably a Single Gloucester that I consider the best English cheese I have ever tasted.

Mr. Hill is a newcomer, replacing John Webber, and with his arrival in late 1985 new, robust flavors have been added to the menu. Try, for instance, his caviar on a potato pancake with sour cream. Or his corned beef hash for breakfast.

Paul Henderson provides the drink to precede, accompany and follow the food: more than a dozen single-malt whiskies (and both Jack Daniel's and George Dickel for the homesick), a glorious collection of marcs and brandies and *eaux de vies*, and a wine list that combines the French classics with excellent specimens from Germany and Italy and the best selection of American wines outside the United States.

To anyone who cares about these things, it is as refreshing to find fifty wines at under $15 a bottle, including several from growers like Ponnelle and Duboeuf and the Marquis de Goulaine, as it is to find a wide range of classics at comparatively reasonable prices: Château Montalena Chardonnay 1978 for $27, Château Gloria 1970 for $45, Beaune Bressandes (Leroy) 1966 for $37, on up to Château Coutet 1934 for $110. The list usually includes more than four hundred items, and Mr. Henderson spends an unusual amount of effort weeding out what seem to him to be "duds."

Gidleigh is a three-and-a-half-hour drive or train trip from London. Its address is Chagford, Devon, its phone number 064732367. The price for a double room with breakfast and dinner for two people, including taxes and service, is about $210.

Even the name of the minuscule village in which it is hidden suggests just how far off the tourist track the Walnut Tree Inn is, and maybe no restaurant with an address like Llandewi Skirrid, Gwent, will ever become a household word. But it is the best place to eat in Wales, that prolix, enigmatic, undervisited principality; indeed, it is one of the best and most winning places to eat in all of Britain.

Franco Taruschio comes from Italy, and that shows in his *brodetto* (a fish stew) and his noodles with pesto and the white truffles he serves in season; also in the wine list, one of the few outside Italy to include Venegazzu and Sassicaia and even Picolit, the semilegendary sweet white wine from the Friuli. He trained in France, and he is as comfortable with the classic (quails Rossini) as with the nouvelle cuisine (salmon with rhubarb). Wonderfully fresh shellfish, kept in tanks; devastating desserts; but what you will remember most, years after you have walked contentedly away from this whitewashed oasis, is the happy Mediterranean hubbub of the dining room—the product of a demonic search for fine ingredients, endless pains in preparing them and real zest in serving them. You will understand what Mr. Taruschio means when he says, "To be a good cook, I believe, one needs to be a caring person; otherwise the soul goes out of the food."

The Walnut Tree, which is closed on Sundays and at lunch on Mondays, at Christmas and for two weeks in February, does not exactly give away this bounty, but the value is remarkable; dinner for two with a good wine will cost less than $50. (Three miles northeast of Abergavenny on route B4521; no credit cards; telephone Abergavenny 2797.) The Angel in Abergavenny, the Bear at Crickhowell and the Crown at Whitebrook, all close by, are plain but perfectly adequate for a couple of nights' stay.

And you will want to stay at least that long, not only for the food, but because the Walnut Tree lies near the valley of the River Wye, one of the most agreeable areas in the country. The valley itself is lovely, best seen perhaps from Symond's Yat, a promontory overlooking a series of serpentine loops. In the same region lie the pink sandstone Hereford cathedral, with an ancient library of fifteen hundred books, each chained to the seventeenth-century oak shelves; Wordsworth's beloved Tintern Abbey, serenaded by the "soft inland murmur" of the "sylvan Wye;" the black-and-white villages of Weobley and Eardisley, full of half-timbered buildings; Raglan Castle, whence the Crimean commander took his name and whence tailors took the name for a kind of rounded sleeve, and Lower Brockhampton, near Bromyard, one of the very few wooden houses from the Middle Ages left in Britain. Built before 1400, it is set in a gentle green glen.

The Wye teems with salmon and foams with rapids, attracting fishermen and boatmen. The surrounding orchards yield some of the world's best cider. But for me, the special treat of a visit to the Borders is the tiny Norman chapel at Kilpeck, my favorite parish church in Britain, which is covered with charming carvings of dogs, men, rabbits and dragons, all gazing wide-eyed at us across eight centuries.

It was in the Lake District of northwestern England that Wordsworth found his "host of golden daffodils" so gaily "tossing their heads in sprightly dance," and that Ruskin came to believe that "the spirit of God is around you in the air that you breathe [and] His glory is in the light that you see."

The beauty of the rocky hills and the long, deep lakes—Ullswater and Derwentwater and Windermere—is undimmed by the fleets of tour buses that choke the winding roads in summer. And the modern visitor will find something that Wordsworth and Ruskin did not: a collection of country restaurants unmatched in any other region of England, except perhaps the West Country. Sharrow Bay Country House, Francis Coulson's and Brian Sack's exuberantly decorated establishment on Ullswater, and White Moss House in Grasmere, with its delicate lovage soup and its hearty hunter's pot of venison and wild duck, and Tullythwaite House at Underbarrow, once the realm of the beloved Mrs. Mary Johnson and now operated by her daughter—it is in places like these, not in London, that one senses how good English cooking can be.

Miller Howe, a small hotel on the brow of a hill overlooking Windermere, seems to me to set the pace for the region. Its chef and proprietor, John J. Tovey, buys the best products he can find for his rather flamboyant place—salmon from Aberdeen, broad beans from a local farmer who picks them the morning they are served, lamb from Yorkshire, lemons from Marks & Spencer in London. ("I know it sounds crazy," he says, "but they are consistently the fattest ones I can find.") Almost everything is homemade, including breads, chutneys and preserves; most of it is very good indeed, although the kitchen has its occasional failures, like any that is totally committed to innovation.

Each night there is a set menu, with no choice except for dessert, and the menu is never exactly repeated. The fiercely energetic and unfailingly affable Mr. Tovey, who once worked in Africa in the British Colonial Service, experiments and adapts, borrows and invents to create a style of cooking that is English but intensely personal.

One evening several years ago, the sixty diners began with mushrooms in a perfectly balanced sauce of Marsala and cream, served in a pastry case. Like the other courses, it was colorfully garnished. A bit of tomato, lettuce, a slice of orange twisted into a small sculpture. Like the other courses, it was small; Mr. Tovey's meals are a parade of miniatures.

Next came a spectacular onion soup, lifted out of the ordinary by careful planning and a last-minute inspiration. This was a Tuesday, and the bones from Sunday's roast beef had given birth to a rich stock; croutons had been made from homemade bread spread lightly with a mixture of brandy and cheddar. While showing a visitor the kitchen and the storerooms before dinner, Mr. Tovey noticed some onion marmalade that he had made after reading Michel Guérard's *Cuisine Minceur*, which had just been published in England. A dollop went into each soup bowl, adding a rich caramel taste.

Cold salmon with olive oil mayonnaise followed. It was the only disappointment. The salmon was a bit dry. "Too late in the season," Mr. Tovey said as he sat down for a midnight post-mortem. "I shouldn't have attempted it."

But the loin of lamb was perfectly pink and juicy, surrounded on the massive service plates by no fewer than seven vegetables, each a rebuke to the waterlogged cabbage and limp beams that have been an English specialty for generations. There was just a bite of each: deep-fried cauliflower, carrots with marjoram, spinach with nutmeg, peas, beans, potatoes and grated zucchini in fresh lime juice, a happy idea adapted from one of Charles Chevillot's dishes at La Petite Ferme in New York. All but the zucchini were from local farms.

Finally, a choice from among nine desserts, six involving a fresh fruit. Nectarine pie and American peach crumble linger in the memory, as does a chocolate freak's delight improbably called Chocolate Rum Squidgy Gâteau.

All of this was served in a setting that rivals the celebrated Père Bise at Talloires in the French Alps. The tapestry-covered chairs and brown-covered tables are set in two tiers in front of a huge window overlooking the lake and the five ranges of mountains beyond. Everyone eats the same thing at the same time, and the dining room's lights are dimmed with appropriate theatricality as the customers file in.

There are no ashtrays on the tables ("If you wish to enjoy the full flavor of your food and drink you will naturally not smoke during this meal," the menu admonishes) and late arrivals are not served. The regimentation is worth it; the food is inspired in its simplicity, the view is magnificent. The price is about $30, not including tips and wine.

"I always have these amazing doubts," said Raymond Blanc as he tasted his coffee. "I chew myself up." Tense, earnest, frail and slim (does he ever eat his own food?), Mr. Blanc was more anxious than ever in 1984. After seven years as chef-patron of Les Quat' Saisons, a tiny restaurant in a shopping center near Oxford, he had just opened a country hotel in a village on the other side of town. It is called Le Manoir aux Quat' Saisons, it cost him and his twenty-nine investors more than one and a half million dollars to create, and he needn't have fretted.

Even before Le Manoir opened, the Michelin guide to Britain broke with precedent and granted it two stars—the only British country hotel to be so honored. Egon Ronay stopped for lunch the day after the opening and commented, "As sparingly as I use the word 'sensational,' that is the only apt adjective for the whole experience." Nico Ladenis also paid an early call and said, in his gruff way, "This food tastes."

With the help of Michael Priest, an interior decorator, Mr. Blanc's English wife, Jenny, has designed ten bedrooms, two dining rooms, a parlor and a private salon that manage to be luxurious and cosseting without ever seeming inappropriate to the English countryside. Add ponds, gardens, tennis courts and the golden beauty of the stone manor house, plus the knowing if not perfectly polished service of a young staff, and it is not surprising that Le Manoir is considered by many not only the best restaurant but also the premier country hotel in Britain.

Perhaps the most astonishing thing about the entire enterprise is that Raymond Blanc is wholly self-taught, wholly self-made. He comes from the Franche-Comté, the mountainous part of France between Burgundy and the Swiss border. Before Oxford, he cooked in a little hotel owned by his wife's parents.

There he perfected his skills as a pastry chef—skills that are as evident at Great Milton in the bread on the table as in the parade of rich desserts (puff pastry lined with ice cream, topped with a pear roasted in ginger butter, for example, or an apple filled with Calvados soufflé, baked and served with apricot *coulis* and vanilla ice cream).

The style of cooking is, of course, strongly influenced by the nouvelle cuisine of Alain Chapel and Fredy Girardet and Michel Guérard—no great cooking in Europe is not—but it has its special characteristics. One is a love of herbs and spices, including coriander and star anise, of mushrooms and of red peppers.

Another is profundity of flavor. If Mr. Blanc indulges in fantasy—say, by serving a tomato sherbet with a lobster salad—he makes sure that the sherbet has the real tang of fresh tomato and is not just there for the color. On occasion, the dishes also display the chef's wit: he delighted in serving both truffles, just going out

86

of season, and morels, just coming in, with a medallion of beef.

There is balance, too: I found that after asparagus tips in puff pastry with a chervil sauce, a plate of seafood—one oyster, salmon twisted into a braid, two scallops and a single, barely cooked langoustine, served with an extraordinary light Pernod sauce—and the aforementioned beef, I still welcomed a bite or two of dessert.

One good way to test a fine restaurant is to look at the little things. At Le Manoir, the nibbles served with cocktails get as much attention as the *plats de résistance*; recently, they have included minuscule brochettes—toothpicks, really—of fish and shellfish, and tiny, savory packets of puff pastry fitted into scallop shells.

The wine list, assembled by the maître d'hôtel, Alain Desenclos, is exhaustive, with 174 items, including such treasures as 1976 Gevrey-Chambertin Clos Saint-Jacques from Armand Rousseau at $57 and 1970 Château Palmer at $63, but it also includes a dozen or more bottles under $15, including Cahors, Savennières and Rully red from outstanding small growers. There is variety, too, in the cheeses, which come from Phillipe Olivier of Boulogne, one of the best *fromagers* in France.

Occasionally there may be a flaw—a vegetable marginally overcooked, a sauce whose taste is ideal but whose color is not—but the food as a whole demonstrates genuine devotion on the part of Mr. Blanc and his brigade of ten. Attention to detail shows not only in the preparation of the food, but in the surroundings as well. The heavy pink tablecloths and napkins and the bouquets of orchids and freesias on the tables are prime examples, to say nothing of the décor and the provision of the bedrooms upstairs.

Each of those is different, some in French fabrics, some in English fabrics, some with exposed beams, some with canopied beds, one blue, one pink, one yellow. The bathtubs have Jacuzzis, the towels are from Descamps, and the beds are made up with antique linen. In each room there are hair dryers, sewing boxes, colognes and fresh fruit.

The prices are stiff. Mr. Blanc says the average price of a meal with cocktails, wine, service and taxes is about $60, although there is a weekday set lunch for $21 without drinks and three- and five-course Sunday set lunches without drinks for $28 and $41, respectively. The rooms cost between $125 and $200 a night, including a light breakfast.

Need I add that the solace of the Cotswolds is less than an hour away?

3. *Fully Cooked*

T o eat well in England," said W. Somerset Maugham, an Englishman born in France who beat it back there to live as soon as he had the money, "you should have a breakfast three times a day."

The "fully cooked English breakfast," as Britons like to call it, has survived the onslaught of Continental eating habits, but barely. Coffee and croissants, or tea and muesli (a Swiss cereal), form the morning meal of many people; according to one national opinion poll, forty-seven percent of the population ate a home-cooked breakfast in 1956, but the figure had dropped to only nineteen percent twenty years later. One person in five makes do with nothing more than coffee or tea.

Even those who do eat something cooked before starting their day's activities often limit themselves to fairly spartan fare. Prime Minister Margaret Thatcher and her predecessor, James Callaghan, begin most days with the same thing: half a grapefruit, a boiled egg, toast and marmalade. Mrs. Thatcher has coffee; Mr. Callaghan prefers Indian tea.

Few follow the advice of Isabella Beeton, the guru of the British kitchen in the nineteenth century, who said in an early edition of her cookbook that "a good meal, if enjoyed and digested, gives the support necessary for the morning's work." For a family breakfast on a Thursday in wintertime, she suggested the following menu: coffee, tea, hot milk, porridge, bread, toast, butter, marmalade, mutton cutlets and fried potatoes, and sardines.

Like their American and Continental cousins, many Britons have come to share the view of the late Morton Shand, an eminent English gastronome, who once described breakfast as "an essentially unsociable meal, an appropriate time to choose for disinheriting one's natural heirs." Few would agree with that New England esthete and sometime American Consul at Liverpool, Nathaniel Hawthorne, that "life, within doors, has few pleasanter prospects than a neatly arranged and well-provisioned breakfast table."

Who, then, keeps alive the tradition of breakfast kippers and haddock, kedgeree (a mélange of fish, rice and eggs) and frumenty (hulled wheat boiled in milk and flavored with cinnamon)? Country people great and small, truck drivers, construction men, children, travelers on long-haul trains and, presumably, Robert Morley.

British Rail takes a lot of stick, as the English say, about its dining-car breakfasts. Lord Olivier, the actor, made a terrible fuss a few years ago when he could no longer get kippers on his morning run from Brighton to London.

More recently, there have been screams about rising prices. But a passenger who asks for the works still gets half a grapefruit or juice or porridge or cereal; a mixed grill containing an egg, mushrooms, a tomato, fried potatoes, bacon and a sausage; toast with marmalade, and tea or coffee.

Breakfasts at Claridge's, one of London's elite hotels, are frighteningly costly. A few years ago, two of us managed to get through $31 without much effort. One had tomato juice, kippers, a croissant, marmalade and coffee; the other had orange juice, two fried eggs and bacon, toast, coffee and a small bottle of Perrier water.

The food was passable, although the orange juice was not freshly squeezed and the toast, as always, arrived on one of those cunning silver racks that positively insure that it will be cold and hard by the time it gets to the table.

Very few Englishmen go to breakfast at Claridge's. They can't afford it. But many of them eat just as well at small storefronts known as transport cafes (hereabouts, the word is pronounced caffs). These are the rough equivalent of the old-fashioned American diner, and every morning, up and down the country, they are filled almost exclusively by men who do hard physical work.

One of the best in London is Fred's, at 40 Aberfeldy Street near the docks of the East End. Fred's doesn't have a headwaiter in a wing collar, like Claridge's. It doesn't have linen napkins; in fact, it has no napkins at all. It doesn't have a big urn of fresh carnations on the sideboard and Art Deco wall lamps; its décor runs to Formica, pictures of Royal Air Force jets and posters showing the stars of such television shows as "Dallas" and "Charlie's Angels."

But Fred's has Fred Cockburn in the kitchen, and his wife, Eileen, behind the counter. She calls almost everyone by their first names, or else she calls them "luv." Every weekday, between 6:00 and 11:00 A.M., she serves seventy-five or more breakfasts, most of them gigantic. You can have two fried eggs and bacon, two slices of toast with marmalade, and a cup of tea for $2.50. There's no service charge.

For those with more exotic tastes, there are kippers, haddock with two poached eggs on top, and bubble and squeak at 60 cents. Bubble and squeak, for the uninitiated, is a cockney creation consisting of last night's mashed potatoes and a bit of last night's cabbage, mixed together and fried.

And at Fred's, the toast always arrives piping hot, buttered, lying on a plate. No racks.

4. Traditional Fare: Cheese, Fish and Chips, Pimm's, Oysters

PATRICK Rance, crusader for farmhouse cheese, was incensed as he told his latest bureaucratic horror story. The Milk Marketing Board, Mr. Rance said, had almost done it again: using its power to set milk prices, it had very nearly obliged the Tuxford & Tebbutt creamery in Melton Mowbray, Leicestershire, to abandon the production of Leicester cheese. Had that happened, he exclaimed with a fine show of indignation, there would have been not a single producer of the traditional deepred forty-five-pound wheels of rich, sharp, close-grained Leicester left in the county of its birth.

Such things matter to Patrick Rance, a sixty-eight-year-old shopkeeper who has loved the hard cheeses of England since he was a child growing up in an Anglican rectory in the East End of London. For more than two decades he has campaigned, often almost single-handedly, to reverse the trend toward characterless factory-produced cheese whose soapy flavor and texture bear little resemblance to farm products.

"The supermarket destruction of English cheese has got a lot of people discontented—a lot of people," Mr. Rance said.

But he is swimming against a strong tide. The cheese that he calls "our most original gift to humanity," Cheddar, is available to most people, Mr. Rance says, only in the form of "some hard-pressed rectangular substitute, often foreign, usually emasculated in character and chilled into irredeemable immaturity." Only eleven farms in southwestern England, where Cheddar originated, still make old-fashioned cheeses.

In his detailed study of the subject, *The Great British Cheese Book* (1982), Mr. Rance calculated that there is only enough real Cheddar to put on two British tables of every three hundred where cheese is eaten.

Given her first taste of the real thing—a slice of tangy, dryish, well-aged farmhouse Cheddar that in some ways resembled a slightly immature Parmesan—my wife protested that it tasted nothing at all like the English, American or Canadian products she had been eating all her life. Most English people react the same way when they first taste a cut from a proper truckle of Cheddar.

The same is true of Cheshire; of Swaledale, one of the best of the Yorkshire cheeses, now made on only two farms, and of many others. Still others, like Dorset Blue Vinney, have disappeared.

In their place new English cheeses are appearing. The pioneers are people like Hilary Charnley, a young farmer in Devon, who makes a herbed cheese called Devon Garland and another, plainer type called Warkleigh. Most such cheeses are not widely available.

One place where nearly all can be bought, not surprisingly, is Mr. Rance's shop. He has spent years traveling the country, sniffing out new producers, encouraging them, selling their cheese and encouraging others to do so. Now his son, Hugh, a quondam sculptor, has joined him in the enterprise.

Their place of business is an anonymous-looking building in Streatley, a quiet village near Reading and a few miles up the Thames from Henley, site of the regatta. The name, Wells Stores, is almost invisible in faded letters on the front. About a fifth of the space is taken up by the amiable clutter of a thousand such shops—"We do a nice line in tinned soups and we're not too bad in bootlaces," Mr. Rance said—but the rest is crammed with cheese, which accounts for eighty percent of sales. Big, small, French, English, smelly, mild, orange, white, soft, hard, jostling one another for space on shelves and counters, the cheeses are displayed and labeled in delightful, unruly profusion. Several hand-lettered signs encourage shoppers: "Please ask for a taste."

More than sixty of the cheeses are English and most are hard, although there are some excellent softer ewe's and goat's milk cheeses. Hard cheeses, Mr. Rance said over a sampling of six or seven of them, were developed in England because winters are harsher than in France or Italy and cheese had to be kept a good deal longer. Nowhere else is such a variety of English cheeses available, although Mr. Rance praises two London shops—Neal's Yard and Paxton & Whitfield—for their efforts to keep the flame burning. He sells to private customers, to mail-order clients and to about twenty-five of the best country restaurants in southern England and Wales. (In New York the cheeses are available at Balducci's, Bloomingdale's, Fairway and Macy's.)

Most shops in England count themselves lucky to have one farmhouse Double Gloucester in stock. Wells Stores has three, and a rare and delicious Single Gloucester, too. (Single Gloucester is only about half as thick—two to three inches—and two-thirds the weight—about sixteen pounds—of Double Gloucester; it is eaten when about six weeks old, while Double Gloucester is ready for the table after six months to a year.) Most days Wells Stores—named for the family that founded the business in the 1830s—offers four or five Cheddars and half a dozen English goat cheeses. Equally well represented is the regal Stilton, blue-veined, with a pebbly consistency, one of the few English cheeses whose production is limited to a single area.

Mr. Rance and his wife, Janet, came to Streatley thirty years ago. He had retired from the army as a major after serving in Italy during World War II and had done a stint in opinion research at Conservative Party headquarters. They moved because they wanted to live in the country and raise their seven children there. The cheese business developed because parents and children wanted "real cheese" for themselves, Mr. Rance said, "not because of any business sense or forethought or genius."

A stocky, handsome man who likes denim work shirts, he must be one of the few shopkeepers who wears a monocle on a black cord around the neck. It seems an appropriately mild eccentricity for one with so gentle a passion.

Despite the precipitate decline of the British fishing industry, and despite the inroads of the American hamburger, fish and chips remain one of England's favorite fast foods.

Properly made, the product bears no resemblance to the lumps served in several franchised chains in the United States. Properly made, that is to say, it bears no resemblance to soggy cardboard. But it is becoming harder to find good fish and chips in London or anywhere else.

The "fish" in fish and chips, for those who might not know, is any nonoily fish dipped in batter and deep-fried, crisp on the outside and moist on the inside. The "chips" are French fries. The English eat them with salt, pepper and a sprinkling of malt vinegar, washed down with tea, and occasionally accompanied by pickled onions the size of a small egg or by "wallies," which are large gherkins.

Traditionally, fish and chips were sold in simple shops in working-class neighborhoods and in seaside resorts. Some of the best were in the East End of London, close to the old Billingsgate fish market, where eel shops and shops specializing in cockles and whelks—small shellfish—also abounded. Relatively few of those are left, and some of London's best places are now owned by Greeks and Cypriots.

Traditionally, both the fish and the chips are cooked in beef drippings, which gives them a rich flavor. (Similarly, some old-fashioned restaurants in the American South and Middle West still cook French fries in lard.) Most shops now use blander corn oil.

Traditionally, fresh cod and haddock were used, or, in the fancier places, fresh Dover sole and plaice, an almost transparent flatfish from the North Sea. Now, many places use frozen fish, with predictably disastrous results, and those that use fresh fish may substitute such expedients as dogfish, an eel-like creature with pink flesh that is sold under such glorified names as rock salmon.

Yet it is still possible to find places that will give you some slight idea of why generations of Englishmen have doted on fish and chips. They use fresh plaice, sole or cod, cooked in fresh drippings. The batter is made (in proportions that the proprietors will never reveal) of flour, water, salt and occasionally a little corn meal for extra crispness.

Fish and chips should always be eaten on the spot; it may be picturesque to carry them home wrapped in a sheet of newspaper, but they will be lukewarm and therefore soggy when you get them there.

In London, by common consent, the best fish-and-chips shop is the Sea Shell, a spotless place at 33 Lisson Grove, near Regent's Park. It is not uncommon to see a string of Rolls-Royces parked outside, and the owners as well as the chauffeurs are usually eating there. Cod and chips (with coleslaw, a solecism but a welcome one) costs about $4; sole and chips about twice that.

Two alternatives are the Fish Inn at 1 Newport Place, a couple of blocks from the Leicester Square movie houses, where plaice and chips is only $3, and the Nautilus, a monument to gaudiness at 27 Fortune Green Road in West Hampstead, with cod and chips at $4.25.

You might also want to evaluate the claims of the northerners, who insist that the best fish and chips in the world are cooked in Yorkshire.

Harry Ramsden's at Guiseley, near Leeds, claims to serve a million meals a year, but it still calls itself a fish-and-chips shop; if it is, it's the only one with chandeliers. Haddock costs $3.50 and plaice $4. Clayton's is one of the best places in Scarborough, a pretty seaside resort famous for this sort of thing; Mrs. Clayton will give you haddock, chips, "a slice" (of bread) and tea for $3.15.

The traditionalists will argue, but I think the best fried fish in England is in restaurants rather than fish-and-chips shops—notably Manzi's, at 1 Leicester Street in Soho, and Sweeting's, an engagingly Victorian place (39 Queen Victoria Street, near the Bank of England) where you sit at a counter and banter with the waiters.

Pimm's Cup is as much a part of the English summer as tennis at Wimbledon, the regatta at Henley, the races at Ascot and the May Week balls at Oxford and Cambridge—and it is a favorite drink at all of those events. James Pimm concocted the formula in the 1840s at his chophouse in a street called Poultry in the City and was soon bottling it for his clients to take on their travels. The last Pimm's restaurant closed in 1967, and Pimm's Nos. 2 through 6 (they were based on Scotch, brandy, rum, rye and vodka) were phased out in 1972.

But Pimm's No. 1, a confection of gin, fruit liqueurs, herbs, spices and bitters, is more popular than ever, and a new vodka version is also sold from the venerable firm's headquarters at 63 Pall Mall, in the heart of London clubland. It is the perfect summer cooler, especially if served in a frosted pewter or silver mug, as at the Garrick and a few other clubs.

The formula is simple: to one part of Pimm's, add two to three parts of mixer, plenty of ice, a thin slice of lemon or lime and a strip of cucumber rind. No maraschino cherries, please. Depending on the sweetness of your tooth, you can use soda water, tonic, dry ginger ale or fizzy lemonade; I like it with Perrier. Or do as the French do: make a Pimm's Royale by adding a slightly sweet Champagne.

In the old days, the company used to give away packets of borage seeds so its customers could grow that pretty blue-flowered herb and decorate their drinks with a sprig or two. The leaves have a taste similar to that of cucumber and a pleasant scent. If you have borage in your garden, by all means use it. And try Pimm's as a picnic drink; I used to take some to softball games in Washington a decade ago, and it always improved the players' moods if not their batting eyes.

If you're willing to take the time to search, and if you can resist the locals' determination to steer you into places where they would rather drape fishnets on the walls than cook, you can find, along most of the seacoasts of the world, honest houses with fresh fish and congenial company.

Galway Bay is like that. If you go into the big hotel in the town, you'll get a beautiful view of the bay, stretching away toward the Atlantic and North America, but you'll also get tough scallops in a plastic shell, covered with a glutinous cheese sauce, rimmed with library paste squeezed through a tube.

So don't go there. Turn off the main road from Shannon, as

you head north up the verdant west coast of Ireland, about twelve miles before you reach Galway, when you see the small sign advertising Moran's Oyster Cottage.

Moran's fishnets aren't much. But you'll find a real Irish cottage, two hundred years old, with a real thatched roof and a real peat fire burning on the hearth, filling the tiny rooms with its special sweet aroma. You may also find young Martin Neylan and his friend Willie Moran, who is the sixth generation of his family to grow up in the harsh, blustery beauty of Kilcolgan.

It is a spot that ranks, in the memory of one exuberant eater, with Sam's Grill in San Francisco, whose charcoal-grilled petrale instantly dispels any lingering temptation to return to Fisherman's Wharf, and with a joint on the beach in Nhatrang, Vietnam, whose name is long since forgotten but whose lobsters are not, and with the Brasserie des Catalans on the *corniche* above Marseille, whose bouillabaisse is the Platonic ideal of fish stew.

At Moran's, this is the menu: "Seafood Specialties: Galway Oysters served with home-made brown bread, butter and Guinness/Smoked salmon/Mussel soup/Irish coffee." Serious students take some of each, though it is socially acceptable to rearrange the order of the first three items.

The oysters are quite simply the best that this fanatic—a man who has eaten Olympias in Seattle, Chincoteagues in Baltimore, Sydney Rocks, Belons and Blue Points, Colchesters and Mobile Bays—ever put in his mouth. Fresh, plump, briny, with none of that unappetizing greasiness that betrays the oyster that left its habitat forever two or three days earlier.

The oysters of Moran's usually reach the table within an hour of the time they are raked into baskets, and moments after Martin or Willie opens them.

Which is something to watch.

The World Oyster-Opening Contest is held a few miles up the road in the village of Clairinbridge each September, and one year Martin came within a whisker of winning. He shucked thirty oysters in two minutes and twenty-nine seconds, by far the best time, but he was penalized for having allowed bits of shell to fall into the oysters. The title went to Cornelius McKall from Saint Marys County, Maryland.

"Our eye-sters," Martin Neylan explained in a rich accent that would pass unnoticed in South Boston, "come from our own beds. They're at the mouth of a little stream, where the water is two-thirds salt, one-third fresh. That's the ideal combination."

The last time I checked, the house record at Moran's—pronounced MORE-ans, not mor-ANN's—belonged to a pair of visiting Englishmen. Hugh Williams and a friend (whose signature, perhaps understandably, is illegible in the guest book) consumed 158 of Galway Bay's best in one hour and fifty minutes.

Presumably they also had plenty of Mother Moran's brown bread, a dense and delicious loaf made with sour milk, and plenty of swarthy Guinness stout from the tap, with a creamy head in which Martin will sometimes write your name if you seem to enjoy the place.

The salmon is no less special, smoked rapidly for only five or six hours, rather than the usual twelve or more, and cut by hand. It is moist without being oily, more the color of a peach than of the nova that New Yorkers dote upon. This is the land of the famine that depopulated Ireland 130 years ago, but one would never know it from the eight or ten slices that cover the plate from rim to rim.

One odd thing: For all its delicacy and subtlety of flavor, the salmon that you'll eat here *smells* like salmon.

Moran's isn't a cooking place, really. The mussel soup is a simple broth, given its savor by the freshness of the shellfish rather than elaborate seasonings and thickenings. Only in the summer, when you can sit on the terrace out front and watch the punters and fishermen at their work, does Mrs. Moran trouble herself with anything complicated—a salmon salad, made from freshly poached local fish. Willie says it's unbeatable.

5. *In a Pope's Eye*

A dish that I do love to feed upon," remarks Kate to Petruchio's manservant, Grumio, in *The Taming of the Shrew*, when he offers her a piece of beef and mustard. The British adored steak in Elizabethan times—the nickname Beefeaters for the Yeomen of the Guard dates from that era—and they continued to adore it in Victorian times. Nathaniel Hawthorne, reaching for a simile, wrote that "Dr. Johnson's morality was as English an article as a beefsteak." Not for nothing is the British equivalent of Uncle Sam called "John Bull."

But like so many things gastronomic in Britain, the steak has fallen on hard times in the twentieth century. It is still possible to find a good roast rib of beef in London or in the countryside, but good steaks are even scarcer than Johnsonian morality.

The typical English restaurant beefsteak is underweight, underage and overcooked, not a patch on its counterpart in New York or Florence or Tokyo; I have been told for at least a decade by Englishmen (and even by Frenchmen) that the best beef in Europe comes from Scotland, but I had never been able until recently to find the evidence to support their argument on my dinner plate.

Now I have. The man who made a believer of me is Clive Davidson, a South African who was so disappointed with the beef offered him by wholesalers that he closed his Edinburgh restaurant and set out to learn butchering. Once he had mastered his new trade, he and his Dundee-born wife, Anne, opened a place called Champany Inn near Linlithgow, about thirty minutes' drive west of Edinburgh. They serve an array of steaks: rib loin, Pope's eye, sirloin and filet (but only reluctantly, because he considers filet "expensive and inferior").

The steaks bear comparison with those of Christ Cella in Manhattan or Peter Luger in Brooklyn or Morton's in Chicago or Sostanza in Florence, which is to say that they are thick, seared black on the outside and dark red in the center, the juices sealed in, the flavor rich and smoky, the texture tender but still chewy. Best of all, they fill the nostrils—indeed the whole restaurant— with their hearty aroma.

Drew Smith, the editor of *The Good Food Guide*, who is a notable campaigner for honest and unpretentious cooking, put Champany on the map. In the 1985 edition of the guide, he said that these are "the best steaks in Britain." And he is absolutely right.

Mr. Davidson cooks his steaks on a massive lava-rock grill that generates enough heat to carbonize a rhinoceros, cooks them rare but not quite blue—if his customers allow him to have his way— and serves them on big oval plates. A trolley holds ten mustards, including a particularly good Scottish one made with honey; Kate would surely smile if she were ever to find her way to Linlithgow.

Clive Davidson, a big, jolly man who is just as serious and just as knowledgeable about his beef as a three-star chef in France is about his sauces, says that there are six main factors that affect the way a steak tastes.

Here they are, together with his comments and a description of the methods used:

1. The breed of steer. "I don't like Aberdeen Angus purebred, so I try to use Angus/Scots blue-grey cross—the ugliest beast you ever saw. Never get near Charolais or a Charolais cross, because it's too fibrous, far too fibrous. Hereford has too much marbling. What you want is a piece of beef that glistens, with creamy-colored fat that flakes off when you scrape it with your nail. It must never be at all rubbery."

2. How the steer is fed. "If possible you want a steer that has had to work for his meals, so the meat is best when they have been battling to find the short grass in June and July. When the grass is too young and tender, they gorge themselves and swell up. Very bad."

3. Aging. "We hang the meat for at least four weeks, and we have had some very good results in hanging it for eight. It goes into a chilled room—thirty-nine degrees, one degree above the European Community limit—where ionizers help to retard the fungus growth and weight loss. Still, by the time we finish, we have lost about a quarter of the original weight—ten percent from aging, fifteen from trimming. An ordinary supermarket steak in Britain hasn't been aged at all."

4. The cut. "My absolute favorite is a Pope's eye, which is cut against the grain from the point where the hind leg connects with the body. It is never flabby and always full of flavor." (There is no direct American comparison, since both the pattern of butchering and the terminology are different. Mr. Davidson said he liked American Porterhouses and T-bones best.)

5. Thickness. "You can't cook a thin steak well. Ours are a minimum of one and a quarter inches, and they should be thicker."

6. Cooking. "I paint the steaks with olive oil, which has a low flash point; that means that the meat cannot burn before it cooks. I use a lava-rock grill, heated with gas, that must be lighted

an hour before cooking. I turn the steak as few times as possible, seldom more than three, because that toughens it. And I never salt the meat before cooking, because if you do that, the juices escape."

Steak isn't everything at Champany. There are several first courses, including frogs' legs cooked over the same grill and served in a tiny copper pan with foamy butter (my wife's favorite) and fine gravlax with mustard sauce (mine). There are deep-fried onion rings, though they don't fascinate me, and baked potatoes that have never seen a piece of foil. There is an ample salad bar, a rarity in Europe, and superb garlic bread, and creditable chocolate mousse and pecan pie for those hardy few who can cope with dessert after an orgy of protein. And there is a first-class wine list offering the full line of Beaujolais from Georges Duboeuf, lots of 1971 and 1972 Burgundies and a selection of South African reds, well served by the amiable and aptly named wine waiter, Andrew Backus.

Not easily satisfied, Mr. Davidson has installed a pool, imported from La Rochelle in western France and the only one of its kind in Britain, to hold live lobsters, oysters and scallops, as well as langoustes, which the Scots call crayfish. The water contains the same salts and trace elements as the Atlantic Ocean. The cocktail lounge, which he dislikes because it tends to decant too many customers into the dining room in no condition to appreciate the cooking, may soon be replaced by a raw bar.

One eats in a round room with stone walls under a six-sided peaked wood roof, served by young waitresses in gingham pinafores. Hunting prints, green velveteen chairs and mahogany tables without cloths give the place something of the air of a London club, but the food in London clubs doesn't taste like this, and London clubs aren't surrounded, as is Champany, by a garden populated by peacocks.

CHAPTER V

France

---

1. No Fuss and No Feathers

AFTER falling head over heels in love in the 1970s with haute cuisine, ancienne as well as nouvelle, Americans seem ready in the 1980s for a more varied diet on their epicurean wanderings. At least my friends and acquaintances are, to judge from their eagerness to swap the names of European restaurants that provide old-fashioned, unadorned regional cooking, and especially the names of good bistros in Paris. Happily for us all, the places are still there, waiting to be rediscovered.

For a while, it seemed that home-style French cooking, the mainstay of the true Parisian bistro, would survive only in the private houses whence it came. Among the majority of critics and customers alike, enthusiasm was reserved for the new, the light, the elegant; no one raved any more about a superlative stuffed cabbage or a classic cassoulet. Many famous old houses either disappeared completely or went up-market (like Bistro 121, whose décor was "improved" by the decorator Slavik) or declined precipitously when the *patron* died (like the much-lamented Lyonnais). That trend seems to have been halted, and although there are comparatively few bistros left, the best among them are as busy as any of the grander establishments. Even Henri Gault and Christian Millau, the high priests of nouvelle

cuisine, began a few years ago to single out for special praise little restaurants that offered sound but simple regional cooking, awarding them a laurel-wreath symbol.

It is not easy to define what is meant by the word *bistro* (or *bistrot*, as it is sometimes spelled). My three French-English dictionaries all translate it as pub, which is absurd. The word comes from a Russian expression meaning fast, which entered the language during the occupation of Paris following the Napoleonic Wars. Even today, the service in most bistros is quick enough, but it is just as speedy in cafés, which specialize in drinks and snacks, and in brasseries, which are distinguished by serving beer on draft and providing both snacks and complete meals.

The classic bistro has a wooden front, usually painted brown or dark red, with sawdust on the floor inside and waiters in aprons; but I know one bistro with a cement-block façade, another with waitresses and a third with a carpet (albeit a shabby one). Most but not all specialize in modest regional wines. All, however, are small, old and cheerfully stuck in the rut of tradition. In his *Dining Out in Paris*, published twenty years ago, the late Waverley Root argued that lack of pretension was the key ingredient in a bistro—no "fuss and feathers."

About five years ago, I put together a list of fifty or so bistros, based on my own experience, the major restaurant guides and the advice of knowledgeable friends, French and otherwise. I have now eaten my way through it, visiting several of the places several times and nearly all of them at least once, with my wife and other trenchermen and trencherwomen, in search of an ideal dozen. In the event, I thought fourteen merited inclusion on my list of favorites, so here it is, offered in the certain knowledge that some will occasionally disappoint, as all restaurants do, and that others ought to be included.

Allard

41 Rue Saint-André-des-Arts, Paris 6
Tel: 4326-4823. Métro: Saint-Michel
Closed Saturday, Sunday, holidays and August
Credit cards: Diners Club, Visa

André Allard, who probably knew more about Burgundy and Beaujolais than any restaurateur in Paris, died in 1983, and his widow, Fernande, no longer presides in the kitchen that confronts you as you enter the door. But for the moment the food—the cucumber salad, the scallops with *beurre blanc*, the *boeuf à la mode*, the duck with baby turnips, the incomparable hen pheasant with cabbage, the chocolate charlotte—remains all that bistro food should be: luscious, copious, unchanging. No change either in the classic décor, complete with tin ceiling and sawdust, or the engaging cheekiness of the waiters. Go now, before the rot sets in.

Chez l'Ami Louis

32 Rue du Vertbois, Paris 3
Tel: 4887-7748. Métro: Temple
Closed Monday, Tuesday and July, August
Credit cards: American Express, Diners Club, Visa

The letters are falling off the signs, the walls haven't been painted in twenty years and you go down a claustrophobic stair to get to the toilet. This is not a place for the squeamish. But Papa Magnin, now eighty-six years old, a great Paris character with his scraggly beard, grubby chef's tunic and neckerchief, is the best *rôtisseur* in town. Try the magnificent *côte de boeuf* or the gigot with its crackling skin; with them, he serves perfect foie gras and a garlic-scented potato cake. Ignore the desserts. What the wine list calls Sauternes and Burgundy are in reality grander wines than the names suggest.

Benoit

20 Rue Saint-Martin, Paris 4
Tel: 4272-2576. Métro: Hôtel-de-Ville
Closed Saturday lunch, Sunday and August
No credit cards

Known to many of its devotees as "the Right Bank Allard," this sparkling little bistro, with potted palms spotted strategically in rooms that still look as they did in 1912, is close to the Tour St. Jacques, where medieval pilgrims gathered for the long trek to Santiago de Compostela, and the Pompidou Center, the target of modern pilgrims seeking out the masterpieces of the School of Paris.

Excellent first-course salads in the style of Lyon (celery-root rémoulade, muzzle of beef) and satisfying main dishes (skate with brown butter, *navarin* of lamb), served on nouvelle-cuisine-size plates but certainly not in nouvelle-cuisine-size quantities. Drink Pouilly-Fumé and Morgon.

Cartet

62 Rue de Malte, Paris 11
Tel: 4805-1765. Métro: République
Closed Saturday, Sunday and August
No credit cards

Debts should be paid; I discovered this place some years ago thanks to Bill Rice, later the editor of *Food and Wine*, in the days when it was open only at lunch because Marie Cartet liked to go to the theater at night. She's retired now, but the style of the kitchen, which is the size of a broom closet, has been carefully preserved. The place holds exactly eighteen people, and everything is homemade: the best *brandade de morue* in town; headcheese; garlicky pâtés; *gras-double* (a form of tripe) and warm sausages as they are made in the Ain, north of Lyon, where Mrs. Cartet came from; and desserts, including a chocolate mousse and a lemon tart. The best wines are a white from Bugey, her village, and a Gigondas from Château Raspail.

Chez Georges

273 Boulevard Pereire, Paris 17
Tel: 4574-3100. Métro: Porte Maillot
Closed Saturday and August
Credit cards: Visa

Some might consider Roger Mazarguil's establishment a little too large to be a bistro, but let's give him the benefit of the doubt, because the food is right, the style is right and it's open on Sunday. You can start with excellent herring (not all that easy to find in Paris) and continue with pickled pork and cabbage, a beef rib cooked the way grandmother did it or a magnificent if slightly undersalted gigot with *flageolets*—all served in formidable quantities. Immense éclairs, either chocolate or caramel, are the special house dessert. The Chiroubles from Paul Beaudet, a small grower, is absolutely first-rate, and Mr. Mazarguil stocks Francis Darroze's glorious Armagnacs.

Chez Josephine

117 Rue du Cherche-Midi, Paris 6
Tel: 4548-5240. Métro: Vaneau
Closed Saturday, Sunday and July
Credit cards: Visa

This sturdy bistro is also known, after its proprietor, as Chez Dumonet. It is a thoroughly Parisian place, almost unknown to tourists, and rather noisy; on the other hand, it retains its warm-hearted turn-of-the-century décor and the smiling service that was more common then than now. Much of the cooking has a southwestern accent, which means you can rely on the foie gras with raisins, the scrambled eggs with truffles and the *confit d'oie* (preserved goose).

Excellent calf's foot and leeks, too, both served with a hearty vinaigrette. This is a good place to try lesser wines from Bordeaux, some of which surpass those of renowned but overconfident chateaus.

Chez Pauline

5 Rue Villedo, Paris 1
Tel: 4296-2070. Métro: Pyramides
Closed Saturday evening and Sunday
Credit cards: Visa

Somehow, a fancy clock, a carpet and fresh flowers crept into Pauline's, but if the face is painted, the heart is still pure. The regular corner place of Curnonsky, the King of Gourmets, is marked by a plaque, and the food is as good as it was in his day—Morvan ham with parsley, shaped into an imposing loaf; truffled Bresse chicken (Tuesday only); old-fashioned blanquette of veal

(Wednesday); and a stupendous stuffed cabbage containing ham, veal, rabbit and two kinds of pork. Perhaps the kindliest service in Paris (they leave the *digestif* bottle on the table). Note the Rhône wines, the rye, walnut and raisin breads available with the fine cheeses (St. Marcellin) and the fact that you can eat here in August. Very nearly perfect.

Le Paillon

4 Cour des Petites-Ecuries, Paris 10
Tel: 4523-0277. Métro: Château-d'Eau
Closed Sunday, Monday and August
Credit cards: Visa

Why, when the welcome is so warm and the food is cooked with such loving care, do some of the best guidebooks omit this charming establishment on a gloomy courtyard near the Folies-Bergère? Maybe it has something to do with the outsize personality of Roger Roux, the chef-*patron*. I happen to like him and his sunny Provençal cooking, and his is one of the few spots in Paris where you will find little stuffed vegetables, Nice-style; rabbit with tomato and polenta; and the mammoth *aïoli* (a garlicky mayonnaise) with cod and ten vegetables. All the fish come direct from the Midi, as do many of the wines. After dinner, have a white alcohol at the memorably turbulent Brasserie Flo across the way.

Chez Philippe

106 Rue de la Folie-Méricourt, Paris 11
Tel: 4357-3378. Métro: Oberkampf
Closed Saturday, Sunday, holidays and August
No credit cards

This is another place with a second name—Auberge Pyrénées-Cévennes—and as that name suggests, it specializes in the intense flavors of the far southwest. The paella and the *pipérade* (scrambled eggs with tomatoes, green peppers and heavily smoked ham) are good; the homemade duck foie gras is excellent; the rich, meat-studded cassoulet is probably the best in Paris, as it was in

Waverley Root's day. Hunting trophies, red tile floors, rustic beams, waiters in blue aprons and the animated talk of habitués give this bistro the feeling of a village café, even if it is on a dingy street where its lights are the only ones to be seen at night. Robust, tangy regional wines (Cahors, Minervois); ask the *patron*, Philippe Serbource, for advice.

Moissonier

28 Rue des Fossés-St.-Bernard, Paris 5
Tel: 4329-8765. Métro: Cardinal-Lemoine
Closed Sunday evening, Monday and August
No credit cards

Hard to get into, for two reasons: the prices are relatively modest, and the regulars—professors from the Sorbonne, provincial politicians and wine merchants whose market used to be across the street—never tire of the place. In an unchanging seedy ambience, with a wicker cornucopia of grapes in the middle of the room, Louis Moisonnier serves good things from Lyon and the Jura. Tripe pounded into a flat sheet and fried, a dish known by the piquant name *tablier de sapeur*, or fireman's apron; air-dried meat called *brezi, cervelas rémoulade*, a wonderful potato gratin and Morbier cheese are a few of the highlights. White Arbois and delectable Beaujolais are drawn unfiltered from the cask and served in heavy glass jugs.

Savy

23 Rue Bayard, Paris 8
Tel: 4723-4698. Métro: F.-D.-Roosevelt
Closed Saturday, Sunday and August
No credit cards

Because it is right across the street from the studios of Radio Luxembourg, Savy is thronged at lunchtime, but in the evenings it reverts to an almost rural calm. Go then, and sit in the front room, with its between-the-wars décor and Art Deco windows, rather than the newer, mock-British back room. Gabriel Savy is from the Auvergne in central France, and his daily specials in-

clude a knuckle of ham with lentils on Wednesday and a pot-au-
feu on Friday. My favorite dish, though, is the succulent shoulder
of lamb, roasted to golden tenderness and served with spinach,
grilled tomatoes and a potato gratin. Drink Cahors, try the regional cheeses (Fourme d'Aubrac, perhaps) and the prune tart
and finish with a fine old Armagnac.

A Souseyrac

35 Rue Faidherbe, Paris 11
Tel: 4371-6530. Métro: Faidherbe-Chaligny
Closed Saturday, Sunday, the week before Easter and during
    August
Credit cards: Visa

Quercy is one of the gastronomically abundant regions of
France, and Sousceyrac is a Quercy restaurant. It comes as no
surprise, then, that its huge menu, handwritten in purple ink
every day, is jammed with rich, hearty dishes such as grilled pig's
trotters, morels in puff pastry, hot rabbit mousse and, during the
hunting season, mignons of doe and mouth-watering hare à la
royale. The hot pear tart is utterly irresistible. Gabriel Asfoux succeeded his father in this unpretentious, wood-paneled bistro, and
he has been at it for thirty-three years; his two sons are already
hard at work. That kind of continuity guarantees quality and the
kind of generosity exhibited in the house's habit of offering reasonably priced "bottles of the day" drawn from a big stock of
regional growths.

Ty Coz

35 Rue St. Georges, Paris 9
Tel: 4878-4295. Métro: Notre-Dame-de-Lorette
Closed Sunday and Monday
No credit cards

As far as I know, this is the only major restaurant in Paris with
an all-woman staff, and for my money it is the best Breton place
in the city. Jacqueline Libois and her daughter Marie-Françoise
buy the freshest fish and shellfish the markets have to offer and

handle them according to traditional precepts. There are Marennes oysters, served with their "hats" on, though of course detached, and available the year round; grilled langoustines, delicious stuffed clams and a wide variety of fish from the Atlantic—sole and turbot, *dorade* and bass and *lotte*—which are listed on a blackboard brought to the table. The Marquis de Goulaine's topnotch Muscadet is the thing to drink.

Chez la Vieille

37 Rue de l'Arbre-Sec, Paris 1
Tel: 4260-1578. Métro: Louvre
Lunch only; closed Saturday, Sunday and August
No credit cards

The "old woman" in question is named Adrienne Biasin, and she is a wonder. I would never have met her had it not been for Jean-Claude Vrinat, the proprietor of Taillevent, perhaps the grandest of the *grand-luxe* restaurants in Paris; I had walked past her tiny corner bistro near the Samaritaine department store a dozen times without noticing it, and even if I had, she keeps a "complet" sign on the door. You must reserve; there are only five tables. Mrs. Biasin will bring things to the table and ask if you want them, and you should taste everything. When I was last there, there were three or four terrines, followed by beef with carrots, which had simmered for hours on the back of the stove, accompanied by salsify and little stuffed cabbage rolls in tomato sauce and Savoy cabbage, then a chocolate floating island. Darting from the dining room to the kitchen across the hall, Mme Biasin will find time to recommend a wine and a *digestif*—probably her Calvados from Madame Tasin, the best I have ever drunk.

Finally, it might be appropriate to add some places that didn't make my list. There were old favorites that didn't live up to their past glories when I most recently visited them, such as La Coquille and Mère Michel; there were hot tips that didn't seem quite good enough, or consistent enough, such as Chez René and Sebillon. Others, like Pierre Traiteur and the Ambassade d'Auvergne, seemed a trifle too elaborate to be classified as bistros, although that is obviously a matter of judgment. A few, such as Artois and the Relais des Pyrénées, were omitted because I haven't tried them yet. And try as I might, I couldn't think how to explain away the fact that Lipp, my favorite haunt for a bistro Sunday supper, is really a brasserie.

2. Machons *and* Bouchons

B USINESS is wonderful," Paul Bocuse was saying recently. "The new train has made Paris part of the suburbs of Lyon."

Well, not quite. Even the Train à Grande Vitesse (TGV), whipping along at 165 miles an hour, takes two hours and forty minutes to complete the run down through Burgundy to the old city on the Rhône that Bocuse, in his understated way, calls "the world capital of gastronomy." But the TGV provides an additional excuse, along with the food and the Beaujolais and the wonderful Burgundian churches in the region, to make the trip to Lyon.

What I hope to persuade you to do while there is to extend your eating beyond the charmed circle of Michelin three-star restaurants—Blanc, Bocuse, Chapel, Troisgros, Pyramide—that get nearly all the publicity. I was fortunate enough to meet most of the stars of the nouvelle cuisine twenty years ago. I liked their cooking then, and I like much of it now, especially that of Bocuse and of Georges Blanc, who seem to me to have avoided most of the excesses of the genre. But even Bocuse, the relentless publicist for himself and for his beloved France, the specialist in shrewd business deals as well as in truffle soup, would be miserable eating nouvelle cuisine six nights a week. Especially in a city that built its reputation on the conversion of humble but first-class products—tripe, sausages, pig's feet, *vins de pays* and so forth—into memorable meals.

Simple cooking flourishes still in Lyon, but it is eaten mostly by the Lyonnais. Everyone else is making a mistake, like the surgeon in Columbus, Ohio, who once proudly showed me his wine cellar, with rack after rack of first growths, and explained that he kept nothing plainer because he preferred Coca-Cola except when he was giving a party.

The most basic meal in Lyon is a *machon*. A typical one might include a salad made of curly endive and bits of bacon, a fat warm sausage with hot potato salad, or a *tablier de sapeur*—a square of breaded tripe, so called because it resembles an old-fashioned fireman's apron—and cheese, preferably the aromatic St. Marcellin, which the great Fernand Point always served, unaccompanied by other cheeses, at the banquets he often cooked in the 1930s. You would be thought daft to drink anything but Beaujolais (either the straight stuff or one of the named growths from such villages as Fleurie or Chiroubles or Morgon or Brouilly)— and you *would* be daft, because all the best Beaujolais flows south to Lyon rather than north to Paris. It is not a question of wine not traveling well but of hoarding.

Where to find a *machon*? There is a place called La Tassée at 20 Rue de la Charité, just behind the Sofitel hotel, that does a splendid one, and serves some of the most delicious Beaujolais I have ever tasted. It's also a good spot to have a glass of wine between meals, or, rather, a *tassée* (tasting cup) of wine, because that's how they serve it. Or you might enjoy eating at one of the stalls in the central market, probably France's finest, where Bocuse and his young protégés often take an early lunch. It's on Cours la Fayette, across the Rhône from the city center. If there is the slightest prospect of a picnic, maybe even if there isn't, don't miss the cheese stand of Mère Richard, considered by the locals and many visitors as a national treasure.

The Lyonnais, who seem to have special words for almost everything, call a small, plain restaurant a *bouchon*. For years, my favorite was a place called La Voute, but known to everyone as Chez Léa. It's still there at 11 Place Gourju; Léa, one of the last of the city's venerable women cooks, a feisty seventy-three-year-old whose insults were as succulent as her *plats du jour*, has sold out, but happily for me, she chose a successor as steeped in tradition as she, Phillipe Rabatel.

A couple of coats of ivory paint have spruced the place up. But the new *patron* has left the old wooden-slat benches in place, and he has preserved the little set menu, which is remarkably good value. In September, 1985, Betsey and I ate the following for

78 francs each (about $10): a *mesclun* salad, composed of five or six lettuces and herbs that gave it a haunting, smoky, anisey taste; the aforementioned *tablier de sapeur*; macaroni and cheese, a dish that somehow made its way from Nice up the Rhone, the only broad north-south passage between the Atlantic and the Danube basin, to become a Lyonnais favorite; *cervelles de Canut*, a dish of soft young cheese, squeezed through a pastry bag in such a way that it looks, lying in a mound on the plate, like brains; and a raspberry tart. With an excellent bottle of Chiroubles and a fine *marc* each, the price for the two of us soared to an unconscionable $39.06. The food was quite delicious.

Le Garet and Chez Georges are on either side of Rue Garet near the city hall, both grubbily wonderful and full of *joie de vivre*. You will almost certainly find yourselves the only foreigners there. Dussaud, in the same neighborhood at 12 Rue Pizay, is the favorite of Jean-Paul Lacombe, of whom more in a moment. All are closed Saturday and Sunday, and Monique Dussaud cooks only at lunch. If a craving for *saucisson chaud* hits you on the Sabbath, try Tante Alice at 22 Rue Remparts d'Ainay.

A somewhat different formula applies at Raymond, a café for most of the day that takes wing at noon for the lucky occupants of its six tables. Located in a run-down neighborhood—21 Rue de Rancy, at the corner of, believe it or not, Rue du Gazomètre—this is the creation of Raymond Caillot, who used to be Bocuse's maître d'hôtel. One day in October, he and his wife put on the big central table a modest assortment of eighteen salads, three terrines and four spectacular sausages—a *jésus*, a *rosette*, a *cervelat* and a spicy one, new to me—a *rouelle*, from the Ardèche. It's always like that at Chez Raymond, and the hors d'oeuvres are always followed by a homey *plat du jour* (sometimes there's a choice, sometimes not). Beautiful cheeses, as many desserts as you could imagine, including, on my visit, some tangerines poached with the loving care of a French grandmother.

A meal Chez Raymond can be had, wine included, for $20, if you're reasonably careful, and they charge nothing for the smiles that come with it.

Those same smiles, so very un-Parisian, are in evidence on the waiters in long blue aprons at Léon de Lyon, which is where I would steer anyone who wanted to know how typical Lyonnais fare tastes when cooked not by a competent operator but by a

major talent. Jean-Paul Lacombe is the young man in question—
a shy and diffident soul when he took over after the untimely
death of his father, a seasoned professional only a few years
later. His *carte* is split in two—tradition on the left, innovation on
the right. Choose one, choose the other, or mix them—you cannot
fail. I have never eaten a single bad dish at Léon de Lyon, and I
am not far from agreeing with David Stevens, the music critic of
the *International Herald Tribune*, who says he could eat at 1 Rue
Pléney every day of his life. Stevens, who has ruined a once-slim
figure through devotion to Lyon cooking, thinks the *gras-double*
is the best dish on the list. Tripe again, but so transformed by
slow simmering with tomatoes and onions that you will be
astounded and delighted even if you avoid tripe the way I avoid
Velveeta.

CHAPTER VI

Italy

1. In Search of Piero

EACH generation makes its own list of the greatest artists of the past; it is not uncommon for someone who was little known in his own lifetime, like Vermeer, to be judged a paragon hundreds of years later. In our own day, perhaps the most dramatic example of the upgrading of a painter's reputation is that of Piero della Francesca, that mysterious genius of the quattrocento from the Tuscan backwater of Sansepolcro. Almost ignored in the nineteenth century (Ruskin barely mentions him), Piero is acknowledged today to be one of the greatest artists who ever lived, worthy of comparison with Leonardo or Rembrandt.

His relatively few surviving pictures appeal strongly to our modern eyes, conditioned as they are by Cubism and Cézanne, because he was a master of geometry and volume. There is something almost abstract in his faces, and there are no grandiose flourishes. As Aldous Huxley, a great admirer, put it: "A natural, spontaneous and unpretentious grandeur—this is the leading quality of all Piero's work. He is majestic without being at all strained, theatrical or hysterical—as Handel is majestic, not as Wagner." To which I would add the observation that Piero infuses his subjects with a timeless serenity that is devoid of sweetness, a quality of which modern man stands in dire need. It is that

which guarantees, in the words of the late Kenneth Clark, that he will remain on the creative pinnacle "even when the tide of taste that carried him there has withdrawn."

"I am tempted to conclude," wrote Bernard Berenson late in life, "that in the long run the most satisfactory creations are those which, like Piero's and Cézanne's, remain ineloquent, mute, with no urgent communication to make, and no thought of rousing us with look and gesture. If they express anything it is character, essence, rather than momentary feeling or purpose. They manifest potentiality rather than activity. It is enough that they exist in themselves."

We know relatively little about Piero's life—not even, for sure, to whom he was apprenticed, although it is thought likely that he first worked with Domenico Veneziano. He was born about 1420 in Sansepolcro (sometimes called Borgo San Sepolcro), a town in the upper Tiber Valley between Assisi and Florence, and spent most of his life there, dying there on October 12, 1492—the very day that another Italian, Christopher Columbus, made his momentous discovery on the other side of the world. But he also worked in Florence and Urbino, in Ferrara and Rimini, and he clearly came into contact with and was deeply influenced by the work of the Florentine Massacio and the Fleming Rogier van der Weyden, who also spent time in Ferrara.

American museums, so rich in the work of so many Old Masters, afford little opportunity to relish the genius of Piero della Francesca. In New York, there is only the Frick Collection's fragment of the great St. Augustine altarpiece, painted for Sansepolcro; two other fragments, one in the Frick, the other in the National Gallery in Washington, were probably done by an assistant. The only other universally acknowledged Pieros in the United States are in New England—a *Virgin and Child with Four Angels* at the Clark Art Institute in Williamstown, Massachusetts, and a powerful *Hercules* in the Isabella Stewart Gardner Museum in Boston.

To see Piero whole, one must devote several days to the project and visit the places south and southeast of Florence where much of his best work remains: Arezzo, a somewhat forbidding place, and Perugia, self-confident on its hilltop, and Monterchi, an out-of-the-way hamlet that most travelers speed past, and Sansepolcro itself, a compact little town of six thousand people with ridged red roofs, and Urbino, the city of Raphael, with its glorious Ducal Palace, and finally Rimini, now a grotesquely overbuilt resort. There are other Piero masterpieces to be seen elsewhere in Europe, but not many; more about them later. A good approach is to take a three-day trip, starting and ending in Florence, including a fine meal or two, traversing some magnificent scenery, but concentrating on this one great artist. (On the way you may not want to miss the Fra Angelicos in Cortona or the Giottos in Assisi; the Blue Guide to Northern Italy will lead you to those delights and many more, but you will have to lengthen your trip accordingly.)

While you are visiting the Uffizi, before setting off, take special note of the Urbino diptych, which depicts Federico da Montefeltro, Duke of Urbino—a celebrated general who was the sworn enemy of Piero's early patron, Sigismondo Malatesta—and his wife, Battista Sforza. They face each other in profile, against a panoramic landscape: she wan and almost lifeless, in jewels and clothes rendered with a Flemish passion for detail, he hook-nosed, dark and powerful, in a simple red cassock and matching flat hat. On the reverse they approach each other in ceremonial chariots, accompanied by various Virtues; beneath are verses extolling his triumphs and her restraint. The handling of color and light is incredibly deft and delicate, never melodramatic.

Arezzo, just fifty miles down the autostrada, was the birthplace of Petrarch, the poet, of Guido, who invented our musical scale, and of Vasari, the artist and biographer of artists. But it owes its modern fame to Piero, who painted a Saint Mary Magdalen in the cathedral about 1466, and covered the choir in the Church of San Francesco with his mighty frescoes of the Legend of the True Cross.

Already hanging in flakes from the walls 140 years ago, they have been repeatedly restored, most recently according to a system whereby heavily damaged areas have been filled in with a distracting, supposedly neutral buff color. The lighting is not all that it might be, the church is often crowded and tour guides deliver their spiels, usually full of misinformation, in voices better suited to the parade ground. But the pictures are great enough to withstand all of that and more. Symmetry vies with irregularity; the paleness of the palette and the skillful and unobtrusive use of

perspective combine to yield a remarkable monumentality. The
Queen of Sheba adores the wood from which the cross was made
and visits Solomon in two of the most famous scenes; Constantine and Heraclius defeat infidels in two others. *The Dream of
Constantine* is usually counted as the most dramatic of Piero's
visions. For me, the most gripping passage in the frescoes is not
any of the hundreds of human figures that are to be seen or
glimpsed, but the rearing gray horse at the extreme left of Constantine's victory, seemingly ready to gallop off the wall, washed
by what Kenneth Clark calls "the most perfect morning light in
all of Renaissance painting."

After lunch, make for Perugia, like Arezzo an old Etruscan
city. As H. V. Morton remarks in A *Traveller in Italy*, the curious,
haughty beauty of Piero's women has an Etruscan quality about
it, and so do many of the faces you will see as you stroll down
the Corso Vannucci, Perugia's main street, to the National
Gallery of Umbria. One of the least-known of the great museums
of Italy, it contains major works by Perugino and Pinturicchio,
a rare if wretchedly preserved example of the work of Domenico
Veneziano and a polyptych attributed to Piero. After Arezzo,
you will have no difficulty in coming to the same conclusion as
the experts—that most of it is the clumsy work of others; but the
Annunciation at the top, especially the brilliant perspective and
the glowing color of the colonnade, is vintage Piero.

Route S3-bis leads north along the Tiber to Città di Castello,
and from there you fork left on S221 to Monterchi, where Piero's
mother was born. Monterchi is relegated to the small print by the
guidebooks, and until recently there were no signs to tell the
traveler that there was anything to detain him. I was taken there
many years ago by an old friend, Raimonda Buitoni, a Piero fanatic who lives in Perugia, and I have been back several times; the
Madonna del Parto in a tiny chapel in the village cemetery, below
the old ramparts, may not be the artist's masterpiece, but it is my
favorite. Only a small altar shares the chapel with the fresco,
which shows two angels drawing back the flaps of a vaguely Arab
tent and, in the center, the Virgin, obviously pregnant, her dress
open down the front and seemingly too small to fit over her swollen belly, to which she points. Her face, as Clark points out, has
the calm, detached beauty of a Buddha. The impact of the paint-

ing itself can only be increased by the knowledge that this icon of birth stands amid memorials to the dead: a beginning among ends.

From Monterchi, it will take you only a few minutes, following route S73, to reach Sansepolcro. The local picture gallery, housed in the town hall, is blissfully relaxed, a world away from the guards and crowds of the Uffizi or the Louvre. Yet it contains, in a single room, a charming portrait of Saint Julian, discovered only in 1954, which may be a fragment of the same work from which the *Hercules* in Boston came; the early *Madonna della Misericordia*, partly by assistants, but with a luminous portrait of the Virgin at the center, in which she shelters worshipers with her cloak; and the *Resurrection of Christ*. The last is a picture of awesome power, perfectly preserved by the whitewash that covered it for centuries. Four Roman soldiers have fallen asleep beside the sarcophagus, three of them with their helmets on, all of them sprawled awkwardly. In the pale light of dawn, Christ towers above them, bold as the Pantocrator in the conch of a Byzantine church yet intensely spiritual, staring straight ahead with one foot poised on His tomb. If any artist ever succeeded in capturing the dual nature of the Saviour, god in man, it was Piero in this painting. Huxley was transported by it; "it stands there before us in entire and actual splendor," he wrote, "the greatest picture in the world."

The S73-bis loops up out of the valley and across the hills toward the coast, a time-consuming if lovely journey today that must have been physically punishing when Piero made it frequently in the fifteenth century. Urbino is forty-two miles away, the seat of the Montefeltros from the twelfth to the seventeenth century and the object of artistic pilgrimages ever since despite its remote location. The town is dominated by the Ducal Palace, the masterwork of Luciano Laurana and one of the greatest of all Renaissance buildings, in which the National Gallery of the Marches is laid out. Curiously, the museum has only one Raphael, and a relatively minor one at that, but it has two Pieros. *The Flagellation of Christ*, one of his most perfect pictures, almost Euclidian in its logic and precision, is not really about the flagellation at all; it is instead a portrait of the three important men in the right foreground, while the abuse of Christ in the left background represents an event in their lives or perhaps the subject of their thoughts. The *Sinigallia Madonna* is much less satisfying, with a Christ child of a strangely middle-aged aspect and an angel who looks more like a school prefect. (The museum has a third picture, the famous *Perspective View of an Ideal Town*, that is sometimes attributed to Piero, but the museum no longer considers it his work. It remains fascinating.)

Our final destination is Rimini, an easy hour's drive up route S423 and then along the coast on the autostrada. There, in Alberti's intriguing Malatesta Temple, a combination of church and temporal shrine, you will find above the door in the Chapel of Relics Piero's heraldic depiction of the tyrant Malatesta kneeling before his patron, Saint Sigismund. He is as hawklike as his enemy, Montefeltro. The fresco has crumbled badly, but Malatesta's face, the architectural frame, the rich green swag across the top and the two magnificently painted hounds in the lower right remain to suggest what once was.

From Rimini, one can take the autostrada to the Forli turnoff, then take S67 back to Florence. That will permit a luncheon stop at Gianfranco Bolognesi's charming restaurant, La Frasca in Castrocaro Terme, before heading across the mountains. The rest of Piero's major works are all in big cities, so you can see them in the course of other trips; the *Saint Jerome* in the Accademia at Venice; the *Madonna* in the Brera Gallery in Milan, with an egg (symbolizing the creation?) suspended over her head, which sprang back to life after an extensive recent restoration, and the *Baptism of Christ*, the *Nativity* and *Saint Michael* (another fragment from the St. Augustine altarpiece)—all in the National Gallery, London. The *Baptism*, with its hovering dove, its keenly observed landscape, its three angels and its shadowless sumptuousness of coloring, is much the finest work by Piero outside Italy.

2. Décor by Palladio

FOR as long as most people can remember, Harry's Bar has been the outstanding restaurant in Venice, celebrated by Hemingway, recognized by Michelin with two stars, chosen as one of the ten best in the country by several Italian guides and, most important, universally named by the finicky Venetians themselves as the only consistently reliable deluxe establishment in town.

But Arrigo Cipriani has been worrying lately. Like the restaurant, he was named by his father after an American benefactor who helped set up the business, and he has maintained its excellence despite all the temptations of celebrity; with Taillevent in Paris, it is one of the few superrestaurants in Europe that gives as warm a welcome to nobodies as to Somebodies. Yet in recent years Venetians, especially the younger ones who will be tomorrow's regulars, have been complaining that the prices are too high and that tables are too hard to get.

Me, I would pay whatever prices he cared to charge, if I had enough lire in my pocket, not only because I love the food but also because the Commendatore, as Arrigo's father was called, had the circumspection to name his specialties—the thinly sliced beef he called Carpaccio and the cocktail he christened the Bellini—after my two favorite Venetian painters and not after those parvenus Titian and Tintoretto.

At any rate, Cipriani (whose family sold the hotel bearing their name some years ago) recently opened a zippy new place called Harry's Dolci. Inside of a week, it was jammed for every meal, mostly, to the delight of the boss, with smart young Venetians. (The menu at Harry's Bar is in three languages, but the one at Harry's Dolci, which means Harry's Sweets, is all in Italian.)

It is a single, woody room, with a few umbrella-topped tables outside, in one of the remoter parts of the city—at the western end of the island of Giudecca, between the church of Sant' Eufemia and the brooding, deserted Teutonic warehouse called the Molino Stucky. Just across the broad Giudecca Canal are anchored, most days, the sleek cruise ships that are calling at Venice, and the view down the canal is closed by the gleaming white bulk of San Giorgio Maggiore; Arrigo Cipriani smiles his double-breasted smile and tells you that "Palladio was my exterior decorator."

The food is simple and ultrafresh. There are antipasti (tiny spring peas, baby artichoke pie and chickpea-and-onion salad one day we were there), soups, *panini* (tiny sandwiches filled with

Cipriani favorites such as Carpaccio, chicken salad and spectacular prosciutto). At first, that was all; but success has prompted Cipriani to add such dishes as a fritto misto of fish, vitello tonnato and linguine with delicious, microscopically small clams from the lagoon. Ice creams and pastries, including a chocolate cake of deadly richness, are produced at a sparkling new Cipriani bakery just around the corner. There is a small kitchen staff, which makes it possible to hold prices down; a pitcher of Venegazzu, the excellent house red at both places, costs $29 at the Bar and $14 at the Dolci. Go Sunday noon if you can, but be sure to call for reservations first (041-24844 or 708337). The restaurant is closed Monday.

Aside from Cipriani's two places, the best food my wife and I have eaten on four recent trips to Venice has been in small, out-of-the-way trattorias suggested to me over the years by local friends. It is in these that you find the most authentic versions of the special local fish dishes, from *coda di rospo* (anglerfish tail) and *triglia* (red mullet) and *spigola* (bass) to *grancevola* (spider crab) and *cicala* (a kind of flat lobster) and *capa longa* (razor clam) and especially the superb scampi.

The Venetians are, of course, a maritime people; they had to be, driven as they were from the mainland to Torcello and finally to the 118 islets of Venice by advancing barbarians, and they have long since lost the taste for most meat—except for calf's liver, which they eat in vast quantities, sliced into thin strips, sautéed with onions and served with grilled cornmeal cakes called polenta. The problem is that most of the restaurants that cater to tourists presume that they have to serve meat, anyway, and they don't cook it very well. I'll tell you about an exception later, but meanwhile here is a short list of places where tradition is served:

Corte Sconta

3886 Castello, Calle del Pestrin
Tel.: 27024
Closed Monday and Tuesday lunch

At the moment, this "hidden courtyard" with its factory décor and tables covered with brown paper is the best fish restaurant in town. Scallops cooked with a bit of broth and seasoned with flat parsley, small clams touched with garlic, fresh sardines, tiny octopus—all that and more as a first course. Then a pair of pastas—on a recent occasion, one with *cicale*, another with fresh anchovies. Then a salad ("our midmeal sorbet," said the owner, Gianni Tegon). Then a platter of six or seven fried fish and shellfish. Everything is fresh, light, understated and washed down with Prosecco, an undeservedly little-known white wine from near Treviso, which comes in sparkling and still versions. There is also an assertive *Grappa di Prosecco* in an unlabeled bottle.

Da Fiore

2202 San Polo, Calle del Scalater
Tel.: 37208
Closed Sunday, Monday, August and Christmas

Tucked away in a small street not far from the Frari, Fiore is a sober bourgeois place that is only now beginning to be discovered by foreigners. Good oysters, which are a rarity in Venice, and excellent risottos, especially those made with *radicchio*. The goal here is quality, not flash, so the selection may be limited. They make their own bread. First-rate service.

Antica Bessetta

1395 Santa Croce, Salizzada Zusto
Tel.: 37687
Closed Tuesday and Wednesday

This place is impossible to find, so have the concierge draw you a map; if he doesn't know it, help him along by telling him that it is near San Giacomo dell'Orio. Nereo Volpe works in the plain front room, his wife, Maurizia, in the back. He is the menu (as well as the producer of the two fine house wines), so pay attention to his advice. Among the memorable dishes she cooks from time to time are tagliatelle with asparagus, fabulous fried soft-shell crabs and razor clams in a gentle, herby broth.

Madonna

594 San Polo, Calle della Madonna
Tel.: 23624
Closed Wednesday and January

Unlike the others on my list, the Madonna is known to almost everybody. Sometimes the pasta is overcooked, though never the *risotto di pesce* and never the grilled fish. Order that, and enjoy the scenery, because the Madonna is the heart and soul of Venice. The interconnecting dining rooms are always full of laughing, gesticulating, fast-talking people and teasing, hustling, smiling waiters. Near the "far" end of the Rialto bridge.

La Furatola

2870A Dorsoduro, Calle Lunga San Barnaba
Tel.: 708594
No dinner Wednesday, closed Thursday and July

Cheerful and inexpensive, this trattoria grills fish as well as any in Venice. Bruno and Sandro, the owners, have a reputation among their peers as canny men at the market, which has a lot to do with the quality of what they put on your plate. Good house white wine.

Now for the exception. When—if—you get tired of fish, head for

Da Ivo

1809 San Marco, Calle dei Fuseri
Tel.: 705889
Closed Sunday and January

A pretty little place with gondolas passing by the windows. The chef is a master of that Florentine delight the *bistecca*, a huge and juicy T-bone steak. Preceded perhaps by *crostini* (rough croutons spread with anchovy paste and chicken livers), ordered rare, squirted with lemon, it will calm the carnivore in you suf-

ficiently to permit a return to the typical briny fare of this noble
city that was once a country.

A Venetian friend suggests that I add the *Trattoria Altonella*
to my list; it is a neighborhood place, rude but good, he says, but
I have yet to try it. If you would like to, you will find it about a
ten-minute walk from the Cipriani Hotel in the direction of
Harry's Dolci. Finally, you might want to share the Venetian
habit of a mid-morning or mid-afternoon nip, a glass of wine
which they call an *ombra* (the word means, in its literal sense,
shadow or ghost). To do so, stop at a *bacaro*, a special local sort
of restaurant with a cold-table at mealtimes and a good stock of
regional wines. An intriguing one is the Osteria Ca' d'Oro, near
the house of the same name, which is newly reopened after more
than a decade of repair.

3. *Ravishing Ravello*

THE forty-one mile trip along the serpentine Amalfi Drive
from Salerno to Sorrento must be one of the world's loveliest. Literary men from the less-favored north—Ibsen and
Nietzsche, Gorky and Gide—have sung the praises of this glorious corner of southern Italy for more than a century, and Gide
confessed in *The Immoralist* that the drive "was so beautiful that
I had no desire to see anything more beautiful on earth." The
coast itself has been little touched by the industrial and commercial blight that has ravaged the areas closer to Naples—
although in this age of mass tourism the narrow, vertiginous highway is packed with cars and buses at the peak of the season. The
best way to enjoy the drive to get away from it—or, more precisely,
to rise above it, by climbing the Valley of the Dragon to Ravello,
the seductive little town huddled on a prowlike ridge some
twelve hundred feet or so above Amalfi.

Ravello is not the place for you if your idea of a seaside vacation is a concrete slab of a hotel, with four restaurants and four

bars, giving directly onto a broad golden strand. The beaches below the town—at Maiori and Marina di Ravello and Amalfi and, a bit farther west, at Positano—are a bit pebbly. The sand at the water's edge is dark. You have to drive down from your aerie to get to them, a fifteen-minute trip to the closest and a forty-minute trip to the farthest. But the surroundings are incomparable, especially at Marina di Ravello, where the beach is hemmed in by towering cliffs and where little has changed in a hundred years. It reminds me a bit of Maine, except that the water is warmer and the wine cheaper.

There are, of course, other differences as well. One is the mosaic of exuberant Latin color that seems to envelop you—broad beach umbrellas in every hue; equally colorful cabanas, in which you can change into swimming gear and, not least, the uninhibited livery of the fishing boats returning to Amalfi and Minori and Praiano with the catch that you may help to eat the next day. You can choose a beach to suit your circumstances. If you are traveling with your family, head for Maiori or Minori; if you aren't, the Lido della Sirena at Amalfi is probably the best choice, with a clientele of sophisticated singles and doubles from all over the world and a snack bar and facilities for snorkelers and wind surfers. If you want something wilder, you can rent a boat at the Sirena and chug along the coast to tiny, unspoiled hideaways that cannot be reached by any other means.

Ravello provides the perfect refuge from the mobs that descend on this coast, like most in southern Europe, in the warmer months. Even in July and August, it is never crowded. It can't be, since there are only 350 hotel rooms in the entire town. You can experience all the joys of the Mediterranean—swimming, sailing in small boats that can be rented in Amalfi, fishing, even water-skiing—without suffering from people pollution. You can experience the sea physically during the day and emotionally during the early mornings and the long, soft evenings, for Ravello is very much of the sea if not on it. And you can combine all of this with a host of excursions—to the island of Capri; to Vesuvius, the only active volcano on the European mainland; to Pompeii and Herculaneum and Paestum, three of the great sites of ancient civilization; to turbulent Naples and its undervalued cultural treasures.

Once you have had your fill of the beaches, and you have run out of opponents at the local tennis club, you can spend a day happily ambling through the town, which retains, despite a century of tourism, its medieval and Renaissance aspect.

The centerpiece is the Villa Rufolo, the grandest of the palaces built by families grown rich in the Levantine trade in the era in which tiny Amalfi, along with Venice, Pisa and Genoa, exercised dominant power in the Mediterranean. Paths lead past two grim old towers and a little courtyard in the Moorish style, with graceful arabesques, to the famous garden with the view toward Cap d'Orso. Wagner was among the admirers of this enchanted spot; after visiting it in 1880, when he was working on *Parsifal*, he exclaimed, "I have found the magic garden of Klingsor!"

You stand there, incredulous, surrounded by palms, cypresses and umbrella pines, with vivid beds of flowers at your feet, and gaze east across hillsides planted with vines and lemon and orange trees, the vista punctuated here and there by the exclamation point of an old campanile, at villages whose whitewashed houses are scattered over the landscape like dotless dice, at gray-brown mountains plunging into the sea and at the blue-green water itself, lapping aimlessly at the little beaches that fill the coves. All is quiet, except for the occasional distant squawk of a tour-bus horn. And if you are both wise and lucky, you can go to bed and wake up to almost the same view from the window or terrace of your room in one of Ravello's little hotels.

A second palazzo, the Villa Cimbrone, is only a ten-minute stroll away; its buildings are largely modern reconstructions but the gardens, clinging to the hillside like a swallow's nest, are extraordinary. The cathedral, which dominates the main square, is an unfortunate mélange of Romanesque and Baroque, but inside are a quite wonderful pulpit (1272), richly inlaid with sparkling mosaics and supported by spiral columns resting on the backs of six fiercely growling lions, and a pair of Romanesque bronze doors (1179), with fifty-four panels depicting the Passion, saints and warriors, made by Barisano da Trani, who also cast the great north door at Monreale in Sicily.

A first excursion might take you to Capri, that tiny island, only four miles long and less than two miles wide, that has so excited the admiration of poets and songwriters, expatriates and jet setters. It was a favorite haunt of the Roman emperor Augustus and a favorite target of the Barbary pirates, and after the abortive St.

Petersburg rising of 1905 it attracted such exiles as Lenin, Chalia-pin and Gorky. For the modern visitor, the great attraction is the motorboat trip to the Blue Grotto (best visited at noon), but I find walking the most satisfying thing to do on the island—starting in the bustling piazza of Capri, the main village, perhaps after an espresso at a café, and heading either through the villas and gardens on Monte Tuoro to the little port of Tragara or up the road to Anacapri through the fragrant dwarf myrtle, juniper, heather and carob.

Another day, drive east along the Gulf of Salerno to Paestum, a trip of about ninety minutes. Founded in the seventh century B.C. by the Greeks, in an area that remained malarial until modern times, the site has three noble and magnificently preserved Doric temples, of which the misleadingly named Temple of Neptune (475 B.C.) is the finest. Equally compelling is the "diver" fresco, preserved in the adjacent museum, which may be the only true ancient Greek painting in existence.

If Paestum reminds us of the grandeur of classical architecture, the excavated Roman towns of Pompeii and Herculaneum ("Ercolano" on the road signs), both of which were buried in the eruption of Vesuvius in A.D. 79, give us our most vivid picture of the ancients' daily lives. Pompeii is the larger and the grander of the two, with an impressive forum and sumptuous villas, but Herculaneum is better preserved (and thus more comprehensible to the layman) because it was buried in mud, while Pompeii was buried in hot lava and cinders. If you haven't time for both, go to Herculaneum, which you can see in about two hours. Pompeii takes at least three. You can combine either with the ascent of Vesuvius by car and then on foot or by chair lift. The panorama from the top is awe-inspiring.

By no means miss a visit to Naples. All the horror stories you have heard about it are true, and you should leave your jewelry and most of your money at the hotel. Naples is a ragamuffin of a town, poor, squalid, noisy, corrupt, a cheap bit of glass in a setting worthy of diamonds. But it is a fascinating place, too, mainly because of its people, who are short, dark, hearty, sentimental, animated and superstitious. They invented spaghetti with tomato sauce and the pizza; they gave us Sophia Loren and Enrico Caruso, and they still sing "Santa Lucia" and "O Sole Mio."

As if that were not enough, there are three wonderful and undervisited museums lurking among the trash and the traffic jams. The National Archeological Museum has one of the world's great collections of classical art, including frescoes and mosaics from Pompeii and Herculaneum and a stunning assembly of statuary, including the twelve-foot-high Farnese Bull, the largest surviving antique sculpture. A mile north is the National Gallery of Capodimonte, with a superb display of porcelain as well as a picture gallery that rivals any in Italy except the Uffizi. Among dozens of other masterpieces, you can see there Brueghel's haunting *The Blind Leading the Blind*, a Bellini *Transfiguration* set in a magical landscape, and Simone Martini's greatest work, *St. Louis of Toulouse Crowning Robert of Anjou*. Finally, the Certosa di San Martino, probably the best example of the exuberant Neapolitan Baroque, houses a well-known collection of *presepi*—Nativity scenes with hundreds of statuettes. The most fantastic of these is called the Cucinello Crib.

All three museums close at 2:00 P.M. on weekdays and 1:00 P.M. on Sundays, so you will need to get an early start for the one-hour drive across the hills into town. Take a break for lunch in Spacca Napoli, the old town, then end your visit with a people-watching (and especially a gesture-watching) stroll—a last taste of frenzy before returning to the soothing calm of Ravello.

The very best times to go are May and June, September and October (July and August are a bit hot, and some of the beaches are apt to be crowded then). There are three choice places to stay, in different price brackets, and none of them is outrageously expensive. The most venerable, the most expensive and the most elegant of the trio is the Palumbo, founded in 1860 and still run by the Vuilleumier family, who originally came from Switzerland. Pasquale Vuilleumier, handsome and patrician, speaks proudly of his Scottish-Swiss-Italian heritage.

Longfellow stayed there, as did Grieg and E. M. Forster and Garbo, and D. H. Lawrence worked on *Lady Chatterley's Lover* in one of the rooms. The celebrity of the moment is Gore Vidal, who spends his summers in Ravello. He often holds court, surrounded by fellow members of the glitterati, at dinner on the Palumbo's terrace, which helps, along with ferns and broken arches and winding staircases, to give the hotel a certain glamour. The food is excellent, though it sometimes seems a bit too modern and "international" for such a tradition-loving region, with dishes like shrimp in puff pastry.

Such things seldom show up down the street at the Caruso Belvedere, which like the Palumbo is housed in a medieval palace rebuilt during the Renaissance, incorporates antique Corinthian columns and produces its own quite palatable wines. But the Caruso Belvedere—now run by Gino Caruso, grandson of the founder, a magnificently mustachioed man named Pantaleone— is a holdout against modernity in almost every respect. The place has the feeling of the 1930s about it, with big, high-ceilinged bedrooms, handsomely but rather sparsely furnished, and sitting rooms with old overstuffed chairs. The only obvious decoration in the hotel is the extraordinary Pompeiian-style painted ceiling in the main lounge, where you have drinks and coffee, and that has been there for ages. Pio Bottone, the chef, cooks simply and very well, and no one should miss his ham- and cheese-filled crepes or his soufflé—half chocolate, half lemon—if they are on the menu. Still farther down the Via Toro, with the same view but less panache, is the warm-hearted little Parsifal.

The food in most of the restaurants up and down the coast has been ruined by a foreign clientele that wants only what it knows. None of the guidebooks, Italian or foreign, is wholly reliable in this region, for some reason, but local friends have steered me to several places where I think you can count on eating a decent and economical seaside lunch. More than that I cannot promise.

Fish will, or certainly should, appear on most menus. Some of the nomenclature may be unfamiliar, so here is a ten-second glossary: *spigola* is sea bass; *orata* is the delicious golden bream that the French call *dorade*; *sarago*, *sarpa*, *dentice* and *marmora* are lesser types of bream; *merluzzo* is hake, a tastier relative of the cod; *pesce spada* is swordfish, and *acciuga* or *alice* is anchovy.

The establishments below are listed in roughly geographical order. At any of them, drink the inexpensive and delicate white wines from Capri or Ischia, or perhaps one of the pale, soft rosés from Ravello. Lunch for two, with such a wine, shouldn't cost much more than $30.

Naples: In a city where the cooking is rapidly improving, three of the best restaurants command grand views of the bay from vantage points to the west: La Sacrestia (81-664-186) in Mergellina, Giuseppone a Mare (81-769-6002) in Posillipo and the simpler Rosiello da Mimi (81-769-4401) farther out at Marechiaro. In the Spacca Napoli quarter, Ciro (81-324-072), a monument to traditional Neapolitan cooking, would be an excellent choice for lunch.

Marina di Cantone: Maria Grazia (81-808-1011), situated almost at the end of the Sorrento peninsula, which points like a rocky thumb at Capri, may be the best restaurant on the whole coast, with especially good *aragosta* (*langouste* or spiny lobster), as well as a heavenly dish of pasta with zucchini.

Capri: La Pigna (81-837-0280) is a good lunch spot.

Positano: The Buca di Bacco (89-875-699), with its veranda on the beach, is not as chic as it was in the 1960s, but it is still extremely pleasant. Try the spaghetti with clam sauce and the swordfish.

Ravello: There is one good independent restaurant in town, the Compo Cosimo (89-857-156), just off the cathedral square, an unpretentious place specializing in what the Italians call "cucina casalinga," or home cooking. Pizza from wood-fired ovens.

Amalfi: Da Gemma (89-871-345) is a good, jolly family trattoria, specializing in fish, either grilled or sautéed.

Paestum: Have lunch at the Nettuno (828-811-928), in the archeological zone, and go for a swim afterward.

4. Cucina Genuina

O F all the great cuisines of the world, Italy's has always been the simplest, built as it is on the prodigal production of the country's rich farms and teeming seas. Dishes like spaghetti with tomato sauce and roast veal owe everything to ingredients—freshly handmade pasta, sun-ripened tomatoes, virgin olive oil and newly picked basil in one case, milk-fed baby veal and fragrant rosemary in the other—and almost nothing to complicated culinary procedures. It is perhaps the hardest food to reproduce outside its native territory, because of the emphasis on ideal ingredients, but at its best there is no better everyday food, in my judgment, to be found anywhere.

Although I have never been lucky enough to live there, I have been lucky enough to visit Italy several dozen times over the last couple of decades. After a stumbling start, I managed to eat wonderfully well by sticking to a few rules: avoid places with starched tablecloths, eat the local specialties, the simpler the better, drink the carafe wine unless you're sitting in the middle of a vineyard, and perhaps even then, and don't take Michelin nearly as seriously as you do in France. But in the last year or so, I have realized that my maxims were out of date; while my attention was elsewhere, all kinds of interesting things have been happening to Italian restaurants.

Not that you can't still eat spectacular regional cuisine in simple trattorias from Udine to Palermo, if you find the right ones; not that all of the innovation has been successful. But a new class of establishment has sprung up, chiefly north of Perugia, with gifted chefs who are no longer content with reproducing the regional classics. The temptation, all too readily embraced by some Italian and foreign food writers, is to call the new style "nuova cucina," after the nouvelle cuisine that has spread from France·across the world, but the name really isn't apt. The cooking in the best of the new places owes something to the modern preference for lighter sauces and clearer tastes, but it also owes something to the rediscovery of old recipes and to the increased availability in one region of products from others. It is simpler, as one might expect, than nouvelle cuisine, though considerably more complex than the traditional style.

The gratifying renaissance in Italian cooking has even acquired a kind of manifesto, drawn up by Franco Colombani, the gentle, self-effacing but fiercely committed proprietor of Il Sole, south of Milan. In his barn, Mr. Colombani brews the best vinegar I have ever tasted, aging it for nine years in a succession of barrels made of different woods—juniper, myrtle, cherry, oak and chestnut. He is that kind of perfectionist. He has also started an association of like-minded restaurateurs, who have agreed to follow several precepts, the most important of which are "to limit the number of dishes on the menu" and "not to invent just for the sake of it, not to play games, and not to slavishly follow fashions." He and his friends are at the forefront of what many Italians are now calling the "cucina genuina."

Some of the restaurants I have in mind are already well known, even to foreigners, but most are not. Here is a list of a dozen such places, all of them in villages or small towns (some so small that they are difficult to locate even on the best Italian Touring Club maps), places where my wife and I ate with pleasure during recent trips to the peninsula. In these establishments you will find, if the gods are smiling, a respect for regional tradition, a passion for ultrafresh ingredients, an interest in lighter sauces and smaller portions and a blessed disdain for clumsy plagiarism.

Locanda dell'Amorosa

1.5 miles south of Sinalunga, near Arezzo; ask locally for directions
Tel.: 679497
Closed Mondays, Tuesdays at lunch and January 20 to February 28
Credit cards: American Express, Diners, Visa

If you were to imagine an Italian country restaurant, it would look like this one: an avenue of cypresses leading to a cluster of low buildings around a courtyard, their walls covered with flowering vines; inside, old tile floors, brick vaults, rough-hewn tables, yellow tablecloths, open fires, wrought-iron sconces. The farm that has been turned into the Sweetheart's Inn has been there for a very long time; in the Museo Civico in Siena there hangs a fresco showing the place as it was in 1300.

I first came across it several years ago, when a group of us who were staying in the neighborhood converged on the place for an Easter gala. We ate all the regional specialties, from *pappa al pomodoro* (a thick tomato-and-bread soup) through *bistecca alla brace* (the very close-grained local Val di Chiana steak, grilled over an open fire). It was delicious, especially when washed down with copious quantities of the excellent, sappy young chianti produced on the property.

The approach has since become altogether more ambitious. The old stand-bys are still there, joined now by such things as lamb roasted with tarragon instead of the usual rosemary; fish from nearby Lake Trasimeno, including grilled eel, smoked *coregone* (a beast without a precise English name, so far as I know) and perch with pasta. On our most recent visit, there was also a stunning apple *mille-feuille*. The cellar now affords a wider choice, including the wonderful 1980 Monte Vertine Chianti, which shows just how complex and satisfying that supposedly common wine can be. The inn remains low-key, unostentatious as always despite its new sophistication.

Antica Osteria del Ponte

Piazza Gaetano Negri 9, Cassinetta di Lugagnano, near Milan
Tel.: (02) 942 0034
Closed Sunday, Monday, Jan. 1 to 15 and August
Credit cards: American Express

Distinctly Mediterranean in feeling, with white walls, dark floors, pink tablecloths and abundant flowers, the Osteria sits in a classically Italian landscape, next to an old canal bridge, with a villa in the distance. Dishes like the wild mushroom soup and the ragout of calf's liver and kidneys with a sauce flavored with black olives flirt dangerously with perfection, and the cellar is stuffed with the triumphs of the new Italian oenology, such as the fabulous Cabernet-based Sassicaia.

This is not the sort of restaurant where four dishes are good and a dozen bad. We ate those mentioned above on our first visit; the next time, we were almost equally enchanted by a meal of hot foie gras, skillfully seared to produce a crisp outside and a melting center, frog's-leg soup, sweetbreads (just slightly too moist), a brilliantly realized risotto with spinach and zucchini the thickness of a pencil, and finally the pistachio ice cream of a lifetime.

135

Working with only two or three helpers in a tiny kitchen, Ezio Santin demonstrates his artistry night after night. Modest to the point of timidity, he speaks constantly of his "piccolo ristorante." His wife, Renata, is a fine judge of Italian wines, and it was she who gave us our first Tignanello. She it was, too, who arranged to have printed for the friends of the house a handsome little volume containing Proust's evocation of a waterside restaurant.

Al Bersagliere

Via Statale 258, Goito, near Verona
Tel.: 60007
Closed Mondays and Aug. 5 to 27
Credit cards: American Express, Diners, Visa

In 1848, the bersaglieri, a flamboyant group of Piemontese riflemen in plumed hats, fought the Austrians beside the River Mincio. The Ferrari family had already been running a restaurant on the spot for eighteen years, and they run it still, with Roberto in the dining room and his brother Massimo in the kitchen.

The cooking is rooted in the traditions of nearby Mantua, where Mantegna's majestic frescoes in the *Camera degli Sposi* survive as evidence of the magnificence of the Gonzaga court. But everything has been made lighter, fresher, zestier—cod with lemon peel, unctuous risotto with snails, grilled eel fresh from the Mincio and lean, moist duck or pigeon breast with honey are among the delights on the Bersagliere's menu. In homage to another pair of brothers who took over an old family business and put it on the gastronomic map, the Ferraris often prepare salmon with sorrel sauce in the style of Troisgros.

Exceptionally among the establishments listed here, this one is slightly formal, with a fair sprinkling of businessmen among its patrons, even though Goito, with 9,149 inhabitants, is not exactly a center of world commerce. Men might be a bit more comfortable in a necktie, but this is Italy, after all, and no one looked askance at my polo shirt or my wife's sundress on an unseasonably warm day in May.

Boschetti

Piazza Mazzini 10, Tricesimo, near Trieste
Tel.: 851230
Closed Mondays and Aug. 5 to 20
Credit cards: American Express, Diners, Visa

Tricesimo is tucked into Friuli, the extreme northeastern corner of Italy, not a region you're likely to be visiting unless you are traveling, as we were, from Venice to Vienna or Salzburg. It is, nonetheless, an area well worth a trip, with the seventh-century relics of Cividale del Friuli and the gentle hills nearby, carpeted with vines that produce superb white wines, both dry and sweet. You can sample them (the aromatic, pale gold Tocai from Schiopetto is especially worthy) at Boschetti, a crossroads mini-Versailles of a restaurant.

The cooking is marked by admirable finesse. Whether the dish is a reinterpretation of an old regional specialty, such as *fagioli* and *orzo* (white beans and rice-shaped pasta, flavored with green olive oil), or a new creation, such as *petto di cappone* (breast of capon, sliced razor-thin and simply sauced), it is likely to be well thought out and carefully balanced. We particularly liked the little *gnocchi* with smoked ricotta.

Giorgio Trentin, the proprietor, has instilled in his staff the kind of devotion that leads to twice-polished cutlery; to good-humored patience with a German family with two restless children; to a "present" of a little dish of the shellfish called sea truffles—"just a taste, in case you've never tried them"; to a suggestion of a wine more modestly priced—"and better, sir, really"—than the one you've ordered. And all of this while a huge and demanding wedding reception is taking place in a private room.

Ca Peo

Strada Panoramica, Leivi, near Rapallo
Tel.: 319090
Closed Mondays, Tuesdays at lunch and Nov. 5 to 30
Credit cards: Visa

In this brightly lighted, almost spartan room, perched high above the resort towns of Portofino and Rapallo, Franco Solari is conducting an undeservedly unheralded crusade for the foods and wines of Liguria. It has not been easy; the mixture of fine crystal and stainless-steel cutlery shows that he has been able to invest only a very little bit of money at any one time.

But there is nothing about the cooking to suggest poverty. Warned that Ca Peo serves only those who have reserved, even if that means that tables go begging, we called several days in advance, asking Mr. Solari to serve us whatever struck his fancy— a request that produced such a cascade of dishes that we could only nibble at the last three or four. His first offering was a typically Genoese *capomagro*, a kind of vegetable tart topped with skewers of shrimps, prawns, lobster and the like. It looked like something out of Carême. There was also a feathery timbale of fava beans and potatoes with a subtle tuna sauce, a roulade of sweetbreads and, of course, the great regional specialty, *trenette al pesto*—noodles with a basil sauce. As always in Liguria, it came with a potato amid the noodles as a reminder, so Mr. Solari explained, of the peasant origins of the dish.

On the sideboard when we arrived was a basket crammed with the jewels of the early Italian fall, porcini mushrooms, some of them as big as a soup plate. We ate them in a half-dozen ways: shaved over a terrine also made of porcini; stuffed into little pasta envelopes; deep-fried; in a clear soup, and so on. All this was served by the owner himself, a burly, hawk-nosed man of serious mien, who my wife said looked like a priest. The dishes combined earthy flavors and delicate textures, which is not common, and the utterly unknown wines that came with them were light, fruity and cheap. When we left, Mr. Solari pressed upon us a couple of bottles of extra-virgin oilve oil (as the Italians inexplicably call it) that his father had made.

Fattoria La Chiusa

Via della Madonnina 88, Montefollonico, north of Montepulciano
Tel.: (0577) 669 668
Closed Tuesday except in Aug. and Sept. and Jan. 20 to Mar. 20
Credit cards: American Express, Diners Club

A meal here is a voyage of rediscovery. Dania and Umberto Luccherini have reactivated farmhouse ovens and a venerable mill in an effort to reproduce authentic old Sienese dishes. In summer, you eat beneath a grape arbor. Minuscule portions of ten or more courses: zucchini flowers stuffed with cheese; matchstick-sized green beans with a sauce of oil and beets; a crouton of fried bread, about the size of a silver dollar, with eggplant and basil; a salad of porcini and herbs; a soup dense with white beans and perhaps several other soups as well; veal with onions and pan drippings; heavenly caramel ice cream. Brunello di Montalcino, the deepest and most complex of Tuscan red wines, is made nearby.

La Chiusa seems to appeal to a wide variety of clients. Not long ago, we ate there with Burton Anderson, the Minnesota-born author of *Vino*, the definitive book on Italian wine, and he told us that there were few places that he would rather eat and drink. That same month, Mrs. Victor Futter, of Port Washington, New York, a reader, wrote to say that her lunch "certainly compared favorably to the Moulin de Mougins," the *grand-luxe*, Michelin three-star establishment in Provence.

Umberto, a droll man with an extravagant mustache, has been "discovered" by so many Americans during the last year that he is learning English.

La Frasca

Via Matteotti 34, Castrocaro Terme, southwest of Ravenna near Forli
Tel.: (0543) 76 7471
Closed 10 unspecified days in August
Credit cards: American Express, Diners Club

Gianfranco Bolognesi, the proprietor of this cozy place in a spa town in the Apennine foothills, used to be a sommelier, and it shows. Empty bottles decorate the stone dining room, and full ones from around the world—Barolo, Chambertin, Ridge Zinfandel—abound in the cellar. He must have most of Italy's best grappas—*digestifs* made according to the same principles as the *marcs* of France, often coarse and biting, but capable of great sophistication, as Mr. Bolognesi's examples from Asti and Barbera and Friuli demonstrate. The food is gloriously inventive without coyness or meaningless baroque flourishes. We particularly admired the lobster ravioli with (sweet) red pepper sauce and the stuffed rabbit, a peasant dish utterly transformed by seasoning too subtle for me to pinpoint. A bit of sage, perhaps?

The pasta dishes seem to me particularly original; two more good ones are green tortelloni with asparagus and tagliatelle with light rabbit stock. And there is a deft touch in the kitchen where vegetables are concerned, as in the asparagus tart and the terrine of green vegetables. Some of these dishes are usually listed on the *menu dégustation* that will be offered to you by Mr. Bolognesi or his very charming wife, Bruna.

Steady progress here in the last three years, with further strides guaranteed by the proprietor's commitment to quality.

Ristorante da Guido

Piazza Umberto I, 27, Costigliole d'Asti, south of Asti
Tel.: (0141) 96 6012
Closed July 15 through Aug. 15 and Dec. 20 through Jan. 20
No credit cards

You pull up to a small, charmless shopping mall, descend dubiously into a basement, discover a décor of bourgeois excess and find yourself welcomed by a sober young boy, perhaps eleven years old. Never mind. Place yourself in the hands of Guido Alciati, the boy's father, and luxuriate in what follows. We arrived on September 24, and we were showered with white truffles—in a mousse, with raw beef, in a timbale of Parmesan cheese, in a woodcock sauce for rabbit. Splendid local wines (Dolcetto, Barbaresco) appeared as if by magic.

Lidia Alciati cooks, aided in the kitchen only by a single *commis*, and she produces dishes of subtlety and savor with humble products as well as with noble ones like truffles and cèpes. Her roast shin of veal—*stinco di vitello* is the provocative name of the dish in Italian—will convince you, once again, that mamma knows best.

As blond and rugged as a panzer commander, Guido will order for you, if you like, and you probably should like, at least on a first visit, because there are always wonderful dishes of the day. By all means let him choose your wines; this is Piemonte, home of Italy's finest vineyards, and Guido knows some of the best of the small growers hereabouts.

Lugana Vecchia

Sirmione, near Milan-Venice autostrada exit
Tel.: (030) 91 90 12
Closed Monday dinner and Tuesday
No credit cards

Sitting on the terrace, sheltered by the vines overhead and by pines planted in old Roman urns, watching the light change on Lago di Garda and on the mountains around it, you might not even notice the food, so supremely relaxing is the setting. That would be a mistake. Start with the "self service"—a breath-taking assortment of antipasti; then take the mixed grill of fish—salmon trout, sardines, pike and eel; finish with woodland berries and vanilla ice cream. Nothing madly creative about it, but everything is done with such finesse that meaning is miraculously restored to clichés.

But if you are in a more flamboyant mood, Luciano Boseggia can accommodate that, too. Try his cold mousse of lake fish, far more delicate than similar dishes made from ocean fish, or his eggplant pie. On Thursdays in winter, Lugana Vecchia produces an enormous *bollito misto*. Everything has a vigor of taste; everything is served with animation and good cheer by young waitresses in this five-hundred-year-old inn, even though it is in the heart of a resort area, the sort of region where standards can so easily slip.

Only one caveat: the prices seem a bit higher than they should be.

San Domenico

Via Sacchi 1, Imola, southeast of Bologna
Tel.: (0542) 29000
Closed Monday
Credit cards: American Express, Diners Club, Visa

Gianluigi Morini is a host of surpassing warmth, his restaurant is a gem of intimacy and elegance, and the service is flawless. San

Domenico's fame has spread quickly, and today it is by far the best known of the new Italian establishments. The food is often brilliant; dishes like the *garganelli* (twisted pasta, a specialty in Emilia-Romagna) with fresh vegetables, and the green *gnocchi* bathed in sage-flavored cream, to say nothing of the pink lamb with rosemary, stick in the memory for months.

But others (the roast pigeon, for example) seem too complicated, too French, and we were depressed to be told there was no cheese but Parmesan, "and that's only good enough for cooking."

Perhaps I quibble too much. Certainly, of all the restaurants cited here, San Domenico is the most splendidly conceived, with waitresses in *fin-de-siècle* uniforms, sumptuous flowers, candles everywhere, silverware and dishes of the finest quality. And when the kitchen is in full stride, it is brilliant; try, for example, the fabulous risotto with meat juices, Parmesan and onions. But should a place that aims so high falter?

Ask Signor Morini to show you his cellar; he will do so with justifiable pride, because he has assembled there Italian and French grands crus stretching back to the 1920s. It is as glittering, in its way, as the Byzantine mosaics down the road in Ravenna.

Il Sole

Via Trabattoni 22, Maleo, near Cremona
Tel.: 58142
Closed Sunday evenings, Mondays, January and August
No credit cards

In my view, this modest place in a trim little village between Cremona and Piacenza serves the best country cooking in Italy; it is good enough to bring back memories of Cantarelli, the extraordinary general-store-cum-restaurant near Busseto that closed a couple of years ago.

A gold sun signboard is the only clue to Franco and Silvana Colombani's charming establishment. Inside are two rooms with wooden ceilings, terrazzo floors, whitewashed walls and long tables. The Colombanis are collectors of old recipes, but they are not above serving something simple, like the salami and ham (both merely perfect) that I had as a first course. Or the colorful salad of diced peppers, beets, carrots and capon, dressed with lemon and olive oil, that Betsey ate.

Every single dish captivated us—*maccheroni alla verdura* (fat pasta tubes cooked with squash, tomatoes, green peppers, zucchini, eggplant, onions and green beans); shin of veal with porcini mushrooms and mashed potatoes made with the drippings from the roasting pan; two of the cheapest bits of beef, muzzle and tail, transformed by slow cooking and served with a purée of polenta not unlike grits; a tart Lodigiano cheese and a sweet Gorgonzola in peak condition; a sliced pound cake with faultless *crema di mascarpone* and a rose-petal tart with a macaroon crust.

We drank two unpretentious wines and one blockbuster—a 1976 Sassicaia, full of spice and balance—and loved all three. As the ideal ending to an ideal meal, we adjourned to a shady loggia overlooking an old courtyard, gazed at the grapevines and the birds' nests and the beds of salvia and impatiens, listened to the church bells, drank our coffee, sipped grappa from di Faedis and envied the bronze statue of a boy fishing, because he got to stay there all the time and we had to leave.

Il Trigabolo

Piazza Garibaldi, Argenta, near Bologna
Tel.: 854121
Closed Monday evenings, Tuesdays
Credit cards: American Express, Visa

Even my wife's direst threats have so far failed to cure me of one of my most irritating traits, a tendency to underestimate the time needed to get from here to there, and it almost cost us the chance to eat at this remarkable restaurant. It was 2:05 P.M. when we pulled into the square where it is set, a square out of a de Chirico painting, in a nondescript town in the rich farm country between Bologna and Ravenna. Lunch had ended and we had no reservation, but I put on my best basset-hound face, and Giacinto Rossetti, one of the two owners, took pity on us. Igles Corelli, the chef, was hastily summoned from a nearby café.

You would have thought that they had been expecting us for a month.

Mr. Rossetti showed us to an immaculately laid table, notable for the pretty wine glasses with long, thin stems, where we were served with old-fashioned propriety by a young woman. Among the dishes we tasted were a fish terrine—bits of sole, bass, scallop and river crayfish, flavored with basil and encased in a crust, which was slightly too heavy; the local pasta, *garganelli*, with a glistening and superb sauce of ham, cream, butter and garlic; a caramelized medallion of veal with a preposterous-sounding but excellent sauce of Gorgonzola cheese and pistachios; and *latte brule*, dense and rich, much the best custard I've ever tasted, along with a soft orange ice cream with orange sauce and candied orange peel, the best orange dessert I've had since my Aunt Anna's nonpareil cookies.

Asked for something local to drink, Mr. Rossetti produced a fine Chardonnay and an even better Cabernet, both made by a relative newcomer to the trade, Dr. Enrico Vallania. (If I understood correctly, he used to be the coroner in Bologna.) To finish, there was a grappa from the house collection of more than two hundred, said to be the largest in all Italy; but if I had left the choice to him, Mr. Rossetti would probably have given me a single-malt Scotch whisky, of which he is an improbably situated connoisseur.

5. *The Heel of the Boot*

WHEN we told people that we planned to spend a week or so in Apulia, we drew a lot of blank stares. Oh, an artistic Italian friend said it was full of Romanesque churches, and a political British friend said he half remembered from his school days a maxim to the effect that "it is better to be a prefect in Apulia than a subprefect in Rome," and someone else said that Luigi Barzini had described it as the undiscovered wonder of his country. But most people we talked to didn't even know where the place was.

Funny, that, because all sorts of people have tramped through Apulia—Puglia to the Italians—in the last two thousand years or so. Greeks, Romans, Byzantines, Franks, Normans, Swabians, Angevins and Bourbons all hoisted their banners there, conquering only to be conquered in turn. In our own time, though, Apulia's site in the heel of the Italian boot, far from Rome and Florence and Venice, has made it a touristic backwater. Most foreigners who know it do so because of its poverty. It is a prime example of the nagging *problema del Mezzogiorno*, the imbalance between the affluent north and the underprivileged south.

Well, the churches are there all right, and a lot more, too. But the first thing we noticed as we drove from Naples across the ankle of the boot was the tomatoes. Millions of them. For two hours, we passed almost nothing but open trucks, heavily laden with crimson globes, shining in the midday sun like the red in the Italian flag, bound for markets in Milan and Munich. My wife, enchanted by the sight, called the highway the "autostrada di pomodoro." I was less jolly; I was afraid there wouldn't be any left for me.

There were. Apulia may not yet have achieved industrial maturity, but its plains and its undulating plateaus once again produce cornucopias of wheat, figs, grapes, olives, almonds and tomatoes, as they did in the Middle Ages. (Somehow, most of the profits never seem to trickle down to the peasants, but profits there must be from all this bounty.) Flat and dry and hot, even in September, Apulia seldom looks scorched, because there are too many fruit and olive trees, too many vines carried on high trellises above the rich, red clay. The cattle look sleek, and so do the horses, some of them wearing little blue beads to ward off the evil eye. And the sea, not wine-dark at all but blue-green, clear enough to pick out stones on the bottom at a depth of twenty-five feet, is never far away.

Every so often a white village looms out of the heat haze, looking like something towed over from the Aegean, seemingly bleached of every last trace of color by the almost frighteningly intense sunlight. Go into one, park the car and walk around—try Cisternino, or perhaps Ostuni—and you will soon discover nuances of color, hidden piazzetas, bits of Renaissance sculpture, tumbling flowers, splashing fountains. There is vivacity, too, in the little town of Alberobello, with its hundreds of trulli—curious windowless limestone dwellings with conical roofs, whitewashed inside and out. In Apulia, Oriental images spring insistently to mind, and the trulli, viewed from afar, resemble a Bedouin encampment. Some of the huts are very old, some brand new; most are still lived in by the townspeople.

The southern three-quarters of Apulia (excluding the mountainous Gargano peninsula, which forms the spur on the boot) is rich not only in fruits and wine, not only in blue skies and soft air and satiny beaches, but also in artistic treasures. They are easy enough to reach, especially for the motorist traveling from Rome or Naples to catch the ferry for Greece. And the region is compact enough so that one can follow its story, if one is so inclined, in rough chronological order. Let us do just that.

Apulia was once part of Magna Graecia—Great Greece, the network of Greek colonies in southern Italy—and Taras was its most opulent and exuberant city. Magna Graecia was to Greece as the New World is to the Old, it seems to many antiquarians, and if that is so, Taras was the New York of the fourth century before Christ. John Boardman, the historian, puts it this way: "The Greek cities in the west were prosperous, nouveaux riches; their temples were that little bit bigger than those at home, their art that little bit more ornate. Artists and philosophers could readily be tempted from Greece by commissions or lecture tours."

Taranto, which rose from the ruins of Taras, is a surprisingly spruce and modern town, with a big naval base and fine broad boulevards, and it has a splendid museum of antiquities that is the best possible place to pick up the thread of Apulia's history. There you will see an Eros and an Aphrodite, both by Praxiteles or one of his pupils; tombs decorated with caryatids and a collection of vases that captivated even a philistine like me, a man who seeks cover at the first mention of the dread words *Greek pot*. These are painted not with endless processions of horses and soldiers and shields but with elegant animal and floral and geometric motifs. The Hellenistic jewelry is even more remarkable, especially a fragile golden diadem decorated with flowers of colored enamel.

After the Greeks came the Romans, of course, and they, too, have left their mark on the land. There are the two columns—one complete, one just a stump now—that marked the end of the Appian Way at Brindisi, the town where the poet Virgil is thought to have died. It was the Romans' chief port for Greece, and it is the Italians'. And there is the curiously clumsy statue up the coast at Barletta, the largest Roman bronze in existence, wearing the armor of a general and holding an orb and a cross. He is an emperor, though no one knows which one, and his odd appearance results from the tribulations he has suffered. Like the four horses of Venice, the Colossus of Barletta was part of the booty from history's greatest robbery, the Sack of Constantinople in 1204; unlike the horses, the Colossus was lost crossing the Adriatic, and when it washed up on the Apulian coast, local priests hacked off the hands and legs and melted them down for church bells. The extremities that we see today are bad fifteenth-century replicas.

Almost nothing remains to remind the visitor of one of the Romans' worst defeats, which was inflicted by the Carthaginian Hannibal in 216 B.C. The battle of Cannae is still studied at West Point and Sandhurst, but about the best one can do at the railway station of Canne della Battaglia, near Canosa di Puglia, is stand on the rising ground south of the river Ofanto and wonder in which field the carnage took place, precisely where the light Carthaginian troops manning the center of the line gave way to the legionaries so that their more heavily armed comrades on the flanks could surround the Romans and tear them to bits. It is beguiling, though, in that remote spot, to consider the fascination that Cannae has always held for generals, even as recently as 1914, when the German army used Schlieffen's modern adaptation of Hannibal's envelopment tactics for its thrust through Belgium into the heart of France—and to recall that the Germans, like Hannibal, won the battle but lost the war.

But the Roman Empire finally fell apart, too, and the south of Italy, including Apulia, was chopped into rival fiefdoms ruled by Lombards and Saracens and Byzantines and Franks. Order was finally imposed by Robert Guiscard, the twelfth son of a modest Norman knight, who with several of his brothers sought fame and fortune in the south because the little family castle in the Cotentin Peninsula was too small to hold them all. By all accounts, he and his warriors were brave but horribly cruel; one Norman, enraged by his wife, told her to put on her wedding dress and burned her at the stake.

Yet like the Normans who settled in England after the Conquest, Robert's followers soon began building cathedrals, not unlike those at Ely and Durham, and parish churches. These now dot the Apulian coast, sometimes no more than five or ten miles apart, Romanesque testaments to a strange marriage of piety and barbarism, a blend of the weighty grandeur of Caen and frothier elements from the Orient—interlaced arcades, the pointed Saracenic arch, fanciful friezes and capitals. "They remain in delightful obscurity," says the English traveler H. V. Morton, "the timeless activity of small harbors going on all round them and weekly markets being held in their shadows." Molfetta's cathedral has its supporters, as does Barletta's, and Bitonto's. See them all, if you can, but if you can see only one I would choose Trani's, because I know of no cathedral that can quite match it for initial impact. It stands behind a broad, barren square on the very edge of the sea, chalk-white against blue, dazzling.

Lions and elephants march across its façade, accompanied by fish and centaurs and griffins and magical birds and one man, only one. Beneath are a pair of bronze doors, with thirty-two panels depicting saints and their exploits; they were carved by a local artist, Barisano da Trani, who as we have seen was also responsible for the famous doors at Ravello and at Monreale in Sicily. Inside, the light is tamed—turned tawny gold—as it passes through thin, narrow alabaster panels.

Most of the cathedrals are based on the design of the church of St. Nicola in Bari, which was founded in 1087 to receive the fruits of one of the more brazen escapades in religious history, the theft of the bones of Saint Nicholas of Myra from Asia Minor by forty-seven Barese sailors. (In addition to his association with Christmas, Nicholas is the patron saint of sailors and fishermen, children, robbers, wolves, pawnbrokers and Russia—an ecclesiastical one-man band.) Although the art historians rave about his church, it disappointed us. Its most noted exterior feature is the Lion Door, but the lions looked suspiciously like pet golliwogs to me; the inside would be boring except for the magnificently carved episcopal throne, which dates from 1098.

Along with Trani's cathedral and Bari's throne, the most fascinating Norman legacy in the region may be the beautiful pavement in the cathedral at Otranto, an ancient port near the tip of the Apulian heel. (This may be a good time to note that, in Apulia, many place names are pronounced irregularly, with the accent on the first syllable and not on the next to last; thus it is

OH-trahn-toe and TAH-rahn-toe and BRIN-dih-zee.) The tes-
sellated pavement, laid by a monk named Pantaleone, fills the
whole nave and choir and shows trees of life peopled not only by
Adam, Eve, and Noah and other Biblical worthies but also by Rex
Arturus—he of the Round Table—and Alexander the Great and
the signs of the zodiac. After eight hundred years and more, the
oranges and tans and blacks still stand out boldly from the gray
background. Like the tireless Morton, I "felt that I might have
been walking on the Bayeux tapestry."

Perhaps the greatest figure in Apulian history was the Emperor
Frederick II, who reigned from 1197 to 1250. A German from
the Swabian royal house of Hohenstaufen with an English wife,
he gave his kingdom just laws, promoted the arts and sciences,
wrote a learned book on falconry and built the Castel del Monte,
probably the finest castle in all of Italy. He was the father of the
ill-fated Manfred, celebrated by both Byron and Tchaikovsky,
and was described by his contemporaries as "stupor mundi et
immutator mirabilis"—the wonder of the world and the mar-
velous innovator.

His monument, the castle, stands in a commanding position on
a conical hillock, its bold outline only lightly touched by time although its rooms have been stripped bare. The honey-colored
structure remains a mystery, a building without kitchens or servants' quarters and almost without windows, an abstruse exercise
in medieval mathematics, octagonal in shape, with eight rooms
on each floor, an octagonal turret at each of the eight corners of
the greater octagon. Only one bit of decoration remains—the
single heroic doorway, clad in a rosy natural conglomerate, full
of marble and other stones, that was laid down in some stream
bed eons ago.

Nothing could be further in spirit from the Castel del Monte
than the youngest of Apulia's masterpieces, the Baroque city of
Lecce. The softness of the yellow local stone, as Osbert Sitwell
explained in 1925, "allows the rich imagination of the South an
unparalleled outlet. The houses seem to be fashioned from snow."
We walked through the city at midday; even cats and dogs take
siestas in Lecce, we noticed, and everything was closed, even
the kiosks. But the buildings provided the animation—here a
wrought-iron balcony supported on brackets and supporting two

beautiful basketwork terra-cotta vases full of palms, there a shady courtyard festooned with coats of arms and a fine octagonal urn set in a circular pool, to the right a church façade topped with elaborate stone baskets full of stone flowers outlined against the sky, to the left another building front fairly exploding with columns and pediments and capitals and oculi and scrolls and swags and baskets of fruit and arches and pilasters and arcades and putti and saints.

It all has a decidedly Spanish flavor, a whiff of the Plateresque, the architectural style that gained its name from its resemblance to the work of silversmiths. "Art, like morality, consists in drawing the line somewhere," said G. K. Chesterton, but Lecce obviously wasn't listening.

A few practical notes now, in case you should decide to explore the Mezzogiorno. Apulia, especially urban Apulia, has a serious crime problem, but it need not bother anyone who takes a few simple precautions. Leave most of your money and your papers in the hotel safe, and at all costs avoid ostentation. That means no flashy jewelry, and it also means hiring a small car. We made the foolish mistake of driving a large German sedan with foreign license plates, and the police had to extract us from a squad of young toughs in Bitonto. But when we parked it and rented a local Fiat, our troubles ceased.

Hotels are not one of Apulia's strengths, but I can heartily recommend the Sierra Silvana in Selva di Fasano (telephone 799322). The hotel is situated in a centrally located village atop a rocky spur, lined with villas, where the rich Barese seek relief from the coastal heat. The rooms are housed in a series of pavilions surrounding a garden of spruce and holly and magnolias. The Sierra Silvana has a sister hotel, the Del Levante, at Torre Canne (720026), just a few miles away on the coast. A free bus links the two, so it is easy to go down for a swim on the private beach and return to Selva later in the day.

The joy of eating in Apulia is the freshness and the quality of the ingredients. The local cuisine cannot compare in inventiveness and subtlety with those of Piemonte or Emilia, but that didn't bother us at all.

Take our very first meal, at Il Brigantino in Barletta (33345), a modern place opening directly onto an immaculate beach. We ate ham with mozzarella, a great local specialty, made fresh every day all over the region; pasta with tomatoes (naturally) and ricotta cheese; *marmora*, or striped bream, the best fish in the area, its skin fabulously crisp and sweet from the wood fire, and fruit from a Lucullan assortment, presented iced on a silver tray, including Persian melon, figs, grapes, and peaches as big as softballs.

That was typical of our daily fare, although the details varied. The most typical pasta is *orecchiette*, or little ears, which is especially good with a sauce of basil and old Pecorino cheese that stings the tongue. Other good fish are the *sarago*, also a kind of bream; *pesce spada*, or swordfish; and *triglia*, or red mullet. Octopus, squid, cuttlefish, black-rimmed apricot-colored mussels and large and small shrimp are also widely served, and for a change from seafood there is good lamb and even better fennel sausage.

All of this can be enjoyed with the sound, inexpensive local wines. For generations, the growers of Apulia have sent their heady products north for blending, but now they are beginning to produce and sell them for their own sake and even to export a few. Take local advice, but try to sample the Rivera wines—red, white and rosé—made at Castel del Monte by Carlo de Corato and those made in the Salento region near Lecce by the Leone de Castris family.

Often we ate for as little as $20. At only one restaurant did our bill, including wine and an occasional aperitif or grappa, exceed $30, and that was at the only place that we didn't like—the Fagiano (799157), right next to the Sierra Silvana. It is one of the few restaurants in the region with a Michelin star, and it is very pretty, but the menu is a tired recital of grand-hotel clichés from the 1950s.

Here are a few suggestions: At Palese, near the Bari airport, da Tomasso (320038), a rustic place without a menu, where a superb assortment of fish is laid out for inspection on a marble slab and constantly sprayed with cold water to keep it fresh; here we had our favorite Apulian meal—a tepid seafood salad, a shrimp risotto, world-class prawns and mullet, and fruit. At Bari, the Mezza Luna, the region's very best pizzeria. At Cisternino, the Aia del Vento (718388), where on a slow night the proprietor opened the dining room just for us, with typical

Apulian warmth. And at Lecce, Gino e Gianni (45888), a snazzy roadhouse north of town that serves good, solid peasant food that is not without subtlety.

The Apulians eat late—2:30 and 9:30 are the fashionable hours.

6. Mia Favorita

THERE is only one man whose house I covet. Not for me a ducal château in the Loire or a penthouse overlooking Central Park or a hideaway on my very own Greek island. I want the Villa Favorita. The man who owns it, I tell myself in my pipe dreams, has lots of other places to live—one in Jamaica, one in St. Moritz, a stately pile near Oxford, a town house in Chester Square in London, a stupendous yacht; surely he could get along with less.

But Baron Hans Heinrich Thyssen-Bornemisza, the man in question, doesn't sell; he buys. So I shall have to content myself with visiting the Favorita whenever I can get there on one of the days when the Baron throws open the gates to us groundlings (at the moment, from Good Friday to mid-October, on Fridays and Saturdays from 10:00 A.M. to noon and from 2:00 to 5:00 P.M., and on Sundays from 2:00 to 5:00 P.M.). "There" is Lugano, that charming Swiss resort town nestled in the Alps alongside a lake of richest blue, perfectly situated to trap the sun's every ray, the jewel of Switzerland's Italian-speaking region, the Ticino.

Baron Thyssen's modest digs are in the suburb of Castagnola, east of the center of town; you can walk there in half an hour, or drive, or take a steamer from the main boat dock. The villa is on a narrow ledge between Monte Brè, whose lower reaches are flecked with the silver-green leaves of olive trees, and the lake shore. After passing through the massive gates, and paying your three dollars or so (Heini Thyssen didn't get where he is by giving things away), you follow a half-mile-long path through the gardens, awash with geraniums, pausing perhaps to sit on one of the shaded benches and look out at the wild mountains framing the lake. The house itself is a handsome, luxurious seventeenth-century building, beautifully kept, of course, that the Baron's father bought in 1932.

One goes there, though, neither for the view nor to see the villa; one goes to see the art collection—or, rather, the core of it, for each Thyssen residence and office has its share of the Thyssen pictures. It is housed in a twenty-room private picture gallery, the only part of the house normally open to the public, and it is quite simply the greatest private art collection in the world, greater than the Queen of England's, greater than all the Rockefeller collections put together, so extraordinary that the Russians agreed in 1983 to lend the Baron forty of the finest modern paintings from the Hermitage in Leningrad and the Pushkin Museum in Moscow in return for the loan of forty of his Old Masters. (More than 260,000 people came to see the Soviet treasures, so many that on several days the opening hours were extended to pacify the huge, eager crowds waiting in the road outside the locked gates.) The collection includes more than fourteen hundred important pictures, worth who knows how much. One hundred million dollars easily, perhaps two or three times that.

The family fortune was founded a century ago in Germany by August Thyssen and based on the steel mills of Düsseldorf; when he died, his son Fritz got the steel mills and his son Heinrich got the rest. Heinrich built up a business empire that now includes hundreds of companies in shipping, trading, farming and almost everything else. It was Heinrich, the present Baron's father, who started collecting art. He bought nothing painted after the eighteenth century and had a weakness for Dutch and German pictures. When he died, in 1947, the collection was split among his three children, but Baron Thyssen bought back much of what went to his siblings and has been buying ever since. He also diversified into Old Masters of other countries, into American paintings (some of which have been shown at the Vatican), and into modern works (some of which have been shown at the Metropolitan Museum of Art and elsewhere around the world).

What bowls you over when you walk into the Thyssen galleries is the sheer size of the collection, which has only been hinted at in the shows abroad, and the sumptuousness of its setting, with marble and pale silk damask on the walls to provide a rich backdrop for the pictures. It contains not one masterpiece, not a half dozen, but twenty or thirty, and there is very little that is second-rate. The Baron has a famous "eye," and although he can afford the best advice, he makes his own decisions and makes them quickly. He is said once to have bought a Holbein and a Jackson Pollock within a minute or two. With forgivable hyperbole, he said at the opening of his exhibition at the Vatican, "When I started to collect, my main capital was my eyes."

The catalogue of the Old Masters contains more than three hundred entries. There is no Leonardo, no Michelangelo or Giotto or Botticelli, and the only picture by Piero della Francesca, an exquisite portrait of Guidobaldo da Montefeltro as a boy, is attributed to others by some art historians. But most of the greatest names are represented—from Altdorfer (his only authenticated portrait) through Zurbarán (a magnificent Crucifixion and two other pictures). There is a portrait of a man by Antonello da Messina, with unforgettably piercing eyes; a glorious Carpaccio, one of the first full-length portraits in European history, with an allegorical landscape; a van Eyck diptych, painted in the technique known as "grisaille," in imitation of marble; a charming representation of the Virgin in a barren tree by Petrus Christus; four Tintorettos and four Titians; a Dürer of *Jesus among the Scribes*, with one of the most beautiful depictions of hands in all of art; a piece of the majestic Duccio altarpiece from Siena; Ghirlandaio's profile portrait of Giovanna Tornabuoni; six El Grecos and two Rembrandts and three Rubenses; a fine *Holy Family with St. John* by Fra Bartolomeo; an exuberant Fragonard; a profusion of major works by Hals, and elegant pictures by a score of lesser-known artists, such as the *Man Holding a Ring* by Francesco del Cossa. It is far too much to grasp, in truth, even in a three-hour visit.

So spend a weekend, and go several times. Between visits you can study the catalogue, which is available in English but contains only black-and-white illustrations; it costs $4.50. The rest of your time can be filled with boat rides on the lake, strolls along its shores, a visit to the church of Santa Maria degli Angioli to see the interesting frescoes by the sixteenth-century Milanese Bernardino Luini and a funicular ride from the Paradiso quarter to the top of Monte San Salvatore.

None of the hotels is extraordinary. The two best, I guess, are the Splendide Royal (Riva Caccia 7, telephone 091-542001), especially its newer wing, and the Grand Hotel Eden (Riva Paradiso 7, 091-542612); both have extensive views. In Castagnola itself, the little Carlton Hotel Villa Moritz (Via Cortivo 9, 091-513812) is very pleasant.

The best restaurant in town is Al Portone (Viale Cassarate 3, 091-235995), which is closed on Sunday, at lunch on Monday and in August. A meal here should begin with the "tartar" of sole and basil, which is delicious. On Sunday or in August, or anytime that you feel like something a bit more relaxed, I would recommend the Locanda del Boschetto on a hillside above town (Via del Boschetto 8, Cassarina, 091-542493), which specializes in simply grilled and succulent fish. It is closed Monday and in January.

CHAPTER VII

The Low Countries

1. Dutch Treats

T H E Netherlands has a utilitarian outlook on food. A Dutch friend once remarked to me, "We've always been a little embarrassed by the amount of attention the French and the Belgians pay to what they eat." As if to prove her point, the concierge at the thoroughly admirable Amstel Hotel told me that he had never heard of a restaurant less than an hour's drive from Amsterdam which French and Belgian colleagues had assured me was the best the country had to offer.

But things are changing, and no wandering *Feinschmecker* need fear an unrelieved diet of smoked eel and pea soup in the Dutch capital—or, for that matter, out in the country. Much of the best food in the Netherlands these days is not Dutch, it must be admitted, but that need bother no one. In Yorkshire, the two best restaurants are both French, and it never particularly perturbed me that the best restaurant I knew in Nigeria was run by a woman who had learned her trade in Shanghai.

That is not to say that there is no good Dutch food to be found in Amsterdam. Indeed, one of my three favorite places there is as Dutch as wooden shoes. Called the Oesterbar (oyster bar), it has that slightly tacky, matter-of-fact quality that often marks the serious seafood house (like Felix's in New Orleans, say, or Crisfield outside Washington, D.C.). There are two floors, and the lower one includes a counter where you can watch them cook your meal—and where, if you happen to be eating alone, you will feel less of a waif than at a table. Splendid Zeeland oysters, delicious small soles cooked with tiny Dutch shrimp, lobsters and, yes, smoked eel, all prepared quickly and simply, as fish should be. No library paste in the sauces here: Wheeler's of London and Brighton, please copy.

The Oesterbar is located on the Leidseplein, the meeting place of the world's young in the summer months, and one of my other Amsterdam haunts is only a few steps away. For a *grande bouffe*, I can think of no place in town better than the De Boerderij at Korte Leidsewarsstraat 69. A warm and welcoming place, with low ceilings and adept waiters, the Farm—to give it its English name—is Amsterdam's best French restaurant at the moment. Birds cooked on a spit are a specialty, but everything else is good, too, and the cellar is first-rate. After you have eaten, ask for a copy of the magazine put out by the Dutch gastronomic alliance, of which this restaurant is a member; it will guide you to places of similar stature in the provinces. No point in going hungry in Eindhoven if you don't have to.

But the one thing you must on no account miss is the Asiatic feast known as *rijsttafel* (rice table), which comes from the former Dutch colony of Indonesia. The Dutch gourmand likes quantity, and in a *rijsttafel* he gets it—perhaps twenty-five small dishes surround the bowl of rice that gives the meal its name. There is *sate*, small cubes of meat on a wooden skewer, served with a fiery pepper-and-peanut sauce; *gado gado*, a vinegary vegetable salad with the same sauce; *rempah*, spicy meatballs with coconut; *nasi goreng*, or fried rice and . . . and . . . The best places to try it are little Sama Sebo (P. C. Hooftstraat 27, near the Rijksmuseum), and Merpatis (at Bilaricum in the far eastern suburbs), an enchantingly converted farmhouse where the unusually refined *rijsttafel* is made with fresh herbs sent weekly from Bandung by the sisters of the proprietress. Go with a group, order the works, and drink plenty of Amstel or Heineken.

Before leaving Amsterdam, a few other random notes: I would strenuously urge you to avoid two establishments of zoological nomenclature, the Five Flies and the Black Sheep. Both are as cutesy as their names would suggest, and both pay more attention to décor than food. Strictly for tourists. For a cup of coffee or a snack, you should go to the American Hotel, whose Art Nouveau café is, rightly, classed as a national monument. And, finally, the aforementioned Amstel Hotel, whose dining room used to specialize in the grand-international-yawn school of cooking, is said by knowledgeable Dutch friends to have blossomed since the chef from the much lamented Auberge took charge.

Now, what about the place the Amstel's concierge didn't know about? It is called Hoefslag, and it is to be found about seven miles north of Utrecht in a forest. I won't pretend that it's easy to get there; the best thing is to call for a reservation, telephone (30) 784-395, and ask for directions. Or take a cab. It is well worth the trouble to taste the cuisine of Gerard Fagel, the most talented of seven brothers who have dotted the Dutch landscape with little sanctuaries of nouvelle cuisine. His specialties include wild mushrooms in several guises, cold oysters with sorrel, and fresh foie gras with tiny vegetables, but if your appetite is in form you should take the *menu dégustation*, which will afford you the opportunity to taste five or six of his offerings. The place looks like a hunting lodge, but there is nothing rustic about the table settings, the service, or the highly skilled cooking.

Elsewhere in the Netherlands, two other places commend themselves: In Delft (a short cab ride from Rotterdam), the Chevalier, a delicious nook along a picturesque canal, installed in an old house and devoted to things French. At Valkenburg, near Maastricht, in the southeastern hook of Holland near the Belgian and West German borders, the Princess Juliana, an old hotel with a tradition of haute cuisine that has been lightened recently by the installation of a young chef of style and imagination.

2. *After Amsterdam*

THE attractions of Amsterdam are manifold: the trip through the canals, the house where Anne Frank kept her tragic journal, and above all the spectacular art galleries. These include not only the Rijksmuseum, with its unmatched Rembrandts and Vermeers and superb Dutch primitives, but also the Vincent van Gogh Museum, which has two hundred of his paintings and five hundred of his drawings, and the relatively little-known Stedelijk (Municipal) Museum, with an excellent modern collection that includes two rooms full of works by the celebrated but seldom exhibited Russian Suprematist painter Kazimir Malevich.

Nonetheless, I would urge anyone who visits the Netherlands to block out two or three days for a trip outside the capital. Because the distances are so small, one can see a great deal in forty-eight to seventy-two hours, and there is a great deal to see in this small country. My first choice would be a journey to the south and east of Amsterdam, one that I have made, in segments, during the course of reporting assignments. It includes wonderfully innovative museums, fine architecture and, inevitably, a shower of flowers. The Dutch have always been a little bit bonkers about flowers—flowers in the parlor, flowers in the garden, flowers for export, flowers in the still lifes of Breughel and other seventeenth-century masters. (Every ten years their infatuation reaches a peak in a horticultural extravaganza called "Floriade," and if you find yourself in Amsterdam in 1992, when the next one is due, by all means go.)

You should leave Amsterdam by car, preferably on a weekday to avoid crowds and Sunday closings, and head for the city of Haarlem, only twelve miles west. The name is a reminder of New York's Dutch origins, as are those of other towns in the Netherlands, such as Breukelen.

Towering over the center of Haarlem is St. Bavo's Church, whose sixty-eight-register organ, built in 1738, was played by Bach and Mozart. The church may still be closed for restoration by the time you arrive, but look at its exterior anyway, and look around the great market square in which it stands. The architecture of five centuries is there to see, including the fourteenth-century town hall and the seventeenth-century meat market, one of the masterpieces of Dutch Mannerism.

For me, however, the great attraction of Haarlem is the Frans Hals Museum, a memorial to the city's most eminent son. It is appealing not only because of the eight monumental Hals group portraits, so different from the pictures of laughing cavaliers for which he is most widely known, not only for the Jan van Scorels and Jacob van Ruysdaels that accompany them, but for the place itself. The museum is housed in an almshouse built in 1608, a building of rare serenity, with slate floors and whitewashed walls, filled with old silver and glass, Delft tiles, brass candelabra and the tintinnabulation of dozens of clocks. It is a quite magical place in which to look at pictures.

You can save a good deal of money, by the way, if you purchase a Holland culture card before you leave home. It costs fifteen dollars, can be obtained through your travel agent or the Netherlands National Tourist Office (576 Fifth Avenue, New York, NY 10036) and entitles you to, among other things, free admission to most museums, discounts on rail and other travel and access to hard-to-get tickets for concerts and ballet and opera performances.

From Haarlem, take the minor road south toward Vogelenzang and De Zilk. In five minutes or so, presuming that you are making the trip during April or May, you will be amid a Kodachrome checkerboard: the bulb fields. Stretching for miles on either side of the road are great blocs of intense color—red, yellow, pink, orange—made up of millions of tulips, grown not for their flowers but for their bulbs.

A few miles farther on, you will see signs for Keukenhof, near Lisse, where the Dutch bulb industry puts on an annual show of a different kind. In seventy acres of beautifully landscaped gardens, a paradise of ponds and swans and old trees, each grower attempts to outdo the other in displaying the best of his tulips, daffodils, lillies and hyacinths. Keukenhof's season begins about April 1 and lasts for roughly eight weeks.

If you visit at some other time of the year, head first for Aalsmeer, which is just south of Schiphol Airport. There, every day except Sunday, the biggest flower auction in the world takes place between 7:45 and 11:00 A.M. The output of thirty-seven hundred nurseries is sold at Aalsmeer, which disposes of almost two billion flowers a year. You can watch the vividly colorful spectacle from a special gallery. Then head west through Hoofddorp to Haarlem and skip the bulb fields.

The next stop, whether you are coming from Haarlem or from Keukenhof, is The Hague, where I would suggest you spend the late afternoon and part of the next morning, staying overnight in or near the city. A good hotel in the center of town is the Des Indes, where a double room will cost about $80; less expensive but also pleasant are the Parkhotel De Zalm, about $60, and the Corona, about $45. If you would prefer to stay outside town, the best choice is the charming and luxurious De Kievet at Wassenaar, only about five miles away. It has much the best food in the area as well, but there are only six rooms, which cost about $65. Dinner for two will cost about $60, including service, tax and wine.

In The Hague itself, you might try the Bajazzo restaurant, which is right across the street from the Des Indes; it is a kind of miniature Maxim's, with wonderful Art Nouveau décor, serving French nouvelle cuisine, as the De Kievet does, at about the same prices. More classic in its ambience and in its cooking is Saur, the best place in town for Zeeland oysters, turbot and sole. If you fancy a *rijsttafel,* a decent one can be had at the Bali in Scheveningen, the beach resort only a ten-minute drive from The Hague. And if the budget pinches, there are numberless pubs scattered around the city where two can eat simply for $20 to $25.

Two museums in The Hague deserve your close attention, both for the pictures they contain and for the buildings themselves. The Mauritshuis, a perfect little Renaissance palace designed by Jacob van Campen, is undergoing restoration, but the façade, which achieves real grandeur despite its small size, can still be viewed. The superb collection of Dutch and Flemish paintings, temporarily housed at the nearby Johan De Witt house, 6 Kneuterdijk, also has an intimacy of scale that makes it easy to assimilate. Among the highlights are the Rembrandts, including *Anatomy Lesson of Professor Tulp* and *The Presentation in the Temple;* the Vermeers, including *Young Girl with a Pearl* and the *View of Delft,* which Proust called the most beautiful painting in the world; Rubens's portraits of his two wives, and a *Descent from the Cross* by Rogier van der Weyden.

You enter an entirely different world at the Municipal (Gemeente) Museum, which was designed by Hendrick Berlage, one of the pioneers of the Modern Movement, and which contains, in addition to other collections, the world's greatest trove of works by Mondrian, about 250 of them. Only here can you trace his development from a painter of relatively conventional landscapes into the genius of primary-color abstraction.

On the second day of your trip, you should head east on the E8 motorway to the cheese town of Gouda, about fifteen miles away. The town hall of the picturesque little city has stepped gables, red shutters and a carillon with small figures that reenact, every half hour, the granting of freedom to the city in 1272. In the summer a cheese market takes place in the square every Thursday between 9:00 and 10:30 A.M.

A few steps from the marketplace is the Church of St. John, built in the fourteenth century and rebuilt in the fifteenth and sixteenth. It is the main reason for going to Gouda, because it boasts seventy stained-glass windows, most notably thirteen by the brothers Dirck and Walter Cravath, which are matched in Europe only by those at York in England and Chartres in France.

Then back to the E8 for the twenty-two-mile run into Utrecht, the fourth-largest city in the Netherlands, which dates from Roman times. It was here that were signed the Union of Utrecht in 1579, creating the Netherlands, and the Peace of Utrecht in 1713, ending the War of the Spanish Succession. The city has much to offer, including the fourteenth-century cathedral tower, 365 feet tall, and lovely canals.

But its prize attraction, still little known outside the Netherlands, is the Het Catharijne Convent Museum at 63 Nieuwe Gracht. Fashioned from a canal house and an old convent, linked by an underground passage, this new museum displays with dazzling skill the relics of six hundred years of Dutch Christianity. It may sound dull, but it isn't; the museum won the 1980 award for European museum of the year.

Ancient chalices, medieval altarpieces, a missal from the twelfth century adorned with ivories and cameos and gold, hundreds of expressive wood sculptures, paintings by Rembrandt, Hals and Geertgen tot Sint Jans succeed as do the displays in few museums in evoking the look and the spirit of another age. The museum is very large, and I would suggest that you confine yourself to the ground floor and basement.

Before returning to Amsterdam, you might want to drive past the Schroeder-Schraeder House, designed by Gerrit Rietveld in 1924 on the Oosterstraat in the southeastern part of the city. Although it is not open to the public, it is worth looking at the exterior, which is probably the greatest architectural achievement of the De Stijl movement. Or, on the way back to Amsterdam, twenty-five miles away, you can stop at the Château De Haar, a castle with fine collections of tapestries and porcelain, which is open until 5:00 P.M., except between August 15 and October 15. It is just off the E9 motorway at the first exit north of Utrecht.

Should you want to extend your trip to three days, you might spend two nights in The Hague and use the extra time to visit the Boymans–Van Beuningen Museum in Rotterdam, which has masterpieces by Bosch, Lucas van Leyden and Rembrandt, in addition to one of the two verisons of *The Tower of Babel* by Breughel, and to spend a few hours in the old town of Delft, with its splendid market square and its historic porcelain factory.

Or you might head east from Utrecht toward the German border for a visit to the remarkable Kroeller-Mueller Museum at Otterlo. Located in the wooded reserve of the Hoge Veluwe National Park, designed by Henri van de Velde, the museum has 272 van Goghs as well as important works by Mondrian, Seurat, Léger and Redon. Stay at the Rijnhotel in nearby Arnhem, site of a great World War II battle; it has fine views and a good dining room.

3. *Art Nouveau Renewed*

T HEY tell us we're difficult," said the tall, courtly old man in his slow, precise French, "and it's true. It's true because we have consciences, and our consciences do not permit us to accept mediocre things."

His name is Louis Wittamer de Camps. He and his wife, Berthe, are couturiers, specializing in debutante and bridal dresses for the Belgian bourgeoisie. But their grand passion in life is Art Nouveau, in particular the work of the Belgian architect Victor Horta (1861–1947), and it is to their passion and their passion alone that the world owes the preservation and restoration of Horta's masterpiece, the Hôtel Solvay in Brussels.

Thanks to the Wittamers, the visitor to Belgium can see this remarkable building, which prefigures so much in modern design. One need only write for an appointment, well in advance, to 224 Avenue Louise, 1050 Brussels, Belgium.

Horta built the Hôtel Solvay between 1894 and 1904 for Armand Solvay, a son of the industrial chemist Ernest Solvay, who earned a fortune from his invention of a process to make sodium carbonate from common salt. His client gave him a free hand, down to the smallest details, such as the house number, carved into the stone in tendrillike digits, with a little roof above them to make sure that the omnipresent rains didn't wash them away.

The Solvay family lived there for more than fifty years, but by the 1960s they were ready to sell. The Belgian government wasn't interested. Horta's reputation was in eclipse, with the leading local architect of the day desciding him derisively as "the inventor of the noodle style." Experts advised against any attempt to preserve the mansion, with its audaciously convoluted wrought-iron staircase, its innovative handling of the flow of air and light, its radically open floor plan, its glowing stained glass, its sunny pointillist murals by Théo van Rysselberghe.

It seemed that the place would be demolished, like two of Horta's other Brussels buildings, his 1902 Aubecq house and his Maison du Peuple, built in 1899 as headquarters for the Belgian Workers Party, or at best mangled, like the celebrated Wolfers jewelry shop, whose 1905 furnishings were ripped out to make way for a bank's computers. The Wittamers were outraged that a prosperous society like Belgium's refused to spend money to keep something so precious, but they finally concluded, as Mr. Wittamer says with disgust, that "when people are crazy, it doesn't matter how rich the country is." They decided to buy the Hôtel Solvay—the Solvays threw in furniture and pictures for almost nothing—and to try to do themselves what other people would not.

Until 1980, they were alone. They spent "several million francs," hundreds of thousands of dollars, of their own money on repairs, until they finally persuaded Intercom, a Belgian company, to spend a great deal more to complete the restoration of the principal rooms. Now Intercom has dropped out and the two couturiers are hoping against hope that someone in the United States will come forward to insure the long-term future of the Hôtel Solvay and to "make it live again."

There can be few buildings of comparable quality in Europe that so few people have seen. The Hôtel Solvay is a milestone not only for its decorative qualities, which burst upon the visitor the minute he steps into the broad hallway and sees the magnificent central staircase, but also for its underlying structural originality. If the swirling, foliate theme is evident everywhere, in the door handles, the racks for pool cues, the wittily handsome radiator covers, so is Horta's eagerness to make use of technical resources.

This was one of the first private houses to be lighted entirely by electricity. It was also one of the first to use partitions of glass, plus skylights, so that even on a dull day the central stairwell is flooded with light. It was one of the first houses with a system of introducing fresh air into a network of ducts. The sinks in the bathrooms rotate, allowing for instantaneous emptying; the rooms are laid out so as to conceal the movements of servants; the interior walls fold and disappear for parties, open and reappear for family intimacy.

Take the extraordinary staircase: Nothing could seem more antithetical to the machine age than the twisting, turning, cascading pattern of the balustrade. But the staircase is mostly iron, then popularly thought of as an ignoble material best suited to factories and railway stations, and the pillars supporting it are held in place by boldly exposed bolts and rivets, not by hidden nails.

At the same time, the architect did not disdain older, warmer materials. He incorporated in the staircase and its surroundings wood and marble and even mosaics, and placed at the first-floor landing richly upholstered settees, surmounted by van Rysselberghe's pastel vision of young women in long dresses and broad-brimmed hats. What Horta achieved was the transformation of the dark, forbidding core of the Victorian house into a warm and welcoming centerpiece.

Horta swept away all the pomposity that rich men of the day thought appropriate to their station and replaced it with airy invention. Like the Scot Charles Rennie Mackintosh and the Catalan Antonio Gaudi, his fellow creators of the new style, he came from simple stock (although he ended life as a baron) and he thought it right to build houses that were beautiful and practical rather than impressive. In Armand Solvay, he found a client interested in both engineering and in art, one of those perfect matches, like Frank Lloyd Wright and Edgar Kaufmann Jr., that come seldom even to great architects.

His vision, wrote Yolande Oostens-Wittamer, the daughter of Louis and Berthe, "was to eschew the static and grandiloquent for dynamism and quality."

"If the staircase is just a shaft," she wrote, "if the living quarters are long rows of poorly lighted rooms, no amount of fine décor can disguise a design which, in its ceaseless repetition, is classic but deadly dull; nor can it mask the pervading misunderstanding of deep human needs which comes from a lack of creative imagination."

The colors inside the house are pale greens, mahogany, oranges, beiges; earth colors, complemented by sunlight. It is a building better seen from the inside out, because the façade, for all its elegant ironwork grilles and balconies, for all the controlled rhythm of its gently swelling bays, is not meant to dazzle. It is quite possible not to notice it as one drives down the street.

Best seen from the inside, too, because there one can appreciate the workmanship of perhaps the last era when such attention was paid to detail. The spiraling chandeliers, the finely framed mirrors and the splendid ceilings: these alone are enough to excite admiration for the genius of Horta and the lonely idealism of the Wittamers.

CHAPTER VIII

Austria and Germany

1. Mit Schlag

T H E Grand Vizier Kara-Mustafa stood at the very gates of Vienna, the green banners of the Prophet waving above his army of 300,000—not only Turks but Slavs and Bosnians and Hungarians, too. Inside the besieged capital of Emperor Leopold I huddled 25,000 defenders.

But the Viennese refused to surrender. Short of food, still recovering from the plague of five years before, they held out until Charles Duke of Lorraine arrived at the head of a relief force of about 80,000 Austrians, Poles, Saxons and Bavarians. He deployed his men on the Kahlenberg Hill and in the Vienna Woods, and on September 12, 1683, he attacked. The Turkish Army broke and ran.

It was a great moment in European history, establishing the authority of the empire and inaugurating a long period of Austrian prosperity. It was also a great moment in gastronomic history, for among the impedimenta left behind by the fleeing invaders the Viennese found bags of dark-brown beans. These, according to tradition, were given to one Franz Georg Kolschitzky, who had spied on the Turks. In due time, so the story goes, he opened Vienna's (and Europe's) first coffeehouse—Zur Blauen Flasche (The Blue Bottle)—in an alley behind St. Stephen's Cathedral.

So it was that not long ago Vienna celebrated the three hundredth anniversary of its most characteristic institution, the café. More than the pastry shop, more than the waltz, more even than the Danube, the café sums up the Viennese approach to life, the leisurely and sometimes solitary contemplation of small pleasures and small sadnesses. A hotel, they say in the Austrian capital, is a sleeping room; a restaurant is a dining room; a café is a living room, where the most important activities of life are conducted—sitting, talking, reading and, in some mysterious way, sharing the flavor of the moment with others.

"In the café you should never rush," explained Peter Langhammer, a thirty-four-year-old coffeehouse owner. "The economy is in a bit of difficulty now, so people take more time; for us, good times are bad and bad times are good. Here you can be alone, but you know you are not alone. You are among old and young, rich and poor, all together, which is rare in our times."

Over three centuries, the Viennese café has acquired an elaborate set of traditions. The waiter—Herr Ober, he is called; there are no Herr Unters—must never hustle the merchandise. He brings what is ordered, always with a glass of water on the side, and he renews the glass of water every half hour, even if the client stays four hours and orders only a single cup of coffee.

An hour in a coffeehouse—a half hour is really cutting it too tight—should not cost more than $3.50 or $4, presuming a person takes two coffees and a pastry. Service is included in the bill, but an extra 50 cents is a good idea if you're well taken care of, which you will be.

The café must supply an assortment of newspapers and magazines, Austrian and foreign, each clipped to a long wooden wand that is hung from a rack near the entrance. The place must have double doors, to keep the winter chill out, and pastry near the front, to whet appetites, and a big mirror in back, to make it look bigger than it is, and benches in the window alcoves, for those who crave more than usual privacy, and marble-topped tables, because there have always been marble-topped tables. The coffee spoon must be balanced on the top of the water glass, so that it doesn't get wet (it could go on the saucer, a graybeard gravely told me, but some kinds of coffee should be served in glasses or in cups without saucers).

Aside from the tortes for which Vienna is famous, the food is uncomplicated—goulash soup, a pair of wieners, two shelled hard-boiled eggs in a glass, that sort of thing, plus wonderful bread, especially the Kaiser rolls and salt sticks. The Viennese use a word of Slovene derivation, *jause*, which means roughly a bite between meals, to describe what they eat in cafés. (Demel's, which most tourists would instantly nominate as the city's greatest café, is not a café at all, but a pastry shop, because it serves rather more elaborate dishes and has no newspapers. By all means go there, but also try to get out to the Kurkonditorei, run by Karl Schuhmacher, whom the local cognoscenti consider the premier pastry chef. Mr. Schuhmacher does the whole range of Viennese specialties, Dobos torte and Sacher torte among them.)

Wines are not the usual drink in cafés or *Konditoreien*, but for those who want them, the best thing is to drink the light whites from the Viennese suburbs; Gumpoldskirchner is the best known, but there are many more. They are usually offered in a carafe and called open wine. There's little beer, although late at night you may be offered a brandy.

But coffee is still the thing. Wonderful, robust coffee, surely the best in Europe, along with Italy's, and available in Vienna in a far greater variety of guises. The classic order is an *einspanner*—coffee in a tall glass with powdered sugar *mit* lots of *schlag*, or whipped cream. But there is also *mocca*, or black coffee; *brauner*, coffee with cream; *kaffee brulot*, coffee with brandy; *kaffee creme*, where the cream is served in a tiny pitcher on the side; *kapuziner*, coffee with a lot of cream, which gives it the color of a monk's robe; *konsul*, coffee with very little cream; *kaffee verkehrt*, with about twice as much hot milk as coffee; *melange*, coffee with less hot milk; *pikkolo*, a small coffee; *Türkischer*, coffee boiled with sugar; *eiskaffee*, coffee with ice cream and whipped cream in a tall glass.

There are still hundreds of cafés in Vienna, but most of them are Italian-style espresso bars, where you drink (the shame of it!) standing up. Only a few traditional places have survived, and many of them have been saved only by government subsidies.

Their leisurely pace does not permit the economically efficient use of space, and none of them produces the kind of revenue required for major repairs. A *melange* in a big café near the city center costs about $1.15. Of that, Mr. Langhammer explained, the beans cost 12 cents, the milk about 4 cents, taxes take about

30 cents, staff salaries take about 50 cents, and incidentals account for another 4 cents. That leaves a profit of 15 cents, and the client may occupy a table for an hour or two.

Mr. Langhammer, who owns a coffeehouse called the Mocca Stuben in the suburbs and heads an association of coffeehouse owners, said: "Prices cannot go much higher because of the competition of the espresso bars, so few of us have the money to renew our places. Landtmann, one of the most famous, cost $500,000 to redecorate a few years ago. The money came from the urban-renewal fund. The only other survivors are the small, family-run places."

Landtmann is one of the cafés on the Ringstrasse, that grandiose boulevard that Frederic Morton described as "a vast stage-set made of concrete, poured and molded to resemble classic stone, a mirage of portals and pediments sweeping around the medieval core of the city." For my taste, Landtmann is a bit too glossy, but its site overlooking the Burgtheater and its rich past recommend it.

A more traditional spot on the Ring is the Schwarzenberg, which is now operated by the city. Other favorites: the Braunerhof, just behind the vast Hofburg, with faded Art Deco light fixtures and concerts on Saturday and Sunday afternoons; the Café Museum, designed by Adolf Loos; the Sirk, modern but correct, across from the State Opera; the atmospheric little Kleines Café, on a quiet side street a few steps from the bustling Kärntnerstrasse; the open-air Central, which is closed during the winter; Sperl, with its relentlessly serious billiard players; Tirolerhof, which is convenient for the Spanish Riding School and the Albertina collection.

Each has its own character. The Braunerhof, for example, seems to attract writers and other intellectuals. The last time I was there, I was remarking to my wife that the people at the next table looked as if they spent their lives discussing Dostoevsky; as I finished the sentence, I overheard a scrap of conversation including the name "Karamazov." The best idea is to visit several cafés until you find one that seems to suit you best.

If I lived in Vienna, I would have my *stammtisch*, or regular table, at an admittedly seedy but thoroughly wonderful place called Café Leopold Hawelka at Dorotheergasse 6, not too far from the site of the old Blue Bottle. With nicotine-stained wallpaper (allegedly changed every couple of years, but I don't believe it), black Thonet chairs and coatracks, upholstered seats in faded red and brown stripes, pictures askew on the walls, a blackened floor and heavy curtains to keep out the sunlight, it is full, day and night, with pensioners, students, artists and tourists.

As you watch the waiters in dinner jackets and black bow ties weave through the throng, balancing overloaded trays above their heads, you will understand why Orson Welles came here thirty-five years ago, when Vienna was a city of spies and black marketeers, to soak up atmosphere for his role in the film *The Third Man*. And when Frau Hawelka, a tiny, tireless, gray-haired sparrow in a frayed blue sweater, stops by just before midnight to ask whether you would like a pear brandy and one of her homemade dumplings, greeting you like old friends on your first visit, you will not say "no."

2. *A Hotel of Operatic Grandeur*

A couple of years ago, a plane on which I was traveling from Budapest to Prague was diverted to Vienna because of bad weather. Congratulating myself on my good luck, I hailed a cab and asked to go to the Imperial, one of my favorites among Europe's grand hotels, hoping that they would have a free room. They did, they made no complaint about my decidedly proletarian Eastern European working clothes, and the concierge on duty, who knew my weakness for opera, called out to me as I registered that there was a particularly festive performance of *Fidelio* that night, starting in about twenty minutes. Were there any tickets? "Go upstairs and change," he replied, "and I'll see what I can do. But everyone you ever heard of is in the cast, so it's been sold out for a month."

As I ran back into the lobby, he slipped a small white envelope into my hand and said, "You'll just have time." Only when I stumbled panting and disheveled into the foyer of the State Opera did I notice that my seat was on the aisle in Row 4.

Like Vienna's, the Imperial's life revolves around music. It sits on the Ringstrasse, the great boulevard laid out in the nineteenth century on the site of the old city ramparts, two blocks from the Vienna State Opera and a block from the Musikverein, the main concert hall. Built by the Italian architect Zanotti for the Duke of Württemberg in 1867 and transformed into a hotel only six years later, it has a claim to be the birthplace of both *Tannhäuser* and *Lohengrin*; Wagner stayed there with his family for two months in 1875. He has been followed by thousands of conductors, dancers and singers—Karajan, Furtwängler, Ormandy; Nureyev, Fonteyn; Domingo, Caballé, Carreras. "I sometimes felt like a musical sandwich," said the Imperial's long-time director, Otto N. K. Heinke, who retired in 1985.

With the musicians have come tens of thousands of music lovers, for most of whom the hotel somehow manages to procure tickets. Erich Benesch, the head concierge, who has spent twenty-seven of his fifty-eight years at the Imperial, after earlier stints in Italy, France and Britain, and Ludwig Wischo, the seventy-two-year-old *Kommissionär*, or ticket agent, whose sole account is the Imperial Hotel, are without question better at their highly specialized trade than anyone else in Europe.

One New Year's, with a couple of month's notice, they managed to get tickets for my wife and me for the gala New Year's Eve performance of *Die Fledermaus* at the State Opera and, even more remarkably, a pair for the New Year's Day concert, seen annually by millions around the world on television but witnessed in person at the Musikverein only by members of the Friends of Music plus about one hundred nonmembers who gladly pay ninety-five dollars each to soothe their hangovers with Strauss polkas and waltzes.

The Imperial is that kind of hotel. Opulent but never stiff, it takes splendid care of nerds and nabobs, and its staff remembers the likes and needs of both. There is a glossy brochure in the rooms recalling the visits of luminaries ranging from Queen Elizabeth II to Thomas Mann, from John F. Kennedy to Elizabeth Taylor (who came with three dogs, two cats, her mother and a retinue of servants, and stayed in the room once occupied by Benito Mussolini). But somehow you never feel you've stepped out of your league, not even (unless you go crazy and ask for a royal suite) when it comes time to pay the bill.

174

The Imperial charges $60 to $95 a night single, $95 to $125 a night double—not Holiday Inn prices, of course, but a good deal less than you would pay at the Ritz in Paris or Claridge's in London. The royal suites cost $450 a night, which is not unreasonable, since they consist of sitting rooms forty or fifty feet long, with ceilings worthy of a Baroque palace, as well as three or four bedrooms and a bath or two.

For your money, you get extraordinary service: a zipper repaired on a Sunday, a rose on the breakfast tray, a greeting by name the first day you come downstairs. Everyone smiles a lot; the only surly employee I ever met was an overworked waiter in the café, and his feet probably hurt. The bedrooms are furnished with antiques and equipped with wall safes, the beds covered with heavy linen sheets, the bathroom floors heated.

All of this is designed to attract not just tourists, musical or otherwise, but also businessmen, who form the backbone of the Imperial's clientele. They account for fifty percent of the turnover and help keep the hotel seventy-three percent full year round (it can break even with only 60 percent occupancy). There are no fewer than 252 employees for the 160 rooms, which can hold a total of 260 guests; on all but the busiest days, there are more people working in the Imperial than staying in it.

World War II was terribly hard on Vienna and the Imperial. The hotel served as a Nazi guesthouse, Hitler staying there several times, and at war's end, badly battered, it was taken over by the Soviet Union, which used it as its headquarters until 1955, when the occupying forces withdrew. It took two years to restore the classical façade, which is painted Hapsburg yellow, and to repair the magnificent central staircase of red, yellow and black marble, supported by reclining gods and goddesses. Only then were the elegant Gobelin tapestries and the Winterhalter portraits of the Emperor Franz Joseph and Empress Elizabeth finally taken out of storage.

For me, winter is prime time at the Imperial. It is the best season to eat in the restaurant and the café; herring and goulash and bread dumplings and sauerkraut and strudel, the kind of good if not great food in which the hotel excels, don't mix well with hot weather. Winter is also the moment when the hotel looks its best, with a Christmas tree dotted with white lights atop the marquee and huge pine Advent wreaths hung with purple ribbons from the chandeliers. And it is the time of the great Viennese events: the Opera Ball, the Philharmonic Ball and New Year's Eve.

I would rather be in Vienna than anywhere else in the world for New Year's Eve, which seems to me to consist too often of forced hilarity. In Vienna, if one is lucky, there is *Fledermaus*, at both the State Opera and the Volksoper, and the Musikverein concert, with midnight balls in between. At the dance at the Imperial, the real point of the ball is not the dancing, which demonstrates how few people waltz well, or the dinner, which demonstrates that Austrian kitchens are better when they don't pretend to be French. The point is the nostalgic warmth with which the evening is suffused. At each place is a glass service plate, engraved to mark the occasion, which you are meant to take home, along with the marzipan mushrooms, four-leaf clovers and pigs which for the Austrians symbolize good luck. Between dances, a waiter dressed as a chimney sweep distributes coins and a kitchen worker carries through the ballroom a live pig with a blue ribbon around its neck.

And who would not be charmed when, at midnight, the lights dim, a gong is sounded, balloons drop from the ceiling and the orchestra, naturally, begins to play the "Blue Danube"?

3. *For the* Feinschmecker

A bleak, granitic presence on the Tauentzienstrasse near the center of West Berlin, the place looks as if it might have been designed by Albert Speer. In fact, the Kaufhaus des Westens—KaDeWe for short (pronounced Kah-Day-Vay)—has been there since 1907, when Albert Speer was a pup. It is called the Department Store of the West not in the interest of political propaganda, but because in its early years it stood in a leafy suburb, well west of the city center of old Imperial Berlin around the Alexanderplatz, in what is now the Communist east.

I had walked airily past it on a half-dozen previous trips to

Berlin, vaguely aware of its presence but dismissing it as just another department store, no more interesting to the likes of me than Selfridge's in London or the Galeries Lafayette in Paris. Then, a few summers ago, Betsey surprised me by insisting that we go there for lunch. My suspicion that she was mad evaporated when we stepped off the elevator on the sixth floor and saw Nirvana spread before us.

The sixth floor at KaDeWe is called the Feinschmecker Etage—the gourmet's floor, although the word *Feinschmecker* carries with it a properly German sense of quantity as well as quality. With the exception of one establishment in Tokyo (where else?), this is the largest food store in the world, dwarfing California supermarkets, Macy's and Fauchon's and Harrods' great food halls. Although I have not (quite) managed to visit them all, it seems to me the best of its kind as well, an astonishingly comprehensive emporium of plain and fancy.

Manfred Breuch, the store's managing director, has a strategy. He wants the best of everything to lure customers into KaDeWe—"You can't find it anywhere else"—and he wants the most complete stock possible so that no one has to make another stop after leaving KaDeWe.

The statistics of the food halls are rather daunting: sixty thousand square feet of sales space; a weekly turnover of roughly one and a half million dollars; twenty-five thousand products on sale, and five hundred sales clerks; twenty tasting stands, where shoppers can sample some of the food and drink on offer and make a mini-tour of the gastronomy of Europe and the Far East in the process.

Gaston LeNôtre, the Parisian caterer, known for his pastries, his ice creams and his candies, ships in chocolate truffles and supervised the installation of a bakery in the store that produces baguettes and other loaves, tortes and tarts and cakes and cookies. In few other establishments would his bread face the competition it faces at KaDeWe, which is also supplied by a bakery elsewhere in Berlin with eighty varieties of pumpernickel and rye and other dark delights, made in the style of Hesse and Westphalia and Bavaria and Pomerania.

Mr. LeNôtre's products can be tasted at one stand, those of Lyon restaurateur Paul Bocuse at another, fresh and an infinite variety of smoked fish at a third, bratwurst and currywurst and Czech Pilsener at a fourth, quite respectable Chinese and Japanese cooking at a fifth.

That summer, my wife and I ate a delicious if imbalanced lunch at three of the counters. It included three raw French oysters each, with glasses of white wine; a pair of bratwurst each, accompanied by sweet Bavarian mustard and steins of Budweiser beer (the original Czech variety); and slabs of a rich LeNôtre cake, followed by coffee. The meal cost $25, but it would have been much cheaper without the oysters.

Lists are boring, but it is impossible to give an adequate idea of the scope of the place without some description of the various departments, all of which are clearly marked on multilingual, multicolored illuminated maps near the elevators. (Many of the clerks speak English, and those who don't do not object to the stand-by of the linguistically underprepared, the pointed finger.)

In the fruit and vegetable departments, I saw chanterelles (wild mushrooms) from Poland, tomatoes from Spain, wax beans from France, Brussels sprouts from Holland, broad beans from Greece, apples from Hungary, avocados from Israel, quinces from Italy, tiny green beans from Kenya, limes from Brazil—to say nothing of the more exotic items like mangosteens from Indonesia and trompettes de la mort (a scarce and succulent variety of wild mushroom) from France.

A few steps away are the cheese counters—one for the choice items from Italy, one for those from France, one for those from other countries—and a dozen racks full of the humbler packaged and processed varieties from around the world. Everything is there, from thirty French goat cheeses to a dozen Italian grating varieties.

Recalling a remarkable Italian mascarpone studded with white truffles that I had once bought for a picnic at Peck's, the great Milan delicatessen, I tried to stump KaDeWe. Didn't work: They produced the cheese and completed my defeat by pointing to the Peck's label.

No one would dream of stumping the sausage department, which consists of more than three hundred feet of gleaming glass showcases, packed with 250 kinds of salami and one thousand other kinds of wurst. Nor, so far inland, could one duplicate the fish department, for which Belons are flown in thrice weekly from Brittany and Colchesters twice weekly from London; eels and trout and carp and crawfish and catfish and lobsters are brought to Berlin in tank trucks, kept alive in glass-fronted tanks, and killed (with a bop on the head approved by the local humane society) only after the customer has made a selection.

Some sample prices from a recent visit: A fat and perfectly ripe mango cost $2.95; a pound of weisswurst (a veal sausage) cost $3.20; a baguette cost $1.10; and a pound of French Brie cost 82 cents.

Don't forget to try the rotisserie chicken and duck, and don't fail to notice the 137 mustards, and don't miss the Dallmayr coffee from Munich, and don't overlook the eighteen kinds of herring salad. They tell me the merchandise on the other five floors is equally outstanding, but I wouldn't know.

4. *Lower Saxony Discovered*

OVER the years, I had satisfied myself that I knew Germany well enough—the Rhineland and the Black Forest, Bavaria and Berlin. So I was a little crestfallen in 1984 when a glorious early medieval manuscript known as Henry the Lion's gospel book was sold—sold, mind you, for $11.9 million, the highest price ever paid at auction for an art object—to a museum in a place I had scarcely heard of, Braunschweig. I resolved to have a look as soon as I could, and when my wife and I went there a few months later, we were surprised and delighted by our first encounter with Braunschweig (its English name is Brunswick) and with Lower Saxony, the uncelebrated region in which it is located.

Lower Saxony lies in the northeastern part of West Germany, alongside Mr. Churchill's Iron Curtain. Its delights are hidden away in small towns like Hameln, where confectioners sell marzipan rats to commemorate the spell cast by the Pied Piper; like Alfeld, with Walter Gropius and Adolf Meyer's 1911 Fagus factory, one of the first buildings with a steel-and-glass skeleton; and like sleepy little Corvey, once a proud monastic center, whose church is composed of two incongruous parts: a frowning façade, one of only three important structures in Germany, along with a gatehouse at Lorsch and the Palatine Chapel at Aachen, that remain to us from Charlemagne's time, and a bubbling Baroque interior, crammed with polychrome wood carvings of inexhaustible charm.

In Braunschweig—I remembered as we drove into town, by the way, that my German-American grandmother always called liverwurst "Braunschweiger"—it turned out that the Herzog-Anton-Ulrich Museum owns not only the multimillion-dollar manuscript but also a noble self-portrait by Giorgione, that most elusive of Venetian painters, and one of the most radiant of our pitifully small hoard of Vermeers. Nearby Hildesheim, the capital of the Ottonian Romanesque, was hideously disfigured by Allied bombers in March 1945, but both St. Michael's Church and the cathedral, two of Germany's greatest medieval buildings, have been restored. The cathedral is a treasure-house of the eleventh century, with an immense polygonal chandelier; a splendidly sculptured bronze column, recalling that of Trajan in Rome, except that this one depicts not the triumphs of the sword but that of the Passion; and a superlative set of bronze doors. The portrayal of the story of Adam and Eve on the doors, so sweet and yet so stern, is for me one of the unqualified masterpieces of European sculpture. Ghiberti couldn't have laid a glove on the unknown genius who carved it.

We made our headquarters in the half-timbered village of Goslar, nestled against the Harz Mountains in the southern part of Lower Saxony. The beguiling Hotel Kaiserworth, a Gothic redoubt overlooking the improbably picturesque square, charges about $60 a night for a room big enough to shelter a family with quintuplets. Along its flank, we were intrigued to notice, are plaques recalling two great German panzer strategists, Erwin Rommel and Heinz Guderian, who commanded local units between world wars; the girl at the desk had, of course, never heard of either of them.

Kassel, about a ninety-minute drive to the south in neighboring Hesse, can also be visited during a stay in Goslar. Its elephantine Schloss Wilhelmshöhe, overlooking the city, houses no fewer than seventeen Rembrandts, a collection arguably finer even than those in Amsterdam and The Hague.

CHAPTER IX

Spain

1. *Legacy of the Moors*

T H E scent of the Orient is everywhere in the Andalusian air—in the heavy perfume of the jasmine and the oleander, in the delicacy of the ornamentation of mosques and palaces, in the look of the people. The buildings of Granada, Córdoba and Seville in southern Spain are the legacy of one of the great conquests of history—a conquest that lasted for almost eight hundred years and came close to changing the course of European history, yet one that most of us never really learned about or remember only vaguely.

The glories of Andalusia are the creation of the Moors, the Moslems who crossed from North Africa in A.D. 711 and pushed steadily north until they were finally halted by Charles Martel in 732 near Poitiers, only two hundred miles from Paris. It took the Christians until January 2, 1492, just seven months before Columbus set sail from Palos, to push the invaders out of their last stronghold on Spanish soil.

To visit the three cities is to partake of perhaps the least Occidental civilization in Western Europe. The best of the buildings are hypnotically beautiful; the first sight of the Court of the Lions in Granada at night, glowing creamily under an inky sky, water trickling into the central fountain and running off through radi-

ating channels, was one of the most breath-taking experiences of my travel lifetime. The food can be quite delicious, especially the gazpacho, another of those clichés of "Continental" cooking, like Wiener schnitzel and spaghetti Bolognese, that one must eat in its place of birth to understand why anyone ever bothered to copy it. The best sangria, the best bullfights and the best (if sadly debased) flamenco are all to be found in Andalusia.

But Cervantes had it right when he remarked that "it seldom happens that any felicity comes so pure as not to be tempered and allayed by some mixture of sorrow."

In Granada and Seville, and to a lesser degree in Córdoba, you will find yourself in the company of tens of thousands of other visitors, especially in summer, and many of them have the capacity to vulgarize the most refined setting. To avoid them, you can go in spring or fall, when the Andalusian gardens are often at their best, and when the heat is less intense; but do not forgo a visit simply because only a summer trip is possible. My wife and I were there one August and missed the worst of the crowds by doing most of our sightseeing early and late. The temperature often approached 100 degrees, but only at midday, when we were usually sitting in an air-conditioned restaurant or taking a siesta. The heat is quite dry and therefore far more tolerable than Washington or New York in the same season, especially since no one is expected to wear anything but the lightest and most informal clothes.

One could easily spend three days in each place without boredom, but five or six days is enough to gain a good feeling for all three. There are plenty of package tours available, but it is far better to go on your own in a car rented in Seville and dropped off at Granada, or vice versa, or rented in Málaga for a circle tour. The trip can be extended with visits to the enchanting old town of Ronda, to Jerez and its sherry *bodegas* (write in advance to the firm that interests you) or to the teeming beach resorts. The driving involved is neither difficult nor costly—86 miles from Seville to Córdoba, 107 from Córdoba to Granada. But be forewarned: The run from Córdoba to Granada, especially the last part, passes through desolate countryside with few gas stations and fewer places to change traveler's checks into pesetas. I came within a couple of miles of fulfilling my wife's longstanding prediction that someday I would strand us in some forlorn place with an empty tank. (I finally did it, a couple of years later, after an excessively well-irrigated lunch in Burgundy.) And be forewarned: If you hope to stay in the government *paradors*, about which more later, you or your travel agent must write months in advance. Others have the same hope.

Seville is the best place to begin, if only because Granada makes the best climax. It is most unforgettable (and most crowded) during Holy Week, so vividly described by James A. Michener in *Iberia*, when rival brotherhoods carry their great *pasos*, litters bearing garlanded and bejeweled polychrome wooden statues, through the streets. A city of art, it is also a commercial center of half a million people. Columbus's discoveries made it rich, and it was from Seville's port on the Guadalquivir that Amerigo Vespucci and Ferdinand Magellan set sail.

The modern traveler goes there either for the festivals or to see the architectural jewels in the Moorish, Gothic and Mudéjar styles. The last is an expression of the lasting impact of the Moors on Spain, created by Christian artists long after the Moslem conquerors had been ousted from Seville in 1248.

Seville's landmark is the Giralda (the name means weather vane), a 322-foot-high minaret, one of the handful of masterpieces surviving from the twelfth-century Almohad dynasty, with restrained ornamentation in keeping with the dynasty's scorn for ostentation. Only a few steps away, across an animated plaza, is the Alcázar, a palace built by Moorish architects for the Christian king Peter the Cruel almost two hundred years later in a far more elaborate style. Here is a first glimpse of the joys of Andalusian art—the brilliantly colored geometric patterns of the azulejos or tiles on the lower walls, the stucco upper walls covered with interlaced Arabic script, the ceilings of mock stalactites. Beyond lie the gardens, cooled by fountains and basins, shaded by exotic trees and shrubs covering the graceful terraces.

For me, that is Seville—that and the wonderful view of the brightly lit Torre del Oro at night from across the river; that and the old Jewish quarter, with its tiny squares planted with orange trees and palms; that and the old tobacco factory, now the university, where Carmen and the other "cigarette girls" once worked. The cathedral, with its immense Flemish altarpiece, struck me as a lily not once but a thousand times gilded, a lily afflicted with elephantiasis.

Its builders are said to have resolved in 1401 to "build a cathedral so immense that everyone on beholding it will take us for madmen." I do. It is the largest Gothic cathedral in the world, but it has none of the majesty of those Baroque behemoths in Rome and London, St. Peter's and St. Paul's. Go anyway, if only to see Columbus's tomb (or is it just a monument?), built in the nineteenth century in the south transept.

The grandest, but in my opinion not the best, place to stay in Seville is the Hotel Alfonso XIII. A three-year, multimillion-dollar renovation has robbed it of some of its old Andalusian charm without giving it a crisp, up-to-date feeling. The little Doña María, decorated in the Hispanic style, has a rooftop swimming pool with a view of the Giralda, only a block away, and some rooms with canopied beds. (Since this article first appeared, I have heard from readers of questionable practices by the management here, which I have had no chance to check.)

Among the restaurants, the Rio Grande has a lovely riverside terrace, smashing views and mediocre food; the Rincón de Curro, southwest of the city center, is probably the best of the more elaborate places; Enrique Becerra is a bistro a couple of blocks from the cathedral that gave us, after the warmest of welcomes, our best meal in Andalusia: green olives cured in herbs and lemon peel to go with the sherry, then tartly silky gazpacho, a glorious platter of tiny deep-fried fish, and chocolate mousse, the lot washed down with an icy, barely sweetened sangria (about $25 for two; no English spoken). If you are picnicking, you will find first-rate supplies at Marciano (Linares 6); if you want to see flamenco dancing, you won't do any better than the nontouristy Tablao de Curro Velez (Rodo 7). Sadly, it is necessary to add the warning that Seville has become one of the worst cities in Europe for purse snatchers, so take every possible precaution, especially after dark.

Present-day Córdoba has only a quarter of a million people; it is not among Spain's half-dozen largest cities. But in the eleventh century, when it had three thousand mosques, three hundred public baths and half a million people, it was eclipsed in magnificence only by Baghdad. Even in Roman times, it was the largest city in Spain, the birthplace of Seneca and the site of a furious battle between Caesar and Pompey the Younger, in which twenty thousand soldiers perished. Today it is hot, dusty and a bit faded; even the exterior of the great Mezquita looks rather dilapidated, with grubby gardens, chipped tiles and cracked stonework.

But the interior of the building, once the most sumptuous of Moslem shrines, remains one of the architectural glories of Europe, with 850 columns of onyx, jasper, marble and granite forming a seemingly endless forest dappled with light. Many of the pillars are topped with exquisite capitals salvaged from the Visigothic church that once stood on the site, and they are linked by horseshoe-shaped arches banded in red and white. In the midst of it all sits a Baroque church, dismayingly inserted in the sixteenth century; the modern visitor can only agree with the Emperor Charles V, who told the canons of Córdoba: "You have destroyed something unique to build something commonplace." But they left untouched most of the columns as well as the gleaming mihrab, or prayer niche, an octagonal recess covered with superlative mosaics.

After visiting the mosque, take a walk through the Judería, the old Jewish quarter, with its languid streets, brilliantly white walls and delicate window grilles. Among the more interesting sights are the old synagogue, one of only two remaining in Spain, and the archeological museum, which is rich in Roman, Visigothic and Moorish sculpture.

Córdoba's best hotel is the Parador Nacional de la Arruzafa, one of the finest of the state-owned inns that provide pretty rooms, often in lovely settings, with limited services and reasonable prices. Situated two miles north of town, it offers swimming, tennis and a garden. As for eating, I strongly recommend the sunny Caballo Rojo, opposite the Mezquita, especially for its braised oxtail and its homemade pistachio ice cream.

And then Granada, sheltering at the foot of the eternally snow-crested Sierra Nevada, with the Alhambra standing guard on its ridge above the modern city. Tarry down below for an hour to see the Capilla Real in the cathedral quarter. It has little to do with the Moors and less to do with Andalusia; it is there because the Spanish monarchs wanted to be buried near the site of their final triumph over the Moslem invaders. But the late Gothic mausoleums are splendidly rich, as is Queen Isabella's personal art collection, which hangs in the sacristy; it includes major works by Memling, van der Weyden, Dierick Bouts and Botticelli. Then up the hill to the Red Fort and to the hotel.

The Alhambra has the most famous of all the *paradors*, the San Francisco, installed in a fifteenth-century convent, and its setting and gardens are unforgettable. But so is its surly, often nonexistent service. Arriving on a weekend, we were told that we could not change any money, that there were no tables left for dinner, that the coffee machine was not yet working. I would not go back; if you take my advice, you will try the Alhambra Palace at the costlier end of the spectrum or the sweet little America. Granada is no gastronomic paradise, but you might go to Cunini for fish or to the Sevilla for meat, both moderately priced and very consistent.

It is imperative that one of your nights in Granada coincide with the illuminations of the Alhambra, which restore to it all of its lush grandeur. Tuesday, Thursday and Saturday nights is the usual schedule, but check before completing your itinerary with the Spanish National Tourist Office (665 Fifth Avenue, New York, NY 10022; 212-759-8822). And while on the subject of imperatives, beware the gypsies in Granada, who will harass you mercilessly unless you rebuff them firmly at the first approach.

You enter the Alhambra through Charles V's palace, a dignified Renaissance building of such perfect proportions, a circle within a square, that it coexists successfully with the utterly antithetical spirit of its Moorish neighbors. It is the only surviving creation of Pedro Machuca, one of Michelangelo's star pupils.

Then, through an underground passage, you reach the Alcázar, the fourteenth-century palace of the Nasrid princes, which is the core of the Alhambra and the most magnificent Moorish building in the world. It is the final expression of a civilization devoted to ornament, built in that fleeting moment before decadence set in. Most remarkably, it gains its effects not from gold and silver but from humbler materials, mainly stucco and tiles, handled in such a way as to create a mood of enchantment.

The Court of the Myrtles, the Hall of the Ambassadors, the King's Chamber, the Hall of the Two Sisters—they are a succession of delights, of intricate kufic and cursive script, of tilework, of honeycomb cupolas, of haunting vistas over the gardens, of fountains and pools. The wonder of wonders is the Court of the

Lions, so named because of the antique fountain, composed of twelve lions in gray marble, at its center. Around the edge runs an arcade of stilted arches, supported by 124 white marble columns, with pavilions at either end. Especially at night, the sense of equilibrium, of perfumed repose, is overwhelming.

Much remains to be seen: the great red walls of the fort itself, the luscious gardens, the nearby Generalife palace and its soothing, terraced water gardens, and, south of town on the road to Motril, the Suspiro del Moro—the Moor's sigh. There, the last Moorish king on Spanish soil, the unfortunate Boabdil, turned and looked longingly back on his former capital, to which he had given the Christians the keys, ending 781 years of Moorish domination. He sighed, then wept. His mother, according to legend, turned furiously upon him and said: "Weep not like a woman for what you could not defend like a man."

2. The Pilgrim's Goal

DURING the 1960s and 1970s, I spent a lot of time exploring the medieval churches and cathedrals of central and southern France, and in many of them I discovered, in some corner or other, a sculptured relief of a scallop shell, the symbol of Saint James the Apostle. The shells were there, a bit of reading revealed, because the buildings had served in the eleventh and twelfth centuries as hostels for the million or more pilgrims who each year walked from France—and from Britain, Germany and Scandinavia—to the great shrine at Santiago de Compostela in northwestern Spain, where the saint's bones are said to have been unearthed in the ninth century.

They wore a kind of pilgrim's uniform of cape, sandals and broad-brimmed hat festooned with scallop shells; they carried staffs with gourds attached to hold water, sometimes spending a year en route, living in fear of robbers and brigands. For a time, the greatest Christian shrines in the world were Rome, Jerusalem and Santiago, which means Saint James in Spanish. Not by chance did Pope John Paul II choose this venerable meeting place at the edge of the Continent to appeal in 1982 to "Old Europe" to "find yourself, be yourself, discover your origins."

It is still possible to follow the route from one of the main gathering points in France, such as the Tour St. Jacques in Paris, between the Bastille and the Louvre. (Saint Jacques is the Apostle's name in French; memories of the great pilgrimages survive not only in the name of the tower but also in the French name for scallops, coquilles St. Jacques.)

The Way of Saint James, as the route is called, divides and reunites several times as it winds from northern France to the southwest, passing Autun and Cluny, Souillac and Conques. It crosses the Pyrénées at Somport or at Roncesvalles, where in 778 the Basques massacred the rear guard of Charlemagne's army under Roland—an episode glorified in France's first epic poem. Then the way leads across northern Spain, through one of the most glorious treasure houses of Romanesque architecture, toward Galicia. All along the Spanish part of the route, the direction signs, each decorated with a scallop shell, give the distance to Santiago for modern pilgrims.

For one reason and another, I never made it to Santiago, despite good intentions, until 1982, when I happened across a pair of newspaper articles that goaded me into action. One, in a French newspaper, reported that that year would be an *año santo*, a holy year, because St. James's Day, July 25, fell on a Sunday. This, the piece said, happened only once every four to eleven years, or some such thing, and would bring tens of thousands to the city. The other article, a profile of Sacheverell Sitwell, the writer and aesthete, in *The Times* (London), quoted him as saying that "there is nothing finer in Europe than Santiago de Compostela," including Venice and Florence.

Not even Sir Sacheverell's enthusiasm prepared my wife and me for the spectacle that greeted us as we drove into the center of the city at midnight, forty-eight hours before the big day, after an exhausting if exhilarating journey over barely adequate roads. We had babbled excitedly after visits to the monastery at Silos, the Romanesque church at Frómista, the Royal Pantheon and the tiny Mozarabic church at León, and the pre-Romanesque buildings on a grassy hillside above Oviedo, but we were stunned into unwonted silence by Santiago de Compostela.

The center of the city is a vast square, the Plaza de España, longer than a football field. Because we had been lucky enough to get a room at the Hostal de los Reyes Católicos, built between 1501 and 1511 by Ferdinand and Isabella and now a sumptuous hotel, we were permitted to drive right into the square and park. As we got out of the car, we could hear young voices somewhere nearby singing hymns; above us towered the softly floodlit Obradoiro façade of the cathedral, a Baroque masterpiece by Fernándo Casas y Novoa, built in 1750 to protect the twelfth-century west front.

The light dramatized the already dramatic—the swirls and curves of the ornamentation, the slender towers, the quadruple flight of rectilinear steps leading up to the door. Splendid buildings, three hundred, four hundred, five hundred years old, stood on other sides of the plaza. George Henry Borrow, the nineteenth-century British traveler, had got it exactly right when he said Santiago was a place "in every respect calculated to excite awe and admiration."

The cathedral is, of course, the focal point of the celebration, which takes place on July 25 every year, although not ordinarily on quite the scale of the holy years. Pilgrims still begin their visit by approaching the Door of Glory, a twelfth-century work by a carver known only as Master Mateo, which ranks as one of the half-dozen greatest pieces of Romanesque sculpture. It remains much as it was eight hundred years ago, a vast composition of three portals opening into the cathedral, embellished with thousands upon thousands of portraits in stone. The eye travels at once to the central opening, which is bisected by a pillar bearing a statue of Saint James, gazing with the utmost serenity at some distant point, and crowned by a tympanum showing Christ the King engulfed by angels. Millions of the faithful, touching the pillar to give thanks for safe arrival, have worn and polished the stone. How many, one wonders, have noticed the kneeling figure of Mateo at the base of the shaft?

From here, the visitor passes down the austere nave to the richly ornamented sanctuary, which seems intolerably gaudy after the serene simplicity of the Door of Glory and the exuberant equilibrium of the façade, to kiss the cloak draped over a thirteenth-century statue of the saint. Silver and precious stones, incredibly elaborate carving—and yet none of the spirituality, for

me at least, that resides in the smallest and least of Master
Mateo's details.

On Saturday, bands play (Wagner, of all things!) in the
streets that feed into the main square, and in the Plaza de la
Quintana, outside the beautifully carved Goldsmiths' Door on
the south side of the cathedral, strong men dance while carrying
on their shoulders gaily colored papier-mâché heads as much as
twelve feet tall. They are accompanied by Galician bagpipes,
whose wail is rather less plaintive than the skirl one hears in
Scotland. It is a brilliantly animated scene, with the fake heads
of Popeye and a pirate and a flamenco dancer bobbing above the
real ones of students at the local university, townspeople and
visitors speaking in a dozen languages. The mood is decidedly secular. Beggars extend their palms, teen-agers play soccer in a
deserted cloister, and young women in spike heels and skimpy
sundresses mix with soberly garbed peasants and bourgeois children dressed to the nines. Many tourists carry wooden staffs
topped by scallop shells and ribbons in the Spanish colors, crimson and gold.

On Saturday night, the Spanish King and Queen appear on a
balcony above the magnificent doorway of the Hostal to the
cheers of the crowd filling the main plaza. The King then lights a
rocket that whizzes along a wire above the crowd and ignites
fireworks attached to scaffolding standing in front of, and in the
shape of, the Obradoiro façade.

Fully thirty-five minutes of spectacular aerial and terrestrial
pyrotechnic displays follow—a giddy prelude to the solemnity of
Sunday, which begins with the concussion of twenty-one aerial
bombs and comes to a climax in an elaborate mass in the cathedral. The Holy Door behind the high altar, into which Master
Mateo's statues of prophets and patriarchs have been incorporated, is flung open, and the *botafumeiro*, a massive incense burn-
er made in 1602, is hung from the transept dome and swung high
by six men heaving on a hawser.

The other hours or days of a visit to Santiago can be spent
wandering through the ancient *rúas*, or streets, admiring the old
walls tufted with the foliage that is encouraged by the damp
Galician air, or shopping for lace, wicker baskets or gold and silver
trinkets in the dozens of tiny shops.

There is good eating aplenty, thanks to the proximity of the sea, at less than ruinous prices. The leading places are Vilas (Rosalia de Castro 88, telephone 59-10-00), Don Gaiferos (Rúa Nova 23, 58-38-94) and Chiton (Rúa Nova 40, 58-53-54); expect to pay $25 to $45 per couple, including local wine, at each. I am particularly fond of Chiton, a gaily decorated establishment with an airy walled garden, where a young waiter took infinite pains to bring to our table a variety of fish and shellfish, whose Spanish names we did not know, so that we could order intelligently. They tasted as good cooked as they looked uncooked.

With the possible exception of the San Marcos in León, a converted sixteenth-century monastery with its own museum, I think the Hostal is the most splurge-worthy hotel in Spain. Rooms cost from $30 for a rather cramped double to $75 for large rooms furnished in considerable style—far from exorbitant, by today's mind-boggling standards. Simpler accommodation is available at the Peregrino (doubles from $30); the Compostela (doubles from $17.50) and the Mexico (doubles from $8.50). In any case, reserve early, especially if you are going in the summer, and without fail if you are going in a holy year; the next is 1988.

3. A Prejudice Shattered

L E T me state my case right away: I think that Spain is the most underrated eating country in Europe. My time there had been limited until 1982, and what I had tasted hadn't impressed me much; I had confidently dismissed Spanish cooking as an oily mediocrity, a compound of gazpacho and paella and excessively heavy red wine. But recent extended stays there have provided a chance to sample the fare of that richly endowed land a lot more thoroughly, and it is clear to me that I didn't know what I was talking about.

Spain isn't France or Italy; the Michelin red guide gives no Spanish restaurants three stars, and neither would I. But below the very top level, Spain's best restaurants, grand and simple, offer fresh and flavorful cooking that bears little resemblance to what is served to package tourists in the seaside hotels and even less to "Spanish cuisine" abroad. You have to do your homework, which means consulting the Michelin or, if you can read a bit of Spanish, one of the local guides, such as the *Guía Gastronómica y Turística*; you can no more choose restaurants at random in Spain than in England or Germany.

The country's greatest gastronomic treasure is its fish and shellfish, of which it has the greatest variety of any country in Europe and, probably, the world. My favorite fish restaurant, a simple place called El Pescador (José Ortéga y Gasset 75, Madrid), sometimes has as many as thirty varieties in its glass cases— old friends like soles and turbots and cod, oysters and clams and mussels, lobsters and shrimp and three different kinds of crab, but also a host of delicious novelties.

There are the big brothers of the shrimp—*gambas, langostinos, cigalas, carabineros* and *santiaguinos*, these last said to bear the image of Saint James on their shells; prehistoric-looking things called *percebes*, a form of edible barnacle; silvery eels no more than an inch long; and fish from both the Mediterranean and the Atlantic that are unknown in American waters: *besugo* and *merluza, rape* and *salmonete* (sea bream and hake, angler-fish and red mullet, which probably won't help very much). The best way to eat most of them is *à la plancha*, grilled with a little lemon, although El Pescador also makes a good fish soup and, as a first course, a fine salpicon, which here is bits of shellfish in light olive oil, and which I could happily eat every noontime for the rest of my days.

Evarista García Gómez, the tall, lean proprietor of El Pescador, has been in the business for almost forty years, and he makes very few mistakes. His more luxurious restaurant, O'Pazo (Reina Mercedes 20), serves turbot baked in oil and garlic, another estimable creation.

El Pescador specializes in fish from Galicia, the northwestern corner of Spain, and brings them down by plane. La Dorada (Orense 66, Madrid) brings its raw material from the Mediterranean in the same way. A fourth Madrid seafood house, also highly reliable, is La Trainera (Lagasca 60). All four seem to have mastered the art of grilling fish and shellfish without drying them out, something that is not often the case, as an old Rome hand remarked to me recently, in Italian places of the same type. I would urge you to accompany your meal in any of these restaurants with an inexpensive wine known by the brand name Monopole. It is a consistently good dry white Rioja.

But there is much more to eating in Spain than seafood. The oranges make the best juice I have ever had outside Morocco, and the raspberries (*frambuesas*) are exquisite. If you like prosciutto or Ardennes ham, be sure to try the Spanish equivalent; it is called *jamón Serrano,* and the very best comes from the village of Jabugo in Andalusia. In the fall, especially in the north, there are glorious wild mushrooms, including some varieties that grow only in Spain, and fresh white *flageolets,* here called *pochas* and stewed with sausage or ham or quail. Game, particularly the partridge, is splendid.

I first discovered how really good Spanish rural cooking can be when we stopped for lunch at a faded-looking restaurant—the kind of place that would have been called a roadhouse in the American Midwest thirty years ago—in Villajuan, south of Santiago de Compostela. It rejoices in the name *Chocolate.* The menu is a sixth or seventh carbon copy of a typed list, tucked into a plastic folder, but there is nothing plastic about the food: mussels and saffron cooked with fresh noodles, beautiful fish and juicy sirloins that are carried into the dining room on the end of a long skewer by the jolly cook and proprietor.

You will be equally pleased, I think, at the Mesón de Cándido (Plaza Azoguejo 5, Segovia), by the roast lamb and roast sweet baby peppers; at Enrique Becerra (Gamazo 2, Seville), by the authentically tart gazpacho and two-inch-long *salmonetes,* deep-fried without batter in some mysterious way that renders them totally greaseless; at the Caballo Rojo (Cardenal Herrero 28, Córdoba) by the oxtail ragout and the homemade ice cream; and at Jaume de Provença (Provenca 88, Barcelona) by almost everything, but especially the nibbles you should order with your drinks, including deep-fried scallions and much the best anchovies I have ever tasted.

You can eat without a necktie at all the places mentioned so far; none of them is uptown in the slightest. But Madrid, in particular, also has a number of quite elegant establishments serving elaborate food, and it is these that most guides award the stars: to Zalacaín (Alvarez de Baena 4), often called the best restaurant in Spain; Horcher (Alfonso XII 6), whose Berlin origins still show in the presence of marinated herring and *Baumkuchen* on the menu, and the Jockey (Amador de los Ríos 6), the favorite of *le tout* Madrid. All are very good (and Horcher gives women a footstool), but none would be on my own list of favorite haute-cuisine restaurants in Spain.

The following four would, because all have refreshed and varied traditional recipes without the banalities of nouvelle cuisine:

El Amparo (Puigcerdá 8, Madrid): a romantically beautiful restaurant in an old alley, with dining rooms on three levels, an innovative Spanish Basque cuisine, a charming polyglot director, Carmen Guasp, and my favorite new dish in some time, roast red peppers stuffed with codfish and napped with a subtle, featherlight sauce.

Arzak (Alto de Miracruz 21, San Sebastián): on the road to the French border, this place is marred by stuttering service, but Juan Mari is such a genius in the kitchen that it barely matters, inventing every week dishes like hot oysters with fennel and lamb stuffed with lambs' kidneys.

Ama Lur (Mallorca 275, Barcelona): this restaurant must be one of the most beautiful in Europe, with miniature plants in bloom on each table, a beautiful garden outside the rear windows, and waitresses in Victorian outfits. I ate a slice of *merluza* that had been roasted with superlative olive oil, garlic and tiny hot peppers, which was as delicious as the uncharacteristically light red Rioja, Gloriosa, that was urged on me by the knowing young sommelier.

Raco d'En Binu (Puig i Cadafalch 14, Argentona): it is worth the trouble pronouncing the name, reserving at least a day in advance and driving forty-five minutes north of Barcelona to eat the world-class cooking in this small, civilized restaurant, which served us a series of delights, including a sea bass cooked in a paper bag and sweet, delicate warm sea urchins. The wine list is an invitation to lose one's prejudices.

Prices (dinner for two, including meals, apéritif, wine and tip) range from $50 at the simpler places, such as Caballo Rojo, to

$200 at the grands, such as the Jockey and Ama Lur. Most of the better restaurants begin dinner later in the evening, often at ten, which is worth noting when making reservations.

Finally, two admissions: despite my best efforts, I have yet to eat at Ampurdán (Route N 11, near Figueras, north of Barcelona), the favorite restaurant of my colleague James M. Markham (for three years the chief of the Madrid Bureau of the *Times*), who steered me toward some of the Spanish places I like best; and hard as I looked, I was unable to find very interesting food in some of the finest of the art towns, notably Toledo, Salamanca, Granada, León and Burgos.

CHAPTER X

Eastern Europe

---

1. Dostoevsky's Leningrad

Fёdor Mikhailovich Dostoevsky died more than a hundred years ago in a country still called Russia and a city still called St. Petersburg. But he remains a vivid presence in Leningrad and the Soviet Union, a presence not so obvious as that of Catherine the Great, whose shade haunts the rich galleries of the Hermitage, or that of Peter the Great, whose famous bronze effigy by Falconet peers steadily toward the West he strove to emulate, but a presence accessible enough to the modestly adventurous foreign visitor.

The Kremlin has never been entirely comfortable with Dostoevsky. Although his masterpieces—*Crime and Punishment, The Idiot, The Brothers Karamazov*—helped to shape the twentieth-century novel in the West, he has never been taken as a model by the practitioners of socialist realism. For Mann, for Gide, for Kafka, he was the father of the psychological novel; for official Soviet critics he has always seemed too morbid, too religious, too conservative.

In the 1930s, Ilya Ehrenburg said that Dostoevsky told "the whole truth" about human nature, "a truth which is undeniable and deadly." It is a truth, he added, that is unmentionable "if one is to a build a state."

Dostoevsky's novels, on sale in paperback at almost any Western bookstore, are all but impossible to obtain in the Soviet Union. A Dostoevsky enthusiast in Leningrad once told me that "the editions are small, and they are all sold out the day that they appear." The official explanation is a shortage of paper. Needless to say, there is no shortage of paper to print the multivolume lucubrations of the Soviet leadership, or to print the tracts on Communism that fill racks in every hotel, airport and railway station in the country.

Likewise, it is noticeable that only one of the many buildings in Leningrad associated with Dostoevsky bears a memorial plaque. Asked why, a guide replied, "Only one plaque per person, except for Pushkin and heros of the revolution."

But it remains Dostoevsky's city—"the most abstract and contrived city on the entire earthly sphere," as he called it—the city whose alleys and canal banks and melancholy stucco courtyards he prowled day after day in search of settings for the books that he wrote at night.

Dostoevsky lived in no fewer than five apartments in St. Petersburg before and after his exile to Siberia and his enforced service in the army. All are still there. They had two curious features in common: all were furnished with borrowed furniture and all occupied a corner position with a view of the spire or cupola of a church.

One of them was at 7 Kaznecheskaya Street, not far from Mira Square, which was known in Dostoevsky's time as the Haymarket. (It has a metro stop.) The surrounding Oktyabrsky District, tucked inside the oxbow bend of a canal, retains much of the shabby gloominess that the writer described in *Crime and Punishment*, which was written in the 1860s when he lived there. The names of the cobblestone streets have been changed since the revolution, of course, but little else has.

Dostoevsky wrote that the student Raskolnikov, the hero of his novel, liked to wander in these streets, mingling with the "many different sorts of tradespeople and rag-and-bone men" who "crowded around the eating-houses in the lower stories, in the dirty ill-smelling courtyards . . . and especially in the pubs."

It was in Mira (Peace) Square that Raskolnikov confessed to murder; along the old canal, at 104 Kanala Griboyedova, that the slain moneylender lived; on Kaznecheskaya Street (at No. 13, perhaps?) that Sonya, the good-hearted prostitute, had her humble lodgings; and at 19 Grazhdanskaya that Raskolnikov himself inhabited a garret.

The garret is filled with an assortment of junk, or so it was when I visited it—an old bicycle wheel, skis, a broken sled, lumber, battered furniture. It sits at the top of thirteen steps, worn and broken as Dostoevsky described them. The courtyard below was littered with garbage, and the stairwell smelled of urine. From the window you can just see the golden dome of St. Isaac's Cathedral above the forest of television antennas.

You will find the great man's footprints in many of Leningrad's neighborhoods, if you know where to look. He studied military science at the Engineer's Castle, near the Russian Museum; he was imprisoned in the Trubetskoy Bastion, a part of the Peter and Paul Fortress, as an enemy of the Romanovs; he began *The Brothers Karamazov* at 5-ya Sovetskaya Street 6/6 in the Smolny District; he is buried—along with Mussorgsky and Glinka and Tchaikovsky and Petipa, among others—in the Tikhvin Cemetery, just at the entrance to the Alexander Nevsky Monastery.

A little less than a mile east of Mira Square (metro Vladimirskaya) is Dostoevsky's last apartment, where he finished *Karamazov* and where he died. Now a small museum with notably irregular opening hours, its address is 5 Kuznechnyy Street.

If you return to the metro station and turn left, you will reach the Theater of Young Spectators in about fifteen minutes. In roughly this location in the nineteenth century stood the parade-ground of the Semyonoysky Regiment, the site of the most bizarre episode of Dostoevsky's life. Early on the morning of December 22, 1849, he and twenty friends were lined up in the snow, surrounded on four sides by soldiers, to be shot for treason. As the drums rolled, the twenty-eight-year-old novelist, still unpublished, pale from eight months in prison, shivered in his light clothes. A white shroud was draped over his head. The marksmen of three guard detachments took aim.

And then a horseman galloped across the square and handed the presiding general a packet. It contained a "last-minute" commutation of the sentences. The whole thing had been a cruel hoax, the Czar's warped notion of how to teach troublemakers a lesson, and Dostoevsky, his life having passed in review through his mind, went off to begin a new one as a prisoner in Siberia.

2. *Samarkand the Golden*

S AMARKAND has been bewitching travelers since ancient times. It was already two hundred years old and known as Maracanda when Alexander the Great conquered it in 329 B.C. He spent a year there before departing for India, a period during which he drunkenly murdered his favorite general, Cleitus, and wrote that "everything I have heard about the beauty of Maracanda is true, except that it is more beautiful than I could have imagined."

In A.D. 712, the Arabs took Samarkand, bringing with them the Islamic faith and its mosques, minarets and madrasahs, or religious schools. In the ninth and tenth centuries, this oasis city on the Zeravshan River was further embellished by the master builders of the Samanid dynasty from Persia. In 1220 the Mongol hordes of Genghis Khan fell upon Samarkand, destroying most of it, so that when Marco Polo passed through with his father and his uncle, following the great Silk Route to China, they saw a sad spectacle.

Samarkand's renaissance came under a Tartar warrior named Timur in the fourteenth century. A cripple, Timur called himself the Scourge of God and Lord of All the Earth; history calls him Timur the Lame, or Tamerlane. It was he who built most of the shimmering, blue-domed, mosaic-encrusted monuments that lure the modern voyager to Samarkand, and imbue its very name—like those of Timbuktu and Lhasa and Angkor—with romance.

Samarkand flourished because of its location as the crossroads of overland trade—on a modern map, the borders of China and Iran and Afghanistan and Pakistan are all less than four hundred miles away. In the days before sail and steam, the quickest routes from Europe to the East led inevitably through Samarkand.

Today the city lies within the Uzbek Soviet Socialist Republic, one of the fifteen component parts of the Union of Soviet Socialist Republics. Most of the ancient monuments are in the eastern and northeastern parts of the town. The west side, with the university, railway station, stadiums, office buildings and movie houses, could be any Soviet city of 400,000, with little that is venerable or even exotic, except for the black skullcaps, embroidered with four white talismans to ward off evil spirits, that are worn by most Uzbek men, and the colorful head scarves worn by many women. The mountains that loom on three sides of the city, although they are often obscured by blowing sand, are another picturesque feature.

Relatively few Americans visit Samarkand, especially in these days of spy dust and suspicion. But there need be no apprehension on political grounds about making the journey, as I found on a recent two-day sojourn: I was made to feel welcome. But this is a trip for travelers, not tourists, because one must put up with a certain measure of inconvenience and discomfort in return for seeing some extraordinary sights.

The only practical way to get to Samarkand is by air, and that means Aeroflot, the Soviet airline. Now Aeroflot is safe enough, but it is also the most miserable major airline in the world. The seats are narrow, and the cushions so thin that you can feel the steel frame cutting into your back and bottom the minute you sit down. The food is a disgrace—desiccated chicken, a piece of bread, a packet of jam whose lid seems welded on, maybe some lukewarm butter. There is only tea to drink, although Samarkand itself produces decent white wine. The stewardesses speak no foreign language and have the demeanor of prison matrons. The planes are often two or three hours behind schedule, and it is difficult, in the case of delays, to discover their cause or probable duration.

Intourist, the Soviet agency that books all foreign travel, will probably put you in the Hotel Samarkand. It is only a decade old, but it reveals the Soviet genius for instant shabbiness; you would swear it was much older. The lobby is gloomy, the elevators fitful and the bathrooms bizarre, with showers bereft of any enclosure. They soak not only the bather but also the toilet, the sink, the towels and whatever else may be in the room. The food is passable, barely, and the dining-room service hopelessly disorganized and slow. But there the list of tribulations ends. The beds are clean and comfortable, the hot water is usually hot and there is a very agreeable bar in the basement with Western booze, for which you must pay in dollars or other hard currency.

More important, Intourist is an efficient organization. You will be met at the airplane on arrival, your bag will be claimed for you and you will be taken to the hotel in a bus or car. The guide who shows you the city will almost certainly be extremely well informed, cheerful, eager to please and curious about the United States. She (more rarely he) will speak excellent English. Intourist guides are one of the Soviet Union's best advertisements for itself.

If you can, stick a packet of luncheon meat and a piece of cheese into your handbag or luggage at your last port of call before entering the Soviet Union. This can be supplemented locally with excellent bread and abundant fruit (melons, grapes, pomegranates, pears) from the bazaar. There are many picnic spots. For dinner, I would suggest the apparently nameless restaurant just across the street from the hotel, where, in the less dressy section, you can get shashlik, rice, beer, fruit and coffee or tea for about $5.

Pack a universal drain stopper, so that you can wash out clothes if need be (few Soviet washbasins have working plugs); a washcloth; a Russian-English phrase book; whatever film you may need; an alarm clock (wake-up calls are erratic), and a few pins or badges from your hometown or from organizations you belong to, which Russians love to collect and exchange. Western credit cards are sometimes accepted, but it is wise to bring to Samarkand a supply of rubles, for use in the bazaar and in local restaurants, and a supply of dollars or other hard currency for use in the hotel bar and in the special souvenir shops (*Beriozka,* or "Little Birch," stores) where rubles are not accepted.

The best months to visit Soviet Central Asia are March through June and September through December. July and August can be extremely hot, January and February extremely cold.

The first thing to see in Samarkand is the least beautiful but in some ways the most impressive: the observatory of Ulug Beg. Only a fragment remains, but it is enough to suggest the intellectual force of this grandson of Timur, a man who was emperor, astronomer, teacher and cartographer.

Ulug Beg aligned his observatory almost perfectly along the sixty-seventh meridian, and did so before the invention of the telescope. He compiled a star catalogue with 1,018 entries that is still used. Decades before Copernicus, he theorized that the planets rotated around the sun. And, perhaps most astonishing, he calculated the length of the solar year to within fifty-eight seconds—a measurement refined only in the nineteenth century.

Approaching through an allée of beautiful trees, the visitor comes across the foundations of the huge observatory, which was 130 feet high and 165 feet in diameter. In the center is a deep trench holding part of the marble track on which rode Ulug Beg's hundred-foot-tall sextant, by far the largest ever built up to his time.

From the observatory, it is only a short drive down Tashkent Street, which follows the route of the old Silk Road, to the extraordinary collection of tombs and mosques known as Shah-i-Zindah. These buildings, which date from the fourteenth and fifteenth centuries (and which incorporate fragments from the tenth-century buildings razed by the Mongols), are grouped along a steep, narrow path.

According to local tradition, the Shah-i-Zindah is built around the site of the grave of Kussam-ibn-Abbas, a Moslem saint and cousin of the Prophet Mohammed. His mausoleum is at the far end of the path, together with a small mosque. Notice especially the beautiful carved wooden door and the elegant calligraphy of the Arabic inscriptions.

The Shah-i-Zindah is a living museum of Islamic art. Each of the little mausoleums is decorated with tilework in dozens of shades of blue, and further adorned with highly geometricized wood and stone carvings. The blue domes are supported from within on squinches that are in turn supported by complex systems of small Islamic arches. Even when thronged by tourists, it is a world apart, and well worth half a day of unhurried strolling and study.

The centerpiece of the old city is the enormous Registan Square, where all the medieval trade routes met. The name means Sandy Place, and in medieval times a bazaar stood here, close to a spring that washed sand into the area. Today it is an enormous paved rectangle, roughly the size of two football fields laid side by side, surrounded on three sides by madrasahs that date from the fifteenth and seventeenth centuries. The Uzbek Republic was announced here in October 1924, and in March 1927 the Moslem women of the city burned their veils here to proclaim their liberation.

Each of the three madrasahs consists of a soaring entrance portal, perhaps seventy-five feet high, set between even higher minarets and leading into a shady courtyard with trees and flowers, around which are grouped dormitories and a mosque. The one on the left, as you stand with your back to the open side of the square, was built by Ulug Beg; the one in the center is called Tilakari, or Covered with Gold, because of its internal gilding; the one on the right is called Shir Dar, or Lion-bearing, although the beasts portrayed above the arch look much more like tigers. But it is the ensemble that most impresses; in size and in aesthetic harmony, it is unparalleled in the Moslem world. Even the fact that some of the minarets lean away from the vertical adds to the sense of linear interplay.

Every Wednesday, Saturday and Sunday evening, from May through September, there is a sound-and-light show at the square—the only one in the Soviet Union. The commentary is given in several languages, English among them, and it, together with lights and music, brings the place alive. (If touring the Registan in the daytime, a pleasant break can be taken at the Jubilee Teahouse next door, where you can buy a cup of green tea for about ten cents and drink it while lounging in the sun on a big rug-covered wooden sofa.)

There are many other sights to see in Samarkand—the ruins of the huge Mosque of Bibi Khanum, Tamerlane's Chinese wife, which was destroyed by an earthquake a century after it was built and is now being restored; three museums; a colorful bazaar just behind the Bibi Khanum Mosque and several other mosques and mausoleums.

One that should on no account be missed is the mausoleum of Tamerlane, just behind the hotel. Some experts believe that it has been overly restored, but that has not affected its elegant fluted dome or the Emperor's tombstone of dark green jade.

The mausoleum, known as the Gur Emir, is a difficult place to leave. I lingered for twenty minutes inside the building, listening to the doves cooing in the rafters, and then I paused for a while outside, studying the dome while sitting on the great block of

gray marble on which the Emirs of Bukhara were crowned—
Samarkand was part of the khanate of Bukhara from 1784 until
1868, when it was conquered by the Russians under Alexander II.
It was easy to forget that this was the Soviet Union; the war in
Afghanistan and the power struggles in the Kremlin seemed
far away.

3. Gulyás *and Other Hungarian Delights*

N o prudent man or woman would travel to Eastern Europe
in anticipation of dining well. The nations of the socialist community, as they call themselves, are places where local
people worry about getting enough to eat, not how well what
they eat is cooked. The visitor is amply enough fed, but he is
usually fed badly, after interminable delays, by waiters and waitresses whose surliness is matched only by their ineptitude.

Hungary is the great exception, in this as in so many other
things. The Hungarians are born eaters, born waiters, born restaurateurs. Some of their patrons may not know it, but the Four
Seasons in Manhattan and The Bakery in Chicago are run by
Hungarians, as is the more obviously ethnic haunt of politicians
and journalists in London, the Gay Hussar. Britain's leading food
critic, Egon Ronay, is Hungarian by birth; his family ran five of
Budapest's leading restaurants before World War II. So is George
Lang, New York's leading consultant on restaurant concepts and
design, who owns the Café des Artistes, near Lincoln Center.

The state runs most of the restaurants in Hungary these days,
and it controls most agricultural output. In all honesty, one must
concede that the consistency of the cooking isn't what it was in
the days of the Hapsburgs. But this is still one of Europe's most
individual cuisines, well worth the trip to Budapest to sample
in its unadulterated form, along with other Hungarian delights.

Hungarian cooking is based on lard, onions, garlic and sour
cream, which are combined in various ways with pork, beef,
freshwater fish and poultry—the country produces wonderful
chickens, ducks and geese—as well as game. (More of the boar,

venison, frogs' legs and snails on Parisian menus come from
Hungary than the French would ever admit, thanks to the industry and talent of the Hungarian peasantry, which produces
enough food for home use and export while farmers in Poland,
the Soviet Union and Rumania find it impossible to keep the
shelves in their own countries filled.)

But the soul of Hungarian cooking is the pepper, or paprika,
as it is known in the Magyar language. What we call the bell
pepper comes in Hungary in ivory, yellow, green or red, depending on the season, and it is stuffed, sliced into stews and pickled.
Smaller varieties, shaped but not flavored the same way as their
North American counterparts, are ground into the spice we call
paprika, which in Hungary has a sweet, gentle piquancy and a
brilliant red color that American commercial versions conspicu-
ously lack. The best comes from south-central Hungary, especially
the towns of Kalocsa and Szeged. In addition, a fiery pepper
called cherry paprika, shaped as its name suggests, is shredded
in a mortar and served as a condiment.

The omnipresence of the paprika in modern Hungary is a
reminder of one of the saddest episodes in the country's history,
the Turkish conquest in 1526. For 150 years, the Turks ruled
most of Hungary and raised in their gardens the peppers they had
imported from India via Persia. When they left, the paprika
stayed and worked its way into a position of dominance in the
cuisine the Magyar nomads had brought with them from Asia.

Outside Hungary, the dish with which Hungary is indelibly
associated, and which constitutes the main Hungarian contribution to that dubious entity known as "international cuisine," is
gulyás or goulash. Many years ago, Karoly Gundel, probably Hungary's greatest chef, wrote that "without wishing to offend my
colleagues abroad, I feel obliged to state that with few exceptions
they ruin this excellent dish." His stricture is no less valid today;
beef goulash is to Hungarian cooking as chicken curry is to Indian
cooking. Gulyás is a soup, not a stew; it contains no flour, no
sour cream, no thickening of any kind. In its pristine form, it
contains beef or pork, tomatoes, onions, potatoes, water or stock,
tiny bits of pasta called csipetke, salt and sweet paprika. A fancier
version might contain sliced green peppers and caraway seeds.
It is never, ever, served with rice.

If you crave a goulashlike dish as a main course, order a pörkölt or a *tokány*. A *paprikás* is similar, too, except that here the meat is likely to be veal or chicken or lamb, and the sauce will be amply laced with sour cream. My own favorite is Transylvanian stuffed cabbage. Even though Transylvania is now a part of Rumania, its stuffed cabbage seems to me the most succulently, extravagantly Hungarian of Hungarian dishes—cabbage leaves filled with rice, pork, bacon and spices, plus sauerkraut mixed with onions, paprika and sour cream, assembled on a platter with a smoked sausage, a slice of cured loin of pork and a piece of pork belly. No dieter's delight, but utterly irresistible as a sequel to a bowl of *gulyás* and a prelude to a piece of pastry.

The Hungarians make other superb soups in addition to *gulyás*, notably *palóc leves*, a surprisingly light combination of mutton (or, better, filet of beef), green beans and sour cream; Jokai bean soup, which contains kidney beans and heavily smoked ham, and, in summer, *meggy leves*, a chilled blend of morello cherries and sour cream. The roast goose and duck are memorable, and be sure, if you see it on a menu, to order *fatányéros*, a mixed grill served on a wood platter. Finally, the *fogas* from Lake Balaton, Europe's largest lake, is an exemplary freshwater fish, firm of texture and mild of taste; it is a relative of the pike-perch, little known in the United States, but called *sandre* in French and *Zander* in German, if that is any help.

You will not lack for things to drink with all this. The Hungarians sometimes take as an apéritif a glass of the brandy made from their apricots, Europe's best. Called *barack*, it is worth trying, but to my infidel tastes, it is better after a meal than before, and the locals won't object if you order a Campari. Harder to find is an excellent plum *eau de vie*, similar to the Yugoslav slivovitz, made under the supervision of local rabbis, which is called Kosher *szilva*.

Among the table wines, I would avoid Egri Bikavér ("Bull's Blood"), the heavily promoted red; according to local experts, it varies widely and is often more Algerian or Bulgarian or Moroccan than Hungarian. Try instead the Pinot Noir or Burgundy from Villány, Hungary's southernmost city. Among the whites, I suggest the richly flavored Kéknyelü (literally, "blue stem") from Badacsony, a basaltic hill on the north shore of Lake Balaton, or the softer, somewhat more deeply colored wine of nearby Csopak.

On no account overlook Tokaji Aszu, the syrupy sweet wine, famous for generations, which owes its character to the same "noble rot" that produces great Sauternes. The slightly oxidized taste, often described as reminiscent of bitter chocolate, is unique. Its sweetness is measured by the number of seven-gallon hods of shriveled, berrylike grapes that are added to a barrel of natural Tokay wine; the sweetest is marked "5 *Puttonyos.*"

A gastronomic tour of Budapest might start at the Kalocsa restaurant of the Hilton Hotel. This may seem an odd recommendation, but the food and service are as good as everything else in this unusual chain hotel, which incorporates in its modern building the tower, nave and cloister of a thirteenth-century Dominican church. For a grand evening, try the nearby Alabardos, in a lovely old building, where meals are served on Herend porcelain. You will find it hard to remember that you are in a Communist country. The kind English-speaking headwaiter, Csaba Szilagyi, will answer your questions. Be forewarned that the gastronomic standards can be inconsistent. In the same category, with especially good venison, is Légrádi Testvérek, which has just eight tables in three vaulted rooms. Although the Gundel family no longer owns it, their restaurant—reborn in 1980 after a three-million-dollar refurbishing—still merits a visit. It is just behind the Fine Arts Museum and is a perfect spot for lunch.

Cheaper than these three, but by no means inferior, are the Regi Orszaghaz (Old Parliament), on Castle Hill near the Hilton, where I ate superb *fogas,* and the Szazeves (100 years old), near the Pest end of the Elizabeth Bridge, which was in fact founded in 1831 and where a band provides subtle gypsy music. Two recent discoveries: Just across the square from the Inter-Continental Hotel, on the Pest side, is the Dunakorzo—a resolutely plain, privately owned place where it seems impossible to order a bad dish. Uncle Joe, the portly, flatfooted proprietor, comes straight out of Lehár. I especially recommend what is described on the German menu as a Schlactplatte and what is in fact the dish of sausages and sauerkraut served in bygone years on the day when pigs were slaughtered. North of town, in the picturesque artists' colony at Szentendre, is the country's most innovative restaurant, the Aranysarkany or Golden Dragon.

The visitor should on one day try to arrive in midmorning or midafternoon at Vorosmarty Square at the north end of the pedestrian shopping street. There stands the Vorosmarty pastry shop, an Austro-Hungarian temple to gluttony, a half-sister to Vienna's famous Demel's, with marble tables, crystal chandeliers and divine Dobos torte, to say nothing of chocolate-and-marzipan royal torte and excellent coffee. Also try the Ruszwurm, a Biedermeier nook that George Lang prefers to the Vorosmarty.

Finally, go to the Hungaria (née New York) Café, a riot of rococo décor where the mediocrity of the food is somewhat offset by the menu. Inside its front cover is a time-machine celebrity register, with the signatures of long-forgotten actors, actresses and other notables, including, believe it or not, those of Rod La Rocque and Maria Jeritza.

4. *Moldavian Masterpieces*

THEY are among the most inaccessible of Europe's masterpieces, even more remote than the great Romanesque church at Conques in southwestern France, but the painted monasteries of Bukovina repay the discomfort and inconvenience tenfold. They can be properly described with that over- and misused word *unique,* because they are the only buildings in the world with medieval frescoes on the outside walls.

The paintings were created in the fifteenth and sixteenth centuries, a fusion of Byzantine and Gothic and purely folkloric traditions, as pictorial Bibles designed to instruct and inspire a people oppressed by their Turkish conquerors. Somehow their brilliant colors, protected only by the deep overhang of the roofs above them, have survived hundreds of rainy springs and snowy winters in far-off northeastern Rumania, hard by the Soviet border, and their bold imagery has come down to us almost unimpaired.

Fifty years ago, Henri Focillon, the great medieval scholar, wrote that "the monasteries, placed in the bosom of nature, covered by an ethereal sky, are masterpieces of archaic poetry and of youthful inspiration." And so they seem today, for all the changes in the country in which they stand.

It would be an exaggeration, but not much of one, to compare the frescoes with those of Giotto in the Scrovegni Chapel at Padua, or with those by an unknown hand in the Royal Pantheon at León in northern Spain, or with the mosaics in Ravenna and in St. Mark's in Venice. The paintings on the five monastery churches of Bukovina are less sophisticated, of course; they were the creations of a provincial culture, not a great civilization, and they were painted in a style that had passed out of vogue in most parts of Western Europe hundreds of years before. The most famous of the churches, Voronet (pronounced Vore-oh-NETS), was painted in 1547, two hundred years after Giotto's death, when Michelangelo was at his peak. But that in no way diminishes their vigor, their piety, their humor or, above all, their directness. There is something about the stiffness of the figures and about the artifice of the composition that adds to their power and to their charm.

Bukovina is part of Moldavia, an ancient region that lies between the Dniester River and the Transylvanian alps; since World War II it has been split between Rumania and the Soviet Union. The main city of the Rumanian portion is Suceava, a wood-processing and furniture center of 100,000 people, and the monasteries lie within easy reach of it to the west. One can, of course, drive directly to Suceava from Vienna or Budapest, crossing some beautiful country, particularly in the Carpathians; it is also possible to drive the 275 miles from Bucharest in about eight hours. The roads are far better than those in the Soviet Union, but there are likely to be stretches of several miles where the pavement has disappeared, to be replaced by muddy gravel.

For that reason, and also because of limited time, I chose to fly to Bucharest and on to Suceava, renting a car there for the monastery tour, then flying back to Bucharest. Tarom, the Rumanian airline, operates two flights a day, morning and evening, in each direction between Suceava an the capital; there are no flights to Suceava from anywhere else. The trip takes a little more than an hour in cramped and spartan Soviet-built Antonov propjets. It is important to note, if you are making connections, that international flights use Otopeni airport and domestic services operate out of Baneasa, eight miles closer to the city.

Once in Suceava, basic but sturdy Dacia sedans (built under license from Renault) can be hired from the local travel office for about one hundred dollars, including adequate gasoline for the 110-mile circuit. I would advise going to Suceava on the evening flight, staying the night at either the Bukovina or the Arcasul Hotel, where a simple double room costs $44 a couple a night, including breakfast, and a single with breakfast costs $32. You can then make the tour and fly back to Bucharest in the evening. Alternately, you can fly to Bukovina one morning and return the next.

This is as good a time as any for a series of caveats. Rumania is a poor country, run by a regime that is repressive even by Eastern European standards, and it faces a dire economic crisis. Food is in especially short supply. You won't by any means starve, but if you are finicky, take a few supplies: cheese, salami, chocolate and fruit. Otherwise, eat at the hotel in Suceava and, in Bucharest, at your hotel or at the Balkan restaurant. Second, don't change much money into lei, the local currency, over and above the ten dollars for each day of your planned stay that you must convert at the airport on arrival; you will need dollars or credit cards for most of your expenses, including hotel, restaurant and car-rental bills. Third, taxis are scarce at the airports, so either use the buses (much easier if you speak a bit of French) or arrange to be met on arrival—in Suceava by the car you are renting, in Bucharest by a hotel car. The Inter-Continental, the capital's best, is very good about this.

If at all possible, nail everything down in advance. This can be done through accredited agents of the Rumanian National Tourist Office, a list of which can be obtained through the office's branch at 573 Third Avenue, New York, NY 10016. If you run into trouble, you can get help from Petr Sipciu of the Carpati Tourist Office in Bucharest, an intelligent, energetic and thoroughly likable young man who speaks fluent English. You can write to him at Boulevard Magheru 7, Bucharest. If time is short, send a Telex; the number is 11270.

When you pick up your car, ask for a copy of the English brochure *Rumanian Historical and Feudal Art Monuments*. Despite the title, it is an introduction to the five monasteries, and it contains an indispensable road map. With that in hand, set off down Route 17, in the direction of Gura Humorului, about twenty-three miles west of Suceava, where signs mark the road leading to the right toward Humor monastery, four miles north.

The route leads through gentle, beautiful hills that are cloaked, in October, with vivid reds and oranges and yellows that reminded me of Vermont. (The local people say that the churches are particularly beautiful with snow on the roofs and that spring is pleasant. The area is warm from May to September, so, provided that one dresses properly, it would seem that a visit any time of the year is feasible.)

Along the way to the Humor monastery, you will no doubt pass people who will greet you with a curious stiff-wristed wave; this is the local hitchhikers' signal, not a gesture of welcome, so don't stop unless you want company. Humor (pronounced Hue-MORE) is painted on the outside from the eaves down to the ground, and on the inside as well. Notice that here, as at most of the monasteries, almost nothing remains on the north wall of the church because of the effects of the weather.

There is a procession of saints, a depiction of the Return of the Prodigal Son and a particularly touching fresco of the Three Kings, riding their horses to Bethlehem and looking over their shoulders at an angel above them. In another scene, the Devil is pictured with considerable wit as a greedy old hag. Of Humor's superb interior frescoes (easier to see with a flashlight and binoculars), the French art historian Paul Henry wrote, "Italian art has nothing more beautiful."

Return now to the main road, Route 17, and drive west for a mile or two. There you should see a turn to the left toward Voronet, whose church was built in fifteen weeks in 1488 on the orders of Prince Stephen the Great, Moldavia's military hero and spiritual father. The frescoes, added in the next century, are dominated by a cerulean blue of such purity that its particular shade is known internationally as "Voronet blue," and of such beauty that it can stand comparison with that of Fra Angelico.

At Voronet, which lies in a shallow valley, surrounded by newly rebuilt ramparts, the south wall is covered with a vast portrayal of the Tree of Jesse, tracing the genealogy of Jesus, and the exterior of the trilobal apse is covered with a hierarchy of saints—both typical Bukovina subjects. The inside of the porch is covered with portraits of 365 saints, one for each day of the year, with Elijah pictured in a crimson cart drawn by two crimson horses.

But it is the doorless, windowless west wall and its buttresses that earned Voronet its fame, for these are covered with a Last Judgment of extraordinary power. From the feet of Christ flows a red tunnel, filled with gray, Boschlike devils; to His right, our left, paradise is peopled by crowned and haloed heads; to His left, our right, turbaned Turks wait in purgatory. Up beneath the eaves, the unrestored colors as bright as the day they were painted, is a panel showing the signs of the zodiac with rare charm (especially poor Taurus, whose hind legs have been replaced by a mermaid's tail).

Again retracing your steps to the main road, continue to the west for ten miles to the village of Vama. There you leave Route 17, taking the right-hand fork toward Moldoviţa (pronounced Mole-doe-VEETS-ah), one of the two monasteries that are still in use as such by the Rumanian Orthodox Church. Here the dominant hue is a reddish-brown; here, too, there is a Last Judgment, with a tiny dove on an enormous throne signifying the Holy Spirit, a hand of God gently cradling seven of His children while holding the scales of justice, and a striking portrait of a group of Armenian wise men. A special feature are friezes of cherubim and seraphim, tiny moon faces framed by wings.

My favorite thing at Moldoviţa is the representation of the Siege of Constantinople on the south wall, which summarizes in its delicious naïveté and rich detail all that is best about these paintings. In the actual siege, of course, the Turks were on the inside, fighting off the Sassanids. But in the Moldavian version, it is the Turks, the oppressors, who are outside; inside are Moldavian saints and archers and gunners, Moldavian churches and nuns, and even Christ himself. The scene is painted with the verve and picturesqueness of a miniaturist.

From Moldoviţa, Route 17A runs northeast to Suceviţa, crossing a low mountain pass. If you have brought a picnic, stop in or near the pass; otherwise, drive a few hundred yards past the monastery to the Suceviţa inn or motel, where you can have a simple grill for lunch.

The monastery at Suceviţa (pronounced Sue-cheh-VEETS-ah) is the largest and most impressive, with great stern battlements and a high wall that has helped to preserve the priceless painting on the north side of the church. This picture shows the ladder of Saint John from Sinai, with the ladder itself dividing the scene from lower right to upper left. On the ladder stand souls striving to reach Heaven; to the right are fifty-two angels urging them on, arranged in six diagonal rows, wings outstretched; to the left are demons dragging people from the ladder and falling with them through seemingly infinite space toward perdition. Everything to the right is bright, neat, rhythmic; everything to the left dim, tangled, discordant. Angels and devils, order and chaos. Linger for a moment also at the south side of the church, where the artist has painted his own version of Jesse's Tree, adding to the Biblical story portraits of Pythagoras, Sophocles, Plato, Aristotle and Solon, all of them clad in rich, almost Byzantine cloaks.

Then proceed along 17A to the village of Marginea (where you can buy the local, rather hideous black pottery), turning south there toward Solca. Do not take the shortcut at Clit, which is all but impassable; continue to Solca, and turn east there toward Arbore, six miles away.

Arbore (pronounced Are-BORE-eh) is perhaps the least dramatic of the churches, smaller than the rest, but it has preserved frescoes dominated by five different shades of green. The best of them are on the west wall—scenes from Genesis and the lives of the saints—in front of which, it is said, priests in medieval times gathered their congregations and preached their sermons. In these paintings the women, especially, seem more graceful than in some others. I also delighted in the scene of Saint Nikita praying before a green, yellow, orange and white church not much taller than he, with a motto in the spiky characters of the Old Church Slavonic alphabet poised in the upper right-hand corner.

From Arbore, it is thirty-three miles back to Suceava; you leave the village, your way perhaps blocked for a moment by a company of geese, on the same road by which you entered, continuing to the east, then turning right at Milisauti, seven miles from Arbore. Four miles farther on, you come onto Route 2 for the run into Suceava.

CHAPTER XI

Scandinavia

1. The Magic of the Fjords

I T is hard to avoid the overripe banalities of the travelogue when looking at, or writing about, the west coast of Norway. It is an expanse of landscape unduplicated anywhere on earth; nowhere else, in a relatively confined area, is there such a prodigal display of mountains and sea, lakes and waterfalls. There are other kinds of superlative beauty—one thinks of the tranquil green hills of Devon, the sere elegance of the East African savannah, the lush color of Moorea and Bora-Bora—but none, for me, inspires the awe that the fjord country always does.

The fjords are what makes western Norway different. These fingers of the sea reaching sixty, seventy, eighty miles inland are so narrow you feel you can touch the mountain walls that rise thousands of feet straight out of the water, with snowfields and glaciers sparkling blue-white far above. They are so deep that the tallest structures in the world could be sunk without a trace in their waters. But the magnificence of the landscape depends also on the rhythmic interplay of rock and water, in which the hundreds of crags and lakes and rivers and waterfalls play a supporting role.

There are many ways to see western Norway, and the fall is a good time for a visit; in high summer, the hotels and transportation facilities are jammed. The classic way is by sea, in one of the mail-and-passenger boats that ply the coastal waters or in one of the cruise ships that sail into the more famous fjords. There are also rail excursions, bus excursions, hydrofoil excursions and combinations of the three. Or, if one prefers to concentrate on one small area, it is possible to spend a holiday in a hotel or a hut in a spectacular setting.

During a recent stay in Norway, I had business in Bergen and in Oslo, Norway's two largest cities, which lie on opposite sides of the country. Rather than fly or take the train across the tundra-like Hardanger Plateau, my wife and I decided to spend a few extra days and make the trip by car, traveling a circuitous route of 550 miles to fit in as much scenic melodrama as possible. The trip can be made in a week in either direction at the beginning of a Scandinavian tour or at the end.

If you arrive in Bergen in the morning, as we did, it is a good idea to spend a few hours exploring that beautiful little city, especially the area around the Vaagen, or inner harbor. At its inner end stands the Torget, a thousand-year-old fish market, and two blocks away is Bryggen (the word means "quay" in Norwegian), with a picturesque collection of warehouses dating from the Hanseatic trading system in the fourteenth and fifteenth centuries. A good place for lunch is the Norge Hotel, Norway's best, which has several restaurants offering everything from an open-faced sandwich and a beer to a full meal.

Then head east toward Voss on Route E-68, which is well posted. Actually, because of the mountains and the sea, you will be driving south and then north before turning east. After a run through the unremarkable Bergen suburbs comes the first startling glimpse of fjords—the Sør Fjord and then the Samnanger Fjord—and you may find it hard to believe that you are looking at an arm of the ocean and not some tranquil lake. At Norheimsund the road comes down to the mighty Hardanger Fjord, with brooding gray mountains keeping watch. Each of the big fjords has its own character, and this one, it has always seemed to me, is the most implacable, the most threatening. It runs from the open sea south of Bergen all the way to the foot of the eerie, rock-strewn Måbø Valley, a distance of almost a hundred miles, but the driver should keep to E-68, which leaves the main fjord at Kvanndal, until reaching the junction of Route 572 to Ulvik, nine miles farther along. The drive into Ulvik, through upland meadows and ponds and down to the Brakanes Hotel at the fjord's edge, takes twenty-five minutes.

Three words of warning before we go any further:

1. Do not try to hurry. The roads are narrow and twisting, and one has to be ready to stop short and sometimes back up to a passing place; besides, you will want to savor the views that unfold at every turn.

2. Bring plenty of sweaters; in the fall it turns cold at night.

3. Avoid the hotel cocktail bars; the prices are almost as awesome as the scenery outside. If you want hard liquor, bring it along; drink beer or a modest wine with meals. Even with that precaution, Norway is never cheap; at most of the hotels along the way, it will cost $75 a night for a double room and $60 for dinner for two. At midday, I advise making a picnic at the roadside areas maintained by the government.

Stay two nights at the Brakanes, a blue-and-white hotel at the head of the narrow Ulvik Fjord. It is more than a century old but thoroughly modernized. Visitors can walk along the water's edge, take a ride in the hotel's launch, explore the fjords and glaciers by light plane or simply sit in the comfortable chairs on the lawn, letting the rigors of an airline journey drain away and watching the changing play of light and cloud on mountains and water.

The next morning, retrace your steps on Route 572 and turn north toward Voss once again on E-68. Shortly before lunchtime, after passing through Voss (where there is a statue to a local boy, Knute Rockne, who emigrated to the United States, developed the forward pass and made Notre Dame into a national football power), one comes to a small road on the left leading to the Stalheim Hotel, which is fifty miles from Ulvik. Look carefully for the turn, which is not very well marked.

There can be few hotels in the world with a more dramatic setting than the Stalheim, which is perched on the lip of the monumental Naerøy Valley. I remember being there one day when showers alternated with periods of bright sunshine; the vista from the lawn in front of the hotel was positively Wagnerian, with clouds rolling up from the valley floor thousands of feet below, then blowing away to reveal brilliantly lit farms on the mountainside. You might have a look through the hotel shop and eat lunch there, or head back down E-68 to Vinje and turn north on Route 13. After a mile or so there is a lakeside picnic spot.

After lunch, continue to Vik, where you should pause for a moment to look at the beautifully preserved stave church. These wooden churches, some of which date from the twelfth century, have long round-tipped shingles and primitive gargoyles. They are remarkable relics of the era when Norway was newly Christianized. Then on to Vangsnes, where one takes the ferry across the Sogne Fjord, with orchards standing along its shores in fields enclosed by stone walls. The trip takes forty minutes, costs only a few dollars and ends at Dragsvik. The Kvikne Hotel, a wood frame building that has been in business for generations, is at Balestrand, five miles south on Route 13.

On the fourth day, take Route 5 north toward Førde, stopping to gaze at the glaciers above the road on the right and turning right onto Route 14. At Byrkjelo, one sees for the first time the characteristic color of the inner Nord Fjord and its subsidiary lakes—a chalky azure blue, caused by algae in the water. Then turn right onto Route 60. After a few miles, the road twists down to Nord Fjord itself like a giant corkscrew, affording one breathtaking view after another, as often as not including a cruise ship at anchor. This is the gentlest of the big fjords, a complete contrast to Hardanger, and the road skirts it for nearly thirty miles before turning inland on the way to the little port of Hellesylt.

From Hellesylt, what must be the most scenic car-ferry route in the world sails down Geiranger Fjord—narrow, its mountain walls dotted with farms clinging to bits of arable land, waterfalls all but dissolving into mist on the long drop into the blue water— to the tiny village of Geiranger. The boats leave only about every two and a half hours, so check the schedules in advance. I would advise spending two nights at the Union Hotel, which offers spectacular views, a waterfall outside the window to lull the traveler to sleep and an outstanding Norwegian cold table at dinner each night.

The village of Geiranger, seventy miles from the open sea, is a settlement of three hundred people, stacked upon the lower slopes of Mount Dalsnibba, which rises nearly a mile above the waters of the fjord. It is in places like this that the Norwegian feels most at home. The fishing village and the isolated farm are the Norwegian's natural habitat; cities are somehow inimical to the national character of a country where mountains, forests, glaciers, islands, rivers and lakes occupy no less than ninety-six and a half percent of the territory.

"Life here is the best in the world," says Karl Mjelva, the lean young man with curly blond hair who manages the Union Hotel, like two generations of his family before him. "We live in the midst of incredible natural beauty. We are free from pollution, free from stress, free from the anxieties of the city."

Most Norwegians who must live and work in the city maintain huts in areas like this, to which they flee for a month each year. There are 300,000 such huts in the country, one for every fourteen people. Like the sauna in Finland, the hut in Norway is believed to have almost unlimited powers to refresh and restore body and spirit, to help a person put things in their proper perspective.

Per Vassbotn, a journalist who owns a hut at the head of the nearby Stranda Valley, a remote, glacier-ringed basin that reminds many Americans of Yosemite, told me: "Here you can find yourself. You must think of the good you've done, and the bad. You sleep, eat, walk, maybe read some Ibsen."

For myself, the ribbon of cobalt-blue water winding between four-thousand-foot cliffs is enough. I feel the magic of the place without Ibsen.

After the grandeur of the fjords, the idyllic beauty of the two-day drive southeast toward Oslo comes as almost a relief, but certainly not as an anticlimax. The road follows the broad Otta and Gudbrands Valleys, which are full of charm, with burbling rivers at the bottom and sod-topped farmhouses on the slopes. From Geiranger, Route 58 climbs almost vertically toward the viewpoint on the slopes of Dalsnibba, where one can take a last look down at the fjord, the toylike ships and boats and the hotel. Then onto Route 15 through Lom to Otta, a right turn onto Route E-6 and down to Vinstra. From there, follow the signs for the Peer Gynt Route—a back road, sometimes unpaved but always well graded and safe, looping lazily through gentle countryside full of artistic associations. This is the region where Ibsen is said to have gained the inspiration for his play, which in turn provided the inspiration for Grieg's music.

Spend the night along that road at one of the excellent mountain hotels, either Skeikampen or Gausdal; the former is notable for its well-stocked cellar, but the latter has better service and more attractive rooms. There is time for a morning stroll before the run into Oslo along Mjøsa, one of Norway's longest and loveliest lakes. In Oslo consider having dinner at the Tre Kokker (Three Cooks) at Drammensveien 30. It has recently emerged as Norway's finest restaurant; its young staff is so enthusiastic that they grow the herbs and collect the wild mushrooms used in the kitchen. And, oh, yes, a gastronomic afterthought: Do not miss breakfast in any Norwegian hotel—a vast buffet of cold meat, cheese, herring, jam, boiled eggs, five or six kinds of bread, hot and cold cereals, juice, coffee, tea, milk and so on. No wonder the Vikings were tough.

2. Clupea Harengus

F o r the peoples who live around the Baltic and the North seas, preserved fish have always been a staple. Scots, Englishmen, Dutchmen, Germans, Danes, Finns, Norwegians and Swedes have devised dozens of ways of salting, smoking and pickling the catch taken off their shores. Salt cod, smoked salmon and mackerel and eel, pickled shrimp, the elegant cured salmon called *gravlax*—all have their honored place on the tables of northern Europe.

But the humble herring (*Clupea harengus*) reigns supreme in Scandinavia. Herring bones have been discovered in Scandinavian mounds dating from Neolithic times; in the Middle Ages it was the herring trade that brought the merchants of Lübeck into the region, giving birth to the Hanseatic League. No visitor should miss the chance to explore the astounding number of changes that talented Scandinavian cooks can ring on this ancient regional theme.

There is such a mind-boggling array of herring recipes in Scandinavia that it is enough to make one believe the story, told by Alan Davidson in his book *North Atlantic Seafood*, that in certain Finnish villages a girl is not considered marriageable until she can prepare the fish twenty-five ways.

Here are just a few of the commoner varieties:

Pickled Herring. Salt herring cut into strips, pickled in a white-vinegar-and-sugar solution that also contains allspice and bay leaves, topped with red onion rings.

Curried Herring. Salt herring in a cold curry sauce.

Matjes Herring with Sour Cream. The only one, curiously enough, that is often encountered in the United States, except in families with Baltic roots.

Stromming or Baltic Herring. Split, battered, fried and then marinated in dill, that most Scandinavian of herbs.

Glassblower's Herring. So called because it is made in a tall glass jar with carrots and onions.

Herring Salad. Herring, beets, cucumbers and sour cream.

Smoked Herring. But enough. You get the idea.

The tiniest of herrings, sometimes no more than six inches long, come from the Baltic, and many people think the most delectable of those come from the waters surrounding the Danish island of Bornholm. They are extremely perishable, so they are caught, cleaned and smoked on the same day, then rushed to Copenhagen. The smoking turns them from silver to reddish-gold. (Smoked herring drawn across a fox's path, the English discovered, destroys the scent and confounds the dogs: hence the phrase "red herring" for diversionary tactics.)

As with other delicacies, the Danes tend to turn Bornholmers into open-faced sandwiches or *smørrebrød*. The herring is filleted, laid on a buttered slice of dark bread and garnished with sliced radishes, chives and sometimes a raw egg yolk. Taken with one or two *smørrebrød* of contrasting taste and texture and, of course, with a glass of potent ice-cold aquavit tamed by beer, they make a splendid lunch.

In the old days, one would have sought such a meal at Oskar Davidsen's, a waterside pavilion in Copenhagen that listed 170 kinds of sandwiches on a five-foot-long menu. Alas, it is no more. But the daughter of the house, a cheery, round-faced woman

named Ida, carries on the tradition in a trim little restaurant
bearing her name, open for lunch only, at 70 Store Kongensgade.
Tell her that you are interested in herring, and especially Bornholmers, and she will help you make an apt selection of *smørrebrød*.

Scandinavians also eat herring for breakfast, along with cheese
and ham and salami. You will probably find a small dish or
two, perhaps one of herring in tomato sauce, another of plain
pickled herring, on the overladen breakfast buffet at your hotel.
They sometimes fry larger fish, if they are not too fat, for dinner.
And at Tre Kokker you will be served herring in a thin, clear,
vinegar-based sauce, garnished with grapefruit.

But it is in the traditional Swedish smorgasbord, it seems to
me, that Scandinavian herring reaches its peak. And the finest
smorgasbord in the world, without question, is the enormous
copper table, fitted with bain-maries and ice chests and a wooden
spindle to hold wheels of flatbread, that dominates the main
room at Stockholm's Operakälleren. This splendid place, all deep
carpets and rich paneling, is not, as the name suggests, a cellar,
but it is, in fact, part of Stockholm's nineteenth-century opera
house.

Each lunchtime, the table is set, with herring at one end,
other fish dishes, cheese, cold meats, salads and so on along the
sides, and warm dishes at the other end. It is not done to heap
your plate with a mishmash of delicacies; you take first as many
sorts of herring as you like, and go to your table to eat them,
accompanied by aquavit (I would suggest a Danish Jubilaeums
or a Norwegian Linie or, for the bold, a spicy Swedish Sten-
borgare) and beer (what else but Tuborg or Carlsberg?). When
you have finished, the waiter takes your plate, and you return for
a second, this time with other fish, a third, with cold meats, cheese
and salads, and a fourth, with hot dishes such as Swedish meatballs and Jansson's temptation, a succulent casserole of potatoes
and anchovies. It is a slow, relaxing process, to be undertaken
when the afternoon presents no greater demand than a long walk
or a nap.

Lunch at the Operakälleren is one of my favorite meals in
Europe. I would no more miss it while in Stockholm, even if for
economic reasons I had to eat hamburgers during the rest of my

visit, than I would miss a beer garden or a *Brauhaus* in Munich. The main reason, aside from the grace of the place and the kindness of the waiters in their old-fashioned, stiffly starched wing collars, is the herring.

3. *Nordic Star*

STOCKHOLM is the most beautiful and most cosmopolitan of the Nordic capitals, but it is a lot like the Swedes themselves. On first acquaintance, it seems a bit austere, a bit unwelcoming—not as jolly as Copenhagen, not as cozy as Oslo, not as hearty as Helsinki. Happily for the visitor, however, the reserve that characterizes the people and the city falls away quickly, revealing an underlying charm.

Walk the twisting medieval streets of the Gamla Stan, or Old Town, many of which are still lined with Renaissance buildings, and you will be reminded that Sweden was once a world power, with a warrior-king, Charles XII, who spent his life in a heroic but ultimately vain struggle against Peter the Great. Walk through the modern shopping quarter, or one of the suburban housing developments, and you will be reminded that Sweden, in our own century, was one of the pioneers of modern architecture, design and town planning, and that its people enjoy one of the most extensive social-welfare systems in the world.

You can get an over-all view of the city from the Kaknas Tower, whose observation platform is more than four hundred feet above the ground. Or take one of the boat tours, which will give you some sense of the layout of a city that is built on fourteen islands near the place where Lake Mälaren meets the Baltic Sea. The best of these, called "Under the Bridges of Stockholm," lasts two hours.

To get up-to-the-minute data on activities in the city, dial 22-18-40 for a recorded announcement in English, which is updated every day. Once you have organized your program, stuff a city map (available at Sweden House) into your pocket and start walking. As with most European cities, Stockholm is best seen on foot, and much of the Old Town is inaccessible to vehicles.

Stockholm's preeminent hotel is the Grand, a dowager establishment perfectly situated on one of the innumerable waterways that give the city so much of its character. Sitting on the glassed-in veranda—where you can eat the staggering Scandinavian breakfast buffet or the best medium-priced lunchtime smorgasbord in town—you look out at the tour boats tied up at the quay just outside. The six-hundred-room Royal Palace is across the water, the National Museum down the street to your left, the Opera House across the square to your right. The Grand has a splendid bar, a winter garden and comfortable if slightly unadorned bedrooms.

Among the more modest candidates, I would strongly suggest a pair of crisp little charmers in the Old Town, the Lord Nelson and the Lady Hamilton. Jointly managed, they are furnished with a mixture of pale modern pieces and country antiques, including gaily painted wardrobes and dower chests. The welcome could hardly be warmer. But be forewarned that they are not cheap; indeed, you are unlikely to find a double room with bath in Stockholm at anything but the most utilitarian sort of place for much less than $60.

I have already enthused about the midday smorgasbord at the Operakälleren. But the Operakälleren itself, the adjoining Opera Grill and the tiny corner snack bar called the Bakfickan (the name means, roughly, Hip Pocket) also offer daily specials, many of which are sophisticated versions of *husmanskost*—home cooking. On my last visit, I ate *kaldomar* (stuffed cabbage) with lingonberries and *ärter med fläsk* (pea soup); both were delicious, and I didn't even get to try the salmon pudding. Ask the waiter to point out the appropriate dishes, which will be expensive if you eat them in the Operakälleren, less so in the Opera Grill and still less if you sit at the Bakfickan's marble counter.

In the last three years, several ambitious restaurants offering a Swedish version of nouvelle cuisine have opened their doors. The most ambitious, perhaps, is Gourmet, which is highly regarded by most of the guidebooks.

But I don't think you will find its food as appealing as that to be sampled at a place called Erik's, which I now consider one of the half-dozen best restaurants in Scandinavia. Erik Laller-stedt opened it five years ago on a refitted barge moored near the National Museum, at Strandvagskajen 17. The cooking? From my notes: "elegant seafood bisque, light but packed with flavor . . . an assortment of fish, sole and turbot poached, salmon very, very lightly sautéed, with two sauces, one lobster, the other made with cream, vermouth (I think) and vegetables chopped into pieces half the size of matchheads . . . perfect coffee." The menu changes every day. About the same prices as the Opera-källeren, and notable for very good wines by the glass—Champagne, Brouilly or Gerwürtztraminer for $5.

Of course, no one would want to eat Erik's-style every day. So here is a short list of relatively inexpensive places, provided by the same canny local who first told me about Erik's: Rodolfo, in the Old Town, for pasta; Prinsen, Master Samuelsgatan 4, Swedish fare; Tennstopet, Dalgatan, a cheery pub with simple food. Or have a hot dog and beer at any of the dozens of street kiosks—about $2.50 to $3.

You will find the major buildings on your own: the red-brick city hall, the Royal Palace, the thirteenth-century Riddarholm Church, where Sweden's monarchs are buried. But you may need help with the museums in a city with more than two dozen of them. If your time is limited, I would suggest four.

A good starting point is the National Museum (open daily, 10:00 to 4:00, later on Tuesday). While not in the class of the Louvre or the Prado, the gallery has a fine collection of European masterpieces, including a ghostlike *St. Veronica* by Zurburán and *Sacrifice to Venus* by Rubens. Room 308, on the second floor, contains no fewer than nine Rembrandts, the highlight of the collection.

Just across a small bridge on the island of Skeppsholmen is the Modern Museum (open Tuesday to Friday, 11:00 to 9:00, and 11:00 to 5:00 on Saturday and Sunday), which advertises itself with an outdoor display of Jean Tinguely's mad, clattering machines and Nikki de Saint Phalle's bulbous amazons. This is one of the best galleries of modern art in Europe, with a small collection of works by the major Cubists and a major collection of works by such later artists as Rauschenberg, Oldenburg, Segal, Warhol and Nevelson.

Recrossing the bridge, you will find a boat landing where you can take a ferry to Djurgården. There you should visit the astonishing royal flagship *Wasa*, which sailed out into Stockholm harbor on her maiden voyage one bright August Sunday in 1628 and promptly sank to the bottom. In 1961, she was raised to the surface and subsequently installed in a specially built museum. The ship herself and the display of grotesque and dramatic sculptures that once decorated her hull provide an unparalleled glimpse into seventeenth-century maritime life. Open daily, 10:00 to 5:00, with longer hours in summer.

A short walk away is Skansen, the seventy-five-acre outdoor Museum of Swedish Life, where more than 150 mostly rural buildings from the eighteenth and nineteenth centuries have been gathered. You visit the buildings, see a glass blower or a weaver at work, eat a simple or elaborate meal, watch folk dancers and visit the zoo. Open daily, 8:30 to 11:00.

There are regular concerts, of course, and the Royal Opera is well worth attending. But the great treat is the opera season at the Drottningholm Court Theater, which runs from May to October. The eighteenth-century opera house is set in the sylvan grounds of the magnificent Drottningholm Palace, to which the royal family moved in 1981. You can reach the site, on an island in Lake Mälaren, by car or by boat. The members of the orchestra wear period costumes and wigs, and the original sets are still used, along with such archaic stage machinery as a wooden box filled with rocks, which is shaken to simulate thunder. Tickets can be ordered by mail (Box 27050, 10251 Stockholm) up to three months in advance of performances and will be held at the box office.

The things to buy in Stockholm are things made in Sweden. Start at the city's best department store, NK, at Hamngatan 18. On the lower level are sections filled with the best Swedish cookware and handicrafts and silver and stainless steel. Another good address for handicrafts is Svensk Hemslöjd, Sveavägen 44; other sources for silver are Georg Jensen, Birger Jarlsgatan 13 (hideously expensive), and Kurt Decker, Biblioteksgatan 12. For the great names in Swedish glass—Orrefors, Kosta, Böda—go to Svenskt Glas, Birger Jarlsgatan 8, or Nordiska Kristallmagasinet, Kungsgatan 9.

Important: ask the clerk at any major store to do the requisite paperwork so you can reclaim the sales tax at the airport; since it amounts to almost twenty percent, it's worth it.

4. *That Tea Trolley*

M A N for man and woman for woman, Finland has probably produced as much good design in the last three decades as any other country on earth. Much of it is available in the United States, but it can be difficult to find and is invariably rather expensive because of shipping costs and duty.

The visitor to Helsinki, on the other hand, can find most of the best on or near a downtown street with the jaw-breaking name of Pohjoisesplanadi, which means, more or less, Northern Boulevard. Almost without exception, the prices will be considerably lower and the selection considerably better.

Pohjoisesplanadi, at least the part that concerns us here, runs four or five blocks from the Swedish Theater to the open public market. Popping in and out of the stores makes a pleasant and unusual half-day stroll through a kind of ad hoc museum of design.

The first cross street as you start out from the theater is called Keskuskatu. A few steps to the north, on the right side at No. 4, you will find the Rautatalo Building, designed by the great Finnish architect Alvar Aalto, and in it, the Artek shop. Artek manufactures furniture, textiles and lamps that he designed, and the retail shop sells these as well as other products.

Without doubt the most famous of all the Aalto designs is the tea trolley, which New York's Museum of Modern Art proposed to its members in 1985 as a luxurious Christmas present. With the member's discount, the museum charged $765 for the trolley, in which Aalto brought to fruition the experiments with curved birch that he began with chairs in the 1920s. In Helsinki, the price is about $350, to which you must add shipping and insurance but from which you can subtract sales tax. It shouldn't add up to more than $450. There is also a more elaborate version with a tile rather than a linoleum top for about $550.

The vase that Aalto designed for the Savoy Restaurant, just across the park from Pohjoisesplanadi, is also available at Artek—not only the one that you see in shops in New York or Milan in clear or milky glass, but also much larger and much squatter versions that I have never seen anywhere else. Aalto's three-legged, round-top birch stools, which nest nicely, to be pulled from a corner when there are more guests than chairs, are remarkably inexpensive and are available with seats in a variety of colors and finishes.

In a section devoted to housewares there are brown ceramic bowls from the old town of Porvoo, just down the coast, roundish chrome steel casseroles designed by Timo Sarpaneva and wonderful oversized Swedish coffee cups in white china.

Finally, be sure to look at the silver jewelry, especially the collars with pendants containing semiprecious stones. They are by no means cheap, but they are a delight to contemplate.

Now, back to the boulevard and turn left, walking toward Marimekko at Pohjoisesplanadi 31. This is the main store of the Finnish textile house founded after World War II by the late Armi Ratia, and it offers an array of items that are either unavailable or more costly at the New York outlet. I also find that it often has more recent and more innovative fabric designs that take months or even years to make their way across the Atlantic, especially those of the gifted Japanese Fujiwo Ishimoto and the equally talented Finn Pentti Rinta.

Marimekko means "a little dress for Mary," and Marimekko clothes are worn by Finnish women of all economic groups. In the main showroom in Helsinki, you will find hundreds of designs, with many of the simple cotton frocks costing less than $100. In the fabric department, the prices vary widely, as do the designs, ranging from the bold, splashy flower prints of Maija Isola, which were so popular in the United States in the 1960s, to the subtle, feathery prints of Fuji. On a recent visit, I particularly liked a brightly colored print of children's toys by Katsuji Wakisaka.

Another favorite of mine, as mentioned earlier, are the carry-alls designed by Ristomatti Ratia, the founder's son, who now manages his own Helsinki design firm. They come in all sizes and shapes, from handbags to duffels to beach bags to a carry-on suit bag. The most practical, in my view, is a bag that looks like a normal canvas sailing bag, with loop handles. It folds flat in the bottom of a traveler's suitcase, then opens up to carry an astonishing amount of accumulated junk for the trip home. Its special feature is a zippered top, invisible unless it is needed, that makes it possible to check the bag on airlines.

In the rear of the store, connected to the main showroom by a corridor, is the Pihastudio, which is full of inexpensive gift items, from scarves to tin trays to place mats to T-shirts, all in Marimekko patterns, plus Ristomatti Ratia's elegant line of hanging lamps.

By now you probably need a rest, so turn into Kluuvikatu, and on your right you will see Fazer, one of the best coffeehouses in town, with good Danish pastry and delicious ice cream. On your way, you will pass Bitco, which has interesting Finnish furniture of a somewhat less classic character than Artek.

Back on the boulevard, you might want to look in at Iittala's new shop at No. 25 (they have a very pretty Sarpaneva decanter for $50) and at Pentik, which makes modish leather and suede coats that cost from $250 to $800 and are worth every penny. But the main goal is the Arabia shop just a few doors farther along, which has some of the most beautiful things in Helsinki, mixed inexplicably with a few that seem more worthy of a dime store.

The store stocks all the Arabia stoneware patterns at good prices: in most, a dinner plate costs $7.50 and a large coffee cup and saucer about $8.50. There are enamel mixing bowls, porcelain soufflé dishes and large numbers of other items by some of the country's best designers, including Kaj Frank and Tapio Wirkkala. Again, if you send the merchandise home, you will save the fourteen percent value-added tax.

Two additional thoughts: If you want to see the newest in Finnish design, that being turned out by the youngsters, you should go to the rather stark Finnish Design Center at Kasarmikatu 19: they sell nothing on the premises, but will give you an address where you can buy whatever strikes your fancy. And if you want lunch at the end of your stroll, I would suggest Havis Amanda, at the corner of Unioninkatu and Pohjoisesplanadi, almost to the marketplace. For about $60 for two, including drinks and service, they will serve you the best fish in town (including, in late July and August, Finnish crayfish). If that price is too steep, there are several small restaurants at the rear of the Swedish Theater.

5. *Meet Alvar Aalto*

T H E Americans at the next table seemed disappointed. They had apparently just returned from a bus tour of Helsinki, or perhaps from a boat tour through the Finnish lake district. They were complaining about "all the raw fish," about the language and about the lack of "interesting buildings and things."

I can offer little help to those who dislike herring (I am addicted to it myself) and even less to those who find the unpronounceable Finnish language unpronounceable. But I know a fair number of interesting buildings in Finland. Most of them were designed by Alvar Aalto, and missing them on a visit to Finland makes about as much sense as missing the sand in Timbuktu.

Aalto, who was born in 1898 and died in 1976, is perhaps the least known of the modern masters. But architectural historians place him alongside the American Frank Lloyd Wright, the Swiss Le Corbusier and the German Ludwig Mies van der Rohe as one of the century's greatest figures.

He designed only two major buildings in the United States— a dormitory for the Massachusetts Institute of Technology in Cambridge and a library for the Mount Angel Benedictine College in Mount Angel, Oregon. But Aalto masterpieces abound in Helsinki and elsewhere in Finland, the land of his birth and the inspiration for his use of blond wood and an undulating line. If you can spare three days during your visit to Finland, you can see much of Aalto's best work and enjoy some of the prettiest and most typical Finnish vistas (lakes, birch, pine) in the process.

Begin on foot in Helsinki at the offices of the Enso-Gutzeit cellulose and paper company (1962), a marble-clad block whose simplicity and symmetry harmonize well with the adjacent Senate Square, the mellow neoclassical heart of the capital. One of the more inventive touches is the set of manholelike skylights on the left side of the building, with lamps above each opening to melt the snow and augment the weak Scandinavian winter sun.

Head next toward Market Square. You are walking down the Pohjoisesplanadi, or Northern Boulevard. At the Helsinki Tourist Office, turn right into Unioninkatu. One block, a glance to your right into the heart of Senate Square, turn left; another block, then left again into Fabianinkatu and, at No. 29, Aalto's Scandinavian Bank (1964).

Aalto was a fussbudget who spent hours on details. In this building, he used the sinuous door pulls and the elegant lighting fixtures that he designed relatively late in life, and he placed on an interior wall a marble relief model of a Finnish landscape.

Fabianinkatu will lead you back to the esplanade, where you turn right again. As you walk along, you can see in the shop windows (and buy inside) examples of the best contemporary Finnish design. Particularly noteworthy are the glass and porcelain of Arabia, at No. 25, and the textiles and clothing of Marimekko at 31. (You will already have seen these, of course, if you have taken the design tour described in the preceding article.)

At 39 is the extraordinarily comprehensive Academic Bookstore, housed in one of Aalto's most satisfying buildings (1969). Entering it, you find yourself in a low-ceilinged room that seems thoroughly unremarkable; but advance a few steps and you are in an airy space three stories tall, surrounded by balconies full of books and browsers and crowned by boat-shaped skylights contrived to maximize natural illumination and minimize glare.

The side door leads to Keskuskatu. Turn right and look up; No. 3, which you are about to pass, is the Rautatalo Building (1955), clad in copper and insulated with cork. A stairway leads to the welcoming lobby, enlivened by a waterfall and potted trees. But the Artek shop, on the street level, is the major interest.

Artek was founded by Aalto and his first wife, Aino, along with Harry and Maire Gullichsen. More about the Gullichsens later. Artek continues to produce Aalto's bentwood chairs, tables and stools as well as other modern furnishings, and the shop shows the most complete selection anywhere.

Now retrace your steps to Northern Boulevard, cross the park and walk back toward Market Place along the Etelaesplanadi, or Southern Boulevard. Lunchtime should be approaching, and on the top floor of 14, a nondescript (and non-Aalto) office building, you will find the Savoy Restaurant.

It has two unassailable virtues: The food is delicious (try the salmon, smoke-cooked in a tin box over birch chips and served with a morel sauce), and the décor is by Alvar Aalto. On every table sits a distinctive vase, free form in cross section. Created for the restaurant, it is now sold all over the world. The top of the serving table in the center of the room has a similar shape.

After lunch, walk to the western end of the esplanade and turn right into Mannerheimintie—the broad boulevard named for Finland's greatest hero—which leads up the hill. In about ten minutes, you will see Finlandia House (1971) on your right.

Aalto managed in this building to create an unmannered, modern concert hall that works acoustically, a combination that has eluded most contemporary architects. Aalto was as fascinated by sound as he was by light, and he began acoustical experiments as early as 1929 in a temporary outdoor theater he designed at Turku. Finlandia House is the culmination of those experiments, a monumental building that nonetheless retains a human scale.

Four other buildings in other parts of Helsinki should be seen during the rest of the afternoon—the House of Culture (1958), a meeting hall for labor unions, built with special bricks that flow magically around tight curves; the Public Pensions Institute (1956), notable for the way in which a series of interconnected blocks are placed to form a quiet garden court, and the main building and the heating plant at the University of Technology at Otaniemi (1964). The university's main building, which is open most afternoons, contains a beautiful auditorium whose sloping and curving roof is fitted with seats, thus forming an outdoor amphitheater as well. All four buildings may be reached easily by car or taxi.

Early the next morning, head north on Route E-4, which leads through lovely lake country to Jyväskylä, 175 miles from Helsinki, where Aalto spent his adolescence and began his career. (If you have plenty of time, take the train to Lahti, then board a lake steamer for a leisurely eight-hour voyage to Jyväskylä, renting a car there for the rest of the trip.)

By all means stay at the Rantasipi Laajavuori Hotel, just northwest of town. It has an adequate restaurant, extraordinary sporting facilities (saunas, tennis and squash courts, swimming pools, ski lifts, jogging track) and splendid views over Jyväskylä and its lake. More to the point, it is the only hotel in the world furnished entirely with Aalto furniture.

In Jyväskylä, you can witness Aalto's struggle to break out of the neoclassicism he learned at the University of Technology. The theater (1925) is rigorously academic, but four years later, in the State Building, the decorative detail has been stripped away. By the time Aalto returned in the 1950s, his style had matured.

Stop at the city tourist office for a copy of its architectural map, then see the two older buildings plus a selection of the newer ones: the Central Finland Museum (1960) and the Alvar Aalto Museum (1973), built next to each other on a hillside (the latter has an exhibition of photographs, plans and furniture); the Police Station (1970), where Aalto again employed his characteristic device of decorating columns with vertical battens, and the College of Education (1957).

Aalto designed eight buildings at the college. None is a masterpiece, but all are worth seeing, especially the student union, whose roof is supported by a graceful, fan-shaped system of wooden trusses. Notice also the way the rear of the main building is designed to serve as a dramatic backdrop for outdoor assemblies.

Just south of town, on a well-marked road branching off Route E-4, is the small town of Säynätsalo. Aalto's summer house was on a nearby island, and he designed for Säynätsalo a town hall that demonstrates his ability to work imaginatively on a small scale as well as a large one. The red-brick building, with a fine council chamber, offices and a library, is a little gem.

The second day's drive is a long one, covering a total of about 375 miles if you take in Aalto's residential masterpiece, Villa Mairea. It is usually open from July 1 to August 14, but before leaving Helsinki, check with the Finnish Tourist Board (telephone 650155) for the latest information.

To reach Villa Mairea and the other buildings on this itinerary, take Route E-4 south to Jämsä, then pick up Route E-80 to Tampere, Finland's second-largest city, which is situated in a pretty setting on an isthmus between two lakes. If Villa Mairea is closed, follow Route E-80 directly to Turku. If not, pick up Route 40 and follow the signs to Pori. Just before Pori, turn north onto Route 2553. After three miles turn west onto Route

255, and after one and a half miles, turn north onto Route 2555, which leads to Normarkku. Once there, and it is less complicated than it sounds, you will see "Villa Mairea" signs.

The house (1938) was commissioned by Harry and Maire Gullichsen, the cofounders of Artek, who told Aalto to experiment as much as he liked. They would understand, they said, if it didn't work out. An architect's dream: wealthy, understanding, architecturally sophisticated clients who were also close friends.

Aalto, a humanist, once said, "It is the task of the architect to give life a gentler structure." He succeeded at Villa Mairea, a house that is luxurious without being pretentious. The details are wonderful: rustic poles holding up the roof of the entryway, a subtle reminder that this is a country house; movable walls to facilitate entertainment and the display of art; an Arp-like shape scooped out of the side of the massive fireplace in the living room; a studio for Mrs. Gullichsen, placed in a turret to guarantee solitude; "Venetian blinds" which are placed outside the ground-floor windows.

Routes 65 and 8 lead to Turku and, at Kauppiaskatu 5, the offices of the newspaper *Turun Sanomat* (1929), one of the buildings that established Aalto's reputation as a master of the international style. After fifty years the façade seems clean but unremarkable.

The interior, though, looks as daring as it must have looked when it was built, particularly the oval reinforced-concrete columns, narrower at the bottom than at the top, that support the roof of the pressroom. You can tour the building if you call Irja Ketonen at *Turun Sanomat* (921-333-600) before you arrive.

Leave Turku on Route E-3, the main road to Helsinki. After about eleven miles, turn north onto Route 234. At Paimio, turn right onto Route 235 and, after about a quarter of a mile, turn left at the sign "Sairaala." That road will take you to the other building that brought Aalto to the attention of his fellow architects, the Paimio Tuberculosis Sanitarium, finished in 1933.

It is almost impossible to believe, as you look at this cool white building, with dark-red iron railings on its balconies, that Aalto completed the plans a half-century ago. Seen from the air, it forms an irregular pinwheel, an arrangement that not only floods the rooms with light but also screens the living quarters of the staff from the areas where the convalescents are housed.

For this building, Aalto devised a system of indirect ventilation so that patients would have the air they need for recovery but would not be exposed to potentially harmful drafts.

Now return to Route 235, turn left and follow it back to Route E-3, which should put you in Helsinki in about an hour and a half. If you can spare an extra half day, it is more comfortable to spend the night in Turku, postponing the visit to the Paimio Sanitarium and the drive to Helsinki until the following morning.

For the insatiable, there is still more to be seen. The trip from Jyväskylä to Villa Mairea can be made by way of Seinäjoki, where Aalto designed the whole city center, including a striking clock tower. A drive toward the Soviet border, northeast of Helsinki, will take you to the vast Sunila cellulose factory at Kotka (for which Aalto owed his commission to Harry Gullichsen) and the dramatic Vuoksenniska church in the town of Imatra.

6. Danish Worth an Ocean Voyage

Y o u can smell it half a block away. Before you see anything, before you taste anything, the aroma prepares you for something extraordinary. And when you turn into the little old-fashioned shop at the sign of the crowned pretzel, at the shabby end of Strøget, Copenhagen's famous walking street, you aren't disappointed.

This is the Valhalla of Danish pastry, the bakery of Reinhard Van Hauen.

American Danish, more often than not, is doughy, heavy, sticky. It often tastes of prunes. It is usually wrapped in cellophane. Danish Danish is light, crisp and buttery. It often tastes of marzipan and raisins; it is seldom wrapped in anything but loving care.

Danes won't eat truly bad pastry, so no one tries to sell it.

In the sorts of places where gastronomes might fear to tread—cafeterias on Danish ferryboats, the café in the Copenhagen railroad station, a college dining hall—the morning Danish is perfectly palatable. Not worth crossing the Atlantic for, mind you, but not bad.

When you start from that kind of base, the best is bound to be brilliant, and the Van Hauen pastry is worth crossing whatever ocean happens to lie between you and the racks of Danish delights at 23 Fredrikberggade.

The search for the perfect Danish, a journalistic task only marginally less rewarding than the quest for the perfect dry martini, began with the names of more than a dozen Copenhagen bakers, supplied by some serious local eaters. Twenty-three cups of coffee and thirty-seven pastries later, Van Hauen emerged as the clear leader on this scorecard.

Søren Gericke, the favorite chef of Danish *Feinschmeckers*, assured me that I was on the right track. Van Hauen's, he said, "makes the best Danish pastry in Copenhagen, and therefore the best in the world."

"They don't play with chemistry sets over there," said Mr. Gericke, who shares with his culinary hero, the French chef Michel Guérard, a passion for natural products. "They use real ingredients, always fresh, always the best that money can buy, and they know how to use the heel of the hand."

The Van Hauen bakery is a family affair. A Van Hauen emigrated from the Netherlands to Denmark in the middle of the last century. His son bought the present shop, which had been a bakery at least since 1732, after World War I and passed it on to his son, Leo, who passed it on to his son, Uggi.

When I visited him several years ago, Leo Mac Van Hauen was seventy-seven, long retired; but he remained as vigorous and voluble as he was in his youth, which included a stint as a cowpuncher in Texas, a bout with yellow fever in the Amazon and a couple of years as a baker of Danish pastry—"the real stuff"—in Montreal.

"There isn't any mystery to it," he said. "The problem is that most people don't want to bother any more."

Van Hauen's does bother—and not only with pastry. For their bread, they buy rye and wheat only from a wholesaler who guarantees that it has been grown in soil untouched by chemical fertilizers or insecticides for fifteen years. In addition, this must be one of the few small bakeries in the world that mills its own flour from whole grains every day.

It is Danish pastry, however, that draws the crowds to the Van Hauen shop, a dignified oasis with travertine walls set amid souvenir shops and pornography palaces not far from Copenhagen's city hall. Or, rather, it is *Wienerbrød* that draws them, for the Danish call Danish pastry "Vienna bread."

Why? You can't find anything resembling Danish pastry in Vienna. Some Danes say the word *Wienerbrød* derives from the fact that their pastry is made from a dough, with its multitude of layers, that resembles Central European puff pastry. Mr. Van Hauen offered a more subtle explanation.

The word, he said, is a tribute not only to the skill of Viennese chefs and to the fact that coffee (with which Danish is usually eaten) was introduced into Europe in Vienna, but also to the courage of the Austrian bakers. The reason for the crown over the pretzel in front of many European bakers' shops, he explained, is that the bakers of Vienna fought so bravely to defend the city against the Turks that the Emperor gave them the right to add a crown to their trademark.

There are three keys to superlative Danish pastry, Mr. Van Hauen believes: freshness, ingredients, temperature.

In the white-tiled basement beneath the Van Hauen salesroom, work begins at 4:00 A.M. and continues throughout the day. It is rare for anyone to buy pastry that has been out of the oven for more than an hour. Because delivery routes would inevitably mean stale pastry, Van Hauen's has no trucks; such bulk customers as banks and hotels must send someone to the bakery every morning to pick up the day's supply.

The central technical problem is the production of a dough with distinct layers of fat that will expand in the oven to produce a light, crisp, multilayered pastry. Butter's flavor is ideal, but its melting point is too low. Ordinary margarine has a high melting point, but it doesn't dissolve instantly in your mouth, and thus leaves an unpleasantly suety aftertaste.

Van Hauen's therefore uses a special margarine in the initial fabrication, made of animal and vegetable fats, and paints the dough with melted butter before it is put into the oven. The ingredients are straightforward enough: high-gluten white flour, preferably from Kansas; the special margarine; "lots of eggs, straight from the henhouse"; sugar, water and yeast.

First, everything but the margarine is mixed together to make a paste. That is then folded over a block of margarine to form a kind of sandwich, which is put through a mechanical roller. The operation is repeated until a ribbon of dough, fifteen feet long and three feet wide, with as many as twenty-seven distinct layers, lies on a long table next to the machine.

"Above all," said Mr. Van Hauen for the sixth or seventh time as he explained the process, "the ingredients must be first class. Fresh. And the mixture must be held as close as possible to fourteen degrees centigrade [fifty-five to fifty-seven degrees Fahrenheit] so the margarine doesn't melt. If it does, you get a soggy mess."

Finally the ribbon is cut into various shapes for the dozen or so varieties of pastry that Van Hauen's sells. (Mr. Van Hauen made as many as seventy-two varieties in Montreal, but his son has sacrificed variety for freshness.) For horns, "burgomeisters," "pretzels" and other types, various flavorings are added—apples, cinnamon, raisins, almonds and marzipan or almond paste, a longtime specialty of Odense, Denmark's second-largest city.

"Smell that?" asked Mr. Van Hauen as he pointed out the items on sale. It was the aroma the visitor had noticed on the street two hours earlier. "You can't fake it," he said. "You won't get it if you use mixes, if you cut corners."

As he said good-bye, he seemed to remember that his caller was an American. "Pecans," he said. "I used them in Montreal. Very good. But we can't find a regular supplier in Denmark."

7. Ærø, as Ever

IN the days, twenty-five years ago and more, before I came to know Europe well, and long before I went there to live, I used to search through travel guides for obscure but interesting places. In one such, I read about an island with the fascinating name of

Ærø, a capital called Ærøskøbing and enough charm to soften a misanthrope.

I went there and loved it. In 1982, I went back and loved it again. It had not changed at all, which is something you cannot say about many of the places that guidebooks are in the habit of praising. In the last twenty-five years Paris has lost Les Halles and gained the Tour Montparnasse; Toledo and San Gimignano and Stratford-upon-Avon have been overrun; the prices at Salzburg and Bayreuth have soared out of the reach of everyone except industrialists from the Ruhr, and Lapérouse is a fading memory.

But Ærøskøbing, where Humperdinck would have staged the premiere of *Hansel and Gretel* if only he had known about it, still has its ships-in-bottles museum and still puts the key to the local jail next to the door, where anyone can reach it. The pastel-colored houses still lean at crazy angles, and the villagers still smile.

Ærø, which is twenty-two miles at its longest and belongs to Denmark, lies in the Baltic Sea between the island called Fyn (also known by its German name Fünen), where Hans Christian Andersen lived, and the coast of Germany. Ærø is only one hundred air miles southwest of Copenhagen, but there are no commercial flights, which is probably the main reason why it has not changed.

It is the perfect one-day antidote to tour blur—you know, two days in Copenhagen, three in London, three in Paris, two in Florence, two in Venice. Break your visit to the great cities, with their great museums, great restaurants and great throngs of people doing exactly what you are doing. See some Europeans.

I say one-day antidote; actually the best thing to do is to combine a visit to Ærø with a visit to Fyn, which you can do comfortably in two days. You can start and finish in Copenhagen, or, if you are driving and it suits your plans, start in Copenhagen and finish in northern Germany or in Jutland, about which more later.

On my last trip, I flew one morning from Copenhagen to Odense, the main town of Fyn. The trip takes thirty minutes and costs little; it is worth the expense to avoid the tremendous backups at the main ferry crossing between Zealand, the island on which Copenhagen is situated, and Fyn. Rent a car at the airport; if you bring a car from Copenhagen, be sure to make an advance booking on the ferry.

Once on Fyn, I stopped in at Andersen's birthplace. He may not actually have been born there, but the house contains a museum full of personal belongings, sketches and letters from Dickens and Jenny Lind. (During the summer the house is open from 9:00 A.M. to 7:00 P.M. daily.) The place provokes thoughts about this strange, gifted man who considered himself the real "ugly duckling" but created stories that have entered the folk culture of the world.

Still in Odense but a couple of miles south is an open-air museum called the Fünen Village. Two items of interest to foreigners here: a group of twenty country buildings—including barns, houses, mills, a smithy and tileworks—brought together to give you some idea of rural life in the days before television and the automobile, and an open-air theater with a Hans Christian Andersen play for the kids in summer. (The Fünen Village is open from 9:00 A.M. to 6:30 P.M. until the middle of August, when it closes at 4:30 P.M.)

Look around town for a while, especially at the old residential quarter, and have a bite of lunch, perhaps at the inexpensive Sortebro Kro in the Fünen Village. The best things to eat there are the open-faced sandwiches, smørrebrød, which might be topped with tiny shrimp or cold roast beef or herring or cheese.

After lunch head to Egeskov, eighteen miles south of Odense. This is, I believe, the most magnificent Renaissance water castle in Europe; it rises on oak piles from, and is reflected in, its serene moat. You cannot go into the castle but you can admire its rose-brick walls and battlements while walking through its well-kept gardens.

To dinner and to bed: you can take your pick of two places, both of which offer that wonderfully European combination of beautiful old buildings, calmly beautiful countryside and good food. Both are near Fåborg, the port town where I caught the ferry the next morning to Ærø.

Steensgård is the more traditional of the two hostelries, a half-timbered manor house set in a twenty-five-acre park. Its oldest portions were built in the fourteenth century, and its five elegantly paneled sitting rooms are filled with antiques, including a two-hundred-year-old Royal Copenhagen Baroque fireplace. A special dinner I once ate there began with half a lobster and went on to asparagus and other delights. It cost $45 a person, including white wine with the lobster and Château Nenin 1974 with the main course; everyday dinners are less.

Almost every village in Fyn has its quota of black-and-white, half-timbered houses with thatched roofs. But only Millinge, thirty miles southwest of Odense, is fortunate enough to have a Frenchman hidden away in the kitchen of one of them. Jean-Louis Lieffroy and his Danish partners, Lene and Sven Gronlykke, have made their fifteenth-century roadside inn, Falsled Kro, the premier country hotel in Scandinavia.

When you walk into the sitting room—"lobby" is altogether too formal a word—the first thing you notice is the huge white fireplace, open on four sides, surrounded by low-slung wood-and-leather chairs. The second is the warmth of the décor—chintz slipcovers, a white wicker birdcage, old plates and pictures on the walls, a magnificent model of a sailing ship, flowers in profusion. The Danes are world-beaters at creating this sort of blissfully rustic ambience, with never a false note, and keeping it looking daffodil-fresh year after year.

There are eight rooms and three suites, all of them full of homely cheer. Equally welcoming on a cold winter's day is the dining room, with its pink tablecloths, scrubbed pine floors and ravishing food. Mr. Lieffroy, who comes from the Vosges, combines the best of local produce—quail, lamb, salmon, mussels—with vegetables and cheeses and other delicacies sent daily by air from the Rungis market outside Paris; the result is a deliciously unhackneyed Franco-Danish cuisine. Among his best dishes are beef cooked in a salty pastry crust and warm foie gras with spinach, wild rice and sweet corn. The inn imports its own wines—well-chosen "little" ones such as Cahors and Jurançon and Rully, as well as blockbusters from Burgundy—and an array of *digestifs* notable for both rarity and quality.

It all goes to show how much can be accomplished, so far off the beaten track, by taste and talent, imagination and perseverance.

The ferry to Ærø takes an hour; start early so you can spend the whole day on the island, which will scarcely be enough. You will arrive at Søby, near the northwest end of the island. Head toward Ærøskøbing, "the Fairy Tale Town of Denmark," as the pamphlets call it, but make your first stop in the little town of Bregninge.

The town's church, or at least part of it, dates from about 1200. The whitewashed building, with a square tower rising into an octagonal steeple, is full of treasures—treasures of a modest sort, to be sure, but nonetheless fascinating for that. The chalk paintings on the arches, for example, in gray and salmon pink; the sailing-ship model suspended in the nave; the retable, which was made in about 1530; Claus Berg's naïve yet evocative triptych of the Crucifixion.

You can have lunch at the Bregninge Kro (as you must have guessed by now, *kro* means "inn"), where the open-faced sandwiches are delicious and reasonably priced, or where you can order a four-course meal. The village is said to make the best rye bread in the country. If you have acquired the habit of drinking aquavit, the fiery caraway-flavored schnapps, have one with a dash of Riga balsam bitters in it. It not only tastes good; you will be taking part in the island's maritime tradition, because the local taste for Riga balsam stems from the days when Ærø men sailed to Riga and other great ports of the Hanseatic League.

Then it is ten miles into Ærøskøbing itself, with its old houses. Many of them are Lilliputian affairs of one story, half-timbered, their walls tilting crazily, capped with tile roofs. Elaborately carved doorways, cobblestone pavements and cast-iron lamps complete the picture, along with the pastel colors that the thirteen hundred residents favor.

There are, of course, some "sights" in Ærøskøbing. Among them are the museum in the house that once belonged to a retired ship's cook known as "Bottle Peter," who must have been the greatest man ever for putting ships under glass. Also worth visiting are the Hammerich House, a museum of porcelain and antiques, and the very fine town church, whitewashed and with a shingle-clad steeple. The antiques are mainly eighteenth-century furniture, and the porcelain and tiles are Danish blue and white, from the same period.

You can swim and sail as well. All of the beaches on the island are open to the public; some are very fine sand, others pebbly. But the joy of the place is simply strolling through it, comparing this house with that, looking for architectural traces of the five hundred years when the island belonged to the German state of Schleswig, stopping in the back garden of a restaurant named Mumm for a beer and the almost inevitable chat with a tableful of convivial Danes. Almost all Danes speak some English, and the younger ones speak it perfectly.

The streets are cobblestone and, though cars are permitted, there is little traffic. For an overnight stay there are several modest hotels—among them Ærøhus and Terrassen—with prices to match. Like all hotels in Denmark, of whatever class, they are clean and they are run by people who will break their backs to help you.

Ærøskøbing is what Disneyland would be like if it were real, I suppose; when you have had enough, head back to Søby, perhaps stopping at the ruins of the old manor called Søbygård, with its dungeons and moat. There you can pick up another ferry, a delightfully ancient craft that plies the strait between Søby and Mommark on Als, an island east of the Jutland Peninsula. The Danish word on the boat's nameplate means "veteran ferry," and it is all of that, but it will carry you and your car without incident to Mommark. From there it takes less than forty-five minutes to drive to the German border at Flensburg and even less to reach the bucolic countryside of Jutland.

Jutland is the peninsula that divides the North Sea from the Baltic Sea, and it was off its coast that the Germans outwitted the British in the most important naval engagement of World War I. Today the peninsula has unspoiled beaches, medieval hamlets and a hospitable population.

For those interested in architecture, there is Ribe, with its twelfth-century cathedral, its wealth of sixteenth- and seventeenth-century houses and its storks, and Ålborg, with its museum designed by Alvar Aalto, the great Finnish modernist. For lovers of the seashore, there is the island of Fanø and the charming old artists' colony of Skagen. For the culturally curious, there is the festival of drama, dance and music, Scandinavia's largest, at Århus in September. For the gastronome, there are succulent and plentiful Limfjord oysters. For the kids, there is Legoland at Billund, a Lilliputian wonder built of fifteen million toy bricks. And for the unashamedly patriotic, there is Rebild National

Park, near Ålborg, where every Fourth of July tens of thousands of Danes and Danish-Americans celebrate Independence Day with speeches and merrymaking.

Jutland is not a place to speed through in a day or even three days; it is a place where one is well advised to emulate the placid cows that dot the flat, green, beautifully tended pastures.

CHAPTER XII

A Few Places in the Sun

1. Morocco's Imperial Quartet

ONLY the nine miles of the Strait of Gibraltar separate Europe from Africa, Spain from Morocco. Cultural, economic and political influences have flowed in both directions; the Moors were in Spain from the eighth to the fifteenth centuries, the Spanish and the Portuguese and finally the French in Morocco from the sixteenth to the twentieth.

"I feel both African and European," an educated Moroccan said to me. Many of his countrymen would agree, and the country's successful transition from the Middle Ages to modern times in only seventy-five years reflects the skills not only of Kings Mohammed V and Hassan II but also of Marshal Louis Lyautey, one of the ablest colonial administrators who ever lived. Up-to-date roads, schools, hospitals, hotels, apartment buildings and factories have been built without spoiling the dignified manners of the people, obscuring the Oriental turbulence of the old towns or threatening the nation's religious and social traditions.

We first went to Morocco because my Virginia-born wife, who was as yet unreconciled to the gloom of northern European winters, wanted some sun, and because I insisted on something more challenging than palm trees and piña coladas. (All three pieces in this chapter, in fact, grew out of such midwinter escapism.)

The compromise plan involved visits to the four *villes im-périales*—Rabat, Meknès, Fez and Marrakech, each of which has served as Morocco's capital—and then a drive across the High Atlas to an oasis in the south for a couple of days of complete torpor, which is about as much as I can usually manage.

We went with some trepidation, but we knew we had got it right the first day as we strolled in seventy-one-degree warmth through the gardens and among the ruined minarets and the tombs of a fourteenth-century walled village called Chella, just at the edge of Rabat. It is a place of enigmatic solitude where the only sound was the clacking of the bills of dozens of storks that had also come south for the winter—in their case, so we later learned, from the chimney tops of Jutland and Saxony and Alsace.

Nine days later, having sampled the joys of the Moroccan table, of the throbbing souks, of sumptuous architecture and uncorrupted handicrafts, of snow-dusted mountain cedars and featureless desert, we no longer wondered why the French have for so long found this most western of Arab countries, in both senses of the word, an ideal winter haven.

We began in Rabat because it is close to Casablanca, more notable on film than in the flesh, where most of the planes from Europe land, as do all of those from the United States. In our rented car, a serviceable if not immaculate Renault, it took less than two hours to drive to the modern capital.

Rabat has a calm and stately air about it, as befits a city whose business is government and not commerce. A good beginning, after visiting Chella to get into the spirit of the thing, is a drive around the twelfth-century pink ramparts, noting the splendid Bab er Rouah, the best of the five surviving gates. Then make for the Casbah of the Oudaïas, the fortified citadel, which you enter (on foot) through a massive gateway that is both a strong-point and a work of art, embellished with bands of Kufic script interwoven with flowers.

Walking up through the narrow streets, you will pass the in-triguing doorways of dozens of houses, some dilapidated, some restored by European and Moroccan owners, before emerging on a platform that affords a view over the city and the sea. Coming back down again, you can tarry in a lovely Andalusian garden and sip a drink in the Café Maure. We skipped the

Museum of Moroccan Art and the souk on local advice, so as to leave more time for two local masterpieces: the Hassan Tower and the madrasah, or school, in nearby Salé.

Only about sixty percent—144 feet—of the tower remains, which gives it a somewhat stumpy appearance. But the sculpture on three sides, subtle, simple and powerful in keeping with the Almohad dislike of flamboyance, plus the sheer mass of the thing, make it the equal of the Giralda in Granada, a great Hispano-Moorish minaret. By comparison, the adjacent modern mausoleum and mosque of Mohammed V, watched over by members of the Royal Guard, seems gaudy despite the workmanship that obviously went into it. The broken columns between the two are all that remains of the never-completed mosque that was to have been the largest in the Moslem world after that at Samarra, Iraq.

Salé, across the river, was established by the Romans and grew to be the main port and commercial center of medieval Morocco. A walk through its twisting streets, crowded with whitewashed buildings, is an utter delight, but you will need help. It is available in two forms. If you can read French, you should arm yourself with the invaluable Michelin green guide to Morocco or the exhaustive Blue Guide, both of which have excellent maps and informative articles on Moroccan history, art and mores. Fodor's *North Africa*, in English, is less detailed though certainly worth taking.

Even with them, however, you would be wise to arrange for an official guide at the hotel, who will save you from the one thing likely to mar your trip—the pestilential small boys who set upon you as soon as you approach the historic center of any town. They won't take no, a smile or even a small tip for an answer, and they can turn nasty; one spat at me before I learned my lesson. Far better to get a trained professional; they charge very little, speak good English or French and will increase your pleasure tenfold.

But to return to Salé . . . The gem of the walk through town, which will take a couple of hours, is the madrasah founded by the Black Sultan in 1341. Its stunning courtyard is decorated with multicolored tiles, slender pillars and elaborately carved cedar. Above are the minute cells once occupied by students and another lovely vista. The madrasah is one of the best (and best-restored) examples of Moorish architecture, in all of its sublime delicacy, that is open to non-Islamic visitors, who are barred from mosques in Morocco.

Rabat's Archeological Museum houses a rich hoard of Roman bronzes—a dog, poised to jump, found at Volubilis, and a famous statue of an adolescent crowned with ivy—but they have not been on view in recent years. Check locally; if you can see them, you should.

There is a good Hilton in Rabat, and the Tour Hassan, though a bit run-down, is highly atmospheric, but I prefer the Farah-Sofitel, part of a French chain. (It is not in some guidebooks because it is new.) Under the direction of Jean-Paul Delacroix, one of the most experienced restaurateurs in the country, and Phillipe Perrichon, a talented chef, the Sofitel's rooftop restaurant has become one of the two or three best French eating places in Morocco; the fish is outstanding, especially the *pageot* (a kind of bream). For Moroccan food, wait for Fez and Marrakech; for lunch, we found the Pizzeria Roma, with outdoor tables, most agreeable.

You can drive from Rabat to Fez in a few hours, which leaves plenty of time to see both Meknès and Volubilis on the way. Meknès is the least known of the imperial cities, but by no means the least impressive; although it was the capital of only one sultan, Moulay Ismail (1647–1727), he built there the largest palace in the world—big enough to house fifty thousand people. Of it, this tyrannical contemporary of Louis XIV said: "I have built this; let them try to demolish it."

It was a ruin within a century of his death, devastated by earthquakes and looted for building blocks. But the miles of massive walls remain, pierced by gigantic gateways that look as if they were put there as the backdrop for one of Valentino's films, and their grandeur is undeniable. You can visit Moulay Ismail's tomb, the only Islamic sanctuary in the country open to non-Moslems, which has considerable charm. It is surprisingly small, and hence out of character with his megalomania; you will sense that quality immediately, however, in the immense and starkly beautiful stables and granary, once filled by twelve thousand horses and their feed, now but an echo of Piranesi.

A pleasant lunch spot lies just east of town on the Fez road— the Hacienda, with a swimming pool, tables under shade trees and excellent Spanish and Moroccan food (try the superb grilled meats). It is well signposted. After lunch, double back and head north to Volubilis, which was the Roman capital of Mauritania.

It is hard to imagine the Romans bustling about in this remote spot, harder even for me than to imagine them manning Hadrian's Wall in blustery Northumbria. But the evidence is there, in the form of a colonnaded shopping street and some very fine mosaics. Spend an hour wandering and dreaming, then head toward Fez, passing en route the hilltop holy city of Moulay Idris, which holds relatively little interest for the foreign visitor.

Fez is the heart and soul of Morocco, the intellectual and religious and artistic capital. By all means visit the sights—the viewpoints over the city along the road that circles it; the Madrasah Bou Inania, with its coolly beautiful courtyard, paved in marble and onyx; the Attarine Madrasah, masterpiece of the Merinid dynasty, thirty years older, smaller, but astonishing in the exuberance of its decoration; the Karaouine Mosque, largest in Morocco, which can be glimpsed through open doors; the Nejjarine Fountain, a kind of shrine to water, beautifully decorated with tiles.

But save at least half a day for the souk and its network of unpaved alleys, each filled with clamoring people and burros and bicycles, with open-fronted shops standing shoulder to shoulder on both sides, for it is here that Fez can be seen whole. You will see sweating men dying thread in vats in a process unchanged for centuries; men embroidering caftans in tiny, ill-lit rooms; men squatting in doorways, operating little lathes with their feet.

Every inch of every shop is crammed with merchandise, and you will want to buy something, whether a caftan or a brass dish or a bunch of fragrant coriander or real kohl to make up your eyes; take along a guide, and begin by offering about a quarter of what is asked. If you are lucky, you will get it for about a third. You must bargain even in the best shops, among which I can recommend the Merveilles de Fez, which has fine rugs, old silver jewelry, porcelain and odd bits of furniture, and where they will ply you with mint tea while you haggle.

Stay, if you can afford it, in the wonderful Palais Jamai, which overlooks the medina or old town. Its fountains and gardens, its swimming pool and its restaurant, the best in Fez, are all truly palatial. Among the good things to eat are an assortment of seven little salads, spicy and delicate, and a chicken *tajine*, or stew, cooked with peppers and onions in an earthenware pot shaped like a dunce cap. The Merinides Hotel, high on a cliff above town, is somewhat cheaper and also good. Another good restaurant is L'Ambre, also with Moroccan cuisine; avoid European restaurants, one of which listed as its sole "green vegetables," on our visit, potatoes and spaghetti.

The drive to Marrakech will take a whole day and offers, frankly, very little interest, except for a brief detour, outlined in Michelin, that will enable you to see a lovely cedar forest. Stop for lunch at the Chems Hotel in Beni Mellal; it is surrounded by orange groves and serves, in season, the best orange juice I have ever drunk. The food is adequate.

And then Marrakech; can there be many cities whose very names so fire the sluggish imagination? Unlike some others, such as Timbuktu, Marrakech never disappoints. It is not quite a Saharan city, the desert proper beginning several hundred miles south, but it is toward the desert that it faces, and it was the desert caravans that first enriched this oasis metropolis.

Marrakech has an enormous medina containing wonderful souks, second only to those of Fez; two outstanding antiquaries, whose wares should be seen if not bought, are the Lampe d'Aladin and Aabdi Nasr Eddine, both known to most guides. Marrakech has its share of architectural landmarks, notably the glorious Koutoubia Minaret; the Madrasah ben Youssef, the largest in the Maghreb but not quite as dazzling as those of Fez and Salé; and the Koubba ba'Adiyn, an elegant little arched building that has somehow survived intact since the twelfth century. It has an evocative palm grove, just ouside the center of town, through which you can drive. And it has an immense and animated central square called Jemaa el Fna, which is not to be missed.

For us, however, the highlights of Marrakech were tombs and gardens. The tombs are those of the Saadians, which were built in the seventeenth century, walled up in the eighteenth and rediscovered only in the twentieth, and they are the last Moorish masterpiece.

Spend as much time as you can gazing into the three main chambers—the Room of the Mihrab, or prayer niche, with its lacy stuccos; the Room of the Twelve Columns, clothed in gold and tiles and honey-colored Carrara marble of indescribable magnificence, and the far simpler Room of Three Niches. Most people miss the light switches and hence the brilliance of the colors; ask someone else's guide for help if you don't have one.

The gardens are those created by the French Art Deco designer Louis Majorelle, and for some reason few seem to know about them. That we can see them at all is due to Yves Saint-Laurent, who has a house nearby. He bought them, spent years looking for a proper Majorelle blue with which to repaint their pavilions, restored them with a loving hand and at last opened them to the public. Palms and bamboos, cedars and banana trees flourish here, but it is the blazing, cascading richness of the bougainvillea that we shall long remember.

If you can, do as Churchill did, and stay at the sumptuous Mamounia; it is an experience beyond compare to arrive at dusk, to be taken to a room both luxurious and Moorish in spirit, to gaze out across the huge swimming pool into a grove of palm trees, lit from below, and to listen to the song of hundreds of birds. The nearby Chems, though far simpler, is not without charm.

Marrakech is the Lyon of Morocco. You will eat superbly at the Mamounia, where I had a perfectly roasted shoulder of lamb; at the legendary Maison Arabe (closed in summer), where you must order your meal at least forty-eight hours in advance, where the sparkling Suzy Sebillon will serve you, among other delights, a feather-light pigeon pie (*bastilla*), flavored with sugar and cinnamon, and where you eat with your right fingers only; and at the more touristic Ksar el Hamra and Riad al-Bahia. For your wanderings in the souks, you could do no better than to phone Mohammed Bouskri, a kind and highly intelligent guide who speaks perfect English, the moment you arrive. His home number is 34240.

You may well decide to call it a trip after Marrakech, in which case you can fly or drive straight back to Casablanca. But if you, too, are in the mood for a bit of sloth, head south out of town toward the village of Ouirgane, stopping there for lunch at a curiously named inn, Au Sanglier qui Fume, or the Boar who Smokes. Put on one of the straw hats that sit on the table (for protection from the sun), order the *boudin* with orange sauce or the roast lamb (*mechoui*) with cumin, and drink in the mountain view.

They gave my wife a daffodil as we left. Then up over the Atlas, on occasionally unpaved and continuously vertiginous roads, and down into the oasis of Taroudant.

The Gazelle d'Or is a kind of miracle, a lovely and supremely comfortable hotel, with bungalows covered in bougainvillea, that entirely avoids chichi. Nothing much happens, nobody organizes shuffleboard tournaments or canasta games; the big event of the day is likely to be a lemon or two falling on your private terrace while you're eating breakfast.

2. *The Fork of Adam*

THE Moroccan is a patient soul. Watch him at work in the souks, carefully operating a little lathe with a foot pedal, turning out the spindles of cedarwood that will be fitted together to form the delicate screens known as *masharabiehs*. Or watch her in the kitchen, preparing *bastilla*, which will require, if the pie is to feed twelve people, about a hundred transparently thin sheets of pastry, eight birds and ample quantities of parsley and pimientos, saffron and coriander, onions and almonds, ginger, cinnamon, eggs and butter.

Moroccan cuisine, like Moroccan handicrafts, has survived the modernization of the country with remarkable success. At its best—and that best can be found in simple rural places, such as the Sanglier qui Fume in the shadow of the Atlas, as well as at fancier places like the Riad in Marrakech—it is untouched by the twin plagues of twentieth-century cooking, convenience foods and misguided "creativity."

As a result of loving attention to traditional methods, and of the continuing availability of fine ingredients, the Moroccan table is the best in the Arab world and by far the best on the African continent. Along with China, Thailand, Indonesia, India, Brazil and Mexico, this is one of the few third-world countries where *gourmandise* thrives.

The classic Moroccan feast, of the kind offered to visitors with all the hospitality of Bedouin tradition, is called a *diffa*. (According to some etymologists, it is from that Arabic word that the Anglo-Indians wrong-headedly evolved "tiffin," their word for an afternoon snack.) All or parts of such a repast can be had not only on great occasions in Moroccan homes but also in the best restaurants of the country.

Take the Maison Arabe in Marrakech, for example—an externally anonymous building on a side street in the old medina, with several small whitewashed rooms grouped around a courtyard, with a simple but spotless kitchen. The Maison Arabe is one of those venerable restaurants that is described by the self-appointed cognoscenti (hotel concierges, taxi drivers) as passé. Pay them no heed. It may not be as good as it was fifteen years ago, when the French food writers Henri Gault and Christian Millau, in a characteristically naughty flight of hyperbole, called it the best restaurant in the world, but it remains very good indeed. Ask Madame Sebillon to prepare a selection from the 162 traditional dishes in her repertory, all of them learned from the chef of the Glaoui, the late pasha of Marrakech.

When my wife and I were last there, she served us an incredibly light *bastilla*, with the sweetness of the sugar and the cinnamon asserting itself at first but then, after a few bites, gradually merging with the more aggressive tastes of coriander and onion; a *tajine* of kefta, a stew in the style of the Berbers, the nomadic people who preceded the Arabs in the northwest corner of Africa, with small meatballs and baked eggs; chicken with ginger; very salty and very spicy chicken livers, and gloriously fresh Moroccan oranges, sliced and flavored with cinnamon and rose water. With it we drank the curious but satisfying wine called Gris de Boulaouane, a very dry pale rosé that copes well with the intense and exotic flavors of the food, and an excellent sparkling water from Oulmès. Afterward, we relaxed with the refreshing, ceremoniously produced staple beverage of the land, mint tea, poured from a big ornamental pot held high above a tiny, fragile cup.

"It takes endless time," said Mme. Sebillon, a tiny, gray-haired Frenchwoman, a resident of Marrakech for forty-five years, who had instructed us carefully at the start of the meal how to eat as the Moslems do with "the fork of Adam"—the thumb and first two fingers of our right hands. "It is a serious and satisfying cuisine, but it must be ordered well in advance, or it is nothing."

We soon found, however, that some of the hotel kitchens, accustomed to dealing with Europeans and Americans in a hurry, could produce simpler but thoroughly delicious meals on a moment's notice or two. The food is slightly less authentic, eaten in a much less authentic manner, with knife and fork, but not so much the worse for all that.

I remember in particular, from the sumptuous hotel dining room of the Palais Jamai in Fez, an Arab fantasy of tiles, low tables and sculptured ceilings, the array of spicy little salads that Betsey ate—especially those flavored with coriander, the flat-leafed herb whose sweet-sharp aroma prefumes the souks. Like the antipasti of Italy, the *tapas* of Andalusia and the *mezes* of Greece and Turkey, these showed the Mediterranean love of a variety of savory nibbles, with one based on tomatoes, another on fennel, a third on cucumbers, a fourth on fava beans and still others on carrots, radishes, green peppers and eggplant. From a number of places, I recall the *tajines*—ragouts steamed for hours over low heat in earthenware vessels shaped like coolies' hats, which can be based on almost anything so long as the bouillon, the olive oil and the butter, which are eventually reduced to a thick sauce, are of prime quality.

(One cookbook I own lists thirty-five varieties, from veal with quinces and honey to lamb with Jerusalem artichokes or turnips or pumpkin.)

But most of all I remember the *mechoui*, the national dish *par excellence*, a whole roast lamb or a part thereof, cooked very slowly over charcoal and basted continually with butter until it falls golden brown from the bone. The best bit, I think, is the shoulder, eaten with a pinch of cumin, as at the El Bahja (The Good Life) restaurant in the Mamounia Hotel in Marrakech. When well prepared, it can hold its own with a herby rack of lamb from the hills of Wales or a juicy pink gigot from the salt marshes of France, which is saying something. And nobody, no matter what war stories anybody has told you, will ask you to eat the sheep's eyes.

There is much, much more in Morocco. You should try *harira*, a hearty soup involving lentils, fava beans and chickpeas, and the simple but often succulent brochettes of lamb and other meats, and the chicken with preserved lemons and olives, and the honey-

and-almond-flavored pastries and, if you are on the Atlantic coast, such fish as fresh sardines, bass, shad and *sar*, which is usually cooked with fennel.

In addition to the wines mentioned, Morocco also has some passable whites, including Semillant, which is made from the sauvignon blanc grape, and considerably better reds, notably the one made from cabernet grapes and called Cuvée du President.

All of this sun-kissed bounty is available at relatively modest prices, even at the country's grandest hotels. We ate and drank copiously at the Palais Jamai in Fez (telephone 34331) for less than $30, at the Mamounia in Marrakech (telephone 32381) for about $40 and at the Maison Arabe (telephone 22604) for less than $50.

3. *Halliburton Was Right*

WHEN I was growing up in Ohio in the 1940s, my most treasured possession was a book with a dark blue cover and impressive pictures of far-off places inside. It was called *Richard Halliburton's Book of Marvels*, and it helped to develop my incipient wanderlust. One of the places Halliburton wrote about was Petra, the ancient Nabatean capital in southern Jordan, which he, like everyone else, referred to as the "rose-red city half as old as time." (A stirring phrase, that, worthy of Ruskin or Wordsworth, but in fact the work of a feeble, long-forgotten nineteenth-century English poet named John William Burgon, who had never been there.)

Halliburton assured his readers that "in the years to come, when the memory of the other wonders you have seen has grown dim, you, too, will still recall clearly, as one of the truly magic moments of your life," the sight of Petra's majestic temples and tombs. I immediately resolved to get there as soon as possible, which turned out to be roughly forty years later.

Petra came into being because of geography. It lies in the great rift valley of which the Dead Sea and the Jordan River and the Sea of Galilee also form a part, a north-south trade route since time immemorial. It commands the only really convenient east-west pass through the mountains that blocked land communications between the ancient civilizations of the Nile and of the Tigris and Euphrates. It also had water, a precious commodity in that parched region.

Through Petra, in the centuries before the birth of Jesus, flowed the wealth of China and India and Egypt and Greece—gold, damask, pearls, spices, cotton, silk, myrrh, ivory. On each shipment, the peoples who lived there levied duty, and with the money thus earned they built their city, culminating in the stupendous Hellenistic monuments we see today. It was the Nabateans, a nomadic Arab tribe, who brought the city to its commercial and artistic peak, but of them we know regrettably little.

What we do know is that they were sculptors of the first order, capable of transforming, with simple tools, a pink rock face into a façade as tall as a ten-story building, adorned with graceful columns and wonderfully delicate garlands and flowers and friezes, and of carving out behind it a cubical hall forty feet on each side. This is the Treasury, the greatest of Petra's two-thousand-year-old buildings. It is the first one that the visitor sees, and so perfect that one wondered how the rest of the place could possibly avoid anticlimax.

I was not let down, nor were my wife and our traveling companions (although one of them, Mark Hampton, a New York interior designer and artist who knows about such things, assured me that most of Petra was not rose-red after all, but cinnamon-colored). After seven hours in that hidden valley—not only dramatic, not only romantic, not only beautiful, but also essentially unchanged since J. L. Burckhardt, an intrepid young Swiss disguised as an Arab, rediscovered it for the West in 1812—two of us found ourselves whistling, spontaneously and simultaneously, if comically, "When You Come to the End of a Perfect Day."

Of few places in the world would I dare to say that they would thrill any sane person, because I know people who hate London and Paris and even Venice, but I would say it about Petra. The world affords few travel experiences to rival the mile-long ride on horseback through the narrow defile called the Siq, the walls of rock rising two hundred feet and more above your head, shutting out the sky, the sound of the horses' footfalls echoing about you, until suddenly, when it seems that the end will never come, you round a last corner and see beyond the mouth of the defile, glowing in the morning sun, the crisp Classical profile of the grandiose Treasury, hewn from the living rock.

"There is a fierce and tragic quality in the scenery," Margaret Alice Murray wrote in her book on Petra forty-five years ago, "which seems to have inspired the hymns to Jehovah which abound in the Bible."

It is possible to visit Petra in a single day. Travel agencies in Amman send buses down the bleak Desert Highway early each morning—four boring hours each way, with less than two hours in Petra itself, which is not nearly enough. If you are going to take the trouble to travel as far as Jordan, take the trouble to rent a car in Amman and devote at least two days to the trip. That way you can take the far more interesting King's Highway south, following in the steps of the Roman emperor Trajan, visit Petra the next day, then head back up the Desert Highway at nightfall. Even better, spend three days, and use the third for a visit to Wadi Rum, the remote desert valley, filled with surrealistic rock formations of every conceivable hue, that T. E. Lawrence celebrated in *Seven Pillars of Wisdom*.

The whole journey can now be accomplished in the kind of comfort undreamed of only a dozen years ago. Both highways are now well paved and graded, and in 1983 a fine little hotel, the eighty-two-room Forum, opened in Wadi Musa, the village nearest Petra. Built in expertly dressed local stone by the Jordanian government and superbly managed by Britain's Grand Metropolitan group, it is an outpost of civilization crouching at the foot of the savage mountains, offering everything that the wandering sybarite could ask for—clean, bright rooms ($45 a night for a double) with well-stocked minibars; a big swimming pool; good meals, prepared by a German chef, including fresh seafood brought from Aqaba by truck (about $40 for two, including decent French wines) and even a quasi-discotheque inside a real Bedouin tent.

The best months to go are March and April, when it's not too hot, the crowds are still small and the fragrant oleanders are in bloom, but the fall is a good second choice. Take a hat, a wrap for the evening, binoculars, insect repellent and a pair of stout walking shoes. In Amman, at your hotel or at any good bookshop, you should buy Iain Browning's *Petra*, which is indispensable despite an intermittently banal style, and the wonderfully relaxed and informative *Antiquities of Jordan,* by G. Lankester Harding, one of the greatest of Palestinian archeologists.

One of the minor tragedies of the continuing strife in the Middle East is the inaccessibility of many of its outstanding archeological sites. Except for the occasional businessman, journalist or diplomat, Americans are effectively barred from Persepolis in Iran, Baghdad and Nineveh in Iraq, Palmyra and the Krak des Chevaliers in Syria, and Baalbek in Lebanon. At the moment, Jordan is one of the safest and most hospitable places in the entire region, eager to prove its virtues to Americans. It is prudent, however, if you are going there or anyplace else subject to political upheaval, to have your travel agent check conditions with the State Department or other informed sources at the last minute.

We left Amman at about 9:30 in the morning, taking a picnic, and headed southwest toward Madaba, about twenty miles away. Just at the edge of town, a spur road leads off to the right toward Mount Nebo, overlooking the Dead Sea, where Moses is thought to have sighted the Promised Land at last, just before his death. It is a barren site, but strangely stirring, like so many in the Holy Land, even for the irreligious.

The Madaba region was the home during the Byzantine period of a noted school of mosaic makers, and one of the finest of their works is on top of the mountain. Now sheltered by a building that looks like an aircraft hangar, it was the pavement of the north aisle of a basilica, from which part of the apse, several chapels and bits of columns also survive. It shows hunting scenes and other scenes of country life, perfectly preserved and full of vigor, with delicious portraits of animals—buffaloes and lions, boars and goats, zebras and dromedaries. There are other good mosaics at Mekhayyat, off to your right as you head back to Madaba on a well-posted road, and in Madaba itself. We particularly liked the sixth-century mosaic map of Palestine at St. George's Greek Orthodox Church in the town, which was shown to us by an old man whose explanation was incomprehensible but who charmed us by dropping our tip into the church's poor box.

From Madaba to Wadi Musa is 150 miles, a comfortable four-hour run. That leaves ample time for a visit to the rugged hilltop citadel of Kerak, built by the Crusaders under Payen le Bouteiller starting in 1142 and rebuilt by the great Arab general Saladin. From the upper court, there is a glorious view over the Dead Sea, and a sickening one down into the valley. Prisoners used to be flung over the sheer precipice, Harding says, with boxes tied securely around their heads so that they would remain conscious and suffer more. South of Kerak, you reach the awesome Wadi al Hasa, a vast dry gorge that marked the ancient boundary of the land of Moab. We ate our picnic on the north wall of the wadi at a spectacularly sited parking area; I don't know whether it was the setting or the cooking, but all hands agreed that the fried chicken (supplied by the Marriott Hotel in Amman) was world-class.

You should arrive at Wadi Musa just in time for the sunset. The next morning, it is only a short walk from the hotel down the hill to the visitors' center, where you buy your tickets and arrange to rent horses (about seven dollars a day each) for the ride into Petra. They are small, docile beasts, and young boys accompany you, holding the lead if you like. Try to start by about 9:00 in the morning so you will reach the Treasury around 10:00, when the sun is shining on it and it is at its most glorious. Down you go onto the trail, passing the Obelisk Tomb and large rectangular funerary monuments on your way to the dam across the mouth of the Siq, the gigantic cleft in the sandstone barrier that leads to the city; before the dam was built, flash floods poured through the defile, endangering anyone trapped there. Once inside the Siq, you can see carved decorations on the walls, which are sometimes only five or six feet apart.

When the final bend has been rounded, you catch a first glimpse of the Treasury—a single column with its Corinthian capital, part of the drum on the top, half of the split pediment. It is hard to believe, even after all the photographs, that it is real; it looks too much like something on a Hollywood back lot. But soon you are off your horse (it will be returned to you at the end of the day near the center of the city), looking up, stunned.

Turning then to the right, you pass a wall of cavelike houses, decorated with ziggurats and pyramids, and then the theater, with a slot that allowed a curtain to be raised and lowered. We sat halfway up, all alone except for a few optimistic goats looking for green shoots on the stage, and drank a bottle of wine we had brought along, just to steady ourselves.

A few steps more, and you come out into the main valley—bigger than expected, dusty, rocky, with only the oleanders and some scrub for relief. There is another surprise, or at least there was for us: up ahead was a Bedouin tent, over on the left a clothesline strung between a stumpy tree and a boulder. Petra is still home to 150 families. Their children cluster around, asking for ball-point pens, offering shards of pottery for sale, but not in the maddeningly insistent way of Egyptian children.

Off to the right lies a series of façades, each worthy of close inspection—the imposing Urn Tomb, high up on the hillside, once used as a Roman or Byzantine church; then, lower down, the Corinthian Tomb, so badly eroded that it looks like melting ice cream, with red and gray and blue and orange striations exposed in the rock, and the Palace Tomb, a broad building that is almost Baroque in its uninhibited handling of the Classical vocabulary.

Farther on is the less interesting, heavily ruined center of the old city, where one should nonetheless notice the ancient paving stones and the inscriptions on the ruins of the Temenos Gate, carved with medallions representing some of the gods of the caravans that brought Petra its wealth. Just beyond is the small museum, which houses fragments of sculpture and a few examples of the elegant, miraculously thin Nabatean pottery, orange with brown and black overglazes.

The Forum will pack a lunch for you, as elaborate as you like (one called the Grand Explorer costs $19 and includes, among other things, smoked salmon from Scotland, pâté and Danish pastries), but we had decided to eat in the new restaurant the Forum had opened near the museum. A handsome, low-lying building that blends perfectly into its surroundings, it has a sunny patio as well as immaculate toilets and everything else you wouldn't expect to find.

An assortment of appetizers, including minty *tabbouleh*, a kebab, drinks and coffee—all delicious—cost us about $12 a head.

Then on to the climax of the visit—the hour-long walk up past the Lion Gate to the largest of all the buildings in Petra: El Deir, the Monastery. Ancient steps cut into the rock and modern stairways make the going easier, and there are benches where you can rest, but it is stiff going all the same, not for those who fear heights nor for those with heart trouble or other infirmities.

The path twists upward through a heroic landscape, much greener than the valley floor, with cactuses and broom and gnarled cedars, past rocks that look like stalagmites. Sometimes the stone resembles petrified redwood. Alone, except for the slight whoosh of the wind, the buzzing of bees and the occasional bird call, we were exhilarated by the way the Nabateans had managed to impose order on nature without destroying it. Finally, puffing embarrassingly, we emerged into a meadow dominated by the huge façade of the Monastery (in fact, a tomb), tallowy in the golden afternoon sun under an improbably azure sky. It is simpler than the Treasury, modified Doric rather than Corinthian, but no less striking; a grown man can barely see over the sill under the front door, and the urn on the top is twenty-five feet high. It is the sort of thing that some German Romantic might have thought up, we decided; that inveterate traveler, Goethe, would have loved it, and so would that most melodramatic of painters, Caspar David Friedrich. We did, too.

The walk down took only thirty-five minutes, and a lot less energy. It ended perfectly. Just before we reached the bottom, we saw a herd of goats, sure-footedly standing on a steeply sloping rock. The old woman tending them snatched her scarf across her face when I approached, but not before I saw the blue tattoos around her eyes and nose, and she thrust out a grubby paw filled with what she hoped I would think were Nabatean coins.

R. W. Apple Jr. has been Chief Washington Correspondent of *The New York Times* since October, 1985. He has worked as a journalist for thirty years, first for the *Wall Street Journal*, then for NBC News, and since 1963 for *The Times*, which he has represented on five continents.

From 1977 to 1985, based in London, he wrote from all the major countries of Eastern and Western Europe not only about political, social and economic issues but also about travel, food and wine, music and art and architecture—subjects that have interested him since childhood. This is his first book.

Mr. Apple has won the George Polk Award and the Overseas Press Club awards for foreign correspondence. He is a founder member and director of the British Academy of Gastronomes and a member of the Confrerie des Chevaliers de Tastevin. He is married with two step-children and lives in Washington, D.C., and Lechlade, Gloucestershire, England.

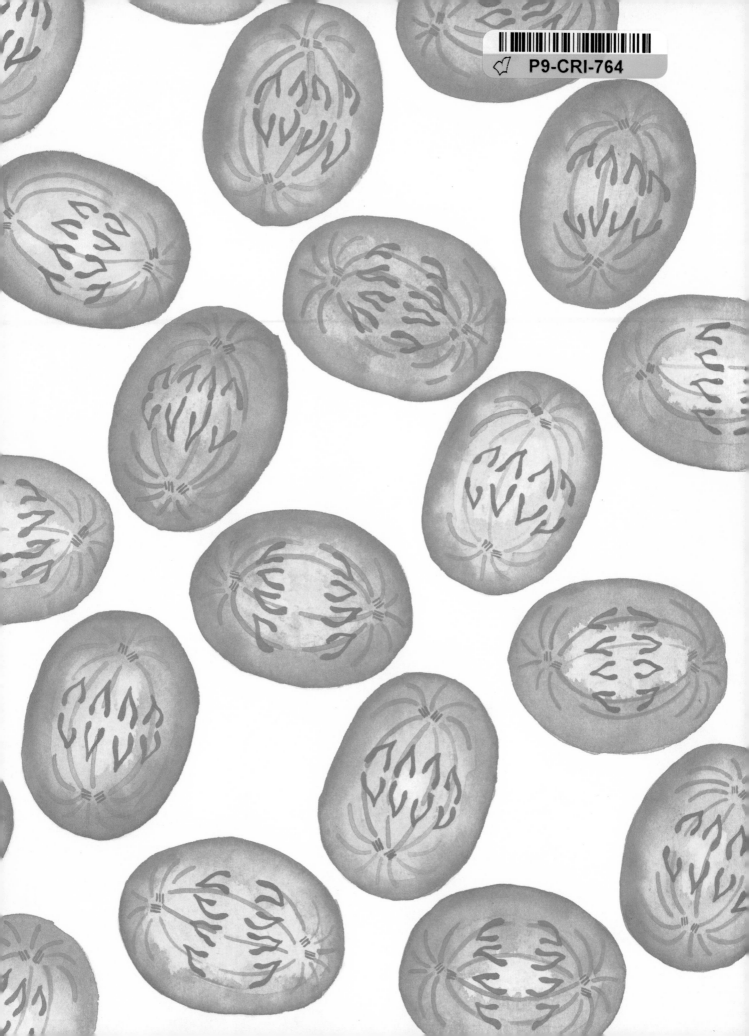

NURSE'S CLINICAL LIBRARY™
NEOPLASTIC DISORDERS

NURSING85 BOOKS™
SPRINGHOUSE CORPORATION
Springhouse, Pennsylvania

NURSING85 BOOKS™

Nurse's Clinical Library™
Other volumes in this series:
Cardiovascular Disorders
Respiratory Disorders
Endocrine Disorders
Neurologic Disorders
Renal and Urologic Disorders
Gastrointestinal Disorders
Immune Disorders

Nurse's Reference Library®
Diseases
Diagnostics
Drugs
Assessment
Procedures
Definitions
Practices
Emergencies

New Nursing Skillbook™ series
Giving Emergency Care
   Competently
Monitoring Fluid and
   Electrolytes Precisely
Assessing Vital Functions
   Accurately
Coping with Neurologic
   Problems Proficiently
Reading EKGs Correctly
Combatting Cardiovascular
   Diseases Skillfully
Nursing Critically Ill Patients
   Confidently
Dealing with Death and Dying
Managing Diabetes Properly
Giving Cardiovascular Drugs
   Safely

Nursing Photobook™ series
Providing Respiratory Care
Managing I.V. Therapy
Dealing with Emergencies
Giving Medications
Assessing Your Patients
Using Monitors
Providing Early Mobility
Giving Cardiac Care
Performing GI Procedures
Implementing Urologic
   Procedures
Controlling Infection
Ensuring Intensive Care
Coping with Neurologic
   Disorders
Caring for Surgical Patients
Working with Orthopedic
   Patients
Nursing Pediatric Patients
Helping Geriatric Patients
Attending Ob/Gyn Patients
Aiding Ambulatory Patients
Carrying Out Special
   Procedures

Nursing Now™ series
Shock
Hypertension
Drug Interactions
Cardiac Crises
Respiratory Emergencies
Pain

***Nursing85* Drug Handbook™**

Nurse's Clinical Library™
Editorial Director
Helen Klusek Hamilton

Clinical Director
Minnie Bowen Rose, RN, BSN, MEd

Art Director
Sonja E. Douglas

Clinical staff
Clinical Editor
Diane Cochet, RN, BSN

Drug Information Manager
Larry Neil Gever, RPh, PharmD

Contributing Clinical Editors
Nan Cameron, RN, BSN; Mary
Gyetvan, RN, BSEd; Sandra Ludwig
Nettina, RN, BSN; Janet Peterka,
RN, BSN, MBA

Acquisitions
Susan Hatch Brunt, Bernadette M.
Glenn

Editorial staff
Senior Editors
Nancy Holmes, Peter Johnson,
Patricia Minard Shinehouse

Managing Editor
Jill Lasker

Associate Editors
Lisa Z. Cohen, June Norris

Assistant Editor
Dorothy L. Tengler

Contributing Editors
Laura Albert, Barbara Hodgson,
Frederick Nohl, Joan Twisdom-Harty

Copy Supervisor
David R. Moreau

Copy Editors
Traci A. Deraco, Diane M. Labus, Jo
Lennon, Carolyn Mortimer, Doris
Weinstock

Production Coordinator
Sally Johnson

Editorial Assistants
Mary Ann Bowes, Maree DeRosa,
Caroline Swider

Design staff
Senior Designer
Matie Anne Patterson

Contributing Designers
Jacalyn Bove, Maryanne Buschini,
Peter Gerritsen, Christopher Laird

Illustrators
Maryanne Buschini, Jerry Cable,
Deborah Camero, David Christiana,
John Cymerman, Design
Management, Jean Gardner, Peter
Gerritsen, Carl Glassman, Robert
Jackson, Adam Mathews, Richard
Oden, George Retseck, Eileen
Rudnick, Dennis Schofield

Production staff
Art Production
Robert Perry (manager), Eileen
Hunsicker, Donald Knauss, Kate
Nichols, Sandra Sanders, Joan
Walsh, Robert Wieder

Typography
David C. Kosten (manager),
Amanda C. Erh, Ethel Halle, Diane
Paluba, Nancy Wirs

Manufacturing
Deborah C. Meiris, Wilbur D.
Davidson (managers), T.A. Landis

Special thanks to Matthew Cahill,
Vonda Heller, Thomas J. Leibrandt,
Diana Odell Potter, and Elaine
Shelly, who assisted in preparation
of this volume.

NCL7-010385

Library of Congress Cataloging in Publication Data

Main entry under title:
Neoplastic disorders.
   (Nurse's clinical library)
   "Nursing85 books."
   Includes bibliographies and index.
1. Cancer. 2. Cancer—Nursing.
I. Series. [DNLM: 1. Neoplasms—
physiopathology—nurses' instruction.
2. Neoplasms—therapy—nurses'
instruction.   QZ 200 N4395]
RC262.N46 1985   616.99′4   84-23627
ISBN 0-916730-73-5

Cover: Color-enhanced mammogram.
Photograph by Howard Sochurek.

Inside front and back covers: Anaphase
stage of cell division.

CONTENTS

CONTRIBUTORS AND CLINICAL CONSULTANTS

Contributors

At the time of publication, the contributors held the following positions:

Nancy Burns, RN, PhD, Associate Professor, School of Nursing, University of Texas at Arlington

Susan Copley Cobb, RN, CS, MSN, Staff Development Instructor, Hospital of the University of Pennsylvania, Philadelphia

Susan Dempsey, RN, MSN, Oncology Clinical Nurse Specialist, Visiting Nurse Association of Northern Virginia, Arlington

Marianne Dietrick-Gallagher, RN, CS, MSN, Chemotherapy Clinical Specialist, Hospital of the University of Pennsylvania, Philadelphia

Kathleen A. Dietz, RN, MA, MS, Hematology Nurse Clinician, Memorial Sloan-Kettering Cancer Center, New York

Jo Ann Huang Eriksson, RN, MS, Practitioner/Teacher, Rush–Presbyterian–St. Luke's Medical Center, Chicago

Sherry P. Greifzu, RN, Head Nurse, Medical Oncology, St. Raphael's Hospital, New Haven, Conn.

Priscilla Houck, RN, MSN, Oncology Clinical Specialist, Philadelphia Hematology/Oncology Associates

Anita Johnston-Early, RN, BSN, Staff Nurse and Protocol Coordinator, Oncology Section, Veterans Administration Medical Center, Washington, D.C.

Brenda Marion Nevidjon, RN, MSN, Director of Nursing, Cancer Control Agency of British Columbia, Vancouver

Peggy Plunkett, RN, MSN, Psychiatric Liaison Nurse, Mary Hitchcock Memorial Hospital, Hanover, N.H.

Nancy J. Ross Gregorcic, RN, Orthopedic Oncology Nurse Clinician, Cleveland Clinic Foundation

Dale Elizabeth Schreffler, RN, BSN, Staff Nurse, Mohs and Laser Surgery Division, Department of Dermatology, Cleveland Clinic Foundation

Regina M. Shannon, RN, BSN, MS, Graduate Student, Medical-Surgical Program, Oncology Tract, Yale University School of Nursing, New Haven, Conn.

Paula S. Vannicola, RN, MS, Oncology Clinical Nurse Specialist, University Hospital, Boston University Medical Center

Ronald G. Wheeland, MD, Staff Physician, Section of Mohs' Histographic Surgery and Oncology, Department of Dermatology, Cleveland Clinic Foundation

Rita Wickham, RN, MS, Practitioner/Teacher; Oncology Clinical Nurse Specialist; Joint Practice, Medical Oncology; Instructor, Rush College of Nursing, Rush–Presbyterian–St. Luke's Medical Center, Chicago

Lyn Cain Zehner, RN, MN, Oncology Clinical Nurse Specialist, Alexandria (Va.) Hospital

Clinical Consultants

At the time of publication, the clinical consultants held the following positions:

Francis C. Au, MD, Associate Professor of Surgery, Temple University Hospital, Philadelphia

Rita S. Axelrod, MD, Assistant Professor of Medicine, Section of Hematology/Oncology, Temple University School of Medicine, Philadelphia

Ron Ballentine, RPh, PharmD, Associate Professor and Chairman, Department of Clinical Pharmacy and Administration, University of Houston

Robert M. Barone, MD, FACS, Associate Clinical Professor of Surgery, University of California School of Medicine, San Diego; Surgical Oncologist, Oncology Associates of San Diego

A. Bruce Campbell, MD, PhD, Attending Physician, Scripps Memorial Hospital, La Jolla, Calif.

Leon E. Clarke, MD, Assistant Professor of Surgery, Medical College of Pennsylvania, Philadelphia

Susan Corbett, RN, Dermatology Nurse, Skin and Cancer Hospital, Philadelphia

Leonard V. Crowley, MD, Clinical Assistant Professor, Department of Laboratory Medicine and Pathology and Department of Family Practice, University of Minnesota Medical School, Minneapolis; Pathologist, St. Mary's Hospital, Minneapolis

Jane Murray Fall, RN, MSN, Oncology Clinical Nurse Specialist, St. Luke's Hospital, Bethlehem, Pa.

Anne Marie Flaherty, RN, BSN, Administrative Nurse Clinician, Adult Day Hospital, Memorial Sloan-Kettering Cancer Center, New York

Catherine Rice Gorrell, RN, MSN, Clinical Nurse Specialist, Cancer Nursing Service, Clinical Center, National Institutes of Health, Bethesda, Md.

Mark R. Green, MD, Professor of Medicine, University of California, San Diego

Richard Evan Greenberg, MD, Assistant Clinical Professor of Urology, Temple University School of Medicine, Philadelphia

Robert D. Harwick, MD, Professor of Surgery and Director of Head and Neck Tumor Clinic, Temple University Hospital, Philadelphia

Anita Johnston-Early, BSN, Oncology Nurse Investigator and Protocol Coordinator, Oncology Section, Veterans Administration Medical Center, Washington, D.C.

Rosaline R. Joseph, MD, Professor of Medicine and Director, Department of Hematology/Oncology, Medical College of Pennsylvania, Philadelphia

Constance S. Kirkpatrick, RN, BA, MS, Assistant Professor, School of Nursing, Pacific Lutheran University, Tacoma, Wash.

Julena Lind, RN, MN, Director of Education, California Hospital Center for Health Education and Research, Los Angeles

Nancy C. Lovejoy, DSN, Assistant Professor, Department of Physiological Nursing, University of California, San Francisco

Terry Mass, RN, MSN, Oncology Nursing Coordinator, Mount Sinai Medical Center, New York

Carolyn Pratt McCarthy, RN, BSN, Radiation Oncology Nurse Clinician, Dartmouth-Hitchcock Medical Center, Hanover, N.H.

Marnie McHale, RN, MS, Assistant Unit Leader, Rush–Presbyterian–St. Luke's Medical Center, Chicago

Gwendolyn Mercer, RN, MS, Clinical Resource Nurse Consultant, Clinical Resource Division, Mount Sinai Medical Center, New York

Robin Miller, MD, Special Fellow, Department of Hematology and Medical Oncology, Cleveland Clinic Foundation

Rose M. Mohr, MD, FACS, Associate Professor of Otorhinology/Bronchoesophagology; Director, Chevalier Jackson Clinic, Temple University Health Sciences Center, Philadelphia

Joseph D. Purvis, III, MD, Staff Physician, Department of Hematology and Medical Oncology, Cleveland Clinic Foundation

Pamela M. Rowe, RN, BSN, MEd, Assistant Director for Nursing Education, Dartmouth-Hitchcock Medical Center, Hanover, N.H.

Carol A. Sheridan, RN, C, MSN, Oncology Clinical Nurse Specialist, Moses Division, Montefiore Medical Center, New York

John H. West, MD, FACP, Private Practice, Hematology and Medical Oncology, Savannah (Ga.) Hematology Associates; Investigator, Piedmont Oncology Association, Winston-Salem, N.C.; Clinical Assistant Professor of Medicine, Medical College of Georgia, Augusta

Peter H. Wiernik, MD, Gutman Professor and Chairman, Department of Oncology, Albert Einstein College of Medicine, Montefiore Medical Center, New York

Morton C. Wilhelm, MD, FACS, Professor of Surgery, Division of Oncology; Assistant Clinical Director, Cancer Center, University of Virginia Medical Center, Charlottesville

Walter G. Wolfe, MD, Professor of Surgery, Duke University Medical Center, Durham, N.C.

FOREWORD

Whether or not you specialize in oncology nursing, recent advances in cancer diagnosis and treatment mean, to put it simply, more effort on your part. More caring and understanding. And more learning. The knowledge required of oncology nurses is broad and transcends the traditional areas of medical-surgical nursing and psychiatric–mental health nursing. It spans clinical settings, from intensive care to community health and from pediatrics to gerontology. Originally hospital-based, oncology nursing is now moving rapidly into the community. Chemotherapy is being administered in the patient's home by the nurse, and home health care is now an option during cancer therapy for many patients. The clinical skills required for effective oncology nursing call for a brand of sophistication that places such practice on the growing edge of the profession. You'll be challenged to constantly update your knowledge and skills to meet the increasingly complex needs of cancer patients and their families and to participate actively in the growing movement toward cancer prevention and early detection.

In addition to specific nursing skills, you'll need to know about prevention, pathophysiology, diagnosis, medical therapy, family dynamics, teaching strategies, counseling, and thanatology. These varied needs are addressed in NEOPLASTIC DISORDERS, a volume in a new reference series for nurses. It supplies both theoretical and practical information about oncology nursing today.

An introductory section, *Fundamental facts,* reviews the anatomy and physiology of normal and cancerous cells, risk factors, tumor growth and spread, grading and staging, and the nurse's role in cancer prevention. It also includes chapters on patient assessment and the latest diagnostic tests, including magnetic resonance imaging (MRI) and hormone receptor assays.

The next section, *Management strategies,* deals with the principles of cancer therapy, including discussions of new treatments, such as bone marrow transplantation and use of interferon and monoclonal antibodies; managing the effects of therapy and symptoms; and—an important feature—managing the psychosocial aspects of cancer for the patient, his family, and the care giver.

The third and last section consisting of seven chapters, *Malignant disorders,* deals with specific neoplastic disorders. Each chapter consists of three major divisions. *Pathophysiology* presents the origins of each disorder (when these are known), distinguishing signs and symptoms, and effects on adjacent body systems. *Medical management* summarizes appropriate diagnostic tests and findings, current treatment, and prognosis. *Nursing management* provides detailed information for assessment, planning, and appropriate interventions, presented according to the nursing process.

This volume is well supplied throughout with useful anatomic drawings, illustrations, charts, and diagrams—many in full color—that clarify and augment the text. Special graphic devices call attention to TNM staging schemes; to patient-teaching aids, such as postmastectomy strengthening exercises; and to emergency management, such as recognizing and treating spinal cord compression. Three appendices add information about rare tumors, oncologic emergencies, and chemotherapeutic agents.

Because oncology nursing is changing so rapidly, you're challenged to keep up with the latest theory and practice. This volume will help you master and organize the available knowledge into a framework for meeting your cancer patients' needs more effectively.

NANCY BURNS, RN, PhD
Associate Professor,
School of Nursing,
University of Texas at Arlington

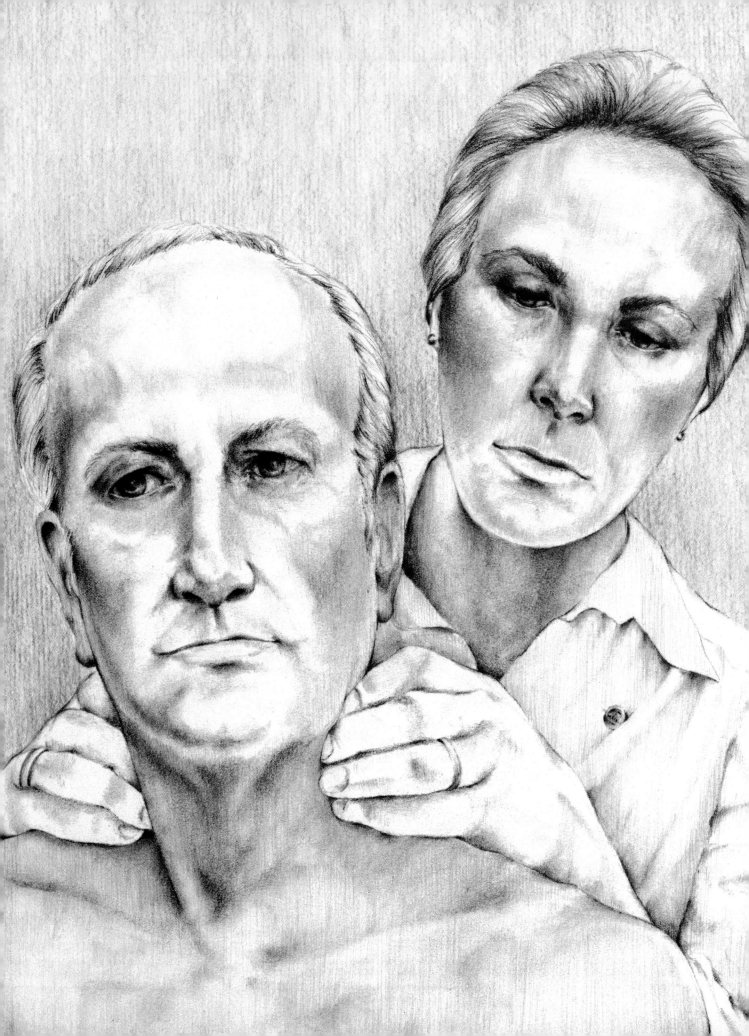

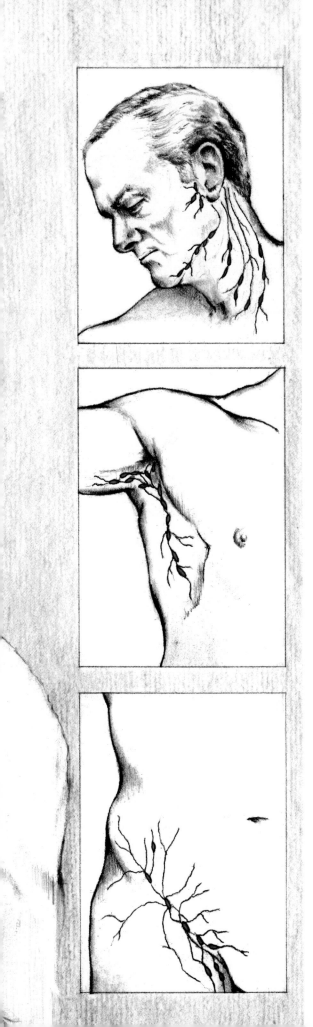

FUNDAMENTAL FACTS

1 REVIEWING FUNDAMENTAL PRINCIPLES

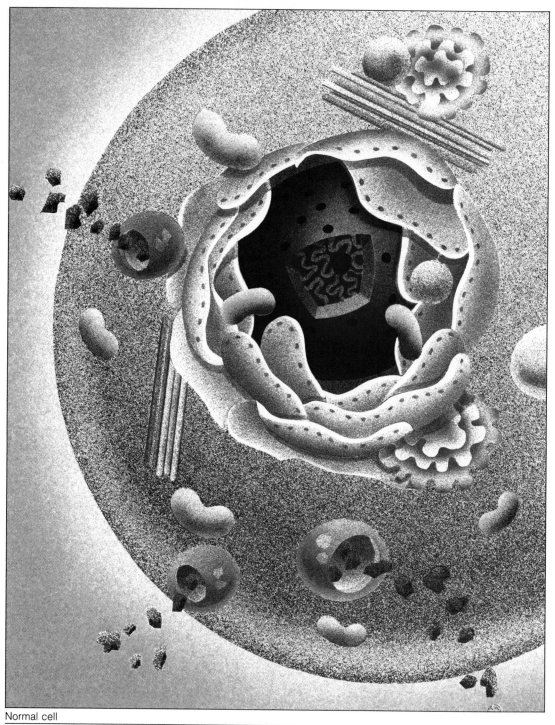

Normal cell

Ask any group of people—nurses or laypersons alike—to say the first word they think of when they hear the word *cancer*. You'll get responses like: *Death. Pain. Fear. Loss.* Few disorders inspire such strong feelings as does cancer. Until about 20 years ago, most people believed cancer was incurable. But recent advances in diagnosis and treatment, coupled with growing numbers of patients considered cured, are beginning to turn this public perception around.

As a nurse, you're a vital part of the battle against cancer. Whatever your professional level and sphere of practice, your responsibilities encompass prevention, detection, and rehabilitation. If you're like most nurses, you contribute most during the curative, rehabilitative, and terminal phases of the disorder. No matter which treatment is used against cancer—surgery, chemotherapy, radiation, hormonal therapy, immunotherapy, or combinations of these—you may be involved, whether in administering chemotherapeutic agents and treating their side effects or in teaching a patient with a laryngectomy how to maintain an open airway.

You'll also be providing psychological support. To accomplish this, you should be able to see your patient as a whole person who happens to have cancer. You can help him and his family to cope with the changes in their lives resulting from the disease and its treatment, and you can help the patient plan realistic goals.

To successfully meet these nursing challenges, you'll need to understand how normal and cancerous cells grow and develop and how tumors can establish themselves and spread in the body.

SOME CAUSE FOR OPTIMISM

Cancer is second only to cardiovascular disease as the leading cause of death in the United States, resulting in some 450,000 deaths annually. If present incidence rates continue, the American Cancer Society (ACS) estimates that about 67 million Americans now living will eventually have some form of cancer and that cancer will strike three out of four American families.

The age-adjusted cancer death rate has been steadily rising. From 1930 to 1980, according to the ACS, this rate rose from 143 to 169 per 100,000. The upward trend results mainly from lung cancer. (The age-adjusted rate results from a statistical method that assumes the same age distribution among the different groups being compared.)

The cancer picture isn't unrelievedly gloomy, however. Death rates for other major cancers are leveling off or declining. In fact, about 5 million Americans with a history of cancer are alive today, and 3 million of these were diagnosed 5 or more years ago. The relative survival rate, or the proportion of people alive 5 years after the initial cancer diagnosis, is now about 48%. This rate is bound to increase with improved diagnostic techniques and more effective treatments.

WHAT IS CANCER?

Cancer is defined as a "malignant neoplasm." The word *neoplasm* means "new growth," and a neoplasm is the mass of tissue (a tumor) resulting from this growth. About 100 neoplastic disorders have been identified.

Malignant tumors are conveniently classified according to their histologic origin. Those derived from epithelial tissues are called *carcinomas;* those arising from connective, muscle, or osseous tissue are *sarcomas;* and those from lymphatic or hematopoietic tissue are *lymphomas, leukemias,* or *myelomas.* The study of malignant neoplasms is *oncology.*

Neoplastic cells differ from normal cells in structure—they have altered morphology and biochemical properties, changes in chromosome structure, and loss of normal external growth controls—and in function, as they serve no useful purpose. The most characteristic difference, however, is the malignant cells' ability to grow and spread throughout the body from the primary site to other tissues and to establish secondary foci called *metastases.* Malignant cells can metastasize by the bloodstream or the lymphatics, by accidental transport or transfer from one site to another during surgery, and by local extension.

RISK FACTORS: INTERNAL AND EXTERNAL

Although cancer can strike anyone, it is predominantly a disease of older adults; its incidence rises geometrically with age.

Internal risk factors

Age, however, is but one of several *endogenous* (internal) *risk factors* that have predictive value in estimating an individual's cancer risk.

Other endogenous risk factors are sexual, racial, hereditary/genetic, immunologic, and psychological.

Sexual factors. Females between the ages of

20 and 40 are three times more likely to develop cancer than men. However, after age 50, men are more likely to develop cancer. The overall death rate is higher for men than for women. In females, the most common cancers are those of the breast, colon, and uterus; in males, cancers of the lung, GI tract, prostate, and bladder.

Racial factors. The incidence of cancer and its associated mortality are greater in blacks as a result of economic, social, and environmental factors that tend to prevent early detection and increase the risk of exposure to industrial carcinogens.

Hereditary/genetic factors. Certain cancers are familial. For example, a woman who has first-degree relatives (daughters or sisters) with breast cancer has a greater risk than the general female population of developing it herself. This tendency may result from common genes, environmental factors, or both.

Certain genetic disorders may predispose the individual to cancer. For example, Down's or Klinefelter's syndromes predispose to leukemia.

Immunologic factors. The immune response may play a role in regulating the development and growth of some tumors. The "immune surveillance" hypothesis states that antigenic differences between normal and neoplastic cells may be an important mechanism allowing the body to eliminate transformed (malignant) cells. From this, some infer that suppressing the immune system may increase susceptibility to cancer. The immune response apparently varies from one type of tumor to another, suppressing metastasis in some but permitting or allowing it in others.

Psychological factors. Emotional stress may increase the patient's cancer risk by leading to poor health habits, such as frequent smoking; by depressing the immune system; or by leading him to ignore early warning symptoms.

External factors
Exogenous (external) *risk factors* include exposure to chemical carcinogens, radiation, or viruses; diet; and use of tobacco and alcohol.

Chemical carcinogens. The most important exogenous risk factor is exposure to a wide range of carcinogens. These agents may exist in the workplace, as from nickel refining; in certain drugs, such as diethylstilbestrol; and in the air, as from asbestos dust.

Researchers believe that chemical carcinogens may cause cancer in a two-step process:

initiation and promotion. *Initiation* consists of exposure to the carcinogen; this irreversible step converts normal cells into latent tumor cells. In *promotion,* repeated exposure to the same or some other substance stimulates the latent cells to active neoplasia.

Potential carcinogens are tested for mutagenic potency (ability to induce mutations). Studies have shown that most carcinogens are also mutagens. However, mutagenesis is not the only carcinogenic mechanism.

Radiation. Ionizing radiations of all kinds are carcinogenic, although their potencies vary. Such radiation includes X-rays as well as nuclear radiation. The exact mechanism of radioactive carcinogenicity is unknown. Fairskinned people are more at risk for skin cancer caused by ultraviolet radiation. The malignancy develops on exposed extremities, and its incidence correlates with the amount of exposure.

Viruses. Through studies of tumors of laboratory animals, some human viruses have been shown to have carcinogenic potential, particularly the Epstein-Barr virus, which has been linked with lymphoma and nasopharyngeal carcinoma. DNA viruses (such as herpes simplex, type 2) have been associated with cancer of the uterine cervix; RNA viruses, with breast cancer in mice. These viruses are thought to exert their oncogenic (tumor-inducing) effects by integrating their genetic information into the chromosomes of infected host cells. According to the *oncogene theory,* the genetic material of oncogenic viruses is present in the normal gene pool of all vertebrates and is transmitted from one generation to the next. This oncogene is normally repressed. It is activated, or derepressed, under certain conditions, such as aging or exposure to radiation or chemical carcinogens. (See *The oncogene: A molecular basis for cancer?* pages 12 and 13.) Another theory proposes that a virus may be transmitted vertically, from mother to child (via cells in utero or via semen or breast milk), or horizontally, from one person to another. The virus then integrates its genetic material with that of the host cell, remaining dormant until activated by the appropriate stimulus.

Diet. Dietary and nutritional factors may also increase the risk of cancer. Certain foods may supply carcinogens (or precarcinogens), affect formation of carcinogens, or modify the effects of other carcinogens. Diet has been implicated in the development of colon cancer, *(continued on page 14)*

Inside the normal cell

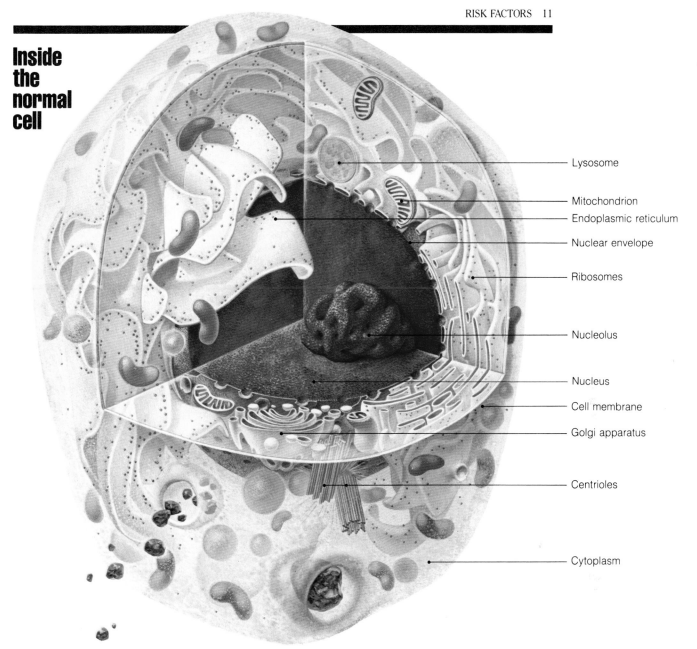

Lysosome

Mitochondrion

Endoplasmic reticulum

Nuclear envelope

Ribosomes

Nucleolus

Nucleus

Cell membrane

Golgi apparatus

Centrioles

Cytoplasm

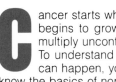

ancer starts when a cell begins to grow and multiply uncontrollably. To understand how this can happen, you should know the basics of normal cellular anatomy.

The *cell membrane* is composed mostly of proteins and lipids. Proteins and other substances embedded in the cell membrane interact to affect cell function.

The cell's interior is divided into two main components, the *nucleus* and the *cytoplasm*. The nucleus contains the cell's DNA, as well as one or more *nucleoli* composed of RNA. The cytoplasm contains many smaller structures, collectively termed "organelles," such as the endoplasmic reticulum, ribosomes, mitochondria, lysosomes, Golgi apparatus, and centrioles.

The *endoplasmic reticulum* is a network of interconnected sacs and canals, forming a miniature circulatory system that moves proteins and enzymes throughout the cytoplasm. Portions of the endoplasmic reticulum are studded with granules, or *ribosomes*, which synthesize proteins. The smooth endoplasmic reticulum, which lacks ribosomes, functions in lipid and steroid metabolism.

Mitochondria, plentiful in most cells, contain enzymes that oxidize nutrients and synthesize adenosine triphosphate (ATP).

ATP is used throughout the cell as its primary energy source.

Lysosomes are small vesicles, surrounded by a protective membrane, containing enzymes that break down engulfed particles into smaller molecules.

The *Golgi apparatus*, another sacculated structure, receives protein from the granular endoplasmic reticulum, bonds carbohydrates to proteins, and assists with cell membrane assembly.

Centrioles are small, cylindrical structures that play an important part in cell division. Each cell has two pairs of centrioles, which migrate to opposite ends of the cell during mitosis.

The oncogene: A molecular basis for cancer?

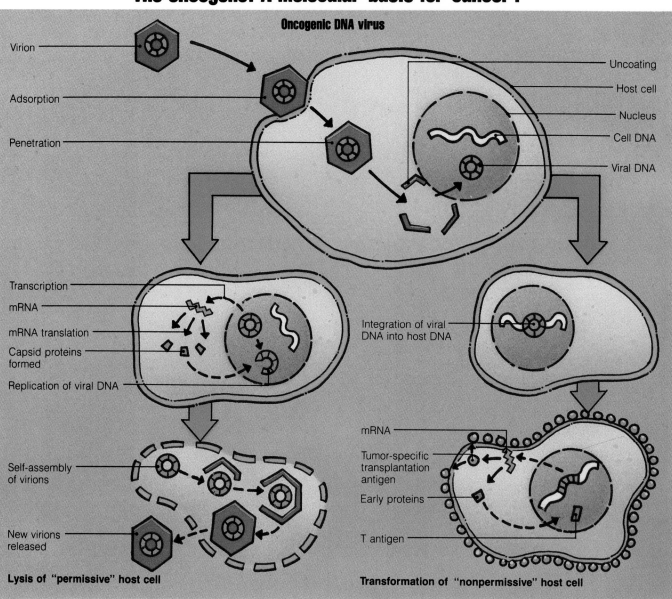

Oncogenic DNA virus

Virion

Adsorption

Penetration

Uncoating

Host cell

Nucleus

Cell DNA

Viral DNA

Transcription

mRNA

mRNA translation

Capsid proteins formed

Replication of viral DNA

Integration of viral DNA into host DNA

Self-assembly of virions

New virions released

mRNA

Tumor-specific transplantation antigen

Early proteins

T antigen

Lysis of "permissive" host cell

Transformation of "nonpermissive" host cell

Cancer genes, called *oncogenes,* have been found in the chromosomes of tumor cells. They are altered versions of normal genes. About 20 different oncogenes have so far been identified, although none have yet been demonstrated in humans. Oncogenes exist in normal cells in a repressed state, when they're known as *protooncogenes.* They may be derepressed by many factors, including certain viral infections; genetic accidents, such as abnormal gene transpositions in chromosomes; chemical carcinogens; or radia-

tion. When activated, the oncogenes interfere with normal gene expression, causing the cell to become malignant.

Sometimes a cellular protooncogene may be incorporated into an invading virus during an infection. When a protooncogene is picked up by a virus, it becomes a part of the viral genetic material but remains repressed. However, when this virus infects another host cell, the viral protooncogene may be activated when the virus takes over the host cell's functions. Once released into the host cell, this activated viral oncogene induces malignancy. On-

cogenic viruses consist of one or more molecules of DNA or RNA. Each induces different cellular effects as shown.
Oncogenic DNA. *Oncogenic DNA viruses* can affect host cells in two ways, depending on whether the host cells are permissive or nonpermissive for infection.

Initially, as an oncogenic DNA virus approaches a host cell, it is adsorbed to the cell membrane; it then penetrates the cell and loses its coating upon reaching the nuclear membrane. If the host cell is *permissive,* replication and transcription of viral DNA takes place to form messenger RNA (mRNA). Trans-

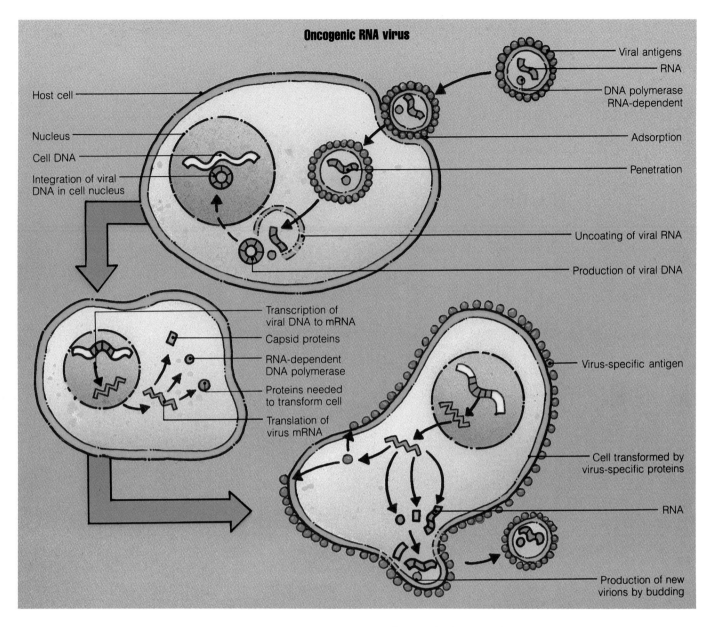

Oncogenic RNA virus

- Host cell
- Nucleus
- Cell DNA
- Integration of viral DNA in cell nucleus
- Viral antigens
- RNA
- DNA polymerase RNA-dependent
- Adsorption
- Penetration
- Uncoating of viral RNA
- Production of viral DNA
- Transcription of viral DNA to mRNA
- Capsid proteins
- RNA-dependent DNA polymerase
- Proteins needed to transform cell
- Translation of virus mRNA
- Virus-specific antigen
- Cell transformed by virus-specific proteins
- RNA
- Production of new virions by budding

lation of mRNA causes the cell to manufacture viral capsid and other proteins. Finally, the oncogenic virus assembles in the host cell nucleus, and the host cell dies, releasing new virions.

If the host cell is *nonpermissive,* the viral DNA integrates into the host cell's DNA. After uncoating, no new viral DNA, capsid proteins, or new virions are produced, and the host cell doesn't die. However, the viral DNA is integrated into the host genome, transforms the cell, and is replicated with subsequent host-cell division. The new genome alters properties of the

host cell, making it a cancer cell. In transformed cells, a *virus-specific tumor antigen* called a "T antigen" is produced and is thought to stimulate DNA synthesis. A *tumor-specific transplantation antigen* (not found in the virus itself) is also produced on the cell surface; it may be responsible for immunospecific rejection of a transplanted tumor by a host animal.
Oncogenic RNA. *Oncogenic RNA viruses* cause cancer by simultaneously transforming host cells replicating themselves. These viruses contain an RNA-dependent DNA polymerase (reverse transcriptase), which

allows a DNA copy of the viral genome to be made. After penetrating the host cell, the oncogenic RNA virus produces its own DNA, which becomes integrated into the host cell's DNA. Then, transcription of DNA to mRNA and translation of mRNA to capsid protein, RNA-dependent DNA polymerase, virus-specific tumor antigens and other proteins take place. The host cell is actually transformed by virus-specific antigens produced on its cell wall. New RNA virions are assembled within the transformed host cell and these are continually shed by budding.

How cancer develops and spreads

This drawing of magnified lung tissue shows how cancer develops and spreads.

Once lung tumor cells grow through the basement membrane of the bronchial epithelium, they spread locally, regionally, and metastatically.

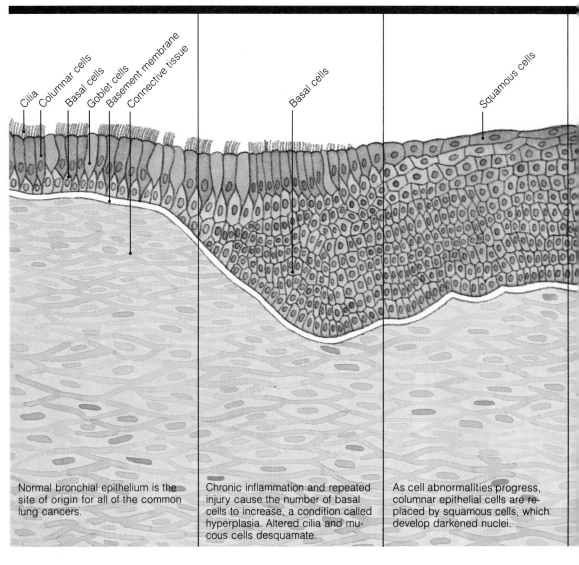

Cilia Columnar cells Basal cells Goblet cells Basement membrane Connective tissue Basal cells Squamous cells

Normal bronchial epithelium is the site of origin for all of the common lung cancers.

Chronic inflammation and repeated injury cause the number of basal cells to increase, a condition called hyperplasia. Altered cilia and mucous cells desquamate.

As cell abnormalities progress, columnar epithelial cells are replaced by squamous cells, which develop darkened nuclei.

which may result from excessive consumption of proteins and fats. Liver tumors may result from food additives such as nitrates (commonly used in smoked and processed meat) and aflatoxin (a fungus that grows on stored grains, nuts, and other foodstuffs).

Cigarettes and alcohol. Lung cancer is the leading cancer in men and is becoming more common in women, too. Cigarette smoking accounts for about 30% of all cancers, and it's implicated in cancers of the mouth, pharynx, larynx, esophagus, pancreas, and bladder. Pipe smoking is associated with lip cancer. In recent years, the risks associated with inhalation of "secondhand" smoke by nonsmokers have become a public concern, but studies have so far produced contradictory results.

Alcohol may act synergistically with tobacco; smokers who drink heavily run an increased risk of head, neck, and esophageal cancers. Heavy beer consumption may increase the risk of colorectal cancers, but the mechanism involved is not known.

Chemotherapeutic agents. Certain agents, such as hormones and anticancer drugs, may themselves be carcinogenic. Some anticancer agents may be directly carcinogenic or may enhance neoplastic development by suppressing the immune system. By altering the body's normal endocrine balance, hormones may contribute to, rather than directly stimulate, neoplastic development, especially in endocrine-sensitive organs such as the breast and prostate. The risk of secondary malignancies due to these agents must be weighed carefully against their benefits.

PATHOPHYSIOLOGY

Uncontrolled cancer cells eventually kill because they compete with normal cells for nutrients and interfere with normal bodily functions. But what makes a normal cell turn cancerous? One way or another, all cancer risk factors affect the normal cell's genetic material, interfering with the normal replication of the genes before cell division (mitosis)

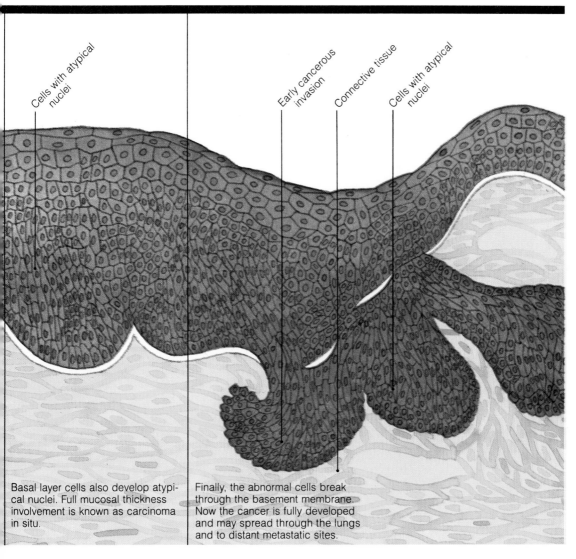

Cells with atypical nuclei

Early cancerous invasion

Connective tissue

Cells with atypical nuclei

Basal layer cells also develop atypical nuclei. Full mucosal thickness involvement is known as carcinoma in situ.

Finally, the abnormal cells break through the basement membrane. Now the cancer is fully developed and may spread through the lungs and to distant metastatic sites.

takes place. Thereby, cancer risk factors enhance the possibility of *mutation*—an abnormal change in some portion of the normal cell's gene complement.

Actually, normal cells may undergo mutation at any time, even without the influence of a carcinogen. If any mistakes in gene replication occur (a misplaced gene, for example), they're usually repaired during the complex process of DNA replication. However, despite this built-in safeguard, perhaps 1 cell in 100,000 may retain a mutant gene. Cancer risk factors may enhance this mutation rate.

The normal cell

The body is made up of about 75 trillion cells, most of which are constantly reproducing to replace dead cells, to repair damaged tissues, and to pursue orderly growth. However much normal cells differ in their assigned roles in the body, they all share these characteristics: they require similar nutrients; they need oxygen for energy; they carry out metabolism

and excretion; and they undergo a reproductive process.

Parts of a cell. Important structural components of the cell include the cell membrane, cytoplasm, organelles, and nucleus. (See *Inside the normal cell,* page 11.) The *cell membrane* encloses the cellular contents (cytoplasm and nucleus) and serves as a selective barrier between molecules inside and outside the cell. Receptor sites on the cell membrane bind exogenous proteins that stimulate specific cellular activities.

The *cytoplasm* comprises the cellular contents, excluding the nucleus. It gives the cell its shape and transports substances to and from various parts of the cell via a network of microtubules. The cytoplasm contains particles such as fat globules and secretory granules, as well as important intracellular structures called *organelles.* These are specialized subcellular structures that are highly organized to perform particular functions within the cell. They include the *endoplasmic reticu-*

Mitosis: How cells divide

Most body cells reproduce themselves by *mitosis*, in which one cell divides into two daughter cells, each having the same number of chromosomes as the parent cell. As shown here, mitosis consists of four major stages.

In *prophase*, the centrioles move to opposite ends of the cell; the spindle begins to form; chromatin material organizes into chromosomes; the nuclear membrane dissolves; and the spindle fibers attach to the chromosomes.

In *metaphase*, the chromosomes line up along the center of the spindle.

In *anaphase*, growth of the spindle fibers pulls the chromosome pairs apart, toward opposite poles of the cell.

In *telophase*, the chromosome pairs are completely separated; a new nuclear membrane forms around each set of chromosomes; the spindle dissolves; and the cell pinches into two.

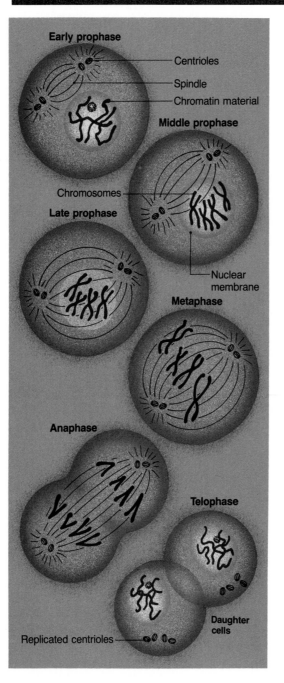

Early prophase — Centrioles
— Spindle
— Chromatin material

Middle prophase

Chromosomes —

Late prophase

— Nuclear membrane

Metaphase

Anaphase

Telophase

Replicated centrioles —

Daughter cells

lum; ribosomes; mitochondria; lysosomes; Golgi apparatus; and centrioles.

The *nucleus* is the cellular control center, containing the cell's genetic material (DNA) and regulating metabolism and cell reproduction. The nucleus also contains one or more smaller *nucleoli,* composed of RNA, which are involved in genetic transcription and ribosome production.

The cell cycle. Most normal cells have the ability to reproduce and do so in an orderly sequence by mitosis. (See *Mitosis: How cells divide.*) But mitosis is only one part of a continuum of biochemical and morphological changes known as the *cell cycle.* For conve-

nience, this cycle is divided into five major phases. Phase G_1 represents the gap between mitosis and DNA synthesis; phase G_0 is a temporary resting phase, during which the cell may or may not continue to proliferate; phase S involves DNA synthesis in preparation for the next cell division; phase G_2 is the gap between the S phase and mitosis; and phase M is mitosis. The point at which the cell "decides" to proliferate or undergo G_0 is called the restriction point (R). If the cell enters G_0, a complex series of events is required before the cell can reenter the cycle. A cell may also be stimulated to leave the cycle entirely and undergo differentiation. Such a cell does not replicate but functions in some other highly specialized manner. (See Chapter 4.)

Environmental factors may affect cell growth and reproduction, although the actual mechanisms involved are not well understood. Depletion of nutrients or accumulated wastes can inhibit normal cell growth and reproduction. A phenomenon known as "contact inhibition" inhibits replication when the number of cells have reached a critical level and "crowding" exists. Recent studies suggest that hypothetical control substances called *chalones* may be secreted by cells and may exert a feedback effect to slow or stop mitosis.

The growth fraction. Only a limited percentage of the body's cells are reproducing at a given time. The proportion of dividing to nondividing cells is called the growth fraction. The net gain of cells (tissue growth) depends on this finely tuned balance between cellular birth and death. Some types of tissue cells are replaced rapidly in the event of a sudden loss; for example, when part of the liver is surgically removed, cell growth and reproduction rates increase until liver mass returns almost to normal.

The cancerous cell

Normal cells can respond to environmental cues that tell them when it's appropriate to grow or differentiate. Cancer cells, because of their altered genetic makeup, cannot.

Cancer cells differ from normal cells in two major respects: they ignore normal growth limitations, possibly because they may not secrete chalones thought to enforce growth limits on normal cells; and their cell walls are less adhesive, which allows them to migrate through the tissues, bloodstream, and lymph system far more easily than normal cells.

Cell structure. The role of the cell membrane in cancer cells is still under study. Some growth factors have been found to agglutinate more readily to neoplastic cells than to normal cells, which may result from alterations of receptor sites or the composition of the cell membrane itself.

Cancer cells use glucose more rapidly, possibly resulting from more rapid transport into the cell or impaired glycolysis regulation. They also synthesize protein faster as a result of highly active anabolic pathways and the larger growth fraction. Cancer cells have larger nuclei than normal cells, and their chromatin frequently clumps irregularly.

In the cell cycle, cancer cells apparently do not enter the temporary resting (G_0) phase as readily as normal cells, but they do follow the same process of replication. Neoplastic cells that do enter G_0 are less likely to be damaged by radiation or chemotherapy. Because of this, scheduling of treatments and combinations of treatments having different sites and mechanisms of action is critical in overall treatment planning.

Tumor growth. Although normal cells stop multiplying when lost cells have been replaced, neoplastic cells continue to grow and multiply. (See *How cancer develops and spreads,* pages 14 and 15.) Initially, tumor growth appears to occur exponentially, but as the tumor grows and tumor cells compete for nutrients, tumor growth declines. Thus, the time required for the tumor mass to double (known as *doubling time*) increases as the tumor grows. Prolonged doubling time is thought to result from a longer cycling time required from one cell division to the next; from a decrease in the number of dividing cells (decreased growth fraction); or from an increased loss of tumor cells resulting from a dwindling nutrient supply.

Benign or malignant? Under favorable conditions, a cancer cell (and, hence, a tumor composed of such cells) may differentiate to some degree. The degree of this differentiation can be used as a prognostic guide at biopsy. Malignant tumors are usually undifferentiated and consist of a high percentage of dividing cells. Benign tumors, in contrast, are well differentiated, grow slowly, and do not spread far from the initial focus. Hence, the less differentiated the tumor, the poorer the prognosis.

Mechanisms of metastasis
If a tumor is malignant, it will *invade,* or encroach upon and destroy, neighboring tissues. Although the mechanism of invasion isn't well known, such a tumor may spread by sheer mechanical pressure, forcing itself into areas of least resistance. The tumor cells may also secrete enzymes that weaken or destroy adjacent healthy cells. Finally, some researchers believe that neovascularization may help the tumor to invade adjacent host tissues.

If a malignant tumor penetrates a vessel, it may metastasize via the bloodstream or the lymphatics. Turbulent blood flow helps eliminate many circulating tumor cells, and the immune system eliminates many more. However few, the surviving cells have the ability to aggregate and form multicellular emboli, which then become lodged in capillaries. After they attach themselves to the capillary endothelium, a thrombus forms, impeding blood flow. There the trapped cells develop into secondary metastases. It's possible that a reduced blood flow, for whatever reason, could favor increased trapping and subsequent survival of circulating tumor cells.

The lymphatic system is another important pathway of metastasis. Moreover, since the lymphatic and circulatory systems interconnect, tumor cells may pass easily from one system to the other. After penetrating a lymph vessel, some malignant cells may lodge in lymph nodes, while others bypass these to form distal nodal metastases.

Metastasis may also occur iatrogenically ("seeding"). An excisional biopsy may implant malignant cells into healthy tissues at the biopsy site, an incisional biopsy may disseminate cells via severed blood and lymph vessels, and a needle biopsy risks depositing tumor cells along the needle track. Surgical manipulation of a friable tumor may also release tumor cells into the operative field.

Some tumors show patterns of metastasis, tending to spread and develop in specific, distant organs. This may result from anatomic and hemodynamic factors, plus numerous interactions between host and tumor cells. Whatever the reasons, effective patient assessment requires knowledge of patterns of metastatic development to guide the diagnostic workup and testing.

THE CHALLENGE OF CANCER
Advances in prevention, detection, and treatment of cancer are giving more and more patients a chance to live longer and fuller lives. Understanding the basic principles of cancer pathophysiology will help you provide these patients with the fullest measure of effective care, counseling, and support.

Points to remember

• Cancer is a group of over 100 diseases, one of which will strike about three out of four families in the United States.
• The age-adjusted death rate for most forms of cancer has risen, mainly because of a sharp rise in lung cancers.
• Risk factors for developing cancer can be classified as endogenous, including age, sex, race, heredity/genetics, immunology, and psychological factors; and exogenous, including carcinogens, radiation, viruses, diet, and use of substances such as tobacco, alcohol, and chemotherapeutic agents.
• The capacity for invasion and metastasis is a unique characteristic of the cancer cell and plays a major role in cancer morbidity and mortality.
• Nurses, whether specializing in cancer treatment or not, have a responsibility and role in the prevention of cancer, as well as in providing effective care, support, and encouragement during the disease process.

2 ASSESSING FOR CANCER

Enlarged lymph nodes

Because early detection of cancer is critical, your role in cancer assessment is critical and can be lifesaving. In assessing a patient who may have cancer, you'll use the basic techniques of history taking, inspection, palpation, percussion, and auscultation. You'll need to know cancer risk factors, such as cigarette smoking and hazardous working conditions. You should also know cancer's seven warning signs (see *Seven warning signs of cancer*) and be able to recognize detectable conditions, such as jaundice or abdominal ascites, which can be, but are not always, signs of cancer. You'll also need to draw on keen perception, which will help you fit together related information and gauge patient reactions as you perform the physical examination.

Your role is actually twofold—screening for cancer, and teaching the patient how to screen for it himself and how to minimize his risks of developing it.

Gather the equipment

Before beginning your assessment, gather the following equipment: penlight, ophthalmoscope, stethoscope with bell and diaphragm, otoscope, tongue blades, blood pressure cuffs, oral and rectal thermometers, pins, reflex hammer, examination gloves, lubricant, vaginal speculum, microscope, slides, Hemoccult paper, tape measure and calipers to obtain anthropometric measurements, and an extra light for the genitalia examination. Arrange to conduct the assessment in a quiet, well-lit room.

Prepare the patient

Introduce yourself to the patient and explain briefly what the assessment will involve. Instruct him to undress and drape, allowing for his privacy. Try to put him at ease.

As you talk to the patient, form an overall impression of his health status. Does he appear overweight or undernourished? Does he appear weak or strong, lethargic or energetic? Note his state of hygiene, how he's dressed, and his level of consciousness.

THE NURSING HISTORY

Structure the nursing interview to obtain as much information as possible, but be flexible enough to allow yourself to establish rapport with the patient. Remember that he is probably nervous, worried that he may have cancer, and hesitant about revealing detailed personal information to a stranger. To help him through the interview, create an atmosphere of trust. Don't hurry him, since this could cause him to leave out important details that he considers insignificant. Remember that he is your best source of information about what's normal for him.

If your health-care facility uses an assessment tool, follow it as a guide without relying solely on it. Assessment tools can facilitate data collection but inhibit spontaneity.

Throughout the history, document the source of information. If the patient is in pain or respiratory distress, your source may be another family member. If the patient is a referral, note the source and reason for referral and any information included in the referral papers.

Record biographical information

Begin the interview with a general biographical sketch. Note the patient's age, sex, race, marital status, socioeconomic position, and occupation. These factors can be significant to cancer disposition. For example, certain cancers, such as cervical, prostatic, esophageal, lung, and colorectal, affect more blacks than whites. Some occupations, especially those associated with low socioeconomic status, expose patients to industrial carcinogens.

Determine the chief complaint

Note the patient's reason for seeking medical attention, preferably in his own words. The chief complaint is often one of the seven warning signs of cancer identified by the American Cancer Society. Determine if the complaint deviates from what is normal for the patient.

If the patient says pain is his chief complaint, know the various sources of cancer pain: infection or inflammation; obstruction of the vascular system or lymphatics; direct compression or infiltration of nerve structures; invasion of bone, fascia, or periosteum; and some cancer treatments. Remember that what one patient calls pain, another may call an ache or discomfort. Help the patient explore and define even a vague complaint.

Ask the patient to detail his chief complaint, outlining his symptoms, their onset, chronicity, location, radiation, severity, and duration. Ask what factors precipitate or relieve them. Record the progress of his illness in chronologic order from development of the first symptom, then fill in missing data with a detailed systemic review.

Seven warning signs of cancer

Because early detection of cancer offers the best chance for cure, encourage all patients to report any of these warning signs.

Change in bowel or bladder habits
A sore that doesn't heal
Unusual bleeding or discharge
Thickening or lump in breast or elsewhere
Indigestion or difficulty in swallowing
Obvious change in wart or mole
Nagging cough or hoarseness.

Review health history

Ask the patient if he has any allergies, has sought treatment for any conditions, or has ever had surgery or been hospitalized. Even the removal of a mole can be significant in cancer assessment because of its possible relationship to melanoma or skin cancer.

Ask if he's had any laboratory tests, radiologic studies (including chest X-ray), nuclear scans, or EKGs, and note the dates. Ask if he's had chemotherapy or ionizing radiation, procedures that have been linked with the development of secondary malignancies. For patients with chronic respiratory disease, note any treatment with nebulizers, atomizers, or oxygen.

Ask the patient about past drug therapy and whether he's currently taking any drugs. Prolonged use of such drugs as phenytoin (Dilantin) or of immunosuppressive drugs, such as azathioprine (Imuran), may lead to cancer. Postmenopausal use of estrogens has been linked with endometrial cancer.

Review family history

Ask the patient about a family history of cancer, especially breast, colorectal, and lung cancers, which demonstrate genetic susceptibility. Ask about incidence of specific inherited conditions, such as colonic polyposis, that have a 100% potential for malignancy.

Review psychosocial history

The patient's living and working conditions can affect his risk of developing cancer.

Environment. Ask the patient if he's been exposed to chemical agents, which can cause cancer long after exposure to them. These include asbestos, asphalt, aniline dyes, herbicides, and fertilizers. Ask about repeated exposure to ultraviolet radiation, which has been associated with skin cancer.

Nutrition and drug use. Ask the patient if he follows any special dietary regimen. For example, diets high in fiber and vitamins A, C, and E or low in animal proteins may aid cancer prevention. Diets that involve daily meat consumption are associated with greater incidence of breast, colon, and uterine cancer.

Ask about alcohol and tobacco use. Both of these substances have been associated with lung, esophageal, and mouth cancer.

Ask the patient about his family situation. Does he live alone? Are finances a problem that will keep him from seeking proper medical care? Ask about religious affiliation and any health beliefs that could influence treatment. Throughout the interview, try to evaluate the patient's emotional state and coping abilities. These significantly influence self-attitude and response to treatment.

Conduct a systemic review

Obtain information about general and specific health changes that the patient may or may not consider significant.

General. Ask the patient to describe all symptoms. Don't ignore general or vague symptoms such as weakness; change in energy level; or unwarranted depression, fatigue, or sweating. Ask about weight gains or losses. Try to establish the amount of weight change and the time period in which it occurred.

Skin. Ask the patient if he's noticed anything unusual about his skin color or texture. Has he noticed any lumps or raised areas, excessive bruising, petechiae, or pruritus? Easy bruising or petechiae may indicate bone marrow suppression or capillary wall defects caused by malignancy. Pruritus sometimes occurs with leukemia, Hodgkin's disease, or malignancies of the liver and kidney.

Head. Ask the patient if he's noticed any hair loss or changes in hair texture. These subtle signs may accompany a latent undiagnosed malignancy. Ask if he's experienced headaches, syncopal episodes, or dizziness. Headaches that are most severe in the morning often accompany intracranial lesions. Ask if he's experienced visual disturbances, such as changes in acuity or fields of vision, or diplopia. These could indicate a primary tumor or metastasis to the brain.

Ear, nose, and throat. Ask the patient if he's noticed any ringing or buzzing in his ears or a feeling that the room is spinning. Has his hearing deteriorated, or have others complained about his hearing? Has he had aural pain or discharge? All of these symptoms can accompany malignant ear tumors.

Ask about changes in the patient's sense of smell, increasing speech nasality, or any problems breathing through his nose, all of which may mean nasal obstruction. Ask about nasal discharge. Bloody, unilateral discharge is a common sign of maxillary and ethmoidal sinus tumors.

Ask the patient if he's noticed any changes in the way food tastes. For unknown reasons, certain malignancies, especially lung tumors, cause taste changes. Also ask if he's noticed sores or swelling on his tongue or cheeks, or if he's had a sore throat, hoarseness, or trouble swallowing. All of these problems should normally resolve within days.

Neck and lymph nodes. Ask about neck swelling or tenderness and continued node enlargement. Cervical lymphadenopathy often pairs with upper respiratory infection, but persistent node enlargement (greater than 1 cm in diameter) may mean local or metastatic disease.

Breasts. Ask if the patient's noticed any breast lumps, nipple swelling, or nipple discharge. Remember that most breast lumps are painless and benign. Ask the female patient if she practices breast self-examination. If she doesn't, make a note to give thorough instruction during the physical examination.

Respiratory and cardiovascular systems. Ask about classic lung cancer symptoms (hemoptysis, coughing, wheezing, dyspnea, or hoarseness). These symptoms may also accompany chronic respiratory disease. If the patient has chronic respiratory disease, try to find out what's normal for him and whether he's seen changes in his symptoms. Remember that chest tumors can compromise cardiac function and mimic congestive heart failure or cause pleural or pericardial effusion.

Gastrointestinal (GI) system. Ask about changes in appetite. Does the patient feel full shortly after beginning a meal? Does he experience nausea, vomiting, indigestion, or a bloated feeling? Stomach cancer involves vague epigastric discomfort and anorexia. Other GI tumors cause dysphagia, weight loss, changes in appetite and energy level, and varying types of pain.

Ask about bowel changes, including stool color, diarrhea, constipation, bloody stools, and hemorrhoids. Don't overlook rectal bleeding, even in patients with hemorrhoids.

Urinary system. Ask the patient if he's experienced difficulty urinating, incontinence, burning or pain on urination, urgency, frequency, hesitancy, or dribbling. Ask if he's noticed a change in the amount, odor, or color of his urine, especially the presence of blood.

Reproductive system. If the patient is male, ask if he's noticed any swelling or lumps in his testicles, and ask if he examines his testicles regularly for lumps. Young male patients and patients with a history of undescended testicles are at high risk for testicular cancer. Ask the patient if he's experienced dysuria, a frequent complaint in prostatic cancer, and if he's noticed any lesions on his penis.

If the patient is female, record her menstrual history and ask about any changes in her menstrual cycle or bleeding between periods. Ask if she's noticed any vaginal discharge, itching, or pain. Ask if she's sexually active and whether she has pain or bleeding with intercourse. Spotting after intercourse can be a sign of vulvar cancer. Ask the date of her last Pap smear. Early detection of cervical cancer increases chances of survival.

Musculoskeletal system. Ask about muscular pain or changes in muscular sensation or function. As soft tissue tumors grow, they interfere with circulation and innervation. Ask about stiffness, swelling, redness, or restricted range of motion in the joints. These symptoms, if persistent and refractory to anti-inflammatory drugs, can indicate a neoplasm or leukemic joint infiltration.

Central nervous system. Ask the patient if he's experienced headaches, dizziness, blackouts, numbness, or tingling or if he's seen spots before his eyes or had trouble maintaining his balance. Behavioral changes accompanying brain or spinal tumors may be subtle. Ask family members if they've noticed any changes in the patient's personality, mental status, or behavior.

Endocrine system. Ask the patient if he has experienced changes in overall energy level, weight, and mental status; or any sexual or metabolic abnormalities. Such symptoms are associated with endocrine disorders. Cancer can affect the endocrine glands directly or as a paraneoplastic syndrome. Tumors can grow within a gland, such as the thyroid, or in a nonendocrine organ, such as the lung, interfering with hormone secretion and even, in some cases, producing a hormone.

Hematopoietic system. Ask the patient if he has a history of bleeding tendencies or anemia and if he's experiencing fatigue or malaise. These factors could suggest a blood dyscrasia, such as leukemia, and warrant a complete blood count with differential. Remember, too, that patients who've been treated with cytotoxic chemotherapy or radiation are at higher risk of developing a second malignancy in the blood-forming system.

THE PHYSICAL EXAMINATION

During the physical examination, you'll carefully assess the patient for clinical evidence of cancer.

First, record the patient's vital signs and anthropometric measurements (height, weight, and arm measurements). (See *Taking arm measurements*, page 22.)

If a patient is experiencing dizziness or other symptoms related to cardiac or pulmo-

Taking arm measurements

Determining the midpoint

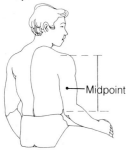

Midpoint

Measuring midarm circumference

Measuring triceps skinfold thickness

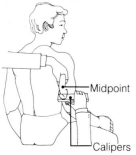

Midpoint

Calipers

Be sure to obtain arm measurements as well as your patient's height and weight. Three arm measurements include midarm circumference (MAC), triceps skinfold thickness (TSF), and midarm muscle circumference (MAMC). These measurements will help you evaluate nutritional status and gross composition of the body.

To take arm measurements, you'll need skinfold calipers, a nonstretch tape measure, and a felt-tipped pen.

Midarm circumference
This measurement refects the body's fat and muscle reserves. To determine it, first find the midpoint of the patient's upper arm. Measure the length of the upper arm, and mark the midpoint with the pen. Then, draw the tape gently but firmly around the arm at the midpoint to determine MAC.

Triceps skinfold thickness
This measurement helps estimate subcutaneous fat reserves, the body's main form of energy storage. With your thumb and forefinger, firmly grasp the skin about 1 cm above the midpoint. (Be careful not to grasp any underlying arm muscle.) Apply calipers at the midpoint and squeeze for about 3 seconds. Then, record the measurement registered on the handle gauge

to the nearest 0.5 mm.
Repeat this procedure twice, and average the results to compensate for error.

Midarm muscle circumference
This measurement reflects the body's skeletal protein (muscle mass) reserves. To calculate the patient's MAMC, multiply the TSF (in centimeters) by 3.143, and subtract this figure from the MAC.

Evaluate measurements
Compare the patient's arm measurements to the standard (see *Standard arm measurement values* below). Then, record your measurements as a percentage of the chart's standard values, using this formula: actual measurement divided by

standard measurement, multiplied by 100. A measurement of less than 90% of the standard indicates caloric deprivation; a measurement of more than 90% indicates adequate or ample energy reserves.

Although arm measurements are important nutritional assessment tools, they have several limitations.
• Measurements fail to consider normal differences in humeral size.
• They do not allow for variations in adipose distribution and skeletal protein stores between individuals.
• They do not account for variations due to edema.
• They may not reflect acute body changes for as long as 3 or 4 weeks.

Standard arm measurement values

| Test | Standard | Percentile of population | | | |
		90%	80%	70%	60%
Triceps skinfold					
Men	12.5 mm	11.3	10.0	8.8	7.5
Women	16.5 mm	14.9	13.2	11.6	9.9
Midarm circumference					
Men	29.3 cm	26.3	23.4	20.5	17.6
Women	28.5 cm	25.7	22.8	20.0	17.1
Midarm muscle circumference					
Men	25.3 cm	22.8	20.2	17.7	15.2
Women	23.2 cm	20.9	18.6	16.2	13.9

nary dysfunction, obtain orthostatic blood pressure readings. These general measurements help assess the patient's state of nutrition and hydration, chronic problem areas for cancer patients.

Conduct the physical examination from head to toe, performing internal examinations last. Throughout the examination, keep in mind the patient's history and chief complaint.

Inspect the skin, hair, and nails
Check the patient's skin for abnormal masses or lesions. To aid detection, shine a penlight at an oblique angle across the skin. Remember that lesions may be elevated or ulcerated,

ranging in appearance from pale, waxy, pearly nodules to red, scaly ones. They may be sharply outlined or have indistinct borders.

Ask about duration of any sores. Note any moles that show evidence of bleeding, plus areas of unusual pigmentation. Look for bruises, petechiae, or purpura, which may indicate bleeding tendencies. Observe skin color for pallor, cyanosis, jaundice, or redness.

Palpate the skin, noting its temperature, especially at the extremities. Cool limbs can result from circulation deficits caused by a tumor. Skin temperature changes occur in diseases involving intermittent fever, such as leukemia. Assess skin turgor, noting areas of edema. Ask if palpation causes pain. Neoplastic tissue invasion may create sensitivity.

Note any unusual hair distribution, possibly suggesting endocrine tumors. Check hair texture for brittleness and nails for unusual configurations, such as clubbing.

Inspect the head and neck

Check the patient's head for asymmetry and the presence of nodules. Be alert for signs of facial paralysis, which may result from tumors with nerve involvement. Examine the patient's neck for masses and asymmetry.

Check the patient's eyes, observing the color of the conjunctiva for signs of anemia or the sclera for icterus. Remember that jaundice may mean cancer of the pancreas, liver, or biliary tract. Assess the patient's ears for drainage, and note any report of pain—two signs of malignancy. Examine the patient's nose, noting any discharge. Assess internal structures for inflammation, swelling, or exudate. Next, use a penlight to examine the patient's mouth for ulcers and growths. Assess the lips, gums, and floor of the mouth for lesions. With gloved fingers, palpate the buccal surface internally and externally for masses and induration. Using a tongue blade to depress the tongue, check the uvula's symmetry and the movement of the soft palate as the patient says "ah." Finally, check for lesions of the oropharynx and swelling or discoloration of the tonsils.

Palpate the thyroid

To palpate the thyroid from the front, face the patient and place your fingers below the cricoid cartilage on both sides of the trachea. Ask the patient to swallow as you palpate the thyroid isthmus. Next, ask the patient to flex his neck toward the side being examined as you gently palpate each lobe. Move the thyroid cartilage toward the side being palpated.

To examine the thyroid from the back, stand behind the patient, with your fingers on either side of the trachea, and ask him to lower his chin. Palpate the isthmus, right lobe, and left lobe as described.

Examine the lymph nodes

Carefully check the lymph nodes, using gentle palpation. (See *The lymphatics: Pathways of metastasis,* page 24.) Begin by palpating the preauricular or parotid gland area, first with the patient's head tilted slightly back, then with his head tilted slightly forward. If you locate enlarged nodes (greater than 1 cm),

note their size; location; and whether they're soft or hard, mobile or fixed, tender or painless. Also check for infection or inflammation in the surrounding area that the node drains. If you find one enlarged node, carefully check other nodes in the same chain.

Examine all nodes in the head and neck region: postauricular, occipital, tonsillar, submaxillary, submental, superficial cervical, posterior cervical, and deep cervical.

Continue by examining the supraclavicular nodes. Ask the patient to relax and bend his head slightly forward, then palpate the shelf above the clavicles, rotating your finger deeply to feel for nodes. An enlarged node in this area could mean Hodgkin's disease.

Next, with the patient still sitting, examine both axillae. Ask him to relax his arm, and hold it, flexed at the elbow, alongside his body. Press your fingers straight up into the armpit, palpating deeply in a sliding motion toward the chest. When you've completed this, ask the patient to lie down. Repeat the axillary examination, and check the inguinal nodes.

Examine the breasts

First, inspect breast symmetry. Breast size may not be identical, but breasts should be symmetrical. Check each breast for dimpling, puckering, erythema, edema, and ulceration. Check for nipple inversion, discharge, and retraction. Check to see if fluid can be expressed from the nipples. Palpate the breasts with the patient in sitting and reclining positions. (See *Examining the breasts,* page 26.) Finally, teach breast self-examination techniques.

Realize that most breast lumps are benign and that malignant masses are usually fixed to underlying tissue and feel immobile and irregularly shaped. Show the location of abnormalities by dividing the breast into four quadrants: upper outer, upper inner, lower outer, and lower inner. Or show the location by approximating numbers on a clock.

Refer the patient for a follow-up examination if you detect any breast mass or nipple discharge.

Assess the respiratory system

Inspect the patient's chest from the front and back, noting size and shape. Check for increased anteroposterior diameter (barrel chest), sometimes a characteristic of patients with emphysema. Note any audible breathing abnormalities, such as dyspnea, wheezing, or coughing. If the patient is coughing, note whether the cough is dry or congested.

The lymphatics: Pathways of metastasis

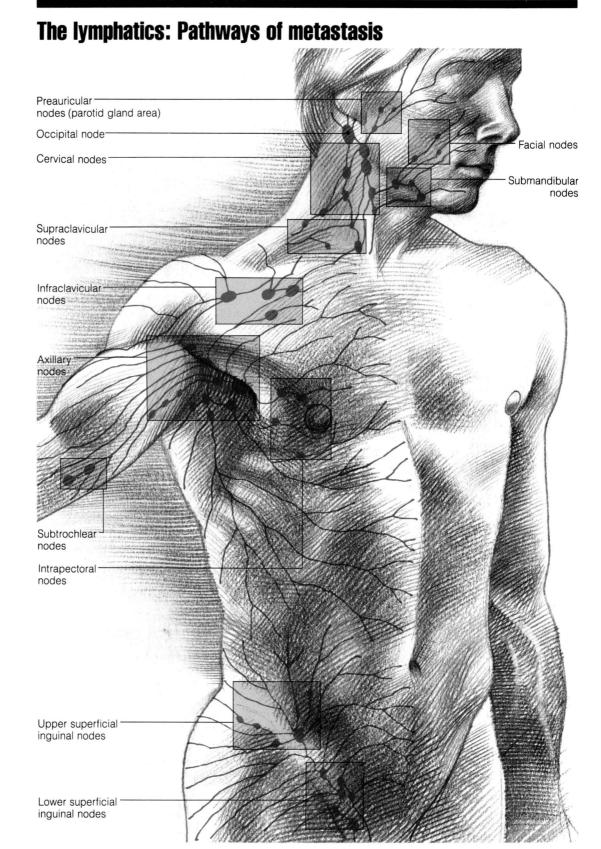

Preauricular nodes (parotid gland area)

Occipital node

Cervical nodes

Facial nodes

Submandibular nodes

Supraclavicular nodes

Infraclavicular nodes

Axillary nodes

Subtrochlear nodes

Intrapectoral nodes

Upper superficial inguinal nodes

Lower superficial inguinal nodes

Cells from a primary tumor can spread, or metastasize, to other body areas through the lymphatic system.

Lymph nodes normally aren't palpable. While palpable nodes usually indicate an inflammatory response to infection, superficial or gross adenopathy occurs in a high percentage of patients with lymphoma and metastatic disease.

Begin palpating lymph nodes in the preauricular, or parotid gland, area; then proceed downward from the head and neck to axillary and inguinal areas.

Next, evaluate respiration symmetry by placing your hands on the patient's back at the thoracic vertebral area, with thumbs abducted toward the spine at the 10th-rib level. Grasp the lateral rib cage with your hands. As the patient inhales, your thumbs should move apart; as he exhales, they should return to midline and touch. Note whether one side moves much more than the other. Asymmetry may indicate lung or pleural disease.

Check for fremitus by placing your palm on the patient's chest at various points over the lungs as the patient repeats the word "ninety-nine." Vibrations should be palpable and more pronounced in the upper chest. Weak or absent fremitus can indicate fluid, a mass, or obstruction in the pleural space.

Percuss the posterior chest, beginning at the shoulders and moving from side to side down the patient's back, avoiding the scapulae. The area over the apices should be resonant; over the diaphragm, dull. Dullness over the lungs indicates fluid or a mass.

Next, auscultate the lungs with the patient sitting upright. Listen to both inspiration and expiration, starting above the scapulae and moving from side to side down the back. You should hear vesicular sounds at the lung bases and bronchovesicular sounds between the scapulae. Decreased or absent breath sounds can mean fluid or tissue obstruction. Note any rales, rhonchi, or other adventitious sounds. Then ask the patient to cough, and auscultate each area again. If abnormal sounds remain, refer him for further assessment.

Assess cardiovascular status
With the patient prone, inspect the chest for unusual movements or visible pulsations. Auscultate for abnormal heart sounds, such as rubs, extra systole, or rhythm irregularities. You'll want to focus on abnormalities that accompany cardiac metastasis, such as dysrhythmias, congestive heart failure, and, rarely, pericardial effusion or tamponade; but also be alert to non-cancer-related cardiac problems that could interfere with cancer treatment. For example, a dysrhythmia or severe angina could contraindicate surgery.

Examine the abdomen
Using the techniques of inspection, auscultation, percussion, and palpation, examine the abdomen.

Inspection. First, inspect the abdomen for shape, skin tone, and symmetry. Distortion in contour may suggest tumor growth or organ enlargement. Abdominal distention with taut skin, bulging flanks, and possibly umbilical eversion accompanies ascites. An abdomen that appears dome-shaped could indicate intestinal obstruction; one that appears concave below the xiphoid process, general wasting.

Auscultation. Next, auscultate for bowel sounds. Hyperactive, tinkling, or high-pitched rushes can occur with intestinal obstruction. A harsh bruit over the liver can mean a vascular tumor such as a hepatoma. A friction rub may indicate surface tumor nodules.

Percussion. Assess for ascites, which is not always detectable by inspection. With the patient prone, percuss the abdomen from the umbilicus toward each flank. Draw a line between areas of dullness and tympany. Then, turn the patient to one side, causing any ascitic fluid to shift, and percuss again from the umbilicus toward the flanks. Again draw a line between areas of dullness and tympany. Any change between the first and second lines means fluid is present. Malignant ascites most commonly occurs with ovarian, endometrial, breast, and colon cancer.

To gauge liver size, percuss the abdomen along the right midclavicular line. Percussion notes over the liver should be dull. A span of dullness along the right midclavicular line greater than 4¾" (12 cm) means hepatomegaly and possibly neoplasm. Continue percussion to assess uterine and bladder size and the presence of ovarian masses.

Palpation. Palpate the abdomen for masses, noting the size, shape, and location of any you find. Describe contour (smooth, rough, nodular, or irregular), consistency (soft, doughy, semisolid, or hard), and whether the mass moves or remains fixed during respiration. Also specify the patient's position when the mass is palpable and whether or not palpation causes tenderness.

Palpate the lower border of the liver beneath the right costal margin as the patient takes a deep breath. If it is hard and nodular, it could be infiltrated with a tumor. Note whether the liver and spleen move during respiration. If they don't, they could be fixed by adhesions or tumor extension.

Palpate under the left costal margin to assess the spleen. The spleen is not normally palpable; enlargement may stem from a neoplasm. If the spleen is enlarged, use light pressure and watch the patient for signs of discomfort. Never use deep palpation on a tender spleen.

Examining the breasts

Breast examination requires skilled use of two assessment techniques: inspection and palpation. No special equipment is necessary.

Breast inspection should be performed in each of the three illustrated sitting positions. Observe each breast for asymmetry, size, dimpling, flattening, redness, ulcerations, edema (orange peel appearance), and venous pattern. Inspect each nipple for location, discharge, inversion, retraction, ulceration, or changes in size.

Breast palpation is done in both sitting and reclining positions. Using your finger pads, palpate using one of the methods below.

If the patient has large breasts, while she is seated, use one hand to support the breast and the other to palpate. Gently press each nipple to find masses or discharge. Note color, consistency, and amount of any discharge, and whether it comes from one or more duct openings. Also, palpate the areola, periphery, and tail.

Positions for breast inspection

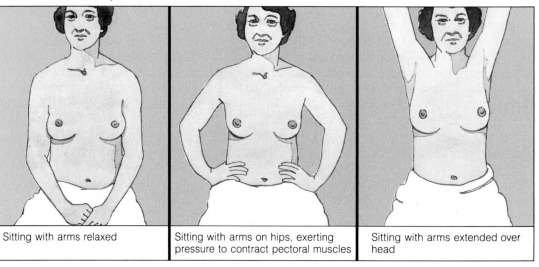

| Sitting with arms relaxed | Sitting with arms on hips, exerting pressure to contract pectoral muscles | Sitting with arms extended over head |

Palpating large breasts

Positions for breast palpation

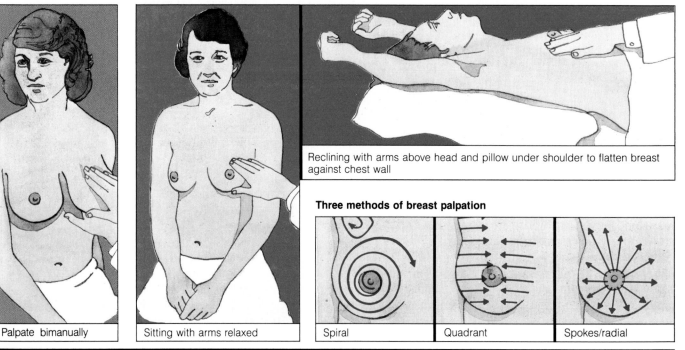

Reclining with arms above head and pillow under shoulder to flatten breast against chest wall

Palpate bimanually

Sitting with arms relaxed

Three methods of breast palpation

Spiral

Quadrant

Spokes/radial

The kidneys are difficult to palpate in adult patients. Use bimanual deep palpation to check for enlargement, which may result from hydronephrosis secondary to obstruction or direct tumor invasion.

Record abnormal findings by quadrants during the abdominal examination. Any tenderness may indicate inflammation or tumor necrosis.

Assess the musculoskeletal system

Inspect the extremities for symmetry and for the presence of edema, unusual contour, contractures, muscle wasting, or enlarged joints. Gently palpate for masses, noting any pain this causes. Most bone tumors involve pain over the lesion site and soft tissue swelling. Bone involvement can also cause nerve compression, resulting in radiating pain. Note any signs of immobility or pathologic fractures, both signs of bone metastasis.

Complete the musculoskeletal examination by performing gentle range of motion in the joints.

Evaluate neurologic function

Conduct the neurologic assessment with the patient sitting upright. Test cranial nerves, motor functions, sensory functions, and reflexes. Cancer patients commonly experience various neurologic problems, such as spinal cord compression and peripheral neuropathies. Refer patients for neurologic follow-up if you detect any of the following: inappropriate affect, lethargy, disorientation, aphasia, apraxia, incoordination, inability to complete simple tasks, or absence of normal sensation.

Examine female genitalia

First, inspect the external labia for growths, lesions, inflammation, or discharge. Then, palpate for masses.

If your institution asks you to perform the internal examination, begin by lubricating the speculum with water. (Other lubricants may interfere with cytologic studies.) Gently insert the closed speculum into the vagina, gently open the blades, and maneuver the speculum until you can see the cervix. Note its color and position and any lesions, masses, ulcerations, nodules, bleeding, or discharge. With the speculum locked open, obtain specimens for a Pap smear and a cervical scrape. Then, unlock the speculum and inspect the vaginal canal as you slowly withdraw the blades. Note any mucosal thickening or white lesions, possible signs of a neoplasm.

Next, put on a glove, lubricate the index and middle fingers, and insert the fingers into the patient's vagina. Palpate the vaginal walls for masses or tenderness. Palpate the cervix for position, shape, consistency, mobility, and tenderness. Palpate the uterus bimanually with your gloved fingers in the anterior fornix and your other hand pushing the patient's abdomen toward the cervix. Find the uterus, noting its size, shape, mobility, and tenderness, and the presence of any masses. Palpate the ovaries, with your gloved fingers in the ipsilateral fornix and your other hand depressing the abdomen. Note the size, shape, and mobility of each ovary and the presence of any masses. Note any pain the patient feels during the vaginal examination, since pain is a frequent manifestation of gynecologic tumors.

Finally, with the patient still in the lithotomy position, perform a rectal examination. Palpate all surfaces of the rectal wall for masses. Then, withdraw your finger and place any adhering stool specimen on Hemoccult paper to test for occult blood. Digital rectal examination is an excellent cancer screening technique and, therefore, an important part of the complete physical examination.

Examine male genitalia

Inspect the skin of the penis for nodules or ulcers that could be cancerous. Examine the skin of the glans, retracting the foreskin on the uncircumcised patient. Note any discharge from the urethral meatus. Next, palpate the scrotum for masses. A painless scrotal mass is the most common sign of testicular cancer. Urge the patient, especially if he's over age 20, to perform testicular self-examinations.

End your assessment by performing a digital rectal examination. Have the patient stand and bend over the examination table, or have him assume a left side-lying position with his knees flexed or in a knee-to-chest position. Check carefully for tissue firmness, a possible sign of prostatic cancer. The rectal examination is the most accurate screening test for this type of cancer.

Devise nursing diagnoses

Based on your impressions and findings, you can now formulate nursing diagnoses specific to your patient's needs. Remember that assessment is the crucial first step in caring for cancer patients. Especially in cancer treatment, where early detection so often determines success, the therapeutic process begins with careful assessment.

Points to remember

- Common chief complaints of patients with cancer include pain, changed bowel or bladder habits, unhealed sores, bleeding, lumps, indigestion, swallowing difficulty, persistent cough or hoarseness, and changes in warts or moles.
- In the patient history, be sure to ask about previous chemotherapy or radiation therapy, since these treatments can cause secondary malignancies.
- Lymph node assessment is crucial, since a superficial or gross adenopathy appears in many patients with lymphoma and metastatic disease.
- Besides taking the patient's history and performing the physical examination, your assessment should include instructions in self-care practices, such as breast or testicular self-examination. Also stress the importance of early detection methods, such as regular Pap smears and rectal examinations.

3 IMPLEMENTING CANCER DIAGNOSIS

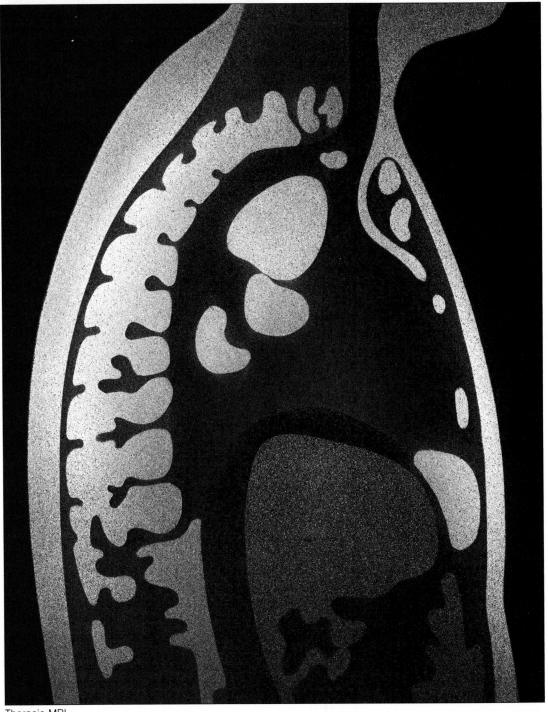

Thoracic MRI

Helping your patient through a diagnostic workup that may confirm cancer is not among your easier nursing tasks. Such a patient is always deeply distressed, whether he shows it or not, and needs your calm reassurance and support. He also needs you to be knowledgeable about the newest high-tech diagnostic methods, such as magnetic resonance imaging and the estrogen receptor assays, which may allow earlier and more effective treatment. If diagnostic test results confirm cancer, you must know what additional tests are needed to help select the treatment and to monitor its effectiveness. Only with such understanding can you provide your patient with a clear explanation of the tests he needs, prepare him thoroughly for them, and anticipate and manage test complications.

Test selection varies
The selection of diagnostic tests depends on the patient history and the results of the physical examination. (See *Detecting cancer: A sample test sequence,* page 30.) Usually, though, the diagnostic workup includes routine blood and X-ray tests to detect the presence of abnormalities. Next, cytologic and histologic tests may follow to confirm or rule out malignancy. Further special tests, such as nuclear medicine scans and endoscopies, help determine the extent of malignancy, predict prognosis, select and monitor therapy, and check for recurrence of the malignancy.

The sequence of tests in a diagnostic workup also depends on the sensitivity and specificity of available tests. *Sensitivity* indicates how reliably the test gives a positive finding for a disease. *Specificity* indicates how often the test is negative when the disease is absent. A bone scan, for example, reliably gives a positive finding when bone cancer is present (high sensitivity). However, it also gives a positive finding in nonmalignant bone disorders (low specificity).

BLOOD TESTS
Blood chemistry studies and a complete blood count (CBC) are routinely ordered when cancer is a suspected diagnosis. (See *Blood chemistry and hematologic findings in cancer,* page 32.) Certain specialized blood tests, such as radioimmunoassays (RIAs) for tumor markers, provide important information about the extent of malignancy and the effectiveness of treatment.

Blood chemistry studies
These studies can include measurement of serum calcium, enzyme, gastrin, and protein levels. Abnormal findings in these studies signal the need for further testing to identify the cause.

Serum calcium. Elevated levels can result from metastatic bone disease, multiple myeloma, or a malignant parathyroid tumor. Elevated calcium levels may also result from secretion of a parathyroid hormone–like substance by tumors such as oat cell carcinoma of the lung or other tumors.

Serum enzymes. Measurement of *acid phosphatase* levels permits early detection of prostatic cancer, promotes accurate staging, and helps monitor treatment. Acid phosphatase, present in large amounts in normal prostatic secretions, increases in approximately 75% of patients when a tumor invades the prostatic capsule.

Sharply elevated *alkaline phosphatase* levels usually indicate liver or bone malignancies, whereas elevated levels of *serum glutamic-pyruvic transaminase* or *serum glutamic-oxaloacetic transaminase* suggest liver metastasis. Abnormally high levels of *lactic acid dehydrogenase* occur in leukemia and in extensive malignancy.

Serum gastrin. Increased levels of this polypeptide hormone result from gastrinoma or Zollinger-Ellison syndrome.

Serum proteins. Total serum protein levels rise in multiple myeloma. Serum globulin levels rise in multiple myeloma and Hodgkin's disease; serum albumin levels also rise in multiple myeloma and Hodgkin's disease and in leukemia.

Complete blood count
This battery of tests includes determinations of hemoglobin concentration and hematocrit, red and white cell counts, differential white cell count, stained red cell examination, and platelet count. Of these, the white blood cell (WBC) count and differential provide the most useful diagnostic information. The WBC count may rise or fall significantly in malignant disorders, but it must be interpreted in light of the differential and the patient's clinical status. (See *Interpreting the differential,* page 31.) The WBC count, for example, rises in leukemia and many other disorders; the differential can confirm leukemia and identify its type. The WBC count also helps determine the need for further tests, such as bone marrow biopsy. The CBC and platelet count help

Detecting cancer: A sample test sequence

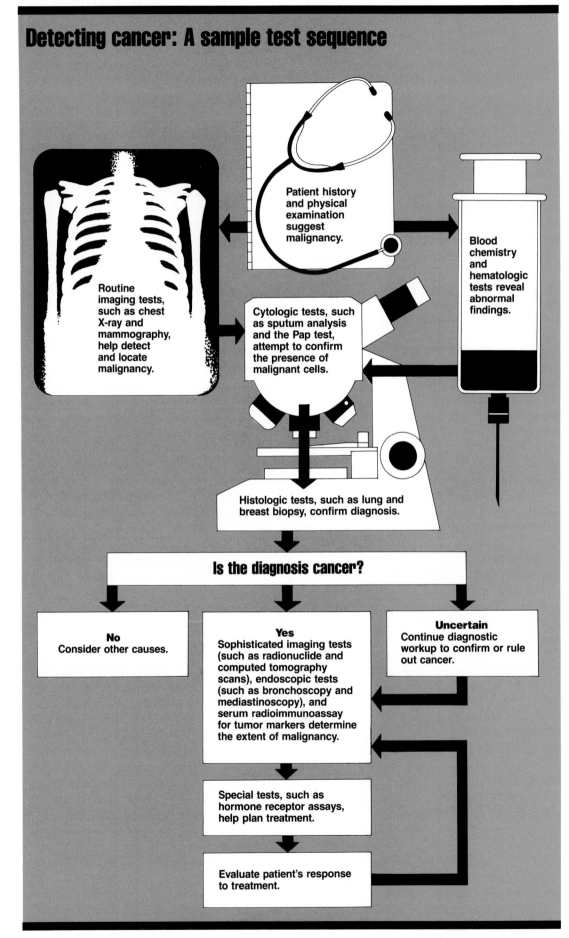

Patient history and physical examination suggest malignancy.

Routine imaging tests, such as chest X-ray and mammography, help detect and locate malignancy.

Cytologic tests, such as sputum analysis and the Pap test, attempt to confirm the presence of malignant cells.

Blood chemistry and hematologic tests reveal abnormal findings.

Histologic tests, such as lung and breast biopsy, confirm diagnosis.

Is the diagnosis cancer?

No
Consider other causes.

Yes
Sophisticated imaging tests (such as radionuclide and computed tomography scans), endoscopic tests (such as bronchoscopy and mediastinoscopy), and serum radioimmunoassay for tumor markers determine the extent of malignancy.

Uncertain
Continue diagnostic workup to confirm or rule out cancer.

Special tests, such as hormone receptor assays, help plan treatment.

Evaluate patient's response to treatment.

monitor chemotherapy and radiation therapy (bone marrow depression is a dose-limiting factor).

Tests for tumor markers
RIA techniques allow precise measurement of oncofetal proteins and ectopic hormones that are secreted by malignant tumors (tumor-derived markers) or by cells of uninvolved tissues (tumor-associated markers). Unfortunately, RIA for tumor markers does not allow early cancer detection because levels of tumor markers usually rise in advanced disease. When these tumor markers are elevated before treatment, periodic measurement during therapy helps monitor the patient's response to treatment and provides early evidence of tumor recurrence.

Oncofetal proteins. These proteins are normally produced during fetal development but repressed thereafter. However, oncofetal proteins may also be produced by some cancer cells. Levels of alpha-fetoprotein (AFP), for example, increase in some hepatomas and germ cell tumors of the testes and ovaries. In germ cell tumors, concurrent measurement of serum AFP and serum human chorionic gonadotropin (HCG) levels helps evaluate response to therapy.

Low levels of carcinoembryonic antigen, a glycoprotein, occur in normal colon tissues. Sharply elevated serum levels occur in metastatic colon cancer; elevated levels of carcinoembryonic antigen also occur in carcinomas involving the large intestine, pancreas, and, sometimes, the breast and lung.

Ectopic hormones. RIA of HCG, normally a product of placental metabolism, aids diagnosis of trophoblastic tumors and tumors that ectopically secrete this hormone. Increased levels of HCG suggest trophoblastic placental neoplasms or HCG-secreting gastric, pancreatic, or ovarian adenocarcinomas. HCG levels rise in approximately 75% of nonseminomatous germ cell tumors and in about 15% of seminomas.

Elevated levels of serum human placental lactogen (HPL), a polypeptide hormone synthesized by placental syncytiotrophoblasts, can indicate various malignancies including carcinoma of the lung, breast, liver, adrenal gland, or stomach, as well as certain sarcomas. Measurement of HPL may help evaluate the effectiveness of chemotherapy and monitor tumor growth and recurrence. Measurement of HPL can also help detect residual malignant tissue after excision.

STOOL TEST
The fecal occult blood test permits early detection of colorectal cancer, providing positive test results in 80% of patients with this disorder. (Consequently, a negative result doesn't rule out colorectal cancer.) This inexpensive, easy-to-use test uses a guaiac-impregnated paper slide to detect minimal amounts of blood in the stool. It requires that the patient refrain from eating meat and fish and taking aspirin and vitamin C for at least 24 hours before the test to minimize false-positive or false-negative test results. The patient also maintains a high-fiber diet for 3 days before the test, since roughage may cause bleeding of friable tumor tissue. The fecal occult blood test requires collection of six stool specimens—two specimens from different areas of three bowel movements. Positive test results require confirmation by a second occult blood test and further evaluation involving digital rectal examination, barium enema, and colonoscopy.

CYTOLOGIC TESTS
These inexpensive, useful screening tests help detect suspected primary or metastatic disease and assess the effectiveness of therapy. However, they fail to determine the location and size of a malignancy and may require further histologic confirmation. Cytologic tests may include the Papanicolaou (Pap) test; tests of sputum and urine; and aspiration of spinal fluid, cell washings, and bone marrow for chromosomal analysis. (See *Common cytologic specimens,* page 33.)

Pap test
The Pap test is most widely recognized for its use in early detection of cervical cancer. In addition, the test may detect endometrial and extrauterine malignancy in an asymptomatic patient. Optimal samplings for cytologic analysis include cervical scrapings, an endometrial swab, and a swab of the vaginal pool. These specimens contain cells that have been exfoliated from the cervix, vaginal wall, endometrium, and, occasionally, the fallopian tubes and ovaries.

The result of a cervical smear is reported by Papanicolaou class: Class I—absence of atypical or abnormal cells; Class II—atypical cells present, no evidence of malignancy; Class III—suggestive of but inconclusive for malignancy; Class IV—strongly suggestive of malignancy; Class V—conclusive for malignancy. An abnormal smear (Class IV or V) requires

Interpreting the differential
To make an accurate diagnosis, consider both relative and absolute values of the differential. Considered alone, relative results may point to one disorder while masking the true pathology that would be revealed by considering the results of the white blood cell (WBC) count. For example, consider a patient whose WBC count is 6,000/μl and whose differential shows 30% neutrophils and 70% lymphocytes. His relative lymphocyte count would seem quite high (lymphocytosis); but when this figure is multiplied by his WBC count—6,000 × 70% = 4,200 lymphocytes/μl—it is well within the normal range. This patient's neutrophil count, however, is low (30%), and when this is multiplied by the WBC count—6,000 × 30% = 1,800 neutrophils/μl—the result is a low absolute number.

This low result indicates decreased neutrophil production, which may mean depressed bone marrow function.

Blood chemistry and hematologic findings in cancer

Test	Normal findings	Implications of abnormal findings
Blood chemistry		
Calcium	*Atomic absorption:* 8.7 to 10.1 mg/dl	*Increased levels:* multiple myeloma, parathyroid tumors *Decreased levels:* alkalosis, hyperphosphatemia
Acid phosphatase	0 to 1.1 Bodansky units/ml 1 to 4 King-Armstrong units/ml 0.13 to 0.63 BLB units/ml	*Increased levels:* bone metastases, prostatic carcinoma
Alkaline phosphatase	1.5 to 4 Bodansky units/dl 4 to 13.5 King-Armstrong units/dl *Chemical inhibition method:* Men: 90 to 239 units/dl Women under age 45: 76 to 196 units/liter Women over age 45: 87 to 250 units/liter	*Increased levels:* bone metastases, Hodgkin's disease, liver metastases *Decreased levels:* hypophosphatemia, malnutrition
Serum glutamic-pyruvic transaminase	Men: 10 to 32 units/liter Women: 9 to 24 units/liter	*Increased levels:* liver metastases
Serum glutamic-oxaloacetic transaminase	8 to 20 units/liter	*Increased levels:* leukemia, liver metastases
Lactic dehydrogenase	45 to 115 IU/liter	*Increased levels:* acute leukemia, extensive cancer, liver metastases
Gastrin	<0.300 pg/ml	*Increased levels:* gastrinomas, stomach cancer
Total protein	6 to 8 g/dl	*Increased levels:* multiple myeloma *Decreased levels:* malnutrition
Albumin	3.3 to 4.5 g/dl	*Increased levels:* Hodgkin's disease, leukemia, multiple myeloma *Decreased levels:* malnutrition
Globulins	1.5 to 3 g/dl	*Increased levels:* Hodgkin's disease, multiple myeloma
Hematology		
Hematocrit	Men: 42% to 54% Women: 38% to 46%	*Increased levels:* cerebellar hemangioblastoma, hepatocellular carcinoma, renal tumor *Decreased levels:* leukemia, lymphoma
White blood cell count	5,000 to 10,000 /µl	*Increased levels:* leukemia, various malignancies *Decreased levels:* bone marrow depression after chemotherapy or radiation
White blood cell differential *Neutrophils*	50% to 70% (1,950 to 8,400/µl)	*Increased levels:* myelogenous leukemia *Decreased levels:* acute lymphoblastic leukemia
Lymphocytes	16.2% to 43% (1,000 to 4,600/µl)	*Increased levels:* lymphocytic leukemia *Decreased levels:* Hodgkin's disease, severe debilitating disease
Monocytes	2% to 6% (100 to 600/µl)	*Increased levels:* lymphomas, monocytic leukemia, multiple myeloma
Eosinophils	1% to 4% (50 to 250/µl)	*Increased levels:* Hodgkin's disease, various malignant tumors, myelogenous leukemia *Decreased levels:* aplastic anemia
Basophils	0.3% to 2% (12 to 200/µl)	*Increased levels:* myelogenous leukemia
Platelet count	130,000 to 370,000/mm^3	*Increased levels:* chronic granulocytic leukemia, various malignant tumors *Decreased levels:* aplastic anemia, bone marrow depression

confirmation by colposcopy, biopsy, or endo-cervical curettage.

The American Cancer Society (ACS) recommends a Pap test every 3 years for women between the ages of 20 and 65 who are not in a high-risk category and who have had two negative Pap smears a year apart. The ACS reasons that cervical cancer is slow-growing, and the number of cases detected at yearly intervals isn't significantly greater than the number detected at 3-year intervals. However, the American College of Obstetricians and Gynecologists (ACOG) disagrees, recommending annual Pap tests. As support for its recommendation, the ACOG cites the test's low cost and the possibility that patients screened at 3-year intervals may neglect regular breast and genital examinations.

Sputum tests

Cytologic examination of sputum helps detect lung cancer. Examination of early morning specimens collected over several days (usually 3) increases test sensitivity because of an overnight accumulation of sputum containing cells exfoliated from the bronchi and lung parenchyma.

Before the test, the patient brushes his teeth or rinses with saline solution to reduce specimen contamination with oral bacteria and food particles; then, he inhales repeatedly to full capacity, and finally exhales with an expulsive cough. In the hospital, if the patient is unable to raise a sputum sample, he may require aerosol inhalation of a saline solution via nebulizer or endotracheal suction with a sputum trap.

Urine tests

Cytologic tests of urine can detect but cannot localize new or recurrent urinary tract malignancies. Cells (mostly transitional) are constantly exfoliated from the renal pelvis, ureters, bladder wall, prostatic ducts, and urethra. The rate of exfoliation increases with cancer or inflammation.

Urine cytology requires collection and refrigeration of 25 to 50 ml of a first-voided morning specimen, using the clean-catch technique. Catheterization may be necessary if the patient can't void voluntarily.

Fluid aspiration

Fine-needle (19G to 23G) aspiration of body fluids permits evaluation of a palpable mass, a lymph node, or a lesion that has been localized by X-rays.

Cerebrospinal fluid (CSF) analysis. Fine-needle aspiration of CSF aids detection of malignant cells and determination of their origin (primary tumors of the central nervous system or metastatic involvement of the meninges). CSF is most commonly obtained by lumbar puncture (usually between the third and fourth lumbar vertebrae) and occasionally by cisternal or ventricular puncture. After the test, the patient lies flat for 6 to 12 hours. Possible complications of CSF aspiration include herniation of intracranial contents, spinal epidural abscess, spinal epidural hematoma, and meningitis.

Cell washing. Occasionally, the bronchial tree, esophagus, stomach, or uterine cavity is instilled (usually during endoscopy) with solutions that are subsequently aspirated. This procedure, called cell washing, loosens exfoliated cells from crevices and suspends them in the solution, thereby increasing the number of cells collected for cytologic examination. The procedure also increases the probability of finding recently exfoliated cells.

Chromosomal analysis. Also called karyotyping, this test allows examination of bone marrow aspirate to identify the Philadelphia (Ph[1]) chromosome, a genetic abnormality present in about 90% of patients with chronic myelogenous leukemia. Ph[1] involves translocation of chromosome 22 (long arm), usually to chromosome 9.

RADIOGRAPHIC AND IMAGING TESTS

Imaging tests visualize internal body structures to help detect, identify, and localize malignancies and, at times, to guide biopsy. Positive findings on imaging tests may require endoscopic, cytologic, or histologic confirmation. Patient preparation includes an explanation of the test; possible drug, food, and fluid restrictions; and, if a contrast medium is used, a check for a history of hypersensitivity to iodine or iodine-containing foods (such as shellfish) or a previous reaction to contrast media.

Chest X-ray

This commonly used test allows visualization of the thorax, mediastinum, heart, and lungs. However, routine chest X-ray is no longer recommended by the ACS as a cancer screening test for asymptomatic patients because of the associated risk of radiation exposure. Nevertheless, the chest X-ray (and bacteriologic examination of sputum) is indicated for the patient with cough, weight loss, or other

Common cytologic specimens

Sputum

Bronchial washings

Lung aspirate

Breast mass aspirate

Bone marrow aspirate

Cul-de-sac of Douglas aspirate

Solid tumor aspirate

Pleural fluid

Ascitic fluid

Spinal fluid

Bladder urine

Vaginal pool scrapings

Cervical scrapings

Endometrial scrapings

Understanding tomography

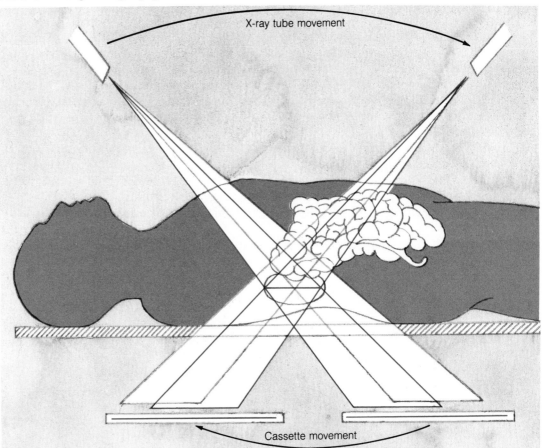

X-ray tube movement

Cassette movement

Tomography provides clearly focused radiographic images of selected body sections otherwise obscured by the shadows of underlying or overlying structures. During this diagnostic test, the X-ray tube and film move around the patient in opposite directions, producing exposures in which a selected body plane appears sharply defined and the areas above and below the plane are blurred.

symptoms of pulmonary malignancy. In addition, this test aids in evaluation of pleural effusions, hilar masses, and mediastinal lymphadenopathy.

Other radiographic tests
Kidney-ureter-bladder radiography detects distortion of renal structures; kidney size; or hydronephrosis from kidney or ureteral masses, including renal cell tumors; Wilms' tumor; and carcinoma, lymphoma, or sarcoma. It can also detect renal displacement resulting from a retroperitoneal tumor. *Bone X-rays* reveal osteolytic lesions (decreased bone density), osteoblastic lesions (increased density), or periosteal reaction with excess bone production. *Spinal X-rays* demonstrate collapse of vertebral bodies or loss of pedicles.

Tomography
Although tomography is more sensitive than plain film in detecting or ruling out a suspected lesion, this test emits high radiation

levels. In tomography, an X-ray tube and film move around the patient (the linear tube sweep) in opposite directions, producing exposures in which a selected body plane appears sharply defined, while the areas above and below this plane are blurred. (See *Understanding tomography.*) Tomography is especially valuable in examining the skull and is also useful in detecting bone, lung, and renal lesions.

Mammography
Mammography evaluates breast cysts and tumors, especially those not palpable on physical examination. This procedure uses standard radiographic film; xeroradiography, another method of performing mammography, uses a selenium-coated plate to record the X-ray image. The plate is developed with a toner that produces a blue image on details of the part examined. Characteristically, xeroradiography records a wider range than standard X-ray film and shows more contrast and

edge detail, permitting identification of smaller structures.

A round, smooth mass with definable edges suggests a benign cyst; calcification, if present, is usually coarse. An irregular shape with extension into adjacent tissue and increased vascularity suggests malignancy; associated calcification is common and occurs as fine, sandlike granules or small deposits. Benign cysts tend to be bilateral, whereas malignant tumors are unilateral. Findings that suggest cancer require further tests, such as biopsy, for confirmation.

The ACS recommends a baseline mammogram, using low-dose mammography (less than 1 rad for two views), for women between the ages of 35 and 40. Afterward, women under age 50 should consult their doctors about their need for mammography; women over age 50 should have an annual mammogram.

Thermography
Breast thermography is an infrared photographic procedure that measures and records heat patterns of breast tissue. Thermography aids detection of breast cancer because the presence of a malignant lesion raises the skin temperature and increases vascularity of the breast. Asymmetric breast changes may also indicate malignancy. Abnormalities of the breast appear on thermograms as white areas, or hot spots. Additional tests, such as mammography and biopsy, are necessary to confirm breast cancer.

Contrast radiography
In radiography, contrast media are frequently used to highlight details of structures with similar densities. Radiopaque contrast media enhance X-ray absorption; radiolucent contrast media reduce it.

Angiography. This test, performed before surgery to map the extent of a tumor, involves the injection of a contrast medium into the arterial circulation of tumors of the head, neck, retroperitoneum, abdomen, pelvis, or extremities.

In *cerebral angiography,* blood vessel displacement reflects the presence and size of a tumor. With the increasing use of computerized tomography (CT) scans, cerebral angiography is usually limited to outlining the vascular supply of a tumor. However, this test can detect some tumors that a CT scan may miss. In *renal angiography,* tumors usually show hypervascularity; cysts typically appear as clearly delineated, radiolucent masses.

Nursing care after the test involves maintaining a pressure dressing on the injection site, watching for bleeding and increased swelling, and checking circulation in the extremities (color, pain, numbness, decreased pulses).

Gastrointestinal (GI) studies. Contrast radiography helps assess the esophagus, stomach, small intestine, and colon. GI studies that involve barium may cause constipation, requiring increased fluid intake and a high-fiber diet. Stool softeners or laxatives may be necessary.

The *barium swallow,* or esophagography, is the cineradiographic examination of the pharynx and the fluoroscopic examination of the esophagus after ingestion of barium sulfate. The barium swallow detects strictures; tumors; diverticula; and functional disorders, including esophageal spasm and achalasia. Further testing confirms diagnosis.

The *upper GI and small bowel series* is the fluoroscopic examination of the esophagus, stomach, and small intestine after ingestion of barium sulfate. As the barium passes through the digestive tract, fluoroscopy outlines peristalsis and the mucosal contours of the respective organs, and spot films record significant findings. X-ray studies of the esophagus reveal strictures and tumors. Benign strictures usually dilate the esophagus proximal to the stricture and show normal mucosa, whereas malignant ones do not dilate the esophagus but change the mucosal contour. All tumors produce filling defects in the barium column, but only malignant ones change the mucosal contour. Biopsy is necessary for definitive diagnosis of both esophageal strictures and tumors.

X-ray of the stomach may reveal malignant tumors and ulcers. Malignant tumors, usually adenocarcinomas, appear as filling defects and usually disrupt peristalsis. Benign tumors, such as adenomatous polyps and leiomyomas, appear as outpouchings of the gastric mucosa and generally don't affect peristalsis. Benign ulcers may demonstrate evidence of healing and are characterized by radiating folds extending to the edge of the ulcer crater. Malignant ulcers usually associated with a suspicious mass generally have radiating folds extending beyond the ulcer crater to the edge of the mass.

Occasionally, X-rays of the stomach detect signs of pancreatic carcinoma, including edematous changes in the mucosa of the antrum or duodenal loop or dilation of the

Predicting prognosis with patient performance

Performance status (PS), as proposed by the American Joint Committee on Cancer, evaluates cancer's effect on the patient's life-style. Measured at the time of diagnosis and with each follow-up visit, PS helps predict prognosis and direct treatment. The PS rating relies on these criteria:
• The patient can carry on normal activities.
• The patient is symptomatic but ambulatory. He can care for most of his personal needs.
• The patient is ambulatory more than 50% of the time. Occasionally, he needs assistance.
• The patient is ambulatory 50% of the time or less and requires nursing care.
• The patient is bedridden and may require hospitalization.

duodenal loop. X-rays of the small intestine may also reveal tumors. In addition, filling defects can occur in Hodgkin's disease and lymphosarcoma.

The *barium enema* is the radiographic examination of the large intestine after rectal instillation of barium sulfate (single-contrast technique) or barium sulfate and air (double-contrast technique). As required, colonoscopy commonly follows the barium enema to detect higher lesions. Carcinoma usually appears as a localized filling defect, involving a sharp transition between the normal and the necrotic mucosa. These characteristics may help distinguish carcinoma from the more diffuse lesions of inflammatory disease. Biopsy or cytologic brushing confirms the diagnosis.

Lymphangiography. This test is the radiographic visualization of the lymphatic system after the injection of an oil-based contrast medium into a lymphatic vessel of each foot or, less commonly, of each hand. Injection into the foot allows visualization of the lymphatics of the leg, inguinal and iliac regions, and the retroperitoneum up to the thoracic duct. X-ray films are taken immediately after injection to demonstrate the filling of the lymphatic system, and again 24 hours later (and occasionally 48 hours later) to visualize the lymph nodes. The dye persists in the nodes for at least 6 months, allowing repeat studies to confirm disease and monitor response to treatment.

Lymphangiography is used for staging lymphomas, Hodgkin's disease, and testicular and prostate cancer. Enlarged, foamy-looking nodes indicate lymphomas. Filling defects or lack of opacification indicates metastasis to the lymph nodes.

Possible complications include incisional infection, lymphangitis (chills, high fever, swelling, pain), pulmonary oil embolism (shortness of breath, pleuritic pain, hypotension), and swelling of the extremity.

Myelography. After injection of a contrast medium, myelography combines fluoroscopy and radiography to evaluate the spinal subarachnoid space. This test can demonstrate or rule out a space-occupying lesion compressing or lying within the spinal canal.

In this test, a lumbar puncture is made between the third and fourth lumbar vertebrae; fluoroscopy verifies proper needle placement in the subarachnoid space. At this time, a sample of spinal fluid may be removed for routine laboratory analysis. The patient is turned to the prone position. Then, with the spinal needle in place, a contrast medium is injected and the table tilted. Fluoroscopy allows visualization of the flow of contrast medium through the subarachnoid space, and X-rays are taken for a permanent record. After the procedure, the patient's position (lying or sitting) depends on the type of contrast medium used. Post-test care involves monitoring for nausea, vomiting, dizziness, pain, and neurologic deficits and encouraging fluid intake.

Ultrasonography

Because ultrasonography delivers no ionizing radiation and is noninvasive, it's considered less hazardous than contrast imaging tests. In ultrasonography, a focused beam of high-frequency sound waves passes into internal organs, creating echoes that vary with changes in tissue density. When these echoes are converted to electrical energy and amplified by a transducer, they appear on an oscilloscope screen as a pattern of spikes or dots. This pattern reveals the size, shape, and position of organs.

Ultrasonography is used to evaluate organs and localize masses, except in the lungs and bone because sound waves cannot travel through air or bone. Ultrasonography is also used to guide biopsy and monitor therapy. The test can evaluate the thyroid, gallbladder and biliary system, liver, spleen, pancreas, and kidneys.

Thyroid ultrasonography. In this test, cysts appear as smooth-bordered, echo-free areas; adenomas and carcinomas appear either solid and well demarcated, with identical echo patterns, or less frequently, solid, with cystic areas. Carcinoma infiltrating the gland may not be well demarcated.

Gallbladder ultrasonography. In this test, polyps and carcinomas within the lumen are distinguished from gallstones by their fixity. Polyps usually appear as sharply defined, echogenic areas; carcinomas appear as poorly defined masses, often associated with a thickened gallbladder wall.

Liver ultrasonography. This test detects metastasis and defines tumors, abscesses, or cysts as cold spots. Characteristics of liver metastasis—the most common intrahepatic neoplasm—are variable, appearing either as hypoechoic or echogenic, poorly defined or well defined. Primary hepatic tumors also present a varied appearance and may mimic metastases. These tumors require angiography and biopsy for definitive diagnosis.

Improving the odds with special procedures

Technologically advanced procedures, such as electron microscopy, monoclonal antibody imaging, and immunohistochemical analysis, allow early and precise detection of certain cancers. Measurement of hormone receptors, another sophisticated procedure, helps predict the breast cancer patient's response to hormonal therapy.

Electron microscopy
Electron microscopy permits examination of cellular structures that are too small for visualization by light microscopy. It may be more useful than light microscopy in demonstrating cytoplasmic differentiation in extremely undifferentiated malignant neoplasms. However, it's most useful for classifying soft-tissue tumors and thymic neoplasms and for identifying neurosecretory granules in endocrine neoplasms and small round-cell tumors in children.

Monoclonal antibody imaging
Monoclonal antibodies, produced by clones of a single cell, are attracted to specific cancer cells. Laboratory production of these antibodies begins with the injection of an antigen into a mouse. Then, antibody-producing cells are removed from the mouse's spleen and mixed with mouse cancer cells, resulting in hybridomas, which are cloned, screened, and purified to make monoclonal antibodies. Radiolabeled monoclonal antibodies are then administered I.V. to patients, allowing detection of malignant tumors too small for visualization by a computerized tomography scan and other tests.

Immunohistochemical procedures
Immunofluorescence and the immunoperoxidase technique, two procedures using specific radiolabeled antibodies, can localize antigens in tissue. In immunofluorescence, fluorescent dyes are attached to antibody molecules. When the antibody is complexed with antigen and viewed under an ultraviolet microscope, it appears as a colored fluorescence.

The immunoperoxidase technique, a method of histologic staining, provides excellent morphologic detail by ordinary light microscopy. It can identify a poorly differentiated metastatic tumor, demonstrate an abnormal distribution or number of cells and loss of normal tissue antigens, and detect oncofetal antigens in a malignant tumor.

Measurement of hormone receptors
In breast cancer, measurement of hormone receptors helps predict patient response to hormonal therapy. The test measures estrogen receptor (ER) and, frequently, progesterone receptor (PR) levels in biopsy specimens. ER levels of less than 3 femtomoles (a femtomole equals 10^{-15} moles of receptor protein per milligram of cytosol protein) are considered negative; levels of 3 to 10 femtomoles/mg are intermediate; and levels greater than 10 femtomoles/mg are positive.

About 50% of ER-positive patients show a favorable response to hormonal therapy. In contrast, less than 10% of ER-negative patients show a favorable response. Also, the presence of PR improves the chances of successful hormonal therapy. Some investigational studies demonstrate that the PR level is more important as a prognostic indicator than the ER level.

Spleen ultrasonography. As a complementary procedure to liver-spleen scanning, spleen ultrasonography identifies cystic or solid lesions as cold spots. Splenic cysts are difficult to distinguish from hematoma or abscess. In leukemia and lymphoma, the spleen appears hard and extremely enlarged with a distinct border. In spleen ultrasonography, dilated pancreatic and biliary ducts and an enlarged nodular pancreas with a homogeneous texture suggest pancreatic carcinoma.

Renal ultrasonography. In this test, cysts have smooth, well-defined borders and don't reflect sound waves. In contract, tumors have irregular shapes and produce multiple echoes.

Radionuclide imaging
This test uses a gamma scintillation camera or a rectilinear scanner to provide images of an organ after I.V. injection of a radionuclide. The scintillation camera or scanner detects rays emitted by the radionuclide—usually technetium 99m pertechnetate—and converts them into images that are then displayed on an oscilloscope screen. A lack of radionuclide uptake by an organ or delay in uptake or excretion denotes loss of function in the organ or part of the organ. The test is sensitive but not specific because areas of inflammation or trauma may also concentrate the radionuclide.

Brain scan. Usually, this scan can detect lesions, such as highly malignant gliomas and meningiomas, since the radionuclide readily accumulates in the presence of such abnormalities. However, the scan is less accurate for identifying certain benign or low-grade malignant tumors that characteristically take up the radionuclide less readily.

Bone scan. This scan can detect bone malignancy, but its findings must be interpreted in light of the patient's medical and surgical history, X-rays, and laboratory tests, since any process causing increased calcium excretion is reflected by an increased radionuclide uptake in bone.

Renal scan. Depending on the patient's clinical status, the renal scan may include dynamic scans to assess renal perfusion and function or static scans to assess structure. Images from perfusion studies can help differentiate tumors from cysts because malignant renal tumors are usually vascular. In the function study, outflow obstruction reduces radionuclide activity in the tubules but increases it in the collecting system. This test can also define the level of ureteral obstruction. Static images can demonstrate space-occupying lesions, such as tumors, within or surrounding the kidney.

Gallium scanning. This test, a total body scan, is usually performed 24 to 48 hours after the I.V. injection of radioactive gallium citrate. Because gallium has an affinity for both benign and malignant neoplasms and inflammatory lesions, exact diagnosis requires confirming tests, such as ultrasonography and CT scans. Abnormally high gallium accumulation occurs in carcinoma of the colon. However, since gallium normally accumulates in the colon, the detection of malignancies is difficult. Other types of tumors that concentrate gallium in detectable amounts include tumors of the lung, breast, cervix, and liver; lymphomas; and melanomas. Gallium scanning may also detect new or recurrent tumors after chemotherapy or radiation therapy.

CT scan

Performed with or without contrast media, CT scanning is an X-ray technique that is far more sensitive than conventional X-ray films in providing images of internal body structures. Multiple X-ray beams travel through organs while detectors record the tissue attenuation of the beams. A computer reconstructs this information as a three-dimensional image on an oscilloscope screen. CT scanning can examine virtually every part of the body, including the head, orbit of the eye, thorax, biliary tract and liver, pancreas, and kidneys. Areas of altered density or displaced vasculature and changes in size and shapes of organs may indicate primary tumors or metastases.

Magnetic resonance imaging (MRI)

Also called nuclear magnetic resonance, this promising noninvasive technique may be superior to CT scanning in detecting cerebellar lesions and metastatic bone marrow disease and in identifying soft tissue masses. Because MRI doesn't employ ionizing radiation, it may permit safe serial studies of children and pregnant women. MRI cannot be used in patients with pacemakers or metal surgical clips in vital areas such as the brain, because metal is affected by the magnetic force.

MRI directs radio and magnetic waves at body tissue to determine the response of test elements, such as hydrogen atoms, that function as tiny magnets. When an external magnetic force is applied, these atoms align themselves within the magnetic field. Then, for a brief period of time, the atoms are bombarded with radio-frequency signals that deflect them from their induced alignment. When the radio signals stop, the energized atoms emit a return signal. A computer analyzes this signal, which varies according to the tissue concentrations of the test element and the time required by the atoms to return to their original alignment. Characteristically, these relaxation times differ for each type of body tissue, but they are sometimes prolonged for malignant tissue.

ENDOSCOPY

In endoscopic tests, a rigid or flexible tube called an endoscope is inserted into a viscus of the body to allow visualization of internal structure. (See *Normal endoscopic landmarks of the upper GI tract.*) All endoscopes contain a light source and channels that can accommodate biopsy forceps, cytology brush, suction, lavage, anesthetic, or oxygen. Most types of endoscopes also allow use of a microscope, camera, and implements for performing minor surgery, such as cauterization of an endobronchial lesion or removal of polyps in the colon.

Rigid endoscopes have a larger internal diameter than flexible endoscopes and allow removal of larger specimens and secretions or excretions that obliterate the view. However, rigid endoscopes cannot be passed beyond strictures, and they usually require a general anesthetic. Flexible endoscopes are tolerated with a minimum of discomfort, can be inserted under a local anesthetic, and carry less risk of trauma from intubation than rigid endoscopes. Also, flexible endoscopes allow visualization of distant structures (such as

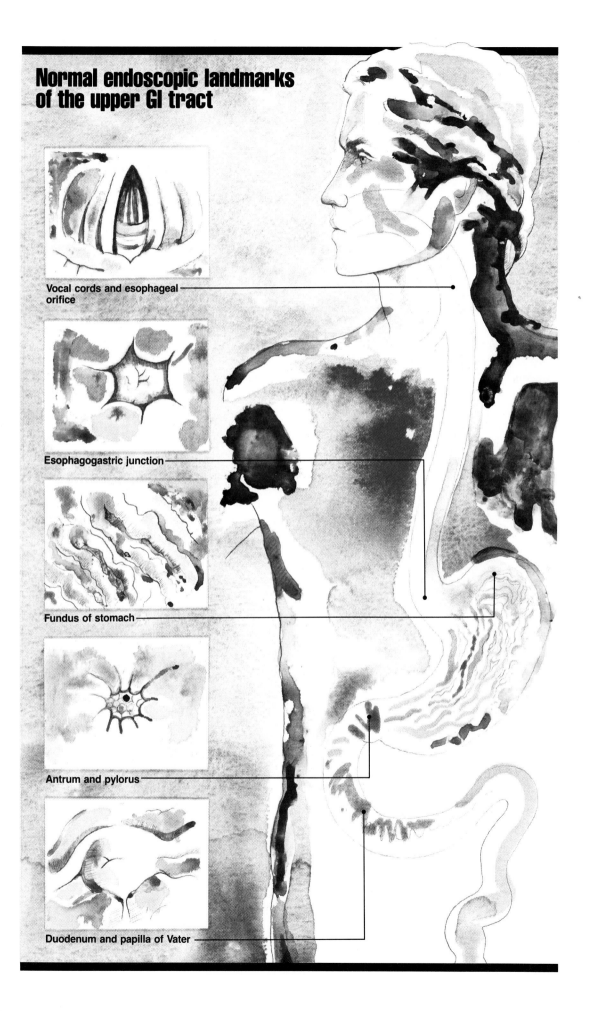

Normal endoscopic landmarks of the upper GI tract

Vocal cords and esophageal orifice

Esophagogastric junction

Fundus of stomach

Antrum and pylorus

Duodenum and papilla of Vater

the bronchial tree and colon), permitting distal biopsy or cytology, and out-of-the-way structures (such as the larynx and the nasopharynx).

Preparation. Preparing a patient for endoscopy involves assessing his anxiety level and ability to follow directions and explaining the purpose of the test, how and where it's done, and what he can expect to experience. It also includes ensuring that the patient signs a consent form, completes the necessary blood tests (such as hematocrit, platelet count, and coagulation studies), and adheres to food and fluid restrictions, as ordered. Finally, pretest care also includes taking baseline vital signs and administering premedication, as ordered.

Post-test care. After endoscopy, nursing considerations involve monitoring the patient for signs of adverse reaction to the anesthetic or sedative (rapid, pounding pulse; hypertension; rapid, deep respirations; euphoria; excitation; and palpitations); administering analgesics, as ordered; and watching for infection, excessive bleeding, and signs of perforation.

After endoscopy of the upper GI tract, nursing care also involves maintaining food and fluid restrictions until the patient's gag reflex returns and monitoring for signs of respiratory difficulty (laryngeal stridor and dyspnea, resulting from laryngeal edema or laryngospasm), hypoxemia (cyanosis), pneumothorax (dyspnea, cyanosis, diminished breath sounds on the affected side), bronchospasm (dyspnea, wheezing), or bleeding (hemoptysis). Keep resuscitative equipment and a tracheotomy tray readily available for 24 hours after this test.

Direct laryngoscopy

In direct laryngoscopy, a fiberoptic endoscope or laryngoscope passed through the mouth and pharynx to the larynx allows visualization of the larynx. Direct laryngoscopy usually follows indirect laryngoscopy, the more common procedure. (Indirect laryngoscopy, normally an office procedure, allows visualization of the larynx, using a warm laryngeal mirror held in front of the mouth and a light source. The larynx is observed at rest and during phonation. A simple excision of polyps may also be performed during this test.) The combined results of direct laryngoscopy, biopsy, and radiography may indicate laryngeal carcinoma. Direct laryngoscopy may reveal benign lesions, strictures, or foreign bodies and,

with a biopsy, this test may distinguish laryngeal edema from radiation reaction or tumor.

Bronchoscopy

Bronchoscopy is the direct visualization of the trachea and tracheobronchial tree through a standard metal or flexible bronchoscope to obtain bronchial washings, brushings, or biopsy. This test allows visual examination of a possible tumor, as demonstrated on an X-ray, and allows fulguration and excision of lesions. Combined results of tissue and cell studies may indicate bronchogenic carcinoma, such as epidermoid or squamous cell carcinoma, adenocarcinoma, or bronchiolar carcinoma. Bronchoscopy may also be used with a laser to open airways that are obstructed by a tumor.

Mediastinoscopy

This surgical procedure allows direct visualization of mediastinal structures and palpation and biopsy of paratracheal and carinal lymph nodes. The mediastinum is the mass of tissues and organs behind the sternum, separating the lungs. Its major contents include the heart and its vessels, the trachea, esophagus, thymus, and lymph nodes. Mediastinoscopy, performed under a general anesthetic, requires an incision over the area to be examined. Examination of the lymph nodes, which drain from the lungs, can detect lymphomas (including Hodgkin's disease) and sarcoidosis and aids in staging lung cancer, which helps determine treatment. For example, extensive nodular involvement can contraindicate surgery in many tumors.

Esophagoscopy and gastroscopy

Esophagoscopy is the visual examination of the esophagus. Although a flexible endoscope is typically used in this test, a rigid endoscope may be used to provide a better view of a tumor, to obtain a larger specimen for biopsy, or to place stents for palliation in advanced esophageal carcinoma. Gastroscopy allows direct visualization of the gastric mucosa. If gastric cancer is suspected, a flexible gastroscope is used to obtain a specimen for biopsy or cytology.

Endoscopic retrograde cholangiopancreatography (ERCP)

This test allows radiographic examination of the pancreatic ducts and hepatobiliary tree after cannulation and injection of a contrast medium into the duodenal papilla. Examination of the hepatobiliary tree may reveal carcinoma of the bile ducts. Examination of the pancreatic ducts may show pancreatic tumor, carcinoma of the head of the pancreas, and carcinoma of the duodenal papilla. Before the test, premedication may include a sedative or narcotic, an anticholinergic to decrease secretions, and a drug such as glucagon to slow peristalsis. A topical anesthetic decreases the gag reflex and permits easier passage of the endoscope; nevertheless, the patient may still vomit when it is passed. After ERCP of the bile ducts, the patient requires monitoring for signs of infection, such as epigastric pain and vomiting.

Colonoscopy

This test allows visual examination of the lining of the large intestine with a flexible fiberoptic endoscope. This instrument is inserted anally and advanced through the large intestine under direct vision, using the scope's optical system.

Colonoscopy can locate the origin of lower GI bleeding, aids diagnosis of colonic strictures and benign or malignant lesions, and can evaluate the colon after surgery for recurrence of polyps or malignant lesions. The test also allows removal of foreign bodies, polyps, or other tissue for biopsy. Preparation for colonoscopy requires a liquid diet for 3 days before the test, a laxative the evening before, and a warm tap-water or sodium biphosphate enema 3 to 4 hours before the test, as ordered. During this test, the patient breathes slowly and deeply during insertion to help relax abdominal muscles and ease the passage of the endoscope.

Proctosigmoidoscopy

Proctosigmoidoscopy is the endoscopic examination of the lining of the distal sigmoid colon, the rectum, and the anal canal. This test is indicated in persistent idiopathic rectal bleeding or as a follow-up to an abnormal barium enema. Malignant masses or polyps, or nonmalignant conditions (benign polyps, hemorrhoids, or inflammatory bowel disease) may cause bleeding.

This procedure involves a digital examination, sigmoidoscopy, and proctoscopy. During digital examination, the anal sphincters are dilated to detect obstructions that might hinder the passage of the endoscope. During sigmoidoscopy, a 10″ to 12″ (25- to 30-cm) rigid sigmoidoscope is inserted into the anus to allow visualization of the distal sigmoid

colon and rectum. (The flexible sigmoidoscope permits an examination up to 20″ [50 cm] from the anus.) During proctoscopy, a 2¾″ (7-cm) rigid proctoscope is inserted into the anus to aid examination of the lower rectum and anal canal. At any step in the procedure, specimens may be obtained from suspicious areas of the mucosa by biopsy, lavage or cytology brush, or culture swab. In addition, rectal and sigmoid polyps may be removed.

Proctosigmoidoscopy requires a liquid diet for 48 hours before the test, a laxative the evening before the test, and a tap-water or sodium biphosphate enema, as ordered. The ACS recommends this screening test for colon cancer every 3 to 5 years after two normal annual tests for all persons over age 50.

Colposcopy

Visualization of the vagina and cervix with a colposcope permits thorough examination and biopsy of small areas of dysplasia, carcinoma in situ, and invasive cancer. Colposcopy is indicated in suspicious Pap test smears, cervical lesions, or abnormal vaginal epithelial patterns. It's also indicated for women whose mothers received diethylstilbestrol during pregnancy.

Abnormal colposcopy findings include white epithelium or punctation and mosaic patterns, which may indicate underlying cervical intraepithelial neoplasia. Other abnormal test findings include keratinization in the transformation zone, which may indicate cervical intraepithelial neoplasia or invasive carcinoma; and atypical vessels, which may indicate invasive carcinoma. Histologic study of the biopsy confirms colposcopic findings. However, if the findings from the examination and biopsy are inconsistent with the results of the Pap test and biopsy of the squamocolumnar junction, conization of the cervix for biopsy may be indicated. Use of the colposcope to perform conization allows removal of a smaller specimen. In carcinoma in situ, colposcopy allows treatment by cryosurgery or laser.

Cystoscopy

Visualization of the lower urinary tract with a cystoscope allows evaluation of painless hematuria, a symptom of bladder cancer, and tumor recurrence in patients with a history of bladder cancer. Passage of a cystoscope allows inspection of the bladder wall for tumors, polyps, or other abnormalities. Passage of ureteral catheters permits evaluation of obstructions. During this procedure, a retrograde

Reviewing histology requirements

Histology, the study of the microscopic structure of tissues and cells, is increasingly important in confirming cancer. Accurate histologic diagnosis requires a representative or complete tissue specimen obtained by excisional, incisional, cone, or needle biopsy. It also requires careful handling, storage, and preparation of the specimen to ensure accurate test results.

Tissue storage and preparation
Biopsy often requires placement of the specimen in a fixative solution (commonly, 10% buffered formaldehyde). If a fixing fluid isn't immediately available, refrigeration of the tissue temporarily (up to 24 hours) prevents its deterioration.

When a tissue specimen arrives in the histology department, a *frozen section analysis* permits an immediate treatment decision during surgery. The histologist quickly freezes a representative section of tissue and then cuts the hardened tissue into microscopic sections for staining and analysis. (Generally, a pathologic diagnosis is available within 10 to 15 minutes after removal.) If a dis-

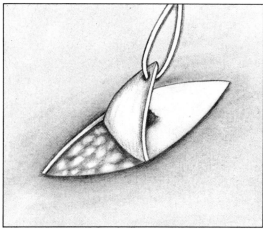

Excisional biopsy is the scalpel removal of an entire lesion, including a margin of normal-appearing tissue. It's used to plan treatment and, for some patients, may be the definitive treatment.

Incisional biopsy, with a scalpel, cutting or aspiration needle, or punch, removes a selected portion of a lesion and, if possible, adjacent normal-appearing tissue. Incisional biopsy is used to plan treatment.

X-ray may be done to visualize the ureters and the collecting system of the kidneys. If a tumor is suspected, cytoscopy permits collection of a urine specimen for cytologic examination; if a tumor is found, the test permits biopsy. The test also allows resection and fulguration of bladder tumors. After the test, urine may appear pink or red-tinged. However, bright red clots, severe pain and anuria, or symptoms of cystitis (fever, chills, increased dysuria) should be reported. Antibiotics may be prescribed after the test to minimize the risk of infection. Increased intake of fluids should increase urinary output. However, if the patient is unable to void, catheterization may be required.

Laparoscopy
This test allows visualization of the peritoneal cavity by the insertion of a laparoscope through a small incision (¾″, or 2 cm) in the anterior abdominal wall. This surgical procedure helps diagnose ovarian carcinoma and is also used to assess the operability of a palpable mass, to obtain biopsy material, to determine the cause of ascites, or to stage lymphomas. The test may also allow evaluation of treatment for ovarian cancer. Laparoscopy does not allow visualization of the retroperitoneal organs (kidneys, ureters, pancreas, and colon).

HISTOLOGIC TESTS
Histology, the study of the microscopic structure of tissues and cells, is vitally important to confirm malignancy and has made biopsy—extraction of a living tissue specimen—a relatively common procedure. Also, if cancer is present, biopsy provides a tissue description that helps classify the malignancy. (See *Reviewing histology requirements.*) Histopathologic diagnosis is usually essential before

torted frozen section results in a questionable diagnosis, surgery may be postponed until permanent sections are made.

Results from a frozen section analysis are usually reliable, but the pathologist routinely performs a standard analysis on tissue from the same specimen to verify the diagnosis. After gross examination, the histologist imbeds the biopsy specimen in paraffin, resulting in a *permanent specimen*. This is thinly sliced and stained to demonstrate cell substances and structures. Slides include different areas of the tumor, especially the edge most likely to contain viable tumor cells. Also, the pathologist examines lymph nodes, veins leading from the tumor, and resection margins for malignant cell changes.

Classifying cancer
The pathologist's report provides both gross and microscopic descriptions, which result in histopathologic classification of the tumor. Typically, results of this analysis are expressed on a scale of four grades: GI—well differentiated; G2—moderately well differentiated; G3—poorly differentiated; G4—anaplastic.

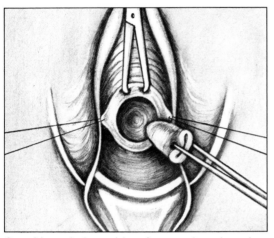

Cone biopsy is the excision of a cone-shaped specimen from the uterine cervix. It's used to diagnose or treat early cervical cancer.

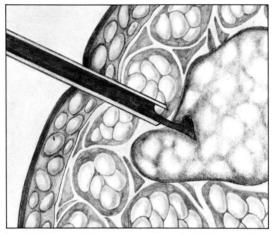

Needle biopsy is the removal of a cylindrical core of tissue (with a larger-bore needle than the fine-bore needle used in aspiration biopsy). Because the tissue specimen is so small, a negative result doesn't rule out malignancy. (Note: Illustration greatly enlarged.)

treatment for malignancy begins.

For all types of biopsy, histopathologic diagnosis relies on removal of a representative or complete tissue specimen and also includes marking of the edges and distinctive areas of the removed tissue (orientation). However, this is not done on small fragments removed by curetting of the uterine endometrium, bladder, or prostate. To prevent spreading the tumor, needle tracts and incisions are carefully placed, and extreme care is taken to avoid excessive bleeding and contamination of surrounding tissue.

Biopsies commonly take place in the hospital, but they may also take place in clinics and doctors' offices. *Open* biopsy, performed in the operating room, usually requires general anesthesia. Open biopsy is required when the results of *closed* biopsy (incision of a hidden lesion) or other diagnostic tests (such as CT scan) suggest the need for complete

excision of a tissue mass.

Before a biopsy, nursing considerations involve ensuring completion of laboratory tests and written consent, if it's necessary. Food and fluids may or may not be restricted. Psychological support is critical. It requires assessing the patient's understanding of the test and his level of anxiety, which may be relieved by distraction, relaxation techniques, or premedication. Psychological support may be especially important if biopsy and surgery are planned as a simultaneous procedure that can have a major impact on the patient's body image and life-style (for example, radical neck dissection or colon resection with colostomy).

Breast biopsy
Although mammography, thermography, and X-rays aid diagnosis of breast masses, only histologic examination of breast tissue

TNM system

The internationally recognized TNM staging system allows an accurate tumor description that can be adjusted as the disease progresses. This system helps direct treatment, predict prognosis, and contribute to cancer research by ensuring reliable comparison of patients in various hospitals.

T for primary tumor
T—the anatomic extent of the primary tumor—depends on its size, depth of invasion, and surface spread.

T_0 No evidence of primary tumor

T_1 A mobile, often superficial tumor (<2 cm in diameter) confined to the organ of origin

T_2 A localized tumor (2 to 5 cm in diameter) with some loss of mobility and deep extension into adjacent tissues

T_3 An advanced tumor (>5 cm in diameter) with complete loss of mobility, involving a region

T_4 A massive tumor (>10 cm in diameter) with extension into another organ (causing a fistula or sinus), major nerves, arteries and veins, or bone

N for nodal involvement
N depends on the size, mobility, and firmness of the tumor; capsular invasion and the depth of invasion; the number of nodes involved; and ipsilateral, contralateral, bilateral, and distant node involvement.

N_0 No evidence of lymph node involvement

N_1 Palpable, mobile lymph nodes, limited to the first station. Involved nodes are usually solitary, larger (2 to 3 cm in diameter), and firmer than normal nodes.

N_2 Palpable, partially mobile, firm-to-hard nodes (3 to 5 cm in diameter), limited to the first station. Involved nodes may show capsular and partial matted muscle invasion, and contralateral or bilateral involvement.

N_3 A node (>5 cm in diameter) with extension beyond the capsule and fixation to bone, large blood vessels, skin, or nerves

N_4 Fixed and destructive nodes (>10 cm in diameter) with extension to second or distant stations

N_x Nodes inaccessible to evaluation

M for metastasis
M refers to the presence or absence of metastasis.

M_0 No evidence of metastasis

M_1 Solitary metastasis

M_2 Multiple metastasis in one organ with no or minimal functional impairment

M_3 Metastasis to multiple organs with no or minimal-to-moderate functional impairment

M_4 Metastasis to multiple organs with moderate-to-severe functional impairment

M_x No metastatic workup done

Stages and survival
Stage I
$T_1 N_0 M_0$
70% to 90% 5-year survival

Stage II
$T_2 N_1 M_0$
50% to 70% 5-year survival

Stage III
$T_3 N_0 M_0$
$T_{1-3} N_1 M_0$
25% to 45% 5-year survival

Stage IV
$T_4 N_{0-1} M_0$
$T_{0-4} N_{2-3} M_0$
$T_{0-4} N_{0-4} M_1$
5% to 20% 5-year survival

---

obtained by biopsy can confirm or rule out cancer. Needle biopsy, which provides a core of tissue or a fluid aspirate, should be restricted to fluid-filled cysts and suspected malignant lesions. This method has limited diagnostic value because of the small and perhaps unrepresentative specimen needle biopsy provides. Open biopsy provides a complete tissue specimen, which can be sectioned to allow more accurate evaluation. Both techniques necessitate only a local anesthetic and can often be performed on outpatients; however, open biopsy may require a general anesthetic if the patient is fearful or uncooperative.

Breast biopsy is indicated in patients with palpable masses, suspicious areas in mammography, or persistently encrusted, inflamed, or eczematoid breast lesions or bloody discharge from the nipples. Breast tissue analysis includes an estrogen receptor assay, which aids selection of therapy if the mass proves malignant. (See *Improving the odds with spe-*

cial procedures, page 37.) Abnormal breast tissue may exhibit a wide range of malignant or benign pathology.

Lung biopsy
In biopsy of the lung, a specimen of pulmonary tissue is excised for histologic examination. Either closed or open technique may be used. Closed technique, performed under a local anesthetic, includes both needle and transbronchial biopsies; open technique, performed under a general anesthetic in the operating room, includes both limited and standard thoracotomies. Possible complications include bleeding, infection, and pneumothorax.

Generally, lung biopsy is recommended after chest X-ray and bronchoscopy have failed to identify the cause of diffuse parenchymal pulmonary disease or of a pulmonary lesion. The chest X-ray is repeated immediately after the biopsy. Histologic examination of a pulmonary tissue specimen can reveal squamous cell or oat cell carcinoma, adenocarcinoma, or large-cell undifferentiated carcinoma.

Percutaneous liver biopsy

Percutaneous biopsy of the liver is the needle aspiration of a core of tissue for histologic analysis. Such analysis can identify hepatic disorders after ultrasonography, CT scan, and radionuclide studies have failed to detect them. The test is performed under a local or general anesthetic.

Because many patients with hepatic disorders have clotting defects, testing for hemostasis should precede liver biopsy. During the test, the patient takes several deep breaths, exhales, and holds his breath while the doctor inserts the needle, aspirates tissue, then withdraws the needle (about 5 to 10 seconds total). After the test, positioning the patient on his right side for 2 hours with a small pillow or sandbag under the costal margin provides extra pressure. Possible complications of liver biopsy include hemorrhage, bile peritonitis, and pneumothorax.

Findings in percutaneous liver biopsy may include primary malignant tumors (hepatocellular carcinoma, cholangiocellular carcinoma, and angiosarcoma), but hepatic metastases are more common. Other findings may include diffuse hepatic disease, such as cirrhosis or hepatitis, or granulomatous infections, such as tuberculosis.

Prostate gland biopsy

Prostate gland biopsy is the needle excision of a prostate tissue specimen for histologic examination. A perineal or transrectal approach may be used; the transrectal approach is usually preferred for high prostatic lesions. Indications for this procedure include potentially malignant prostatic hypertrophy and prostatic nodules. Histologic examination can confirm cancer and can also detect benign prostatic hyperplasia, prostatitis, tuberculosis, and lymphomas.

Lymph node biopsy

This diagnostic test involves the surgical excision of an active lymph node or the needle aspiration of a nodal specimen for histologic examination. Both of these techniques employ a local anesthetic, and both usually sample the superficial nodes in the cervical, supraclavicular, axillary, or inguinal region. Excision is the preferred technique because it provides a larger, more representative specimen. Stor-

ing the specimen in normal saline solution instead of 10% formaldehyde solution allows part of the specimen to be used for cytologic examination.

Lymph node biopsy is indicated to determine the cause of lymph node enlargement, to distinguish between benign and malignant lymph node tumors, and to stage metastatic carcinomas. When histologic results aren't clear or nodular material isn't involved, mediastinoscopy or laparotomy can provide another nodal specimen.

Bone marrow biopsy

Bone marrow, the soft tissue contained in the medullary canals of long bone and in the interstices of cancellous bone, may be removed by aspiration or needle biopsy under local anesthetic. (Be aware that the patient may experience significant pressure or pain despite the use of anesthetic.) In aspiration biopsy, a fluid specimen in which bone spicules are suspended is removed from the bone marrow. In needle biopsy, a core of marrow— cells, not fluid—is removed. Occasionally, needle biopsy and aspiration biopsy are employed concurrently to obtain the best possible marrow specimens.

Because bone marrow is the major site of hematopoiesis, the histologic and hematologic examination of its contents provides reliable diagnostic information about blood disorders. Bone marrow biopsy can help diagnose leukemias; thrombocytopenias; granulomas; aplastic, hypoplastic, and pernicious anemias; and primary and metastatic tumors. In addition, this procedure can aid staging of disease, such as Hodgkin's disease; evaluate the effectiveness of chemotherapy; and help monitor myelosuppression.

Furthermore, biopsy may be used to provide specimens for the histologic examination and confirmation of malignancy in the thyroid, kidney, pleura, bone, synovial membrane, and skin.

Diagnostic complexity

Today, an ever-increasing number of diagnostic tests are being used in the diagnostic workup for suspected cancer. Many of these tests are routine, such as the CBC and chest X-ray. But many more require complex equipment, specially trained technicians, and a team of interpreters. As the complexity of tests has increased, so too has your responsibility for thorough patient preparation and attentive post-test care.

Points to remember

• Because the sensitivity and specificity of diagnostic tests vary considerably, several tests are often required to detect and stage malignant disorders.
• Accurate diagnosis and staging are essential for appropriate selection and evaluation of treatment. Histologic diagnosis is usually essential before treatment begins.
• In diagnostic tests, nursing management includes preparing the patient physically and psychologically for testing. It also includes careful monitoring for possible complications after tests.

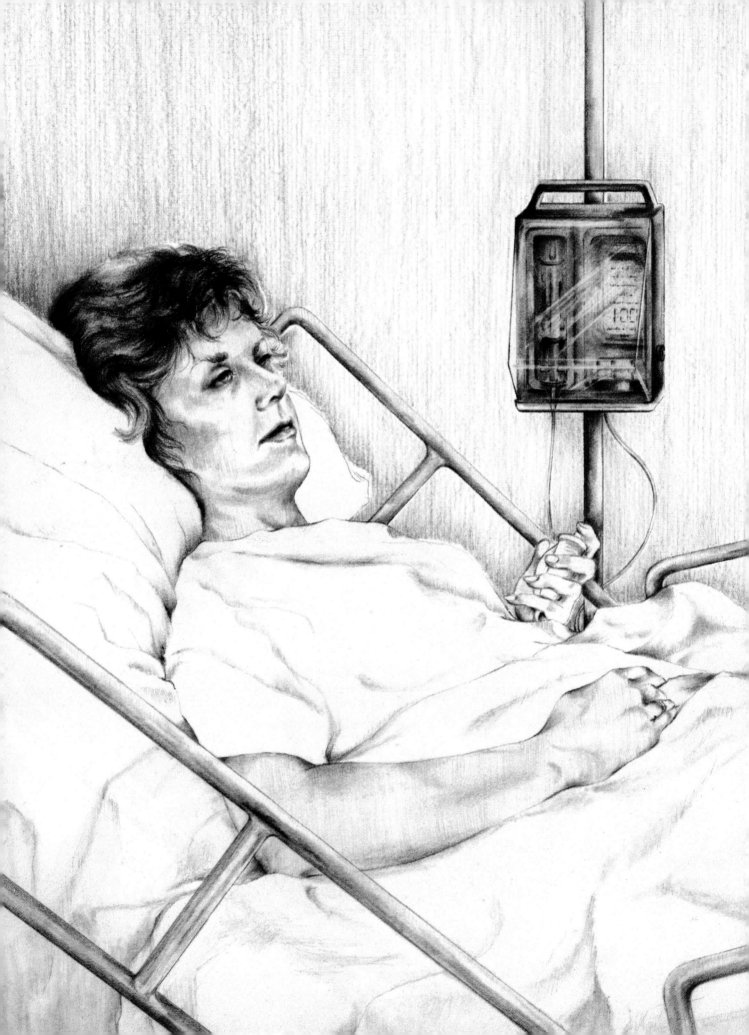

MANAGEMENT STRATEGIES

4 UNDERSTANDING PRINCIPLES OF THERAPY

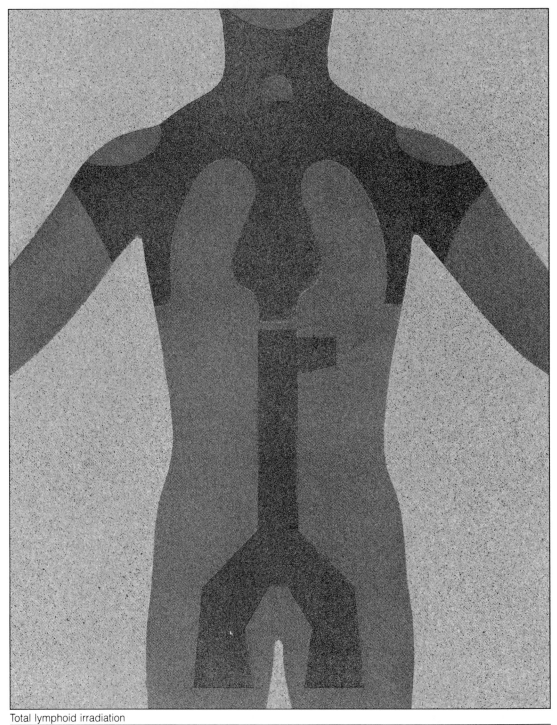

Total lymphoid irradiation

Thanks to treatment advances, cancer cure rates have improved dramatically; many patients have enjoyed longer remissions and survival, and treatment side effects have been managed better. But the battle against cancer is not over, and researchers vigorously pursue new treatments.

The goal of cancer treatment is to destroy malignant cells while minimizing damage to normal ones. To do this, a single primary treatment or a combination of treatments may be used. Today, primary treatments include surgery and radiation, which give local or regional treatment. (Surgery may also be done to *prevent* cancer in certain high-risk patients.) Chemotherapy, the third form of primary treatment, allows a systemic attack on cancer cells. When used together, these treatments can provide local *and* systemic therapy and offer the advantage of attacking cancer cells by a combination of mechanisms.

Surgery removes tumors or reduces their size (which also makes other treatment more effective because there are fewer cancerous cells to combat). *Radiation* inhibits the ability of cancer cells to divide and spread by causing breaks in the DNA strands or by cell membrane lysis. And *chemotherapy* interrupts the cells' life cycle, also inhibiting or destroying their ability to divide.

New cancer treatments—currently in limited use or under investigation—include bone marrow transplantation, immunotherapy, and monoclonal antibody therapy. (See *Three new cancer treatments,* pages 56 and 57.)

While you may not be directly involved in administering cancer treatment, you'll routinely assist and prepare the patient and his family. This chapter will help you know what the treatment selected for the patient involves and understand how it fits into his overall therapy. You must be able to:
• explain the purpose of treatment
• describe the procedure involved and its potential effects
• listen to the patient's and family's concerns about treatment and its side effects
• provide accurate answers to their questions
• provide emotional support to help the patient and his family
• monitor the patient for side effects.

SURGERY
The first—and for many years the only—cancer treatment, surgery has since developed dramatically. Today, surgical techniques exist for preventing cancer in certain high-risk patients, for detecting it, and for treating it.

Value in cancer prevention
When a patient has a disorder that's associated with a type of cancer or has a family history of a specific cancer, his doctor may suggest that he have surgery to decrease the likelihood that cancer will develop. For example, if a patient has ulcerative colitis, familial polyposis, or a family history of colon cancer, a preventive colectomy or proctectomy may eliminate the risk of colorectal cancer. Similarly, a child under age 6 with cryptorchidism (failure of the testes to descend into the scrotum) may undergo orchiopexy (not effective after age 6) to fasten the undescended testicle in the scrotum; this will reduce his risk of testicular cancer later in life.

Value in cancer diagnosis
Surgical biopsy is done to confirm cancer; laparotomy and other types of exploratory surgery are done to diagnose cancer and to assess the extent of spread.

Biopsy techniques. Definitive cancer treatment can begin only after analysis of biopsy results. The biopsy technique is chosen according to the type and location of the suspected tumor. The two types of biopsy are:
• *Aspiration.* A scalpel, cutting or aspirating needle, or punch is used to remove a portion of tissue from large, multiple, hidden lesions.
• *Excisional.* A scalpel is used to remove abnormal tissue from the skin or from subcutaneous tissue.

After the tissue specimen is obtained, it is prepared for analysis. In the past, analysis that indicated malignancy meant that definitive surgery would begin immediately. For example, a woman with positive breast biopsy results would immediately have a mastectomy while she was still under anesthesia. But today, many doctors separate biopsy and surgery. This allows patients time to adjust to the diagnosis and to evaluate their options; it also allows time for standard biopsy results to be returned, confirming the diagnosis.

Laparotomy and other exploratory surgery. Usually, laparotomy is done to detect visceral cancer, to stage malignant lymphoma such as Hodgkin's disease, and to stage ovarian cancer. Later, in a few tumor types such as ovarian cancer, if the patient's condition allows, a "second-look" laparotomy may assess recurrent cancer or the patient's response to chemotherapy. Exploratory surgery may also precede scheduled radical surgery to find occult metastases that would rule out radical surgery. For example, if exploratory surgery in a patient with esophageal cancer shows that he also has intraabdominal metastases, a scheduled esophagectomy probably won't be done. In these cases, the exploratory surgery is done immediately before the planned radical surgery, eliminating the need for the patient to undergo anesthesia twice.

Value in cancer treatment
Surgery may be used alone or in combination with other forms of treatment, depending on the treatment goal:
• cure
• pretreatment surgery to facilitate other treatments
• resolution of a cancer-related emergency
• palliation of symptoms
• reconstruction after radical surgery
• rehabilitation (restoration of function in body areas previously irradiated or surgically treated for cancer).

Curative surgery. With a solid tumor that hasn't metastasized, curative surgery is done to remove the tumor and a margin of normal tissue (regional lymph nodes may also be removed). Although this surgery is termed curative, the surgeon can't remove *every* cancer cell, so cure is hoped for rather than predicted. To reduce the risk of recurrence by destroying remaining cancer cells, postoperative patients often receive radiation treatment, chemotherapy, or both.

Debulking surgery. When a malignant tumor is too large to be excised completely, most of it may be removed using debulking surgery. This decreases the number of malignant cells so that radiation, chemotherapy, and the patient's own immunologic response will be more likely to control the cancer.

Ablative surgery. When the growth of a tumor is hormonally dependent, ablative surgery may be done to remove the organ or organs involved in producing the hormone. Then, in the absence of hormonal stimulation, the tumor will presumably grow more slowly. For example, if a woman has estrogen-dependent breast cancer, then oophorectomy, adrenalectomy, hypophysectomy, or all three, may decrease the level of circulating estrogen and retard the tumor's growth.

Surgery for cancer-related emergencies. Cancer patients can have such emergencies as hemorrhage or colon perforation. Hemorrhage may be initiated by drug therapy associated with gastritis; emergency surgery usually involves ligating a blood vessel or removing the involved portion of the affected organ. GI tract perforation can stem from direct tumor extension or from tumor cell lysis from systemic therapy. Surgery for perforation may include resecting the involved colon portion and reanastomosis or creation of an ostomy.

Pretreatment surgery. Certain types of chemotherapy and radiation need preliminary surgery for access. For example, surgery is needed to insert a Hickman or Broviac catheter for venous access or to put a Silastic catheter in the abdominal cavity for chemotherapy. Such surgery is also needed to insert applicators for internal radiation implants.

Palliative surgery. When cancer-related pain (especially unilateral caudal pain) can't be controlled by narcotics or radiation, palliative surgery may be done. The procedure used depends on the site of the patient's pain.

The most common neurosurgical procedure for permanent pain control is *cordotomy,* which may be unilateral or bilateral. This procedure involves cutting the spinothalamic fibers above the site of pain. But surgery to control pain is usually a last resort because of potential complications, such as sexual dysfunction and urinary retention.

Dorsal rhizotomy involves laminectomy, sectioning of dorsal roots, and interruptions of sensory fibers. This procedure permanently relieves pain but also anesthetizes areas previously innervated by the severed nerves.

When such neurosurgery is contraindicated, subarachnoid injection of phenol usually provides rapid—but temporary—pain relief, lasting from 2 weeks to 6 months.

Palliative surgery is indicated when obstructions pose problems with a normal organ function, cause pain, or do both. Obstruction of the biliary tree, of the ureteral system, or along the GI tract is treated by resection and reanastomosis or division.

Reconstructive or rehabilitative surgery. After radical surgery or radiation therapy, the patient may need reconstructive surgery. Depending on the area excised or irradiated, such repair can range from skin graft to reconstruction—for example, postmastectomy breast reconstruction. Cancer patients face the same emotional adjustments as other patients who have reconstructive surgery: they must accept the cosmetic and sensory differences of the reconstruction.

When radiation therapy or prior surgery causes function loss, rehabilitative surgery

Radiation effects on normal tissue

Tissue	Immediate side effects	Intermediate side effects	Late side effects
Brain	Edema	0 to 1 year: reversible edema	1 to 2 years: necrosis
Spinal cord	Edema, compression, pain if tumor is present	6 months to 1 year: reversible transverse myelitis	1 to 2 years: paraplegia
Heart	None	None	1 to 2 years: pericarditis
Major blood vessels	None	Arterial fibrosis	None
Lung	None	0 to 3 months: pneumonitis 8 months to 1 year: fibrosis	1 to 2 years: fibrosis
Liver	Altered liver function	7 months to 1 year: radiation hepatitis	None
Kidney	None	6 months to 1 year: nephrosclerosis, radiation nephritis	1.5 to 3+ years: chronic radiation nephritis, vascular sclerosis
Ureter	None	None	1 to 2 years: fibrosis, obstruction
Bladder	Cystitis	7 to 8 months: contraction	1+ years: atrophic ulcers
Oral mucosa	Mucositis, moist desquamation	2 to 3 months: atrophy 6 months to 1 year: fibrosis	1 to 5+ years: ulcers, deep necrosis, atrophy
Esophagus	Dysphagia	None	1 to 5 years: stenosis
Stomach	Anorexia, nausea, reduced acidity	1 to 2 months: superficial ulcers	1+ years: chronic atrophic gastritis
Small intestine	Diarrhea, colic, malabsorption	6 months to 1 year: obstruction	1 to 11 years: obstruction (may require surgery)
Colon and rectum	Diarrhea, colic	6 months to 1 year: diarrhea, necrosis	2 to 3 years: slow stenosis, fibrosis, induration
Skin	Erythema, desquamation	6 to 8 weeks: desquamation, pigmentation 6 months to 1 year: atrophy, ulcers, deep fibrosis	1 to 5 years: atrophy, ulcers, deep fibrosis

may be done to lyse contractures or to transpose muscles. Common complications of reconstructive or rehabilitative surgery include infection, soft tissue ischemia, and hematoma.

RADIATION THERAPY
About half of all cancer patients need primary or adjunctive radiation therapy. Introduced in the 1890s, this technique uses X-rays, gamma rays, or electrons to destroy malignant cells or retard their growth. However, it also damages normal cells within the irradiated area—especially those that divide rapidly and need constant renewal, such as red and white blood cells, platelets, and GI mucosal cells.

Despite its long-standing and widespread use, radiation therapy poses some hazards, and your patient may express concern about its safety, side effects, and effectiveness. Understanding the principles of radiation therapy will help you explain it to your patient and correct any misconceptions he may have.

How radiation works
Radiation of body cells impairs DNA synthesis via ionization and cell membrane changes, which cause physical changes within the cells.

Radiosensitivity. Radiation therapy has random cellular effects: it damages some cells and leaves others with no discernible change. Which cells respond to radiation depends on their mitotic potential, tissue of origin, and extracellular environment, as well as on the radiation dosage they receive.

Mitotic potential directly relates to radiosensi-

Safety precautions for administering chemotherapy

• Wear surgical or polyvinyl chloride gloves when priming I.V. tubing, dispelling air bubbles from syringes or I.V. tubing, and administering chemotherapy. This prevents any drug from coming in direct contact with your skin.
• For 24 hours after drug administration, wear disposable gloves when handling patients' excreta.
• Dispose of used needles and syringes carefully. To prevent aerosol generation of chemotherapeutic drugs, don't clip needles. Place them intact in a leakproof, puncture-resistant container to be incinerated.
• Dispose of I.V. bags, bottles, and tubing in a covered trash container. Chemotherapy trash should be incinerated.
• Even though you've used gloves, you need to wash your hands thoroughly after giving any chemotherapeutic drug.

tivity. The mitotic potential reflects the number of cells in mitotic cycle phases. Because cells are more sensitive to radiation when they are dividing, a high mitotic potential makes a tumor more responsive to radiation.

Tissue of origin also influences cell radiosensitivity. For example, lymphomas arise from lymphoid tissue, which is relatively sensitive to radiation, so they can be treated with comparatively low doses of radiation that do little or no damage to surrounding healthy tissue. Tumors that arise from neuromuscular tissue, however, are less radiosensitive.

Extracellular environment affects radiation effectiveness. Radiation therapy is more effective in a well-oxygenated extracellular environment. Because of their distance from capillary supply, however, many tumor cells are hypoxic.

Radiation dosage is critical to response. The total dose of radiation is determined by the tumor's sensitivity to radiation, the sensitivity of surrounding tissue, and the patient's response as treatment progresses. An excessive dose may unnecessarily damage healthy cells; an inadequate one may not be effective.

Radiation side effects

Radiation can cause side effects, including mucositis (for example, tracheitis), skin changes, and bone marrow depression. The type and severity of side effects depend on the total radiation dose, the fractionated doses, the location of the treatment field, and the adequacy of protection for healthy tissue in the treatment field. Most side effects arise directly from the irradiated site. For example, when the head and neck area is radiated, patients may experience mucositis. Some side effects, such as tracheitis, can be minimized by using a lead barrier to shield the patient's normal tissue within the treatment field. (See *Radiation effects on normal tissue,* page 51.)

Acute side effects. These occur during radiation therapy in response to immediate cellular death. To minimize these side effects, a total radiation dose is divided into smaller units (fractions) given over a period of time.

Intermediate side effects. These occur in cells with high mitotic potential shortly after radiation therapy is done. Damage to these cells isn't detectable until cell division occurs.

Late side effects. These may occur months or even years after treatment, probably resulting from damage to supportive tissue structures. Whether late side effects occur depends mainly on the total radiation dose.

Undetectable chromosomal damage from radiation can cause somatic or germinal mutations. *Somatic mutations* may cause malignancies later in life: for example, Hiroshima survivors have a very high incidence of leukemia. *Germinal mutations,* which can occur if the patient's ovaries or testes are exposed to ionizing radiation, are usually recessive; their effects appear in future generations.

Radiation delivery: External or internal

Most radiation is delivered via external beam therapy, using megavoltage and supervoltage machines such as the cobalt-60 and the linear accelerator. These deliver maximum doses to a depth of 10 cm, dramatically reducing the risk of skin changes from radiation. These machines also deliver accurate dosages with less side-scattering of radiation. Prior to treatment with external beam radiation, patients undergo a process called simulation, which delineates the treatment field and helps them adjust to the treatment setting.

Internal radiation is typically used to treat patients with cancer of the head or neck, cervix or endometrium, or breast—locally, using radioactive implants, or systemically, using radioactive solutions or suspensions.

To place a radioactive implant, an applicator is surgically inserted in interstitial tissue or into a body cavity. After placement is confirmed with an X-ray, the implant is placed in the applicator for several hours or days, depending on the radioactive source. (Common sources include cesium 137, iridium 192, and iodine 125.) To give systemic internal radiation therapy, a radioactive solution or suspension (such as iodine 131) is given to the patient intravenously, orally, or by instillation.

When you're caring for a patient who's receiving either form of internal radiation therapy, be sure to take every precaution against radioactive contamination. Abide by the principles of time and distance. Spend no more time with the patient than is absolutely necessary and maximize your distance from him. If your institution provides radiation badges, be sure to wear one. But remember, it simply measures exposure and does not offer protection. If your patient's receiving systemic therapy, his body excretions are potentially radioactive, so dispose of them carefully.

CHEMOTHERAPY

Like other cancer treatment, chemotherapy aims at destroying cancer cells or suppressing their growth with minimal damage to non-

How chemotherapeutic agents disrupt the cell cycle

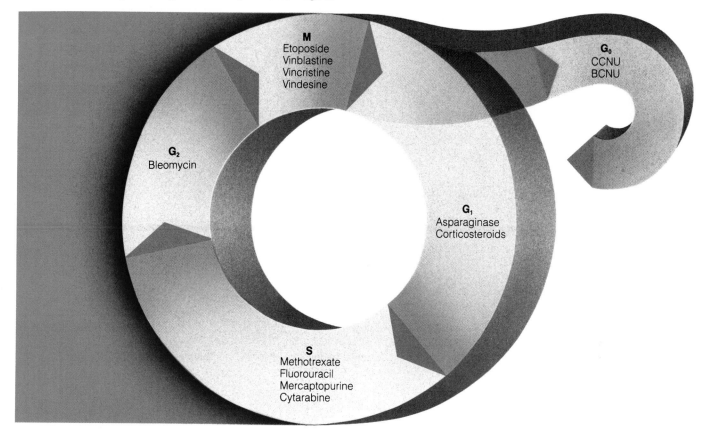

cancerous tissue. The drugs used, which work by interrupting the cancer cells' life cycle, are especially useful as primary treatment for curing Hodgkin's disease, choriocarcinoma, testicular cancer, and childhood leukemia. They can also put certain other cancers, such as adult leukemia and breast cancer, into remission. These drugs are also palliative. For example, chemotherapy may relieve the pain of bone metastases or of tumor pressure on lymphatics, nerves, or vascular elements.

As adjunctive treatment, chemotherapy is commonly administered after surgery or radiation therapy to destroy remaining cancer cells and to prevent recurrence of cancer.

However, these drugs also affect the reproduction of certain normal cells that multiply rapidly, such as cells of the bone marrow, GI tract, reproductive system, and hair follicles. This is why chemotherapy may be associated with so many side effects, such as bone marrow depression, nausea, vomiting, stomatitis, and alopecia. But normal body cells may recover after chemotherapy is finished.

Effects on the cell life cycle

Chemotherapeutic agents attack cancer cells directly and depending on whether they inter-

rupt the cell life cycle, these drugs may be cell-cycle-specific or -nonspecific. (See *How chemotherapeutic agents disrupt the cell cycle.*)

Drugs used in cancer chemotherapy generally fall into four categories: alkylating agents, antibiotic antineoplastic agents, antimetabolites, and plant derivatives. *Cell-cycle-specific drugs,* such as antimetabolites and plant derivatives, affect cells only in the developmental phases and act only at one or more specific phases of the cell cycle. *Cell-cycle-nonspecific drugs,* such as alkylating agents and some antibiotic antineoplastic agents, act on cells at all phases of the cycle.

Alkylating agents. One of the largest chemotherapeutic groups, alkylating agents inhibit cell growth by cross-linking DNA strands. These cell-cycle-nonspecific drugs are primarily used to treat cancer of the breast, lung, ovary, and bladder, as well as multiple myeloma, lymphoma, and leukemia. Because they can cross the blood-brain barrier, alkylating nitrosoureas, such as carmustine (BCNU) and lomustine (CCNU), are used to treat primary brain tumors.

Major side effects of alkylating agents include bone marrow depression, skin rashes, nausea, vomiting, and gonadal dysfunction.

Chemotherapeutic agents stop cancer cell production by interrupting the cell cycle.

The cell cycle is divided into these distinct phases:
• phase G_0: the resting phase in which cells are not committed to division
• phase G_1: RNA and protein synthesis
• phase S: DNA synthesis
• phase G_2: RNA and protein synthesis
• phase M: mitosis—the process of cell division.

Chemotherapeutic agents may be either cell-cycle-specific or cell-cycle-nonspecific. Cell-cycle-specific drugs, such as methotrexate, act at one or more specific cell-cycle phases. Cell-cycle-nonspecific drugs, such as busulfan, can act on both replicating and resting cells.

Note: Drugs shown in diagram are only examples.

High-dose methotrexate therapy with leucovorin rescue

Methotrexate interferes with cell division by inhibiting dihydrofolate reductase (DHFR), an enzyme involved in DNA synthesis. Usually, methotrexate enters cells via the active transport system in cell membranes. But in high doses, methotrexate can also enter by passive diffusion.

High-dose methotrexate is most effective against cells that have a high metabolic rate, such as leukemia cells. But if not interfered with, high-dose methotrexate will eventually affect normal cells as well, causing a high risk of severe toxicities.

To protect normal cells, methotrexate is often given with leucovorin (folinic acid). Leucovorin rescues cells by bypassing methotrexate inhibition of DHFR, as well as by other mechanisms that are not completely understood. In order for leucovorin to rescue the largest number of normal cells, it is essential that it be given exactly on time, as ordered. When administered properly, leucovorin rescues cells before they begin active growth and division.

Since leucovorin cannot completely prevent methotrexate toxicity, closely monitor any patient on high-dose methotrexate for toxicities, such as bone marrow depression, stomatitis, pulmonary complications, and renal damage (from precipitation in tubules). Keep the patient's urine alkaline to avoid precipitation in tubules, and watch his urine output closely.

Common protocols for combination chemotherapy

Sometimes the best way to kill cancer cells with chemotherapy is to combine several antineoplastic drugs that attack different cell-cycle phases or act throughout the cycle. To be effective, drugs used in combination chemotherapy should:
• show some effectiveness against the tumor type when used alone
• act at different phases of the cell cycle
• interact with other drugs to enhance overall toxicity
• produce different, complementary toxicities at one time or the same toxicity at different times.
Note: All dosages and schedules are subject to change. Always follow your hospital's protocol, and check current literature for new dosing information.

Hodgkin's disease

MOPP (repeated every 28 days)
mechlorethamine (Mustargen): 6 mg/m² I.V. push on days 1 and 8
vincristine (Oncovin): 1.4 mg/m² (2 mg maximum) I.V. on days 1 and 8
procarbazine (Matulane): 100 mg/m² P.O. daily for 14 days
prednisone: 40 mg/m² P.O. daily for 14 days
(optional) bleomycin (Blenoxane): 2 to 4 mg/m² I.V. on days 1 and 8

BCVPP (repeated every 28 days)
carmustine (BCNU): 100 mg/m² I.V. on day 1
cyclophosphamide: 600 mg/m² I.V. on day 1
vinblastine: 5 mg/m² I.V. on day 1
procarbazine: 100 mg/m₂ P.O. on days 1 to 10
prednisone: 60 mg/m₂ P.O. on days 1 to 10

ABVD (repeated every 28 days)
doxorubicin (Adriamycin): 25 mg/m² I.V. on days 1 and 14
bleomycin (Blenoxane): 10 mg/m² I.V. on days 1 and 14
vinblastine (Velban): 6 mg/m² I.V. on days 1 and 14
dacarbazine (DTIC-Dome): 150 mg/m² I.V. on days 1 to 5

CVP (repeated every 21 days)
cyclophosphamide: 400 mg/m² P.O. on days 1 to 5
vincristine: 1.4 mg/m² I.V. on day 1

prednisone: 100 mg/m² P.O. on days 1 to 5

CHOP-BLEO (repeated every 21 or 28 days)
cyclophosphamide: 750 mg/m² I.V. on day 1
*doxorubicin (Adriamycin): 50 mg/m² I.V. on day 1
vincristine (Oncovin): 2 mg I.V. on days 1 and 5
prednisone: 100 mg P.O. on days 1 to 5
bleomycin: 15 units I.V. on days 1 and 5
*H is for hydroxydaunorubicin, a chemical synonym for doxorubicin.

Acute nonlymphocytic leukemia (induction therapy for adults)

AMSA-AZA
amsacrine: 150 mg/m² I.V. on days 1 to 5
5-azacytidine: 150 mg/m² I.V. on days 1 to 5

DAT
daunorubicin: 60 mg/m² I.V. on days 1 to 3
cytarabine (ara-C): 25 mg/m² I.V. push, then 200 mg/m²/day continuous I.V. infusion on days 1 to 5

One alkylating agent, cyclophosphamide, may also cause hemorrhagic cystitis.

Antibiotic antineoplastic agents. Usually, these drugs disrupt cell functioning by inhibiting DNA and RNA synthesis. They are used primarily to treat cancer of the breast, lung, ovary, and testes, as well as leukemia and lymphoma. Although each drug in this category affects cancer cells differently, most antibiotic antineoplastics are cell-cycle-nonspecific. These drugs usually cause similar side effects—bone marrow depression, nausea, vomiting, and alopecia. Also, many are vesicants that can severely damage tissues if extravasation occurs. Bleomycin causes less bone marrow depression than the other antibiotic antineoplastics, but it may cause pulmonary toxicity, anaphylaxis, fever, and chills. Doxorubicin may cause cardiac toxicity.

Antimetabolites. These cell-cycle-specific drugs interfere with DNA and RNA synthesis either by blocking metabolic pathways or by replacing certain essential metabolites.

Based on how they interfere with DNA and RNA synthesis, these drugs are classified as folic acid antagonists, purine antagonists, or pyrimidine antagonists. *Folic acid antagonists,* such as methotrexate and methotrexate sodium, interfere with biosynthetic enzymes. Both *purine antagonists* (such as azathioprine and mercaptopurine) and *pyrimidine antagonists* (such as cytarabine, floxuridine, and fluorouracil) replace normal cell components during DNA and RNA synthesis.

Antimetabolites primarily treat cancer of the breast, colon, testes, stomach, liver, ovary, and pancreas, along with osteogenic sarcoma, lymphoma, choriocarcinoma, and acute leukemia. Their major side effects are bone marrow depression, nausea, vomiting, diarrhea, mucositis, and hepatic dysfunction.

Plant derivatives. These cell-cycle-specific agents, also called *vinca alkaloids,* stop mitosis in metaphase (the second cell division

6-TG: 100 mg/m² P.O. every 12 hours on days 1 to 5

VAPA
vincristine: 1.5 mg/m² I.V. on days 1 and 5
doxorubicin (Adriamycin): 30 mg/m² I.V. on days 1, 2, and 3
prednisone: 40 mg/m² P.O. every 12 hours on days 1 to 5
cytarabine (ara-C): 100 mg/m² continuous I.V. infusion on days 1 to 7

Acute lymphocytic leukemia (induction therapy for adults)

VP
vincristine: 2 mg/m² I.V. weekly for 4 weeks
prednisone: 40 mg/m² P.O. daily for 28 days, then taper over 1 week

Breast carcinoma

FAC (repeated every 21 days)
5-fluorouracil: 500 mg/m² I.V. on days 1 and 8
doxorubicin (Adriamycin): 50 mg/m² I.V. on day 1
cyclophosphamide (Cytoxan): 500 mg/m² I.V. on day 1

CAF (repeated every 28 days)
cyclophosphamide (Cytoxan): 100 mg/m² P.O. daily for 14 days
doxorubicin (Adriamycin): 30 mg/m² I.V. on days 1 and 8

5-fluorouracil: 400 mg/m² I.V. on days 1 and 8

CMF (repeated every 28 days)
cyclophosphamide (Cytoxan): 100 mg/m² P.O. daily for 14 days
methotrexate: 30 mg/m² I.V. on days 1 and 8
5-fluorouracil: 400 mg/m² I.V. on days 1 and 8

Upper gastrointestinal tumors

FAM (repeated every 8 weeks)
5-fluorouracil: 600 mg/m² I.V. on days 1, 8, 28, and 35
doxorubicin (Adriamycin): 30 mg/m² I.V. on days 1 and 28
mitomycin (Mutamycin): 10 mg/m² I.V. on day 1

Bladder carcinoma

CISCA (repeated every 21 days)
cisplatin: 100 mg/m² I.V. on day 2
cyclophosphamide (Cytoxan): 650 mg/m² I.V. on day 1
doxorubicin (Adriamycin): 50 mg/m² I.V. on day 1

Testicular tumors

VBP Einhorn regimen (repeated every 3 to 6 weeks)
vinblastine (Velban): 0.2 to 0.4 mg/kg I.V. split into two doses
bleomycin (Blenoxane): 30 units/day I.V. on days 2 to 6 as con-

tinuous infusion
cisplatin (Platinol): 20 mg/m² I.V. on days 1 to 5

Multiple myeloma

VCAP (repeated every 3 weeks)
vincristine (Oncovin): 1 mg I.V. on day 1
cyclophosphamide (Cytoxan): 100 mg/m²/day P.O. on days 1 to 4
doxorubicin (Adriamycin): 25 mg/m² I.V. on day 2
prednisone: 60 mg/m²/day P.O. on days 1 to 4

VBAP (repeated every 3 weeks)
vincristine (Oncovin): 1 mg I.V. on day 1
carmustine (BCNU): 30 mg/m² I.V. on day 1
doxorubicin (Adriamycin): 30 mg/m² I.V. on day 1
prednisone: 100 mg/day P.O. on days 1 to 4

Soft tissue sarcoma

CY-VA-DIC
cyclophosphamide (Cytoxan): 500 mg/m² I.V. on day 1
vincristine (Oncovin): 1 mg/m² (maximum 1.5 mg) I.V. on days 1 and 5
doxorubicin (Adriamycin): 50 mg/m² I.V. on day 1
dacarbazine (DTIC-Dome): 250 mg/m² I.V. daily for 5 days

Giving intravenous chemotherapy

Follow these guidelines for safe I.V. administration of chemotherapeutic drugs.
• Observe safety precautions. (See *Safety precautions for administering chemotherapy,* page 52.)
• Give sclerosing chemotherapy medications only if you have been properly instructed.
• Keep emergency medications handy to treat hypersensitivity reactions or extravasations.
• Give the patient any premedications, such as antiemetics, as ordered.
• Alert the patient to immediately report any adverse reactions, such as burning or irritation at the treatment site, nausea, or vomiting.
• Examine the patient's veins for a viable route of drug administration, starting with his hand and proceeding to his forearm. (Remember, the use of veins in the dorsum of the hand is controversial if you are giving a sclerosing agent.)
• Do not use an existing I.V. line. Make a new venipuncture: this will ensure proper needle placement and vein patency. Never use a chemotherapeutic drug to test vein patency. Infuse 10 to 20 cc normal saline solution to ensure patency. Administer nonsclerosing agents I.V. push or admixed in a bag of I.V. fluid. Give sclerosing agents I.V. push through the sidearm of a rapidly infusing I.V.
• During drug administration, watch closely for signs of a hypersensitivity reaction or extravasation. Check for blood return after each 5 cc of medication are injected.
• If you suspect extravasation, stop the infusion immediately, leave the needle in place, and notify the doctor. Know your institutional policy for treating drug extravasations.
• Infuse 20 cc normal saline solution between all chemotherapeutic medications and prior to discontinuing the I.V. line.

---

phase) by damaging spindle protein. The most commonly used plant derivatives are vinblastine and vincristine—both derived from the periwinkle plant. Although these drugs are structurally similar, their clinical indications and toxicities differ. For example, vinblastine is usually used to treat lymphoma and testicular cancer, whereas vincristine is used to treat lymphoma and acute lymphocytic leukemia. Similarly, severe bone marrow depression may occur with vinblastine but usually doesn't occur with vincristine. And although both drugs may cause neurotoxicity, this occurs most often with vincristine; symptoms may include peripheral neuropathies (numbness, tingling, and arm and leg weakness), paralytic ileus, and constipation. These drugs are vesicants and may cause severe tissue damage if they extravasate.

A new chemotherapeutic plant derivative, etoposide, is active in the S and G₂ cell division phases. Its mechanism of action isn't fully

understood, but etoposide seems to damage DNA directly by breaking both single and double strands and DNA protein cross-links.

Etoposide is used to treat small-cell lung cancer, lymphoma, testicular carcinoma, and some forms of leukemia. The most dangerous side effect associated with this drug is myelosuppression, but this effect is dose-related and reversible. Other side effects include GI toxicity, anaphylaxis, and hypotension.

Other chemotherapeutic agents. Some chemotherapeutic drugs, such as asparaginase and procarbazine, have mechanisms of action that are either unknown or unlike those of other classified drugs.

Asparaginase, an enzyme that occurs naturally in guinea pig serum, destroys asparagine, an amino acid that's essential for cell protein synthesis in acute lymphocytic leukemia. Asparaginase is associated with severe toxicity, especially central nervous system, hepatic, or GI toxicity.

Procarbazine inhibits DNA, RNA, and protein synthesis by causing chromosomal breakage. It's used to treat lymphoma, melanoma, brain tumors, and oat cell tumors of the lung. Its major side effects include bleeding tendencies, alterations in level of consciousness, nausea, and vomiting.

Why chemotherapy sometimes fails

Chemotherapy isn't always effective; some cancer cells either have or develop resistance to the drugs used, and some may receive doses that are too low to be effective. Resistance to chemotherapy is classified as follows:
• *Type I resistance* occurs if a certain number of cancer cells are permanently resistant to a specific drug or class of chemotherapeutic drugs.
• *Type II resistance* occurs if cancer cells undergo long resting phases, when they temporarily resist chemotherapy. The use of combination chemotherapy, incorporating specific agents, can reduce Type II resistance.
• *Type III resistance* occurs if cancer cells receive ineffective amounts of drugs. This may occur when malignant brain cells are protected from drugs that can't pass the blood-brain barrier or when an inadequate blood supply prevents drug delivery to cells in the center of a large tumor. Intrathecal administration or tumor reduction by radiation or surgery can oppose Type III resistance.

Combination protocols

Generally, a single chemotherapeutic drug doesn't achieve cure or long-term remission. Combining three or more of these drugs permits administration of smaller, less toxic doses of each and may kill the same number of cancer cells that a larger, possibly more toxic dose of a single drug would kill. Combining drugs also inhibits tumor resistance. And when drugs that act in different parts of the cell cycle or by different mechanisms are used together, their combined effectiveness may exceed the sum of their individual effectiveness. Typically, at least three drugs are given together. Different types of cancer are treated with specific protocols of drugs, doses, and schedules. But these protocols are also calculated individually, using body surface calculations to ensure patient safety and optimal drug dose. (See *Common protocols for combination chemotherapy,* pages 54 and 55.)

How chemotherapy is administered

Chemotherapy is extremely toxic. When giving

Three new cancer treatments

Bone marrow aspiration sites

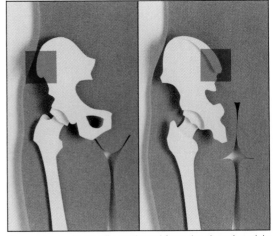

Bone marrow is usually aspirated from the donor's pelvic bones.

How interferon enhances immune response

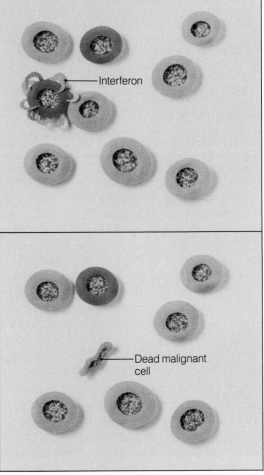

Killer T lymphocytes release interferon when they contact malignant cells (see top drawing). Interferon release stimulates killer cells and destroys malignant cells (see bottom drawing).

Researchers are constantly exploring new cancer treatments. Three new treatments currently under investigation are bone marrow transplantation, immunotherapy, and monoclonal antibody therapy.

Bone marrow transplantation

In this procedure, bone marrow is aspirated from a human-leukocyte-antigen–compatible donor, usually the patient's twin or sibling. The patient first receives chemotherapy, total body irradiation, or both, to kill any residual cancer cells. Then he's placed in reverse isolation, and the donated bone marrow is infused through a Hickman catheter. After 2 to 4 weeks, the patient's bone marrow should be engrafted. But until the new marrow functions he receives transfusions (platelets, red blood cells, and granulocytes) to prevent hemorrhage and infection. Another potentially life-threatening complication, graft-versus-host disease (GVHD), occurs when lymphocytes from the donor's marrow recognize the host as foreign and attack host cells. GVHD can be treated with corticosteroids and immunosuppressives such as azathioprine.

Immunotherapy

In immunotherapy, antigens and other materials are introduced into the patient's body to try to make his immune system respond to his illness. The major types of immunotherapy include:

Passive specific: Cancer cells containing specific tumor antigens are taken from the patient or another source. Then they're modified and injected into the patient to stimulate antibody production. The resulting immune response is directed specifically at the tumor.

Active nonspecific: Antigens, such as bacille Calmette-Guérin (BCG) vaccine, are used to stimulate nonspecific immune response. For example, BCG vaccine mainly stimulates cellu-

lar immune response—which includes the cancer-fighting T cells.

Passive: Immune serum from an immunologically competent patient is transferred to one who's not. Unfortunately, this immunity is short-lived because the transferred serum is broken down and eliminated.

Adoptive: Active immune lymphocytes from a compatible donor are transferred to a cancer patient, whose body will eventually accept these new immune cells and use them in its immunologic defenses.

Mediator and hormonal: Extracts of chemical mediators and hormones are used to stimulate the immune response. For example, interferon—a human leukocyte extract—inhibits cell multiplication, increases the expression of tumor surface antigens, and stimulates lymphocytes to attack cancer cells.

Immunotherapy may produce local, systemic, and anaphylac-

tic reactions. Common side effects include mild erythema and induration at the treatment site, pruritus, necrosis, fever, chills, mild malaise, and anaphylaxis. Interferon can also cause muscle aches, fatigue, and decreased blood cell production.

Monoclonal antibody therapy

Produced from the cloned cells of mice, monoclonal antibodies offer two new ways to detect and treat cancer. When radioactive tracers are attached to monoclonal antibodies that are specific for selected cancer cells, they can accurately locate areas of that cancer in the body. And when used with antineoplastic drugs, monoclonal antibodies can selectively destroy cancer cells while leaving normal ones alone. Use of monoclonal antibodies is still experimental, however. Side effects include fever, chills, hypotension, and allergic reactions.

How monoclonal antibodies are produced

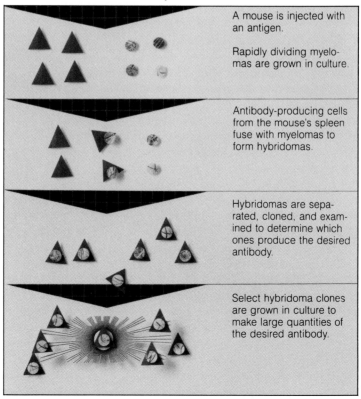

A mouse is injected with an antigen.

Rapidly dividing myelomas are grown in culture.

Antibody-producing cells from the mouse's spleen fuse with myelomas to form hybridomas.

Hybridomas are separated, cloned, and examined to determine which ones produce the desired antibody.

Select hybridoma clones are grown in culture to make large quantities of the desired antibody.

Key

▲ Spleen cells

● Myeloma cells

Alternative treatments: Hazardous to your patient's health

Fear of the planned treatment or feelings of despair as his cancer progresses despite treatment may make a patient with cancer consider undergoing treatments that haven't gained medical acceptance—so-called alternative treatments. When a patient chooses to try such alternative treatment, he risks delaying needed medical treatment, and he may also suffer damaging side effects.

What can you do to help your patient make an informed decision? Listen to his concerns about his disease and treatment plan; if he mentions that he's considering an alternative treatment, be sure to provide accurate information and help him evaluate the alternative form.

Here are some of the most common alternative methods of cancer treatment.

Laetrile. Also known as amygdalin, laetrile produces cyanide and is derived from such foods as apricots, peaches, plums, almonds, cloves, and lima beans. Two theories exist concerning laetrile's actions against cancer cells. These postulate that:
• cancer cells contain an enzyme that releases cyanide from laetrile, and this kills the cancer cells.
• cancer is a vitamin deficiency disease, and laetrile is the missing vitamin B_{17}.

Extensive testing shows that laetrile is not effective as a cancer treatment. Also, it can cause cyanide toxicity, hypotension, vomiting, and motor disturbances. But its myth endures, and it remains popular.

Dimethyl sulfoxide (DMSO). Widely used as an industrial solvent and a veterinary pharmacologic agent, DMSO is believed, but not proven, to decrease pain, increase the therapeutic effects of chemotherapy, and decrease its side effects. But the only FDA-approved use of DMSO is for bladder instillation in interstitial cystitis.

Macrobiotic diet. This diet is based on the eastern philosophy of keeping a proper balance between one's self and the environment. Its supporters believe that cancer is related to an excess intake of so-called yin or yang foods. Macrobiotic diets usually include cereals, vegetables, and beans, with limited fluids. Besides having no proven effect as cancer therapy, such a diet can cause decreased levels of essential vitamins, iron deficiency anemia, and decreased bone maintenance.

Metabolic therapy. Based on the idea that cancer is a result of metabolic contamination due to inadequate elimination of waste, metabolic therapy involves attempting to cleanse and purify the body through special diets, internal irrigation, and the "proper" spiritual attitude. Again, no proof exists that metabolic therapy benefits patients with cancer.

Vitamin therapy. Vitamins A and C are popular because they're widely available and thought to be generally beneficial and nontoxic. But when taken in large doses, vitamin A *is* toxic—it causes vomiting, fatigue, and abdominal discomfort. And large doses of vitamin C can cause nausea and diarrhea. But because the body's need for vitamin C increases with stress and wound healing and in response to certain drugs used in cancer treatment, patients with cancer may benefit from eating more vitamin C–rich foods or from taking dietary supplements. Vitamin C also aids immune system function, and it may help the body fight infection.

it, observe your hospital's precautions carefully. The following guidelines will help.

Intravenous (I.V.). The most common route, it provides ready access to most body tissues. But this method is also hazardous. (See *Safety precautions for administering chemotherapy,* page 52, and *Giving intravenous chemotherapy,* page 55.)

Oral. Although oral administration generally causes inconsistent drug absorption, such drugs as hydroxyurea, procarbazine, methotrexate, and cyclophosphamide are well absorbed when given orally. However, side effects of these drugs include nausea and vomiting—if these occur, expect oral administration to be discontinued if antiemetics are ineffective.

Intramuscular (I.M.) or subcutaneous (S.C.). These routes may be used if patients have poor veins or if they will be receiving their chemotherapy at home. But many chemotherapeutic drugs are too irritating to surrounding tissue to be given by either route. In addition, I.M. or S.C. administration is usually contraindicated in patients with thrombocytopenia or other bleeding disorders because of possible bleeding at the injection site.

Intrathecal. Because most chemotherapeutic agents can't cross the blood-brain barrier, such drugs as methotrexate and cytarabine may be given intrathecally to reach cancer cells in the central nervous system. Intrathecal drugs are injected via the theca of the spinal cord into the subarachnoid space. To avoid multiple lumbar puncture sites, antineoplastic drugs can also be administered directly into the ventricles of the brain via an implantable pump called an Ommaya reservoir.

Intraarterial chemotherapy (IAC). In IAC, drugs are perfused into a major artery leading directly into a tumor. Used to treat cancer of the liver, lung, head, and neck, IAC permits localized drug absorption and helps eliminate diffuse toxicity. But because some systemic absorption may still occur, the patient may show diarrhea, nausea, and vomiting. Also, IAC may cause severe local side effects, such as edema, hemorrhage, necrosis, and infection.

Regional perfusion. This still-experimental technique involves temporarily isolating the tumor site from general circulation, then giving high concentrations of chemotherapy through an extracorporeal pump oxygenator.

HORMONAL THERAPY

Some types of tumors seem to need a specific hormonal environment for growth. For example, breast tumors are most likely to grow and develop in an estrogen-rich environment. Administering an antihormone, such as the estrogen antagonist tamoxifen, may inhibit neoplastic growth by preventing hormones from nourishing tumor cells.

Certain types of tumors may respond to *additional* hormones. For example, a patient with prostate cancer may be given an estrogen called diethylstilbestrol, which creates an unfavorable environment for cancer growth. Similarly, a corticosteroid such as prednisone may be given to treat leukemia, lymphoma, multiple myeloma, and breast cancer. (Because they produce mild euphoria and often stimulate appetite, corticosteroids may also be given to palliate cancer symptoms.)

Although most of the drugs used in hormonal therapy have unknown mechanisms of action, they don't seem to be cytotoxic.

COMBINED THERAPY

Surgery, radiation, and chemotherapy are often combined for more effective treatment because combining treatments increases the effect of each individual method *and* increases the probability of success. These treatments have different targets: surgery and radiation affect local or regional tissues, whereas chemotherapy affects cells throughout the body. And each treatment combats cancer in a different way: surgery removes tumor growth or reduces its size; radiation impairs cancer cells' ability to divide; and chemotherapy interrupts the cell life cycle, also affecting cell division.

Combining treatments can also provide alternatives for the patient to consider (depending on his cancer's type and extent). For example, for many years the Halsted radical mastectomy was almost always selected to treat breast cancer. Now, however, the combination of a modified surgical approach with radiation can produce equivalent local control of disease with less disfigurement.

Surgery and radiation

When these two treatments are combined, radiation therapy may take place either pre- or postoperatively. Preoperative radiation shrinks large tumors so they're more resectable; postoperative radiation attacks remaining cancer cells and may prevent recurrence.

Besides their primary effects, surgery and radiation can increase each other's effects. For example, if complete tumor excision is impossible because of the need to preserve surrounding tissue, radiation can combat the remaining growth. And since radiation is most effective in a tumor's periphery (where cells are well vascularized), surgical removal of the tumor's main body will allow radiation concentration where it's most effective.

Unfortunately, some disadvantages are associated with this combination.
• Preoperative radiation, along with delaying surgery, may interfere with surgical staging by altering the original extent of the tumor.
• Postoperative radiation, by altering the vasculature of any residual tumor, may impair its response to further treatment.

Surgery and chemotherapy

Performing surgery to decrease the size of a large tumor increases the effectiveness of chemotherapy against the remaining cancer cells. Thus, depending on the stage, most patients with ovarian cancer receive combination chemotherapy immediately after surgery.

Chemotherapy and radiation

These forms of treatment may be combined to increase tumor responsiveness to therapy, but the drug dose may need to be modified to avoid enhancing toxicity. For example, doses of doxorubicin or cyclophosphamide must be reduced during or after radiation therapy.

A FINAL WORD

Understanding how cancer treatments work, you can feel confident about explaining them to your patients and knowing how to keep your patient as comfortable as possible during treatment. You can do a great deal to help him and his family cope more effectively before, during, and after treatment.

Points to remember

• The primary treatments for cancer are surgery, radiation, or chemotherapy, or a combination of these.
• Combining surgery, radiation, and chemotherapy maximizes the effectiveness of each individual method.
• Researchers are constantly looking for new cancer treatments. Three new treatments currently in use or under investigation are bone marrow transplantation, immunotherapy, and monoclonal antibody therapy.
• You're responsible for preparing the patient for treatment; for providing treatment, as ordered; and for performing therapeutic care. This includes explaining the purpose and procedure of treatment, providing emotional and physical support, monitoring the patient for side effects, and teaching him how to manage side effects.

5 MANAGING THE PATIENT WITH CANCER

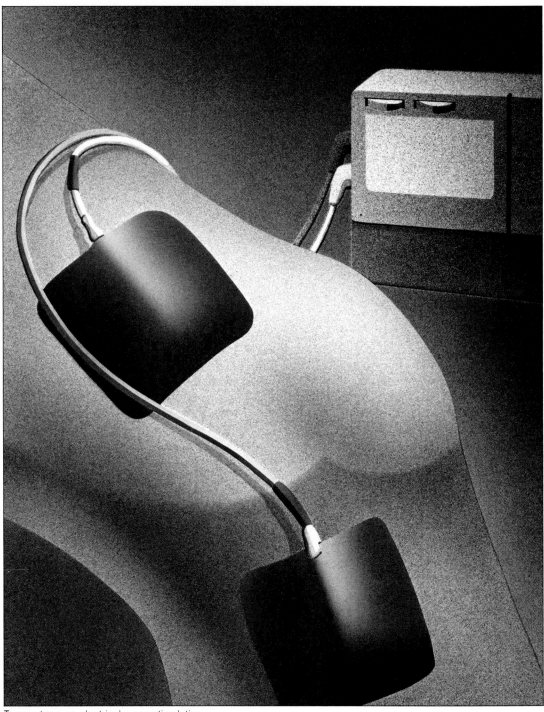

Transcutaneous electrical nerve stimulation

One of the most difficult aspects of managing cancer is that complications of its treatments—including those designed to combat pain, protein-calorie malnutrition, and infection—can threaten the patient's life and well-being as much as the disease itself. Fortunately, these complications aren't inevitable, and you can often prevent or minimize them if you're willing to take these three steps:

• Identify the high risk factors that make your patient susceptible to complications. This means you should consider their physiologic, psychological, and sociologic causes.

• Assess your patient thoroughly, keeping in mind his uniqueness, the characteristics of his cancer, and the treatments ordered for him. Above all, determine your patient's perception of his cancer, especially as it bears on his ability to participate in treatment programs.

• Use assessment findings to plan and initiate precautions that will prevent complications. If complications develop despite your best efforts, take remedial measures at once—before complications can overwhelm your patient both physically and psychologically.

You can help manage the complications of cancer and its treatment. Just how will become clear as you read on.

MANAGING PAIN

Not all patients with cancer experience pain, but, in those who do, it can be difficult to manage. You can manage pain better if you take into account current knowledge, views about the nature of pain, its pathophysiology, and the latest invasive and non-invasive pain-relieving methods.

Pain perception varies

Pain has a sensory component and a reaction component. The sensory component involves an electrical impulse that travels to the central nervous system, where it's perceived as pain. The response to this perception is the reaction component.

People differ widely in their reactions to pain, mainly because of different pain thresholds and tolerances. A person's pain threshold, mainly of physiologic origin, is the intensity of stimulus he needs to sense pain. His pain tolerance, mainly of psychological origin, is the duration or intensity of pain he'll tolerate before openly expressing pain. (See *The gate control theory of pain,* page 62.)

Acute and chronic pain

Patients with cancer may experience acute or chronic pain, or both, during the course of their illness.

Acute pain is usually sharp, intense, and easily localized. It sets in suddenly; is transient; and prompts autonomic responses such as heavy perspiration, rising blood pressure, and rapid pulse and respiratory rates.

Chronic pain may start as acute pain, but usually its beginnings are slow and insidious. Typically, it's poorly localized, generates no autonomic responses, and may persist for months or even years. Although dull and achy, chronic pain can nevertheless be severe; it can dominate a patient's every thought and action, causing insomnia, fatigue, depression, appetite loss, and sexual malfunction.

What causes cancer pain?

Contrary to popular opinion, cancer pain doesn't result from the tumor itself, but from the growing tumor's intrusion on normal tissues. Such intrusion can take many forms:

• infiltration of nerves, blood vessels, or lymphatic channels

• compression of nerves

• obstruction of hollow organs or ductal systems such as the trachea, the ureters, and the GI or biliary tract

• occlusion of blood vessels, resulting in venous engorgement with edema or arterial ischemia, or both

• necrosis, inflammation, or infection of tissue

• distension of tissues such as fascia or periosteum.

Pain may also result from diagnostic procedures associated with cancer, such as lumbar puncture, and from treatments for cancer, including surgery, chemotherapy, and radiation therapy.

A patient's emotional state can profoundly influence his perception of pain. Fear and anxiety about the future, body image and role changes, financial problems, social isolation—all can exaggerate the frequency and intensity of pain.

Pain may be minimal at rest but becomes intolerable with any kind of motion. This may cause the patient to avoid motion, which can lead to decubiti, constipation, contractures, osteoporosis, renal calculi, and impaired ventilation and circulation.

Careful assessment critical

Begin by asking the patient to describe his pain. What exactly does it feel like? When

The gate control theory of pain

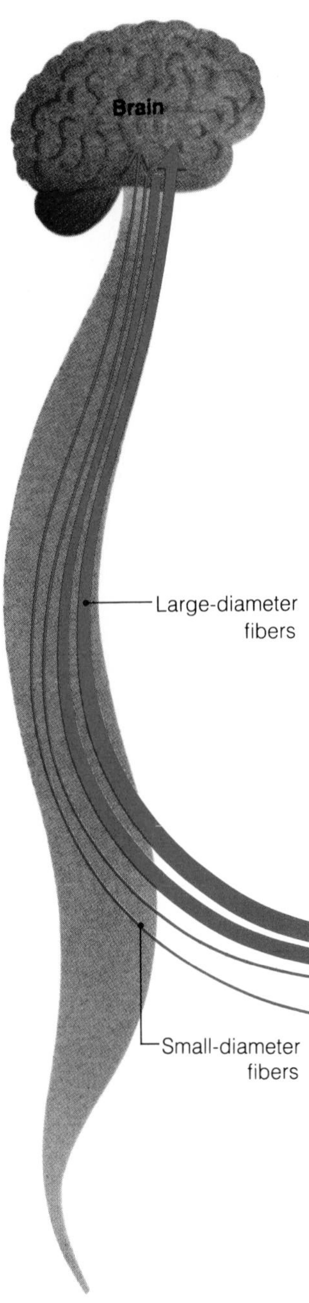

Intensive research on the pathophysiology of pain in recent years has resulted in several new theories of pain perception. Among these is the Melzack-Wall *gate control theory.*

According to this theory, pain and thermal impulses travel over small-diameter, slow-conducting afferent nerve fibers to the spinal cord's dorsal horns (see below). There, they terminate in an area of gray matter called the *substantia gelatinosa* (SG). When sensory stimulation reaches a critical level, a so-called gate in the SG opens, allowing nearby *transmission (T) cells* to transmit the pain impulse to the brain via the *interspinal neurons* to the *spinothalamic tract,* and thence to the thalamus and cerebral cortex (upper left). Thus, the small fibers function to enhance pain transmission.

Large-diameter fibers, in contrast, function to inhibit pain transmission. Stimulation of these large, fast-conducting afferent fibers opposes the smaller fibers' input and activates the SG gate to close, blocking the pain transmission. In addition, descending (efferent) impulses along various tracts from the brain and brain stem can enhance or reduce pain transmission at the gate. For example, triggering selective brain processes, such as attention, emotions, and memory of pain, can intensify pain by opening the gate.

Unlike earlier pain theories, the gate control theory explains how external methods and cognitive techniques can modulate pain transmission. For example, stimulation of the large fibers—through massage, heat or cold applications, acupuncture, transcutaneous electrical nerve stimulation, or dorsal column stimulation—can override sensory input and block pain transmission at the gate. Techniques such as biofeedback, distraction, and relaxation training, which operate through the descending fibers, can reduce pain by closing the gate.

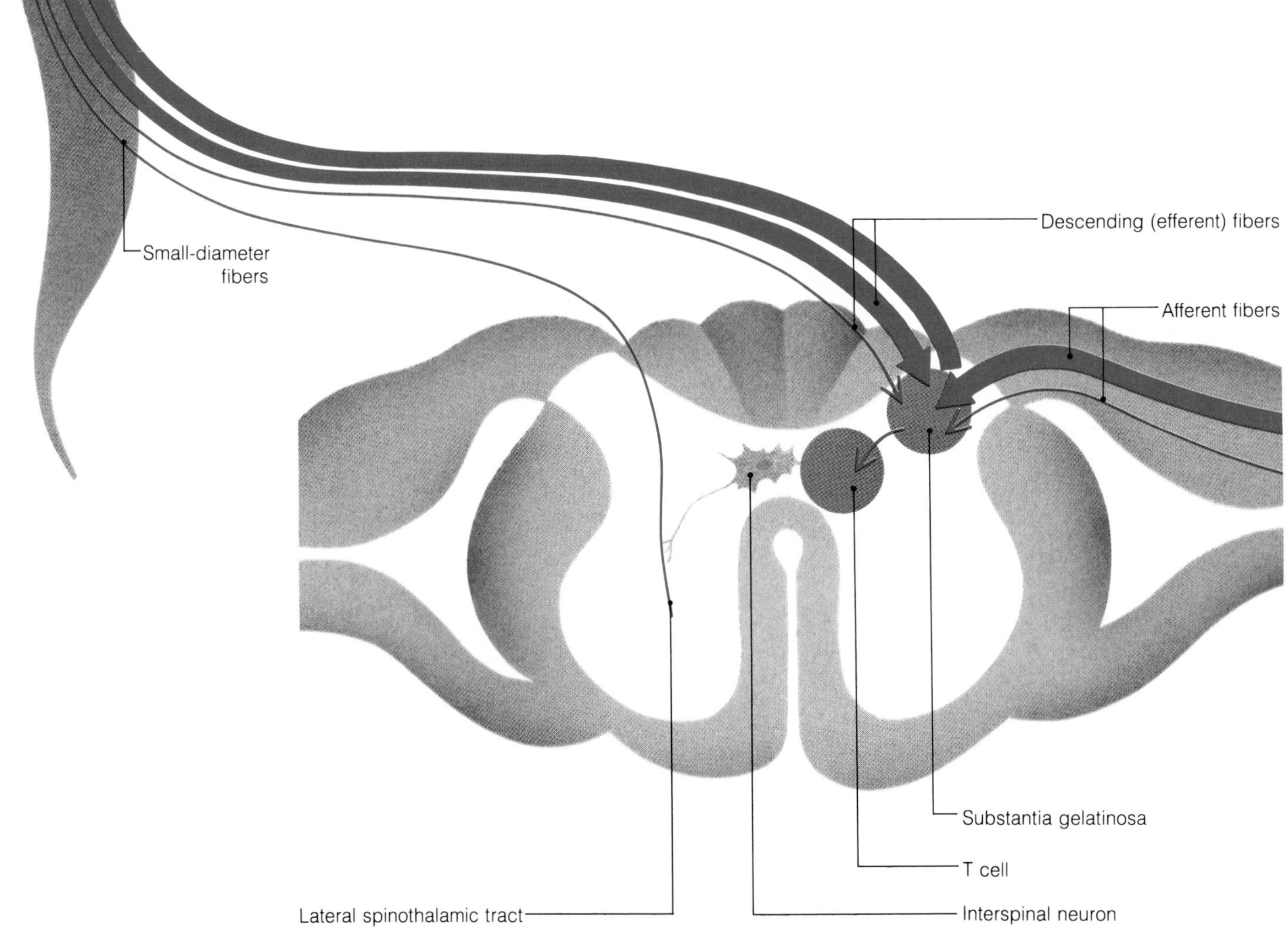

Brain

Large-diameter fibers

Small-diameter fibers

Descending (efferent) fibers

Afferent fibers

Substantia gelatinosa

T cell

Lateral spinothalamic tract

Interspinal neuron

does it start, how long does it last, and how often does it recur? What provokes its onset? Encourage the patient to use a pain-rating scale to report pain intensity and relief. Also ask: What actions does he find help relieve his pain? What actions seem to make it worse? Carefully define its location.

Ask the patient to point to the place(s) on his body where he feels pain. Remember that localized pain is felt only at its origin; projected pain travels along the nerve pathways; radiated pain extends in several directions from the point of origin; and referred pain occurs in places remote from the site of origin.

Factors that influence a patient's ability to localize his pain include its duration, severity, and source. Its source is usually categorized as cutaneous, which includes skin and sub-skin tissue; deep somatic, which includes nerve, bone, muscle, and their supporting tissue; or visceral, which includes the body trunk organs.

Find out how the patient responds to pain. Does his pain interfere with eating? With sleeping? With working? With his sex life? With his relationships to others?

Watch for any physiologic responses to pain. These may include nausea, vomiting, and changes in vital signs. Look for behavioral responses to pain. These may show in facial expressions, body movement, or what the patient says or doesn't say. Also note psychological responses such as anger, depression, and irritability.

Be sure to assess attitudes about pain. Ask: How does he usually handle pain? Does he tell others when he hurts or does he try to hide it? Does his family understand his pain and try to help him deal with it? Does he accept their help?

Realistic goals and interventions
Include the patient when planning interventions for pain relief. Determine what pain-relief measures he wants to use and what he expects them to do for him.

Caution: Remember that a patient overcome by severe pain may be unable to cooperate with your assessment and may have trouble establishing pain-relief goals. You may first have to provide some pain relief to help him think clearly and work with you.

When the patient has established his goals, discuss measures to achieve them. If he's using a measure that affords adequate pain relief, continue it so long as it's not harmful.

Determine whether the patient wants to participate actively or passively in pain-relief activities. If he prefers to be active, consider using relaxation techniques. If he prefers to be passive, consider cutaneous stimulation. Which pain-relieving measures you select must depend on your patient's preferences and on the severity and chronology of his pain. Generally, several pain-control measures used simultaneously work better than one, through an additive effect.

Noninvasive measures
Noninvasive measures to relieve pain generally have a low risk of complications, are less costly, and don't produce serious adverse effects. They can be used alone for mild to moderate pain or can be combined with drug therapy for severe pain. Popular noninvasive measures include methods of cutaneous stimulation, relaxation, distraction, and guided imagery.

Cutaneous stimulation. This is thought to work by stimulating large-diameter nerve fibers, thereby closing the "gate" to pain impulses in the substantia gelatinosa. (See *The gate control theory of pain.*) It may also increase the release of endorphins.

Cutaneous stimulation can be achieved in various ways, including:
• *Massage.* Apply firm or light pressure with the hands, using a circular or stroking motion. (Be careful to apply light pressure over tumor sites.)
• *Acupressure.* Apply pressure at traditional acupuncture sites.
• *Lotion or ointment.* If the mixture contains alcohol or menthol, first test it on a small normal area, then apply it over the painful area.
• *Vibration.* Run an electric vibrator over the painful area or over acupressure points, but not directly over the tumor.
• *Heat.* Use a heat lamp or heating pad to apply dry heat, or hot packs or tub baths to apply moist heat. (Don't apply heat directly over tumor sites or over an area exposed to radiotherapy.)
• *Cold.* Apply an ice pack, an ice cube, or cold water to the painful area.
• *Transcutaneous electrical nerve stimulation* (TENS). This requires a doctor's order and involves use of a battery-driven, solid-state pulse generator connected by cables to electrodes on the patient's skin. The generator can be attached to the patient's belt.

TENS works by transmitting electrical im-

Patient-controlled analgesia system
A new method of pain relief, the "patient-controlled analgesia system" (PCA), is now being used in some centers. This system permits the patient to self-administer his own analgesic by pressing a button at the end of a cord that's attached to a pump fitted with a pre-filled syringe containing an analgesic (see photo).

Small intermittent doses of the analgesic administered intravenously maintain blood levels that assure comfort and minimize oversedation. Dosages and time intervals (usually 8 to 10 minutes) allowed for the patient to determine his comfort level are preset by the doctor or the nursing staff. The syringe is locked inside the pump as a safety feature. The system will only dispense the analgesic until the correct (preset) time interval has elapsed.

Clinical studies report that patients on PCA tend to titrate analgesic drugs effectively and maintain comfort without oversedation. They tend to use less of the drug than the amount normally given by I.M. injection.

PCA provides other significant advantages.
• Patients are alert and active during daytime hours.
• Patients no longer need to suffer pain while awaiting their injections.
• Patients are free from pain caused by injections.
• The nursing staff is free for other clinical duties.

Neurosurgical procedures for pain control

Nerve block

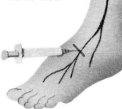

Peripheral neurectomy

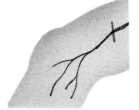

Sensory rhizotomy

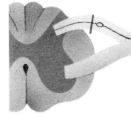

Cordotomy

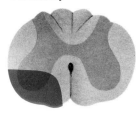

Midline myelotomy

Stereotaxic thalamotomy

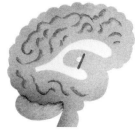

When chemotherapy, narcotics, or other measures fail to relieve cancer pain, neurosurgery may be an appropriate alternative. Six common neurosurgical procedures are:

• *Nerve block:* interrupting sensory nerve transmissions by injecting either local anesthetics (lidocaine) or neurolytic agents (alcohol). This procedure eases pain in the injection area but may cause loss of function of tissues and organs served by the blocked nerve. The resulting pain relief is temporary, lasting from hours (after injecting a local anesthetic) to 6 months or more (after injecting some neurolytic agents). An occasional long-term side effect is peripheral neuritis of the injected nerve.

• *Peripheral neurectomy:* sectioning peripheral nerves supplying the painful area. This procedure is useful if the pain is localized in a small area. Its hazards include complete loss of sensation in the involved area, possible paralysis, and recurrence of pain. Cranial nerve neurectomy may be useful against the pain of head and neck cancer.

• *Sensory rhizotomy:* sectioning the sensory root of a spinal or cranial nerve proximal to the dorsal root ganglion. This procedure works best to control pain originating in the thorax or abdomen. Sensory rhizotomy causes permanent loss of sensation in the affected area but allows motor responses to continue. Cranial nerve rhizotomy is more effective than spinal nerve rhizotomy.

• *Cordotomy:* sectioning the spinal cord's anterolateral quadrant to destroy spinothalamic pain pathways. The procedure may be unilateral on the side opposite the pain or bilateral. It may be done surgically or percutaneously with an electric needle. Its benefit is selective loss of pain and temperature sensation in the involved area; its possible disadvantages include hemiparesis on the lesion side and sexual and bladder dysfunction.

• *Midline myelotomy:* interrupting spinothalamic nerve tracts at the anterior commissure where the tracts cross the spinal cord. This procedure eradicates pain and temperature sensation in the affected area. It involves microsurgery and extensive laminectomy and reportedly causes less bowel and bladder dysfunction than the classical cordotomy.

• *Stereotaxic thalamotomy:* creating an intracranial lesion with an implanted electrode. This procedure stops transmission of pain impulses through the thalamus and is typically used only when other therapy has failed to relieve pain. Side effects result from difficulty in isolating the lesion site.

pulses that produce a pleasant tingling, tapping, or massaging sensation, thereby relieving pain. The unit is under the patient's control; he can adjust the intensity, rate, and duration of impulses to suit himself.

TENS works best on well-localized moderate pain. It does little to relieve visceral pain, and it's of little value to narcotic-tolerant patients. Up to 2 weeks of treatment may be needed before TENS takes effect; meanwhile, watch for possible skin irritations.

Relaxation techniques. Yoga, meditation and progressive relaxation are examples of techniques that decrease muscle tension and increase blood flow. By themselves, these techniques won't relieve pain (except that caused by muscle tension), but when used with other measures, they can increase in effectiveness.

Distraction. This venerable old measure still has its place in pain relief. It works by focusing the patient's attention on something other than his pain. Distracting foci may include watching TV, playing electronic games, doing rhythmic breathing, and listening to music.

Guided imagery. Essentially another form of distraction, guided imagery calls on the patient to imagine a positive image that will help take his mind off the pain. The most effective images involve most or all of the five senses; for example, savoring the sight, sound, smell, taste, and touch of a gentle rainshower or a gracious banquet. Successful imagery, of course, requires concentration. So it's usually preceded by a relaxation technique, especially if the patient's tense or anxious.

Two new noninvasive pain-relief methods are therapeutic touch and the Simonton technique. (See *Therapeutic touch: A controversial new treatment,* page 65, and *The Simonton technique: A new psychological approach,* page 67.)

Invasive measures

Invasive measures to control cancer pain can take various forms. An obvious one is surgery—for example, removing all or part of a tumor in hopes of relieving pain or effecting a cure. Radiation therapy or chemotherapy may also relieve pain by shrinking a tumor.

Neurosurgery relieves pain by interrupting

nerve pathways that transmit painful impulses. Many neurosurgical procedures have serious adverse effects, so be sure to teach your patient what they are and how to manage them. (See *Neurosurgical procedures for pain control.*)

Analgesic drugs

Analgesics are the most familiar way to control pain. Nonnarcotic analgesics, which act at the peripheral level, are best for mild pain; narcotics, which act at the central level, are best for severe pain. Often, a combination of narcotic and nonnarcotic analgesics is more effective than either drug alone. Keep in mind the following guidelines for effective use of analgesic drugs.

Remember that preventing pain is easier than curing it. Analgesics are more effective when given before pain sets in or before it becomes severe. Avoid a p.r.n. approach, which tries to eradicate pain that has already taken hold; instead, determine the patient's pain pattern, then establish a regular schedule of around-the-clock administration to maintain effective blood levels of analgesics that don't allow pain breakthrough.

Whenever possible, give oral analgesics, which allow your patient's independence and also reduce his risk of infection and tissue damage from intramuscular or subcutaneous injections. Remember, when switching a patient from parenteral to oral analgesics, to give an equianalgesic dose; if you don't, the patient's pain won't be relieved, and he may quickly lose faith in oral analgesics. (See *Narcotic and opioid analgesics,* page 66.)

Titrate the dose. Before administering morphine or other narcotics, assess the patient's condition. Begin with the standard drug dosage; if the patient's pain isn't relieved within 30 minutes, reassess the need for additional medication, and if ordered, titrate it to the smallest dose that controls pain. Administer these drugs intravenously to relieve severe pain, and if possible, follow a continuous rather than an intermittent schedule to avoid pain-control peaks and valleys and possible pain breakthrough. Check dose limits carefully; the correct I.V. dose is usually one half to one third of that required for an I.M. or subcutaneous dose.

Watch for tolerance and adverse effects. An important disadvantage of narcotics is the development of patient tolerance to the original dose. The first sign of tolerance is a shorter duration of pain relief; the second, a diminished analgesic effect. Report signs of tolerance to the doctor.

Also observe for other adverse effects of narcotics, and take preventive steps. Constipation is common, as are nausea and vomiting. Elderly patients and those with underlying lung disease or tumor-induced depression of the brain's respiratory center are especially vulnerable to respiratory depression.

If the patient's respiratory rate falls below 10 breaths/minute, hold the narcotic and notify the doctor. Simple techniques such as stimulating the patient frequently, changing his position, and encouraging him to cough and to breathe deeply can minimize the risk of respiratory depression.

Avoid oversedation. If narcotics are involved, caffeine or dextroamphetamine may be used as counteragents. Check with the doctor.

Evaluate analgesic effectiveness. Before discarding an analgesic, give yourself enough time to evaluate its effect thoroughly. Usually, this will take at least 24 to 48 hours.

If you find the patient's pain relief incomplete, be sure to discuss this with his doctor. For example, if an analgesic relieves pain only for 2 hours but is prescribed only every 4 hours, the doctor will need to adjust the schedule accordingly. In the meantime, use noninvasive measures to help alleviate pain.

Tricyclic antidepressants may also be prescribed as part of the pain-relief regimen. If so, expect an analgesic effect after about 4 days and an antidepressant effect after about 2 weeks.

MANAGING PROTEIN-CALORIE MALNUTRITION

Among patients with cancer, the most common complication is protein-calorie malnutrition, a condition marked by weight loss, decreased fat and muscle stores, depleted visceral protein stores, and depressed cellular immunity. Untreated, it can result in cachexia and even death.

Cancerous cachexia, a catchall term, is still not completely understood. However, its characteristic signs are well known; they include anorexia; reduced food intake; weight loss; weakness; anemia; increased basal metabolic rate; and fluid, electrolyte, taste, and olfactory abnormalities. Fortunately, cancerous cachexia can often be prevented. And even when it can't, its severity can be significantly diminished if you provide nutritional support that can prevent or correct protein-calorie malnutrition.

Therapeutic touch: A controversial new treatment

Therapeutic touch, a modern adaptation of the ancient practice of "laying on of hands," is being used in some centers to alleviate pain, including that of patients with cancer. In this pain-relief technique, the care giver (known as a healer) uses his hands to detect abnormal changes in the patient's energy field, which surrounds his body. When the healer detects areas of increased tension in the patient's energy field—an indication of pain—he "channels" this tension out of the field with appropriate hand movements.

Therapeutic touch consists of 3 phases: *centering, assessment,* and *energy transfer.* In centering, the healer attains a meditative state by focusing all his thoughts on the patient's condition. Once this state is achieved, assessment begins. Using his hands as sensors, the healer passes them over the patient's body (usually without touching it) to passively assess his energy field and detect differences in energy rhythm and flow, which may be felt as heat, a tingling sensation, or pressure. After assessment, the healer formulates a care plan with the patient and his family.

In the third phase, energy transfer, the healer again passes his hands over areas of accumulated tension in the patient's body and redirects these energies. This appears to involve a transfer of energy from the healer to the patient, dubbed "electron transfer resonance."

This technique is being used in a growing number of nursing care settings.

Narcotic and opioid analgesics

Drug	Action times			Equianalgesic doses	
	Onset	Peak	Duration	I.M.	P.O.
alphaprodine	5 to 10 min	30 to 60 min	1 to 2 hr	50 mg	‡
Brompton's cocktail*	10 to 15 min	2 to 3 hr	3 to 8 hr	‡	Depends on preparation
butorphanol	10 min	30 to 60 min	3 to 4 hr	2 to 3 mg	‡
codeine	15 to 30 min	60 to 90 min	4 to 6 hr	130 mg	200 mg
fentanyl	5 to 15 min	Within 30 min	1 to 2 hr	0.1 mg	‡
hydromorphone	15 to 30 min	30 to 90 min	2 to 4 hr	1.5 mg	8 mg
levorphanol	Within 1 hr	60 to 90 min	4 to 5 hr	2 mg	4 mg
meperidine	10 to 15 min	30 to 60 min	2 to 4 hr	75 mg	300 mg
methadone	10 to 15 min	1 to 2 hr	6 to 8 hr †	10 mg	20 mg
morphine	Within 20 min	30 to 90 min	2 to 4 hr	10 mg	60 mg
nalbuphine	10 to 15 min	30 to 60 min	3 to 6 hr	10 mg	‡
oxycodone*	10 to 15 min	60 to 90 min	4 to 5 hr	‡	30 mg
oxymorphone	5 to 10 min	30 to 90 min	4 to 5 hr	1 mg	5 mg (rectal)
pentazocine	10 to 15 min	30 to 60 min	2 to 3 hr	40 mg	100 mg
propoxyphene*	15 to 60 min	2 to 3 hr	4 to 6 hr	‡	About 300 mg

*Oral administration. (Other values in chart are for I.M. or subcutaneous administration.)
†Increases with repeated use because of cumulative effects.
‡Not available in this form.

Assess nutritional status

Begin by determining if your patient's at high risk for protein-calorie malnutrition. Risk factors to look for include:
• weight loss of 7% to 10% within 6 months
• major surgery, chemotherapy, or radiation therapy in the past 6 months
• active cancer or other illness lasting more than 3 weeks
• inability to feed himself or to prepare food because of weakness, pain, or motor or sensory loss
• drugs (such as steroids) that may cause protein breakdown or GI dysfunction
• inability to chew or swallow food
• GI dysfunction causing stomatitis/mucositis, dysphagia, nausea, vomiting, constipation, or diarrhea
• decreased nutritional intake because of anorexia or taste alterations.

To assess your patient's *somatic protein stores,* which when depleted account for fat and muscle wasting, evaluate his weight and weight index. Compare his actual weight with the ideal weight obtained from a standard height-weight chart. Calculate your patient's percentage of ideal body weight, using the following equation:

$$\frac{\text{Actual weight}}{\text{Ideal weight}} \times 100 = \frac{\% \text{ ideal}}{\text{body weight}}$$

Next, compare your patient's current weight with his usual weight. To determine the percentage of weight change, use this equation:

$$\left(\frac{\text{Usual weight before illness} - \text{actual weight}}{\text{Usual weight before illness}} \right) \times 100 = \frac{\% \text{ weight}}{\text{change}}$$

Remember that weight loss greater than 2% in 1 week, 5% in 1 month, and 10% in 6 months greatly increases your patient's risk of deterioration and even death. Check his weight regularly, preferably every week.

Anthropometric measurements, which are easily done, can also help you assess somatic protein stores. Obtain these measurements every 2 weeks. (For an explanation of how to do this, see Chapter 2.)

To assess the patient's *visceral protein compartment,* examine results of plasma protein blood tests such as serum albumin levels. Or use serum transferrin results, which are unaffected by hydration status or surgery as is serum albumin. Also note the total lymphocyte count, with the following equation:

$$\frac{\text{\% lymphocyte} \times \text{white blood cells}}{100} = \frac{\text{Total lymphocyte count}}{}$$

(See *Evaluating visceral protein depletion,* page 68.)

Continue to monitor blood test results at least weekly.

While assessing the patient, and as you continue to care for him, look for clinical signs of malnutrition. Common signs include poor dentition; bleeding or receding gums; beefy, scarlet tongue; and dry, red fissures at lip angles (angular cheilosis). Also look for thin, dull hair; brittle nails; and dry, flaky skin. You'll also need information about the patient's nutritional patterns, including who normally prepares his meals; what stimulates his appetite; which foods he likes and dislikes; and what effects religious, cultural, or financial factors have on his diet. You may need a 3-day oral-intake record so you can calculate protein, carbohydrate, fat, and calorie intake and make recommendations for improvement.

Nutritional intervention

If your patient has protein-calorie deficiencies, use assessment information to help determine his diet requirements. Also consult with his dietitian and doctor, and with the patient decide how best to provide nutritional support.

If your patient can ingest nutrients and has a functional GI tract, encourage oral feeding. Teach him the basics of a well-balanced, protein- and calorie-enriched diet. Identify specific foods and products that help support adequate nutrition. For example, foods and drinks may be enriched with glucose polymers, which add 32 calories/tablespoon and don't affect food taste. Also useful are commercial high-protein and high-calorie supplements, which can be slowly sipped between meals. If these supplements cause diarrhea, suggest diluting them with more water or cutting back on the amount.

Common causes of malnourishment

Some patients will have trouble ingesting, digesting, or absorbing nutrients because of the following conditions:

Anorexia. Loss of appetite is a common byproduct of cancer. You may be able to minimize this and promote eating with one or more of these techniques:
• Serve all meals in a pleasant environment (such as group meals in a patient lounge).

• Accompany meals with music and, if allowed, a glass of wine to help stimulate the patient's appetite.
• Encourage eating five, six, or more small meals daily rather than three large meals.
• If the patient's appetite is best at breakfast (which it usually is), have him eat at least one third of his daily requirements then.
• Encourage and help the patient to exercise before meals.
• Don't serve water or other drinks with meals because they may cause a feeling of fullness before the patient takes in enough calories.
• Have the patient avoid gas-forming foods.
• Encourage the patient to wash his hands and face and to rinse his mouth with a mouthwash before meals.
• Control symptoms that contribute to anorexia, such as pain, nausea, and taste alterations.

Nausea and vomiting. A calm, reassuring approach to the patient can help control nausea, as can the following procedures:
• Modify the environment to eliminate noxious odors and sights.
• Ventilate the room, keep an emesis basin handy but out of sight, and provide distractions such as TV or radio.
• Serve foods the patient prefers.
• Have the patient avoid eating up to 2 hours before and after chemotherapy or radiotherapy to the abdomen or brain.
• Administer an antiemetic as ordered, and evaluate its effectiveness.
• Avoid therapies or activities during episodes of active vomiting.
• Elevate the head of the bed to 45°.
• Encourage the patient to eat low-fat meals, to avoid overly sweet or spicy foods, and to eat dry foods such as toast or crackers after getting up in the morning. Allow some salty foods.
• Encourage the patient to drink soups or clear, cool beverages slowly with a straw, but only between meals.
• If the patient is sedated or has a decreased level of consciousness from disease effects, take measures to prevent aspiration.
• Offer frequent mouth care.
• If possible, administer chemotherapy by I.V. drip infusion rather than I.V. push and at a time of day that doesn't interfere with meals (try early morning or night).
• Maintain intake and output records and confer with the doctor about the need for I.V. fluid supplements.

Taste alterations. Cancer may disrupt a pa-

The Simonton technique: A new psychological approach

Developed by a radiation oncologist and a psychotherapist, the Simontons' self-awareness technique combines traditional medical management with psychological treatment. This new treatment is based on a concept which suggests that:
• The patient's negative psychological processes can cause or aggravate physical illness.
• Positive thinking can control or cure physical illnesses.
• These psychological mechanisms function by aiding or impeding our body's natural immune system.
• The patient can learn to control these mechanisms.

The Simontons' method consists of several phases:
• Taking responsibility for one's own health.
• Learning to relax and visualize recovery. The patient combines Progressive Muscle Relaxation exercises with personalized mental imagery of his own immune system and of his medical treatment attacking and overcoming the cancer cells. The patient is then instructed to envision himself as a healthy, strong, and physically invincible person.
• Living a healthy, goal-directed life.

Although the effectiveness of this method is yet to be proven, the technique has been gaining popularity because it causes no harm, is simple to do, and has shown some effectiveness.

Evaluating visceral protein depletion

Serum albumin levels

Normal
4.5-3.8 g/dl

Mild depletion
3.7-3.0 g/dl

Moderate depletion
2.9-2.5 g/dl

Severe depletion
<2.5 g/dl

Serum transferrin levels

Mild depletion
200-150 mg/dl

Moderate depletion
150-100 mg/dl

Severe depletion
<100 mg/dl

Total lymphocyte count

Normal
>1,800/mm³

Mild depletion
1,500-1,200/mm³

Moderate depletion
1,200-800/mm³

Severe depletion
<800/mm³

tient's sense of taste, causing him to refuse certain foods. Avoid serving the foods he finds offensive, but also take other steps to encourage eating. For example:
• If the patient has an aversion to meat, teach him how to substitute nonmeat protein sources.
• Suggest that he try cold foods, which are usually preferred, and new spices to improve taste, especially those that smell inviting and help stimulate appetite. Having food prepared and arranged on a plate or tray in ways that are visually appealing also helps stimulate appetite.

Stomatitis/mucositis. Obviously, a painful mouth discourages eating. So be sure to examine the patient's mouth at least once daily. Early signs and symptoms of stomatitis and mucositis include dry lips and mucous membranes, and mild erythema and edema along the mucocutaneous junctions. At early stages, the patient may not feel severe pain, but he may complain of mild burning. Later signs and symptoms include pain, bleeding, ulceration, and necrosis.

The patient with thrombocytopenia is at special risk for bleeding; the one with leukopenia, for oral infection. Watch for candidiasis, which is common and causes soft, white patches on the mucous membranes.

To help combat mouth soreness, encourage intake of fluids to 3,000 ml daily unless contraindicated. If the patient has loose fitting dentures, have a dentist correct them. In the meantime, have the patient remove the dentures when not eating or leave them out entirely.

Help him select soft, moist foods such as eggs, ricotta cheese, yogurt, pasta, and bananas. Tell him to avoid citrus fruits and hot, spicy, or coarse-textured foods. Encourage a high-protein diet to promote tissue repair, but discourage alcohol and tobacco use.

Some patients with sore mouths experience less pain when foods and liquids are served at room temperature; others tolerate cold foods better and benefit from popsicles, frozen yogurt, or iced drinks.

Pay close attention to mouth care. For preventive purposes, giving the patient mouth care after each meal and every 4 hours while he's awake may suffice. But if stomatitis is severe, increase the frequency of mouth care to as often as every 2 hours while the patient is awake and once or twice during the night.

Depending on the severity of stomatitis, suggest that the patient clean his teeth with either a soft-bristle toothbrush, a sponge-tipped swab, an irrigation syringe, or a spray. Tell him to avoid dental floss and drying agents such as glycerine, lemon, and alcohol-based mouthwashes. Instead, suggest a solution made up of equal parts hydrogen peroxide, normal saline solution or water, and a mild mouthwash. To maintain the hydrogen peroxide's oxidizing properties, prepare the mixture just before use.

For lip care, apply a water-soluble lubricant or a commercial lip moisturizer. Topical analgesics (for example, a combination of Xylocaine 2% Viscous Solution, Benadryl Elixir [12.5 mg/5 ml]), and an antacid may be used as a comforting rinse. If infection is present, systemic analgesics may be needed, also. Administer nystatin oral suspension as ordered for candidiasis or a broad-spectrum antibiotic as ordered for bacterial infections.

Esophagitis. To help the patient with esophagitis, consider the following measures:
• Determine the consistency of foods your patient can swallow. Soft, semisoft, cool foods are usually easily tolerated and minimize pain. Firm, slippery foods such as pasta may also be tolerated.
• If the patient has trouble moving food to his pharynx, try using a long-handled spoon to place his food on the back of his tongue.
• If the patient has trouble swallowing during the pharyngeal phase of swallowing, have him inhale, place a small bite of food on his tongue, swallow, and then exhale or cough. He should then wait 30 seconds before the next bite.
• Offer a straw for liquids and semisoft foods.
• Offer antacids or soft dairy products to coat the mucous membranes of the pharynx or esophagus.
• Tell the patient to avoid hot or highly spiced foods, citrus fruits, and alcoholic drinks.
• Help the patient use a topical analgesic, or administer systemic analgesics as ordered.

Xerostomia. For the patient with dry mouth, try these suggestions:
• Encourage oral irrigations with normal saline solution or bicarbonate of soda every 2 hours.
• Apply artificial saliva to moisten mucous membranes.
• Encourage the patient to eat moist foods.
• Provide humidified air in the patient's room. Always humidify oxygen.
• Tell the patient to avoid alcohol, which dries mucous membranes.
• Moisten the patient's lips with a water-solu-

Preventing infection in hyperalimentation

Because the intravenous hyperalimentation solution is a good medium for bacterial growth and the central venous line gives systemic access, contamination and sepsis are always a risk when this mode of therapy is chosen to combat malnutrition. However, the patient with cancer is at even greater risk because of her already debilitated state and suppressed immune response.

To avoid this life-threatening complication, strict aseptic during solution, dressing, tubing, and filter changes is essential.

To properly care for the patient receiving hyperalimentation, change the dressing on her insertion site at least three times weekly or immediately if it becomes loose or wet.

Before you begin, explain to your patient exactly what you're about to do. Then prepare her for the procedure as follows:

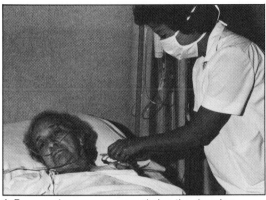

1. Face masks are necessary during the dressing change to keep the hyperalimentation site uncontaminated. Slip your mask on, and place the other loosely over her mouth. However, do not put a mask on a patient who needs oxygen or who has a nasogastric tube in place. Put the patient in a supine position. Turn her head away from the dressing to make the insertion site more accessible and to minimize the risk of contamination. Remove the old dressing, taking care not to disturb the catheter.

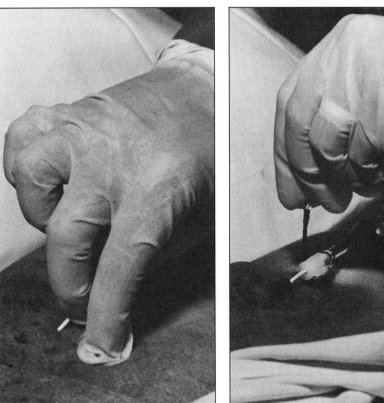

2. Now, examine the site for any signs of infection; for example, discharge, inflammation, or soreness. If you suspect infection, notify the doctor and culture the drainage.

3. Put on sterile gloves and clean around the insertion site with acetone. Work in a circular motion from the site outward, taking care not to jostle the catheter. (*Caution:* Acetone will corrode the catheter and may cause skin irritation or breakdown predisposing to infection. If acetone contacts the catheter, wash it off with saline solution. Use of acetone has been discontinued in some centers.) Now, clean the site with povidone-iodine, again using a circular motion. The catheter connection should also be cleansed. Let it dry naturally. Don't fan your hands over the site; doing so increases the risk of contamination. Place a 2″ × 2″ sterile gauze pad under the catheter connection. Insert the new primed tubing into the hub, making sure it's secure.

4. Apply antimicrobial ointment to the insertion site. Dress the site according to hospital policy.

Controlling infection odors

In some patients with cancer, draining infected wounds, caused by fungating tumors, may develop offensive odors. Manage this problem by keeping the wound as clean as possible.

After removing the old dressing, irrigate the wound to remove debris and secretions. Depending on your hospital's protocol, irrigation may be done using half-strength hydrogen peroxide and normal saline at room temperature; or it may be done with a pulsatile water-jet system, such as a hand-held shower head or pulsating shower massage; or in a hydrotherapy tub that's equipped with pulsatile jet wands. Ten to 15 minutes of pulsatile jet therapy, applied to the wound 2 to 3 times daily, significantly reduces odor-causing bacteria.

With pulsatile jet irrigation, debriding agents are not necessary. Products such as absorption dressings are indicated for cleansing, deodorizing, and protecting the wound. Skin barriers protect the surrounding skin from potential irritation. A hydrophilic wound dressing such as Vigilon can be used to relieve pain resulting from denuding of the epithelial surface caused by tumor invasion.

A drainage pouch can be used to contain copious wound drainage. Pouching the wound also controls the odor and protects the skin. The pouch can be opened and closed for wound irrigation without being removed.

ble lubricant or a commercial moisturizer.
• Suggest sugar-free gum or hard candy to stimulate salivation.

Diarrhea. Try the following methods to combat diarrhea:
• Serve a soft, low-residue, high-protein, high-calorie diet as ordered.
• Suggest that the patient avoid alcohol; tobacco products; caffeine products; milk and milk products; hot, cold, spicy, fatty, or fried foods; and commercial supplements with a high osmolarity.
• Encourage adequate rest.
• Help the patient keep a record of bowel movements.
• Administer antidiarrheal agents as ordered.
• Initiate measures to protect rectal skin and mucous membranes.
• If diarrhea becomes severe, consult the doctor about parenteral nutrition.

Enteral hyperalimentation preferred
When patients with cancer can't get enough food orally, enteral or parenteral hyperalimentation may become necessary. The preferable route is determined by the condition of the patient's GI tract, by his ability to sustain potential complications, and by the duration of treatment.

The enteral route is usually safer and better tolerated. Tubes used for enteral feedings include orogastric, nasogastric, esophagostomy, pharyngostomy, gastrostomy, and jejunostomy tubes. Most patients tolerate slow, continuous feedings better than bolus feedings.

Prevent aspiration. When feeding patients through a nasogastric tube, be alert for possible aspiration pneumonia, which may result from incorrect positioning of the tube or the patient and from large residual volumes. To minimize the risk of aspiration, check the tube for position before each intermittent feeding or every 4 hours if you're using continuous feeding. Also check the patient's gastric residual volume; if it's greater than 200 to 250 ml, hold feedings for 4 hours and then resume them after residual volume has diminished. While feeding the patient, elevate the head of his bed from 30° to 45°; maintain this elevation for 1 hour after a bolus feeding or continuously if the infusion is constant. If aspiration occurs, discontinue feedings and notify the doctor.

Watch for metabolic complications. Such complications may include hyperglycemia, glycosuria, and hyperosmolar hyperglycemic nonketotic coma (HHNC). They are especially

common in patients with diabetes mellitus, those receiving steroids, those under acute stress, and those who receive chemically defined formulas.

To identify these complications promptly, monitor urine glucose and acetone every 4 hours, blood glucose as ordered, intake and output (noting carefully negative fluid balance), and daily weights. You may have to increase the patient's fluid intake if osmotic diuresis occurs in response to glycosuria. This intervention is important to prevent rapid onset of HHNC.

Prevent diarrhea. This complication, associated with tube feedings, can result from formula hypertonicity, lactose intolerance, too rapid start-up or advancement of feedings, and contaminated formula.

To prevent or treat diarrhea, dilute the feeding, provide a fresh feeding every 4 to 8 hours, dispose of uninfused formula before adding fresh formula to the bag, and change the feeding bag and tube daily. Also consult with the doctor about possibly reducing the feeding rate and shifting from continuous to intermittent feedings (or vice versa). If you suspect lactose intolerance, notify the doctor, who may prescribe a lactose-free formula. Monitor patient intake and output; administer antidiarrheals as ordered.

Minimize nausea, vomiting, abdominal distension, and cramping. These can result from too rapid feedings, too cold formula, or intolerance to the formula's volume or concentration. Obviously, slowing the rate of feeding, administering the formula at room temperature, and temporarily decreasing the volume and concentration are actions you can take to minimize such patient discomfort.

Reduce possible nasal or pharyngeal irritation. Make sure the tube is positioned and secured without pressure. Offer the patient frequent mouth care and, if possible, have him gargle with a water or saline solution. Obstruction of the feeding tube may require its removal and uncomfortable reinsertion. To avoid this, flush the tube between feedings; thoroughly crush and dissolve solid, dry preparations in water before administering them through the tube; or substitute liquid forms of medication whenever possible.

Parenteral hyperalimentation
When enteral feedings prove inappropriate many patients respond well to intravenous hyperalimentation (IVH), which is designed to meet all protein and calorie demands.

Essential fatty acid requirements are provided by infusing lipids peripherally two to five times a week. Calories are provided by adding hypertonic dextrose (D-glucose) to the solution.

If the prescribed solution contains dextrose, administer it through a central vein, preferably the superior vena cava. By using a central rather than a peripheral vein, you'll minimize the risk of sclerosis and phlebitis.

Generally, patients started on IVH are seriously debilitated and are thus vulnerable to serious complications. Take special care to prevent these complications, whether they be technical (related to catheter insertion), metabolic, or septic. (See *Preventing infection in hyperalimentation*, page 69.)

MANAGING INFECTION

Infection is the leading cause of morbidity and mortality in patients with cancer. Patients with leukemia are at highest risk, but the risk is growing for those with solid tumors who are receiving today's more intensive therapies. So one of your highest priorities is to prevent infection or, failing that, to detect infection early and then to provide appropriate care.

Check first for malfunctioning protective mechanisms. In a healthy person, various external and internal mechanisms protect against infection. But in a patient with cancer, these mechanisms often fail, either because of the cancer itself or because of debilitating treatments. (See *Cancer and cancer therapy: An open door to infection*, page 72.) Common failures—and their causes—include the following:

• *A break in the integrity of skin, mucous membranes, or connective tissue.* This may result from tumor-caused obstructions, effusions, or ulcerations that encourage bacterial growth. It may also result from cancer therapies or from diagnostic or supportive therapies (for example, central venous, urinary, or peripheral I.V. catheters; I.M. injections; drainage tubes; or bone marrow aspirations).

• *Leukopenia: A decrease in white blood cells (WBCs) to less than 5,000/mm³.* This condition may result from myelosuppressive and lymphosuppressive therapies such as chemotherapy, corticosteroids, and bone marrow irradiation.

Among the various WBCs, the neutrophils, essential for infection control, are most sensitive to the effects of chemotherapy. Their destruction, a condition called neutropenia, is most severe at 7 to 10 days after administra-

tion of most antineoplastic drugs. About 3 weeks later, the neutrophil count usually returns to normal. Note, however, that repeated chemotherapy will diminish the functional reserve of neutrophils and that radiation therapy to productive bone marrow tissue also destroys the stem cells and may cause neutropenia. A combination of chemotherapy and radiation therapy that involves functional marrow, whether administered concurrently or separately, will induce even more severe and prolonged neutropenia.

• *Malignancies of the reticuloendothelial or hematopoietic systems.* Myeloproliferative malignancies are marked by inadequate neutrophil production; multiple myelomas, by decreased production of immunoglobins (antibodies); and lymphomas, by defects in cell-mediated or humoral immunity that exaggerate susceptibility to yeast and fungal infection.

• *Protein-calorie malnutrition.* Whether related to the cancer itself or to its treatment, this condition weakens immunocompetence.

• *Fluid accumulation, dead air space, and decreased blood supply.* This condition commonly results from surgical resection of large amounts of tissue.

• *Fistula formation.* These abnormal passages, often induced by irradiation of the cervix, bladder, or intestinal tract, may lead to cross-contamination.

• *Diminished immune response.* This may result from high levels of stress, especially the kind that results in intense depression, anger, and anxiety.

• *Diminution of the immune system.* In many patients, this normally accompanies the aging process.

Assess cellular immunity

To assess your patient's *cellular immunity*, recall antigens may be intradermally injected. Those most commonly used are *Candida*, mumps, purified protein derivative (PPD), streptokinase-streptodornase (SKSD), and *Trichophyton*.

Most people have been exposed to these antigens at some time. So, assuming the immune system is intact, an antigen injection will produce erythema and a raised, indurated red wheal at the injection site within 48 hours. The smaller the induration, the less competent the patient's immune system, and consequently, the greater the risk of infection. A wheal induration smaller than 5 mm suggests severe depletion; 5 to 10 mm, moderate depletion; and 10 to 15 mm, mild depletion.

Helping your patient through a granulocyte transfusion

If the doctor has ordered a granulocyte transfusion, remember first that granulocytes (neutrophils, basophils, and eosinophils) are short-lived—about 6 hours. So after they're collected, they must be administered as soon as possible.

Explain the procedure to the patient, and obtain baseline vital signs.

Infuse granulocytes with isotonic saline solution through a Y-type blood administration set with a standard blood filter. Infuse the first 50 to 75 ml slowly (at least 1 hour). Depending on the volume, a transfusion should take 2 to 4 hours.

Check vital signs every 15 minutes for the first ½ hour, then every ½ hour during the rest of the transfusion, then every 4 hours for 24 hours.

During the transfusion, assess for complications and take needed action.

• *Fever and chills.* Reduce the transfusion rate, call the doctor, and plan to administer acetaminophen. *Caution:* If the patient is also thrombocytopenic, chills may trigger intracranial bleeding.

• *Allergic reactions.* Discontinue the transfusion. Call the doctor at once. Anticipate an order for corticosteroids or antihistamines and possibly epinephrine.

• *Hypotension.* If severe, and associated with other signs of shock, call the doctor, and if ordered, stop the transfusion. If slight or moderate (a drop of 10 mm Hg or less), continue the transfusion and monitor vital signs frequently.

• *Respiratory distress.* Discontinue the transfusion. Call the doctor and administer oxygen, or provide other respiratory care measures.

After the transfusion's completed, rinse the transfusion bag with about 30 ml isotonic saline solution to remove adherent granulocytes.

Cancer and cancer therapy: An open door to infection

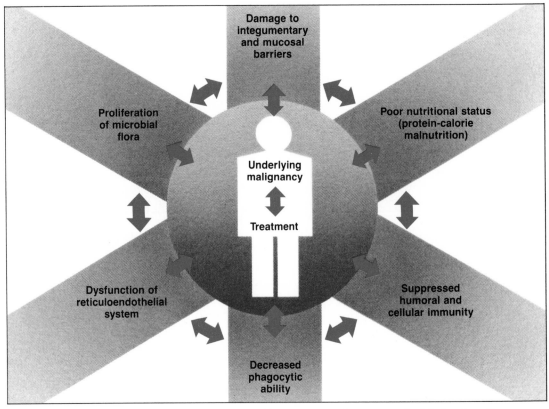

The body's defenses against infection, already stressed by cancer, may be compromised further by anticancer measures such as radiation and chemotherapy.

Assess for infection

Because infection poses such a serious threat, assess the patient frequently for signs and symptoms. Obviously, you need to check his temperature often. Consider infection a real possibility when the temperature rises to 100.4° F. (38° C.) or higher, especially if the patient's neutropenic. Remember, though, that cancer may alter physiologic processes related to infection; either the tumor itself or therapy (such as corticosteroids) may alter the patient's inflammatory response. As a result, the patient with significant infection may develop no fever at all, his temperature may be lower than normal, or fever may develop in late stages of infection.

Consider that fever may be related to factors other than infection. For example, it may be a response to blood transfusions or drugs. It may also result from a pulmonary embolus or from the tumor itself, as in leukemia.

To confirm infection, check the patient's WBC count regularly. Typically, an increase of 4% above the normal 4,100 to 10,900/μl reliably indicates infection. However, if the patient's tumor or treatment is causing bone marrow depression, you won't see an elevated WBC count. In such a patient, a better indicator of infection is the neutrophil count.

Neutrophils make up about 50% to 70% of the total WBC count (normal neutrophil count, 1,950 to 8,400/μl). To obtain a patient's neutrophil count, multiply his total WBC count by the sum of the segmented and band neutrophils divided by 100. If the result shows less than 500/μl, consider the patient at severe risk for infection, which develops rapidly and can quickly become overwhelming. Be sure to check daily the total WBC count and neutrophil count of myelosuppressed patients.

Check vulnerable body sites

Regularly assess body sites that are most prone to infection:
• *Skin.* Inspect daily for cracks, erythema, warm or tender spots, and purulent or serous drainage. Pay special attention to I.V. insertion sites, surgical incisions, skin folds, nares, the umbilicus, bony prominences, and the anal margin.
• *Oropharyngeal cavity.* Inspect it daily, using a flashlight. Assess for stomatitis and for secondary infection (look for exudate; ulcerations; and white, patchy areas). Listen to the quality

of the patient's voice for new hoarseness or raspiness. Note his complaints of sore throat and difficult or painful swallowing.

• *Perianal-vaginal region.* Ask about vaginal itching or rectal pain and tenderness, and check for vaginal discharge. Look for other signs of inflammation—redness, induration, and swelling.

• *Respiratory system.* Check the nasal mucosa for ulcerations and exudate, and watch for changes in respiration rate, rhythm, and depth. Be especially alert for dyspnea on exertion. Note the presence of (or change in) cough, and observe the color, consistency, odor, and amount of sputum. Note the use of accessory muscles or flaring of nares during respirations. Auscultate the lungs every shift, remaining alert for changes in the usual breath sounds.

• *Genitourinary system.* Assess for frequency of urination and for patient complaints of a burning sensation. Note whether urine is voided in small amounts, and check for the presence of foul odor, mucous threads, or blood in the urine.

When assessing any body site, remember that if the patient has neutropenia, local infections may not produce pus or abscesses.

Watch for septic shock
Be alert for signs and symptoms of septicemia, especially if your patient's neutropenic. Monitor temperature frequently; also monitor pulse, respiration, and blood pressure. The first clue to septicemia—and to septic shock—may be a change in the patient's sensorium. He may be confused, irritable, or vaguely aware that something's wrong. Other early signs include fever; warm, dry skin; lowered systolic and diastolic blood pressure; tachycardia with weak peripheral pulses; and tachypnea.

As septic shock proceeds, the patient will look toxic, his breathing will be labored, his urine output will drop, and he'll develop glycosuria. Serum potassium levels will be elevated. He'll look cyanotic and you may note either facial pallor or a dusky reddish hue over the upper chest and face. Septic shock is a life-threatening emergency that demands immediate consultation with the doctor.

Prevention: A primary goal
When caring for a patient who's vulnerable to infection, your first goal is prevention. To achieve this, you can use two general strategies: maintain the patient's optimal health,

and protect him from exposure to environmental contagions.

To maintain optimal health, provide a high-protein, high-calorie diet. Maximize intake by using the techniques described earlier in this chapter. Also encourage oral fluids to hydrate the patient and to prevent bacterial proliferation in the bladder.

Preserving skin integrity is essential. If possible, avoid I.M. and subcutaneous injections, and minimize I.V. injections. As much as possible, avoid the use of urinary catheters.

Minimize trauma to the rectal mucosa by avoiding rectal thermometers, suppositories, and enemas; suggest stool softeners to reduce straining. Provide sitz baths two or three times a day. Encourage or help the patient to do perianal cleansing after elimination.

Keep the skin clean and dry, and use soaps that minimize drying and cracking. Apply lubricating lotions liberally, and encourage frequent oral hygiene. If the skin is broken, consult with the doctor about applying a topical antibiotic and protective dressing.

Impose a regimen of pulmonary hygiene that includes regular coughing, turning, and deep breathing. If the patient is severely debilitated or has especially tenacious secretions, try postural drainage, vibration, and percussion to remove them.

Restrict visitors and exclude everyone with an infection, including staff, from contact with the patient. If the patient has severe neutropenia, have him wear a mask when leaving the room, and keep him away from plants, cut flowers, or fresh fruits or vegetables because these carry gram-negative organisms.

Place the patient in a private room, if possible. Take measures to prevent infection at I.V.-line sites, and use strict aseptic techniques when changing the dressings at the sites or when performing any other invasive procedure. Some doctors order protective or reverse isolation. Some favor placing the severely neutropenic patient in a laminar airflow room, which provides a unidirectional air flow, thereby establishing a barrier between the infection-prone patient and exogenous microorganisms. Others avoid such rigorous isolation, believing that normal preventive measures provide adequate protection and that infection is most likely to stem from the patient's own flora anyway.

Prompt treatment essential
If infection develops, report it to the doctor promptly. Get an order for urine, sputum,

Scalp hypothermia

Scalp hypothermia reduces blood flow to hair follicles, reducing their uptake of chemotherapeutic agents and thereby reducing alopecia.

This treatment appears to be most effective against alopecia caused by doxorubicin (Adriamycin). However, it is contraindicated in patients with certain lymphomas, leukemias, or other neoplastic disorders in which tumor cells may be circulating in the scalp. It is commonly used with a variety of cancers, such as breast, ovarian, pancreatic, gastric, and thyroid cancers; osteosarcomas; and Hodgkin's disease.

Scalp hypothermia may be applied using crushed ice; polyethlyene bags containing gel that crystallizes at 5° F. (-15° C.) held together with waterproof tape; or a commercial product, such as a Kay Kold Kap. Ice or gel bags should be applied 10 to 15 minutes or more (depending on dosage) before I.V. chemotherapy and kept in place for at least 30 minutes afterward. The patient's ears should be protected by foam, cotton wool, or gauze pads. Follow the manufacturer's directions when using commercial products.

throat, and blood cultures, as well as cultures of I.V. sites, wound drainage, and other potential sources of infection. Next, administer broad-spectrum antibiotics as ordered, taking precautions against side effects. Take measures to reduce fever as ordered. Usually this means standard cooling techniques as well as use of antipyretics such as acetaminophen. Also use standard comfort measures, and give additional analgesia as ordered.

Cleanse infected wound sites frequently. As part of wound care, follow suggestions in *Controlling infection odors,* page 70.

If your patient's infection doesn't respond to antibiotics, his doctor may order a *granulocyte transfusion.* Hospital rules differ as to when such transfusions may be given, but most specify the following criteria:

• presence of neutropenia (<500 cells/μl)
• clinical sepsis as determined by fever and a positive blood culture
• anticipated prolonged recovery from marrow suppression (>3 days)
• failure to respond to antibiotic therapy.

For an explanation of your role in this procedure, see *Helping your patient through a granulocyte transfusion,* page 71.

MANAGING SKIN DISORDERS
After chemotherapy, alopecia and various dermatologic impairments are common.

Alopecia: Effects vary with treatment
Most people, regardless of age or sex, consider their hair essential to their appearance. So alopecia, whether temporary or permanent, has devastating psychological effects.

The specific drug used determines the degree and duration of alopecia. Other variables include the duration of treatment and, for some drugs, the route of administration.

Chemotherapy. Alopecia usually begins about 2 weeks after the first chemotherapeutic drug dose and is complete after 1 or 2 months of therapy. Its severity can vary from slight thinning to complete baldness.

Alopecia resulting from chemotherapy is usually reversible. Hair regrowth may begin during the later stages of therapy but usually isn't complete until about 2 months after therapy stops. Commonly, the new hair has different texture and color.

Radiation. Radiation therapy can also produce alopecia. Its severity and duration depend on the radiation dosage and the extent of the treatment field. After administration of 1,500 to 3,000 rads, expect temporary alo-

pecia, either partial or complete; after 3,000 to 4,500 rads, expect variable effects; above 4,500 rads, expect complete and permanent alopecia.

Hair loss typically begins 5 to 7 days after treatment begins. But if the patient has previously lost hair because of chemotherapy, the loss will begin earlier, will be total, and may be permanent. Regrowth usually won't begin until about 2 months after the last radiation treatment.

Other factors that may contribute to alopecia include protein malnutrition, hormonal changes, and drugs such as phenytoin sodium, hydrochlorothiazide, and propranolol (Inderal). Use of certain antibiotics, including gentamicin, minocycline, streptomycin, and tetracycline, may also promote alopecia.

Assessment and intervention. Identify aspects of the therapy and the patient's condition that may contribute to hair loss. Also try to determine the intensity of the patient's feelings about losing some or all of his hair. Understanding his feelings will help guide your interventions, especially patient teaching.

As soon as possible, tell your patient when his hair loss might begin, and give him some idea of its severity and duration. If you expect his hair to regrow, let him know that, and tell him that the new hair may look different in color and texture. Suggest ways to cope with hair loss and to reduce the stress related to body-image changes. For example, before hair loss begins, recommend and help with selection of a hairpiece, wig, covering hat, or scarf. (*Note:* Some health insurance plans cover the cost of hairpieces and wigs for this purpose. Government funds may also be available for these items; check with the National Cancer Institute, Bethesda, Md. 20205, phone [301] 496-4000.)

Prevention. Some patients may be scheduled for short-term, I.V.-administered chemotherapy. In this case, the doctor may try to minimize hair loss by ordering peripheral scalp constriction using a tourniquet. This procedure constricts scalp blood vessels, reducing both the amount of drugs that reach the hair follicles and the cellular uptake of drugs.

A recently developed alternative to peripheral scalp constriction is scalp hypothermia, which aims to reduce blood flow rather than occlude it. (See *Scalp hypothermia.*)

Peripheral scalp constriction is contraindicated in patients with hypertension, platelet counts below 50,000/mm^3, or a diagnosis of leukemia or lymphoma. In the case of leukemia or lymphoma, tumor cells may be present in the blood vessels and scalp tissue; therefore, reducing the dose delivered to the area is hazardous. For this reason, peripheral scalp constriction is controversial. Some also consider it too time-consuming, too uncomfortable, ineffective, and a possible cause of compression damage to underlying nerves.

Skin damage common

Because epidermal basal cells, like hair follicles, have a rapid turnover rate, they are highly susceptible to damage. Consequently, chemotherapy and radiation therapy also commonly cause generalized and local skin damage. Common generalized effects include pruritus, erythema or urticaria, photosensitivity, hyperpigmentation, and acne.

Local effects usually appear at I.V. drug infusion sites or along the veins used to administer drugs. Chemotherapy's most serious effect is extravasation (infiltration into subcutaneous tissue) of I.V. drugs, which can cause severe tissue damage, especially with the use of vesicant drugs such as doxorubicin (Adriamycin).

Apparently, vesicants cause such damage because of their low pH. Doxorubicin compounds the damage by also complexing with the cells' DNA and thus exerting a prolonged vesicating action. Vesicant extravasation is painful and potentially life-threatening; over joints, tendons, or neurovascular structures, it can cause permanent disability. (For more on extravasation and its management, see *Oncologic emergencies*, in the Appendix.)

Radiation recall

When chemotherapy accompanies or follows radiation therapy, patients may develop radiation recall months or even years later. This condition, which progresses from dry desquamation with erythema to moist desquamation, results in permanent hyperpigmentation after the injury heals. Agents most often associated with radiation recall include dactinomycin, bleomycin (Blenoxane), cyclophosphamide (Cytoxan), doxorubicin, and 5-fluorouracil (Adrucil, 5-FU).

Of course, radiation therapy damages the skin even without chemotherapy. Fortunately, today's radiation equipment, which transmits maximum energy below the skin surface, has done much to reduce the severity of skin reactions. But reactions still occur, especially when the radiation dose is high and the treatment field includes vulnerable areas, such as

the axilla, groin, perineum, inframammary area, or wherever two skin surfaces touch.

Typically, the first reaction to radiation is erythema in the treatment field, which usually occurs when the accumulated dose is 3,500 rads. This gradually progresses to dry desquamation, marked by pruritus, dryness, and peeling. Hyperpigmentation may follow dry desquamation and may be permanent. A few patients progress to yet another stage: wet desquamation. This usually reflects severe skin damage and, like a bad sunburn, may involve blistering. Other late reactions, all related to radiation-induced vascular changes, include telangiectasia, fibrosis of the portal area, and impaired lymph drainage.

Frequently assess all patients undergoing chemotherapy or radiation therapy for the color, texture, and integrity of their skin. Also carefully evaluate patient complaints of dryness, pruritus, or pain. If skin reactions do occur, assess their effects on the patient's emotional state.

Interventions. Begin with patient teaching. Explain possible skin reactions well before therapy begins and suggest preventive measures. Encourage optimal nutrition, especially adequate protein intake for tissue repair and adequate hydration. Promote optimal hygiene and take measures to prevent breaks in the skin. Evaluate erythema or urticaria and report it promptly. A severe reaction may require discontinuation of treatment.

To minimize pruritus associated with dry, scaly skin, use mild soaps, colloidal baths, and water-soluble lubricants. Keep the patient's fingernails short to prevent damage from scratching. Maintain cool room temperatures, apply topical drugs (for example, steroids), and administer antihistamines or antipruritics as ordered.

To prevent photosensitivity, encourage the ambulatory patient to keep out of the sun as much as possible. If he can't avoid such exposure, urge him to apply total blocking sunscreens and to wear protective clothing.

If the patient develops acne, remind him that it'll probably disappear when treatment stops. Keep lesions clean. If they're severe, administer antibiotics as ordered.

Emotional support critical

Above all, provide emotional support. Just knowing he has cancer is stress enough for any patient. When cancer therapies add their own stresses, your sustaining help and encouragement are all-important.

Points to remember

• Pain associated with cancer can be controlled—or at least minimized—with various invasive and noninvasive techniques.
• Optimal nutrition in the patient with cancer is critical. It often requires special management of conditions that interfere with adequate oral intake and the administration of balanced enteral or parenteral hyperalimentation.
• Cancer patients with neutropenia are vulnerable to life-threatening infections. They require diligent assessment and measures that promote optimal health and prevent exposure to environmental contagions.
• Both chemotherapeutic drugs and radiation therapy often cause alopecia and skin damage. Patients need preparation for these adverse effects and help in dealing with their potentially devastating physical and emotional consequences.

6 COMPREHENDING PSYCHOSOCIAL IMPACT

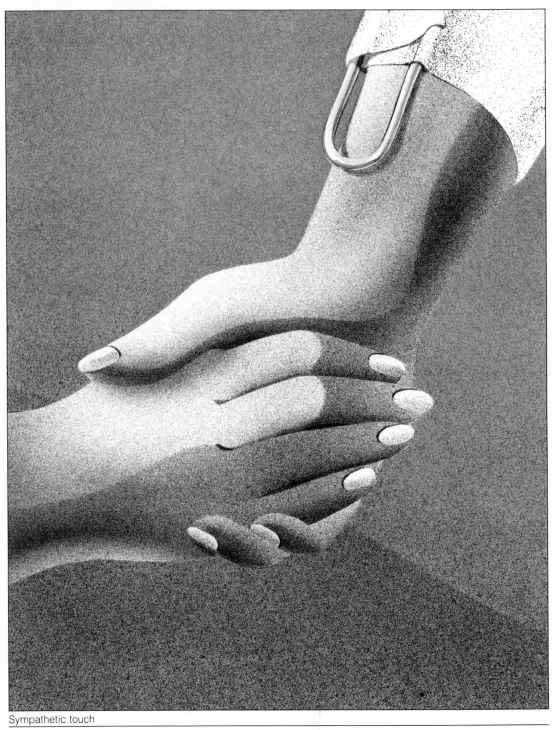

Sympathetic touch

Cancer. Despite the millions (probably billions) of dollars spent for research, we still don't know what causes it or how to prevent or cure it. And despite the efforts of nurses and other health-care professionals to educate the public about it, fear of this dreaded disease still stops many people from seeking early (and possibly lifesaving) treatment. Because cancer can be so frightening, we shouldn't be surprised that its psychological impact can devastate patients, their families, and sometimes the health-care team, as well.

As a nurse, you can do a great deal to help the cancer patient cope with the psychosocial aspects of his illness. This chapter explains how, by debunking myths about cancer, you can reduce your patient's fears. You'll learn how to identify the stages of the grieving process that cancer patients and their families usually experience and to respond appropriately. You'll also learn how to protect yourself from stress and burnout as you care for these profoundly distressed patients.

Myths about cancer
Our society's fear of cancer has created and perpetuated a series of myths. For example:

Cancer is always fatal. Actually, the survival rate has consistently been improving since the turn of the century, when few patients survived. Today, three out of eight patients diagnosed as having cancer can expect to be alive 5 years later.

Cancer is always excruciatingly painful. Unfortunately, the media support this myth by portraying most cancer patients as writhing in pain or drugged into comas. Of course, some cancers—metastatic bone cancer, for example—may be extremely painful. However, some cancer patients (for example, those with basal cell carcinoma) never have any pain. And many cancer patients who do have pain find adequate relief with analgesics.

Cancer is contagious. Even though cancer occurrence is widespread—and this widespread occurrence is sometimes mistakenly termed as epidemic—no evidence exists that cancer is an infectious disease.

Cancer always mutilates the body. The key word here is *always*. Yes, patients with cancer that destroys external body tissues and those who need disfiguring surgery for removal of malignancies do suffer mutilation. (For example, some bone cancer patients may need amputation.) These realities help fuel the myth that cancer patients *always* look horrible or are horribly mutilated. Our hero worship of physical perfection and athleticism exacerbates the problems that stem from this myth.

Cancer has a miracle cure. Desperate patients or their families may turn to faith healers or to alternative therapies that don't have medical approval (such as laetrile). These patients usually die unless they get the care they need. When a patient who's received both a "miracle cure" and medical care survives, he may credit his cure to the former, perpetuating the myth of the "miracle cure." Also, a rare, spontaneous cure from an unknown cause may occur. Such a cure can easily be confused with a miracle cure.

THE PATIENT'S RESPONSE
Individual responses to cancer vary according to ethnic, religious, cultural, and personality factors; personal interpretation of diagnosis; and past history of coping (see *Factors that affect coping with loss,* page 78). Despite these variables, you can expect cancer patients to share some common responses—for example, fears about their illness. And if their cancer progresses, you'll find that these patients go through predictable stages of grieving. Understanding these shared responses will help you to understand your patient and to individualize his care.

Fears that cancer patients share
The fears that cancer patients share aren't unique—they're mostly what any seriously ill patient experiences. But our society's myths about cancer's hopelessness tend to intensify these fears. If you are informed, you can help the cancer patient to control his fears by demythologizing his outlook, by keeping him informed about his treatment (including possible side effects, so he won't think his cancer is causing them), and by being accepting and empathetic with him.

Cancer patients usually fear rejection and isolation, death, the unknown, dependence, loss of self (such as by surgical amputation), treatment, pain, and becoming a financial burden on their family. If your patient expresses any of these fears, note the circumstances, the time he spoke to you, and the intensity of his emotions. Your experience offers the best guide as to whether a reaction is normal or unusual. If you have doubts or concerns, consult a more experienced nurse or a professional counselor.

Fear of rejection and isolation. These are

Factors that affect coping with loss

A cancer patient may face actual loss or the threat of future loss—or both. You can't usually predict a patient's initial response to loss. But you can use your assessment of his initial response to predict how he'll cope with loss over time. Assess the following factors:

Perception
• Does he understand his illness?
• What does the loss mean to him? Does he view it as a challenge, a punishment, or fate?
• How does he see his illness affecting his lifestyle?

History
• What other losses has he experienced? Did he cope well? If so, could these same strategies be useful now?
• Does he know other people who have had cancer? How did they cope?

Timing
• At what stage in life is he encountering this loss?

Support
• Does he have family and friends who can offer him emotional support?

Spiritual beliefs
• What are his current spiritual beliefs? What are the beliefs he was raised with? Does he believe in God or in an afterlife? How does he view death? Does he have a religious explanation for his illness?

Familial, cultural, and societal factors
• What familial or cultural beliefs, values, and practices help or detract from his coping ability? For instance, has he been taught to be openly emotional or stoic?
• How is he influenced by societal attitudes? For instance, does our society's emphasis on youth, health, and industriousness make coping with illness difficult for him?

the cancer patient's greatest fears. Having cancer may make him feel "different," soiled, or contagious, as if he should be quarantined. This feeling is reinforced if he perceives that his family and friends are avoiding him. He may say his friends "look the other way," or that they never call him. His family may be visiting him less often. To help him, try to find out how he feels about having cancer, and try to pinpoint reasons why his family and friends are distancing themselves from him. Encourage him to discuss his feelings and needs with his loved ones, and do what you can to clarify misconceptions that the patient and his family or friends may have. Explain that cancer patients are typically irritable or withdrawn at moments when they actually need their family's and friends' support.

Beware of unknowingly contributing to the patient's sense of isolation; he may especially fear rejection from hospital staff. Avoid such unwitting statements as "There is nothing else that we can do" or "We have nothing else to offer." To increase his sense of security, explain how the health-care system—inpatient, outpatient, and community services—is coordinated to supply his care. Stress the key roles that his primary nurse and doctor play in helping him cope.

Fear of death. Although cancer is not invariably fatal, most patients interpret a cancer diagnosis as a death sentence. A patient whose death is certain may fear the dying process more than death itself. He can think of death abstractly, but he knows that the physical and emotional pain of dying will be real.

Be sensitive to your patient's need to talk about death; he may not be able to speak about it with his family. If you sense that he's having difficulty discussing this *taboo* subject, try remarking that most patients think about death even when they're doing well. If he doesn't respond, try arranging for him to speak to other cancer patients, or refer him for individual or group counseling.

Fear of the unknown. Of course, a patient who has a life-threatening illness with an unknown cause and an unknown outcome is anxious, irritable, even panicky. In his desperate search for stability, even slight delays or changes may irritate him. If this occurs infrequently, overlook it. But be prepared to intervene if his anxiety deepens. Help him to focus his concerns (be careful not to waste time discussing unrelated complaints). Fear of the unknown may cause him to quiz you about why he got cancer—or he may create

his own reason (for example, he may believe God is punishing him). As you know, such misconceptions can reduce his ability to cope with his illness. Make sure he realizes cancer has no clear-cut cause.

Fear of dependence and loss of control. We all struggle with issues of dependence and independence, from birth through old age. A person who's very old or very ill will become increasingly dependent on others to care for him. A patient with advanced or terminal cancer may be offered no chance to participate in his own care beyond his initial agreement to treatment. As a nurse, your goal is to prevent this while remaining sensitive to his appropriate dependency needs. You can encourage him to be more independent and to gain control of his own care by giving thorough patient teaching, including written material that will help him to make informed decisions. Tell your colleagues to include him in decisions about his care, as well. But when the patient's energy is low, expect that he'll become more dependent and may want you or the doctor to make more of the necessary decisions.

Fear of loss of self. Loss of self can refer to death, to surgical amputation or body alteration, to loss of a familiar role with family or friends, or to loss of mental capacity or consciousness. After surgery, for example, the suture line is a constant reminder that the patient's body is altered. And weakness and discomfort may rule out activities that previously maintained his self-esteem. If he has to reduce the hours he works or quit his job, his family role may also change, further eroding his self-esteem. In this situation, encourage him and his loved ones to focus on other ways in which he contributes to the family's well-being.

If your cancer patient can no longer follow his normal exercise routine, this will also reduce his self-esteem. With his doctor's approval and the help of your hospital's physical therapy department, plan a program of modified calisthenics.

To distract him from his fears of self-loss and to prevent further loss of self-esteem, encourage him to talk about his past accomplishments and good times. Sometimes just listening can be the best intervention; the patient may simply want reassurance and acceptance. Also, to build his sense of self, encourage him to wear his own clothes and have his family bring personal belongings, such as pictures, to the hospital. Respect his modesty and privacy, especially while he has visitors. If the patient's loss of self-esteem affects many areas of his care or his interactions, refer him for counseling.

Fear of treatment. All of the different types of cancer treatment—surgery, radiation, and chemotherapy—cause discomfort and body alterations, sometimes even mutilation. So you can't expect to eliminate your patient's fear of treatment. But you can help him adjust to therapy's discomforts with patient teaching. For instance, make sure he realizes that not all patients who undergo chemotherapy experience uncontrollable nausea and vomiting, or any at all. Explain that, for those who do, drugs, relaxation exercises, and diet can minimize or prevent these problems. With a patient who's heard that chemotherapy is "poison," explain its benefits and the measures available to relieve any discomfort it may cause. If his treatment includes radiation, be sure he knows that he'll be protected from potentially harmful effects. When appropriate, put him in touch with patients who've had (or are undergoing) similar treatment.

Fear of pain. Just as most people think all cancer is alike, most also think cancer always causes excruciating pain. Many patients remember one or more friends or family members who died in agony from cancer. The cancer patient also may interpret pain as a sign that his disease is progressing.

To lessen his fear, explain that many effective treatments are available to help manage pain (but don't promise to relieve pain completely because this may be impossible).

Fear of becoming a financial burden. Cancer treatment is very costly. Although health insurance generally pays most costs of hospitalization, the patient and his family may worry about what will happen if his illness is prolonged. Will his medical insurance run out? If he doesn't have disability insurance, will loss of income from his job mean hardship for his family? Even when he leaves the hospital, his care at home may require costly home modifications, equipment, or nursing care. Find out whether such financial burdens (or fear of them) are adding to the family's stress. Consider referring the family to your hospital's social service department or to another appropriate agency.

The grieving process

If a patient's cancer progresses to advanced or terminal stages, expect him to go through a grieving process related to the stages of acceptance of death that Elisabeth Kübler-Ross has detailed. The patient's grieving, which begins at diagnosis, doesn't progress smoothly or methodically, however. A patient may stay in one stage for a long time, then rapidly move through several stages; he may experience several stages at once; or he may unexpectedly return to an earlier stage. This lack of a smooth progression is due to the continued separate losses that a cancer patient experiences throughout his illness. He must grieve for each one.

Denial. At first, the patient may deny his diagnosis. This can be harmful if it stops him from getting the treatment he needs—but if he isn't denying his need for treatment, don't force him into accepting his cancer before he's ready. Realize that his denial is a necessary part of the grieving process, which will help him cope throughout his illness.

Once he fully realizes the impact of his illness, he may panic, feel hopeless, or even reject treatment and try to leave the hospital. If you've been his nurse for a while, try to persuade him to calm down and stay; if not, ask another nurse he knows to talk to him. If he's extremely panicky, avoid long explanations. Instead, briefly stress the importance of staying in the hospital. Help him to focus on the concept that cancer is manageable.

Awareness and anger. The patient's first response, once he's past denial, is usually "Why me?" Such questioning is an attempt to control his illness and to make it less frightening. He may blame himself, stating that he didn't see a doctor soon enough or didn't demand tests soon enough. Accept his understandable concern, but reassure him that his self-blame is unfounded. Point out to him that self-blame is common.

At this point, the patient may also become angry. Anyone who is healthy may be a target; but he's likely to direct his anger toward care givers or even relatives, who, because of their love, are less likely to reject or abandon him. During this period, the patient may also temporarily regress, becoming more childlike and dependent until he can sort through his feelings. In his anger, he may withdraw from those closest to him and seem unreachable. Explain to his family that withdrawal is needed (it enables him to conserve his emotional energy and to think and restructure his life) and that it doesn't mean rejection.

Whether he shows self-blame, anger, withdrawal, or regression (or a combination), encourage him to talk—even if he is angry

Nursing pediatric cancer patients

Caring for a child with cancer requires special expertise and sensitivity. The issues are much the same as those adult patients and their families face—including separation, pain, altered body image, and death—but you'll adjust your care according to developmental status.

Reaction according to development

As a nurse, you know that a child's stage of development influences how he and his family react to psychosocial issues. This is also true at each stage of the cancer continuum from prediagnosis, through treatment, to cure or death.

For example, a 5-year-old child views death as reversible, centering his anxiety on fear of separation from his mother. A 5- to 10-year-old personifies death, imagining it as a separate person. (A child this age also experiences mutilation anxiety, so he may find treatment very threatening.) It's not until age 9 or 10 that a child sees death as irreversible.

Expect a child with cancer to regress at first and to react to his illness the way a much younger child would. However, eventually he should move on to a more appropriate developmental stage. If he doesn't, refer him for counseling.

Consider the child's stage of development when you determine how much to tell him about his illness (see *Erikson's stages of childhood development,* at right). In general, don't try to shield him from the seriousness of his illness. Even young children seem to be aware of the seriousness of their illness, although they may not be able to discuss it in adult terms.

While the child is undergoing treatment, try to support his psychosocial development. Encourage parents to have their child attend school, if possible, or to keep up with his schoolwork at home or in the hospital.

Special problems of adolescence

A seriously ill adolescent has special adjustment problems because the main developmental task of adolescence, achieving independence, conflicts with the forced dependence of illness. Also, although he is old enough to understand the implications of his diagnosis and prognosis, he has not yet developed adult coping mechanisms. So he may become rebellious, angry, and uncooperative.

Be particularly alert to the adolescent's typically fragile body image and self-esteem. According to Erikson, adoles-

and you're the target. Try to be nonjudgmental, open, and compassionate. If he seems to want no more than silent support, comfort him by sitting quietly with him. If you feel uncomfortable just sitting, offer him a back rub or a bath. If his reaction becomes extreme, consider referring him for counseling.

Bargaining. When the patient is no longer withdrawn, he may try to change his fate by bargaining, usually with God. He may promise to "be good"—in an abstract way or by specifying actions he will take if he is cured. The danger in this is that he may feel abandoned if his bargain doesn't work. What should you do if you see a patient in the bargaining stage of grieving? Ask if he'd like to see a clergyman, who may help him through this stage so he doesn't feel abandoned later.

If the patient shares with you any bargains that he made, don't remind him of them. Once he feels better, he may want to forget his bargains. That's all right.

Depression. If the patient's cancer advances, the stages of denial, anger, and bargaining will often be expressed less often. He may instead become increasingly discouraged and depressed, sleeping for long periods, refusing food and visitors, and (if he talks at all) expressing sadness and hopelessness. Support him by listening. But be ready to suggest counseling if his depression seems to be interfering with his family interactions or important physical care activities.

Be sensitive to suicidal intent, too. A patient in severe pain who says "I'd be better off dead" probably isn't suicidal, but a patient who says he wants to kill himself and has a plan may be. Even though the suicide rate among cancer patients is very low, take all expressions of suicidal intent seriously. Try to find out why the patient's life is unbearable. If he says, "Too much pain," talk to the doctor about a change in pain medication. If he tells you that his family has withdrawn from him, try to reinvolve them. If this is impossible, a hospice worker, a volunteer trained in helping dying patients, or frequent staff visits may ease his loneliness.

Acceptance. Eventually, most cancer patients come to accept their diagnosis and its effects on their lives, and in the terminal phase of illness they accept death. The patient's family—and you—should take cues from the patient when offering support. For example, he

Erikson's stages of childhood development

cents are primarily concerned with who they appear to be as compared with who they actually are. Belonging is essential to them, so the feeling of being different that's produced by cancer causes feelings of inferiority, loss of self-esteem, and even depression. This can result in withdrawal from previous social activities and refusal to return to school.

To counteract these problems, try to give an adolescent patient as much control over his treatment as possible, even if you must deviate slightly from strict hospital protocol. Encourage him to wear street clothes, to attend school, to participate in organized activities, to eat in communal dining areas, and to return to his normal activities as soon as possible. When you can, give him a choice of body sites for blood tests, injections, or I.V.s, and plan treatment ahead so you can accommodate his schedule. Your flexibility will foster his cooperation.

Under normal conditions, an adolescent has difficulty communicating with adults, particularly his parents. Illness can make this problem even worse. To help, encourage open discussion of his illness and its treatment between him and his parents. But you may get better results if you set up a peer support group, because an adolescent is extremely peer-oriented. Such a group provides social contact as well as support.

Problems of parents
The parents of a child with cancer generally find that problems develop with him *and* with their other children.

Managing discipline. Parents commonly have more difficulty disciplining their child after he's diagnosed as having cancer. Nevertheless, encourage them to discipline him (and their other children, as well) as they normally would. They all need the security of consistent limits and loving but firm discipline; overprotectiveness may be harmful.

Meeting needs of siblings. In the early postdiagnosis period, parents are upset and sometimes have little time to spend with their healthy children, who may feel frightened, jealous, and guilty. Teach the parents the importance of spending time with their healthy children and of bringing them to the hospital soon after the patient's diagnosis is made, so they can adjust to the situation with a realistic outlook. The parents should also make sure their healthy children know that cancer is not contagious and that nothing anyone in the family did caused the patient's cancer.

Age 0 to 1
Trust vs. mistrust
Needs maximum comfort with minimal uncertainty in order to trust himself, people, and environment

Age 2 to 3
Autonomy vs. shame and doubt
Tries to master physical environment while maintaining self-esteem

Age 4 to 5
Initiative vs. guilt
Develops conscience

Age 6 to 11
Industry vs. inferiority
Tries to develop a sense of self-worth through industry

Age 12 to 18
Identity vs. role confusion
Integrates life experiences; begins to establish identity and place in society

Age 19 to 25
Intimacy vs. isolation
Tries to make personal commitment to another

may discuss future plans, even though he knows he won't live to fulfill them. Or he may simply want you or his family to stay with him and to give silent support. Don't try to second-guess his needs; now that he's accepted the inevitable, he's in control of his feelings and able to ask for what he needs.

THE FAMILY'S RESPONSE
Cancer forces changes within the patient's family, who typically respond much as the patient himself does. Family members may initially deny the truth of the diagnosis so they don't have to consider how it will affect their roles and the family's overall balance.

The family's coping mechanisms in this crisis may be similar to their ways of coping in past crises. Members of a close-knit family will probably bind together and support each other; in other families, members may be so caught up in grieving that they can't support the patient or each other. (In fact, if they are locked into denial as a coping method, they may not even let the patient discuss his illness.) Even if they recognize his illness, family members reacting with anger may press him to question his treatment. They may also give him upsetting contradictory advice, the result of their own ambivalence or disagreements.

Of course, you recognize these reactions as signs of the family's need for support and guidance. Their sense of loss is as profound as the patient's and just as deserving of intervention. And if you can help them adjust to needed changes in family roles, you'll be easing the patient's burden of concerns.

Keeping in mind that the patient's family is likely to go through stages of grieving similar to the patient's, try to stay a step ahead of their reactions. This will allow you to offer support before their reactions can become a problem for the patient.

To help you predict their responses, evaluate the patient's family and the quality of his relationships with them. What was his role in the family prior to his diagnosis? For example, was he the breadwinner and the one who generally made the family's major decisions? If so, his family faces a difficult adjustment if he becomes a passive, dependent recipient of care. By indicating that you understand their problems, you'll help the family to give the patient the support he needs.

Stress the importance of open communica-

Roles of the hospice nurse

The goal of hospice care is to give the dying patient and his family as much control of his care as possible. The primary roles of the hospice nurse are teaching the patient and his family to perform the physical care he needs and preparing them emotionally to cope with his approaching death (see top photo). Skills taught include treatment to control cancer symptoms—for example, injections for pain management (see bottom photo), skin care, and catheter care. Personal care techniques, such as bed baths, turning, and ambulating, are also stressed. After the patient dies, the nurse continues supporting the family throughout the grieving period.

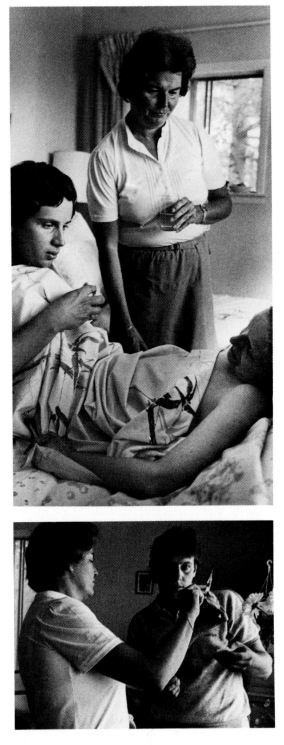

tion. You can be an effective model by consistently using understandable language and by openly communicating your own thoughts and feelings. Avoid euphemisms such as "the growth" (cancer) and "passing away" (dying). Also be aware of other problems that can inhibit communication. For example, the patient and his family may feel intimidated by hospitals and health-care professionals, or they may not speak English very well.

Planning for care

The patient may have physical care needs that continue after he leaves the hospital. With his cooperation, help the family to design a care plan. Remember, there is no one right way to care for the patient; don't try to influence him and his family with your own ideas and biases. They may need to try several of the following options. Remember, too, that what works now may not work in the future. Remind the family to be flexible and forgiving, and take care that they don't view the plan as a test of their love and caring.

The family as care givers. For this plan to work, the family must be ready to assume the care-giver role; the patient, the care-receiver role. Some families may feel these roles alter their relationships too drastically, causing resentment and alienation, or they may be afraid they won't be able to give adequate care. Other families insist on caring for the patient themselves. (Such families may even help care for the patient in the hospital.) Still other families may verbally express the desire to provide care but, in their behavior, may show reluctance to participate in teaching or in discharge planning. You may need to question such a family, nonjudgmentally, about any second thoughts or doubts they may have.

If you're the primary nurse for the patient while he's in the hospital, you may be encouraged to be available for continued consultation and support after discharge. Also, you may need to refer the patient and his family for visiting nursing, private-duty nursing, or community support. If private-duty nursing is affordable, the patient may be able to remain a member of the family with less strain for all involved. Also, having nursing help at home means the family can assist as much as they feel able to but can also take needed time for themselves.

Extended-care facility (ECF). ECFs include nursing homes and rehabilitation centers. This option can be valuable for stable but debilitated patients, those requiring specialized care, those who lack the option of family care, and those whose finances prohibit home care. If the patient chooses an ECF, send a nursing summary to the facility.

Hospice care. When all curative medical therapies are discontinued and the patient is receiving only palliative treatment, he may be referred for hospice care. As you may know, hospice care involves an interdisciplinary team concentrating on the dying patient's emotional and physical comfort and on the

Understanding legal and ethical issues

Caring for a cancer patient may raise a number of legal and ethical issues. Use your hospital's patient bill of rights as a guideline. Most hospitals have such documents listing rights such as the patient's right to know about his care, to make decisions about his care, and to have his health-care records kept confidential. Even with such guidance, however, you're apt to find gray areas—with no clear-cut answers—that test your judgment.

Informed consent
Considering the complexity of the information the patient must understand to give informed consent, he may turn to you for advice or answers. Refrain from giving him advice, but try to answer his questions. When you can't, refer him to his doctor.

Adequate information is not the only requirement for an informed consent. The patient must be considered competent; that is, he must be able to understand the information that he needs to make his decision. It is the doctor's responsibility to determine competence when soliciting consent.

The cancer patient is usually competent. However, sometimes a patient is temporarily incompetent either because of the disease process or because of medications that alter his ability to think clearly and to comprehend fully.

If you feel the patient is incompetent, question him on his understanding of the outcome of signing for treatment, and document any evidence of incompetence.

In such a situation, family members can often help determine what the *patient's wishes* would be. Sometimes, the court appoints a legal guardian, particularly if the patient remains incompetent for a long time or if family members disagree.

Sometimes a cancer patient refuses treatment, whether it be a dose of chemotherapy, his entire chemotherapy regimen, or even all traditional treatment. Such rejection can occur at any point. When it does, make sure the patient's refusal is informed. Then, respect his refusal.

Decisions to withhold CPR and life support
As the cancer progresses, the patient and his family may be confronted with decisions about dying and life support. Some states have legalized living wills so that a patient may indicate his desire not to be kept alive by artificial support.

Also, according to the wishes of the patient or his family (if the patient is incompetent), the doctor may write a "Do not resuscitate" (DNR) or a "no-code" order. The precise meaning of this order may differ from hospital to hospital, but it usually means cardiopulmonary resus-

citation will not be performed when the patient stops breathing or his heart stops. It usually doesn't indicate any other decisions. Document the patient's and family's choices for or against other treatment. Such documentation will help the doctor in his ongoing discussion of their wishes.

According to the law, you cannot perform euthanasia or do anything that would cause death. However, withdrawing or withholding life support from a patient with terminal cancer is not euthanasia. Instead, it is allowing the patient to reach the inevitable end of his terminal illness without prolonging his suffering.

Suicide
Suicide presents another difficult ethical issue. Occasionally, the cancer patient may view suicide as his only escape. Along with the emotional trauma of such an act, if the patient harms himself under your care, you may be subject to prosecution. You would be judged on whether you knew, or should have known, that the patient was likely to harm himself; and whether, knowing he was likely to harm himself, you used reasonable care to help him avoid injury or death. However, although cancer patients may contemplate suicide as a way out of their difficult situation, the incidence of suicidal acts is fairly rare.

family's emotional adjustment to his death. Hospices may be inpatient-based, home-care–based, or a combination. (See *Roles of the hospice nurse.*)

THE NURSE'S RESPONSE
As a cancer nurse, besides giving care and support to the patient and his family, you help to coordinate his care between the health-care team and outside organizations. But you need to care for yourself, too, as you cope with the stresses of cancer nursing.

Coordinate care. Coordination is particularly important in planning the patient's care since so many care providers may be involved. Nurses are often key people to guide and promote coordination of efforts.

Plan discharge. With the aid of the health-care team, plan for your cancer patient's discharge with written care plans. At discharge, his needs may center on issues identified during hospitalization, which are partially addressed or resolved, or he may develop new needs. Many decisions depend on whether his cancer is terminal or progressing toward a cure or prolonged remission.

Burnout: Causes and solutions

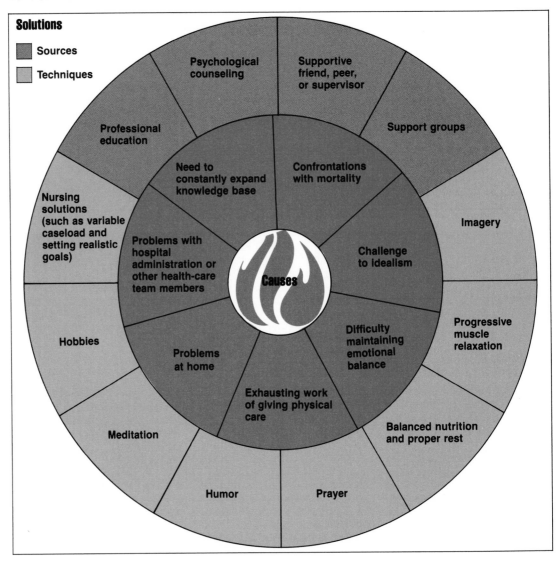

Make referrals. When you make appropriate referrals for your cancer patient, you're helping to ensure that he gets the complete care he needs. If emotional issues threaten to overwhelm him or his family, refer them to your hospital's social service department or to the appropriate community mental health resource. Provide the referrals he needs for physical care, as well.

Before you can make referrals, you need to know the availability of resources in your hospital and community. For cancer patients and their families, potentially helpful groups include the American Cancer Society (ACS), the American Red Cross, the Leukemia Society of America, and the United Ostomy Association. Helpful agencies include social service agencies, mental health centers, hospices, visiting nurse agencies, the Social Security Administration, the United States Veterans

Administration, and cancer clinics and centers.

Counseling referrals. You may need to refer the patient or his family for more formal therapy; this may involve only the patient or his family and may include a support group. Support groups give the patient a sense of belonging and the benefit of a shared experience. Nationwide support groups include Candlelighters, for parents of children with cancer, and Make Today Count, a general support group. (Contact your local ACS office for information on these groups.)

Carry out follow-up. Use follow-up contacts to find out how well your referrals worked and to reinforce the coping and communication skills the patient learned during his hospitalization. Sometimes a brief telephone call provides adequate follow-up; however, some cancer patients need more extensive follow-up—including additional referrals.

Coping with stress

Everyone knows that cancer nursing is stressful. Here are some of the reasons why.

• *You must constantly expand your knowledge base.* Keeping up with continual advances in cancer treatment and with the many different techniques required to give nursing care to cancer patients is stressful.

• *The work can be exhausting.* Sometimes you won't have enough hours in the day to meet the urgent needs of your cancer patients. What's more, you may have too little energy left to maintain a satisfying personal life.

• *Working closely with other health-care members may generate conflict.* Because cancer treatment involves so many decisions, teamwork can be stressful. You may disagree with doctors and other nurses about appropriate treatment for a patient. Or, because of factors beyond your control (such as short staffing), you may not always be able to meet your own high standards of care.

• *Keeping your emotions in balance can be difficult.* Because a cancer patient is likely to return to the same unit, you risk overinvolvement. Unchecked, this can progress to the point where you can't distinguish between what is happening to him and what is happening to you. Be especially careful when a patient is close to your age or if he reminds you of a relative or friend. To keep your balance, try to be sensitive but objective. Also, beware of overinvolvement in patient-family conflicts. To be sure you're meeting these goals, continually reevaluate your therapeutic relationship.

• *Cancer may also challenge your idealism.* Idealism may sustain you during difficult times, but it stresses you when it conflicts with cancer's realities. While you strive for the ideal, realize that it is not always possible.

• *You frequently confront your own mortality.* This may be your biggest challenge. How well you handle it depends on how well you have explored your personal outlook on death.

Physical signs of stress. You probably know that stress has physical as well as emotional effects. And eventually, chronic stress may cause burnout—listlessness; worry about work, even when at home; difficulty making decisions; a feeling of powerlessness; guilt; irritability; anger; and emotional withdrawal from patients and co-workers. When this occurs, you need help. Other nurses, a mental health professional, or a personal friend outside of work may be supportive.

Techniques to relieve stress. You may want to try one of the following techniques and may want to recommend these techniques to patients as well.

• *Hobbies* provide helpful diversion. Some hobbies, such as exercise and sports, also provide energy release.

• *Balanced nutrition and proper rest* help maximize energy.

• *Progressive muscle relaxation* promotes overall relaxation through conscious tensing and relaxing of various parts of the body.

• *Imagery* involves creating a tranquil scene in the mind, then concentrating on what it feels like to be there and enjoying the peacefulness of the scene.

• *Meditation,* a brief, but highly structured mental escape from everyday routine, aims to reduce blood pressure and oxygen requirements through calm, restful concentration.

• *Humor* has tension-relieving effects, according to some specialists in stress management.

• *Prayer,* of course, can be helpful in achieving peace of mind.

• *Nursing solutions:* Other ways of dealing with stress include varying your patient caseload (for instance, balancing self-care patients with total-care patients), teaming up with an associate nurse in a buddy system for the care of primary patients (if your hospital uses primary nursing), and requesting emotional support and feedback from nursing peers and supervisors. Feedback is needed to ensure that your goals are realistic. Your department may want to organize support groups. Informal networking and mentorship from unit leaders or other nurses can also help you gain perspective. Consider attending a professional seminar on managing your emotions. Such seminars can help you gain important knowledge and peer support while taking a break from your daily work routine. Taking frequent vacations is another good way to break from the daily routine.

The rewards of cancer nursing

Unquestionably, nursing cancer patients can be stressful. These patients typically need all the care and support you're able to give. But nursing these patients can also be unusually rewarding. Your care can make the difference between a despairing patient and one who courageously accepts his fate; between a family shattered after a patient's death and one that continues on toward a rewarding life together. Of all nursing's many rewards, these may be among the most satisfying you'll experience.

 **Points to remember**

• Societal myths about cancer can make its psychological impact on the patient, his family, and even the health-care team devastating. These myths are that cancer is always fatal; it always causes excruciating pain; it's contagious; it always mutilates the body; and a "miracle cure" exists.

• To adjust to having cancer, the patient must deal with his fears of rejection and isolation, death, the unknown, dependence, loss of self, treatment, pain, and becoming a financial burden. And both he and his family must work through the grieving process, which includes stages of denial, awareness and anger, bargaining, depression, and acceptance.

• The family's reaction to the cancer diagnosis can range from sensitivity to the patient's needs to grief-stricken immobilization. Their reaction affects the patient's adaptation to his diagnosis.

• One of your major roles as a cancer nurse is coordinating the patient's care between the resources of the health-care team and the community. Tasks involved include assessing needs, planning discharge, making referrals, and evaluating the effectiveness of these plans.

• Caring for the cancer patient means acting as a supportive but objective care giver, not as an emotionally overinvolved friend.

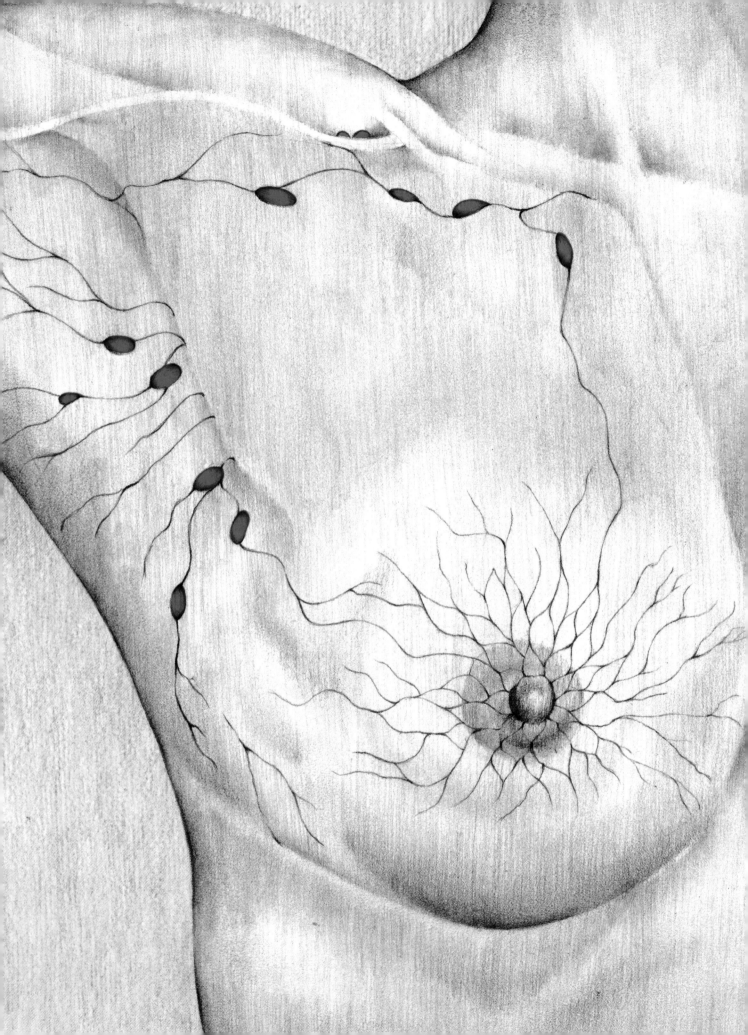

MALIGNANT DISORDERS

7 TREATING CANCERS OF SKIN, BONE, AND SOFT TISSUE

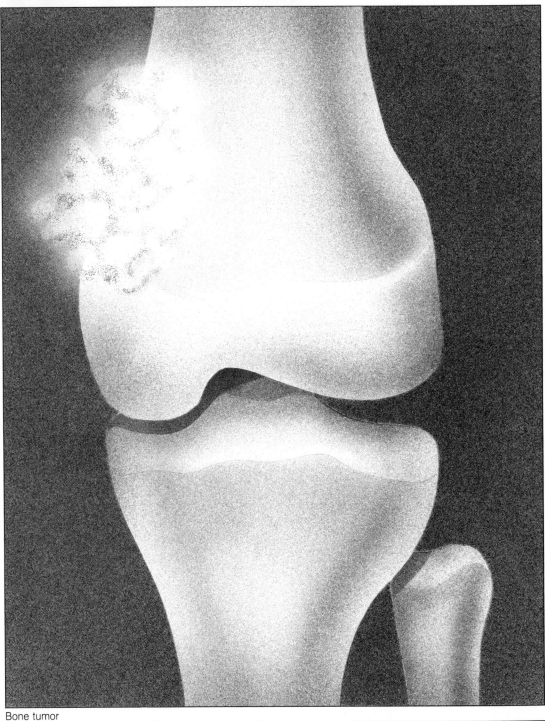

Bone tumor

Because physical appearance and the ability to move about freely profoundly affect a patient's self-image, cancer of the skin, bone, or soft tissue—which may cause disfiguring lesions or limit mobility—severely challenges his identity as well as his physical health. As a result, nursing care for such a patient must recognize psychological needs as well as the need for physical care.

Fortunately, you can often assure the patient a good prognosis. Cure rates for skin, bone, and soft-tissue cancers are continually improving—provided these cancers are detected and treated early. In fact, the cure rate for most skin cancers already exceeds 90%. Clearly, your role in educating patients about risk factors is more important than ever to promote early detection or, better still, prevention of these cancers. When prevention fails, your understanding of pathophysiology and current treatment will help you provide support and expert care at every stage of disease.

Identifying risk factors

Skin cancer affects about 600,000 individuals each year and ranks as the most common neoplasm. It usually appears in fair-skinned individuals with blond or red hair, is less common in Orientals, and is rare in blacks. Although skin cancer is more prevalent in the elderly, its incidence is rising in younger age-groups. Associated with its development are prolonged excessive exposure to sunlight, arsenic ingestion, radiation therapy, burns, chronic skin irritation, premalignant lesions (such as actinic keratosis), exposure to local carcinogens (tar and oil), and heredity.

Bone cancer most commonly affects males, especially children and adolescents. It may be related to aberrant metabolism during periods of rapid skeletal growth. Other predisposing factors may include Paget's disease, radiation, heredity, and some benign precursors such as osteoblastoma and fibrous dysplasia.

Soft-tissue cancer is more common in adults and affects both sexes. Its predisposing factors may include radiation and chronic lymphedema (after radical mastectomies).

PATHOPHYSIOLOGY

Before discussing the pathophysiology of skin, bone, and soft-tissue cancers, it's important to recognize how each is classified histologically. Skin cancer arises from epithelial tissue and is known as carcinoma; bone and soft-tissue cancers arise from connective tissue and are known as sarcomas.

The major types of skin cancer are malignant melanoma, basal cell carcinoma, and squamous cell carcinoma; the latter two are also called nonmelanoma skin cancers. The major types of bone cancer are osteogenic sarcoma, chondrosarcoma, and Ewing's sarcoma; of soft-tissue cancers, fibrosarcoma, liposarcoma, and rhabdomyosarcoma.

Patterns in skin cancer

Malignant melanoma arises from pigment-producing melanocytes in the epidermis or dermis. Nonmelanoma skin cancer develops in the epidermis of the skin and produces characteristic lesions. Basal cell carcinoma arises from the basal layer, whereas squamous cell carcinoma begins higher up in the epithelium.

Malignant melanoma. These pigmented lesions appear in shades of black, gray, blue, brown, or red and are usually less than 2.5 cm in size. They may be flat or elevated and may have an irregular, notched border. Malignant melanoma commonly develops on the upper back in men, on the legs in women, and on the head, neck, and back of the hands of persons exposed to excessive sunlight. Less common sites include the nailbeds, palms of the hands, and soles of the feet. It's classified into lentigo maligna melanoma, superficial spreading melanoma, nodular melanoma, and acral lentiginous melanoma.

Basal cell carcinoma. This most common skin cancer typically occurs as a small, waxy or pearly, semitranslucent nodule with a depressed center. Like melanoma, it's sometimes pigmented. Its surface may be smooth, ulcerated, crusted, or bleeding; telangiectatic blood vessels commonly mark its borders.

Basal cell carcinoma usually develops on the face, ears, and neck and occasionally on the trunk. It's described as nodular, superficial, or morphea-like and often produces multiple lesions.

Squamous cell carcinoma. This cancer characteristically appears on a site of actinic keratosis as a discrete, hard, opaque, reddish-brown, dome-shaped, scaly papule that may resemble a wart. It may also appear on sun-damaged skin as a painless, erythematous, hard, scaly plaque that enlarges and ulcerates in a few months. In advanced disease, the tumor may resemble a cauliflower-like mass. Squamous cell carcinoma usually develops on the face, back of the hands, lips, and mucous

Growth phases of malignant melanoma

Malignant melanoma typically stems from pigment-producing melanocytes. This lesion may extend radially (horizontally), vertically, or both. Vertical growth penetrates the deeper cutaneous tissues and risks widespread metastasis.

In *lentigo maligna melanoma*, melanoma cells first extend horizontally, causing minimal epidermal hyperplasia. This radial growth phase may continue for decades before vertical growth begins.

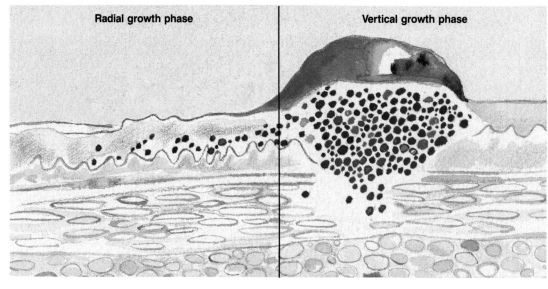

In *superficial spreading melanoma*, melanoma cells may proliferate for several years within the epidermis and papillary dermis during the radial growth phase. The vertical growth phase, which may occur within a few weeks to months, is marked by the development of a nodule.

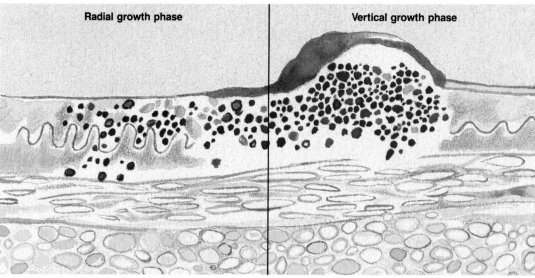

In *nodular melanoma*, the most virulent form of melanoma, melanoma cells extend almost exclusively by vertical growth.

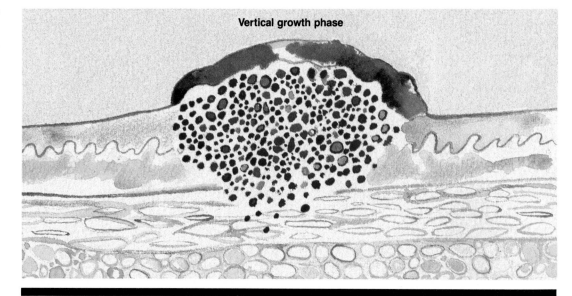

membranes.

Besides producing characteristic lesions, skin cancers also follow specific growth patterns. After developing within the epidermis, melanoma extends locally by radial, then vertical, growth (see *Growth phases of malignant melanoma*). Generally, prognosis becomes increasingly grim when melanoma cells penetrate the basement membrane that separates the epidermis and dermis, risking widespread metastasis via the lymphatic and blood vessels.

Conversely, basal cell and squamous cell carcinomas typically extend only locally to involve adjacent structures. Although they usually grow slowly, these carcinomas may become large, destructive tumors if neglected. However, prompt treatment usually guarantees an excellent prognosis. Primary basal cell carcinoma has a 95% to 99% cure rate; squamous cell carcinoma, a 90% to 95% cure rate. One exception is squamous cell carcinoma of the lip, which is potentially a markedly invasive metastatic lesion with a poor prognosis.

Patterns in bone sarcoma

Bone sarcoma may originate in osseous or nonosseous tissue. Osteogenic sarcoma and chondrosarcoma stem from the bone; Ewing's sarcoma arises from the bone marrow.

Each bone cancer produces a characteristic tumor.

Osteogenic sarcoma. This tumor favors the rapid growth areas of the metaphysis and typically occurs in the long bones, especially the distal femur, proximal tibia, and proximal humerus. Tumor growth is marked by proliferation of spindle cells, which first invade the bone's medullary cavity, then penetrate the cortex and invade adjacent soft tissues. Here spindle cells form osteoid tissue that later calcifies, producing a bulky, gray-white mass with hemorrhagic areas. The tumor causes obvious swelling of the involved extremity. Osteogenic sarcoma usually first metastasizes to the lungs via the blood.

Chondrosarcoma. This slow-growing, bulky cartilage tumor usually occurs in the pelvis, ribs, femur, spine, scapula, or tibia. Because chondrosarcoma is centrally located, tumor growth expands the bone cortex, causing marginal sclerosis within the long bone shafts.

Ewing's sarcoma. A gray, cystic tumor, Ewing's sarcoma commonly occurs in the diaphyses of the femur, humerus, ribs, scapula, and pelvis. Tumor growth is marked by prolif-

eration of small round cells, which extend through the marrow interstices, causing marrow displacement. The tumor spreads insidiously within the marrow, then usually penetrates the periosteum and extends into adjacent soft tissue, producing a palpable mass. An intense inflammatory response may occur simultaneously, causing the characteristic fever of this sarcoma. Regional lymph node metastasis occurs more commonly in marrow-cell tumors such as Ewing's sarcoma than in other sarcomas. However, it usually metastasizes to the lungs via the blood.

Metastatic cancers more common

Primary cancers elsewhere in the body, particularly from the kidney, prostate, lung, breast, ovary, and thyroid, often metastasize to the bone. In fact, metastatic bone tumors outnumber primary bone sarcomas. These metastatic tumors are histologically classified according to the site of origin.

Patterns in soft-tissue sarcoma

Soft-tissue sarcoma originates in mesenchymal cells that form muscle, fat, fibrous tissue, nerve sheaths, blood vessels, and synovia. Typically, this tumor is described according to its site of origin (see *Classifying soft-tissue sarcomas*). Soft-tissue sarcoma extends by local radial growth, forming a palpable mass that compresses surrounding structures. Tumor pressure on nerves may cause pain, paralysis, or paresthesia, and on blood vessels tumor pressure may cause ischemia. Soft-tissue sarcoma is markedly aggressive and may metastasize to the lungs early in the disease via the blood.

MEDICAL MANAGEMENT

Accurate evaluation of the patient with skin, bone, or soft-tissue cancer requires a thorough history and physical examination with diagnostic tests to detect, locate, and stage tumor growth.

Detecting and sizing cancer

In patients with skin, bone, or soft-tissue cancers, the results of several laboratory tests help narrow the diagnosis and assess physical status. Baseline laboratory tests may include complete blood count with differential; erythrocyte sedimentation rate (ESR); platelet count; liver function tests; and urinalysis, including lactic dehydrogenase (LDH) and blood urea nitrogen.

Blood tests. In sarcoma or metastatic dis-

Classifying soft-tissue sarcomas

These malignant tumors may be classified by their tissue of origin as listed below.

Adipose: liposarcoma
Fibrous: fibrosarcoma
Histiocytic: malignant fibrous histiocytoma, giant cell sarcoma
Mesothelial: malignant mesothelioma
Neural: neurofibrosarcoma
Smooth muscle: leiomyosarcoma
Striated muscle: rhabdomyosarcoma
Synovial: synovial sarcoma
Vascular and lymphatic: angiosarcoma, lymphangiosarcoma, malignant hemangiopericytoma, Kaposi's sarcoma.

Recognizing potentially malignant nevi

Nevi (moles) are skin lesions that are often pigmented and may be hereditary. Many patients with melanoma have a history of a preexisting nevus at the tumor site.

Suspect possible malignant transformation of a nevus that changes:
Color: red, white, and blue; sudden darkening to dark brown or black
Size: sudden enlargement
Shape: rapid elevation; irregular, notched border
Consistency: softening, friable, or nodular
Surface characteristics: bleeding, crusting, erosion, scaling, oozing, ulceration, or a mushrooming mass
Surrounding skin: inflammation, redness, swelling, satellite pigmentations, or spread of pigmentation into the normal skin
Symptoms: pruritus, tenderness, pain.

ease, a decreased red blood cell count or decreased hemoglobin and hematocrit levels may reflect tumor necrosis. In Ewing's sarcoma, an increased white blood cell count may reflect an intense response to inflammation. Also common in Ewing's sarcoma, elevated ESR and LDH levels correlate with a poor prognosis. In primary bone cancer, elevated serum alkaline phosphatase and calcium levels may result from malignant proliferation of new bone.

Radiologic tests. These tests outline tumor size and show metastasis. *Tomograms* and *computerized tomography scans* may help diagnose large skin cancers or sarcomas near vital structures. *Chest X-rays* help detect metastasis to the lungs. *Bone X-rays* outline new bone formation and destruction. *Angiography* reveals distorted blood vessels caused by tumor extension into soft tissues. A *bone scan* demonstrates bony involvement throughout the body. It may also detect "skip lesions" beyond the expected tumor margins. *Magnetic resonance scans* produce computerized images that reveal inflammation and bony or soft-tissue masses. *Ultrasound* evaluates soft-tissue masses in the abdomen or pelvis but fails to penetrate bone. *Biopsy* (incisional, excisional, or needle aspiration) establishes definitive diagnosis of cancer by allowing histologic study of tumor tissue.

Staging and grading

Correct staging of skin, bone, and soft-tissue cancers is the first step toward effective treatment. The internationally known TNM-staging system—which correlates tumor size, nodal involvement, and metastatic progress—is frequently used. (See *Staging cancer: Skin, bone, and soft tissue,* page 95.) In bone and soft-tissue cancers, a surgical staging system may be used that classifies these cancers according to grade (high or low), site (intra- or extra-compartmental), and the presence or absence of nodal involvement and distant metastases. Generally, more invasive tumors such as malignant melanoma carry greater risk of nodal involvement and metastases and a correspondingly poor prognosis. Two methods are currently used to measure tumor depth in skin cancer: the Clark level and the Breslow level. The Breslow level measures lesion depth from the top of the granular layer to the base of the tumor. Melanoma lesions less than 0.76 mm deep have an excellent prognosis; deeper lesions are at risk for metastasis (see *Classifying malignant melanoma* for more on

Clark level). Tumor location, particularly in soft-tissue sarcomas, is also significant. Tumors near the trunk of the body tend to metastasize sooner than those of the extremities.

Grading describes a tumor by its degree of differentiation, primary cellular makeup, and established growth rate. For example, soft-tissue sarcomas are graded from G1 to G3, or well differentiated to undifferentiated. Typically, well-differentiated tumors have a better prognosis than poorly differentiated ones.

Tumors are also graded or named according to their most differentiated tissue: bone—osteo; cartilage—chondro; fiber—fibro; fat—lipo; blood vessels—angio; nerve—neuro; and no differentiation—spindle cell, round cell.

Combined treatment

Treatment for skin, bone, and soft-tissue cancers involves surgery, radiation, chemotherapy, or a combination of these measures. Immunotherapy to bolster the immune response to cancer is considered adjuvant therapy for skin cancer. Treatment depends on the type, stage, location, and responsiveness of the tumor, and on the patient's ability to withstand the treatment protocol.

Skin cancer. Treatment of malignant melanoma involves wide surgical excision, including a ¾″ (2-cm) margin of normal tissue for thin lesions and a 2″ (5-cm) margin for thicker lesions. The larger excision requires a split-thickness or full-thickness skin graft, or a local rotation flap to provide closure. Also, regional lymph node dissection may prevent metastasis via the lymphatics in early disease but is of little or no benefit once metastasis has occurred.

Adjuvant chemotherapy is usually limited to use in metastatic disease or for palliation in malignant melanoma. Intraarterial infusion of chemotherapeutic drugs may allow higher tissue levels of chemotherapeutic drugs without systemic toxicity. Dacarbazine (DTIC) is the most commonly used single drug; other drugs, such as carmustine (BCNU), semustine, thiotepa, melphalan, and cisplatin, are used in combination.

Immunotherapy includes bacille Calmette-Guérin (BCG) vaccine and dinitrochlorobenzene (DNCB) to stimulate the patient's immune response. When injected into metastatic melanoma nodules, these vaccines produce lesion regression with little, if any, systemic effects. Injecting the patient's irradiated melanoma cells into other lesions may also cause tumor regression.

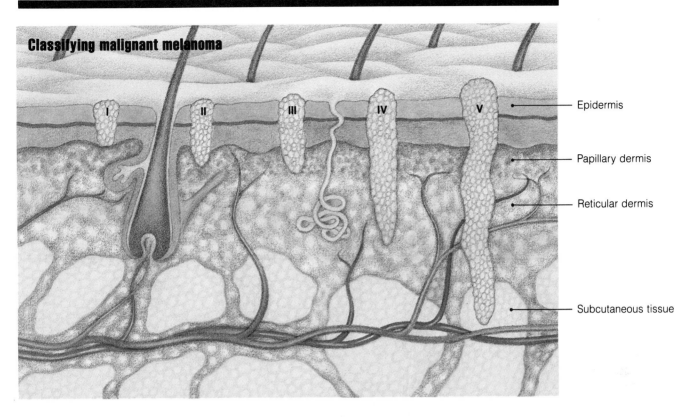

Classifying malignant melanoma

Epidermis

Papillary dermis

Reticular dermis

Subcutaneous tissue

Treatment of basal cell carcinoma and squamous cell carcinoma depends on the lesion's size, depth, and location. Topical 5-fluorouracil is often used for superficial basal cell carcinoma. It produces marked local inflammation with necrosis and sloughing of malignant tissue. Deeper lesions may require surgical excision, perhaps followed by skin grafting. Radiation may be an effective treatment for nonmelanoma skin cancer; it's often useful for older or debilitated patients. Since radiation itself is carcinogenic with a latent period of about 20 years, careful selection of patients is crucial. Also, adequate shielding is necessary, particularly for ear and nose lesions, to avoid chondritis (cartilage inflammation).

Other treatments for nonmelanoma skin cancer are also being used. *Electrosurgery* via needle, blade, or disk electrodes cuts and coagulates the lesions. *Cryosurgery* uses liquid nitrogen to freeze the lesion, resulting in necrosis. *Chemosurgery,* the most effective treatment for nonmelanoma skin cancer, involves microscopic control of skin excision with examination of all margins and the base of the lesion. The *carbon dioxide (CO_2) laser* vaporizes superficial basal cell carcinoma rapidly and allows faster reepithelialization than do other types of treatment.

Bone cancer. Surgery involving amputation or limb salvage, radiation, and chemotherapy are the primary treatments in bone sarcoma. Although amputation may be necessary, tumor resection combined with radiation and chemotherapy often saves the limb. Resected bone is replaced with metal prostheses, autografts, or allografts. Unfortunately, radical surgery, such as hemipelvectomy, is sometimes mandatory. Surgical removal of pulmonary metastases, which typically develop early in disease, may also improve prognosis.

Adjuvant chemotherapy helps minimize micrometastasis to the lungs. Drugs, given pre- and postoperatively, include doxorubicin (Adriamycin); cisplatin; methotrexate; leucovorin calcium; and the combination of bleomycin, cyclophosphamide (Cytoxan), and dactinomycin.

Surgery and adjuvant chemotherapy is the primary treatment in Ewing's sarcoma. Such chemotherapy involves combinations of drugs including vincristine, dactinomycin, cyclophosphamide, and doxorubicin.

Soft-tissue cancer. Surgery, the primary treatment, varies with the sarcoma's location; accordingly, it may involve muscle resection, limb amputation, or radical local excision. In any case, the sarcoma must be excised en bloc (in one piece) with adequate margins on all sides. Skin grafts or myocutaneous flaps may be necessary to repair the defect.

Adjuvant radiation therapy given pre- or postoperatively or for palliation in metastatic

Malignant melanoma may be classified at biopsy by its depth of invasion (Clark level). This helps determine prognosis, which tends to worsen with deeper invasion.

I Tumor cells are confined to the epidermis.

II Tumor cells penetrate the papillary dermis.

III Tumor cells accumulate between the papillary and reticular dermis.

IV Tumor cells extend between collagen bundles of the reticular dermis.

V Tumor cells invade the subcutaneous tissue.

EMERGENCY MANAGEMENT

Hypercalcemia

A potentially life-threatening complication, hypercalcemia occurs most commonly in metastatic carcinoma to bone. Hypercalcemia results from excessive calcium release associated with tumor destruction of bone. When this calcium level exceeds the renal and gastrointestinal capacity to excrete it, the calcium blood level rises above normal. Early symptoms of hypercalcemia may include lethargy, anorexia, nausea and vomiting, constipation, and dehydration. Pathologic fractures may accompany weakening of involved bone, while kidney stones reflect excessive glomerular filtration of calcium. Because hypercalcemia interferes with normal conduction and muscle contraction, markedly elevated levels (above 15 mg/dl) may cause cardiac dysrhythmias, coma, and eventually, cardiac arrest. Prompt treatment of hypercalcemia is crucial. Here's what you should do.

• Immediately hydrate the patient to reduce the risk of renal damage and to help dilute the serum calcium level. Infuse 1,000 ml of normal saline solution every 4 to 6 hours to promote diuresis. Monitor the patient's urinary output and adjust the infusion accordingly.

• Perform an EKG to check for cardiac dysrhythmias, and carefully monitor the patient's vital signs.

• To decrease serum calcium levels, administer drugs such as calcitonin, mithramycin, and corticosteroids, as ordered. Sodium bicarbonate is also used occasionally.

• If infusion of saline solution fails to promote adequate diuresis, give furosemide, as ordered. Avoid thiazide diuretics which inhibit calcium excretion.

• Continue to watch for signs of impending cardiac arrest. Repeat the EKG and serum calcium determination, as ordered. Also observe for drug side effects and for rebound hypocalcemic tetany.

---

bone disease reduces local recurrence and distant metastasis, but side effects may include radiation fibrosis of the adjacent joint or of underlying muscle and bone.

Adjuvant chemotherapy involves combinations of dactinomycin, dacarbazine, doxorubicin, methotrexate, cyclophosphamide, and vincristine, given pre- or postoperatively.

In bone and soft-tissue cancer, adjuvant chemotherapy or radiation given preoperatively can shrink tumor size before excision.

NURSING MANAGEMENT
Thorough assessment is critical in the recognition of cancer. Nursing management also involves knowledgeable patient teaching and caring psychological support to help the patient adapt to the effects of his illness.

Determine the chief complaint
Begin with a nursing history. Obtain biographic information; then address the patient's chief complaint. If he complains of a skin lesion, find out when it was first noticed. Has it changed size or color? Does it itch? Is it sore or inflamed? Basal cell or squamous cell carcinoma may start as an elevated nodule or a rough-surfaced lesion that crusts over, ulcerates, and heals; then repeats the cycle.

In suspected nonmelanoma ask about pain around the lesion. If the lesion arises near the eye, also ask about loss of eyelashes, bleeding, crusting, and excessive tearing.

If the patient complains of an enlarging mass, find out when he first noticed it. Is it tender or swollen? Ask about abnormal sensations (dysesthesias or paresthesias) that may indicate the mass is compressing neural structures. Ask about coolness, numbness, swelling, or cyanosis of the involved extremity, which may indicate vascular compression. Also ask about muscle weakness, fatigue, or atrophy, indicating compression of muscles, tendons, or nerves, or disuse due to pain.

If a sacral or pelvic tumor is suspected, ask about altered bowel or bladder habits or sexual dysfunction.

If the patient complains of pain, determine its onset, location, and character. When does it occur? Does he have night pain? Does it radiate from the primary site? Is it severe? Does pain occur with walking, climbing stairs, or sitting? Can the patient readily move his arms and legs in a wide range of motions? Do such motions cause pain? Abnormal gait or impaired joint mobility may result from pain or tumor invasion of the joint capsule, muscle, or articular cartilage. Are any joints swollen?

Ask about chills, sweating, or fever, indicating infection. Also investigate complaints suggesting tumor metastasis, such as pulmonary symptoms, malaise, or weight loss.

Complete the history
Ask the patient about risk factors such as chronic exposure to sunlight or chemical car-

STAGING CANCER

Skin, bone, and soft tissue

Melanoma of the skin
Primary tumor (T)
T_0 Tumor confined to the epidermis (Clark level I)
T_1 Tumor invades the papillary dermis (level II), or tumor of 0.75 mm thickness or less
T_2 Tumor extends to the interface between the papillary and reticular dermis (level III), or tumor of 0.76 to 1.5 mm thickness
T_3 Tumor extends into the reticular dermis (level IV), or tumor of 1.51 to 4.0 mm thickness
T_4 Tumor invades the subcutaneous tissue (level V), or tumor of 4.1 mm or more thickness, or satellite within 2 cm of a primary melanoma

Nodal involvement (N)
N_0 No evidence of regional lymph node involvement
N_1 Movable nodes (5 cm or less in diameter), involving one regional lymph node station, or no regional lymph node involvement and the presence of less than five in-transit (between primary tumor and primary lymph node drainage site) metastases beyond 2 cm from primary site
N_2 Involvement of more than one regional lymph node station, or regional nodes more than 5 cm in diameter or fixed, or five or more in-transit metastases or any in-transit metastases beyond 2 cm from primary site with regional lymph node involvement

Distant metastasis (M)
M_0 No evidence of metastasis
M_1 Metastasis to skin or subcutaneous tissues beyond the site of primary lymph node drainage
M_2 Metastasis to any distant site other than skin or subcutaneous tissues

Squamous cell and basal cell carcinoma of the skin
Primary tumor (T)
Tis Carcinoma in situ
T_0 No evidence of tumor
T_1 Superficial or exophytic tumor 2 cm or less in its largest dimension
T_2 Tumor 2 cm to 5 cm in its largest dimension, or tumor of any size with minimal infiltration of the dermis
T_3 Tumor more than 5 cm in its largest dimension, or tumor of any size with deep infiltration of the dermis

Nodal involvement (N)
N_0 No evidence of regional lymph node involvement
N_1 Involvement of movable homolateral regional lymph nodes
N_2 Involvement of movable contralateral or bilateral regional lymph nodes
N_3 Involvement of fixed regional lymph nodes

Distant metastasis (M)
M_0 No evidence of metastasis
M_1 Evidence of distant metastasis

Bone
Primary tumor (T)
T_0 No evidence of primary tumor
T_1 Tumor confined within the bone cortex
T_2 Tumor extends beyond the bone cortex

Nodal involvement (N)
N_0 No evidence of regional lymph node involvement
N_1 Metastatic deposits in regional lymph nodes

Distant metastasis (M)
M_0 No evidence of metastasis
M_1 Evidence of distant metastasis

Soft-tissue sarcoma
Primary tumor (T)
T_0 No evidence of tumor
T_1 Tumor less than 5 cm in diameter
T_2 Tumor 5 cm or more in diameter
T_3 Radiographic evidence of cortical bone destruction, or histopathologic confirmation of major artery or nerve invasion

Nodal involvement (N)
N_0 No evidence of regional lymph node involvement
N_1 Histologic verification of regional lymph node involvement

Distant metastasis (M)
M_0 No evidence of metastasis
M_1 Evidence of distant metastasis

---

cinogens and previous radiation therapy to the skin. Radiation exposure may predispose the patient to basal cell carcinoma, squamous cell carcinoma, and osteogenic sarcoma. Check for a history of Paget's disease of the bone, which is frequently complicated by chondrosarcoma, fibrosarcoma, or osteogenic sarcoma. Also, ask about recent bone infection, because osteomyelitis can mimic Ewing's sarcoma on an X-ray. Similarly, previous injury or surgery may cause excessive normal bone growth that mimics tumor formation. Finally, ask about a family history of cancer, and determine the patient's psychosocial needs.

Perform the physical examination
Begin by observing the patient's overall appearance. Is he well nourished or cachectic, overweight or underweight? Does his skin color reflect pallor or jaundice that may accompany anemia or metastatic disease?

Take vital signs. Elevated temperature may occur with inflammation in Ewing's sarcoma.

Note skin tone and hair and eye color. Ask about recent sun exposure. Observe the skin for actinic damage, such as reddish-brown color and telangiectasias on the nose, cheeks, and chin. Inspect for hypo- or hyperpigmented scars and determine their cause. Also look for lesions, plaques, or crusts, and for redness, irritation, or other signs of infection.

Note the number, color, and distribution of nevi (see *Recognizing potentially malignant nevi,* page 92). Report those with irregular borders; unusual color; or signs of chronic irritation, such as those on the neck, where a collar or jewelry may cause friction. Also check for sores, ulceration, warts, discoloration, nodules, or changes in sensation. Note fever and red, swollen, or tender lymph nodes, suggesting systemic metastasis.

If the patient has a mass, inspect its surface for rashes, nodules, redness or discoloration,

PATIENT-TEACHING AID

How to use your prosthesis

Dear _____

Now that you're ready to go home, follow these steps to help speed your recovery and ensure that your new prosthesis fits and functions properly.

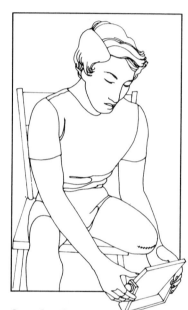

Care for the stump
Inspect your stump once a day. Use a mirror to help you see all surfaces. Call your doctor if your incision appears to be opening, looks red or swollen, feels warm, or is painful to the touch, or if you see drainage.

If you see a blister, raw spot, or cut on your stump, your prosthesis may need an adjustment. Call your prosthetist immediately. Don't cover the irritated area with gauze, tape, or an adhesive bandage. Never try to adjust the prosthesis yourself.

Clean your stump daily, using a washcloth and mild soap. Rinse the area with warm water and dry it thoroughly. To ensure that the prosthesis fits properly, do not apply rubbing alcohol, oil, or body lotion to your stump.

Choose a properly fitted sock
Before applying your prosthesis, slip a specially made sock (synthetic or woolen) over your stump. Make sure the sock fits properly, and smooth out any wrinkles. To avoid skin irritation, never apply a sock that's been mended or has tears, holes, or seams. Wash the sock daily and dry it thoroughly. If your sock's woolen, allow it to air-dry. (A woolen sock shrinks in a dryer.)

Expect periodic adjustments
When the doctor advises, you'll begin wearing your prosthesis all day. Doing so helps mold your stump. However, expect your prosthesis to need adjustments from time to time. Remember, as your stump heals, it should shrink, because the swollen tissue is returning to

normal. But if your prosthesis begins to feel too tight, remove it, and elevate your stump for short periods during the day. If the prosthesis continues to feel too tight and you notice increased swelling, call your doctor. If the prosthesis feels too loose, make an appointment to see your prosthetist.

Care for the prosthesis
When you remove your prosthesis after a day's wear, wipe out the inside with a damp cloth. Thoroughly dry it with a towel. Never immerse your prosthesis in water. Eventually, water causes the prosthesis' leather and joints to deteriorate.

Don't forget to read and follow the manufacturer's instructions that came with your prosthesis. Also, be sure to return to your prosthetist for a yearly check.

Finally, continue the arm or leg exercises the nurse taught you in the hospital.

swelling, and abnormal pulsations. Gently palpate the mass for consistency (hard, firm, or soft), mobility (mobile or adherent to underlying muscle or bone), and tenderness. Then measure it. Note if borders are well demarcated or undetectable. If the mass is located in the soft tissues of the trunk, do adjacent organs feel involved? Auscultate for a bruit, which may occur in a vascular mass.

Observe the extremities for muscle atrophy, joint swelling, and generalized edema. Atrophy may result from disuse due to pain, joint swelling, pathologic fracture, or tumor invasion. Generalized edema points to venous compromise. Measure leg length bilaterally from the anterior superior iliac spine to the medial malleolus to detect shortening caused by tumor impingement on bone or muscle.

Next, palpate the extremities for tenderness. Assess range of motion of the upper extremities. Because sarcomas are more prominent in the legs, focus special attention there. Assess range of motion of the hips with internal and external rotation, flexion, extension, abduction, and adduction; assess the knees with flexion and extension; assess the ankles with dorsiflexion, plantar flexion, inversion, and eversion.

Plan your nursing care
After completing your assessment, begin to formulate appropriate nursing diagnoses like the following.

Knowledge deficit related to causes, signs and symptoms, and treatment of skin cancer. Explain to the patient the risk factors, causes, signs and symptoms, and treatment for skin cancer. Advise him to avoid excessive sun exposure and to use a sunscreen or sunshade. Stress prompt diagnosis and treatment of suspicious lesions. Describe the biopsy procedure. Also, tell the patient what to expect before and after surgery, what the wound will look like, and what type of dressing he'll have. Warn him about the possible side effects of radiation and chemotherapy.

Anxiety related to fear of death, pain, amputation, immobility, or life-style changes related to disease. Inform the patient about the prognosis of his disease, including the extent of disability. Try to instill a positive attitude toward recovery. Urge the patient to resume an independent life-style. Refer him to appropriate health-care professionals for answers to his questions about rehabilitation and prosthetic devices. Encourage him to express his concerns openly; try to be accessi-

ble when he's experiencing intense anxiety. Take measures to relieve pain; administer prescribed drugs; and use comfort measures, such as proper positioning, massage, and relaxation exercises.

Impaired physical ability related to orthopedic surgery to treat cancer. Consult with the prosthetist and physical therapist to plan a teaching program that restores mobility. Instruct the patient in the use of crutches, canes, walkers, limb prostheses, or braces. Reinforce the need for range-of-motion and muscle-strengthening exercises (see *How to use your prosthesis*). Examine the patient's life-style and help him learn self-care techniques to master his daily activities.

Potential for impaired skin integrity related to surgical treatment. After surgery, monitor the wound carefully; observe for erythema, necrotic skin margins, purulent drainage, dehiscence, tenderness, and scaling. Report signs of skin graft nonviability, and give antibiotics as ordered in signs of infection. Also, prevent pressure on the graft site. Carefully follow orders for postoperative wound care. Observe aseptic technique when cleansing and redressing the graft site.

Knowledge deficit related to importance of follow-up care to detect recurrence or metastasis of skin, bone, and soft-tissue cancers. Stress the importance of keeping follow-up appointments with the doctor, taking medication as prescribed, and reporting symptoms of recurrence. Explain that recurrences and metastases, if they occur, may be delayed, so follow-up must continue for at least 5 years. Consider your care plan and interventions successful if the patient:
• understands his disease and its treatment
• expresses his fears and concerns
• plans calmly and realistically for the future
• adapts to functional body changes
• performs self-care effectively
• demonstrates safe mobility, using crutches, walker, cane, or prosthetic devices
• incorporates his disability into his life-style.

Making a difference
Effective nursing care can make all the difference in managing cancer of the skin, bone, or soft tissue. In patients with suspicious lesions, you can promote good prognosis by teaching and encouraging early recognition and prompt treatment. In patients with overt cancer, you can help by teaching effective ways to cope with disfigurement or limited mobility.

Points to remember

• Most basal cell and squamous cell carcinomas have a cure rate exceeding 90% and little risk of metastasis.
• Malignant melanoma is curable in its early stages but lethal in advanced disease.
• Soft-tissue sarcomas are aggressive tumors with a high recurrence rate.
• Surgical resection is the treatment of choice for many cancers of the skin, bone, and soft tissue.
• The patient history should include questions about overexposure to solar radiation, since this is a major contributing factor in skin cancer.

8 IDENTIFYING HEMATOLOGIC CANCER

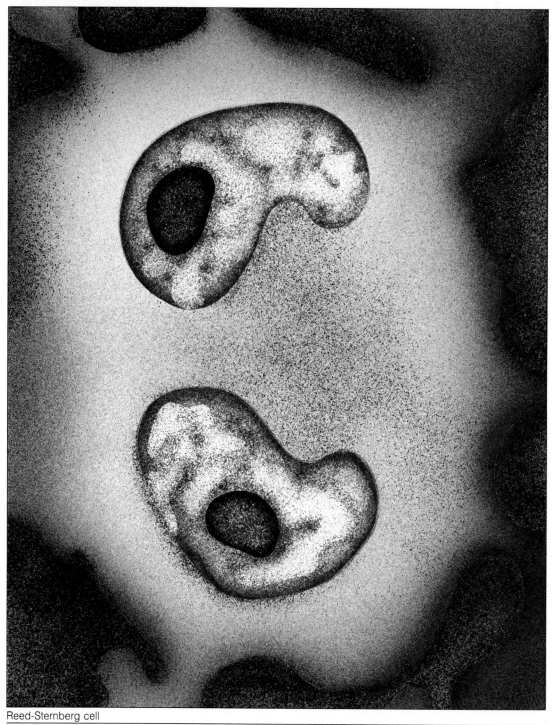

Reed-Sternberg cell

Leukemia and lymphoma account for a slim 8% of the total number of cancers. Nevertheless, you undoubtedly consider them an important clinical problem—because leukemia and lymphoma often strike children, because they often follow a relentlessly terminal course, and because these diseases generally require extended therapy. In the course of such therapy, you'll typically have an opportunity to get to know the patient and his family well and to significantly influence how they cope with cancer. By understanding the pathophysiology, diagnosis, and current treatment of leukemia and lymphoma, you can help them minimize complications of bleeding and infection and make the most of remissions.

Identifying risk factors

Current research has yet to decipher the causes of leukemia and lymphoma; however, several factors may contribute to the development of these cancers. Among the predisposing factors of leukemia are ionizing radiation; occupational exposure to the chemical benzene; exposure to certain drugs, such as the alkylating agents (especially melphalan) and nitrosoureas used in chemotherapy, and chloramphenicol and phenylbutazone, which cause bone marrow depression and aplasia; genetic and congenital disorders, such as Down's syndrome, Fanconi's syndrome, and ataxia-telangiectasia; and viruses. Predisposing factors of lymphoma include ionizing radiation, infection, and immunologic defects resulting from illness (such as Wiskott-Aldrich syndrome) or from treatments (such as kidney allografts).

PATHOPHYSIOLOGY OF LEUKEMIA

A brief look at the classification of leukemia sets the stage for discussing its pathophysiology. By definition, leukemia is the malignant proliferation of white blood cells (WBCs); it's classified according to the type and maturation of these aberrant cells. (See *Blood cell differentiation,* page 100.)

In *acute lymphocytic leukemia,* the aberrant cells are lymphoblasts produced in the lymph nodes and other lymphoid organs. In *acute nonlymphocytic leukemia* (also called *granulocytic* or *myelogenous leukemia*), the cells are myeloblasts, monoblasts, erythroblasts, or (rarely) megakaryoblasts, produced in the bone marrow. Acute leukemias involve immature cells that tend to divide and proliferate quickly; chronic leukemias involve mostly mature cells and some immature cells that exist in a steady state until development of the blast crisis phase.

Types of leukemia

The major types of leukemia are acute lymphocytic leukemia (ALL), acute nonlymphocytic leukemia (ANLL), chronic lymphocytic leukemia (CLL), and chronic myelogenous leukemia (CML).

Acute lymphocytic leukemia. The most common leukemia of childhood, ALL is characterized by the abnormal proliferation of lymphoblasts, which typically cannot be distinguished as T cells or B cells. It usually begins abruptly and, if untreated, becomes fatal within about 4 months.

ALL accounts for about 80% of leukemias in children and about 20% in adults. It typically appears between ages 2 and 10, and 30 and 50. With treatment, about 90% of children survive at least 5 years. Adults require more aggressive treatment; about 50% survive at least 5 years.

Acute nonlymphocytic leukemia. An umbrella term for several leukemias, ANLL includes acute myeloblastic leukemia (AML), acute monoblastic leukemia, and acute promyelocytic leukemia, among other morphologic types. Each leukemia is named according to its aberrant cell type: myeloblastic for abnormal proliferation of myeloblasts, monoblastic for monoblasts, and promyelocytic for promyelocytes.

In children, ANLL accounts for about 20% of leukemias. In adults, it occurs more commonly than ALL and typically appears between ages 30 and 60. Like ALL, ANLL begins abruptly and progresses rapidly. Even with treatment, prognosis is poor in children and adults.

Chronic lymphocytic leukemia. CLL is characterized by the abnormal proliferation of early B-cell lymphocytes or, occasionally, T-cell lymphocytes. It typically appears near age 60 and rarely occurs in children.

When anemia or thrombocytopenia develops in this leukemia, expected survival time is less than 2 years; otherwise, survival time may exceed 70 months.

Chronic myelogenous leukemia. CML is characterized by the abnormal proliferation of granulocytic precursors. It most commonly appears in middle-aged adults and the elderly and rarely occurs in children. Nearly all patients with CML have a small acrocentric

All blood cells derive from a pluripotent stem cell located in the bone marrow. This stem cell differentiates into a lymphoblast or myeloblast, the parent cell of the lymphoid or myeloid cell line, respectively.

Lymphoid cell line

T cells, the most numerous lymphocytes, travel from the bone marrow to the thymus where they mature. These cells initiate cell-mediated immunity, directly attacking foreign substances in the body. B cells mature within the bone marrow before entering the bloodstream where they initiate humoral immunity. Antigen-stimulated B cells differentiate into plasma cells that produce antibodies to disable or destroy foreign substances.

Myeloid cell line

Granulocytes and monocytes act as phagocytes, ridding the body of bacteria, viruses, and other pathogens; foreign or defective cells (including malignant cells); and foreign or defective organic structures, such as proteins. These white blood cells (WBCs) normally outnumber the lymphocytes.

Although erythrocytes (red blood cells) do not participate in the immune response, they play a pivotal role in oxygen transport and prevention of anemia.

Also part of the myeloid cell line, small, disklike platelets break off from megakaryocytes in the bone marrow, circulate in the bloodstream, and congregate at rupture or trauma sites. Here they clump together, promoting coagulation to stop bleeding. Platelets also participate in the inflammatory response by releasing serotonin, which increases blood vessel permeability, allowing easier passage of WBCs.

Blood cell differentiation

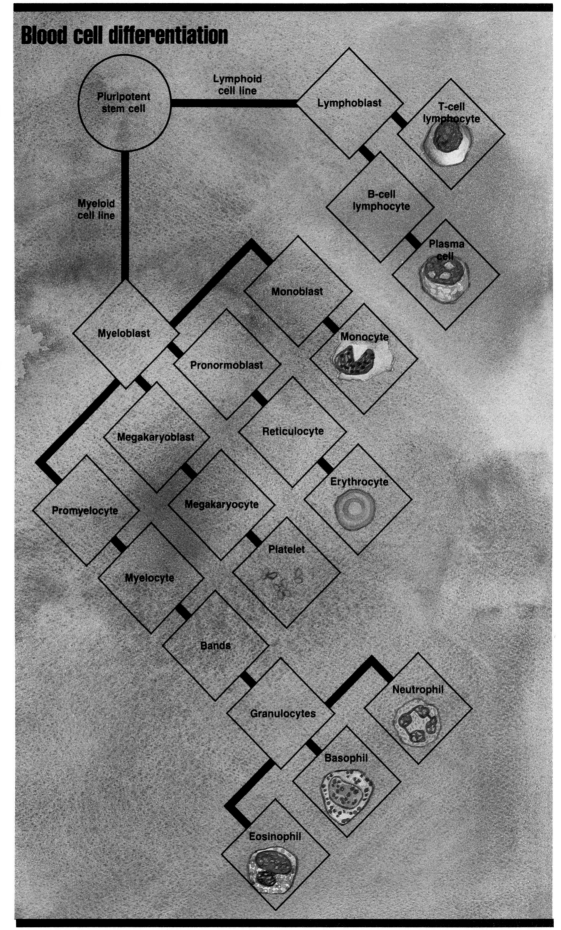

chromosome known as the Philadelphia chromosome. This leukemia has two distinct phases: the chronic phase, which continues about 4 years, and the acute phase (blast crisis), which is invariably fatal within 3 to 6 months.

Effects of leukemia

In leukemia, nonfunctional WBCs accumulate in the bone marrow or lymph tissue, then spill into the bloodstream and infiltrate other organs, interfering with normal function. Leukemic cell infiltration of the bone marrow impairs hematopoiesis, although the mechanism is not yet clear. These cells may cause overcrowding of the marrow space or may release unknown inhibitory factors. Impaired hematopoiesis is responsible for various characteristic cytopenias, such as anemia and thrombocytopenia. In fact, associated hemorrhage or overwhelming infection is frequently the cause of death in leukemia.

Other common signs of leukemic cell infiltration are lymph node enlargement and liver and spleen hypertrophy.

PATHOPHYSIOLOGY OF LYMPHOMA

Like leukemia, lymphoma affects a body system that communicates with every other organ system. However, instead of arising in the blood system, this cancer arises in the lymphatic system, a network of nodes, vessels, and organs that provides a major defense against infection. The lymphatic vessels carry lymph, a clear, colorless fluid containing infection-fighting WBCs, throughout the body. Along these vessels, small oval glands (lymph nodes) trap and help destroy foreign particles and disease-causing agents. Lymphoma usually originates in these nodes but occasionally arises on other lymphoid tissues, such as the spleen or the intestinal lining.

Types of lymphoma

Lymphoma is broadly classified into Hodgkin's disease and non-Hodgkin's lymphoma.

Hodgkin's disease. Accounting for about 40% of all lymphomas, Hodgkin's disease typically occurs between ages 15 and 35 and after age 50. Hodgkin's disease is classified by one of the following four histologic patterns: lymphocyte predominance, nodular sclerosis, mixed cellularity, and lymphocyte depletion. All of these histologic patterns are marked by a scattering of Reed-Sternberg cells. (See *Recognizing leukemic cells,* page 102.)

Treatment in early Hodgkin's disease

achieves complete remission in about 80% to 90% of patients, with a relapse rate of about 10%. Even in advanced disease, treatment achieves complete remission in about 88% of patients; however, the relapse rate is slightly greater—20% at 66 months.

Non-Hodgkin's lymphoma. This lymphoma commonly arises from a monoclonal population of B cells. Non-Hodgkin's lymphoma is classified by nodal architecture (nodular or diffuse) and cell type (lymphocytic, histiocytic, small, or large cell). Although non-Hodgkin's lymphoma occurs in all age-groups, incidence of this disease rises with increasing age.

Effects of lymphoma

How lymphoma spreads—and thus causes symptoms—is not exactly clear; its cells may disseminate through the lymphatic system or the bloodstream, or by direct invasion of adjacent tissue. Hodgkin's disease tends to follow a more predictable and limited growth pattern than non-Hodgkin's lymphoma; as a result, prognosis in Hodgkin's disease is more hopeful.

Nodular non-Hodgkin's lymphoma typically follows a more indolent course than the aggressive, diffuse form of the disease. In fact, nodular lymphoma may wax and wane for months to years before obvious symptoms demand treatment.

Nonspecific signs and symptoms of lymphoma include fever, malaise, weight loss, and night sweats. Specific signs and symptoms vary with the degree and location of lymphomatous infiltration. Painless swelling—most commonly of one or more cervical nodes—characterizes lymph node infiltration; however, alcohol ingestion in Hodgkin's disease makes swollen nodes painful for unknown reasons. Additional signs and symptoms arise when enlarged lymph nodes obstruct or compress an adjacent structure, such as the superior vena cava (causing edema of the face, neck, and right arm) or the ureter (causing renal failure).

A dry, nonproductive cough may accompany lymphomatous infiltration of the lung parenchyma or mediastinal lymph nodes. Asymptomatic mediastinal masses also commonly appear in Hodgkin's disease. Gastrointestinal symptoms, such as fullness or increased girth, may reflect abdominal infiltration. Infiltration of the liver and spleen, marked by hepatosplenomegaly, and of the bone and bone marrow may also be evident.

Recognizing leukemic cells

The photographs below show abnormal cells in blood samples taken from patients with leukemia.

1. Acute lymphocytic leukemia

2. Acute nonlymphocytic leukemia

3. Chronic lymphocytic leukemia

4. Chronic myelogenous leukemia

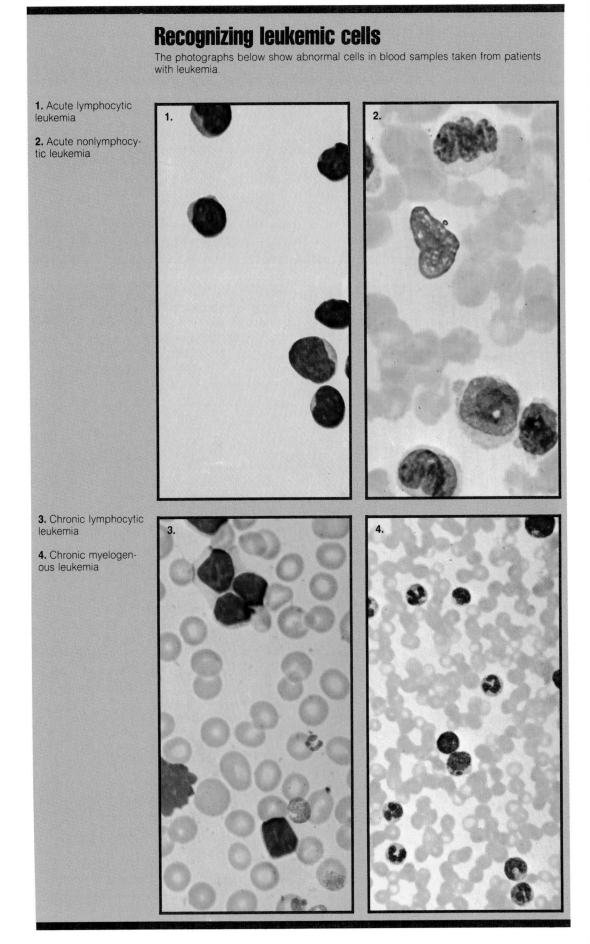

MEDICAL MANAGEMENT

Medical management of leukemia or lymphoma begins with a detailed history, followed by a thorough physical examination with special attention to the lymph nodes, liver, and spleen. Diagnostic tests then confirm the presence of disease and delineate its extent.

Laboratory tests confirm diagnosis

Various laboratory tests help narrow the diagnosis of leukemia and lymphoma. Blood tests, obviously, are most significant.

Blood tests. An abnormality in the complete blood count and differential is often the first diagnostic clue. In acute leukemia, thrombocytopenia and the presence of blast cells are characteristic. In lymphoma, leukocytosis and mild anemia may be present.

Blood chemistry tests typically reveal hyperuricemia and elevated lactate dehydrogenase levels in acute leukemia; the latter reflects extensive bone marrow infiltration. Liver enzymes may also be elevated in leukemia and lymphoma, thereby reflecting hepatic infiltration. Elevated blood urea nitrogen and creatinine levels suggest renal disease or ureter obstruction due to lymph node enlargement.

Blood cultures and cultures of urine and sputum screen for infection, which may be life-threatening in leukemia and lymphoma. Another blood test measures leukocyte alkaline phosphatase, an enzyme in granulocytes. Decreased levels usually occur in CML. A direct Coombs' test may be positive in CLL or lymphoma.

Skin tests. Tuberculin skin tests and DNCB (dinitrochlorobenzene, a chemical allergen) tests are used to evaluate cell-mediated immunity; cutaneous anergy frequently exists in lymphoma.

Bone marrow tests. Bone marrow aspiration confirms a diagnosis of leukemia by revealing marrow composition and cellularity and by identifying aberrant cell types.

Biopsy. Lymph node biopsy establishes histopathologic classification of lymphoma, distinguishing Hodgkin's disease and non-Hodgkin's lymphoma. Needle biopsy and frozen section analysis of the biopsy fail to yield suitable material for accurate diagnosis.

Radiographic tests. After confirming a diagnosis of leukemia or lymphoma, various tests help evaluate the extent of the disease. (See *Staging cancer: Hodgkin's disease and non-Hodgkin's lymphoma.*) Chest X-ray detects lung infiltration, mediastinal adenopathy, and

initial infection. Whole chest tomography or computerized tomography (CT) scans provide more detailed evaluation. A complete skeletal survey and bone scan can help evaluate bone infiltration.

If acute renal failure develops in leukemia or lymphoma, intravenous pyelography, CT scan, or renal ultrasound identifies ureter obstruction from enlarged retroperitoneal nodes. A liver-spleen scan and percutaneous liver biopsy help stage Hodgkin's disease. Also, CT scan is especially accurate for identifying enlarged mesenteric and upper abdominal lymph nodes. Ultrasonography may outline intraabdominal masses and distinct sonolucency of lymphomatous nodes. However, accurate staging of Hodgkin's disease frequently requires laparotomy and bipedal lymphangiography, unless contraindicated. (See *Laparotomy: Surgical staging of Hodgkin's disease,* page 104.)

Treatment varies

Treatment, of course, depends on the specific diagnosis in leukemia and lymphoma. Also, evaluation of the patient's medical history and cardiovascular and renal function is necessary to determine his ability to tolerate aggressive treatment. The patient who has major organ dysfunction or is elderly may require specific modification of treatment.

Acute leukemia: Three-phase chemotherapy

The treatment of choice for acute leukemia, chemotherapy involves three phases: induction, consolidation, and maintenance.

The induction phase, an intensive course with chemotherapeutic drugs, aims to achieve complete remission. The consolidation phase then begins to eliminate remaining occult disease. The maintenance phase consists of low-dose combinations of chemotherapeutic drugs administered every 3 or 4 weeks to prevent possible relapse. Chemotherapy varies for ALL and ANLL.

ALL. Currently, the most effective chemotherapeutic drugs for ALL are vincristine (Oncovin) and prednisone. These drugs specifically destroy lymphoblasts yet spare normal marrow cells. Other drugs frequently used include doxorubicin (Adriamycin); methotrexate; cytarabine (Cytosar-U), also known as ara-C and cytosine arabinoside; asparaginase; and cyclophosphamide (Cytoxan). ALL is associated with a significant risk of central nervous system (CNS) leukemia, particularly if the WBC count exceeds 20,000/mm³. When

Hodgkin's disease and non-Hodgkin's lymphoma

Correct staging is the first step toward effective treatment of Hodgkin's disease and non-Hodgkin's lymphoma. These four stages are currently used.

Stage I: Disease is limited to a single lymph node region or to a single extralymphatic organ.

Stage II: Disease involves two or more lymph node regions on the same side of the diaphragm, or involves an extralymphatic organ and one or more lymph node regions on the same side of the diaphragm.

Stage III: Disease involves lymph node regions on both sides of the diaphragm and may also be accompanied by localized involvement of an extralymphatic organ or site or by involvement of the spleen, or both.

Stage IV: Disease shows diffuse or disseminated involvement of one or more extralymphatic organs or tissues with or without associated lymph node involvement.

Each stage is further divided into A and B categories. A refers to asymptomatic patients; B refers to those with symptoms such as fever, night sweats, and weight loss of more than 10% of body weight.

Laparotomy: Surgical staging of Hodgkin's disease

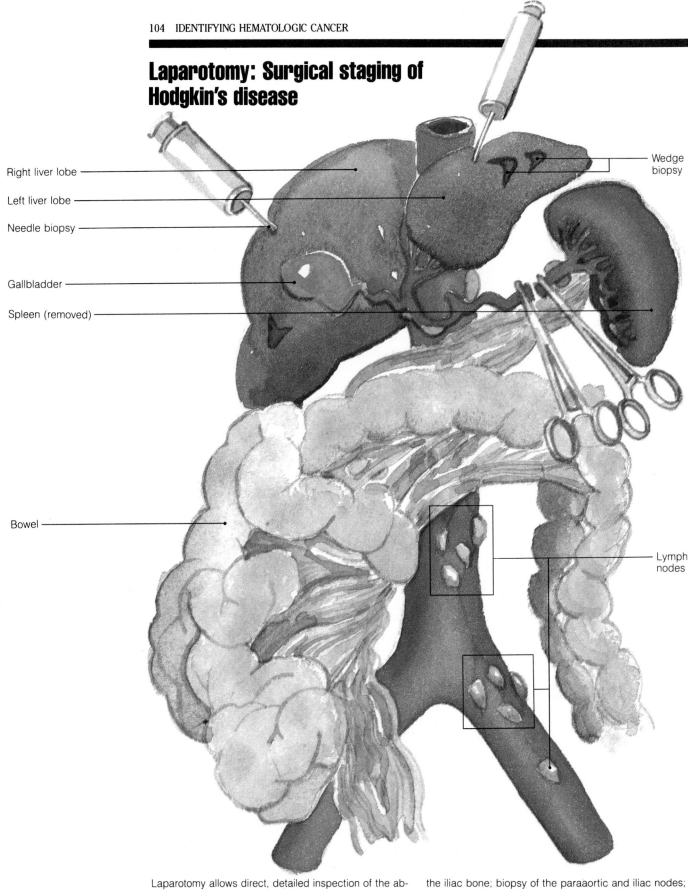

Right liver lobe

Left liver lobe

Needle biopsy

Gallbladder

Spleen (removed)

Bowel

Wedge biopsy

Lymph nodes

Laparotomy allows direct, detailed inspection of the abdomen. Although laparotomy is a controversial procedure, it excels even the most sophisticated diagnostic techniques for staging abdominal involvement in Hodgkin's disease. This procedure involves splenectomy; wedge and needle biopsy of the liver; wedge biopsy of the iliac bone; biopsy of the paraaortic and iliac nodes; and removal of nodes from the splenic hilar, celiac, porta hepatis, mesenteric, and iliac regions. In addition, fixation of the ovary (oophoropexy) may be performed to prevent sterilization during subsequent radiation therapy.

leukemic cells cross the blood-brain barrier, they escape the effects of intravenous chemotherapy at conventionally prescribed dosages. However, intrathecal instillation of methotrexate may be effective for treatment or prophylaxis. Cranial radiation is another option for CNS leukemia. Other uses of local radiation in ALL include treatment of bulky, mediastinal infiltration and of testicular infiltration, which occurs most frequently in children.

ANLL. Chemotherapy for ANLL typically involves an anthracycline agent—usually daunorubicin—in combination with cytarabine. Current understanding maintains that the bone marrow must become markedly hypocellular for complete remission to occur. If hypocellularity has not developed within 7 to 10 days after therapy ends, a second course may be administered. Approximately 2 to 3 weeks after chemotherapy, the marrow repopulates with either normal or leukemic cells, a response confirmed by bone marrow aspiration and biopsy. If the patient's in remission, a rest period of about 3 weeks is given before the consolidation phase begins. Treatment then continues with the same drugs at a lower dosage or with different drugs. Generally, two or three consolidation courses are administered before maintenance therapy.

Bone marrow transplant: A treatment option for some

Allogeneic bone marrow transplantation may be a treatment option for either ALL or ANLL. In this procedure, marrow cells from an HLA-identical sibling or twin are administered intravenously. The patient receives large doses of cyclophosphamide and total body irradiation beforehand to help eradicate leukemic cells and to impair his tendency to reject donor marrow cells. Typically, a series of low-dose, fractionated radiation treatments are given to reduce pulmonary toxicity and to avoid interstitial pneumonitis. Marrow transplantation failure may result from recurrent leukemia, graft-versus-host disease, or uncontrollable infection.

Chronic leukemia: Chemotherapy plus adjuvant measures

Although chemotherapy is also the treatment of choice for chronic leukemia, various adjuvant measures are frequently used.

CLL. Treatment for CLL is primarily palliative; it aims to relieve symptoms of bulky lymphadenopathy with splenomegaly or hepatomegaly. Alkylating agents (chlorambucil or cyclophosphamide) are usually given to decrease symptoms. Oral prednisone is given daily as an adjunct when anemia or thrombocytopenia develops. Since lymphocytes are radiosensitive, total body irradiation or local radiation to the spleen may also be beneficial. Splenectomy increases the platelet count in patients with splenomegaly and thrombocytopenia.

CML. Treatment of CML in its chronic phase aims to control leukocytosis and thrombocytosis. The most widely used chemotherapeutic drugs are busulfan (Myleran) and hydroxyurea (Hydrea), administered orally. Unfortunately, treatment of its acute phase (blast crisis) is less successful. Use of acute leukemia regimens rarely causes the marrow to revert to the chronic phase; however, chemotherapeutic drugs effective against ALL may achieve brief complete remission.

Bone marrow transplant is currently under investigation for use in the chronic phase of CML. If painful splenomegaly develops, local radiation therapy or splenectomy may relieve symptoms.

Leukapheresis—the selective removal of leukocytes from the blood—may be performed to lower the WBC count quickly; however, the effects of leukapheresis are temporary. Platelet pheresis may be performed for marked thrombocytosis.

Hodgkin's disease: Radiation and chemotherapy

Effective treatment of Hodgkin's disease depends on accurate histologic evaluation and subsequent clinical staging. Stages range from I to IV and each has an A and a B category; A refers to asymptomatic patients, B to those with unexplained fever, night sweats, and weight loss of more than 10% of body weight.

Radiation is the primary treatment for stages I, II, and in some cases, IIIA. (See *Radiation therapy: Two techniques for Hodgkin's disease,* page 106.) Adjuvant chemotherapy may be given to patients at high risk of extranodal spread. Megavoltage radiation (linear accelerator) and extended fields to include adjacent uninvolved nodal sites are crucial in achieving high cure rates. Appropriate shielding and field shaping protect the lungs, spinal cord, larynx, heart, kidneys, gonads, and iliac crest marrow.

Chemotherapy, the primary treatment for stages IIIB and IV, is most effective with combinations of drugs; in fact, it sometimes induces complete remission.

Radiation therapy: Two techniques for Hodgkin's disease

Typically, radiation is the primary treatment for localized Hodgkin's disease (stages I, II, and IIIA). Using the two-field or three-field technique, all or most of the lymph nodes can be irradiated within sets of matched anterior and posterior fields. The mantle field covers the cervical, supraclavicular, intraclavicular, axillary, hilar, and mediastinal nodes down to the diaphragm. The inverted-Y field covers the spleen or splenic pedicle and the celiac, paraaortic, iliac, inguinal, and femoral nodes. In the three-field technique, the inverted-Y field is split into two.

Two-field technique

Three-field technique

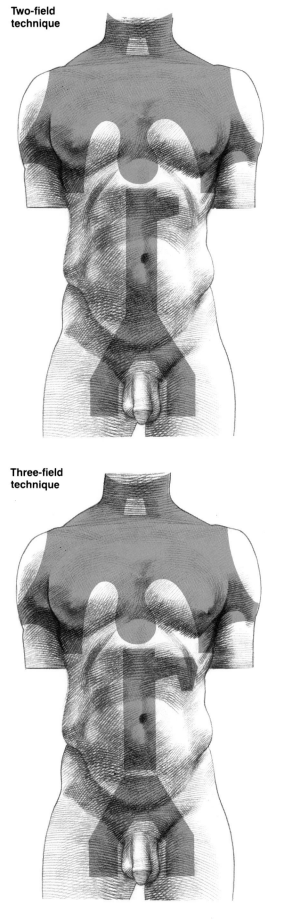

Non-Hodgkin's lymphoma: Mainly chemotherapy

Radiation therapy is most effective in the early localized stages of non-Hodgkin's lymphoma. However, the radiation fields used to treat Hodgkin's disease are frequently inappropriate for non-Hodgkin's lymphoma. Because widespread extranodal disease commonly occurs at relapse, extra care must be taken to preserve adequate marrow function so that the patient can tolerate chemotherapy. Total body irradiation is sometimes used in non-Hodgkin's lymphoma and may achieve complete remission.

Chemotherapy is the primary treatment for stages III and IV, although radiation may be used as an adjunct.

When to initiate chemotherapy and what drugs to use depend on the stage and histologic classification of non-Hodgkin's lymphoma (favorable and unfavorable) and on the patient's age and general health, including bone marrow function. (See *Classifying non-Hodgkin's lymphomas,* page 108.)

Non-Hodgkin's lymphomas of favorable histology include nodular, lymphocytic, well differentiated; nodular, lymphocytic, poorly differentiated; nodular, mixed, histiocytic-lymphocytic; and diffuse, lymphocytic, well differentiated. Slowly progressive, asymptomatic non-Hodgkin's lymphoma may be initially observed without treatment, particularly in the elderly. In fact, these elderly patients may not require treatment for 2 or 3 years. Several investigational studies indicate that delaying treatment during asymptomatic disease achieves survival rates similar to survival rates for early, intensive treatment. When enlarged nodes become tender or encroach on organ systems, appropriate treatment usually involves an alkylating agent with or without prednisone.

Non-Hodgkin's lymphomas of unfavorable histology include nodular, histiocytic; diffuse, histiocytic; diffuse, lymphocytic, poorly differentiated; diffuse, mixed, histiocytic-lymphocytic; and diffuse, undifferentiated. Typically, these lymphomas follow a more virulent course and are more likely to relapse within the first year of treatment. Primary treatment—early, intensive chemotherapy—involves various combinations of cyclophosphamide, doxorubicin, vincristine, and prednisone. Such chemotherapy improves remission rates, but it may also cause toxicity, particularly increased myelosuppression, alopecia, and fatigue.

Blood transfusions: Indispensable supportive therapy

In advanced disease or during radiation and chemotherapy, the patient may require transfusions of red blood cells (RBCs), white blood cells (WBCs), or platelets. Knowing the purpose and steps for preparing each transfusion helps ensure correct administration.

RBCs
Transfusions of packed RBCs help maintain the patient's hematocrit. Packed RBCs are produced by centrifuging a unit of whole blood, forcing the RBCs (which are heavier than plasma) to the bottom of the container. After the plasma is removed, the percentage by volume of packed RBCs (called hematocrit) increases. Whole blood has a hematocrit of about 40%; a unit of RBCs has a hematocrit of about 70% to 80%. RBCs may be refrigerated up to 35 days.

WBCs
WBC (granulocyte) transfusions treat patients with severe granulocytopenia. Granulocytes are obtained by filtration or by differential centrifugation of donor blood. Granulocytes are infused

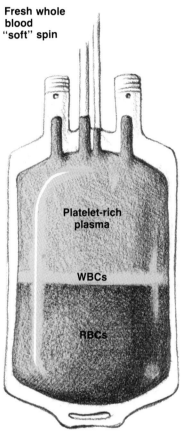

Fresh whole blood "soft" spin

Platelet-rich plasma

WBCs

RBCs

daily for 4 or 5 days. HLA matching of donors to recipients helps avoid adverse WBC transfusion reactions (chills, fever, and possibly, anaphylaxis). Premedication with corticosteroids, acetaminophen, or meperidine (Demerol) may also minimize reactions.

Platelets
Platelet transfusions treat patients with thrombocytopenia or active bleeding. Platelet concentrates are prepared from whole blood by a series of differential centrifugations. Initially, centrifugation is a soft spin—a slow spin for a short time. Platelets remain suspended in the plasma, while the heavier RBCs and WBCs settle to the bottom. The plasma is then transferred to another bag and respun at a faster speed, which separates the excess plasma from the platelet concentrate.

Platelet concentrate is best preserved at room temperature in a plastic container with gentle agitation to prevent clumping or aggregating. Proper storage guarantees the shelf-life of platelet concentrate for 3 to 5 days. Refrigerated platelet concentrate lasts only 2 days.

Supportive therapy improves prognosis
Investigational treatments for leukemia and lymphoma have been largely disappointing. Immunotherapy alone or in combination with chemotherapy has failed to improve long-term survival rates. Modified leukemic cells, bacille Calmette-Guérin (BCG) vaccine, *Corynebacterium parvum,* and mixed bacterial endotoxins have also been tested without success. Interferon occasionally achieves remission in patients with leukemia, but the remission is short-lived.

However, advances in supportive therapy have done much to improve remission and survival rates. Use of broad-spectrum antibiotics for bacterial infections and amphotericin B for fungal infections has minimized mortality from treatment-related sepsis. Trimethoprim-sulfamethoxazole (Bactrim) given prophylactically during withdrawal from ste-

roids has reduced the incidence of *Pneumocystis carinii* pneumonia, a potentially lethal protozoan infection. Random, single-donor platelet transfusions have helped control hemorrhage in prolonged thrombocytopenia, and leukocyte transfusions may help control antibiotic-resistant infection. (See *Blood transfusions: Indispensable supportive therapy.*)

NURSING MANAGEMENT
The patient with leukemia or lymphoma faces a difficult prognosis and certainly requires much physical and emotional support. Your nursing history and physical examination are essential to formulate a care plan that provides this support.

Explore the chief complaint
Begin the nursing history by obtaining biographic data. Then have the patient describe

Classifying non-Hodgkin's lymphomas

These lymphomas are described by the Rappaport histologic classification listed below, which notes the degree of cellular differentiation and the presence or absence of nodularity. Nodular lymphomas carry a more optimistic prognosis than the diffuse form of non-Hodgkin's lymphoma.

NH: Nodular, histiocytic
NM: Nodular, mixed, histiocytic-lymphocytic
NLPD: Nodular, lymphocytic, poorly differentiated
NLWD: Nodular, lymphocytic, well differentiated
DH: Diffuse, histiocytic
DM: Diffuse, mixed, histiocytic-lymphocytic
DLPD: Diffuse, lymphocytic, poorly differentiated
DLWD: Diffuse, lymphocytic, well differentiated
DU: Diffuse, undifferentiated

his chief complaint. Document the complaint, using the patient's own words; for example, "I've been very tired and my throat's sore."

Ask the patient when he first noticed the symptom. How often does it occur? Do other symptoms occur at the same time? What makes it better or worse? Have the patient describe any treatment he's received, and note its effectiveness.

Record the medical and family history

Obtain a chronologic record of previous hospitalizations, surgical procedures, and significant illnesses or accidents. Note allergies and list drugs the patient is currently taking. Determine if he's ever taken alkylating agents or other immunosuppressive or marrow-suppressive drugs. Also ask about exposure to radiation and hazardous chemicals such as benzene.

Obtain a family history of lymphatic, immunologic, hematologic, or genetic disease. This history helps identify other family members at risk; for example, a member with Down's syndrome may be more susceptible to leukemia.

Finally, have the patient describe activities of a typical day to evaluate his diet and other habits.

Physical examination: Systematic and thorough

Carefully examine all body systems to uncover signs and symptoms that the patient may have forgotten or overlooked. During the physical examination, be especially alert for generalized complaints, such as fever, sweats, chills, weight change, fatigue, and weakness. Also note headaches, which may indicate a hematologic disorder such as leukocytosis or bleeding.

Begin by taking the patient's vital signs and measuring height and weight. Briefly describe his overall appearance, then assess each body system. Clearly document all of your findings.

Head and neck. Examine the scalp for infection. Ask the patient if he's noticed any hair loss or texture change. Observe the face and neck for swelling, which may be due to lymph node compression (superior vena cava syndrome).

Examine the eyes with a light for blood flecks. Also ask about vision changes or spots in front of the eyes, which may signify hemorrhage or leukemic infiltration. Inspect the nose and sinuses for tenderness and bleeding; nosebleeds and sinus pain may be related to

thrombocytopenia and infection. Inspect the gums for gingival hypertrophy secondary to leukemic infiltration or bleeding, which may result from thrombocytopenia. Examine the throat with a flashlight. Note erythema, swelling, white patches, yellow coating on tongue, or ulcerations, which may point to infection. Also ask about sore throat and dysphagia.

Lymph nodes. Carefully assess for lymphadenopathy, which may signify leukemic or lymphomatous infiltration. Enlarged nodes are often painless, and the patient may be unaware of them. Measure enlarged nodes in centimeters, and check for tenderness and mobility.

Respiratory system. Auscultate and percuss the lungs, noting the depth and character of respirations, unusual breath sounds, and percussion tone. Note if the patient experiences discomfort during percussion. Ask about shortness of breath, dyspnea on exertion, cough, or pain, which may indicate infection, effusion, or mediastinal infiltration.

Cardiovascular system. Auscultate the heart, noting cardiac rate, rhythm, and sound. Observe the patient's skin color. Palpate the jugular, carotid, and peripheral pulses.

Gastrointestinal system. Observe abdominal contour, then auscultate bowel sounds. Explore abdominal complaints; early satiety points to splenomegaly, and increased girth suggests hepatosplenomegaly. Determine liver and spleen size by percussion and palpation. Inspect the rectum externally for signs of infection and bleeding. Do not perform a digital examination, which may cause bleeding and lead to infection. Ask about tarry stools (melena), which may indicate thrombocytopenia. Also ask about nausea, vomiting, and abdominal pain; these symptoms may indicate abdominal infiltration.

Genitourinary system. Inspect the genitalia externally, noting drainage or lesions. Palpate testicular masses for size and consistency. Ask about urinary habits. Dysuria or frequency points to infection, while anuria suggests ureter obstruction by enlarged lymph nodes. Hematuria may indicate thrombocytopenia, as may menorrhagia or vaginal spotting between periods.

Integument. Ask the patient if he bruises easily, and note petechiae and ecchymoses, which may indicate thrombocytopenia. Estimate the size of bruises, petechiae, and other skin lesions. Observe for erythema, swelling, tenderness, or drainage, which may signify infection. Describe the amount, color, and

Understanding multiple myeloma

Multiple myeloma is a disseminated neoplasm of plasma cells that invade the bone marrow. It strikes about 7,000 people yearly—mostly men between the ages of 50 and 69.

Although its cause remains unknown, some studies suggest that multiple myeloma reflects an inappropriate response to an antigen or a viruslike particle. Prognosis is usually poor, because diagnosis of this disease is often made after multiple myeloma has already infiltrated the vertebrae, pelvis, skull, ribs, clavicles, and sternum. In fact, most patients die within 2 years of diagnosis following such complications as infection, renal failure, hematologic imbalance, fractures, hypercalcemia, hyperuricemia, or dehydration.

Plasma cell proliferation
In multiple myeloma, malignant plasma cells proliferate within the hematopoietic tissue of the bone marrow, then infiltrate the rest of the bone to produce osteolytic lesions. Bone destruction leads to hypercalcemia and pathologic fractures, most commonly in the ribs, spine, skull, and pelvis.

Plasma cell proliferation within the bone marrow crowds the marrow space, usually inhibiting red blood cell production. Also, plasma cells synthesize and secrete abnormally few immunoglobulins, which increases the risk of infection. Rarely, a marked increase in a single immunoglobulin increases blood viscosity, leading to the occlusion of small blood vessels, especially those of the brain, retina, and glomeruli.

The hallmark of multiple myeloma is the production of an abnormal immunoglobulin, typically indicated by the presence of Bence Jones protein in the urine (appearing in about 50% of patients). It is filtered by the glomeruli, then reabsorbed and metabolized. Bence Jones pro-tein spills into the urine when it exceeds the tubules' capacity to reabsorb it, thus severely damaging the kidneys.

The diagnostic workup
After a thorough physical examination and medical history, the diagnostic workup consists of blood and urine tests, bone marrow aspiration and biopsy, and X-rays.

A *complete blood count* shows moderate or severe anemia. The differential may show 40% to 50% lymphocytes but seldom more than 3% plasma cells. Rouleaux formation seen on the differential smear results from elevation of the erythrocyte sedimentation rate.

Urine studies may show Bence Jones protein and hypercalciuria. Bence Jones protein confirms multiple myeloma, but its absence does not rule it out.

Bone marrow aspiration confirms multiple myeloma by revealing an abnormal number of immature plasma cells. *Serum electrophoresis* shows an elevated globulin spike that is electrophoretically and immunologically abnormal.

X-rays show multiple, sharply circumscribed osteolytic (punched out) lesions, particularly on the skull, pelvis, and spine; vertebral compression fractures; and demineralization.

Chemotherapy: Mainstay of treatment
Long-term treatment consists of chemotherapy and adjuvant local radiation therapy to alleviate pain and reduce acute lesions. Combinations of melphalan (Alkeran) and prednisone given at monthly intervals achieve remission in about 50% of patients.

Recently, combinations of vincristine (Oncovin), cyclophosphamide (Cytoxan), doxorubicin (Adriamycin), and prednisone have improved remission to about 65% to 70%. Other agents used to treat multiple myeloma include human leuko-cyte interferon and intermittent combinations of vindesine and prednisone.

Major nursing goals
Nursing care aims to ensure adequate hydration, to promote exercise, to prevent complications, and to provide emotional support.

Ensure adequate hydration. Encourage the patient to drink 3,000 to 4,000 ml of fluids daily. Adequate hydration helps prevent hypercalcemia, hyperuricemia, and renal insufficiency. Monitor fluid intake and output. (Daily output should be at least 1,500 ml.)

Promote exercise. Encourage walking to help prevent bone demineralization and hypercalcemia. Give analgesics, as ordered, to lessen pain. Since the patient is particularly vulnerable to pathologic fractures, he may be fearful of exercise. Reassure him and allow him to move at his own pace.

Prevent complications. Watch for fever or malaise, which may signal the onset of infection, and for signs of other complications, such as severe anemia and fractures.

If the patient is bedridden, be sure to change his position every 2 hours. In addition, perform passive range-of-motion exercises, and encourage deep breathing.

If the patient is taking melphalan (a phenylalanine derivative of nitrogen mustard that depresses bone marrow), make sure his blood count (platelet and white blood cell) is taken before each chemotherapy treatment.

If he is taking prednisone, watch closely for infection since this drug often masks it.

Provide emotional support. Help relieve the patient's anxiety by truthfully informing him and his family about diagnostic tests (including painful procedures such as bone marrow aspiration and biopsy), treatment, and prognosis.

Bone marrow dysfunction in aplastic anemias

Aplastic anemias result from injury to, or destruction of, stem cells in bone marrow or the bone marrow matrix, causing pancytopenia (anemia, granulocytopenia, thrombocytopenia) and bone marrow hypoplasia. In some patients, the bone marrow lacks platelet and red and white (myeloid) blood cell precursors. In others, its cellularity is reduced, or areas of acellularity mix with areas of normal cellularity or hypercellularity.

Sometimes puzzling etiology
About half of aplastic anemias result from drugs (such as chloramphenicol), toxic agents (such as benzene), or radiation. The rest may result from immunologic factors or severe disease, especially hepatitis. Idiopathic aplastic anemias may also be congenital, as in congenital hypoplastic anemia and Fanconi's syndrome.

Variable signs and symptoms
Clinical features of aplastic anemias vary with the severity of pancytopenia but often develop insidiously. Symptoms of anemia include progressive weakness and fatigue, shortness of breath, headache, pallor, and ultimately, tachycardia and congestive heart failure. Thrombocytopenia leads to ecchymoses, petechiae, and hemorrhage, especially from the mucous membranes or into the retina or central nervous system. Neutropenia may lead to infection, but without characteristic inflammation.

A series of diagnostic tests
Several tests together confirm aplastic anemia. *Red blood cells* are normochromic and normocytic (rarely, macrocytic). *Reticulocyte levels* and *platelet, neutrophil,* and *white blood cell counts* are decreased. Aspirated bone marrow is acellular. *Serum iron levels* are elevated.

Bone marrow transplant
Aplastic anemias rarely respond to marrow-stimulating agents, such as androgens. Consequently, the treatment of choice is bone marrow transplant.

odor of any drainage. Note skin rashes, which may be related to leukemic infiltration.

Musculoskeletal system. Perform passive range-of-motion exercises to detect joint or bone pain, which may accompany leukemic infiltration. Myalgia may indicate infection or thrombocytopenia.

Neurologic system. Assess cranial nerves, sensory and motor function reflexes, and mental status to rule out CNS infiltration, particularly in acute lymphocytic leukemia. In addition, note facial palsy, paresthesia, and hyperesthesia.

Care plan: Supportive and instructive
In patients with leukemia or lymphoma, your care plan focuses on meticulous supportive care, psychological support, and sound patient teaching to make the most of remissions and to minimize complications. The following nursing diagnoses will likely be part of your plan.

Anxiety related to knowledge deficit about disease and its treatment. If possible, be with the patient when the doctor explains the disease and outlines treatment. Assess his understanding of this explanation later by asking direct questions. Consider the patient's readiness and ability to learn; also find out how he's coped with stress in the past. Then reinforce the doctor's explanation, making sure to define terms—such as relapse and remission—that will be used to describe the effects of therapy.

Arrange group or individual learning sessions and provide written educational material. If possible, arrange for someone with a similar diagnosis to visit the patient with leukemia or lymphoma. Involve the family and significant others in the teaching to establish a firm support group. Inform them that the local chapter of the American Cancer Society is available for additional information, financial assistance, and supportive counseling.

Knowledge deficit related to potential infection in immunosuppression or neutropenia. Explain to the patient why immunosuppression and neutropenia increase the risk of infection. Stress the importance of promptly reporting signs and symptoms of infection, including fever of 100.4° F. (38° C.) or higher, chills, sweats, or flushing; sore throat, oral sensitivity or ulcerations, white patches or plaques in mouth, esophageal burning, or dysphagia; cough, shortness of breath, or dyspnea on exertion; burning on urination or urinary frequency; vaginal discharge; rectal tenderness or pain; erythema, edema, tenderness, heat, or drainage at sites where skin has been broken; myalgias or arthralgias; abdominal pain, cramping, diarrhea, or nausea and vomiting (unrelated to treatment).

Emphasize the importance of meticulous hygiene to prevent infection. Tell the patient to bathe or shower daily, giving special attention to the axillae, groin, and perineal areas. Instruct him to rinse his mouth with normal saline solution and to brush his teeth and tongue gently with a soft brush or sponge-tipped swab four times daily. Have him avoid commercial mouthwashes containing alcohol. Advise him to take oral antifungal drugs only as prescribed and not to visit the dentist without his doctor's approval.

Urge the patient to wash his hands before meals and after using the commode. Suggest that he use stool softeners or laxatives, as needed, to avoid straining, which may traumatize rectal tissue and lead to infection. If the patient experiences rectal pain or discomfort, suggest a sitz bath three times daily. Avoid administering rectal suppositories or enemas and using rectal thermometers to prevent introduction of trauma and bacteria. Instruct the female patient to cleanse the perianal area from front to back, away from the meatus and vaginal introitus, to prevent fecal contamination of the urinary tract. Also tell her to avoid vaginal tampons and commercial douches, which may cause trauma or introduce chemical irritants and bacteria. Instruct the patient to soak swollen or tender skin areas and to keep such areas clean and comfortable.

Warn the patient about activities that may lead to infection, such as close contact with obviously ill persons or those exposed to contagious illnesses; contact with animal excretion, such as litter boxes; using sharp utensils or straight razors; sewing without a thimble; eating raw meats or unwashed fruits and vegetables; and immobility.

Inform the patient that some infections are associated with treatment and that they may occur despite careful preventive regimens. Encourage him to resume as many social activities as possible, such as going to the movies and dancing. Many patients wrongly feel that such activities may lead to infection; as a result, they may isolate themselves unnecessarily.

Knowledge deficit related to potential bleeding in thrombocytopenia. Explain to the patient why thrombocytopenia increases the risk of bleeding. Then stress the importance of reporting signs and symptoms of bleeding, including headache, loss of vision or black spots in front of the eyes, or conjunctival hemorrhage; nosebleed; bleeding gums; he-

moptysis; hematemesis; hematuria; frank melena; menorrhagia or vaginal spotting between menstrual periods; petechiae, particularly on legs, and ecchymoses; and excessive bleeding at broken-skin sites, such as the venipuncture site.

Teach the patient how to prevent bleeding or how to detect it promptly. Have him immediately notify the doctor of excessive vomiting, coughing, or straining during defecation so that the problem may be treated early. Instruct him to avoid aspirin and aspirin-containing products, such as Percodan, which may cause GI irritation and bleeding. Advise him to blow his nose gently and to brush his teeth with a soft toothbrush or sponge-tipped swab. Have him notify the doctor before any dental work; it may be contraindicated, or if not, prophylactic bleeding precautions may be necessary.

Encourage the patient to shave with an electric, instead of a straight-edged, razor. Instruct him not to walk after taking drugs that may potentially cause orthostatic hypotension. Also, tell him to avoid contact sports. Suggest wearing a glove or mitt when handling sharp utensils. Advise the patient against forceful sexual intercourse, and stress the necessity for adequate lubrication to prevent trauma.

Fatigue secondary to anemia related to disease process or treatment. Explain to the patient that fatigue results when disease or its treatment lowers hemoglobin and hematocrit levels. (See *Bone marrow dysfunction in aplastic anemias.*) Monitor the patient's hemoglobin and hematocrit levels; transfuse blood products, as ordered.

Determine if other factors, such as depression, may be contributing to fatigue. Also, schedule physical care, meals, and required tests or procedures to allow adequate rest. Encourage the patient to eat a high-protein, iron-rich diet. Explain the complications of immobility; encourage him to change position often, to perform deep-breathing and isotonic exercises, and to increase his level of activity as tolerated.

Effective interventions
Caring for the patient with leukemia or lymphoma will undoubtedly tax your emotions and challenge your nursing skills. But your interventions can help the patient to understand his disease and its treatment, to minimize complications, and to cope with the stress of illness.

Points to remember

- Leukemia involves malignant proliferation of immature white blood cells; it's classified according to the type and maturation of these aberrant cells.
- Lymphoma—the malignant proliferation of lymphoid cells—is broadly classified into Hodgkin's disease and non-Hodgkin's lymphoma. Typically, prognosis is less hopeful in non-Hodgkin's lymphoma.
- Leukemia and lymphoma are systemic cancers that can potentially affect all organs and tissues of the body.
- Diagnosis of leukemia depends on blood tests and bone marrow examination.
- Diagnosis of lymphoma must include accurate staging to ensure appropriate treatment.
- Nursing care focuses on meticulous supportive care, psychological support, and sound patient teaching to minimize complications. Teaching patients how to prevent infection and bleeding is especially crucial.

9 DETECTING CANCER OF HEAD, NECK, AND C.N.S.

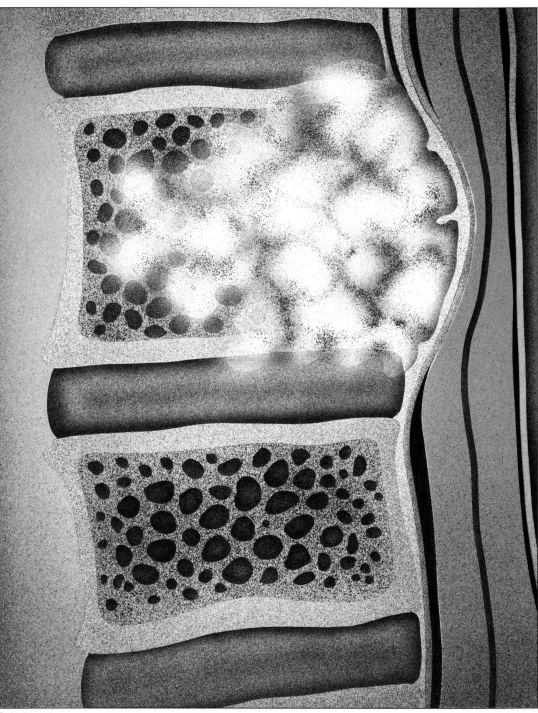

Spinal cord tumor

Cancers of the head, neck, and central nervous system (CNS) are less common than other cancers and are highly curable if discovered early. Unfortunately, several factors militate against early discovery. Most head and neck cancers cause no symptoms or cause symptoms that may easily be attributed to benign conditions. Moreover, the people at greatest risk—the elderly, heavy tobacco users, and those of poor socioeconomic backgrounds—seldom visit their doctors and dentists regularly so that a premalignant or easily detected cancer could be found early.

Because the head and neck form an anatomic crossroads where the great blood vessels and the air and food passageways converge in a confined area, malignancy in this area can have serious and far-reaching effects. Malignancy can cause cosmetic and neurologic deformities, crippling the patient both physically and psychologically. (See *Five-year survival rates in common head and neck cancers,* page 114.)

You have a better chance of detecting head, neck, and CNS cancers early and participating successfully in their cure or control if you understand their pathophysiology, current treatment, and probable aftermath.

The high risks
The cause of head, neck, and CNS cancers remains elusive, but in head and neck cancer cigarette smoking, tobacco chewing, and high alcohol intake are considered major risk factors, especially in combination. Also strongly implicated are poor oral hygiene, prolonged focal dental irritation, betel nut chewing, and certain occupational exposures (such as wood-dust inhalation). In addition, heredity may influence certain cancers in that Oriental men show increased incidence of nasopharyngeal carcinoma. What's more, radiation received years before for noncancerous conditions of the head, neck, and upper chest has been linked to thyroid tumors.

The role of trauma in head and neck cancer has not been established, and no known environmental carcinogen has thus far been linked to CNS tumors. Childhood tumors are believed to be developmental or hereditary. For instance, neurofibromatosis (von Recklinghausen's disease) is associated with schwannomas and rare sarcomas of cranial nerves and spinal nerve roots. And tuberous sclerosis (Bourneville's disease) is associated with certain CNS tumors.

PATHOPHYSIOLOGY
Clinical behavior of head, neck, and CNS tumors depends on their location and tissue type. Staging tumor growth and establishing histologic grade are the chief means of determining treatment and prognosis.

CNS tumors: Largely intracranial
About 80% of CNS tumors occur intracranially and 20% occur within the spinal canal. Of the intracranial lesions, about 60% are primary and the remaining 40% are metastatic lesions, often multiple and most commonly from the lung, breast, kidney, and GI tract.

CNS tumors still carry a high mortality, despite advances in treatment with surgery and radiation. Brain tumors strike young and old alike, with peak incidence at ages 5 to 10 and ages 50 to 55. They are second only to leukemia as a cause of death in children.

Virtually every cell type within the CNS may give rise to a neoplasm. However, tumors commonly develop from the neurons themselves. Glial, or support, cells give rise to gliomas, and meningeal cells give rise to meningiomas. Gliomas alone comprise 40% to 50% of primary brain tumors. Less frequently, they occur within the spinal canal where they're predominantly benign.

Any CNS tumor, even well differentiated and histologically benign, is potentially dangerous due to numerous factors, such as the lethal effects of increased intracranial pressure and tumor location near critical structures. For example, a small, well-differentiated lesion in the pons or medulla may be more rapidly fatal than a massive liver cancer.

Primary CNS tumors rarely metastasize outside the CNS, since no lymphatic network drains this system. Also, hematogenous spread is unlikely. In almost all cases, CNS spread is contained in the cerebrospinal axis, involving local invasion or CNS seeding through the subarachnoid space and the ventricles.

Brain. Malignant brain tumors can destroy functional tissue or cause pressure effects since little room for tissue growth exists within the cranial vault. Pressure effects of brain tumors, even benign ones, generally involve structure displacement and ventricular obstruction resulting in hydrocephalus. However, the most dreaded pressure effect is brain herniation.

The most common symptom of brain tumor is headache, usually deep, dull, and worse in the morning due to differences in CNS drainage in the supine and prone positions. The second most common symptom is seizure, a generalized tonic-clonic seizure or a focal jacksonian seizure. Focal neurologic symptoms usually mean a well-developed mass. Next come personality changes. Motor dysfunction, sensory loss, and speech, smell, vision, or hearing deficits may occur depending on tumor location.

Generalized signs and symptoms reflect increased intracranial pressure—the early consequence of a rapidly expanding mass—or impaired cerebrospinal fluid flow or reabsorption. Sudden increases in tumor volume by intralesional hemorrhages or extensive perineoplastic edema may also provoke rapid and severe increase in intracranial pressure. Its symptoms include headache; nausea and vomiting; depressed level of consciousness with lethargy, drowsiness, and irritability; seizures; and papilledema.

The CNS can better accommodate a slowly expanding mass, such as a meningioma. This tumor can become quite large without much change in intracranial pressure.

Spinal cord. Tumors of the spinal cord cause cord compression, since the bony vertebral canal allows little room for displacement. As with brain tumors, a small mass (1 to 10 g) may cause extensive dysfunction.

Cord tumors are classified by anatomic location (see *Spinal cord tumors*). They favor the thoracic segment, most likely because of its length, the thoracic spine's proximity to the mediastinum, and its attractiveness to direct metastatic extension from lymph nodes involved with lymphoma, breast, or lung cancer. The level of spinal involvement and the lesion's size and extent determine spinal cord tumor symptoms. Cord compression most often produces pain. An intramedullary, intradural tumor may produce deep, severe pain and, depending on the tracts involved, a radiating pain. An extramedullary intradural tumor, such as a neurofibroma, may be restricted to one nerve route, producing radicular pain confined to that particular root distribution.

Motor and sensory losses commonly develop later and affect areas distal to the lesion. When bowel and bladder dysfunction appears, cord compression may already be irreversible.

Histopathology crucial to treatment
Histopathology surpasses anatomic staging in predicting the clinical behavior of tumors and in determining treatment and prognosis. Growth rate correlates with histologic grade

for all tumor types—intrinsic, extrinsic, and metastatic. High-grade (Grade 4) tumors are poorly differentiated, grow rapidly, and create more edema. Low-grade (Grade 1) tumors are well differentiated and grow more slowly. Heterogeneous tumors are commonly graded according to the least differentiated tissue present, usually permitting prediction of the tumor's clinical course.

Intrinsic tumors. Gliomas are intrinsic tumors histologically classified according to their prominent cell type—most commonly, astrocytes, oligodendrocytes, and ependymal cells. Most intracranial tumors are gliomas; about 75% of these are astrocytomas. Malignant astrocytomas range from well differentiated to poorly differentiated and highly anaplastic. Anaplastic astrocytomas carry a poor prognosis since their rapid tumor growth causes death within months to a few years. Unfortunately, the highly malignant Grade 4 astrocytoma (glioblastoma multiforme) is the most common brain tumor. It is highly vascular, often produces edema in surrounding normal tissue, and may be multifocal in origin. Seldom circumscribed, it usually infiltrates widely and may cross the midline by way of the corpus callosum.

Oligodendrogliomas arise predominantly in the cerebral hemisphere; rarely in the diencephalon and cerebellum. These tumors may be well circumscribed and grow slowly so their symptoms may span a period of years.

Ependymomas arise from cells lining the ventricular surfaces and the spinal cord's central canal. They represent only 5% of all intracranial gliomas but 63% of intraspinal gliomas. Though well differentiated and of low-grade malignancy, they can be fatal when they obstruct the cerebrospinal fluid pathway.

Medulloblastomas, also intrinsic tumors, are classified by some as tumors of primitive undifferentiated cells and by others as primitive neuronal tumors. These embryonal tumors occur most commonly in the first decade of life. They are almost exclusively tumors of the vermis of the cerebellum in childhood and comprise about 1.5% of all brain tumors. They are rapidly growing, infiltrative neoplasms, and they tend to disseminate throughout the subarachnoid space and to seed meningeal foci.

Extrinsic tumors. Meningiomas are extrinsic tumors that arise in the connective tissue layers (meninges) covering the CNS. These encapsulated, superficially situated tumors grow slowly, do not usually invade neural pa-

Spinal cord tumors

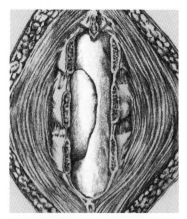 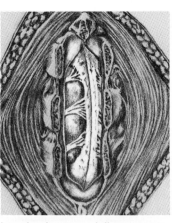 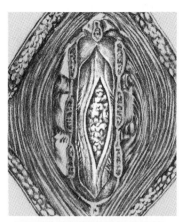

Extradural tumors, usually secondary metastatic tumors, arise in the vertebrae, extradural space, or paraspinal area. They compress but do not invade the spinal cord.

Intradural extramedullary tumors arise idiopathically in the nerve roots or meninges. These superficially situated tumors compress but do not invade the spinal cord.

Intradural intramedullary tumors arise idiopathically within the spinal cord. They invade and destroy motor and sensory tracts and central gray structures.

renchyma, and are usually amenable to excision depending on the location and accessibility for surgery. Most common in the fifth decade of life, meningiomas comprise about 16% of all brain tumors but are the second most common spinal cord tumor after metastatic disease. Compared with gliomas, they are relatively benign and highly curable.

Metastatic tumors. The most common type in the spinal cord, metastatic tumors derive their histologic classification from the primary tumor (spinal cord, lung, breast, melanoma). Most metastatic masses originate as circulating tumor emboli, yet some may directly extend into CNS structures from adjacent sites. They're sharply circumscribed, highly invasive, destructive growths.

Head and neck tumors: Primarily laryngeal

More than 80% of head and neck cancers are squamous cell carcinomas arising from the mucosal epithelium. Most of these tumors present as malignant surface mucosa ulcerations with raised, indurated edges and underlying infiltration. These infiltrative growths are more aggressive and difficult to control than less common fungating, elevated growths. They spread predominantly by local extension to adjacent muscles and periosteum. Bone and cartilage act as initial barriers to spread, and their involvement usually occurs late.

Head and neck cancers commonly disseminate through lymphatic channels. Nodal involvement tends to follow normal lymphatic drainage, although skips and random involve-

ment may occur. Hematogenous dissemination is uncommon and appears late. Metastasis most commonly occurs to the lungs (about 52% of first recognized sites) but may spread to the bone and other sites.

Oral cavity. Tumors of the oral cavity may appear on the lips, floor of the mouth, anterior two-thirds of the tongue, buccal mucosa, upper or lower gingiva, upper or lower alveolar ridge, or hard palate. The lip is the most common site, followed closely by the tongue. Early premalignant changes in the mucous membrane are generally asymptomatic and typically first noticed by the patient's doctor or dentist. Leukoplakia (white patches or speckled red and white patches on nonkeratinizing surfaces) has been overemphasized; only about 5% become malignant over a 20-year period. Erythroplasia (red plaques or well-defined red patches with a velvety consistency) has been underemphasized; 80% to 90% of these lesions are severe epithelial dysplasia, carcinoma in situ, or invasive carcinoma. However, most oral-cavity carcinomas first appear as chronic, nonhealing, painless ulcers. Localized pain, a late symptom, can indicate deep invasion or perineural or bone involvement.

Tumor spread depends on location. Direct tumor extension to adjacent structures is possible. For example, carcinoma of the lip may spread to the orbicularis oris muscle, and alveolar ridge carcinoma may spread to the bone. With the exception of glottic cancers, oral cancers have the lowest incidence of cervical metastasis of all head and neck cancers. In about 15% to 20% of patients, hematogenous metastasis occurs, most typically with poorly differentiated, locally advanced tumors involving cervical lymph nodes.

Oropharynx. Oropharyngeal tumors may appear on the base of the tongue, tonsillar region, soft palate, or lateral or posterior pharyngeal walls. Such tumors are common head and neck cancers; tonsillar malignancy is most common.

Two factors render prognosis poor for oropharyngeal cancer. First, the oropharynx occupies a central anatomic region tightly packed with vital structures, rendering it relatively inaccessible to surgery. Second, cancers in this region, particularly those at the base of the tongue, may escape clinical detection until far advanced. The most common symptoms include sore throat or pain on swallowing and referred otalgia. By the time dyspnea, dysphagia, hoarseness, or dysarthria appear, the disease is advanced.

Again, spread pattern depends on tumor site, and widespread regional infiltration is common. Occasionally, wall carcinomas may spread laterally and directly into the neck around the carotid sheath, disrupting arterial integrity. Oropharyngeal carcinoma has a high incidence of cervical node involvement, often to surgically inaccessible nodes. Bilateral nodal involvement is not uncommon. Hematogenous metastasis occurs with advanced primary disease or massive or bilateral cervical node deposits. The lung is the most commonly affected site.

Larynx. Laryngeal carcinomas are the most common head and neck tumors. About 90% are squamous cell in origin; leukoplakia or other premalignant epithelial changes may appear. Laryngeal disease progression patterns depend on the tumor's location. (See *Regional classification of laryngeal tumors.*)

Salivary glands. Salivary tissue tumors arise

Regional classification of laryngeal tumors

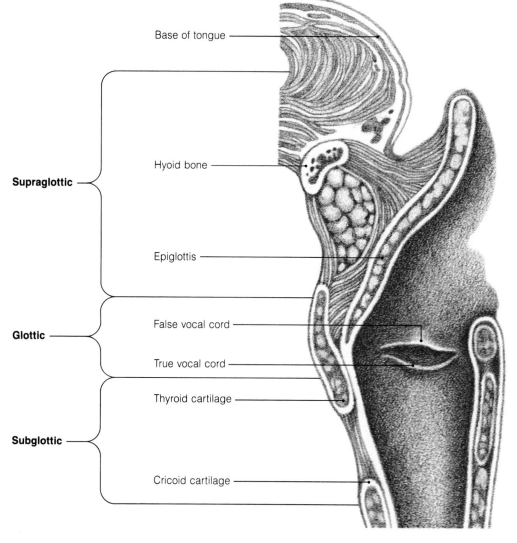

Base of tongue

Supraglottic

Hyoid bone

Epiglottis

Glottic

False vocal cord

True vocal cord

Thyroid cartilage

Subglottic

Cricoid cartilage

Laryngeal cancer is classified according to its location.

Glottic carcinoma occurs in up to 65% of patients with laryngeal cancer. Lesions are well or moderately well differentiated and usually arise in the anterior portion of the vocal cord. The sparse lymphatic network makes cervical node metastasis rare. Because even small lesions produce symptoms, such as hoarseness, they're usually detected early and prognosis is good. However, tumor invasion of underlying muscles impairs cord mobility and worsens prognosis. Further extension favors a supraglottic rather than subglottic route.

Supraglottic carcinoma occurs in up to 35% of patients with laryngeal cancer. Lesions are less well differentiated and produce symptoms later in the disease's course. A mild pain on swallowing is usually the first symptom; hoarseness occurs with an extensive tumor.

The richer lymphatic network in this area may result in lymph node metastasis. Prognosis depends on cervical node involvement.

Subglottic carcinoma is rare, occurring in less than 5% of patients with laryngeal cancer. Lymph node metastasis occurs in about 30% of extensive lesions and in about 2% of localized lesions.

most commonly in the parotid gland, less commonly in the submandibular gland, and rarely in the sublingual or numerous minor salivary glands. The parotid accounts for about 80% of salivary gland tumors in adults; of these, two thirds are benign. Local pain or tenderness and rapid growth indicate malignancy. Malignant tumors are marked by their histologic diversity, including adenocarcinomas and squamous cell carcinomas. They vary in site of origin and have an unpredictable course, characterized by stubborn chronicity and multiple recurrences.

Malignant tumors commonly invade the surrounding tissues including nerves, bone, and skin, causing pain and facial paralysis. Although characterized by direct extension and infiltration, malignant neoplasms may also metastasize locally to cervical nodes or distantly to the lungs. Recurrences 10 to 15 years after treatment are not uncommon.

Thyroid gland. Most thyroid malignancies are glandular-epithelial in origin and are characterized by slow growth, delayed symptoms, and low morbidity and mortality. A solitary thyroid nodule is the typical presenting sign.

Histologic classification includes four main types. *Papillary carcinoma,* the most common form, usually affects women under age 40. The tumor remains localized for years, frequently metastasizes to cervical lymph nodes, but rarely spreads hematogenously. Later, however, this type of carcinoma becomes more aggressive and metastasizes widely.

Follicular carcinoma, the second most common thyroid malignancy, also grows slowly but has a greater tendency to invade blood vessels and metastasize distantly to bone and lung. It shows a lesser tendency for lymphatic spread to local nodes. This tumor can also spread locally and adhere to surrounding structures including the trachea, muscles, skin, and great vessels of the neck; it often traps the recurrent laryngeal nerves, leading to hoarseness and cough.

Medullary carcinoma accounts for about 5% to 10% of all thyroid malignancies. The tumor grows slowly but metastasizes to regional lymph nodes. Distant metastasis is not unusual and most commonly causes death. Sporadic and familial forms of this neoplasm occur as part of a multiple endocrine neoplasia syndrome characterized by tumors in several endocrine glands (adrenal medulla, parathyroid). The parafollicular or C cells that produce this tumor produce excess calcitonin

and, less commonly, adrenocorticotropic hormone, prostaglandins, and serotonin.

Anaplastic carcinoma, a highly malignant and aggressive thyroid tumor, grows rapidly and produces severe local symptoms. It invades lymphatic and blood vessels early and may be fatal within 1 to 2 years.

MEDICAL MANAGEMENT
The patient with suspected head, neck or CNS cancer requires thorough evaluation to verify and localize disease, identify appropriate treatment, determine prognosis, and rule out other cancer. Such evaluation must include a detailed medical and social history emphasizing symptoms and predisposing factors, a physical and neurologic examination, and diagnostic tests.

Diagnostic tests locate and type tumors
The patient with suspected head or neck cancer will undergo various tests to locate and stage the tumor and to direct treatment.

Blood work. A complete blood count helps assess overall health. It's typically normal in the otherwise healthy patient with a primary brain tumor, but polycythemia may accompany cerebellar hemangioblastoma. Renal and liver function tests help detect metastasis and evaluate the patient's ability to metabolize or excrete chemotherapeutic drugs to avert toxicity.

Thyroid tests, primarily thyroxine (T_4) and thyroid-stimulating hormone (TSH) tests, gauge thyroid function. (They are usually normal with a primary thyroid tumor but may be abnormal after treatment.) Elevated serum calcitonin levels suggest medullary thyroid carcinoma. Abnormal levels of alkaline phosphatase may indicate metastasis to the liver or bone. The presence of serum antibodies to Epstein-Barr viral capsid antigen suggests nasopharyngeal cancer.

Radiographic tests. X-ray studies help localize the tumor. Plain films of the skull, base of the skull, sinuses, and a lateral soft-tissue view of the neck are routine in suspected head and neck cancers.

Skull X-ray may show bone erosion secondary to tumor, abnormal vascular channels, tumor calcification, pineal gland position if calcified, and evidence of increased intracranial pressure. *Mandible X-ray* may help detect bone erosion or mental nerve foramen enlargement, indicating perineural invasion.

Spinal X-ray may determine tumor site and extension. *Chest X-ray* can detect primary tumor or metastasis to the lung. *Barium swallow* may help evaluate some head and neck tumors; *laryngogram,* laryngeal and hypopharyngeal tumors.

Cerebral angiography precisely delineates a brain tumor, its relationship to surrounding blood vessels, and its intrinsic vasculature, thus helping to plan resection. *Pneumoencephalography* and *ventriculography* can detect midline tumors, such as pituitary and posterior fossa tumors. *Myelography* confirms spinal cord tumor and reveals the tumor's relationship to the spinal cord and dura.

Nuclear imaging. *Computerized tomography* (CT) of the brain has become the preferred screening procedure for diagnosing and localizing brain tumors. CT scan visualized directly or following I.V. contrast material infusion shows tumor displacement of tissue and the degree of cerebral edema, ventricular blockage, and hydrocephalus. CT scan with gas or radioopaque contrast injection into the subarachnoid space of the cerebral ventricles can detect spinal cord and paraspinal tumors, including those of the nasopharynx, oropharynx, and paranasal sinus, and can evaluate and stage laryngeal tumors.

Brain scans with radioisotope injection help clarify CT scan findings but may not detect benign and low-grade malignant tumors because of poor radioisotope uptake.

Thyroid scans evaluate solitary thyroid nodules. A hypofunctioning (cold) nodule may be malignant but a hot nodule usually isn't. *Bone scans* may show bone metastasis.

Magnetic resonance imaging can differentiate normal from diseased tissue with greater sensitivity than CT scan. *Xenon cerebral blood flow studies* demonstrate abnormal perfusion patterns correlating to tumors located on a CT scan.

Other essential tests. *Lumbar puncture* permits cerebrospinal fluid analysis for tumor cells, elevated protein levels (indicating cerebrospinal fluid block), and decreased glucose levels, suggesting highly malignant CNS tumors or meningeal metastasis. *Lumbar puncture is contraindicated with increased intracranial pressure because of the danger of precipitating brain herniation by lowering intraspinal pressure.*

Direct *laryngoscopy,* essential in suspected laryngeal tumor, helps distinguish tumor from edema or radiation reaction.

Biopsy and histologic examination can confirm tumor and help plan treatment. Tissue diagnosis of CNS tumors is appropriate when-ever anatomically feasible and essential when no evidence of a primary lesion appears elsewhere.

Staging and grading: Determining prognosis

The classification of the initial tumor's extent (T classification) varies for each region of primary head and neck cancers. (See *Staging cancer: The head, neck, and brain.*)

Prognosis depends on the tumor location, type, and, especially, histologic grade (G classification). Grading extends from G_1 (well differentiated) and G_2 (moderately well differentiated) to G_3 (poorly differentiated) and G_4 (extremely poorly differentiated). Generally, the better the differentiation of the tumor, the better the anticipated response to treatment and overall prognosis.

Treatment: The hopes and goals

The twin goals of treatment are eradication of tumor and maintenance of optimal physiologic function. Attempts to achieve these goals, however, must follow realistic assessment of the disease and of the patient's age, general health, nutritional status, and emotional stability. Limitations of life-style and evidence of alcohol or tobacco abuse may influence treatment decisions. For instance, lack of transportation may make daily radiation sessions impractical, or the high probability of complications related to alcohol intake may make radiation undesirable. Any treatment decision must also take into account available support systems and the potential for treatment-associated morbidity.

Surgery when possible. Tradition favors resection of most accessible malignancies as initial treatment and as a backup when radiation fails. Small malignancies of the head, neck, and CNS are excised when confined to the site of origin. Deeply invasive tumors and tumors extending into bone or lying adjacent to bone also yield well to surgery. Large primary lesions and extensive lymph node disease typically require surgery to remove the bulk of the disease, with follow-up radiation to destroy peripheral cancer cells.

Excision of a primary head or neck tumor usually involves radical or modified neck dissection to prevent tumor extension and cervical node metastasis. Dissection removes all nonvital neck structures and the cervical lymph nodes on the tumor side and may be followed by radiation.

Follow-up radiation is essential, especially

STAGING CANCER

The head, neck, and brain

Brain
Primary tumor (T)
T_0 No evidence of tumor

Supratentorial tumor
T_1 A tumor 5 cm or less in diameter confined to one side
T_2 A tumor over 5 cm in diameter confined to one side
T_3 A tumor 5 cm or less in diameter that involves the ventricular system
T_4 A tumor that crosses the midline, invades the opposite hemisphere, or extends infratentorially

Infratentorial tumor
T_1 A tumor 3 cm or less in diameter confined to one side
T_2 A tumor over 3 cm in diameter confined to one side
T_3 A tumor 3 cm or less in diameter that involves the ventricular system
T_4 A tumor that crosses the midline, invades the opposite hemisphere, or extends supratentorially

Nodal involvement (N)
Does not apply to this site

Distant metastasis (M)
M_0 No evidence of metastasis
M_1 Distant metastasis

Oral cavity
Primary tumor (T)
T_0 No evidence of tumor
Tis Carcinoma in situ
T_1 A tumor 2 cm or less in diameter
T_2 A tumor 2 to 4 cm in diameter
T_3 A tumor over 4 cm in diameter
T_4 A tumor over 4 cm in diameter that involves the antrum, pterygoid muscles, base of tongue, and skin of neck

Nodal involvement (N)
N_0 No positive node

N_1 A positive homolateral node 3 cm or less in diameter
N_2 A positive homolateral node 3 to 6 cm in diameter; or multiple, positive homolateral nodes, none over 6 cm in diameter
N_3 Massive homolateral, bilateral or contralateral nodes

Distant metastasis (M)
M_0 No evidence of metastasis
M_1 Distant metastasis

Oropharynx
Primary tumor (T)
T_0 No evidence of tumor
Tis Carcinoma in situ
T_1 A tumor 2 cm or less in diameter
T_2 A tumor 2 to 4 cm in diameter
T_3 A tumor over 4 cm in diameter
T_4 A tumor over 4 cm in diameter that involves bone, soft tissues of neck, or root of tongue

Nodal involvement (N)
N_0 No positive node
N_1 A positive homolateral node 3 cm or less in diameter
N_2 A positive homolateral node 3 to 6 cm in diameter; or multiple, positive homolateral nodes, none over 6 cm in diameter
N_3 Massive homolateral, bilateral, or contralateral nodes

Distant metastasis (M)
M_0 No evidence of metastasis
M_1 Distant metastasis

Larynx
Primary tumor (T)
T_0 No evidence of tumor

Supraglottic tumor
Tis Carcinoma in situ
T_1 A tumor confined to region of origin with

normal mobility
T_2 A tumor that involves adjacent supraglottis or glottis without fixation
T_3 A tumor confined to the larynx with fixation or that involves the post-cricoid area, medial wall of piriform sinus, or preepiglottic space
T_4 A tumor that extends beyond the larynx to the oropharynx, soft tissues of neck, or thyroid cartilage

Glottic tumor
Tis Carcinoma in situ
T_1 A tumor confined to the vocal cords with normal mobility (includes involvement of anterior or posterior commissures)
T_2 A tumor that involves the supraglottis or subglottis with normal or impaired cord mobility, or both
T_3 A tumor confined to the larynx with cord fixation
T_4 A tumor with thyroid cartilage destruction or extension beyond the larynx, or both

Subglottic tumor
Tis Carcinoma in situ
T_1 A tumor confined to the subglottis
T_2 A tumor that involves vocal cords with normal or impaired cord mobility
T_3 A tumor confined to larynx with cord fixation
T_4 A tumor with cartilage destruction or extension beyond the larynx, or both

Nodal involvement (N)
N_0 No positive node
N_1 A positive homolateral node 3 cm or less in diameter
N_2 A positive homolateral node 3 to 6 cm in diameter; or multiple, positive homolateral nodes, none over 6 cm in diameter
N_3 Massive homolateral, bilateral, or contralateral

nodes

Distant metastasis (M)
M_0 No evidence of metastasis
M_1 Distant metastasis

Salivary glands
Primary tumor (T)
T_0 No evidence of tumor
T_1 A tumor 2 cm or less in diameter without significant local extension (skin, soft tissues, bone, or lingual or facial nerves)
T_2 A tumor 2 to 4 cm in diameter without significant local extension
T_3 A tumor 4 to 6 cm in diameter without significant local extension
T_{4a} A tumor over 6 cm in diameter without significant local extension
T_{4b} A tumor of any size with significant local extension

Nodal involvement (N)
N_0 No regional lymph node involvement
N_1 Regional lymph node involvement

Distant metastasis (M)
M_0 No evidence of metastasis
M_1 Distant metastasis

Thyroid
Primary tumor (T)
T_0 No evidence of tumor
Tis Carcinoma in situ
T_1 A tumor 3 cm or less in diameter
T_2 A tumor over 3 cm in diameter
T_3 A tumor with multiple intraglandular foci
T_4 A tumor with fixation and extension through the thyroid capsule

Nodal involvement (N)
N_0 No positive nodes
N_1 Positive nodes

Distant metastasis (M)
M_0 No distant metastasis
M_1 Distant metastasis

---

after wide resection. Modern reconstructive techniques include newer prostheses and myocutaneous flaps (pectoralis major, trapezius, and latissimus dorsi). These techniques allow for better physiologic and cosmetic reconstruction after ablative head and neck surgery. (See *Restoring form and function after head*

and neck surgery, page 121.)

Total laryngectomy is favored for deeply infiltrative laryngeal tumors with cord paralysis, since these tumors aren't radiotherapy curable, and for tumors unresponsive to radiotherapy. Combined with laryngoplasty to connect the pharynx and trachea (Serafini procedure), laryngectomy preserves normal speech and respiration and eliminates permanent tracheostomas in glottic tumors of both vocal cords. Conservative surgery, such as hemilaryngectomy, or radiation therapy can cure early laryngeal cancer (T_1, T_2, or early T_3 lesions).

Surgical excision is the treatment of choice for all salivary gland tumors. An attempt is made to spare the facial nerve in parotid gland lesions. In low-grade malignancies, neck dissection is reserved for patients with palpable nodes. High-grade malignancies permit elective neck dissection, depending on the extent of disease. All high-grade malignancies require radiation following surgery.

Surgery is the more common therapy for thyroid cancer, with procedures varying according to histologic type and disease extent.

Surgical excision is also the mainstay in managing CNS tumors, limited by tumor location and invasiveness. Surgery establishes the diagnosis and improves neurologic symptoms by reducing tumor bulk and decreasing intracranial pressure; in some cases, it may be curative. However, metastatic brain lesions are treated with radiation and drugs and are rarely excised. In patients with spinal tumors, decompressive laminectomy may relieve cord compression.

Laser surgery, which eradicates tumors by vaporizing them, now offers a cure for early head and neck cancers and palliative treatment for advanced cancers. With CT scan to direct the beam, it's being used to treat certain brain tumors, such as deep or highly vascular tumors or tumors adjacent to large blood vessels. This technique decreases hemorrhagic risk because it coagulates small vessels, causes less edema, and limits destruction of adjacent cells.

Ultrasonic aspiration is another new treatment for brain tumors. Ultrasonic wave vibration breaks the tumor into small pieces, and aspiration removes it. Like laser treatment, this may permit removal of some brain tumors inaccessible to surgery.

Radiation an option. Radiation therapy is the most common alternate treatment for head, neck, and CNS tumors. It's usually successful with small head and neck malignancies confined to the site of origin or with nodal metastasis of 2 cm or less. In these tumors, the field must cover an area comparable to wide-field surgical excision, including regional nodes draining the tumor. The curative radiation dose approaches the maximum

dose tolerated by the normal tissues near the tumor, except for extremely small lesions. Surgically inaccessible sites, such as the nasopharynx, are always irradiated.

When radiation and surgery promise equal effect, radiation is better used with high-grade tumors. Large primary tumors and extensive lymph node disease usually require postoperative radiotherapy to destroy malignant cells undetected in the surgical bed. X-ray therapy also follows radical neck dissection to avert recurrence when three or more lymph nodes show cancer. If the cancer is far advanced at the primary site and considered unresectable, radiation alone or combined with chemotherapy may preserve life and voice.

External beam radiation is probably indicated as adjuvant therapy after surgery for undifferentiated thyroid cancers that resist radioisotope uptake. Radiation after surgery in CNS tumors generally prolongs survival and may allay symptoms when tumors recur. Metastatic brain lesions are traditionally treated with radiation and corticosteroids.

Some authorities now advocate radiation therapy with corticosteroids as the treatment choice in spinal cord compression from extradural metastatic disease. They believe that most patients might be spared the discomforts and morbidity of decompressive laminectomy without compromising results. Radiation may also be used when brain tumors are centrally located and surgery aggravates the problem or when the tumor involves vital structures, making surgery hazardous.

Traditional radiation therapy, with X-rays and gamma rays, presents a major problem in treating brain tumor. The brain tumor core is hypoxic; its cells are not actively dividing; therefore, they are not sensitive to radiation. After radiation therapy, these surviving cells can receive oxygen and begin dividing, causing tumor regrowth. New treatments now undergoing research may overcome this problem. Hypoxic cell radiosensitizers include a new class of drugs, the nitroimidazoles. Another available treatment is fast neuron radiation, which depends less on oxygenated cells to cause damage; however, this type of radiation produces far more damage to normal tissues than traditional radiation.

Interstitial radiation (brachytherapy) is another new treatment for brain tumors that implants a radiation source directly into the tumor, thereby minimizing damage to normal tissue.

Chemotherapy not yet proved. Chemothera-

Restoring form and function after head and neck surgery

Successful restoration of appearance and function depends on the patient's physical condition and psychological makeup. After treatment, many patients fail to return to work, becoming socially isolated and experiencing feelings of shame, worthlessness, and dejection, even when they've been fitted with prostheses. These patients require psychological support throughout treatment and rehabilitation.

Site and defect	Disabilities	Rehabilitation
Face Orbital exenterations; excision of all or a part of the nose, ear, or cheek; or oral and facial defects combined	Severe disfigurement	Surgical reconstruction is limited by lack of available tissue, damage to the vascular bed, the need for periodic inspection of the defect, and the patient's physical condition. Prosthodontic restoration is limited by inadequate materials, movable tissue beds, difficulty in retaining large prostheses, and the patient's resistance to accepting the result.
Maxilla Partial or total resection of hard or soft palate due to tumors that arise from the paranasal sinus, palatal epithelium, or minor salivary glands in the submucosa	Unintelligible speech, difficult mastication, awkward swallowing, dessicated nasal membranes, collection of nasal and sinus secretions in defect area, facial disfigurement	A temporary prosthesis placed soon after surgery and relined periodically during healing compensates for tissue changes. After healing (usually 3 to 4 months), a definitive prosthesis restores the physical separation between oral and nasal cavities. This restores normal speech and swallowing and provides support for the lip and cheek.
Mandible Resection of the mandible and large portions of the tongue, floor of the mouth, and regional lymphatics due to squamous cell carcinomas that arise from the lateral margins of the tongue and the floor of the mouth. This predisposes the mandible to tumor invasion.	Impaired speech, difficult swallowing, mandibular deviation during functional movements (usually impossible to restore), poor control of salivary secretions, severe disfigurement	Prosthetic prognosis varies. In some patients, only appearance can be improved; in others, improved mastication is possible. Since most patients do not depend on their prostheses for oral function, some prefer not to wear a removable prosthesis if the resection doesn't involve anterior teeth.

py's place in treating head, neck, and CNS cancer remains under clinical investigation. Whether it can improve local control and eradicate metastatic foci has yet to be proved. Its effectiveness has been limited by the advanced stage and poor nutrition of most patients referred for chemotherapy. Using it at an earlier stage as an adjuvant to surgery or radiation may improve survival.

The most active chemotherapeutic agents for treating head and neck cancers include methotrexate, vincristine, bleomycin, and cisplatin. Complete response to a single drug is rare; partial response lasts for an average of 3 months.

Multiple drug regimens achieve higher response rates—50% to 95%—than single agents, although complete remission occurs in fewer than 30% of patients. Remission usually lasts only 6 months or less, but a few patients achieve control beyond 1 year. Previously treated patients have a lower response rate than untreated patients.

Intraarterial infusion of chemotherapeutic agents may be used to treat advanced disease. For example, doxorubicin (Adriamycin) by this route proves most useful in metastatic thyroid cancer unresponsive to other therapy.

Antineoplastic drugs commonly enhance results of surgery and radiation in CNS disease. Effective agents include the nitrosoureas (such as carmustine [BCNU]), which are lipid-soluble and therefore cross the blood-brain barrier (although the tumor itself may disturb the normal blood-brain barrier); procarbazine; etoposide; vincristine; and cisplatin. These drugs have been used singly and in combinations with encouraging results. However, the nitrosoureas have cumulative toxic effects; these effects may require dosage reduction, which may be associated with tumor relapse. A new technique that involves giving mannitol before chemotherapy to alter the blood-brain barrier and permit reduced drug dosage may overcome this problem with toxic effects.

Other drugs prescribed for head, neck, and CNS cancer include *corticosteroids* (usually dexamethasone) to reduce edema surrounding the tumor and thus help control intracranial pressure; whether corticosteroids also have an antitumor effect has not yet been established. *Anticonvulsants* may also be necessary with CNS disease. Another option involves prophylaxis. For example, *radioactive iodine* may be useful in treating metastatic thyroid lesions capable of concentrating sufficient isotope—chiefly follicular carcinoma and mixed papillary-follicular carcinoma, but not undifferentiated carcinoma, which fails to take up the isotope. Before this treatment, surgery removes all normally functioning thyroid tissue, if possible, to boost pituitary production of endogenous TSH. This induces tumor affinity for the radioactive iodine by using the endogenous TSH stimulus that develops after ablation of functioning thyroid tissue.

Complications of treatment or disease
Hypothyroidism may result from thyroid resection; external beam radiation to the gland; or therapeutic doses of radioactive iodine, which cause glandular degeneration, perivascular fibrosis, and damage to the fine thyroid vasculature. Replacement therapy is needed for clinical hypothyroidism and for asymptomatic elevation of TSH. TSH levels must be controlled by daily exogenous thyroid medication to minimize TSH's stimulating effect on the growth of an incompletely resected tumor.

CNS infections can follow surgery or can develop later, with symptoms mimicking tumor progression or recurrence. Fever and rapidly progressive neurologic symptoms indicate an infection and require bacterial and fungal cultures.

Early delayed radiation encephalopathy may stem from temporary demyelination and resolves spontaneously. Symptoms of anorexia, somnolence, lethargy, and headache occur 2 to 6 weeks after therapy and usually last about 6 weeks. *Late delayed radiation encephalopathy* stems from brain necrosis and small vessel occlusion. Its symptoms can mimic disease advancement and may include intracranial hypertension and focal neurologic dysfunction, both irreversible and potentially fatal complications.

Corticosteroid therapy predisposes the patient to *cushingoid symptoms* and GI ulceration. Concomitant administration of antacids and cimetidine can minimize the risk of GI bleeding.

Immediate postoperative complications are rare but may include *wound infection, fistula formation, skin flap sloughing* (especially at trifurcation points), *exposure and rupture of the carotid artery, aspiration* (when the trachea remains connected to the esophagus), *peptic ulceration and gastritis with hematemesis,* and *pulmonary embolism.*

Local complications are more common if the patient receives preoperative radiation; in these patients, surgical techniques, especially skin incision, need modification. Delayed surgical problems include physiologic dysfunctions of deglutition and speech and tracheitis sicca after laryngectomy. Shoulder disability and chronic neck pain may follow radical neck dissection.

Radiation complications include *dryness of the mouth* (xerostomia), which is universal in patients receiving more than 5,000 rads to major salivary glands. Bothersome at first, it tends to diminish after 1 to 2 years. Loss of the sense of taste is also universal, but this sense usually returns within 1 year. Dental caries can be severe but is preventable with comprehensive dental care.

NURSING MANAGEMENT
Optimal nursing care of the patient with head, neck, or CNS cancer centers on recognizing and managing the complications of treatment (see *Nursing care after head, neck, and brain surgery,* page 124), teaching the patient to cope with physical and neurologic deficits, and providing information and emotional support for the patient and his family.

Assessment first
Assess the patient and include the family in the assessment if possible. Family members may add vital information the patient has omitted because he has forgotten, is too anxious or depressed to articulate, or is mentally impaired.

After obtaining biographic information, ask about the chief complaint. Remember, however, patients with head and neck tumors may be asymptomatic in the early stages. Commonly, the tumor is detected during a routine dental examination.

If symptoms exist, find out when they started. Are they persistent or intermittent? What aggravates or relieves them? A patient with head or neck disease may have noticed a lesion or mass, sore throat, swallowing difficulty, earache, inability to chew, pain or discomfort, mouth odor, voice changes, or weight loss. Perhaps he's experienced unusual bleeding from his mouth, occurring spontaneously or after light contact.

Ask about headaches, and suspect CNS cancer if the patient describes a pain that's dull, deep, and worse in the morning. Ask about seizures, and have the patient's family describe them if possible. How often do they occur? Always suspect brain tumor when an apparently healthy middle-aged adult has a first seizure, especially a localized one. Ask about signs of increased intracranial pressure, such as vomiting, which may occur particularly with a tumor in or near the fourth ventricle. Ask if the patient's experienced speech problems or loss of smell or hearing. Has he noticed decreased visual acuity, double vision, or a visual field defect? Inquire about weakness, paresis, and sensory defects, which may occur with an intracranial lesion or a spinal cord tumor. If the patient reports back pain with these complaints, suspect a spinal cord tumor with cord compression and take immediate action. (See *Emergency management: Recognizing spinal cord compression.*)

Probe the patient's medical history. Find out if he's ever been treated for a malignancy and when. Remember that metastasis to the brain and spinal cord is common.

Has the patient ever received radiation therapy to the head or neck for a benign condition? Previous radiation therapy may result in thyroid tumor.

Thoroughly assess the patient's psychosocial and family health history. Ask the family if they've noticed a change in the patient's personality or mental functioning. Unusual irritability, forgetfulness, and sleeping more than usual may indicate a brain tumor. Has the patient ever been hospitalized or otherwise treated for a psychiatric problem that may actually have been a brain tumor syndrome? Has he avoided seeking medical care because he couldn't afford it? Does he visit the dentist regularly? Has he neglected oral hygiene because of pain or bleeding?

Find out about the patient's activities of daily living, especially use of alcohol and tobacco, that predispose to head and neck cancer. Have his symptoms interfered with daily activities? Determine his nutritional intake; malnutrition related to possible tumor growth can intensify with depression, alcoholism, pain, or anorexia.

Next, the physical examination

In CNS tumor, the physical examination and the history help pinpoint the site of tumor. (See *Brain tumors: Site-specific symptoms,* page 125.) You may carry out your mental status examination throughout your assessment to evaluate cerebral function. Is the patient alert? What is his attention span? How complete does his memory seem as you question him? What is his present mood? Is he frequently confused? Determine if he's oriented to time, place, and person, and check his judgment and insight. Does he seem to have hallucinations or seizures?

Assess motor function. Note the patient's body position and any asymmetries. Observe his gait. Is he unsteady, or does he have difficulty moving one leg?

Also evaluate the patient's muscle strength, tone, and size and his deep tendon and superficial reflexes. Deep tendon reflexes may be hyperactive with upper motor neuron involvement, but superficial reflexes disappear. Abnormalities can help pinpont tumor location. For example, muscle weakness and then paralysis commonly occurs on the side of the body opposite a tumor in the motor area of the cerebral frontal lobe. You can simultaneously evaluate cerebellar function by testing the patient's coordination and equilibrium. Unlike the cerebral hemispheres, cerebellar hemispheres control the same side of the body.

Test for asymmetry in pain, temperature, and touch sensations and for vibratory and position senses. Sensory disturbances may result from sensory cortex involvement of the parietal lobe or with a spinal cord lesion. Be sure to evaluate the cranial nerves by assessing the motor and sensory function of head and neck structures.

Evaluate the patient's speech for content, clarity, and coherence. Aphasia often occurs with lesions of the dominant cerebral hemisphere involving the frontal, parietal, or temporal lobes. The deficit may be expressive (difficulty forming words or verbalizing ideas), receptive (inability to understand written or oral expression), or a combination.

If you suspect head or neck cancer, perform a thorough oropharyngeal examination (see *Assessing the oropharynx,* page 126). Also inspect the patient's neck, looking for swelling or asymmetry related to a primary tumor mass or lymph node involvement. Does he have any open lesions with potential for further ulceration? Palpating the neck may delineate tumor extent, associated tenderness, and the tumor's proximity to vital structures.

Assess his nutritional status. Uncorrected malnutrition can interfere with treatment and impair prognosis (see Chapter 5).

Recognizing spinal cord compression

Assess all cancer patients for signs and symptoms of spinal cord compression due to a tumor. Early diagnosis and emergency treatment are mandatory to prevent or delay permanent paraplegia. Once spinal cord compression symptoms begin, paraplegia may develop in hours or days. Complete paraplegia is irreversible; however, patients with mild-to-moderate signs often maintain or regain spinal cord function.

Be alert for back pain, an early symptom of spinal cord compression from an extradural tumor, the most common spinal cord tumor. Local pain precedes radicular pain and other symptoms by weeks or months, but occasionally the tumor is painless.

Watch also for other symptoms, such as paresthesias, posterior column sensory losses, and weakness, spasticity, and hyperreflexia (indicating corticospinal tract involvement). Symptoms usually appear distally first (in the legs) and progress proximally. Bladder and bowel dysfunction are usually late signs. Document and report signs and symptoms immediately.

Prepare the patient for diagnostic tests, including spinal X-ray, CT scan, and lumbar puncture. Myelography confirms and localizes spinal cord compression. Immediate treatment includes radiation and, if ordered, chemotherapy. In some patients, laminectomy may also be performed. Administer corticosteroids, as ordered, to decrease spinal cord edema.

Nursing care after head, neck, and brain surgery

Surgery for head, neck, and brain tumors requires special preoperative and postoperative care. For all types of surgery, preoperative care involves psychological support and an accurate baseline assessment. Postoperative care involves careful monitoring for possible life-threatening complications.

To prepare the patient, reinforce the doctor's explanation of anticipated surgery, describe postoperative care measures, and be sure to answer any questions. Encourage the patient to express his concerns about possible disfigurement or loss of function.

In head and neck surgery, also suggest alternate methods of communication if a communication problem is anticipated.

In intracranial surgery, tell the patient that his head will be shaved before surgery and that he'll awaken with a large bandage on his head, temporary swelling and discoloration around his eye on the affected side, and possibly a headache. Reassure him that he'll receive pain medication as needed.

Head and neck surgery
After surgery, position the patient to facilitate drainage and promote respirations. Place him in Fowler's position when he's recovered from the anesthetic.
• Ensure adequate breathing. Observe the patient's respirations closely, and immediately report any signs of respiratory distress (such as dyspnea, cyanosis).
• Encourage deep breathing and coughing. Help the patient sit up and cough while you support the affected area with your hands. Suction gently, if needed, to prevent tension on sutures. Give endotracheal tube or tracheostomy care.
• Check vital signs frequently, and watch for signs of infection and hemorrhage. *If sudden hemorrhage occurs, immediately apply pressure over the common carotid and internal jugular vessels. Notify the doctor immediately and treat the patient for shock.* After blood vessel repair, replace lost fluid and blood as ordered. Continue to monitor vital signs until they're consistently normal.
• Check dressings for signs of hemorrhage and constriction. Reinforce pressure dressings, as needed, and maintain suction devices to promote drainage (up to 120 ml the first day after a radical neck dissection). During dressing changes, maintain aseptic technique and provide privacy.
• Administer analgesics, as ordered, while avoiding respiratory depression.
• Give frequent mouth care using normal saline solution, diluted hydrogen peroxide, an alkaline mouthwash, or sodium bicarbonate. Lavage carefully with a catheter placed between the cheek and teeth; use a power spray for inaccessible areas.
• Administer I.V. fluids and enteral or parenteral feedings, if ordered. Encourage oral fluids, when permitted, and watch for difficulty in swallowing, indicating nerve damage. After mouth surgery, serve small, frequent, bland feedings (liquid or soft), as ordered. Serve meals in a pleasant, odor-free environment.

Intracranial surgery
After surgery, position the patient on the unaffected side to avoid any pressure on the brain. To prevent increased intracranial pressure (ICP), elevate the head.
• With a supratentorial incision, elevate the head of the bed 30°, and turn the patient every 2 hours to facilitate breathing and venous return. With an infratentorial incision, keep him off his back for at least 48 hours and elevate the head of the bed 30°, as ordered.
• Observe the patient's respirations closely, and immediately report any signs of respiratory distress (dyspnea, cyanosis). Suction gently, if needed, since suctioning raises ICP. Make sure arterial blood gases are measured regularly.
• Monitor the patient's fluid and electrolyte status. To reduce the risk of increased ICP, restrict fluids to 1,500 ml every 24 hours and avoid overly rapid I.V. infusions. Be sure to withhold oral fluids since they may provoke vomiting, which could raise ICP.
• Watch for signs of diabetes insipidus (severe thirst, frequent urination, dehydration) or inappropriate antidiuretic hormone secretion (decreased urination, hunger and thirst, irritability, decreased level of consciousness, muscle weakness). Report these signs and symptoms immediately and adjust fluid balance, as ordered.
• Monitor neurologic status, (level of consciousness, pupil checks) every half hour or as ordered until the patient's condition stabilizes. Then, monitor every 2 hours. Watch for and report seizures, deteriorated level of consciousness, increased ICP (characterized by headache, vomiting, altered level of consciousness, limb weakness and paralysis, and visual disturbances or pupillary changes).
• Check the patient's dressing at least hourly and report any abnormalities. If the patient has a surgical drain, note the amount, color, and odor of drainage. Notify the doctor if bleeding is excessive, if drainage is clear or yellow (possible cerebrospinal fluid leakage), or if signs of infection appear.
• Give drugs, as ordered (usually steroids to prevent cerebral edema, anticonvulsants to prevent seizures, stool softeners to prevent increased ICP from straining during defecation, and mild analgesics to control pain).
• To prevent infection, keep the scalp clean, and clean and dress the incision site daily using sterile technique and an antiseptic, as ordered.

Tailoring the nursing diagnoses

Now, formulate the nursing diagnoses, your care plan, and appropriate nursing interventions.

Knowledge deficit related to disease treatment. Your goal is to help the patient and his family learn about the disease and therapy and thereby gain some control, to help them participate in therapy, and to attain optimal quality of remaining life and, possibly, peaceful death.

Explain the disease and its management at a level consistent with the intellectual and emotional states of the patient and his family. To ease anxiety, explain the diagnostic tests and their significance.

If surgery is scheduled, explain what will be done and why. Be sure the patient understands the risks and the functional deficits that may follow. If surgery will change his physical appearance, prepare him for this. Be sure he understands rehabilitation options.

Brain tumors: Site-specific symptoms

Brain tumors—both benign and malignant—usually produce signs and symptoms specific to their location. Recognizing these helps you identify tumor site; plan pre- and postoperative treatment; and spot life-threatening complications, such as increasing intracranial pressure and imminent brain herniation.

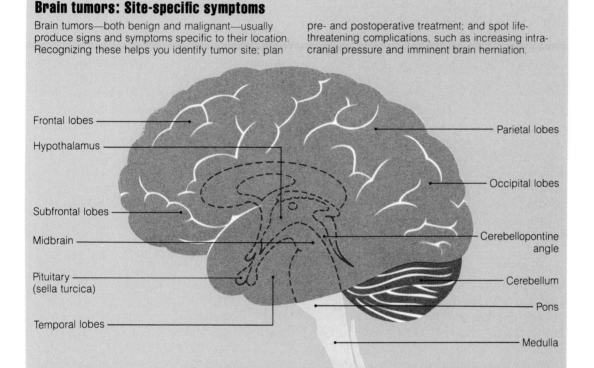

Frontal lobes
Broca's aphasia (dominant hemisphere)
Contralateral seizures
Motor weakness (on side opposite tumor)
Personality changes

Subfrontal lobes
Olfactory nerve: loss of smell

Hypothalamus
(possibly in pituitary area extending upward)
Diabetes insipidus
Loss of temperature control

Midbrain
Cranial nerve III (oculomotor) on side with tumor: ptosis; diplopia; dilated pupil; inability to gaze down, up, in

Cerebellum
Gait disturbance
Impaired balance
Incoordination

Pituitary (sella turcica)
Amenorrhea
Cushingoid symptoms
Galactorrhea
Impotence
Visual field deficits

Cerebellopontine angle
Cranial nerve VII (facial): drooping of facial muscles on same side as tumor
Cranial nerve VIII (acoustic): tinnitus, hearing loss

Occipital lobes
Visual agnosia (inability to name objects)
Visual field deficits

Medulla
Cranial nerve IX (glossopharyngeal): difficulty swallowing
Cranial nerve X (vagus): loss of gag reflex, difficulty swallowing, loss of cough reflex, hoarseness
Cranial nerve XI (spinal accessory): inability to shrug shoulders or turn head toward side of tumor
Cranial neve XII (hypoglossal): protrusion of tongue toward side of tumor

Parietal lobes
Dyslexia (left side)
Loss of position sense
Perceptual problems
Sensory disturbances (on side opposite tumor)
Visual field deficits

Pons
Cranial nerve V (trigeminal): loss of sensation in face or forehead on same side as tumor; no corneal reflex
Cranial nerve VI (abducens): inability to move eye out on same side as tumor
Cranial nerve VII (facial): drooping of facial muscles on same side as tumor

Temporal lobes
Auditory hallucinations
Impaired memory (if bilateral)
Personality changes
Psychomotor seizures
Visual field deficits
Wernicke's aphasia (dominant hemisphere)

Assessing the oropharynx

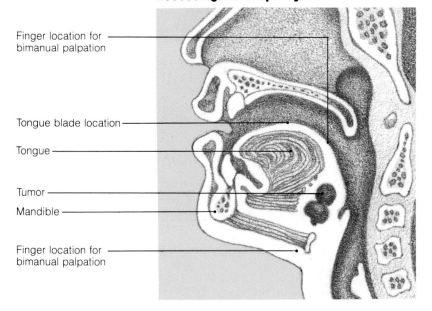

Finger location for bimanual palpation

Tongue blade location

Tongue

Tumor

Mandible

Finger location for bimanual palpation

First, *inspect* the lips, using a penlight or flashlight. Then check all surfaces for possible premalignant changes of the mucous membranes, such as white or red patches, masses, or ulcerations. Use two tongue blades, one to retract the cheek, the other to lift or push the tongue aside. Prevent gagging by applying the tongue blade only to the anterior two thirds of the tongue. When examining the floor of the mouth, always elevate the tongue and carefully inspect all areas, particularly the base of the frenulum. Check the base of the tongue, hypopharynx, nasopharynx, and larynx with a mirror or an endoscopic device. Carefully inspect the tonsils and the palate. Note any bleeding, odor, or pain.

Palpate all indurated and tender areas. Bimanual palpation, with the second hand beneath the mandible, helps assess possible tumor contours and the depth and extent of infiltration. Keep in mind that multiple primary tumors may coexist. In the anterior floor or alveolar ridge areas, check for involvement of the submandibular gland or local nodes and for fixation to the mandible.

Provide physical and psychological support before and after surgery. Have a health professional (plastic surgeon, dentist, speech therapist) speak to the patient about any question you can't answer.

If the patient's having radiation for a brain tumor, explain the procedure and prepare him to expect hair loss. If he's having radiation for head and neck cancer, prepare him for possible xerostomia (when the salivary glands lie within the radiation field) and stomatitis, and tell him how to deal with these problems (see Chapter 5). Have the patient report other adverse effects, such as nausea and vomiting, so intervention may begin.

If the patient's taking chemotherapeutic drugs, explain their purpose, dosage, route, and schedule. Discuss adverse effects; tell the patient to report them. Explain ways to prevent or minimize adverse effects, such as taking antiemetics on a regular schedule.

Teach self-care procedures, such as dressing changes, suctioning, nasogastric or gastrostomy tube feedings, and laryngectomy care. Accompany your verbal explanations with written material.

If the patient will have radical neck surgery, teach him how to perform exercises to regain maximum shoulder function and neck motion.

Later, in your follow-up care, teach the patient the signs of cancer recurrence, and urge him to call his doctor promptly if any occur. Patients with head and neck cancer need to know that recurring cancer can be cured if detected early.

Let the patient know that continued smoking or alcohol consumption magnifies the risk of recurrence and may compromise treatment. Remember that changing such habits isn't easy, so the patient needs your support and that of his family. Encourage him to participate in appropriate self-help groups, such as a smoking clinic or Alcoholics Anonymous.

Consider your interventions successful if the patient and his family ask questions, demonstrate knowledge of the disease and treatment, participate in the care plan, and effectively deal with the disease and treatment-related problems.

Potential for injury related to sensory or motor deficits. Your goal is to prevent injury.

Because the patient with a CNS tumor frequently has sensory or motor deficits, encourage him to use a night-light and to use his call light so you can provide assistance. Keep his bed at the lowest level with the wheels locked and siderails up; if seizures are likely, pad the siderails. Remove unused equipment and obstacles from the patient's path, and keep floors clean and dry. If the patient has decreased tactile sensation due to a CNS tumor, practice and teach preventive measures, such as checking the temperature of heating pads before use; using bath thermometers to avoid hot water burns; keeping his feet warm and dry and his skin softened with lanolin or mineral oil. If the patient's gait is unstable, instruct him in using a cane or walker. If he uses a wheelchair, teach him to lock and unlock the wheels. If the patient has impaired vision but not loss of vision, make sure that his room is adequately lit. Teach him to reduce glare. Place needed articles nearby. Suggest that he have bright colors put on doorknobs and on the edges of steps when he goes home.

Consider your interventions successful if the patient avoids injury and can identify and practice prevention.

Impaired physical mobility related to CNS tumor or its treatment. Your goals are to promote optimal mobility and prevent the complications of impaired mobility.

Perform passive range-of-motion exercises, or if the patient is capable, explain and encourage active range-of-motion exercises, progressing to functional activities if possible. Provide optimal skin care, and position the patient in proper alignment. Use proper transfer techniques and teach them to the family. Instruct the patient, if he is capable, in the use of crutches, a cane, or a walker. Paraplegic patients require a detailed rehabilitation program. Some may use braces and crutches to walk a short distance, but many rely on motorized wheelchairs and specially equipped vans to maintain independent mobility. Secure the services of a physical therapist to help you with such patients, if possible.

Consider your interventions successful if the patient remains free of complications secondary to decreased activity and maintains optimal mobility.

Impaired speech related to the disease or treatment. Your goal is to promote optimal communication.

Oral, facial, or neck deformities from cancer and its treatment may interfere with intelligible speech. Traditional total laryngectomy results in permanent loss of voice; tracheostomy following head or neck surgery causes temporary loss. Cranial nerve damage from a CNS, head, or neck tumor can produce garbled speech (dysarthria). Cerebral damage from a brain tumor can result in expressive or receptive aphasia.

Regardless of the cause, speech difficulties interfere with the patient's ability to express needs and feelings, leading to a loss of self-esteem and causing depression, frustation, confusion, anger, fear, and isolation.

Obtain the help of a speech pathologist to evaluate the patient's ability to communicate. For temporary communication problems, suggest alternate methods, such as blinking, nodding, and using a pad and pencil or letterboard. Avoid shouting or talking down to the patient; a speech problem doesn't presuppose impaired hearing or intelligence. Allow silence; the patient may need to gather his thoughts, or he may just not wish to comment.

If the patient has had a total laryngectomy, he needs your support and encouragement. He needs to know how much can be done for him through rehabilitation. Encourage him to learn esophageal speech. If he can't learn for reasons such as advanced emphysema, asthma, or esophageal stricture, inform him about artificial larynxes. One type consists of a battery-powered vibrator placed against the side of the neck that vibrates the air inside the mouth while the patient articulates. Another battery-powered device uses a plastic tube inserted into the side and well to the back of the mouth. This provides a continuous sound source within the mouth.

Tracheoesophageal puncture, a relatively new technique, uses a prosthetic device (duck-bill). A fistula is developed in the posterior trachea and anterior esophageal wall, and a one-way valve is created through the fistula. During speech, the patient closes the stoma with a finger.

Consider your interventions successful if the patient learns to communicate effectively.

Alteration in body and self-image related to disease or therapy. Your goal is to help the patient cope with his altered self-image.

Encourage the patient to verbalize his fear, anger, or sadness concerning disfigurement or physical impairment. Foster a caring and accepting atmosphere among the family members and staff. Respect the patient's privacy, but remember that he might gain needed support from visits with patients having similar problems.

Begin rehabilitation as soon as possible. The patient with a CNS tumor may have neurologic deficits; the one with head or neck cancer may have functional deficits as well as disfigurement. Reconstructive surgery or a prosthesis may help improve the patient's self-image.

Since head, neck, or CNS cancer may tax a patient's emotional resources to the limit, help him secure the services of a multidisciplinary team, including the surgeon and radiotherapists and when appropriate, the social worker, vocational rehabilitation counselor, dietitian, physical therapist, speech pathologist, and dentist or dental hygienist. Encourage him to participate in hospital and community-based support programs. For instance, laryngectomees across the country have formed the Lost Chord Club and New Voice Club.

Consider your interventions successful if the patient and his family openly express their feelings, assume responsibility for care in the home, and participate in group sessions and if the patient does not withdraw from social contacts.

Alteration in comfort (pain) and alteration in nutrition related to tumor. The patient with any of these tumors, especially with spinal cord involvement, may suffer severe pain. In addition, his nutritional status may be poor. The methods described in Chapter 5 may help you relieve or minimize these problems.

A final word
For the patient with head, neck, or CNS cancer, physical deformity and neurologic deficit exacerbate depression and induce isolation. Providing nursing care places you in a prime position to reach out to him. You can serve as his link to recovery, offering the motivation to take control of his life once again.

Points to remember

- Head and neck cancers are curable if detected early. Thus, public education about risk factors and warning signs and symptoms is essential.
- Head, neck, and CNS tumors result in progressive disfigurement and physical or neurologic impairment.
- Because head and neck cancers commonly develop second primary tumors, follow-up is imperative.
- Head, neck, and CNS tumors metastasize distantly in advanced stages, if at all. Typically, complications arise from progressive local disease.
- Surgery is the traditional treatment for these tumors, with radiation a frequent option. Each is a backup treatment when the other fails.
- Nursing care involves postoperative monitoring to detect complications, instruction in rehabilitation and coping techniques, and psychological support.

10 GIVING SUPPORTIVE CARE IN BREAST CANCER

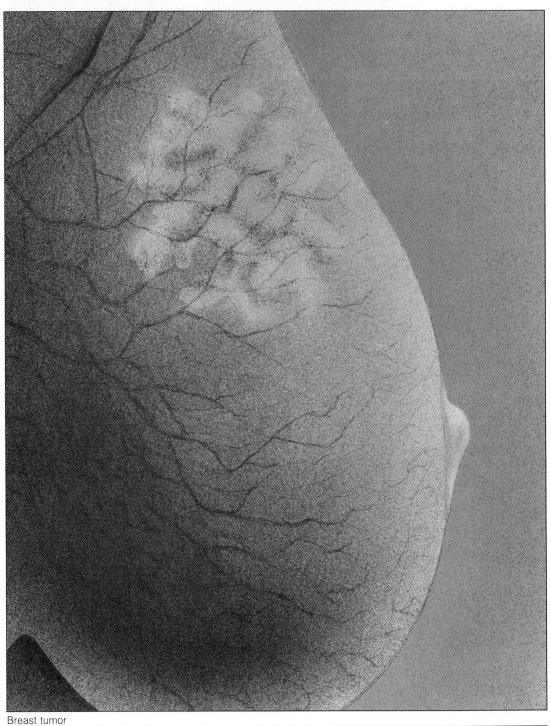

Breast tumor

Breast cancer threatens a woman's self-image perhaps more than any other disorder. Its incidence is rising, producing about 115,000 new cases every year that will eventually cause 31,000 cancer deaths. Roughly 1 woman in 11 will develop breast cancer sometime in her life.

These are certainly daunting statistics. Nevertheless, there are some positive things to say about breast cancer: it's curable if detected early; longer survival rates have offset mortality; its risk factors are probably better defined than for most other cancers; it can be diagnosed early; and its treatment options are more varied today than they were even 10 years ago.

As a nurse, you can help make the most of these positive aspects. You can promote early detection by identifying and screening women at high risk for breast cancer and by teaching them to perform the monthly breast self-examination (BSE). You can help patients with physical and emotional rehabilitation after mastectomy; you can help patients and their families cope with the physical and psychological impact of cancer; and you can provide skilled physical care for patients with recurrent or terminal illness. These varied responsibilities demand that you learn all you can about breast cancer.

Risk factors
The family and health histories of patients with breast cancer suggest various contributing factors, including the following:

Heredity. First-degree relatives—daughters or sisters—of patients with breast cancer have two to three times the risk of developing breast cancer that the general female population does; relatives of patients with *bilateral* breast cancer have five times the normal risk. About 10% to 15% of patients describe a family history of breast cancer, indicating the presence of some genetic influence in breast cancer development.

Hormonal influences. Reproductive histories suggest that hormonal influences may also be important. Nulliparous women and women who deliver after age 30 are at increased risk. Those who have a full-term delivery before age 18 have only one third the risk of women who bear their first child after age 30. Early menarche or late menopause increases the risk of breast cancer. However, an oophorectomy before menopause decreases the risk by one third.

Although long-term estrogen replacement therapy for menopausal symptoms increases the incidence of breast cancer, use of oral contraceptives has not yet been shown to have this effect.

Age. Age itself represents a risk factor because breast cancer incidence is highest in women over age 50.

Radiation. Women who were exposed to large doses of ionizing radiation during their adolescent or childbearing years, such as Japanese atomic bomb survivors, and those who received multiple fluoroscopies for tuberculosis or radiation treatment for mastitis are also at increased risk.

Other factors. Women with a history of benign fibrocystic breast disease have four times the risk of breast cancer as women without this disorder.

Viruses, immunologic processes, and high-fat diets are being investigated as potential risk factors.

PATHOPHYSIOLOGY
Varying widely, breast cancers are classified by site of origin and by histologic type. Over 90% arise from the epithelium of the mammary ducts; these are called *ductal* carcinomas. The remainder arise from the mammary lobules and are called *lobular* carcinomas. (See *Reviewing breast basics,* page 130.) Breast cancer usually has a single focus in one breast. Almost half of breast tumors arise in the upper outer quadrant. (See *Incidence of breast cancer by quadrants,* page 131.)

Ductal carcinomas
Infiltrating ductal carcinomas, which spread beyond the ductal basement membrane, account for almost 70% of breast tumors. These tumors generally feel stony and hard on palpation and seldom grow very large. Most male breast cancers resemble this type of tumor. (See *Male breast cancer,* page 132.)

Regional metastasis to the axillary lymph nodes occurs in many cases. Infiltrating ductal carcinomas have the poorest prognosis of all breast cancers.

Inflammatory carcinomas are a special manifestation of breast cancer, marked by extensive local lymphatic involvement. Lymph vessels draining local skin areas may clog with neoplastic cells. The resulting lymphedema causes the classic "orange peel" appearance as well as skin warmth, redness, and induration. This disorder does not produce a palpable, discrete mass.

Reviewing breast basics

Mammary glands overlie the pectoral muscles. Each gland contains approximately 20 lobes, which are divided into lobules and alveoli. Ducts extend from the lobes through breast tissue and converge in the nipple.

Each mammary gland has an elaborate lymphatic system, which drains primarily into the axilla. This accounts for axillary node enlargement common in malignant breast disease.

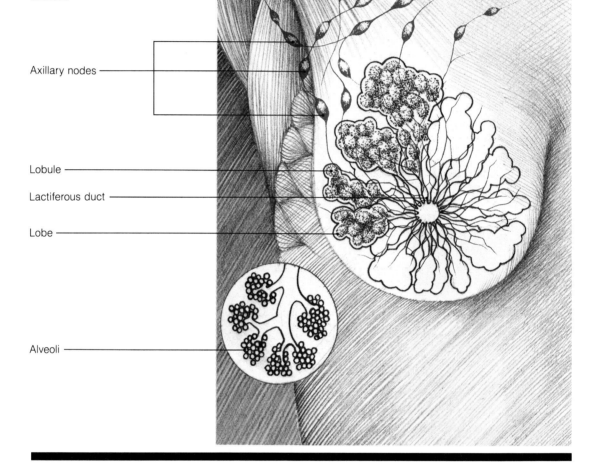

Axillary nodes

Lobule

Lactiferous duct

Lobe

Alveoli

Medullary carcinomas. Of infiltrating ductal carcinomas with special histologic features, medullary carcinomas occur most often. These tumors tend to be large, fleshy, and circumscribed—up to 10 cm in diameter—which makes them more yielding on palpation. They contain large numbers of infiltrating lymphocytes. Because these tumors demonstrate low-grade invasiveness, they're associated with a better prognosis than less-differentiated infiltrating ductal carcinomas.

Mucinous tumors. These colloidal intraductal tumors tend to be large, bulky, gelatinlike masses that are marked by copious pro-

duction of intra- or extracellular mucin. They occur in older women and develop over the course of several years. The prognosis is somewhat favorable, particularly when the tumor is of true colloidal form.

Intraductal carcinomas, such as comedocarcinoma and papillary carcinoma, are confined to the ductal basement membrane. Cancer cells grow from the ductal epithelium and eventually fill and plug the ducts. If the tumor grows into the duct in a papillary configuration, it's called a papillary carcinoma. Such a tumor is a movable, circumscribed lesion, having a soft consistency within the breast due to dilation and solidification of ducts; however, in some cases, no change in breast consistency may be detected. It rarely invades the surrounding tissue; but if it does, it grows slowly, becoming quite large and bulky. Axillary node involvement occurs in late stages.

Comedocarcinomas. These tumors produce cordlike ducts filled with necrotic, cheesy, tumorous growth. In some instances, they take on a glandular or papillary configuration; however, with tumor extension, only solid cords of cancer cells may be distinguished. Like pure papillary tumors, comedocarcinomas can become infiltrative.

Lobular carcinomas

Lobular carcinomas arise from terminal ductules in a breast lobule and occur as in situ or infiltrating tumors. The infiltrating variety accounts for about 5% of all breast carcinomas. Incidence of the in situ variety is speculative.

Lobular carcinomas have relatively distinct characteristics. The tumor cells may appear in a sharply linear pattern or cluster in a circular pattern around normal ducts, making differentiation from infiltrating ductal cancer difficult. In situ lobular cancer is of particular significance because it may be mistaken for the tissue hyperplasia that often accompanies benign fibrocystic breast disease.

Both invasive and in situ lobular carcinomas have a high incidence of bilateral involvement. The invasive type tends to be multifocal in the same breast and carries a poor prognosis.

Pathways of extension

Breast cancer was originally thought to grow and spread sequentially, beginning with local growth in the breast, proceeding to penetration of axillary lymph nodes, and ending in metastasis to distant sites. Recent research suggests that such cancer spreads to the lymph nodes and to distant organs more or less simultaneously. This means that treating breast lymph nodes may control only local or regional recurrence and have no effect on metastasis to distant sites, which may have already occurred at diagnosis.

Local pathways. Breast cancer spreads locally along three pathways: by direct infiltration of surrounding tissue, along mammary ducts, and along breast lymphatics. Direct infiltration occurs when the primary tumor extends small cellular projections into surrounding tissue. If untreated, this local infiltration may extend to the underlying pectoral fascia or the overlying skin, causing fixation to the chest wall, skin dimpling, or nipple retraction.

Local spread along the mammary ducts may involve large areas of the breast. Whether this results from true primary tumor extension along the duct or represents multiple foci spreading simultaneously and producing widespread ductal dissemination, or both, is not known.

Local lymphatic spread occurs along the extensive lymphatic system, toward the pectoral fascia underlying the breast.

Lymphatic extension. Because breast cancer may spread regionally to the surrounding lymph nodes, careful examination of the *axillary nodes* must precede treatment decisions and prognosis.

These nodes, which drain much of the breast, are frequently involved; about 40% to 50% of patients have axillary lymph nodes that are positive for cancer at initial surgery. The tumor's location may influence the pattern of lymphatic involvement, since outer quadrant breast tumors frequently involve only the axillary nodes. However, tumor size may be an even more important factor.

The *internal mammary lymph nodes* lie at the anterior ends of the intercostal spaces and alongside the internal thoracic artery. This chain of nodes commonly becomes involved when the tumor is large and is located centrally or in the upper and lower aspects of the inner quadrant, and when axillary nodes contain cancer cells.

The *supraclavicular lymph nodes* are another common site of lymphatic involvement. Positive supraclavicular nodes indicate a poor prognosis because their involvement is believed to result from extensive axillary node involvement.

Metastatic spread. In metastatic breast cancer, small clusters of cells have broken off from the primary tumor and spread as emboli through the blood or lymph systems to distant sites. These distant metastases can affect practically any organ in the body or several organs simultaneously. The most common sites of metastasis are the bones, lungs, liver, and adrenal glands.

Complications of breast cancer

Complications associated with breast cancer relate directly to the organ systems involved and may include the following:

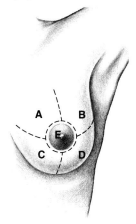

Incidence of breast cancer by quadrants

A Upper inner 15%
B Upper outer 48%
C Lower inner 6%
D Lower outer 11%
E Central area (within 1 cm of areola) 17%

Diffuse with multifocal origin (not shown) 3%

Male breast cancer

This disorder accounts for about 1% of all breast cancers, with the average age of onset at 60.

Men with Klinefelter's syndrome (a genetic disorder causing hypogonadism) or those who have a history of radiation to the breast area are more susceptible to this type of cancer. Bilateral gynecomastia is sometimes associated with the disorder.

Since the male breast has considerably less tissue than the female breast, the malignancy rapidly infiltrates, extending to the overlying skin and underlying pectoral muscles. As a result, ulceration through the skin is more common in the male than in the female.

Tumor spread generally follows the same pattern as in females, and axillary lymph node involvement is present in about one half the cases of male breast cancer at diagnosis. Common signs and symptoms include breast mass, bloody nipple discharge, nipple retraction, axillary mass, and distant or local pain. Primary treatment and prognosis in operable cases are similar in both male and female breast cancer.

Labels: Muscle (pectoralis major), Adipose tissue, Tumor, Areola, Ulcerating carcinoma

• bone pain, pathologic fractures, or hypercalcemia related to bone involvement
• liver failure or hepatic encephalopathy secondary to liver involvement
• pulmonary insufficiency and pleural effusions resulting from pulmonary or pleural involvement or lymphangitic spread in the lungs
• adrenal insufficiency with metastatic adrenal involvement.

In some cases of advanced breast cancer, local chest wall lesions occur. Less common complications include central nervous system or spinal cord involvement, metastasis to the eye, and pericardial tamponade.

MEDICAL MANAGEMENT

The diagnostic workup for breast cancer begins with the patient history and physical examination. Questions should elicit information about breast cancer risk factors, as well as about other symptoms or complaints referable to the breast.

The breast examination should include careful inspection in more than one position and thorough and systematic gentle palpation to detect any abnormalities. If a mass is found, a full description—including tumor size (in centimeters), shape, consistency, and location, as well as any adjacent structural involvement—should be recorded on the patient's history. Palpable lymph nodes must also be completely described. (See Chapter 2.)

Diagnostic tests

Routine diagnostic procedures include screening tests and other procedures to determine the extent of local, regional, or distant spread of tumors. When the problem has been defined, tumor staging accurately determines the severity and extent of disease.

Routine studies. These include chest X-ray, complete blood count, urinalysis, and electrolyte and liver enzyme studies. Routine tests provide basic information on the patient's general health and may suggest the possibility of metastatic disease.

An abnormal chest X-ray may reveal lesions in lung fields, indicating metastasis to the lungs. Although the bones and liver are other common sites of breast cancer metastasis, radiologic examination of these organ systems is controversial unless the patient is symptomatic.

Elevated liver enzymes, such as lactate dehydrogenase, serum glutamic-oxaloacetic transaminase, and serum glutamic-pyruvic transaminase, may reflect metastasis to the liver, especially when associated with liver enlargement.

Mammography. A radiographic technique that is 85% to 90% accurate, mammography is used to identify cysts and small masses in breast tissue, especially those not palpable on physical examination. Cysts usually appear as well-defined and regular clear spots, whereas malignant tumors appear as poorly outlined and irregular opaque masses.

Breast thermography. In this procedure, infrared photography measures and records heat patterns within breast tissue. Abnormalities appear as asymmetrical, white hot spots, which represent increased tissue vascularity and suggest inflammatory or malignant lesions. While this procedure is not specific for cancer, an abnormality may increase the risk of breast cancer.

Breast ultrasonography. This technique is most valuable in differentiating cystic and solid masses found on mammography. However, it is not yet as effective or reliable a screening tool as mammography and is not considered a substitute for it.

Tissue biopsy. Once a breast mass has been confirmed, a sample must be obtained for an accurate diagnosis, histologic typing, and tumor grading. Breast tissue for microscopic examination can be obtained by percutaneous needle aspiration or by incisional or excisional biopsy.

Hormone receptor assay. At biopsy, a portion of the tissue is evaluated for estrogen and, usually, progesterone receptors. Estrogen receptors appear in about 30% of breast cancer patients under age 50 and in about 60% of breast cancer patients over age 50. Knowing

whether or not the tumor binds and retains estrogen helps the doctor predict the effectiveness of hormonal manipulation therapy, such as the removal of ovaries or adrenal glands or the use of antiestrogenic drugs.

The diagnostic workup concludes with an axillary node dissection done at mastectomy or after the lumpectomy to evaluate possible extension.

Scans. Bone, liver, and brain scans are also done to detect and evaluate distant metastasis or to evaluate related symptoms. However, whether or not these studies should be done during pretreatment evaluation, particularly with early disease, is controversial. The yield may be too minimal to justify the expense or the necessary delay in definitive treatment.

Biologic markers. The use of biologic markers, such as carcinoembryonic antigen (CEA), has been suggested during pretreatment to serve as a prognostic indicator. Normally, CEA levels are measured by radioimmunoassay to monitor therapeutic response in metastatic breast cancer. Growing evidence shows that serial determinations may be used to detect early tumor recurrence.

Clinical staging. When the results of the physical examination and diagnostic tests have been collected and evaluated, the doctor can stage the breast tumor. Staging depends on the extent of cancer spread found in preoperative evaluation. It's vital for planning appropriate therapy, evaluating disease status, and comparing the effects of various therapies.

One staging system in common use ranks breast disease in four general stages. In stage I disease, the tumor is localized, lymph nodes are negative, and there is no distant metastasis. In stage II disease, the tumor is localized, with no distant metastasis, but nodes are positive. In stage III, no distant metastasis occurs, but the tumor is locally extensive, with nodes positive and fixed. In stage IV, distant metastasis is also evident. The TNM system, developed by the American Joint Committee on Cancer, is explained in Chapter 3. See also *Staging cancer: Breast.*

Treatment: Many choices
The choice of treatments for breast cancer (surgery, radiotherapy, chemotherapy, hormonal therapy, and combinations thereof) is based primarily on the stage of the disease at diagnosis, the patient's age and health status, and the hormone receptor study results. The treatment decision must also take into account the patient's clinical status and ability to tol-

Surgical options in breast cancer

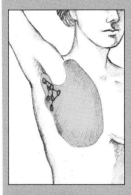 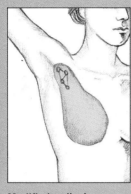 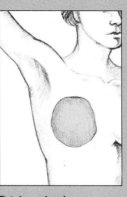 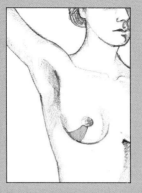 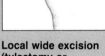

Halsted radical mastectomy
The Halsted radical procedure removes the entire breast, major and minor pectoral muscles, axillary lymph nodes, and fat. This procedure is used when the tumor is large or invasive or when there is lymph node involvement.

Modified radical mastectomy
This modified Halsted procedure involves removing the entire breast, some fat, and most of the axillary nodes. However, the pectoral muscles are not removed.
   This procedure is often preferred over radical mastectomy because it may be just as effective without causing severe functional and cosmetic losses.

Total or simple mastectomy
This involves removing the entire breast and some fat tissue. Muscles and axillary lymph nodes are left in place. This procedure is used when a large tumor exists without muscle or lymph node involvement.

Partial or segmental mastectomy
This involves removing the tumor, overlying skin, and a wedge of breast tissue (2 to 3 cm of tissue surrounding the tumor) and is used when there is a small, self-contained tumor near the nipple.

Local wide excision (tylectomy or lumpectomy)
This involves removing the tumor and a small amount of surrounding breast tissue but leaves muscles and most of the skin intact. This procedure is used for very small, self-contained cancerous or precancerous tumors or fibroid tumors that don't respond to conservative treatment.

erate the recommended treatment.

Surgery more conservative. Surgery for breast cancer once involved the classic Halsted radical mastectomy, aimed at curing local and regional breast cancer. Today, radical surgery is most often a modified Halsted procedure. Modified versions now retain one or both pectoral muscles; conservative management involves removing the tumor and a generous margin of normal tissue.

Modified radical surgery has become the most widely used procedure for operable breast cancer. (See *Surgical options in breast cancer.*) Long-term data comparing the effectiveness of conservative and radical surgery in local-regional eradication or control are not yet available. However, preliminary reports indicate comparable results in patients with negative lymph nodes but somewhat poorer results in patients with positive nodes.

All forms of surgery for breast cancer must include axillary lymph node dissection. Nodal status is the most commonly accepted criterion for adjuvant therapy and the single most important prognostic indicator.

Breast reconstruction. Mastectomy patients should be informed of the possibility for breast reconstruction to help them cope with their altered body image. Reconstruction is usually considered about 6 months after surgery, when other therapies, such as chemotherapy or radiation, have been completed and healing and other skin changes have occurred. Breast reconstruction may also be done 10 years or more after the primary surgery, if necessary.

Reconstructive technique varies with the plastic surgeon's preference and expertise and must be individualized for the patient. Generally, a silicone gel implant is positioned beneath the skin. Skin flaps are recommended for patients with tight skin or with radiation-related skin problems. However, some surgeons are reluctant to attempt breast reconstruction in patients who have received radiation therapy, because of associated difficulty with healing.

Complications of surgery. Conservative primary breast surgery has reduced the incidence of significant complications. However, severe edema and restricted shoulder mobility are still common complications of radical mastectomy, especially after postoperative radiation. Necrosis of skin edges and accumulation of fluid in the axilla or under a skin flap may follow total or segmental resection; however, adequate postoperative suction technique usually can minimize this complication.

Radiation therapy. Radiation has been used in several ways to control local and regional breast cancer. An important early use was as *adjuvant therapy* following radical mastectomy to eliminate occult residual deposits of cancer cells at the operative site. However, this has largely been abandoned because it has not significantly improved survival rates despite a reduction in local-regional disease. Recently, radiation has been combined with lumpectomy to treat patients with clinically negative axillary nodes as an alternative to mastectomy, with comparable success in preventing local recurrence. Preliminary results also show comparable success in women with positive nodes.

External beam radiotherapy may be delivered to the chest and axilla in divided doses for 5 weeks. To provide additional radiation directly to the tumor area, external radiotherapy may be followed by a temporary interstitial implant of radioactive seeds. (See *Interstitial irradiation: An alternative to surgery.*)

Locally advanced breast cancer (stage III, with no evidence of distant metastasis) has a high recurrence rate following radical mastectomy. External beam radiation helps prevent or control its local-regional spread and recurrence.

Combined with chemotherapy, radiation may be used to treat most locally advanced carcinomas not amenable to resection. Radiation is also useful for local treatment of symptomatic metastasis and is the most effective palliative treatment for easing pain resulting from metastasis to bone. However, metastatic bone lesions are not usually irradiated unless they are causing symptoms or are likely to cause pathologic fractures.

Complications of radiation. External beam radiation is generally well tolerated. However, it may cause temporary skin irritation and increased skin pigmentation; skin changes may include dry or moist desquamative reddened areas, which may clear up in 1 to 3 weeks. Fibrosis of the affected breast rarely results. Late reactions, occurring months after treatment, include rib fracture; nonproductive cough; and mild shortness of breath, suggesting radiation pneumonitis.

The risk of radiation-induced tumor is quite small and depends on the dose and the patient's age at treatment.

Chemotherapy. Systemic chemotherapy is

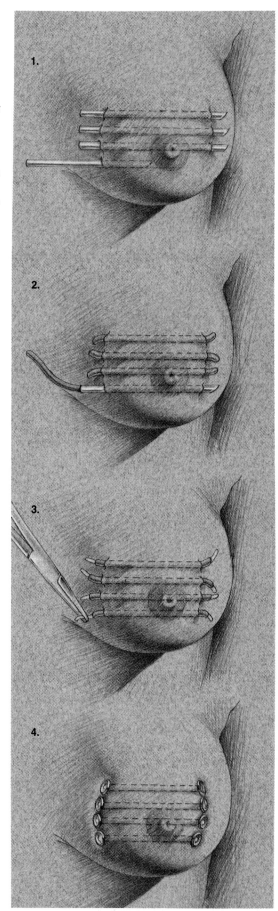

Interstitial irradiation: An alternative to surgery

Interstitial implants are used to treat breast cancer in combination with lumpectomy and external beam radiotherapy. The implants provide additional radiation directly to the tumor bed with decreased side effects. This treatment combination obviates mastectomy and gives good cosmetic results.

Since mastectomy is unnecessary, the patient will not experience complications such as the severe psychological trauma associated with altered body image and loss of function in the arm.

This invasive procedure is relatively quick and painless and can be performed under local or general anesthesia.

1. Stainless steel guide needles are threaded through the tumor area at 1-cm intervals.

2. Flexible nylon tubes are inserted in the guide needles. The guide needles are then removed, leaving the nylon tubes in place.

3. Strands of radioactive iridium seeds are threaded through the tubing at 1-cm intervals to form a grid with seeds above and below, to irradiate the tissues evenly.

4. The nylon tubes are cut and secured with buttons to prevent the seeds from falling out. Implant placement is verified by X-ray. The treatment lasts about 48 hours and delivers an average of 2,000 rads to the tumor.

most often combined with surgery, radiation therapy, or both. In breast cancer, it may be used for one of three reasons: to provide adjuvant therapy, to control metastasis, or to palliate symptoms.

Adjuvant chemotherapy, a relatively new approach, is based on the rationale that micrometastases may already be established by the time the primary tumor is clinically visible. Used with local-regional treatment, surgery, or radiation, adjuvant chemotherapy destroys small metastatic lesions, thus forestalling later recurrences. Adjuvant chemotherapy is most effective for treating histologically proved axillary metastasis that has a high risk of recurrence, as in patients with stage II or stage III disease with one or more positive nodes. Stage I patients usually do not undergo chemotherapy.

Breast carcinomas respond to many cytotoxic agents, especially when used in combinations. Chemotherapy is given intermittently for prolonged periods (6 to 24 months). Several cyclical drug regimens are being tried as adjuvants. All combinations include an alkylating agent, such as cyclophosphamide (Cytoxan), chlorambucil, or doxorubicin (Adriamycin). Doxorubicin, the best single agent for breast cancer, is not widely used for prolonged therapy because of its cardiotoxicity. The combination of cyclophosphamide, methotrexate, and 5-fluorouracil (CMF) is used most often. Alternative combinations usually contain doxorubicin, perhaps with vincristine. Although they produce a higher initial response rate than CMF, they don't prolong remission or overall survival.

NURSING MANAGEMENT

Successful management of breast cancer requires a thorough history and accurate physical assessment. The history should help you formulate an impression of the patient's concerns and attitudes about her breasts and the number of significant risk factors she faces. Then you can proceed to the physical assessment.

Thorough patient history

Begin the patient history by determining the chief complaint. For most women, the first and perhaps only symptom is a painless, palpable lump or mass discovered accidentally or during BSE. Breast pain without a lump occurs in about 10% of patients; nipple discharge in about 7%. Skin changes or palpable axillary lymph nodes occur in few cases.

Ask every woman whether she practices BSE. If she doesn't, stress its impact on early detection and teach her how to perform it.

Now you're ready to ask specific questions related to the breasts and axillary areas. If the patient is premenopausal, is the lump or thickness in her breast related to her menstrual cycle? Has she felt any masses in the axillary area or noticed any skin changes, such as redness or swelling, or any nipple changes, such as retraction or inversion?

Next, check for a history of breast disease. Has she ever had fibrocystic disease? Has she sustained any breast injuries? Has she ever had any diagnostic breast studies, such as mammography, thermography, breast ultrasound, or biopsy? If so, ask where, when, and with what results.

Also, get a reproductive history. Find out her age at the onset of menstruation and, if applicable, her age at menopause and at the birth of her first child; also determine the number of full-term pregnancies she has had and whether or not she's used estrogen replacements, oral contraceptives, or other hormonal therapy.

You'll also need to take a family history. Check to see if any family members have had breast cancer. If so, find out the age at diagnosis, breast cancer type, treatments received, course of the disease and, if cancer was fatal, age at death.

Finally, ask about exogenous and endogenous risk factors, such as previous exposure to radiation or to environmental carcinogens, obesity, diabetes, or hypertension.

If the patient has already been diagnosed as having breast cancer, ask her about any new local lesions or pain. If she is receiving radiation therapy, ask her about skin changes. If she is receiving chemotherapy, ask about the intensity of side effects, such as nausea and vomiting, and about her compliance with her chemotherapy schedule. If she has had surgery, ask about pain or swelling at the mastectomy site.

Examine the breasts

This part of the physical examination offers another opportunity to instruct the patient in BSE. The procedure requires no special equipment. (See *Examining the breasts,* page 26.) Conduct your examination of the breasts in a warm, well-lit, private room. The patient should disrobe to the waist and sit on the side of the examining table. Observe her breasts in each of the following positions: with arms hanging at her sides, with arms over her head, with hands pressed against her hips, with arms held straight ahead and leaning forward, and with her lying down. Then, note breast size and symmetry and the shape, color, and surface characteristics of the skin, such as dimpling, edema (orange peel skin), striae, lesions, rashes, unilateral dilated veins, abnormal bulging, or ulcerations. Check the areolae and nipples for inversion, retraction, discharge, crusting, thickening, and redness.

Next, palpate each breast. If the patient has discovered a lump, have her demonstrate it to you; then palpate the other breast first. Begin with the patient seated and facing you; with her arms at her sides and her head bent slightly forward, palpate the neck and supra-clavicular areas for enlarged lymph nodes. With her arms slightly abducted, palpate for axillary lymph nodes. Note the size, consistency, and mobility of palpable nodes.

Next, have her lie down. Gently palpate her breasts with the pads of two or three fingers held together. Begin with the upper outer quadrant and axillary tail. Press the breast gently against the chest wall using circular motions around the breast to make significant masses more distinct. Usually three or more circles are needed to cover the entire breast. Palpate the areolae and nipple areas.

If the examination reveals a mass, evaluate it and record which quadrant it's in; its size in centimeters; its shape; its consistency; its mobility; and any tenderness, erythema, or dimpling. Draw a diagram to help describe the lesion.

If your patient is already under treatment for primary or recurrent cancer or if she has advanced metastatic disease (characterized by local recurrence with fungating skin lesions or by metastasis to distant organs), focus your assessment accordingly. If she is being treated by surgery, radiation, chemotherapy, or a combination of these, assess the treatment site for wound healing or skin changes. Check for any newly enlarged lymph nodes, and palpate the incisional area for evidence of local recurrence, which is usually in the form of small lumps. Evaluate and record local recurrence by size, location, and amount of drainage or infection. Evaluate bone pain, a sign of metastasis, for location, duration, intensity, and impairment of the patient's daily activities.

Formulate nursing diagnoses
After collecting subjective data from the patient interview and objective data from the breast examination, you're ready to formulate nursing diagnoses that clearly explain the patient's problem and help you establish goals and interventions.

Knowledge deficit related to prevention and early breast cancer detection. Your goals are to help the patient understand the importance of BSE, to have her demonstrate it correctly, and to enable her to identify follow-up care for a mass discovered during BSE.

Emphasize the connections between BSE, early diagnosis, and improved outcome. Then instruct the patient in BSE and describe follow-up care for a suspicious lump.

Consider your intervention successful if the patient understands the importance of BSE, demonstrates her competence in performing it, and understands appropriate follow-up for any lump she may find.

Knowledge deficit related to breast cancer disease, the diagnostic workup, and treatment. Your goal is to help the patient understand her disease and the rationale, risks, and benefits of diagnostic procedures and the prescribed treatment program.

Identify and discuss the patient's present knowledge of and past experience with breast cancer, its diagnosis, and treatment. Then, accordingly, discuss her disease and its treatment. Explain the procedures and rationales for diagnostic tests, such as blood tests, chest X-ray, bone scan, mammography, thermography, breast ultrasonography, and biopsy. Be present when the patient meets with her doctor so that you can clarify and reinforce unclear terms and concepts. Help her formulate any questions she may have regarding the disease and its treatment.

Your intervention is successful if the patient understands what she needs to know about breast cancer, the diagnostic workup, and necessary treatment.

Ineffective coping by the patient or family related to the impact of the diagnosis, treatment, or disease itself. Assess the patient's and her family's methods of coping during previous crises and their patterns of communication and interaction. Help them identify their strengths and weaknesses to enable them to cope and adjust. Also identify current perceptions, attitudes, and fears concerning breast cancer. If needed, refer the patient to a psychiatrist, clinical specialist, social worker, or social agencies.

Consider your intervention effective if the patient and her family are communicating

Preventing post-mastectomy complications

With the removal of lymph nodes and lymph vessels in a radical mastectomy, the patient's arm may swell, and the body's ability to fight infection in that arm is greatly reduced. The following list of do's and don'ts will help the patient prevent complications.

Do
• Contact the doctor if the affected arm becomes red, warm, or unusually hard or swollen.
• Protect hand and arm on affected side.
• Order and wear Medic-Alert tag engraved: *Caution—lymphedema arm—no tests—no injections.*
• Use a thimble while sewing.
• Wear loose rubber glove while washing dishes.
• Stay out of strong sunlight.
• Apply lanolin hand cream several times a day.

Avoid
• Holding a cigarette
• Injury to cuticles or hangnails
• Strong detergents
• Reaching into a hot oven
• Cuts, bruises, insect bites
• Digging in the garden or working near thorny bushes
• Having blood drawn; injections
• Having a blood pressure cuff applied
• Wearing jewelry or a wristwatch
• Carrying heavy bags or purse.

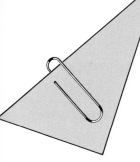

Strengthening exercises

Dear ⎯⎯⎯⎯⎯⎯⎯⎯⎯⎯⎯⎯⎯⎯⎯⎯⎯

After your mastectomy, it is important that you exercise the involved arm and shoulder to prevent muscle shortening, to maintain muscle tone, and to improve blood and lymph circulation.

Wall climbing
Stand facing a wall, with your toes as close to the wall as possible and your feet apart. Bending your elbows slightly, place your palms against the wall at shoulder level. Then, flexing your fingers, work your hands up the wall until your arms are fully extended. Work your hands back down to the starting point.

Pendulum swing
Place your uninvolved arm on the back of a chair. Let your involved (free) arm hang loosely.
1. Swing your arm from left to right. Be sure the movement comes from your shoulder joint and not your elbow.

2. Swing your arm in small circles. Again, be sure the movement is coming from your shoulder joint. As your arm relaxes, the size of the circle will probably increase. Then, circle in the opposite direction.
3. Swing your arm forward and backward from your shoulder, within the range of comfort.

1.

2.

3.

Pully
Toss a rope over your shower curtain rod and hold an end of the rope in each hand. Using a seesaw motion and with your arms outstretched, slide the rope up and down over the rod.

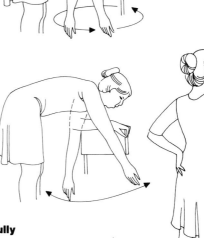

Rope turning
Stand facing the door. Take the free end of a rope in the hand of the operated side. Place your other hand on your hip. With your arm extended and held away from your body, turn the rope, making as wide a swing as possible. Start slowly, and increase your speed as your arm gets stronger.

and meeting each other's needs, their fears are under control, their misconceptions are corrected, and they have been referred for any necessary additional support.

Alteration in comfort related to pain. Your goal is to help the patient learn how to control pain.

Identify the source of pain, such as postoperative incisional pain or bone pain from metastasis. When needed and ordered, give narcotic analgesics around the clock. Identify the patient's perception of and solutions for pain. Assess the effectiveness of the present pain-control program. Accordingly, instruct the patient in alternative or adjunctive pain control methods, such as relaxation, guided imagery, or transcutaneous electrical nerve stimulation.

Your intervention is effective if the patient's pain is under control and she understands alternative pain control methods.

Alterations in skin integrity related to local malignant lesions. Your goal is to have the patient understand how to prevent bleeding and infection and how to control odor from local skin lesions.

Evaluate local lesions for location, extent, and general appearance. Teach the patient how to cleanse the wound, recognize the need for debridement, reduce bacteria, control odor, and dress the wound.

Your intervention is effective if the patient identifies the proper care of local malignant lesions.

Impaired mobility on the affected side related to radical mastectomy. Your goal is to encourage exercise to improve mobility.

After mastectomy and axillary node dissection, teach the patient a postmastectomy routine she can perform daily at the hospital and continue at home. If needed, encourage her to take pain medication before exercising. Also, if possible, alert other health-care team members to avoid drawing blood or taking blood pressure readings on the affected side.

Your intervention is effective if the patient is exercising to improve her mobility.

Impaired mobility related to lymphedema in the affected arm. Your goal is to have the patient understand the causes and symptoms of lymphedema, how to reduce or prevent it, and how to treat it.

Discuss the causes and symptoms of lymphedema. Teach her to prevent lymphedema by elevating her affected arm frequently, by avoiding restrictive clothing, by maintaining good hand and arm care (see *Preventing postmastectomy complications,* page 137), by performing postmastectomy exercises regularly (see *Strengthening exercises*), and by massaging her affected arm to increase circulation. Discuss treatment options such as diuretics, an arm-length elastic glove, or an alternating pressure sleeve. Tell the patient to notify the doctor if she experiences lymphangitis or cellulitis (which may be indicated by warmth, swelling, redness).

Your intervention is successful if the patient understands signs and symptoms of lymphedema and knows how to prevent and treat it.

Alteration in self-concept and body image related to diagnosis and treatment of breast cancer. Your goals are to have the patient identify the impact of breast cancer's diagnosis and treatment on her self-concept and body image and to help her develop ways to cope with it.

Identify and discuss the patient's fears and attitudes concerning breast cancer diagnosis and treatment. The patient may want to discuss her concerns with another breast cancer patient from the American Cancer Society or Reach for Recovery. Help the patient improve her body image by teaching her where she can buy a breast prosthesis and how she can dress appropriately to conceal her mastectomy. Also, explore the possibility of breast reconstruction. Your intervention is successful if the patient understands and is coping with physical changes.

Sexual dysfunction related to effects of breast cancer disease or treatment. Your goal is to have the patient develop strategies for coping with sexual dysfunction. Evaluate the level of sexual dysfunction the patient and her partner experience as a result of breast cancer. Provide information regarding the effects of the disease and of any hormone manipulation therapy on sexuality. Discuss strategies for correcting sexual dysfunction.

Your interventions are effective if the patient reports improved sexual gratification.

Evaluate your interventions

The physical and psychological impact of breast cancer on a woman and her family can be devastating. And sometimes, given such overwhelming impact, achieving all your nursing goals may be impossible. Nevertheless, if your patient begins to face the reality of the situation, takes an interest in her care and treatment, and is learning to live with cancer, you can feel confident that you're providing her with the best possible care.

Points to remember

- Approximately 1 out of 11 women will develop breast cancer sometime in her life.
- Breast cancer is the most common malignancy in women. The most common symptom of breast cancer is a painless lump.
- Diagnosis of breast cancer depends on clinical, radiologic, and histologic evaluation of the breast mass.
- The single most important factor in early diagnosis, and thus in a possible cure, is monthly breast self-examination.

11 INTERVENING IN LUNG AND THORACIC CANCER

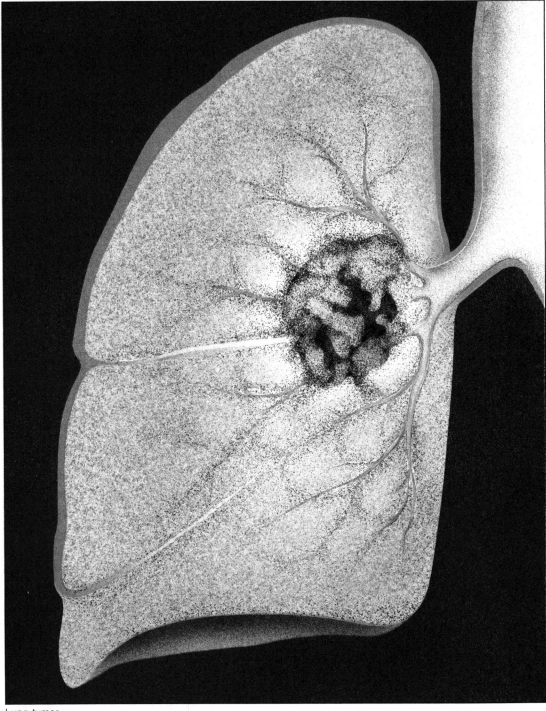

Lung tumor

The most prevalent primary carcinoma of the thorax is bronchogenic carcinoma, or lung cancer. In fact, lung cancer is the leading cause of cancer death in American men and is rapidly approaching this status in American women as well. Why? While lung cancer has been clearly linked to various respiratory carcinogens, such as asbestos and coal dust, its major cause is cigarette smoking. The American Cancer Society (ACS) estimates that cigarette smoking causes about 83% of lung cancer cases among men and about 43% among women.

Prognosis is poor because lung cancer is not usually diagnosed until it's in an advanced stage. (See *Lung cancer prognosis by cell type*, page 143.)

The associated mediastinal structures are also sites of various tumors; however, these are very rare. (See *Thoracic tumors: Primary tumors of the mediastinum*, page 144.)

The nursing challenge

How can you, as a nurse, help to combat this growing health problem? You can help your patient and his family cope with the physical and emotional costs of the disease once it's been diagnosed. You can warn workers who are exposed to occupational respiratory carcinogens of the need for on-the-job protection and of the dangerous synergistic effects of combining such exposure with smoking. You can also support efforts to screen smokers for early lung cancer detection, promote the use of smoking withdrawal clinics, and help educate young people to prevent them from starting the habit.

Smoking and other causes

Although smoking has been implicated as the most significant cause of all types of lung cancer, many others have been identified, including the following:
• *Genetic predisposition.* Smokers related to lung cancer patients have about 11 times more risk of developing lung cancer than smokers who have no family history of the disease.
• *Respiratory carcinogens.* Smoking greatly increases the risk of lung cancer when combined with exposure to carcinogens such as asbestos; the ACS states that exposure to asbestos, when combined with cigarette smoking, multiplies the cancer risk nearly 60 times.

Also, growing evidence shows that even passive smoking (inhaling cigarette smoke generated by others) increases the nonsmoker's cancer risk.

Not everyone who smokes develops lung cancer, however; only about 12% to 15% do. Other factors under investigation that influence a person's chances of developing the disease include the role of vitamin A, necessary for normal growth and development of bronchial mucosa; the role of aryl hydrocarbon hydroxylases, a series of enzymes that activate chemical carcinogens; and the possible predisposing effect of tissue scarring from unrelated previous lung injuries.

Can lung cancer be arrested or prevented?

Progressive irritation of the respiratory tract by cigarette smoke and respiratory carcinogens results in proliferation and alteration of the bronchial mucosa (hyperplasia and metaplasia) and may ultimately cause neoplastic transformation. Some researchers believe that eliminating carcinogens and administering vitamin A may check the disease before it progresses to carcinoma in situ. However, they've not yet determined at what point such measures would be effective, before pathologic changes become irreversible.

If a patient stops smoking, his risk of getting cancer doesn't fall to that of a nonsmoker for 5 to 10 years after he stops. This is largely because of the time the tumor needs to reach detectable size. If a single malignant cell develops the day before a patient stops smoking, that cell may progress to clinically evident disease anywhere from 2.4 to 15.5 years later, depending on the type of tumor. (See *Lung tumors: Average times of diagnosis and death*, page 142.)

Early diagnosis may also improve prognosis. An approach currently being evaluated is a program of quarterly chest X-rays and sputum cytology as routine screening measures for cigarette smokers over age 45. In this type of screening, chest X-ray detects peripheral cancers in the alveoli and smaller airways, while sputum cytology detects central cancers in the bronchi and hilum. However, such screening is costly and is not widely used. Future screening tests may also involve use of radiolabeled monoclonal antibodies specific for lung cancer.

PATHOPHYSIOLOGY

The term *lung cancer* actually refers to several types of cancer. The four most common are:

Lung tumors: Average times of diagnosis and death

This table assumes that lung cancer arises from a single cell. The time for the single cell to double sufficiently to form a 1-cm tumor (earliest diagnosis) or a 3-cm tumor (usual diagnosis) is determined by its mean doubling time. When a tumor is 3 cm in diameter, an additional seven doublings will usually cause death.

Elapsed time between diagnosis and death varies with the histologic cell type of lung tumors.

(Insufficient data was available for large-cell carcinomas.)

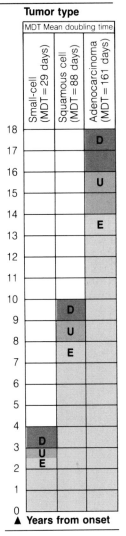

Tumor type

MDT Mean doubling time

	Small-cell (MDT = 29 days)	Squamous cell (MDT = 88 days)	Adenocarcinoma (MDT = 161 days)
18			D
17			
16			U
15			
14			E
13			
12			
11			
10		D	
9		U	
8		E	
7			
6			
5			
4			
3	D		
2	U E		
1			
0			

▲ Years from onset

Key:
E Earliest diagnosis
U Usual diagnosis
D Death

• *squamous cell* (epidermoid) carcinoma
• *small-cell* (including intermediate cell and lymphocytic or oat cell) carcinoma
• *adenocarcinoma* (including bronchoalveolar)
• *large-cell* carcinoma.

Histologic cancer classifications were developed in 1958 and revised in 1967 by the World Health Organization (WHO). In 1972, the pathology panel of the Working Party for Therapy of Lung Cancer modified the WHO classifications. Accurate histologic classification of cancer is important because cell types respond differently to anticancer treatments. (See *Chief histologic classifications of lung cancers.*)

How lung cancer develops and spreads

All common lung cancers originate in the bronchial epithelium. Generally, tumor growth and development progress in three stages.
• *Hyperplasia.* Onset occurs with proliferation of basal cells in the bronchial mucosal epithelium. As hyperplasia progresses, normal epithelium disappears.
• *Metaplasia.* Loss of epithelial cells is accompanied by loss of normal columnar ciliated cells, which are gradually replaced by squamous epithelium.
• *Dysplasia.* Nuclei of squamous cells become progressively more atypical as these cells progress to carcinoma in situ.

With continued tissue injury, cancer cells penetrate the basement membrane of the bronchial epithelium to become invasive. Small-cell tumors may progress to carcinoma in situ in as few as 2.4 years, while adenocarcinomas may take 15.5 years to reach the same stage.

Once lung cancer cells grow through the basement membrane, they spread locally, regionally, and metastatically.

Local spread refers to growth within the lung and to direct extension of the primary tumor into nearby intrathoracic structures. The tumor may spread endobronchially via the submucosal lymphatics within the walls of the bronchial tree, or it may spread transbronchially by growing directly through the bronchial walls and thus to the peribronchial lymphatics and connective tissue.

Both endobronchial and transbronchial extensions of the primary tumor usually follow a centripetal course toward the mediastinum. However, if the tumor blocks lymphatics, lymphatic flow reverses, resulting in a centrifugal course toward the chest wall. Local tumor growth may also extend to intrathoracic or-

gans such as the heart and pleura if the primary tumor is located nearby.

Regional spread refers to extension of the tumor into hilar and mediastinal lymph nodes via either submucosal or peribronchial lymphatics. Once tumor cells are established in a node, they may extend through its capsule to involve adjacent mediastinal structures.

Metastatic spread occurs when the tumor grows beyond the involved lung and mediastinal lymph nodes. Cancer cells may then travel through the blood or lymph to any organ in the body, but the most common sites of metastases are the brain, liver, bone, contralateral lung, adrenal glands, and extrathoracic lymph nodes.

Tumor growth patterns. As cancer cells develop, their local and regional growth pattern and their propensity to metastasize depend ultimately on tumor histology and location within the lung. (See *Characteristics of common lung cancers,* page 146; and *Major bronchogenic carcinomas,* pages 144 and 145.)

Squamous cell and small-cell carcinomas. These tumors tend to grow centrally within the bronchial lumen. As they grow, they form large, polypoid, friable tumors that tend to bleed easily and obstruct the lumen, causing atelectasis and pneumonitis. These friable tumors may shed malignant cells into bronchial secretions, which yield positive results on cytologic sputum examination.

As squamous cell carcinoma enlarges, it may outgrow its blood supply and develop central necrosis (cavitation). These carcinomas sometimes form apical (Pancoast's) tumors, which may invade nearby structures. Squamous cell tumors are the least likely of all lung cancer histologies to metastasize to distant sites, whereas small-cell tumors often metastasize early to involve many different organ systems.

Adenocarcinoma and large-cell carcinoma. Since these tumors usually grow peripherally, in the smaller airways and alveoli near the pleura, they may interfere with lung expansion by causing pleuritic pain. This may result in shortness of breath. Because they grow in the bronchial submucosa, these tumors don't shed cells into the bronchial tree. Regional lymphatic spread to hilar and mediastinal lymph nodes is common.

Lung cancer symptoms

The symptoms of lung cancer differ according to the location of the primary tumor, locations of metastases, paraneoplastic syn-

Lung cancer prognosis by cell type

Characteristic	Squamous cell (epidermoid)	Adenocarcinoma	Large-cell	Small-cell
Approximate incidence	25% to 30%	30% to 35%	15% to 20%	20% to 25%
5-year survival	25%	12%	13%	1%
Operability	43% to 50%	35%	35% to 43%	Rare
Potential for metastasis	Low to moderate	Moderate	Moderate	High
Response rate to systemic treatment	Low	Low	Low	Moderate

dromes, and ectopic hormone production.

Central tumors. Primary tumors that are centrally located often cause coughing; wheezing and stridor; dyspnea; or diffuse chest pain that can involve the chest, shoulder blades, and back. The pain stems from peribronchial or perivascular nerve involvement. In many patients, squamous cell and small-cell tumors also cause hemoptysis, and squamous cell cancer can be associated with fecal breath odor, a result of secondary infection within a necrotic tumor mass. Central tumors also commonly cause postobstructive pneumonia, the result of infection behind an occluded airway. Its symptoms are those of a bronchopulmonary infection: cough, fever, chills, malaise, and dyspnea. This condition often becomes chronic because antibiotics are relatively ineffective without drainage. After treatment shrinks the tumor enough to allow drainage, such infection subsides.

These central tumors, particularly the small-cell type, occasionally extend to the pericardium, causing pericardial effusion and tamponade. In cardiac tamponade, circulation becomes progressively more inefficient and the body compensates through peripheral vasoconstriction and diversion of its limited blood supply to the vital organs. Resulting signs and symptoms are the sudden onset of dysrhythmia (sinus tachycardia or atrial fibrillation), paradoxical pulse, distant heart sounds, weakness, anxiety, dyspnea, and shock.

Peripheral tumors. Peripherally located primary tumors are more often asymptomatic at diagnosis than central tumors. An exception may be the bronchoalveolar variant of adenocarcinoma, in which distal bronchial and alveolar involvement causes a productive cough.

Symptoms appear as peripheral tumors extend through the visceral and parietal pleura to the chest wall, irritating local nerves and causing crippling pleuritic pain. Such pain tends to be localized and sharp and increases upon inspiration, unlike the dull, diffuse pain associated with central tumors. Restricted lung expansion, interfering with ventilation, results from pain or the accumulation of pleural fluid.

Pancoast's tumors. These tumors, usually squamous cell but sometimes adenocarcinomas, present in the apex of the lung. Usually asymptomatic while confined to the pulmonary parenchyma, they can extend into surrounding structures and frequently involve the first thoracic and eighth cervical nerves within the brachial plexus. This produces neuritic pain in the arm and shoulder on the affected side and atrophy of the muscles of the arm and hand. Further local tumor growth may erode the first and second ribs and the vertebrae, causing bone pain, and may also involve the sympathetic nerve ganglia, which are located paravertebrally. Sympathetic nerve ganglia involvement leads to Horner's syndrome, which causes miosis, partial eyelid ptosis, and anhidrosis on the affected side of the face.

Regional lymph node metastasis. Extension of the tumor to the hilar lymph nodes alone doesn't usually cause symptoms. Mediastinal lymph node involvement, however, produces various signs and symptoms, any one of which may indicate that surgery is no longer a treatment option. Vocal cord paralysis, caused by entrapment of the recurrent laryngeal nerve, leads to hoarseness. Compression of this nerve may also cause dysphagia. Compression of the phrenic nerve causes paralysis

Chief histologic classifications of lung cancers

World Health Organization
Squamous cell (epidermoid) carcinoma
Small-cell carcinoma
  Fusiform
  Polygonal
  Lymphocyte-like (oat cell)
  Others
Adenocarcinoma
  Bronchogenic
    Acinar
    Papillary
  Bronchoalveolar
Large-cell carcinoma
  Solid tumor with mucin
  Solid tumor without mucin
  Giant cell
  Clear cell

Working Party for Therapy of Lung Cancer
Squamous cell (epidermoid) carcinoma
  Well differentiated
  Moderately differentiated
  Poorly differentiated
Small-cell carcinoma
  Lymphocyte-like (oat cell)
  Intermediate cell
Adenocarcinoma
  Well differentiated
  Moderately differentiated
  Poorly differentiated
  Bronchopapillary
Large-cell carcinoma
  With stratification
  Giant cell
  With mucin formation
  Clear cell

Thoracic tumors: Primary tumors of the mediastinum

Although mediastinal tumors are quite rare, they may include germ cell, mesenchymal, and neurogenic tumors; thymic, pericardial, bronchogenic, and enteric cysts; and thymomas, adenomas, lymphomas, and carcinomas.

Most mediastinal masses are detected initially by chest X-ray; mediastinoscopy, mediastinotomy, thoracotomy, or needle biopsy is used to establish malignancy, depending on the tumor location. Symptoms, if present, suggest a malignant lesion; 95% of asymptomatic patients have benign lesions, while 47% of symptomatic patients have malignant tumors. Most symptoms result from direct tumor invasion or compression of adjacent mediastinal structures.

Mediastinal tumors occur almost equally often in males and females and may be diagnosed at any age. Prognosis depends on the tumor stage, histologic differentiation, and response to surgery or other anticancer therapies.

Surgery is the treatment of choice for most mediastinal tumors. Radiation therapy may be the primary treatment for Hodgkin's disease, and it may also be used postoperatively. Chemotherapy may be the primary therapy for various lymphomas and for germ cell lesions, and it is often used to palliate advanced disease.

of the diaphragm on the affected side, followed by dyspnea.

Mediastinal node involvement may also cause superior vena cava syndrome, a result of vena caval compression by enlarged nodes and invasion of tissues around the vena cava by the growing tumor. If the obstruction occurs distal to the junction of the superior vena cava and the azygous vein, it causes distention of arm and neck veins; suffusion or edema of the face, neck, and arms; and the appearance of tortuous collateral vessels on the upper chest and back. Obstruction of the superior vena cava proximal to the junction leads to the development of extensive collateral circulation along the anterior and posterior abdominal walls and, possibly, to venous stasis with secondary thrombus formation. Superior vena cava syndrome on occasion is a life-threatening emergency, requiring palliative radiotherapy.

Tumors infiltrating the mediastinal lymph nodes and adjacent tissues can also compress the esophagus, causing dysphagia. Extensive mediastinal lymphatic obstruction can block lymphatic flow and lead to pleural effusion.

Distant metastasis. Metastasis to the brain, long bones, liver, and supraclavicular lymph nodes is common.

About 10% of all patients with lung cancer have central nervous system (CNS) involvement; those who don't risk developing it eventually. Such involvement is most common in patients with small-cell carcinoma and adenocarcinoma, and the brain is the most common site. The major symptoms of brain metastasis result from increased intracranial pressure and include headache, nausea, vomiting, malaise, anorexia, weakness, and altered mentation.

Metastasis to the weight-bearing long bones causes dull bone pain and a tendency toward fractures. The liver is the most common site of abdominal metastasis and is chiefly associated with small-cell carcinoma.

Paraneoplastic syndromes. While not directly related to metastasis, paraneoplastic syndromes mimic metastatic involvement. Up to 20% of all patients with lung cancer develop these syndromes. Signs and symptoms of paraneoplastic syndromes often precede those of tumor presence and may trigger diagnostic studies; they often disappear when the disease is cured or in remission. Typical signs and symptoms include skin rash, clubbing of the fingers, pigmentation disorders, arthralgia, thrombophlebitis, and muscle

Major bronchogenic carcinomas

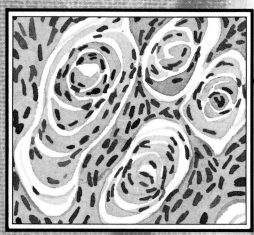

Well-differentiated adenocarcinoma. Characterized by enlarged cuboidal or columnar cells with prominent nuclei and excessive cytoplasm, this tumor usually develops in the peripheral submucosa and forms glandlike structures or sacs.

Well-differentiated squamous cell (epidermoid) carcinoma. Characterized by intracellular keratinization, intracellular bridges, and shrunken nuclei, squamous cell carcinoma is usually located centrally in the large bronchi.

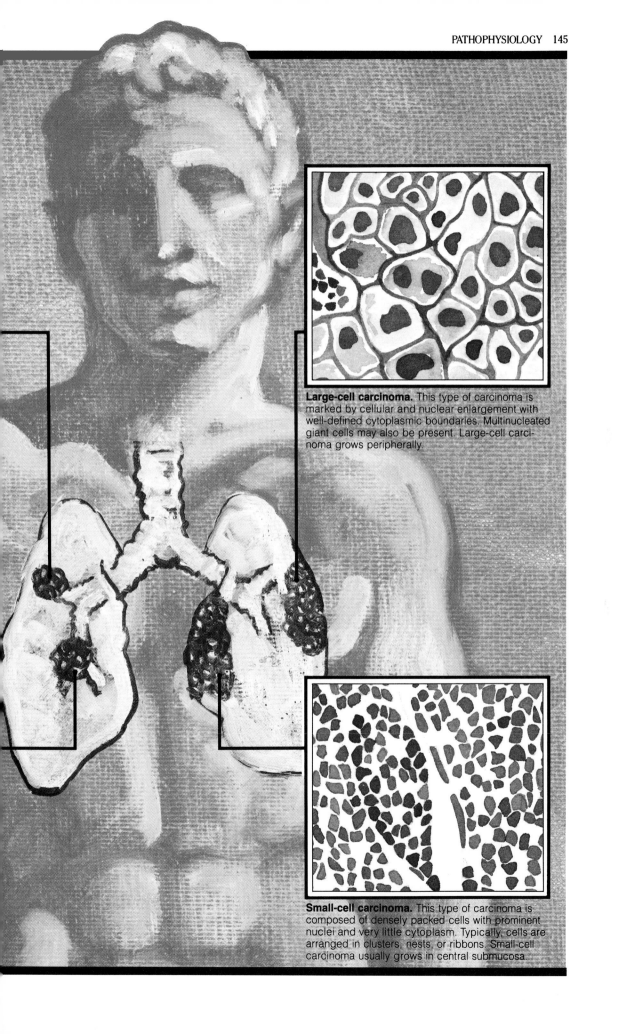

Large-cell carcinoma. This type of carcinoma is marked by cellular and nuclear enlargement with well-defined cytoplasmic boundaries. Multinucleated giant cells may also be present. Large-cell carcinoma grows peripherally.

Small-cell carcinoma. This type of carcinoma is composed of densely packed cells with prominent nuclei and very little cytoplasm. Typically, cells are arranged in clusters, nests, or ribbons. Small-cell carcinoma usually grows in central submucosa.

Characteristics of common lung cancers

Growth patterns and primary tumor locations vary according to the tumor cell type. Pulmonary abnormalities resulting from lung cancer also vary according to the primary tumor location. The major pulmonary abnormalities you'll encounter in patients with lung cancer are lung restriction, decreased ventilation:perfusion ratio, and airway obstruction.

Histologic type	Location	Lesion character	Growth pattern
Squamous cell (epidermoid)	• Central • Grow in bronchial lumen • Involve hilar lymph nodes	• Enlarge within pulmonary parenchyma • Friable, bleed easily • Shed cells into bronchial secretions • May develop central lesion necrosis (cavitation)	• Formation of Pancoast's tumors, which grow by local extension • Late lymphatic spread • Late hematogenous spread
Small-cell	• Central • Grow in bronchial lumen • Involve hilar and mediastinal lymph nodes	• Enlarge within pulmonary parenchyma • Large, polypoid, friable, bleed easily • Shed cells into bronchial secretions	• Early submucosal spread • Early lymphatic spread • Early hematogenous metastasis to many organ systems
Adeno-carcinoma	• Peripheral • Grow in smaller airways and alveoli, near pleura	• Well-defined nodules • Enlarge within bronchial mucosa • Often involve pleura and chest wall	• Direct local extension to pleura • Lymphatic spread to hilar and mediastinal nodes • Hematogenous spread
Large-cell	• Peripheral • Grow in smaller airways and alveoli, near pleura	• Large, poorly defined mass • Grow rapidly • Hilar node involvement common • May develop central lesion necrosis	• Direct local extension to pleura • Early lymphatic spread • Early hematogenous spread

weakness, especially of the pelvic girdle.

Ectopic hormone production. This complication produces symptoms that may suggest CNS metastasis, such as mental changes, or may produce gynecomastia. Examples of ectopic hormone syndromes include Cushing's syndrome (ectopic secretion of adrenocorticotropic hormone), inappropriate secretion of antidiuretic hormone, and hypercalcemia secondary to production of a parathyroid hormone-like substance.

MEDICAL MANAGEMENT

When lung cancer is strongly suspected, usually because of a shadow on a chest X-ray and sometimes because of a persistent cough, a thorough physical examination and patient history may provide further clues. However, comprehensive diagnostic tests must confirm diagnosis and describe the extent of the disease for staging.

Diagnostic tests

Chest X-ray is the most important method of initially detecting lung cancer, but X-rays usually fail to detect tumors smaller than 1 cm in diameter, and they can miss larger tumors hidden by other organs.

Sputum cytology aids early diagnosis, since it can detect atypical cells before irreversible malignancy occurs and sometimes before the tumor is large enough to appear on a chest X-ray. However, this test is not always specific for lung cancer, since head and neck malignancies may also shed tumor cells into the sputum. Ideally, cytologic specimens are obtained from bronchoscopic brushings and washings.

Computerized tomography (CT) scan helps evaluate a pulmonary nodule and check the pleural, hilar, and mediastinal regions for masses. It shows the exact dimensions and internal composition of a mass, revealing benign calcification, additional nodules, and other subtle densities not apparent on a chest film. CT scan can also localize the site of a mass for biopsy.

Biopsy confirms a diagnosis. Tumor tissue can be obtained for histologic identification through flexible fiberoptic bronchoscopy, mediastinoscopy, mediastinotomy, needle biopsy (using fluoroscopy or CT guidance), or thoracotomy. The last two procedures are used only when other diagnostic tests fail to provide accurate diagnosis: needle biopsy carries a slight risk of seeding tumor cells along the needle track; thoracotomy has the risks and disadvantages of a major surgical procedure.

Bronchoscopy can also be used to visualize a tumor mass and to detect signs of nonresectability such as carina involvement. (Resectability refers to the prospects for complete removal of the cancer.)

Tests to detect metastasis include liver function studies and biopsy; bone marrow biopsy; mediastinoscopy; CT scan of the brain, thorax, and abdomen; and radionuclide bone and liver-spleen scan.

Staging procedure

Once the medical history, physical assessment, and diagnostic test results are collected and analyzed, tumor stage can be determined. Except for cases of small-cell carcinoma, clinical diagnostic staging is based on the anatomic extent of the disease, using the TNM system. (See *Staging cancer: Lung cancer*.)

Treatment often palliative

Because lung cancer is often advanced at diagnosis, treatment tends to be palliative rather than curative. Surgery remains the treatment of choice for resectable carcinomas other than small-cell, and it can cure limited disease. Other treatments sometimes combined with surgery include radiation, chemotherapy, and immunotherapy. For small-cell cancer, nonsurgical treatment with combined-agent chemotherapy has been progressively more successful. Radiation therapy might be combined with chemotherapy for patients with disease confined to the thorax. Most patients receiving either chemotherapy alone or both radiation and chemotherapy achieve at least 50% tumor shrinkage; in others, the tumor disappears. Unfortunately, such remission is almost always transient.

Surgery. A tumor is resectable if it's well contained, with no apparent metastasis, and if the patient's ability to tolerate surgery isn't limited by cardiac disease, chronic obstructive pulmonary disease, or some other debilitating condition. Surgical options range from wedge and segmental resections through lobectomy to pneumonectomy with removal of regional lymph nodes.

At diagnosis, about 40% of lung cancer patients have resectable tumors. Prospects of surgical resection and five-year survival are highest for squamous cell cancer (25%) and lowest for small-cell cancer (less than 1%).

Radiation. The major purpose of radiotherapy today is to relieve tumor symptoms. Radiation can offer weeks to months of relief from cough; dyspnea; hemoptysis; and bone, chest, and liver pain. Some clinical studies also suggest that prophylactic brain irradiation reduces the incidence of CNS metastasis in some types of tumors, especially small-cell carcinoma and possibly adenocarcinoma. Squamous cell cancer may respond to radiation because the tumor is often confined to the chest. Small-cell cancer is also radiosensitive, but metastasis often makes chemotherapy its primary treatment. Recent research has shown significantly improved median survival rates when thoracic radiotherapy is combined with chemotherapy in the treatment of small-cell cancer patients with local-regional disease.

Radiotherapy may also be used to reduce tumor size before surgery, especially for patients with Pancoast's tumor. Recently, interstitial placement of radioactive gold seeds has been used in patients refractory to other treatments and has typically produced significant symptom palliation.

Chemotherapy. Chemotherapy is indicated when lung cancer is extensive and surgery and high-dose radiation treatments are infeasible or the patient has ceased to benefit from them. In small-cell carcinoma especially, chemotherapy has improved the formerly poor prognosis, providing a 65% remission rate when coupled with other forms of treatment. However, long-term prognosis with chemotherapy remains poor. The most effective drugs, used singly or (more often) in combination, include doxorubicin, lomustine (CCNU), cyclophosphamide, methotrexate, cisplatin, mitomycin, and vincristine. Cyclophosphamide and methotrexate combined are particularly effective against small-cell cancer. Chemotherapy may also relieve cancer symptoms, chiefly pain and pressure; relieve effects of paraneoplastic syndromes; and help control metastasis.

Immunotherapy. Still experimental, immunotherapy may prolong survival rates by counteracting the immunosuppression that accompanies lung cancer. Administration of live vaccines, such as bacille Calmette-Guérin) or *Corynebacterium parvum*, is used in an attempt to stimulate the immune system to destroy residual tumor cells after surgery.

Laser therapy. This new method for local

Respiratory carcinogens: Who's at risk?

Carcinogenic substance	Workers at risk
Radioisotopes	Uranium miners Iron ore miners Hard rock miners Nuclear waste workers
Mustard gas	Research workers WWI veterans
Polycyclic aromatic hydrocarbons (coal dust, carbonization products)	Gas workers Steel workers Coal miners Roofers
Halo ethers	Chloromethyl ether production workers
Nickel	Nickel ore processors
Chromium	Chromium ore processors Pigment workers
Inorganic arsenic	Metallurgic workers Insecticide applicators Copper smelters Sheep dip workers Gold miners Crop dusters
Iron ore	Hematite miners Steel workers
Vinyl chloride	Rubber workers Chemical workers

tumor destruction uses laser energy directed through a bronchoscope. Still largely experimental, it is used for palliation of symptoms caused by obstruction or bleeding in large central bronchi.

NURSING MANAGEMENT

The patient with lung cancer faces an uncertain future filled with physical difficulties, extensive medical treatments, and psychosocial adjustments. Careful nursing assessment is the key to developing the nursing interventions that will provide patient support and improve his quality of life.

Compile a nursing history

Gather information covering the patient's medical and psychosocial history. Include the following areas:

Chief complaint. In most instances, the patient will complain of a productive or nonproductive cough, dyspnea, and pain. Explore these symptoms to establish a history of the present illness.

Cough. Ask the patient how and when the cough occurs. Is it more common in the morning? Is it related to activity or present all the time? Is the cough dry and hacking or congested? When did it start? Has it become progressively worse? If the cough is productive, how much sputum is usually produced? Copious amounts of sputum are associated with the bronchoalveolar type of adenocarcinoma. Is the sputum bloody? Hemoptysis suggests a friable central tumor. Sputum with a foul odor suggests central tumor necrosis.

Dyspnea. If the patient complains of dyspnea, find out when it started, if it's getting worse, and which of the patient's daily activities, if any, precipitate it. Is dyspnea associated with other symptoms, such as fever, chills, malaise, or diaphoresis? Dyspnea associated with signs of pleural effusion suggests peripheral tumor and invasion of the pleural wall, chest wall, or both. Dyspnea with tachycardia and neck vein distention could mean pericardial tumor involvement from a central tumor.

Pain. Complaints of pain vary with the type of tumor and the extent of the disease, so try to determine the nature and exact location of pain. Is it dull or sharp? Diffuse or localized? Is the pain associated with respiration? Sharp, localized pain that increases on inspiration is a sign of pleural involvement by a peripheral tumor. Does the patient experience shoulder and arm pain in the ulnar nerve distribution area? This suggests Pancoast's tumor, particularly when associated with pain in the rib and vertebral areas. Local or radicular back pain indicates possible spinal cord involvement. Be especially alert to a history of pain in weight-bearing bones and the pelvic girdle, indicating osteolytic involvement and the potential for pathologic fractures.

Find out how these symptoms affect the patient's life-style. Do dyspnea and cough interfere with his activities and nutritional patterns? Does dyspnea affect his appetite or ability to eat? Does eating exacerbate dyspnea? Is the patient able to rest and sleep?

Signs of tumor spread. Since lung cancer is typically advanced when the patient becomes symptomatic, investigate other symptoms that may suggest regional tumor growth and metastasis; for example:
• Dysphagia may be caused by either compression or invasion of the esophagus by lung tumor growth or by enlarged mediastinal lymph nodes.
• Hoarseness alone or accompanied by dys-

Promoting an effective cough

Splinting with pillow

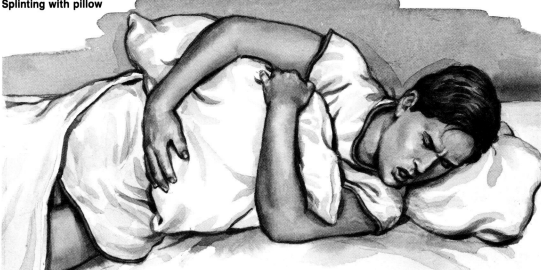

Splinting with hands

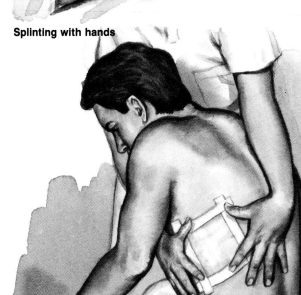

You can help your patient cough efficiently to mobilize secretions that otherwise would result in atelectasis and pneumonia.

First, instruct the patient to sit up straight for maximum ventilation; or if he cannot tolerate sitting, help him assume a sidelong position with his knees flexed to support his abdominal muscles.

Next, splint the affected area with your hands, a pillow, or a folded blanket to reduce pain.

Then have him take a deep breath to increase coughing pressure. He should tighten his abdominal muscles while coughing vigorously. Repeat this procedure at least hourly at first, then as needed.

phagia suggests tumor involvement of the recurrent laryngeal nerve.
• CNS symptoms, including anorexia, muscle weakness, and changing mental status, may indicate brain, meningeal, or spinal cord metastasis.
• Weight loss, loss of strength, and abdominal pain suggest liver involvement.
• Hyperpigmentation of exposed body areas and skin creases, gynecomastia, central obe-

sity, and altered mentation may result from ectopic hormone production.

Smoking history. If the patient smokes or has smoked in the past, at what age did he start? How many packs of cigarettes did he smoke a day? How many does he smoke now? Do other family members smoke?

Medical history. Has the patient had previous lung disorders that might have caused fibrosis or localized pulmonary scarring? Such

Smoking prevention: How you can help

Undoubtedly, the best time to encourage patients to stop smoking is before they sustain any damage to the bronchial epithelium; but even after they've been diagnosed as having cancer, withdrawal from cigarettes can help.

Try a multifaceted approach to help patients stop smoking.
• Educate patients about the harmful effects of smoking. Remind them there is no safe cigarette. Smokers who switch to low tar and nicotine cigarettes often smoke even more to compensate for the lower levels of tar and nicotine.
• Suggest nicotine-containing chewing gum as a way to wean themselves from cigarettes. You may also want to suggest hypnosis or support groups as alternatives.
• Discourage young people from starting to smoke.
• On a community level, encourage industries, organizations, and medical facilities to sponsor smoking cessation programs.

injury may predispose to adenocarcinoma. Has he had any heart or kidney disease? Is there a family history of lung cancer?

Social factors. Ask about family relationships and the patient's socioeconomic position. Does he live in an area of industrial pollutants? Does his job put him in contact with known carcinogens? (See *Respiratory carcinogens: Who's at risk?* page 148.)

Perform a physical assessment

After obtaining a comprehensive history, begin your physical assessment. First, give the patient an overall inspection. What is his general respiratory status? Does he look dyspneic or anxious? What's his mental status? Can he communicate and understand? Is he oriented to time and place?

Next, inspect the skin for central or peripheral cyanosis, ecchymoses, petechiae, and hyperpigmentation. Also be alert for digital clubbing from chronic hypoxia; neck vein distention from right ventricular failure or superior vena caval obstruction; and foul breath odor, a possible sign of tumor necrosis. Look for signs of Horner's syndrome (ptosis of the upper eyelid, pupil constriction, and enophthalmos). These suggest sympathetic nerve ganglia involvement.

Perform palpation. Palpate over bony areas, particularly the spinal vertebrae, pelvic girdle, and long bones, and ask if this causes any pain. Palpate for enlarged supraclavicular nodes. Look for diminished diaphragmatic excursion, indicating phrenic nerve involvement or pleural effusion, and decreased or absent tactile fremitus, which occurs over areas of tumor or lung compression. Increased tactile and vocal fremitus can accompany Pancoast's tumors or occur above pleural effusion.

Perform percussion and auscultation. When you percuss, listen for any dull sound, indicating an area of tumor growth or pleural effusion. Percuss the abdomen for liver enlargement, which could signify tumor involvement. Listen for decreased or absent breath sounds, indicating areas of tumor growth, atelectasis, or pleural effusion. Wheezing indicates airway obstruction; rales may indicate fluid in the alveoli or reexpansion of collapsed alveoli.

Develop nursing diagnoses

Once you've completed your assessment, you can begin to determine goals and a nursing care plan that best meet the patient's needs. In setting up your nursing care plan, consider both the nursing responsibilities important for collaboration with the doctor in providing medical and surgical treatment and the nursing diagnoses necessary to ease the adverse effects of cancer or its treatment.

An important nursing aspect of medical treatment for lung cancer is the need to observe for signs that may indicate tumor extension or metastasis. Be alert for evidence of complications, such as airway obstruction by tumor, superior vena cava syndrome, cardiac tamponade, infection in necrotic lung tissue, laryngeal nerve involvement, phrenic nerve paralysis, Horner's syndrome, esophageal compression, esophageal invasion with secondary bronchoesophageal fistula, aspiration pneumonia resulting from bronchoesophageal fistula, brain metastasis, carcinomatous meningitis, spinal cord compression, and paraneoplastic syndromes.

Your nursing interventions for these complications include identifying their signs and symptoms; reporting them to the doctor; and participating with the doctor in medical treatment, which may involve assisting with diagnostic studies, such as bronchoscopy, and administering treatments.

Continually assess the patient to identify problems. Your nursing diagnoses and the interventions you implement can significantly improve the quality of the patient's life. Nursing diagnoses often used in lung cancer include the following.

Ineffective airway clearance related to tumor obstruction. Your goal is to help maintain oxygen to all body cells by helping the patient gain maximum benefit from respiration, removing secretions that block airways, and promoting tumor shrinkage by implementing the treatment plan.

To meet this goal, provide oxygen as ordered and elevate the head of the bed for maximum thoracic excursion. Instruct the patient in breathing and coughing exercises, initiate pulmonary physical therapy or postural drainage, and suction the patient as ordered. Also administer and monitor antibiotic and antineoplastic drugs as ordered. Teach the patient to reduce exertion, and make any necessary arrangements for a wheelchair or walking aids.

Consider your interventions successful when the patient's skin, nail beds, and mucous membranes regain their normal color; when he breathes comfortably; when his arterial blood gases (ABGs) show improved to normal oxygen, carbon dioxide, and pH values; and when tests show evidence of tumor shrinkage.

Alteration in nutrition caused by tumor-related dyspnea, cough, or anorexia. Your goal is to provide adequate nutrition to maintain body weight.

After assessing the patient's nutritional status and appetite, consult the doctor and dietitian for optimum caloric intake. Have the dietitian talk with the patient to determine his food preferences and to plan an appealing nutritional program. Provide small, frequent meals; high-calorie supplements; and, if appropriate, home-cooked meals to promote optimum food intake. Weigh the patient daily.

Consider your interventions successful when the patient consumes smaller, more frequent meals and his weight stabilizes.

Anxiety related to dyspnea and fear of inability to breathe. Your goal is to reduce the patient's anxiety during dyspneic periods by using relaxation techniques, body positioning, and energy conservation.

First, assess the effect of body position and activity on dyspnea. Encourage the patient to proceed with activities slowly and to rest frequently. Raise the head of his bed, and teach him how to use body positions, such as the tripod position, to facilitate chest expansion. Help him to conserve energy by placing needed objects within easy reach. Teach relaxation techniques to reduce muscle tension and unnecessary oxygen consumption. Calm and reassure him during severe dyspneic periods by staying with him.

Consider your interventions effective when the patient can talk with you and family members about his fears, when he can use effective measures to relieve dyspnea and anxiety, and when he can accept recurring dyspnea without extreme anxiety.

Impairment of skin integrity related to radiation therapy. Your goal is to help the patient maintain intact skin.

Assess the patient's skin regularly for redness, burning, tenderness, or tanning. Avoid use of powders, creams, or lotions that can irritate irradiated areas. Tell the patient to avoid restrictive clothing and direct sunlight on irradiated areas. Advise him to not wash off markings and to keep the area dry.

Consider your interventions effective when, after completion of treatment, the patient's skin is pink and without pain or excoriation in irradiated areas.

Impaired gas exchange related to loss of lung parenchyma from lobectomy or pneumonectomy. Your goals are to maintain a patent airway, to maintain adequate oxygenation, and to minimize oxygen demand.

To maintain a patent airway, clear secretions from bronchial passages by endotracheal suctioning and by teaching the patient to cough effectively. (See *Promoting an effective cough,* page 149.) Administer prescribed medication and help him to support his incision during coughing. Administer oxygen by face mask or nasal cannula, and monitor serial ABGs to evaluate oxygen therapy. Elevate the patient's head with pillows to facilitate diaphragmatic excursion. Turn him every 2 hours and encourage early ambulation to promote lung expansion and mobilize secretions. Implement postural drainage, chest physiotherapy and breathing exercises, as ordered. To minimize oxygen demand, gain the patient's cooperation during treatment by explaining all procedures to him beforehand.

Consider your interventions successful if the patient coughs effectively to clear his airway of secretions, if auscultation reveals normal breath sounds, and if ABG results indicate effective oxygenation.

Alteration in comfort caused by pain from tumor involvement of the lung, parenchyma, lung pleura, or bones. Your goal is to relieve the patient's pain.

To do this, assess the type, amount, and location of his pain; administer analgesic drugs, as ordered, and monitor their effects; and intervene with the doctor on the patient's behalf. Teach the patient relaxation techniques, and involve family members in using distraction and guided imagery pain-control techniques. You'll know your interventions are successful when the patient uses pain management techniques to relieve pain.

Your support can make the difference

As the person who sees the patient daily and intervenes with other health-care professionals on his behalf, you can have tremendous influence in improving the quality of medical and nursing care he receives. Through all the stages of this intractable disease—from first remission to relapse, further treatment, and finally, relapse into terminal stages—you can ensure the ever-increasing supportive care the patient needs so desperately. Through your daily involvement and sensitivity, you can recognize the patient's often subtle mental, emotional, and physical changes and react promptly to their implications. Thus, by preventing avoidable complications, you may add comfortable, productive time to the patient's life.

Points to remember

• Lung cancer, the leading cause of cancer death in American men, is rapidly assuming similar status in American women.

• Cigarette smoking is the most significant cause of all types of lung cancer; it also multiplies the cancer risk when combined with exposure to occupational carcinogens.

• Tumor growth patterns, prognosis, and treatment vary according to the cell type of lung cancer. The four major cell types are squamous cell (epidermoid) carcinoma, small-cell carcinoma, adenocarcinoma, and large-cell carcinoma.

• Because lung cancer is generally not detected until it's in an advanced stage, prognosis is usually poor.

• Although chest X-ray is the most important diagnostic tool, the diagnosis is confirmed by positive histologic identification of tumor tissue.

• You can help educate people not to smoke, promote the use of smoking withdrawal clinics, and support efforts to screen smokers for early signs of lung cancer.

12 RECOGNIZING GASTROINTESTINAL CANCER

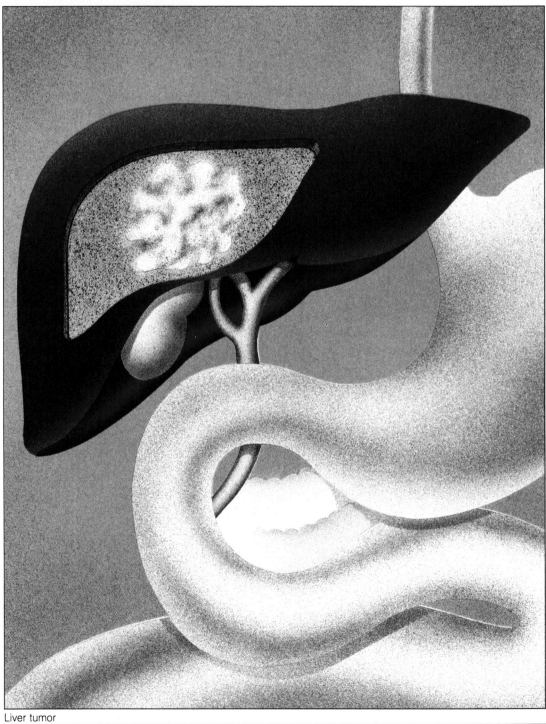

Liver tumor

Gastrointestinal (GI) cancer is a furtive killer. This disease typically overwhelms the patient silently, generating few or no signs and symptoms until its progress is irreversible. For such a patient, only palliative treatment can be given; nursing care focuses on making him as comfortable as possible until he dies. Your skill in giving such care, based on your knowledge of palliative treatment techniques and of the pathophysiology and course of GI cancer, can help ensure the patient's comfort. And your generous support can help improve the quality of the patient's life and ease his family's struggle to cope with his illness.

PATHOPHYSIOLOGY

Malignant tumors of the GI tract may be adenocarcinomas, carcinoid tumors, or squamous cell (epidermoid) carcinomas. The majority occurring in the upper digestive tract or the anus are squamous cell carcinomas. In the stomach, small intestine, large intestine, rectum, gallbladder, bile ducts, liver, and pancreas, malignant tumors are predominantly adenocarcinomas. Carcinoid tumors generally occur in the small intestine.

Patterns of metastasis

As in any form of cancer, the tumor is localized at first, involving the primary GI organ. After extensive local growth, the tumor extends quickly into adjacent lymphatics and lymph nodes. Rapid and direct extension to other GI organs follows, facilitated by these organs' closeness to one another and by the absence of intervening bone or tumor-impeding tissue. Metastasis to distant sites occurs via lymphatic and portal system transport of malignant cells. (See *Understanding gastrointestinal tract cancer,* pages 154 and 155.)

GI interconnecting structures share a rich lymphatic network that permits cells to disseminate rapidly. This can result in areas of new tumor growth or in areas of normal tissue separating tumor growth sites. These so-called skip areas occur primarily in esophageal cancer.

The veins of the GI tract (including the pancreas) and the biliary tract drain through the portal system, which carries blood to the liver. For this reason hematogenous metastasis from GI tract carcinoma most commonly involves the liver (the lungs are the second most frequently involved site). (See *Progression of colon cancer,* page 156.) Malignant

tumor cells may also spread from the primary GI site to distant tissues during resection that transfers tumor cells into the peritoneal cavity.

Clinical manifestations

Direct obstruction of an affected organ—or disruption of its secretory or absorptive functions—is the primary medical problem a GI tumor causes. The resulting signs and symptoms may be vague and nonspecific (indigestion, abdominal or back pain, epigastric distress, changes in bowel habits) or may include weight loss, anorexia, and nausea. Generally, tumors of the esophagus, stomach, small and large intestines, rectum, anus, hepatobiliary system, and pancreas don't produce signs and symptoms until they're well advanced.

MEDICAL MANAGEMENT

In patients with GI cancer, which so often progresses insidiously, early diagnosis generally offers the only chance for survival. Nevertheless, the vague, nonspecific signs and symptoms that are typical of early GI malignancy militate against early detection. At the earliest suspicion of GI cancer, the patient should have a complete diagnostic workup, including a thorough physical examination and detailed history; hematologic, biochemical, and radiographic tests; and any necessary surgical exploration.

Blood studies

In GI cancer, blood studies provide useful but nonspecific diagnostic information.

Complete blood count. This test helps to determine the patient's hematologic status and to detect anemia—a hallmark of GI cancer no matter where it arises.

Erythrocyte sedimentation rate. An increased rate indicates the presence of an inflammatory disorder: infection, failure of an immune mechanism, or malignancy.

Alkaline phosphatase level. Alkaline phosphatase is the most commonly elevated liver enzyme in patients with primary or metastatic liver cancer.

Bilirubin levels. Elevated bilirubin levels indicate metastasis to the liver in patients with cancer of the hepatobiliary system, stomach, pancreas, or small or large intestine.

Prothrombin time. Prolonged prothrombin time is a common finding in patients with cancer of the pancreas, extrahepatic ducts, or liver. This occurs once primary or metastatic *(continued on page 157)*

Understanding gastrointestinal tract cancer

Site	Risk factors	Growth and metastasis
Esophagus	Excessive use of alcohol or tobacco, long-chronic achalasia (25 years), *tylosis palmaris et plantaris*	Fungating and infiltrating tumors (98% squamous cell) encircle and occlude the lumen, resulting in dysphagia. Lack of a serosal layer allows invasion of intrathoracic organs via the submucosal and muscular lymphatic systems. Distant metastasis occurs in the lungs and liver. Death results from fistula formation, destruction of adjacent structures, or esophageal obstruction.
Stomach	Diets high in starch and low in fruits and vegetables; occupational exposure to coal, nickel, asbestos, and rubber; pernicious anemia	Ulcerative, polypoid, scirrhous, or superficial lesions (95% adenocarcinomas) occur most often in the antral and lesser curvature of the stomach. Gastric carcinoma extends to the omentum, liver, pancreas, esophagus, bile ducts, or large intestine. Proximal lesions metastasize to the pancreatico-lienal, pericardial, and superior diaphragmatic lymph nodes; distal lesions, to the inferior gastric, subpyloric, and celiac axis nodes. Tumor cells spread via the thoracic ducts to the cervical nodes or retrogradely to other abdominal areas. Vascular metastasis may involve the liver and later the lungs, bone, and brain. Lymphatic spread or tumor implantation may involve the peritoneum, causing bowel obstruction and death.
Liver	Cirrhosis, positive response to hepatitis B antigen, hepatic cell dysplasia, steroids	Nodules, a mass, or diffuse tumors (90% adenocarcinomas) most commonly arise from parenchymal cells or less often from bile duct cells. Tumors invade the portal and hepatic veins, causing thrombosis; they can extend into the vena cava and as far as the right atrium. Metastases involve the periportal lymph nodes, lungs, and occasionally bone, the adrenals, and the brain. Death results from liver failure.
Bile duct	Parasite infestation (such as *Clonorchis sinensis*), ulcerative colitis	Nodular or diffuse infiltrating adenocarcinomas frequently involve the duct wall and extend directly to the liver, portal vein, hepatic artery, pancreas, and duodenum. Metastasis involves regional lymph nodes and the liver. Death results from liver failure or infection secondary to biliary obstruction.
Gallbladder	Cholelithiasis	Infiltrative, scirrhous, or (less commonly) papillary lesions (95% adenocarcinomas) involve the lymphatic system and extend to the liver; they may also extend to the cystic and common bile ducts, stomach, colon, duodenum, and jejunum, producing obstructions. Cancer also spreads via the portal or hepatic veins, causing hepatic metastasis. Distant metastasis involves the peritoneum, ovaries, and lower lung lobes.
Pancreas	Chronic pancreatitis, diabetes mellitus, cholelithiasis, exposure to industrial chemicals, smoking, alcoholism	Adenocarcinomas of the head invade the bile duct, duodenum, stomach, adjacent transverse colon, kidney, superior mesenteric vessel, or inferior vena cava, causing common bile duct obstruction. Tumors of the body involve the portal vein or mesenteric vessels, causing portal hypertension (from compression of the portal vein), splenomegaly, and esophageal or gastric varices. Tumors of the tail may involve splenic vessels and the spleen. Pancreatic cancer metastasizes early, involving the regional lymph nodes and the liver, then the peritoneum, lungs, adrenals, bone, and spleen. Ultimately, it may involve any body area, progressing to death from liver failure.
Small intestine	*Adenocarcinomas:* familial polyposis (Gardner's syndrome, Peutz-Jeghers syndrome) *Carcinoid tumors:* Crohn's disease, celiac disease, neurofibromatosis	*Adenocarcinomas:* Ulcerative, polypoid, or stenotic lesions arise from glandular epithelium. They spread via the lymph or blood or by peritoneal seeding, involving the regional lymph nodes and the liver. *Carcinoid tumors:* Small, multicentric lesions arise from Kulchitsky's cells in the intestinal lining. They grow and metastasize slowly by invading the muscular layer, then the peritoneum and the mesentery, causing small-intestine obstruction in advanced disease.
Colon and rectum	Diets high in fat and low in fiber, bacteria, history or family history of colorectal cancer, history of female genital or breast cancer, familial polyposis (Gardner's syndrome), ulcerative colitis, Crohn's disease	Sessile or polypoid lesions (98% adenocarcinomas), usually in the rectosigmoid region, progress slowly to finally constrict the colon lumen and extend through the submucosa, muscle, and serosa. Cancer spreads to the mesentery and periaortic lymph nodes. Distant metastasis involves the liver. Rectal cancer extends to the urinary tract, the abdominal wall, and the small intestine. Distant metastasis commonly involves the liver and lungs.
Anus	Chronic irritation from condylomata, fistulas, fissures, abscesses, hemorrhoids	Early anal cancer resembles nonmalignant fissures, progressing to ulcerative, nodular, or polypoid lesions (90% squamous cell). They invade adjacent tissues, then the sphincter muscles, vagina, prostate, urethra, and bladder. Metastasis occurs via the lymph and blood to the liver, lungs, bone, and peritoneum. Death results from extension into the pelvis or from metastasis.

Signs and symptoms

Dysphagia and weight loss in 90% of patients, odyno-phagia (pain with swallowing) in 50% of patients, anorexia, persistent cough, hematemesis, cervical or supraclavicular adenopathy, paralysis of the left vocal cord, hemoptysis

Vague epigastric discomfort, weight loss, iron deficiency anemia, fatigue, pain

With cirrhosis: Rapid deterioration with cachexia, right upper quadrant pain, jaundice, ascites, hemorrhage
Without cirrhosis: Less rapid deterioration with dull or aching pain in the right upper quadrant, jaundice, ascites, hemorrhage

Pruritus preceding jaundice, hepatomegaly, vague and gnawing epigastric or right-upper-quadrant pain or discomfort

Pain in the right upper quadrant or epigastrium (often radiating to the back, more severe at night) in 80% of patients, nausea, vomiting, weight loss, jaundice

Weight loss; pain, especially in the epigastrium (worse at night, may radiate to the back); anorexia; nausea; vomiting; weakness; jaundice; upper abdominal mass

Pain (cramps or diffuse, dull aches) in 65% of patients, weight loss, obstruction, hemorrhage, carcinoid syndrome, cyanosis, chronic diarrhea

Right side of colon: abdominal pain, weakness, melena, anemia, nausea, abdominal mass
Left side of colon: abdominal pain (cramps), melena, constipation, nausea, vomiting
Rectum: melena, constipation, tenesmus, diarrhea, abdominal pain

Rectal bleeding in 60% of patients, pain or a sensation of pressure in the perineal area, anal mass, change in bowel habits

Progression of colon cancer

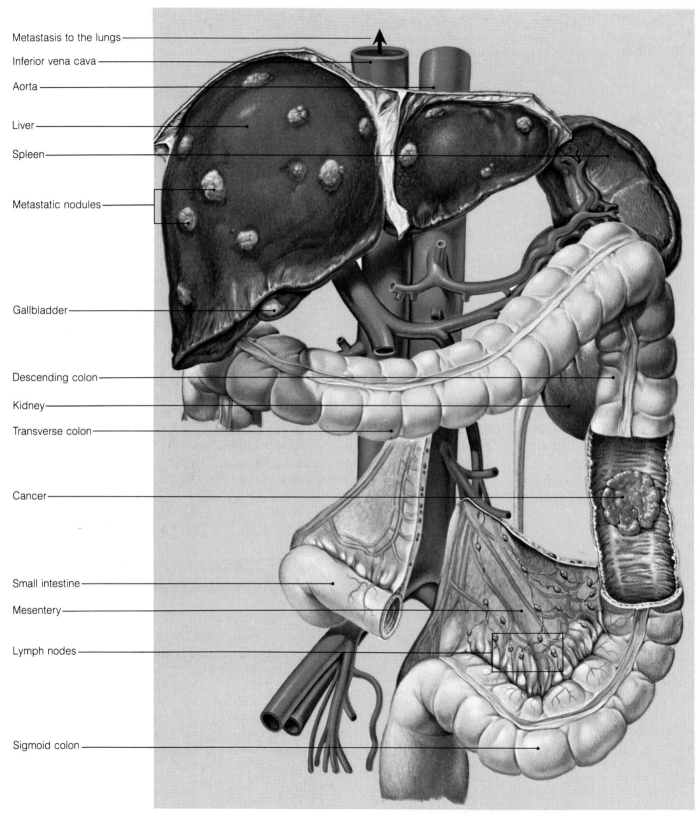

Colon cancer progresses slowly, so it remains localized for a long time. Eventually, however, it may spread to adjacent organs and through the bloodstream or the lymphatic system to distant sites, such as the liver and lungs.

disease has disrupted liver function.

Serum protein and blood sugar levels. Abnormal results in tests of serum proteins and blood sugars generally indicate liver failure. Two oncofetal proteins, carcinoembryonic antigen (CEA) and alpha-fetoprotein (AFP)—used as biological tumor markers—have proved to be of limited significance in diagnosing specific GI cancer. This is because their levels are not consistently elevated in specific neoplastic processes. Also, CEA and AFP levels may be elevated in patients with nonmalignant conditions, such as hepatitis and pancreatitis, and in patients who are heavy smokers. Nevertheless, in a patient with diagnosed colorectal cancer, a CEA level greater than 20 ng/ml indicates a poor prognosis and may also indicate recurrent disease after resection. AFP is used mainly to monitor the growth of primary liver cancer and its response to therapy.

Feces and urine tests
Examination of feces and urine can suggest GI cancer.

Feces examination. This screening test is performed to detect occult blood from hemorrhage due to tumor invasion or GI mucosa ulceration. It is also done to detect steatorrhea, a characteristic finding in cancer of the gallbladder, pancreas, extrahepatic duct, and small intestine. (Excessive lipid excretion in feces also occurs with various malabsorption syndromes.) Melena is a common finding in cancer of the esophagus, stomach, and colorectal area.

Urine tests. Hematuria most consistently occurs in colorectal cancer when the tumor invades the bladder or ureter.

Radiographic studies
Various forms of radiographic tests are employed to detect and localize tumors and metastases.

Chest X-rays. The doctor may order chest X-rays if he suspects metastasis of GI cancer to the patient's lungs. Also, elevation or an uneven appearance of the right diaphragm may indicate compression or invasion by liver cancer.

Tomograms and computerized tomography (CT) scans. These highly sensitive tests aid in detecting minute or subtle evidence of malignancy. For example, they can detect small pulmonary metastases. In esophageal cancer, a CT scan of the mediastinum and upper abdomen helps to identify mediastinal nodal involvement or mediastinal extension of the tumor. In stomach cancer, a CT scan can locate metastatic sites as well as epigastric extension to adjacent organs or lymph nodes. In pancreatic cancer, these tests are used for diagnosis, follow-up, and treatment planning and to define enlarged peripancreatic lymph nodes, biliary system abnormalities, and liver metastases. In primary liver cancer, tomograms and CT scans can show whether the tumor is solitary and confined to one lobe. In gallbladder cancer, these radiographic tests reveal stones, thickening of walls, and tumor extension outside the gallbladder. In small-intestine cancer, they help locate large tumors extending beyond the bowel wall and reveal metastatic liver disease, retroperitoneal lymphadenopathy, or ascites from peritoneal implants. (However, fluid and gas in the small intestine can interfere with visualization of intestinal masses.)

Ultrasonograms. In GI cancer, ultrasonography detects tumors and aids in evaluating them. For example, in pancreatic cancer, it can distinguish a tumor from a cyst or pseudocyst; in bile duct cancer, obstructive from nonobstructive jaundice. Ultrasonography can also evaluate intraabdominal masses; differentiate solid from cystic masses; and detect metastases, particularly in the liver. (Liver scanning can detect liver metastases, too; however, in patients with cirrhosis, interpretation is difficult because of incomplete isotope uptake in the liver parenchyma.)

Esophagograms. Results of esophagograms in patients with esophageal cancer are useful in determining the tumor size, extent of obstruction, and resectability and in determining whether the tumor represents esophageal fistulization, fixation, or distortion from locally invasive cancer.

Barium studies. An upper GI series using double contrast techniques aids in evaluating the proximal stomach, an area where tumor growth is commonly overlooked. An upper GI series with small-intestine follow-through can help diagnose tumors of the small intestine, and barium enemas can reveal tumors in the large intestine.

Percutaneous transhepatic cholangiography. In biliary duct cancer, this test, using a contrast medium, can distinguish obstructive from nonobstructive jaundice and help localize biliary duct obstruction.

Endoscopic studies. Esophagoscopic examination and manipulation can determine the degree of fixation and tumor length. Laryngoscopy and bronchoscopy can determine esophageal extension into the tracheobronchial tree. Endoscopy can be used to establish tissue diagnosis of gastric cancer (biopsy or exfoliative cytology), to examine the duodenum, and to obtain biopsies and cytologic samples. Sigmoidoscopic or colonoscopic examination can aid in the diagnostic and preoperative workup of large-bowel cancer. About one third of colorectal cancers can be visualized with a sigmoidoscope.

Endoscopic retrograde cholangiopancreatography can help diagnose pancreatic carcinoma and obtain a tissue sample in pancreatic and bile duct carcinoma. Fine-needle percutaneous aspiration biopsy techniques can help diagnose intraabdominal tumors under CT localization and obtain pulmonary and liver parenchymal tissue. This is performed either by blind sampling of tissue or by localization of the lesion with ultrasound, CT scan, or fluoroscopy.

Laparotomy: Conclusive diagnosis

When other tests are inconclusive, laparotomy provides direct diagnosis of cancer involving the bile duct or small intestine. (Most colorectal, gastric, and esophageal cancers can be diagnosed without surgery.) Laparotomy can also reveal whether the cancer has spread to lymph nodes and adjacent organs, and to what extent, so the doctor can determine whether resection is possible.

Staging: Correlation with prognosis

After positive diagnosis of GI cancer, including histologic grading, TNM staging determines the extent of disease. (See *Staging cancer: Gastrointestinal tract.*) The degree of cellular differentiation has not been found to affect the survival rate in patients with esophageal or pancreatic cancer. However, in gastric cancer, the grade is considered prognostic—from well differentiated (good prognosis) to undifferentiated (poor prognosis).

Treatment considerations

A patient with GI cancer may be treated with surgery, radiotherapy, or chemotherapy. Before therapy begins, however, the patient's general condition and ability to undergo treatment are assessed. This includes determining if he has anemia from blood loss; hypoalbuminemia from malnutrition; or electrolyte imbalance from vomiting, diarrhea, or intestinal absorption defects. His age, medical history, and treatment preference are also considered. Pre-

operative malnutrition may require vigorous enteral or parenteral nutrition treatment, which can minimize postoperative complications, improve response to therapy (and the patient's outlook), and increase his strength.

Surgery. Surgical removal of the tumor offers the best chance for survival in patients with GI cancer. But unfortunately, GI cancer is often beyond hope of cure at diagnosis. Consequently, surgery is usually performed to palliate signs and symptoms; it may or may not remove the primary tumor. Surgery may also be done to remove a solitary metastasis to the liver or lung; to reduce tumor burden in colorectal cancer; to relieve alimentary or hepatobiliary obstruction; or to place catheters into the hepatic artery for chemotherapy.

Esophageal surgery. Esophagectomy involves removing all or part of the esophagus, then immediately reconstructing it. If palliation is the goal, an alternative procedure, esophageal bypass, may be done by using a segment of the GI tract to bypass the primary tumor and esophagus.

Stomach surgery. High subtotal gastrectomy (Billroth II) is the usual procedure for primary gastric carcinoma; proximal subtotal gastrectomy is done for extensive and diffuse disease. In poor-risk patients with obstruction, for whom palliative resection is impossible, small-bowel bypass to the stomach (above the obstruction) may be done.

Colorectal surgery. Small-intestine surgery entails wide mesenteric resection of the primary tumor and regional lymph nodes. Palliative treatment for unresectable carcinoid tumors involves bypassing the obstructed site; this will halt abdominal pain and diarrhea for extended periods.

Adenoma of the large intestine requires radical resection. The procedure of choice, if no obstruction is present, is one-stage resection and primary anastomosis. The extent of resection is determined by lymph drainage patterns and blood supply. A patient with rectal cancer may need abdominoperineal resection and permanent colostomy. Bladder and rectum resection may be done for lesions involving the base of the bladder.

Anal cancer, if diagnosed as in situ or as a superficially invasive perianal skin lesion, may require only simple local excision. In extensive disease, abdominoperineal resection may be needed. A bilateral groin dissection may be needed if suspicious nodes are palpable.

Hepatobiliary system surgery. When possible, resection is the treatment of choice. Hepato-

STAGING CANCER

Gastrointestinal tract

Esophagus
Primary tumor (T)
T_0 No evidence of tumor
Tis Carcinoma in situ
T_1 Tumor involves 5 cm or less of esophageal length, produces no obstruction, and does not involve the circumference
T_2 Tumor involves more than 5 cm of esophageal length; or a tumor of any size that produces obstruction or involves the entire circumference
T_3 Any tumor that spreads beyond the esophagus

Lymph node involvement (N)
N_0 No palpable nodes
N_1 Movable, unilateral, palpable nodes
N_2 Movable, bilateral, palpable nodes
N_3 Fixed nodes

Distant metastasis (M)
M_0 No evidence of distant metastasis
M_1 Distant metastasis

Stomach
Primary tumor (T)
T_0 No evidence of tumor
Tis Carcinoma in situ
T_1 Tumor limited to the mucosa and submucosa
T_2 Tumor involves the mucosa and the submucosa and extends to or into the serosa
T_3 Tumor extends through the serosa
T_{4a} Tumor extends through the serosa and involves adjacent tissues
T_{4b} Tumor extends through the serosa and involves the liver, diaphragm, pan-

creas, abdominal wall, adrenal glands, kidney, retroperitoneum, small intestine, esophagus, or duodenum

Lymph node involvement (N)
N_0 No regional lymph node involvement
N_1 Perigastric lymph node involvement within 3 cm of the primary tumor along the lesser or greater curvature
N_2 Regional lymph node involvement more than 3 cm from the primary tumor (permits resection)
N_3 Involvement of other intraabdominal lymph nodes (does not permit resection)

Distant metastasis (M)
M_0 No evidence of distant metastasis
M_1 Distant metastasis

Colon/rectum
Primary tumor (T)
T_0 No evidence of tumor
Tis Carcinoma in situ
T_1 Tumor confined to mucosa or submucosa
T_2 Tumor limited to the intestinal wall
T_{2a} Partial invasion of muscularis propria
T_{2b} Complete invasion of muscularis propria
T_3 Tumor invades all layers of the intestinal wall with or without invasion of adjacent tissues (A fistula may or may not be present.)
T_4 Tumor extends beyond adjacent tissues or organs

T_- Multiple tumors (The most extensive are classified and the number of nodes indicated.)

Lymph node involvement (N)
N_0 No lymph node involvement
N_1 Involvement of one to three regional nodes adjacent to the primary tumor
N_2 Involvement of regional nodes, extending to the line of resection or ligature of blood vessels
N_3 Involvement of unidentified lymph nodes

Distant metastasis (M)
M_0 No evidence of distant metastasis
M_1 Distant metastasis

Liver
Primary tumor (T)
T_0 No evidence of tumor
T_1 Tumor < 2 cm, confined to one lobe
T_2 Tumor > 2 cm, confined to one lobe
T_{2a} Single tumor nodule
T_{2b} Multiple tumor nodules
T_3 Tumor involves both major lobes
T_{3a} Single tumor nodule with direct extension
T_{3b} Multiple tumor nodules
T_4 Tumor invades adjacent organs

Lymph node involvement (N)
N_0 No evidence of regional or distant lymph node involvement
N_1 Involvement of regional lymph nodes in the porta hepatis
N_2 Involvement of lymph nodes beyond the porta

hepatis

Distant metastasis (M)
M_0 No evidence of distant metastasis
M_1 Distant metastasis

Gallbladder
Primary tumor (T)
T_0 No evidence of tumor
Tis Carcinoma in situ
T_1 Tumor limited to the lamina propria or to the muscle layer
T_2 Tumor limited to perimuscular connective tissue
T_3 Tumor involves all layers and extends beyond the serosa or into one adjacent organ, or both (must be less than 2 cm into the liver)
T_4 Tumor involves all layers and extends 2 cm or more into the liver or into two or more adjacent organs

Lymph node involvement (N)
N_0 No evidence of regional lymph node involvement
N_1 Involvement of first-station regional lymph nodes
N_2 Involvement of second-station regional lymph nodes

Distant metastasis (M)
M_0 No evidence of distant metastasis
M_1 Distant metastasis

Bile duct
Primary tumor (T)
T_0 No evidence of tumor
Tis Carcinoma in situ
T_1 Tumor limited to the bile duct wall

T_2 Tumor limited to the periductal connective tissue
T_3 Tumor involves all layers and extends into one adjacent major vessel or organ
T_4 Tumor involves all layers and extends beyond secondary ductal bifurcation or into two or more adjacent organs

Lymph node involvement (N)
N_0 No evidence of regional lymph node involvement
N_1 Involvement of first-station regional lymph nodes
N_2 Involvement of second-station regional lymph nodes

Distant metastasis (M)
M_0 No evidence of distant metastasis
M_1 Distant metastasis

Pancreas
Primary tumor (T)
T_1 Tumor limited to the pancreas
T_2 Tumor with limited extension to the duodenum, bile ducts, or stomach (may permit resection)
T_3 Further direct extension (does not permit resection)

Lymph node involvement (N)
N_0 No regional lymph node involvement
N_1 Involvement of regional lymph nodes

Distant metastasis (M)
M_0 No evidence of distant metastasis
M_1 Distant metastasis

---

mas can usually be excised by total hepatic lobectomy if the lesion is solitary or localized, with no evidence of lymph node or distant metastasis.

Pancreatic surgery. Typically, pancreatic cancer has already metastasized or is unresectable at diagnosis, so potentially curative treatment is restricted to tumors involving the head of the pancreas. The Whipple procedure (pancreatoduodenectomy)—a resection of the proximal pancreas, distal stomach, common bile duct, and entire duodenum—or total pancreatectomy may be done.

Radiation. Except in patients who are poor candidates for surgery, radiation therapy is seldom used alone to cure GI cancer. Exceptions are patients with esophageal cancer and, at times, those with anal epidermoid cancer. These cancers are radioresponsive, so radiation may eradicate local tumors. In cervical esophageal cancer, radiation is favored because it produces less cosmetic distortion and because this cancer's surgical mortality is high.

Radiation is more commonly used to palliate the dysphagia and pain of esophageal cancer

The dumping syndrome

When a patient who's had a gastric resection eats a meal, his gastric contents subsequently empty too rapidly—are "dumped"— into his small intestine. This causes major intravascular fluid shifting. Signs and symptoms of this dumping syndrome (which may worsen if the patient has eaten a high-carbohydrate meal) include epigastric fullness, hyperperistalsis, cramps, nausea, vomiting, diarrhea, diaphoresis, weakness, dizziness, and tachycardia.

Early dumping occurs about 15 minutes after eating and may be actively symptomatic for up to 45 minutes. Late dumping (with less severe signs and symptoms) occurs 2 to 3 hours after eating. Be sure your patient understands that he may suffer attacks of dumping syndrome for a year or more following surgery—and possibly for the rest of his life.

and the pain of bone metastasis from gastric cancer; to control symptoms of carcinoid tumors of the small intestine; to reduce pain and repress tumor growth in colon adenocarcinoma; to relieve obstruction and hemorrhage due to inoperable lesions; and to palliate symptoms of unresectable anal, pancreatic, gallbladder, or bile duct cancer. Primary liver cancer is not radiosensitive, so palliative radiation treatment is not effective.

Radiation therapy may also be used before or after surgery to increase the patient's chances for survival. Preoperatively, it's used in esophageal and rectal cancer to retard local recurrence and to shrink the primary lesion so it will be easier to resect. Postoperatively, radiation is used in esophageal and rectal cancer to destroy microscopic tumor cells in lymphatic nodes or deposited at the suture line, again to retard local recurrence. Intraoperative radiation therapy, involving interstitial implants or carefully placed electron beam therapy through surgical wounds, is used investigatively in pancreatic carcinoma and other inoperable intraabdominal tumors.

Chemotherapy. In patients with GI cancer, chemotherapy is used primarily as palliative or postoperative adjuvant treatment. It may also be combined with radiation therapy. Drugs used to treat esophageal cancer include 5-fluorouracil, mitomycin-C, bleomycin, and cisplatin; 5-fluorouracil is also used to treat cancer of the small and large intestines. For palliation, a combination of such drugs as 5-fluorouracil, mitomycin-C, and doxorubicin is useful in stomach and pancreatic adenocarcinomas; streptozocin combined with such agents as 5-fluorouracil, cyclophosphamide, and doxorubicin is used in carcinoid tumors of the small and large intestines. Floxuridine, 5-fluorouracil, mitomycin-C, and the nitrosoureas are used in colon, rectal, gallbladder, and bile duct cancer. For primary liver cancer, doxorubicin is commonly administered systemically or by way of a cannulated hepatic artery. Drugs used to treat anal cancer include bleomycin and the nitrosourea lomustine (CCNU).

Many possible complications

Possible complications of esophageal cancer include inability to control oral secretions and regurgitation of gastric contents, which may be due to malignant obstruction, tracheoesophageal fistula, or lost control of the lower esophageal sphincter. Aspiration pneumonia may result.

Surgery-related complications of stomach cancer include steatorrhea, malnutrition, and dumping syndrome. (See *The dumping syndrome.*) In addition, several metabolic complications may be associated with GI cancers or their treatment. For example, a late complication of gastric resection is megaloblastic anemia from vitamin B_{12} malabsorption. And resection of the pancreas causes deficiencies in the organ's endocrine or exocrine function, so patients develop insulin-dependent diabetes. Patients also require pancreatic enzyme replacement after total pancreatectomy.

Disrupted liver function due to primary liver cancer or metastatic disease impairs the synthesis of coagulation factors and may lead to inadequate hemostasis.

NURSING MANAGEMENT

After obtaining biographic information, elicit the patient's chief complaint and the date of onset. If he complains of dysphagia, have him specify the kinds of foods causing it. Initially, dysphagia from esophageal cancer is mild and intermittent, but it progresses to difficulty with swallowing coarse foods—such as raw vegetables and meats—and eventually to difficulty with swallowing liquids. Get a family and medical history; a medical history of gallstones, liver disease (such as cirrhosis or hepatitis), pernicious anemia, or other high-risk factors should alert you to potential GI problems.

Systems review

Ask about the patient's general well-being. He may report weakness, fatigability, weight loss, changes in bowel habits, and vague pain and discomfort. He may also have anemia and malnutrition, common in GI cancer. Ask about his past and present dietary habits. Check carefully for changes in his skin; for example, jaundice, turgor, pruritus (associated with biliary obstruction and resultant hyperbilirubinemia), a change in thickness of palms and soles (a rare syndrome related to esophageal cancer), or pigmented lesions associated with stomach cancer.

Respiratory symptoms, such as shortness of breath and hemoptysis, may be due to metastatic spread to the lungs, causing bronchial hemorrhage and destruction of lung parenchyma. Direct extension of esophageal cancer may cause an esophagotracheobronchial fistula with persistent cough.

A patient with GI cancer may experience multiple changes in alimentary and hepatobiliary system function due mainly to mechanical obstruction, hemorrhage, and malabsorption. He may complain of appetite loss, taste aversions, abnormal taste sensations, early satiety, nausea, vomiting, indigestion, dysphagia, excessive belching, bloating or flatulence, and, infrequently, hematemesis. If your patient's bowel habits have changed, find out if the changes include stool size or color, constipation, diarrhea, or a feeling of incomplete evacuation. Any of these may be due to obstruction or hemorrhage within the large or small intestine.

Vague abdominal pain accompanies most GI malignancies. Explore the location, duration, severity, changing characteristics, and timing of your patient's pain. Cramping, gaseous abdominal pain may be associated with colorectal cancer. Pain due to pancreatic cancer may be relieved by changing body position. Right upper quadrant pain may be associated with hepatobiliary system cancer.

Explore your patient's social habits, including use of alcohol or tobacco and possible drug abuse. Investigate the family situation to find out about their religious beliefs, coping abilities, financial status, and knowledge and attitudes concerning the disease.

Physical assessment

Observe the patient's general appearance—his personal hygiene and grooming as well as any signs of distress, such as dyspnea—to determine the disease's possible effects on his other body systems. Does the patient appear his stated age? Is he frail, acutely ill, or chronically ill? Obtain vital signs, take his blood pressure, and weigh him. A patient with liver cancer is likely to have an elevated temperature. Increased pulse and respiratory rate may signal respiratory dysfunction associated with metastatic spread to the lungs.

Check his breathing pattern. Do you note an abnormal or irregular rate or rhythm? Does dyspnea occur when the patient tries to talk? If his breathing is labored, is he using accessory muscles to breathe? Find out what body position is most comfortable for him. Check his lips and nail beds for cyanosis. Palpate the anterior and posterior chest wall for areas of tenderness, pain, and asymmetrical movement; these may indicate direct tumor invasion into the chest wall.

Assess for tactile fremitus. A localized increase in a patient with esophageal cancer may indicate a consolidated area associated with aspiration pneumonia. An area of de-

creased tactile fremitus may be caused by a large tumor obstructing the airway. The percussion sound in a consolidated lung area is dull, and you may hear adventitious breath sounds on auscultation. If sputum is produced, check the amount and whether it's blood-tinged, which may indicate esophagotracheobronchial fistula.

Examine the skin. Note jaundice or pallor of the patient's skin, mucous membranes, or sclera. (Use skin areas protected from the sun to observe skin color.) Pallor may result from chronic blood loss and anemia. Inspect the skin for hyperpigmentation, marked wrinkling, or tissue sagging from excessive weight loss. Palpate the skin for dryness and for areas of thickened epidermis; poor skin turgor may indicate malnutrition. Degenerative skin and muscle changes with edema, erythema, and increased melena (dermatomyositis) may occur in stomach and large-intestine cancers.

Palpate for pain and tenderness. Check for peripheral edema; this may indicate decreased plasma albumin levels in liver dysfunction and malnutrition. Assess for pressure sores in a cachectic patient, and check for muscle wasting, especially in interosseous and supraclavicular areas. Estimate muscle mass and fat stores by measuring triceps skin-fold thickness and midarm circumference.

Inspect the hair and nails. Thinning, brittle hair, as well as brittle nails with ridges, may indicate malnutrition.

Inspect the abdomen. Note the general contour and symmetry of the abdomen. Look for distended or bulging areas, abnormal pulsations, peristaltic waves, prominent venous patterns, or ascites. The abdomen may be markedly hollowed, if the patient's severely debilitated with significant weight loss, or protuberant from gaseous distention and ascitic fluid. Asymmetry may be caused by an enlarged diseased organ or by the tumor itself. Increased peristaltic waves may indicate intestinal obstruction.

Auscultate for bowel sounds. They may be increased from diarrhea or early obstruction or decreased or absent if the patient has peritonitis. Rushes of high-pitched sounds coinciding with abdominal cramps may occur in intestinal obstruction. Before documenting absence of bowel sounds, auscultate in one area for 5 minutes or longer. A friction rub over the liver may indicate a liver tumor.

Percuss the abdomen. This will reveal whether the patient's liver is enlarged; if it is, you'll note an increased span of liver dull-

Managing colostomy

Colostomy facts

A colostomy allows excretion of body wastes through an opening created between the colon and the surface of the body. The intestinal mucosa is brought through the abdominal wall, and a stoma is formed by suturing the mucosa to the skin. An ileostomy allows elimination of fecal content from the ileum through the stoma.

An ileostomy and a colostomy may be temporary or permanent. A temporary ostomy allows the intestine to repair itself after inflammatory disease, some types of intestinal surgery, or injury. Temporary colostomy (often double-barrel, forming two stomal orifices) is commonly performed in the transverse colon. A permanent ostomy is usually performed as the result of debilitating intestinal disease or cancer of the colon or rectum.

Before surgery, assess the patient's knowledge about colostomy and his willingness to learn more about it. This will help you individualize your teaching. Keep in mind that the patient bears the burden of coping with the emotional impact of cancer and adjusting to a colostomy. Enlist the support of his family and friends, other health team members, and people who've had similar experiences.

Give physical care first

After surgery, the patient with a colostomy requires specific physical care.

Intake and output. Measure and record the patient's intake and output every 4 hours for the first 3 days after surgery. Report decreased output promptly. Check the ostomy appliance for quantity and characteristics of discharge.

Odors. Keep the patient free of odors, if possible. Apply a temporary appliance after surgery or during the first dressing change to help eliminate fecal

odor. Empty it frequently.

Stoma care. Check the patient's stoma regularly (normally it's dark pink to red, with minimal bleeding around the stoma and its stem). Report any abnormal color or bleeding or excessive edema promptly. If the patient requires an abdominal dressing, check it frequently for drainage and bleeding. Keep the skin around the stoma clean and dry.

Help the patient adjust

After meeting the patient's immediate physical needs, teach him what he needs to know when he begins self-care.

Gradual self-care. Be supportive. Be available, listen, and answer questions. The patient usually begins to accept his altered body image when he is willing to look at the stoma, makes neutral or positive statements concerning the ostomy, and expresses an interest in self-care.

Choice of an appliance. In 2 to 3 weeks, after the stoma shrinks, the patient chooses a permanent appliance. Before

this, he's shown several kinds and told of their advantages, disadvantages, and cost. Stress that an appliance is usually unnoticeable under clothing. Also, assure him that he can minimize odor with an appropriate diet, thorough cleansing of the bag at regular intervals, a proper-fitting appliance, and deodorizer (if needed), which may be sprayed inside the bag.

Diet and bowel control. The patient can usually resume his normal diet after a colostomy except that he must avoid foods that cause diarrhea, such as beans and cabbage. (Since the colostomy has no sphincter, the artificial opening doesn't retain flatus.) If the patient is constipated, encourage him to drink more fluids, eat fruits and vegetables, and exercise.

Sigmoid colostomies produce a formed stool, allowing bowel control by diet alone. Patients who are least likely to achieve satisfactory bowel control are those with a liquid or semisoft fecal stream, those who respond to stress with diarrhea, and those whose bowel habits were irregular before surgery. For patients whose fecal stream remains semisoft or liquid, develop a plan to prevent water and electrolyte imbalances by balancing fluid intake and fecal losses.

Activity. Within 3 months, most patients resume normal activities, including such sports as swimming and tennis. However, the patient should avoid contact sports, such as football.

Sexual function. Be alert for the patient's indirect cues about his concern for normal sexual functioning. Tell him that he can resume sexual relations with allowance for placement of the bag, if one is worn.

Community resources. A representative from a local ostomy club may visit the patient before and after surgery, if requested. Encourage the patient to continue his contact with this group to help him adjust to living with his colostomy.

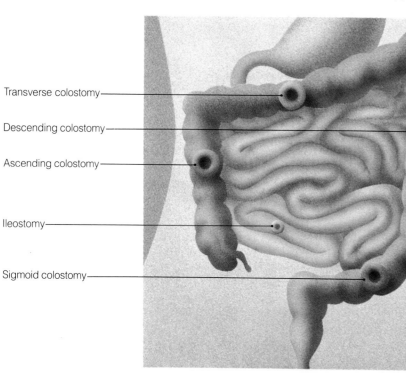

Transverse colostomy

Descending colostomy

Ascending colostomy

Ileostomy

Sigmoid colostomy

ness. Ascitic fluid sounds dull on percussion, whereas percussion over flatulence causes an enhanced tympanic sound. (This may occur in partial obstruction from a constricting lesion.) Lightly palpate to identify specific organ tenderness, areas of rigidity, and masses. Rigid abdominal muscles and rebound tenderness may occur in peritoneal irritation from tumors and internal bleeding. If you identify a mass, deeply palpate to assess its consistency and mobility. A hard liver with an irregular edge or surface may indicate malignancy. Keep in mind that a stool-filled colon can feel like a tubular abdominal mass and that the sacral promontory—easily felt in thin patients—can mimic a hard tumor.

Inspect and palpate the perianal area. Look for lumps, pressure sores, inflammation, anorectal fistula, external hemorrhoids, or excoriated areas. Palpate the anus and rectum to note sphincter tone and any tenderness, irregularities, or nodules.

A rectal malignancy may appear as a polypoid mass or as a firm, nodular ulceration with rolled edges. Inspect any stool returned on the glove for necrotic debris, blood flecks, and occult blood.

Common nursing diagnoses
Your nursing diagnoses for patients with GI cancer may include the following:
• alteration in nutrition related to disease or treatment
• alteration in bowel elimination related to fecal or urinary diversion caused by disease or treatment
• disturbance in self-concept related to disease spread or treatment.

Nursing interventions
In collaboration with the dietitian, teach the patient with GI cancer the importance of a diet high in protein and calories (2,500 to 3,500 calories per day). A dysphagic patient may need high-calorie beverages and enteral or parenteral supplementation. Teach the patient with an altered sense of taste the use of spices and alternate protein sources, such as eggs, dairy products, poultry, and fish. Encourage him to eat with others and to maintain good oral hygiene by using nonalcoholic mouthwashes and brushing his teeth before and after meals. If he's had surgery, explain that he will have I.V. feedings until peristalsis resumes and he can tolerate oral food. Avoid giving him high-carbohydrate foods and fluids between meals to prevent the dumping syn-

drome. For a patient with postoperative diabetes after pancreatic resection, replace digestive enzymes with meals, as ordered, and teach the patient how to manage diabetes.

If the patient has esophageal reflux, explain that sitting up and taking frequent, small feedings will help prevent this problem. To minimize stomatitis, esophagitis, nausea, and vomiting, provide the patient with a diet of liquids and soft foods, and teach oral hygiene to be done before and after meals and every 4 hours during the day. He (or you) should cleanse his teeth with a soft toothbrush and rinse his mouth with a 1:3 solution of hydrogen peroxide and normal saline or a solution of 1 teaspoon of sodium bicarbonate in 8 oz of salt water. (Don't offer alcohol-based, lemon, or glycerin rinses; these promote dryness.) Have him avoid alcohol; tobacco; and very hot, cold, or irritating foods. As ordered, give systemic or topical analgesics if mouth soreness inhibits eating. (Nursing care and interventions for nausea and vomiting are discussed in Chapter 5.)

If the patient has an ostomy, instruct him in caring for it. Include his family in the discussion of factors contributing to skin irritation; careful cleansing of the skin around the stoma; irrigation methods; and selection and application of the appropriate appliance. Help the patient and his family learn how to recognize signs and symptoms of infection and inflammation and how to cope with these complications. Refer the patient to the American Cancer Society or the United Ostomy Association, as appropriate. (See *Managing colostomies.*)

Meeting the challenge
Your concern for the patient's well-being is a key element in his care. Establish a trusting relationship with him by encouraging him to ask questions about his problems. Don't let him withdraw; instead, promote social interaction with others. Help him to acknowledge the changes taking place in his body, and suggest realistic ways to cope with them. For example, if a male patient has become impotent because of resection, discuss this frankly with him and his partner, and suggest alternate means of sexual expression. By following the guidelines this chapter provides, you can help your patient meet the challenge of living with GI cancer or its aftermath. Remember, the quality of your nursing care can make a vital difference in the quality of the life that remains for your patient.

Points to remember

• Most malignancies of the GI tract are in advanced stages at diagnosis. Consequently, their treatment is commonly palliative.
• GI cancer rapidly invades adjacent organs because of their proximity and the lack of tumor-impeding bone or tissue.
• Endoscopic examination allows biopsy or exfoliative cytology to establish a tissue diagnosis in GI cancer.
• An important nursing management goal in GI cancer is teaching the patient to maintain adequate nutrition.

13 COPING WITH UROGENITAL CANCER

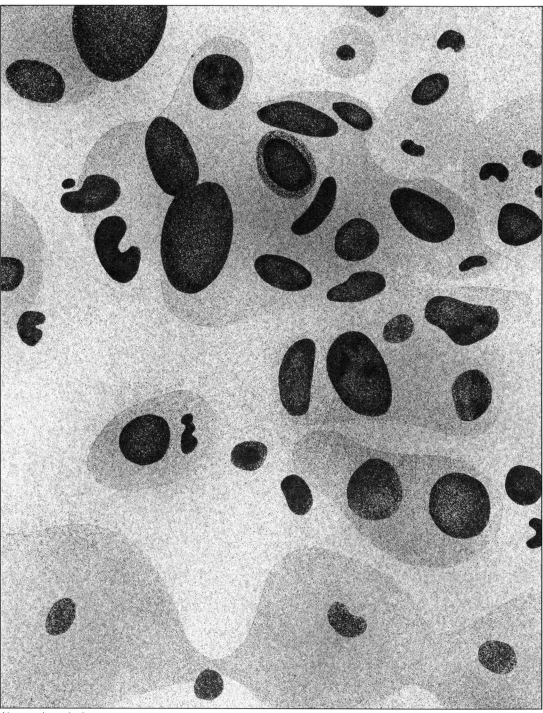

Abnormal cervical smear

Urogenital cancer is especially difficult to deal with because it threatens its victims' survival and often forces difficult psychosexual adjustments as well. These adjustments stem from the location of the tumor and the aftermath of its removal, the resulting threat to the patient's body image, and the effect on his sex role.

This patient needs an extra measure of compassion, sensitivity, and tact, as well as skillful nursing interventions for assisting in early detection and treatment of the disorder and for preventing or treating complications.

A gradually receding threat

Urogenital cancer accounts for about 15% of all cancer deaths in males and 14% in females, but the prognosis is improving. Relative 5-year survival rates have increased significantly since 1960. For example, the 5-year survival rate for prostate cancer in 1960 to 1963 ranged from 50% for whites to 35% for blacks. In 1970 to 1980, these rates were 68% and 58%, respectively. These higher figures clearly suggest significantly improved diagnoses and treatments. However, prostate cancer is still second among leading types of cancer in males. Among other urogenital cancers, ovarian cancer is the fourth most frequent cause of death in females, and testicular cancer ranks among the leading causes of death in young adult males.

What causes urogenital cancer?

No one knows but researchers have identified many apparent predisposing *risk factors*, including chemical carcinogens, viruses, ionizing radiation, hormonal manipulation, drugs, cancer-promoting substances in the urine, and socioeconomic factors.

Industrial carcinogens. Exposure to certain substances increases cancer risk, especially in the transitional epithelial cells lining the renal pelvis, ureters, and bladder.

Viruses. Certain viruses, including herpesvirus type II and human papilloma virus, may play a key role in cervical, vulvar and prostate cancers.

Ionizing radiation. Exposure to ionizing radiation is the only known risk factor for endometrial sarcomas and is also associated with squamous carcinomas of the vagina and vulva. Patients treated with radiotherapy for cervical cancer may develop vulvar and vaginal cancer, and renal adenocarcinomas may develop after exposure to radioactive contrast agents such as Thorotrast (colloidal thorium dioxide), formerly used to visualize the kidneys and liver.

Hormones. Hormonal imbalance has been linked to several urogenital cancers and has also resulted in development of renal adenocarcinomas in animals. Endometrial cancer may result from deranged estrogen metabolism and continuous endometrial stimulation from prolonged use of exogenous estrogens.

The use of diethylstilbestrol by pregnant women, especially during their first trimester, has been linked to vaginal clear cell adenocarcinomas in their offspring; these neoplasms tend to appear in the late teens and early twenties. Nurses can play an important role in educating patients about this risk, thereby helping in early detection.

Drugs. Chronic users of phenacetin have a high incidence of renal pelvic malignancies. Phenacetin metabolites place the ureters and bladder at risk as well.

Promoters. Certain substances in the urine may promote growth of bladder cancer, especially when a carcinogenic initiator, such as a foreign body, is present in the bladder. The initiator may cause development of a neoplasm when stimulated by the promoter substance or substances. (See Chapter 1.)

Socioeconomic factors. Higher incidence of cervical cancer has long been associated with patients of low socioeconomic status and patients with early age of first coitus, regular sexual activity before age 20, and continued exposure to multiple sexual partners. Theoretically, protamine in the sperm ejaculate affects cervical epithelium when these cells change from columnar to squamous type during the early teen years. Exposure to multiple sexual partners and to venereal disease increases the risk of prostate cancer.

Other factors. Cancers of the renal parenchyma and mucosal epithelium are linked to tobacco use and chronic infections, with or without associated calculous disease.

Chronic irritation and proliferative lesions, such as papillomas, caruncles, polyps and adenomas, may increase incidence of urethral cancer in females. Cryptorchidism (especially if orchiopexy is not performed before age 6) is associated with testicular cancer.

PATHOPHYSIOLOGY

Knowing the various tumor cell types involved in urogenital cancer is very important, because they guide the selection of treatment. For example, a testicular seminoma requires an inguinal orchiectomy (removal of the testis) and radiation therapy. However, nonseminomatous or germ cell carcinoma of the testis requires inguinal orchiectomy, plus retroperitoneal lymph node dissection and possibly chemotherapy.

Histologic origins

Several major cell types are involved in urogenital cancer. Because the epithelium of the vagina, vulva, and female urethra consists mainly of squamous cells, most vaginal, vulvar, and urethral cancers are squamous in origin, although adenocarcinomas and other epithelial cancers may develop.

The cervix consists mostly of squamous cells and some glandular cells. Cervical cancers tend to develop at the squamocolumnar junction of the endocervical canal and the portio of the cervix, where epithelial metaplasia places these cells at risk. Squamous cell carcinomas are prevalent on the exocervix, whereas adenocarcinomas tend to develop in the endocervix.

Transitional cells line the renal calyces, renal pelvis, ureters, and bladder. Up to 90% of urothelial cancers occur in these cells, and the cancers are often multifocal in origin. Squamous and glandular cancers may also develop in the urothelium.

Adenocarcinomas are the primary tumor type occurring in the renal parenchyma, prostate gland, endometrium, and ovaries.

Tumors of germ cells (arising from ova or spermatozoa) arise in the testes and ovaries. Ovarian cancers are mainly epithelial and originate in the ovary's visceral peritoneum.

Tumor growth patterns

Urogenital tumors may exhibit different growth characteristics according to their individual histologic type.

Renal parenchymal carcinoma arises from the renal tubule cells. At biopsy, its tumor cells may be clear, granular, or sarcomatous in appearance. This carcinoma may spread by local extension through the renal capsule; by extension into the renal vein and vena cava, leading to hematogenous metastases in the lungs and bones; or by lymphatic spread to the hilar and paracaval nodes. (See *Renal adenocarcinoma: Potential sites of metastasis.*) The disease may also spread to the adrenal glands, the contralateral kidney, and to the brain, heart, spleen, bowel, and skin.

Renal pelvic, ureteral, and bladder cancers occur most commonly in men in their forties,

fifties, or sixties. Predisposing factors include exposure to dyestuffs, rubber, leather, print, or petroleum; a long history of using phenacetin; Balkan nephritis; bladder calculi; and infection with the parasite *Schistosoma haematobium.* Urothelial cancers spread by direct extension. Bladder cancer infiltrates through the bladder wall to other pelvic structures. Lymphatic and hematogenous metastases occur to the liver, lungs, and skeleton.

Prostate cancer is often diagnosed only when the disease is far advanced. It spreads by direct extension to the seminal vesicles, bladder, membranous urethra, and pelvic side walls; by lymphatic spread through the pelvic lymph nodes; and by hematogenous metastasis to the bone. In many patients, bone pain, joint stiffness, and bone metastases are present at diagnosis. An important sign of bone metastasis is pathologic fracture at the tumor site, which occurs easily.

Testicular cancer develops as an enlarging mass, spreads through local invasion and extension to adjacent scrotal structures, and metastasizes primarily through the lymphatic system. Hematogenous spread to the liver, brain, lungs, and bone may follow lymphatic metastases. *Germ cell tumors* constitute 90% to 95% of testicular neoplasms. They are seldom bilateral and occur more often on the right testis.

Female urethral and vulvar cancers afflict postmenopausal women over age 50. Leukoplakia of the vulva may progress to carcinoma in situ and eventually to invasive carcinoma. In the male, urethral cancer is extremely rare.

About 90% of vulvar cancers originate in squamous cells on the labia. These tumors are usually localized and well demarcated, though multicentric in origin. They spread by lymphatic metastasis in a predictable progression, involving first the inguinal lymph nodes and deep femoral nodes and finally the pelvic lymph nodes. This progression allows a confident assessment of response to treatment.

Vulvar squamous cell carcinoma may also involve adjacent organs, such as the vagina, urethra, and anus. Except for melanoma, vulvar cancer rarely spreads hematogenously.

Chronic irritation and proliferative lesions, such as papillomas, caruncles, polyps, and adenomas, are associated with female urethral cancer.

The urethral tumor, usually a small papillary mass, progresses to a fungating, soft mass that may ulcerate, become infected, and progress to a foul-smelling lesion that bleeds

Renal adenocarcinoma: Potential sites of metastasis

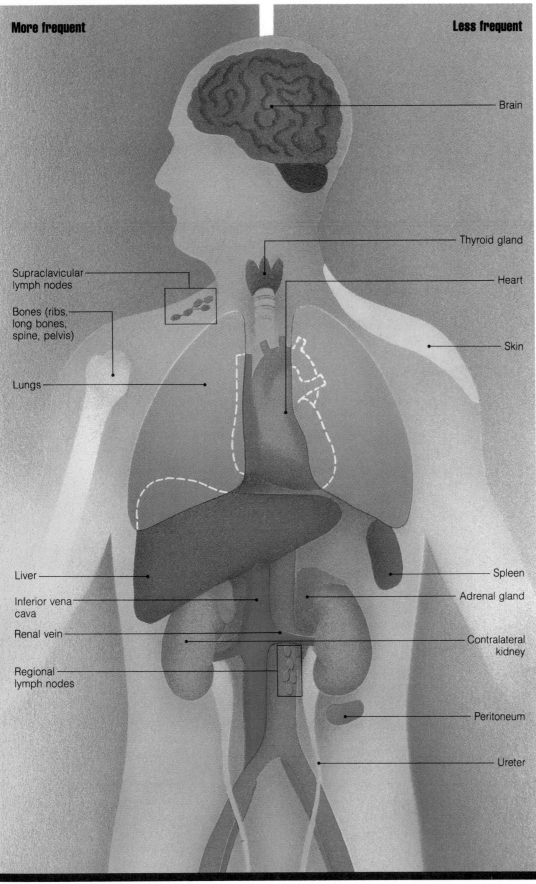

More frequent

Less frequent

Brain

Thyroid gland

Heart

Supraclavicular
lymph nodes

Skin

Bones (ribs,
long bones,
spine, pelvis)

Lungs

Liver

Spleen

Inferior vena
cava

Adrenal gland

Renal vein

Contralateral
kidney

Regional
lymph nodes

Peritoneum

Ureter

Adenocarcinoma, the most common kidney malignancy, occurs most often after age 50. It usually arises in one kidney but may occasionally be bilateral. Because it's so closely involved with the circulation, this malignancy may spread through the bloodstream and sometimes via the lymphatics as far as the ureters, the lungs, and even the bones.

easily. Urethral cancer extends to the bladder neck and vulva, ultimately eroding into the vagina to produce a urethrovaginal fistula. In advanced stages, this form of cancer metastasizes to the lymphatic system; from there, it's most likely to spread to the lungs, liver, bone, or brain.

Vaginal cancer, though rare, occurs most often on the posterior wall of the upper third of the vagina in women age 50 to 70. Typically, early dysplastic changes progress to cervical or vaginal carcinoma in situ that becomes invasive. It may spread to the paravaginal and parametrial tissues, with extension into the obturator fossa and cardinal ligaments, the lateral wall of the pelvis, and the uterosacral ligament.

Cervical cancer originates as a localized epithelial lesion that penetrates the epithelial basement membrane and invades the cervical stroma. It may then spread to the adjacent vaginal fornices and into parametrial tissues, eventually invading the bladder or rectum. It may also extend into the lower uterine segment and endometrial cavity, with increased incidence of distant metastasis.

Lymphatic dissemination may occur, but not always in a predictable, orderly progression. Cervical carcinoma may spread to the paracervical and parametrial lymphatics; may involve the obturator, external iliac, and hypogastric lymph nodes; and may spread to the common iliac or paraaortic lymph nodes. It may also spread hematogenously through the venous plexus and paracervical vein in advanced stages. The most common metastatic sites are the lungs, mediastinal and supraclavicular lymph nodes, the bones, and the liver.

Endometrial cancer usually affects women age 60 to 70. Adenomatous hyperplasia may be a precursor of this disease, which usually originates in the fundus and extends into the endometrium, but it may also originate in the endometrial cavity. Endometrial tumors may involve the lower uterine segment and endocervix. The cancer may spread by microscopic extension into the endocervical canal or by gross extension and exocervical ulceration.

Myometrial infiltration commonly involves the broad ligament, pelvic lymph nodes, and parametrium. These tumors may involve the fallopian tube and ovaries and rarely involve the vagina. Hematogenous metastasis to the lungs, liver, bone, and brain commonly occurs, and metastasis to the peritoneal cavity and omentum has also been reported.

Ovarian cancer. Epithelial tumors account for about 90% of all ovarian malignancies; tumors of the germ cells, sex cord, and stroma account for the rest. Ovarian cancer has been linked to exposure to asbestos or talc, which may move into the female reproductive tract (for example, during application of talc on a diaphragm or on the vagina after bathing). Incidence is lower in multiparous women and those who use oral contraceptives.

Ovarian tumors disseminate primarily by surface implantation, or seeding, in the peritoneal cavity. Thus, they threaten all intraperitoneal structures, such as the bowel, diaphragm, liver, and omentum, and this small implantation makes early detection difficult. Ovarian tumors also spread by lymphatic metastasis to the pelvic and paraaortic lymph nodes.

MEDICAL MANAGEMENT
The effects of urogenital cancers sometimes mimic those of other disorders and can make accurate diagnosis difficult. Consequently, diagnosis requires careful interpretation of physical findings in light of laboratory test results, which are also important in staging the disorder.

Except for ovarian cancers, which are surgically staged, urogenital cancers are staged according to clinical status. (See *Staging cancer: Urogenital cancer*, page 170.)

Diagnostic tests useful
A wide range of diagnostic tests is available to detect and identify urogenital cancers. After diagnosis, additional tests are needed to accurately stage the disorder.

Blood tests. A complete blood count and sequential multiple analysis (SMA) provide much information on the patient's bone, tissue, and hematologic status, as well as liver, kidney, and parathyroid function. Anemia commonly occurs in patients with renal cell cancer. It also occurs with bone metastasis, which is common in renal, ureter, bladder, testicular, and prostate cancers. Erythrocytosis occurs in about 2% of patients with renal cell cancer; the adenocarcinoma produces erythropoietin, which stimulates bone marrow to produce more red blood cells.

The SMA evaluates renal and liver function and provides clues to metastatic involvement of these organs. Elevated *alkaline phosphatase* levels may indicate bone metastasis. An elevated *acid phosphatase* level may indicate advanced prostatic disease (elevation may not

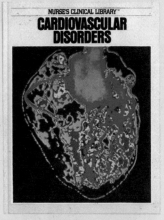
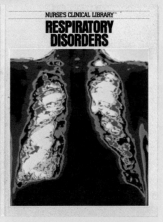
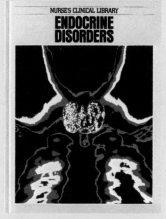
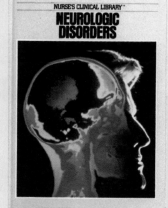

Introduce yourself to the new NURSE'S CLINICAL LIBRARY™ series.

A comprehensive book for each specific body system disorder. That's what makes this set of books so valuable to nurses. No longer will you have to go to one book for drug information, then another for pathophysiology, and still another for diagnostics. Each book in the NURSE'S CLINICAL LIBRARY is a complete source for each body system disorder. And as a subscriber to the series, you save $3.00 off the single-copy price of each book. Act now. Send the postage-paid card above today!

Mail the card at left to get your trial copy of *NursingLife.*

Send no money now. Just mail the card at left and we'll send you a trial copy of *NursingLife,* the fastest growing nursing journal in the world. You'll discover how to avoid malpractice suits, answer touchy ethical questions, get along better with doctors and other nurses, work better under pressure, and much more. Send for yours today!

occur in early stages). Levels of alpha-fetoprotein and the beta subunit of human chorionic gonadotropin are useful for detection and monitoring of treatment and disease progression in nonseminomatous testicular cancer, germ cell tumors of the ovary, and choriocarcinoma. Diminishing serum renin and liver function levels may indicate a response to treatment in renal adenocarcinomas.

Urine tests. Urinalysis screens for bacteria, proteins, and gross or microscopic hematuria. About 30% of patients with bladder cancer have bacterial infections; about 70% of patients with renal cancer have hematuria, and as many as 90% have proteinuria.

Cytology. Urine cytology aids detection of urothelial malignancies, such as renal pelvic, ureteral, and bladder cancers, but doesn't detect renal parenchyma or prostate malignancies unless mucosal invasion has occurred. Pap smears can detect cervical and vaginal cancers.

Radiographic and contrast studies. These include X-ray studies, tomography, intravenous pyelography (IVP), barium studies, and various forms of angiography.

Radiology. Chest X-ray studies help detect metastatic disease; radiopaque nodules may indicate metastasis from any urogenital cancer, since the lungs are a common site of metastasis in testicular, prostate, renal, and endometrial cancers.

Intravenous pyelography. IVP is used in urogenital disorders to demonstrate obstruction resulting from calculi, tumor involvement, and blood clots, and it may also reveal urinary system compression secondary to metastatic disease or tumor extension. IVP may also detect defects in the urinary tract; for example, dye leakage into the abdomen indicates a rupture in the tract. Retrograde pyelograms may further define the site of pathology after an abnormal IVP has been obtained. IVP can detect metastatic sites in staging cervical and endometrial cancer and is used routinely in ovarian cancer to outline the urinary tract and define the extent of disease. It's also used before surgical manipulation of the ureter to establish and evaluate baseline function. Comparing baseline and postoperative IVP films can help identify tumor progression and other postoperative changes.

Tomography. Tomograms more clearly define kidney and lung lesions detected by routine X-ray studies; help determine the cystic or solid component of a renal mass and the ex-

tent of tumor involvement in the renal parenchyma; and can be used in patients allergic to IVP dye.

Barium studies. The barium enema is commonly used to visualize colonic involvement in ovarian and cervical cancers. Barium examinations of the upper GI system and the small bowel are used less frequently.

Angiography. This test provides support for radiologic diagnosis of renal cancer. It allows clearer understanding of tumor vasculature, especially in highly vascular renal cell carcinomas. A preoperative angiogram prepares the surgeon for radical resection; before removing the kidney, he must identify and ligate the renal artery and vein to prevent hematogenous spread. In another preoperative use, angiography also identifies the renal artery for *embolization.* In this procedure, a piece of Gelfoam, copper coil, or other obstruction is inserted into the renal artery to infarct the kidney and reduce its size before nephrectomy. In nonsurgical therapy, embolization can be used to control advanced complications, such as severe bleeding or pain.

In patients with gynecologic tumors, angiography can rule out thrombus formation and detect choriocarcinoma of the uterus when it infiltrates the myometrium.

Venacavography. This test helps identify renal carcinomas obstructed by clots. Results can significantly alter the surgeon's approach to renal tumor resection.

Lymphangiography. Although this procedure provides a clear assessment of the paraaortic lymph node chain, the contrast material may not reach the hypogastric or obturator lymph nodes, the first to be involved in tumor dissemination in many urogenital cancers.

Ultrasonography. These noninvasive studies can distinguish solid and cystic masses in the kidneys, ovaries, endometrium, and testes; help determine the size of the mass and its relationship to other structures; and detect ascites in advanced gynecologic tumors.

By providing information about the size of tumors in the abdomen, sonograms can guide the course of treatment.

Scanning studies. Computerized tomography (CT) scans of the abdomen and pelvis can determine the extent of disease and lymph node involvement. However, CT scans are not particularly useful for detecting small foci, such as metastatic peritoneal cavity lesions, in patients with ovarian cancer.

The magnetic resonance imaging (MRI) scanner uses magnetic fields to delineate ana-

STAGING CANCER

Urogenital cancer

Kidney
T_1 Small tumor/no tumor enlargement
T_2 Large tumor/cortex not broken
T_3 Perinephric or hilar extension
T_4 Extension to neighboring organs
N_1 Single, homolateral regional
N_2 Contra- or bilateral/ multiple regional
N_3 Fixed regional
N_4 Juxtaregional nodes
M_0 No known distant metastases
M_1 Distant metastases present

Bladder
TIS Carcinoma in situ
T_1 Mobile mass, absent after transurethral resection (TUR); lamina propria
T_2 Infiltrated wall, absent after TUR; superficial muscle
T_3 Mass/induration, remains after TUR
T_4 Fixed/extension to neighboring organs
N_1 Single, homolateral regional
N_2 Contra- or bilateral/ multiple regional
N_3 Fixed regional
N_4 Juxtaregional
M_0 No known distant metastases

M_1 Distant metastases present

Prostate
T_0 Incident carcinoma
T_1 Intracapsular/normal gland
T_2 Intracapsular/deformed gland
T_3 Extension beyond capsule
T_4 Extension fixed to neighboring organs
N_1 Single, homolateral regional
N_2 Contra- or bilateral/ multiple regional
N_3 Fixed regional
N_4 Juxtaregional
M_0 No known distant metastases
M_1 Distant metastases present

Testes
T_1 Body only
T_2 Beyond tunica albuginea
T_3 Infiltrating epididymis
T_4 Infiltrating cord/scrotum
N_1 Single, homolateral regional
N_2 Contra- or bilateral/ multiple regional
N_3 Fixed regional
N_4 Juxtaregional
M_0 No known distant metastases
M_1 Distant metastases present

Vulva
T_1 Diameter of tumor < 2 cm
T_2 Diameter of tumor > 2 cm
T_3 Extension into lower urethra, vagina, perineum/ pelvis
T_4 Extension into upper urethra and bladder
N_1 Unilateral/movable
N_2 Bilateral/movable
N_3 Fixed or ulcerative nodes
N_4 Juxtaregional node enlargement
M_0 No known distant metastases
M_1 Distant metastases present

Cervix
TIS Carcinoma in situ
T_1 Confined to cervix
T_2 Extension from cervix to vagina (not lower third) or to parametrium, but not pelvic wall
T_3 Extension to lower third of vagina or to pelvic side wall and parametrium
T_4 Extension into bladder/ rectum, beyond true pelvis
M_0 No known distant metastases
M_1 Distant metastases present

Vagina
T_1 Absence of penetration

into subvaginal tissue
T_2 Penetration into subvaginal tissue
T_3 Extension into side wall
T_4 Extension into bladder or rectum
N_1 Unilateral/movable
N_2 Bilateral/movable
N_3 Fixed or ulcerative nodes
M_0 No known distant metastases
M_1 Distant metastases present

Endometrium
TIS Carcinoma in situ
T_1 Confined to corpus
T_2 Extension to cervix
T_3 Extension beyond uterus within true pelvis
T_4 Extension to bladder/ rectum beyond true pelvis
M_0 No known distant metastases
M_1 Distant metastases present

Ovary
T_1 Limited to ovaries
T_2 With pelvic extension
T_3 Extension into small bowel/omentum, in true pelvis or intraperitoneal metastases/retroperitoneal nodes
M_0 No known distant metastases
M_1 Distant metastases present

---

tomic structures. It produces a computerized image similar to CT scan films and also provides sagittal views. Unlike the CT scan, MRI does use radiation or contrast material to delineate structures.

Endoscopic studies. These studies, including colposcopy, proctosigmoidoscopy, and laparoscopy, allow direct visualization of internal structures and provide a channel for biopsy or treatment.

Colposcopy, performed primarily in the doctor's office, allows closer examination of the vulva, vagina, and cervix when a Pap smear is abnormal, when gauging a lesion's extent, and when identifying the most suspicious part of a lesion for biopsy.

Proctosigmoidoscopy helps identify rectal and sigmoid colon involvement in cervical cancer and rules out primary rectal malignancies or other abnormalities.

Laparoscopy allows examination of the

peritoneal cavity in gynecologic disorders. In some centers, it occasionally replaces "second look" laparotomy for ovarian cancer.

Cystoscopy and tissue biopsy. Cystoscopic examinations evaluate bladder disorders by visualizing the bladder mucosa and ureteral orifices and may also reveal secondary invasion from other malignancies. Cystoscopy provides a channel for biopsy of suspicious lesions and resection of superficial lesions. Transperineal or transrectal prostate biopsies are basic to diagnosing prostate cancer. (See *Prostate biopsy: Highly accurate.*)

A colposcopically directed punch biopsy diagnoses vulvar, vaginal, and cervical malignancies. Fractional dilatation and curettage of the endometrium and endocervix most accurately diagnoses endometrial cancer. Endocervical dilatation is performed first, followed by endocervical curettage and endometrial curettage. The resulting tissue specimens are analyzed separately to determine the tumor's site of origin.

Surgical exploration. Inguinal exploration is the main diagnostic tool for testicular cancer and allows immediate excision of suspected lesions by inguinal orchiectomy.

Treatment: Surgery, radiation, chemotherapy

Urogenital cancers are primarily treated surgically. However, since they commonly affect older patients who are likely to have other illnesses, treatment may involve severe risks. Consequently, selection of treatment depends on the patient's general health, his ability to cope with body changes, the stage of the disease, tumor cell type and degree of tumor differentiation, and the treatment goal.

Surgery

Resection may be extensive due to the need to perform an "en bloc" dissection, or removal of all tissue in one mass, to prevent tumor dissemination during the procedure. Specific surgical treatment varies as reviewed below.

Vaginal and cervical cancers. Vaginal cancer is treated with surgery only when radiation fails; however, because this surgery is often ultraradical, it's seldom appropriate for elderly patients. *Cervical conization* may be used to treat cervical carcinoma in situ; *abdominal or vaginal hysterectomy* is the preferred treatment for cervical dysplasias and carcinoma in situ when future childbearing is not desired. *Extrafascial hysterectomy* may be used for microinvasive cervical cancers and may also be used for cancer confined to the cervix after external and intracavitary radiation therapy. *Radical hysterectomy* or definitive radiotherapy may be used for invasive carcinoma extending beyond the cervix with no obvious parametrial involvement.

Endometrial cancers. Stage I endometrial cancer is treated with total abdominal hysterectomy (TAH) and bilateral salpingo-oophorectomy (BSO), which are used alone or after intracavitary radiotherapy. Stage II disease, involving the cervix, requires both external beam and intracavitary radiation before hysterectomy.

Ovarian cancers. TAH and BSO, omentectomy, tumor debulking, and paraaortic lymph node sampling constitute primary therapy. Exploratory (second look) laparotomy, with multiple biopsies and fluid cytology, is performed after chemotherapy to gauge response to treatment and amount of residual disease.

Prostate biopsy: Highly accurate

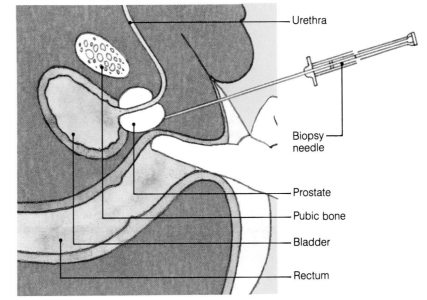

Female urethral and vulvar cancers. Squamous cell carcinomas and adenocarcinomas of the whole urethra may be treated with surgery, radiotherapy, or both. Such tumors have a poor prognosis, with 46% to 64% local recurrence. *Partial urethrectomy* can be used to treat squamous cell carcinomas of the anterior urethra. These tumors metastasize infrequently, and no further treatment is needed.

Laser ablation or *wide local excision* can be used to manage localized unifocal preinvasive lesions of the vulva. Multifocal lesions can be treated by *skinning vulvectomy* with a split-thickness graft to the denuded area. This can be used for younger patients with good cosmetic and functional results.

Radical vulvectomy and inguinofemoral lymphadenectomy are used to treat invasive vulvar carcinoma.

Testicular cancer. *Inguinal orchiectomy* is used to diagnose testicular cancer. External beam radiotherapy is combined with this procedure to treat seminoma. *Retroperitoneal lymphadenectomy* is recommended to achieve good local control in other germ cell tumors.

Prostate cancer. *Radical prostatectomy* is required for extensive disease. It may be performed through a perineal or retropubic approach. *Retropubic prostatectomy* is sometimes preferred since the pelvic lymph nodes are accessible for accurate tumor staging.

Renal cancer. *Radical nephrectomy* with early ligation or embolization of the renal artery or vein to prevent hematogenous dissemination is the treatment for renal cell cancer. The kidney is removed en bloc with perinephric

When prostate cancer is suspected after completion of a rectal examination and other tests, a small portion of tissue is removed for biopsy by needle aspiration. In the transperineal approach shown here, the patient, under general anesthesia, has been placed in lithotomy position. The doctor makes a small stab wound in the perineum and inserts the needle and obturator.

He guides the needle into the prostate by palpating the prostatic abnormality with the index finger of his other hand. When he positions the needle, he removes the obturator and withdraws a core of tissue. Tissue biopsy has a high degree of diagnostic accuracy. Prostate cancers are almost always adenocarcinomas.

Intracavitary radiation

In an effort to deliver high doses of radiation to the endometrium, radium is inserted into the uterus. In this procedure, radiation sources known as Heyman's capsules are packed into the uterine cavity to create as uniform a dosage of radiation as possible. By twisting the capsule inserter and moving the capsule tags to one side, the doctor clears a parallel path for the next capsule.

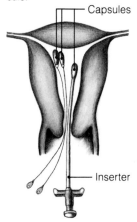

Capsules

Inserter

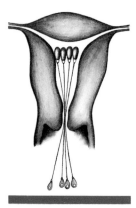

fat, the adrenal gland, and the regional lymph nodes to prevent metastasis.

Renal pelvic, ureteral, and bladder cancer. Removal of a cuff of the bladder with bladder mucosa, ureter, kidney, and regional lymph nodes *(radical nephroureterectomy)* is the treatment for renal pelvic and ureteral cancers. The extensive resection is done to prevent metastasis to the lower urothelium.

Transurethral resection and fulguration of the bladder (TURB) is done to treat small, superficial, low-grade bladder tumors.

Partial cystectomy may be used if the bladder tumor is small, solitary, and located far enough from the bladder neck and base to allow resection of a 3-cm margin of normal bladder tissue. *Radical cystectomy* is required for large, high-grade, multifocal tumors. This should include all perivesical adipose tissue as well as the regional lymph nodes.

Radiation therapy

External beam radiation may be used as curative or adjunctive treatment. It's used pre- and postoperatively in renal adenocarcinoma to improve survival and to control local tumor and preoperatively in advanced bladder cancer. In urogenital malignancies with bone metastases, radiation can relieve pain. Low-dose external beam radiotherapy may prevent or minimize estrogen-induced gynecomastia in advanced prostate cancer.

Intracavitary radiation. When administered along with external beam therapy, this procedure may control regional cervical and uterine cancers. Intracavitary radiation may also follow external beam radiation in treatment of vaginal and cervical cancers. (See *Intracavitary radiation.*) In this procedure, high radiation doses can be delivered to target areas with minimal exposure to the bladder and rectum. Occasionally, surgical resection may follow.

Interstitial radiation. Vaginal and female urethral cancer are treated primarily with interstitial implants of cesium 137, radium 226, or iridium 192. The prostate gland may also be treated with interstitial implants of iodine 125, usually in the operating room immediately after a negative pelvic lymph node dissection (during the same laparotomy). In late stages, external beam radiation therapy may supplement the interstitial implants.

In some centers, therapy may include intraperitoneal instillation of chromic phosphate or radioactive gold. The radioactive substance is infused into the luminal cavity through a

catheter inserted into the patient's abdominal cavity. (See *Intraperitoneal chemotherapy.*) This treatment is reserved for low-stage ovarian cancer or microscopic disease limited to the abdominal cavity after conventional chemotherapy. The treatment is effective solely against microscopic peritoneal disease, because the chemotherapeutic agents penetrate only a few millimeters into the tissues.

Chemotherapy

No chemotherapeutic agent has been truly effective for renal, prostate, and urethral carcinomas. Thiotepa, bleomycin, mitomycin C, and doxorubicin (Adriamycin) have been instilled intravesically for superficial bladder cancer but have produced mixed results. Other drugs tried for this disorder include teniposide (VM-26), ethoglucid, and bacille Calmette-Guérin (BCG) vaccine. Several systemic agents are often combined with surgery to treat invasive bladder carcinoma.

Although few studies have been done, initial evidence indicates that systemic and intraluminal agents most effective in bladder cancer may be equally effective against renal pelvis and ureter cancers.

In nonseminomatous testicular germ cell tumors, the cure rate for Stage I and II disease approaches 100% with surgery and chemotherapy with cisplatin, vinblastine, and bleomycin, and 70% for Stage III disease with the same drug combination and surgical resection of residual disease. This drug combination, when used with vincristine, dactinomycin (actinomycin D), and cyclophosphamide (Cytoxan), has also proved effective against ovarian germ cell tumors.

Dinitrochlorobenzene (DNCB) and other agents are being investigated for treatment of persistent, progressive vulvar cancer. For vaginal cancer with a high risk of invasion or recurrence, chemotherapy may be adjunctive to primary radiation therapy. Cervical cancer requires chemotherapy when it recurs or resists radiation therapy. Agents considered radiosensitizers (such as hydroxyurea, 5-fluorouracil, and cisplatin) are also being tried for improving response to radiation therapy, as, for example, in combination with hyperfractionation radiotherapy.

Chemotherapy for endometrial cancers is not usually applied until radiation, surgery, and hormonal treatments fail. Doxorubicin produces a 37% response rate in endometrial cancers resistant to other therapy. Cisplatin is most effective for ovarian tumors; it's used routinely in combination with doxorubicin and cyclophosphamide in advanced stages. Single alkylating agents, such as melphalan, are also used in early stages.

Because ovarian cancer usually remains confined to the intraabdominal space, treatment with large-volume, continuous intraperitoneal administration of chemotherapeutic agents (methotrexate, 5-fluorouracil, and cisplatin) is being tested. This "belly bath" therapy is based on the observation that the peritoneal permeability of many anticancer drugs is less than plasma clearance. Thus, when given in large volumes to ensure adequate distribution, significantly greater drug concentrations may be maintained in the peritoneal cavity than in the plasma.

Interferon, BCG vaccine, and other drugs that enhance or alter the immune response to treatment are also being studied for use against urogenital cancers.

Hormonal therapy
Antiestrogens or progestins are used to palliate advanced vaginal, cervical, and ovarian cancers and to treat prostate and endometrial cancers. Also, since adult prostatic epithelium may be androgen-dependent and atrophies when androgenic hormones are removed, androgen ablation or suppression is being used to manage prostate cancer. These treatments have slowed tumor growth and temporarily relieved bone pain.

Endometrial carcinomas may be related to deranged estrogen metabolism and exogenous estrogen. This is the theoretic basis for hormonal manipulation in late-stage, recurrent, and metastatic disease. Bilateral oophorectomies, progestins, and antiestrogens are commonly used together. When these hormone treatments fail, chemotherapy follows.

The usefulness of estrogen and progestin receptor levels in predicting treatment response in endometrial cancers is also being investigated.

Complications of treatment
Complications are specifically related to surgery or progression of urogenital cancers. Permanent impotence almost always follows radical cystectomy and prostatectomy, and urinary incontinence may follow radical prostatectomy. Urinary frequency and urgency, bladder spasms, and hemorrhagic cystitis may follow chemotherapy or pelvic radiation. Proctitis, rectal bleeding, and radiation enteritis may follow pelvic or whole abdominal radia-

tion therapy. Other complications of radiation therapy include impotence; uterovaginal, vesicovaginal, and rectovaginal fistulas; tissue necrosis; abscess; urethral strictures; and sterility (from irradiation of the ovary and testis).

Vaginal surgery may cause a significantly shortened, obliterated, or stenosed vagina. Radiotherapy may cause loss of natural secretions, making coitus difficult or impossible. Vulvar, prostatic, and cystic surgery may also cause sexual problems. And, in advanced stages of disease, disfiguring procedures, such as ostomies to relieve bowel complications or catheters for venous access, may be required.

NURSING MANAGEMENT
A good history and physical assessment are important for developing accurate nursing diagnoses, setting care goals, and planning interventions.

Obtain a patient history
Determine the chief complaint, and obtain a medical history to ascertain other medical problems and risk factors. For example, vaginal bleeding in an older woman may indicate endometrial cancer; at the same time, hypertension in this patient may be related to an underlying cardiovascular disease so severe that it rules out surgery. A history of orchiopexy after age 6 should alert you to do a more careful testes examination. A family history of cancer should alert you to be more conscious of the patient's physical state and of early symptoms that suggest cancer.

While you're obtaining a psychosocial history, also gather information on the patient's sexual function. He'll probably be reluctant to bring up the subject voluntarily, but if you approach it in a matter-of-fact way early on, he'll be more likely to broach the subject when concerns arise. You might ask questions like these: Has your illness interfered with your being a parent or spouse? Has it changed the way you see yourself as a man (or woman)? Has it affected your sexual function? With careful questioning, you reassure the patient that he can discuss such personal matters confidently.

Perform a physical assessment
Review the body systems to gather pertinent facts about the disease. Check for fever, chills, fatigue, weight loss, and malaise. In advanced malignancies, severe inanition and malnutrition may be noted. Carefully assess organs

Intraperitoneal chemotherapy (IPC)
A new method of treating ovarian cancer currently in use in some centers, IPC involves instillation of anticancer agents through a Tenckhoff catheter into the peritoneal cavity. This route of administration decreases the systemic toxicity that usually accompanies I.V. and oral chemotherapy. In IPC, most of the drugs are cleared from the peritoneal cavity via the portal circulation, avoiding the destructive effect of the high doses used in systemic chemotherapy.

The primary treatment of ovarian cancer remains surgical—transabdominal hysterectomy and bilateral salpingo-oophorectomy are performed whenever possible. However, IPC is useful in helping to eradicate residual malignant cells after surgery.

and systems.

Breasts. Examine breast tissue in nulliparous, obese women suspected of having endometrial cancer. In men, gynecomastia may indicate testicular cancer.

Cardiovascular system. Cardiovascular involvement may be prominent in renal adenocarcinoma. Hypertension and anemia are common in renal cancer; anemia also commonly results from bone metastasis of renal, ureteral, bladder, and prostate cancers. Hemorrhage secondary to tumor erosion of a vessel may occur and is a medical emergency. Signs and symptoms of hemorrhage include bleeding, increased respiration rate, rising pulse rate, diminishing blood pressure, and altered level of consciousness.

Respiratory system. Palpate, percuss, and auscultate the lungs to detect pleural or pulmonary involvement. Abnormalities may result from extensive pulmonary metastases, obstructing pulmonary bronchioles or restricting pulmonary expansion, and may appear in testicular, renal, cervical, and endometrial cancers.

Gastrointestinal system. Assess abdominal girth and the presence of ascites. Assess bowel function, abdominal masses, and liver size (the liver may be involved in renal, bladder, and prostate carcinomas). Check for anorexia, nausea, vomiting, early satiety, diarrhea, constipation, abdominal bloating, and bowel obstruction, all common in gynecologic malignancy.

Renal and genitourinary systems. Check for flank pain, pelvic pain, bladder irritability, urinary frequency or urgency, dysuria, nocturia, gross or microscopic hematuria, slow stream, dribbling, bladder distention, pelvic fullness, and complete urinary retention. In testicular cancer, assess the scrotum for testicular masses; in prostate cancer, prostatic nodules may be present.

Reproductive system. Perform a testicular and rectal examination in men and a pelvic and rectal examination in women. In the female patient, check for pruritus; ulceration; foul, watery vaginal discharge; bleeding between menses; bleeding after coitus; peri- and postmenopausal bleeding; and dyspareunia. Also check the age of onset of menses, its regularity, the number of pregnancies, the age of onset of menopause, and treatments for problems related to menses. Irregular menses and a difficult menopause may result in treatment with estrogens. Exogenous estrogens given without progestins increase the risk of endometrial cancer. Older, nulliparous, white women with a long, uninterrupted history of menstrual problems are at high risk for ovarian and endometrial cancer.

A history of sexual exposure to multiple partners and early age of coitus, especially with a history of venereal disease, raises the risk of cervical cancer. Herpesvirus type II and condylomata acuminata are associated with vulvar, vaginal, cervical, and prostate cancers. In male patients, note a history of cryptorchid testes or impotence.

Neurologic system. Assess central and peripheral neurologic involvement. Neurologic symptoms in urogenital cancers include pain due to nerve compression from metastatic disease, numbness, tingling, and weakness of the arms and legs. Muscular atrophy also results from neurologic motor nerve destruction or from inanition in advanced disease. Brain metastasis can cause CNS symptoms.

Skeletal system. Osseous involvement occurs in renal, ureteral, bladder, prostate, and cervical cancers. Metastatic disease may replace bone marrow, leading to anemia, weight loss, and pain. Pathologic fractures and spinal compression may develop.

Lymphatic system. Assess all lymph nodes. The inguinal node is important in testicular, vulvar, and distal vaginal cancer. The supraclavicular node may be involved in prostatic, testicular, renal, and cervical carcinomas. Lymphatic obstruction of the legs may appear in urogenital malignancy. Significant lymphedema may result from surgical resection of lymph nodes and from extrinsic compression and lymphatic system infiltration by a tumor.

Formulate nursing diagnoses

With detailed knowledge of the patient's disease, its risk factors, natural history, and treatment, you can establish your nursing diagnoses and prepare effective nursing interventions. You can expect the following nursing diagnoses in patients with urogenital cancer.

Alteration in urinary elimination pattern related to altered structures and reduced micturition control resulting from surgery or manipulation. Assess voiding patterns (time, voluntary or involuntary control, sensation of need to void, amount voided, and amount of residual urine). Explain to the patient the cause of incontinence and altered structures, the treatment rationale, and the need for hydration to prevent urine stasis. Emphasize that stress, anger, anxiety, and pain inhibit urinary sphincter relaxation and that loss of bladder tone can result from bladder overdistention and continuous catheterization. When teaching bladder training, focus on communication, fluid intake, and voiding patterns.

To improve the patient's urinary control, teach pelvic floor muscle–strengthening exercises. To exercise posterior pelvic floor muscles, ask the patient to imagine he is preventing the passage of a stool: ask him to tighten his anal muscles without tightening the leg or abdominal muscles, and have him squeeze the muscles tight for 4 seconds. Ask him to repeat the exercise 10 times.

To exercise anterior pelvic floor muscles, ask the patient to imagine he is stopping the passage of urine: have him squeeze the anterior muscles tight for 4 seconds, and ask him to repeat the exercise 10 times. During micturition, have him start and stop the urinary stream several times.

Teach intermittent self-catheterization, if ordered. Teach the patient and his family about physiology and care of the urinary stoma and how to change a urostomy pouch. (See *Patient-teaching aid: Home urostomy care,* page 176.) Provide information on ostomies and ostomy support groups.

Consider your interventions successful if the patient controls urinary elimination, has less than 50 ml of residual urine, or maintains skin integrity at the urostomy site.

Potential injury related to intracavitary and intrastitial radiation implants. Follow your hospital's policy for specific procedures and precautions, which may vary with the isotope being used. If the patient is receiving radium 226 or cesium 137 treatments, place him in a private room with his bed separated from all others by at least 6′ in all directions. Patients treated with phosphorus 32 or iodine 125 don't require isolation because radioactivity does not travel further than a few centimeters. Discuss the procedure with the patient and tell him what to expect.

The day before the implant, give the patient a low-residue diet. Administer an enema the night before, and expect to insert an indwelling (Foley) catheter before or during the implant. Give nothing by mouth the day of the implant. After implantation, maintain complete bed rest. Elevate the head of the bed 15°, and allow the patient to move his legs and turn his upper body freely. Attach the Foley catheter to allow free drainage. Maintain the low-residue diet to prevent bowel movements, especially with vaginal implants.

Give medications for diarrhea, nausea and vomiting, pain, and sleep, as ordered. Elevated temperature accompanying nausea and vomiting may indicate infection or perforation.

Restrict visitors to no more than 10 minutes, and be sure they stand at least 10′ away from the patient. Do not admit pregnant women or minors, and limit the number of staff attending the patient. Perform only necessary tasks as efficiently as possible; give minimal perineal care. Omit complete bed baths, but allow the patient to freshen up. Change bed linens only if they are soiled.

Following infection-control protocol, change and carefully discard dressings around the implant insertion site, to prevent dislodging the radioactive source. In some institutions, only the doctor changes the dressings. Post any special precautions for sputum, vomitus, urine, feces, or eating utensils.

If a radioactive source loosens or falls out, pick it up with a long forceps and place it in a lead container in the patient's room. Do not touch it with a bare hand. Notify the radiation safety officer and the doctor immediately.

Strain the urine of patients on iodine 125 to catch seeds that may be dislodged after removal of the Foley catheter. Place the loose seed in the proper container with long forceps and notify the radiation safety officer. If phosphorus 32 leaks out of the peritoneal cavity onto the patient's gown and bed linen, isolate these items, and notify the radiation safety officer and the doctor.

Consider your interventions successful if no one sustains radiation injury.

Alteration in nutrition related to intestinal obstruction, stomatitis, anorexia, depression, or altered sense of taste or smell. Assess the patient's weight, dietary history, treatment, emotional state, perception of the problem and desire to change, knowledge of nutrition, and support systems. Check for nausea, vomiting, anorexia, fatigue, pain, and stomatitis. Explain the need for adequate nutrition. Provide the patient with alternative diet suggestions.

Encourage socialization at mealtimes by having the patient eat with other patients or by having family visit him.

Schedule activities so that painful procedures do not precede meals. Medicate for pain and have the patient rest before eating.

Provide small, frequent meals, and have the patient eat slowly and sit rather than lie down after eating. Provide mouth care after eating.

Arrange to have the highest protein foods served when the patient feels most like eating. For example, serve a large breakfast before

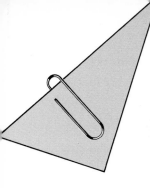

PATIENT-TEACHING AID

Home urostomy care

Dear _____

Your enterostomal therapist or nurse has taught you to care for your stoma and pouch when you go home. Here's a list of other things you should know.

Urostomy care tips and reminders
• Call your doctor if your temperature rises to 100.8° F. (38.2° C.) or more.
• If you become constipated, take a mild laxative. If the problem continues, tell your doctor. Also call him if you develop diarrhea.
• Don't lift objects heavier than a folding chair for at least 4 weeks after surgery.
• Don't drive or ride in a car unnecessarily for 4 weeks. A sudden stop could strain your abdominal muscles.
• Clean the area around your stoma daily, as mucus can collect and cause irritation. Check your stoma to make sure it's as pink and moist as the inside of your cheek. Report any change, such as black spots, to your doctor.
• You may notice a slight bulging to one side of your stoma. Don't become alarmed. This can result from a weakness in the abdominal muscles. Notify your doctor at your next appointment.
• Drink _____ to _____ 8-oz glasses of water daily to help your urinary tract function properly. If your urine output seems scanty or stops completely, call your doctor immediately.
• If the skin around your stoma becomes red or sore, the area's probably been irritated by urine. Prevent or correct this by keeping the area clean and dry and by applying your urostomy pouch carefully.
• Several types of urostomy pouches are available, including disposables. If you're using a reusable pouch, always carry an extra pouch and faceplate in your car, in case your faceplate comes loose.

Applying a reusable pouch
To apply a reusable urostomy pouch, follow these steps:
• Begin by gathering this equipment: a reusable pouch, faceplate and O-ring, a double-sided adhesive disk, gauze pads, and a skin barrier. (You'll also need scissors if you're using a skin barrier that must be cut to size.)
• Drain the urine from your pouch and wash your hands.
• Lay the clean pouch on a flat surface, with the cup facing up. Slip the O-ring around the cup, with the O-ring's protruding edge against the pouch. Then fold the cup down over the ring of the faceplate. Firmly press the faceplate against the ring. Snap them together to provide a tight seal.

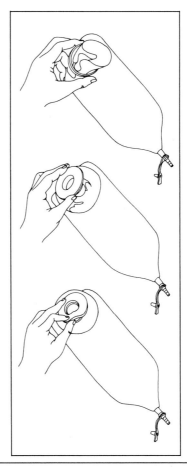

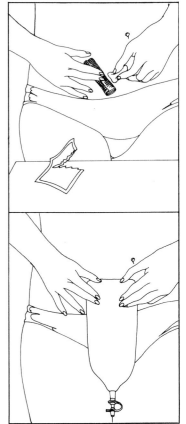

• Peel off the paper backing from one side of the double-sided adhesive disk. Center the disk, sticky side down, over the faceplate. Firmly press the disk onto the faceplate.
• Remove the old pouch. If necessary, use warm water to loosen the adhesive. Then, set the pouch aside for cleaning.
• Cover the stoma with a rolled gauze pad to absorb any leaking urine. Gently wash your stoma and peristomal area with warm water and pat dry.
• Now, still holding the rolled gauze pad over the stoma, apply the skin barrier of your choice.
• Finally, remove the paper backing from the foam pad on the faceplate. Center the faceplate over the stoma and gently press down on it. Make sure you don't wrinkle the seal.

radiation treatments. Encourage the family to bring food from home except for overly sweet, rich, greasy, or fried foods. Use commercial supplements when necessary. Teach ways to add proteins and calories to the home diet.

Consider your interventions successful if the patient attains ideal body weight.

Alteration in comfort related to acute and chronic pain resulting from surgery, tests, and progression of disease and its complications. Convey your acceptance of the patient's response to pain, and explain its causes. Prepare him for painful procedures by telling him what to expect. Reduce his fears of addiction, tolerance, or loss of control. Explain the difference between these problems to the patient and his family.

Teach the patient relaxation techniques, progressive muscle exercises, guided imagery, and breathing exercises. Promote relaxation with back rubs, massage, and warm baths. Provide cutaneous stimulation with hot or cold applications, menthol preparations, or transcutaneous electrical nerve stimulation, if ordered. Give optimal relief with prescribed analgesics. To avoid severe pain, medicate the patient on a regular rather than p.r.n. basis. Immobilize painful body parts.

Include the family in the pain-relief program. Have them assist with massage or guided imagery.

Consider your interventions successful if the patient has less pain, and if he and his family intervene to achieve effective relief.

Alteration in bowel elimination pattern (constipation) related to obstruction, side effects of treatment, medications, malnutrition, or surgery. Determine the patient's previous elimination pattern and whether constipation results from bowel obstruction. Persistent nausea and vomiting, and diminished or absent bowel sounds may indicate obstruction; notify the doctor. (In early mechanical obstruction, however, bowel sounds may be present or hyperactive.)

Encourage a well-balanced diet high in fiber; adequate hydration; and physical activity, as tolerated. Provide privacy, a regular time, and a comfortable setting for defecation. Whenever possible, have the patient use the bathroom for elimination. Administer enemas or suppositories, as ordered.

Consider your interventions successful if the patient recovers his previous elimination pattern and experiences fewer uncomfortable symptoms.

Disturbance in self-concept related to al-tered body function and inability to meet role responsibilities. Assess the meaning of the illness and associated body-image changes and function loss to the patient in light of his sociocultural background. Be aware of the responses of family and significant others; try to incorporate these into patient care, and promote sharing of mutual concerns. Correct misconceptions about the disease, self-care, and caregivers. Encourage the patient to familiarize himself with, and care for, the operative site. Allow him time to accept changes in body image and function, and make sure he receives support to deal with these problems after discharge. For example, arrange for outpatient visits or contact with a visiting nurse or psychologist.

Consider your interventions successful if the patient expresses confidence and self-satisfaction and begins to assume role-related responsibilities.

Alteration in sexual satisfaction related to altered anatomic structures, decreased vaginal lubrication, depression, fatigue, altered self-concept, fear of rejection, or medications. Provide privacy for your discussion with the patient. Explain the physiology of the altered anatomic structures and the causes of decreased vaginal lubrication or impotence. Question him about past sexual experiences, and, after determining his social, cultural, and religious views toward alternate sexual techniques, discuss appropriate alternative means of satisfaction for the patient and his partner. Teach the patient to change his ostomy bag or dressings before sexual activity and to use perfume or after-shave lotion if needed.

Encourage the couple to experiment and enjoy each other. Inform the patient of self-help groups and other information resources to help him gain self-confidence.

Consider your interventions successful if the patient and his partner express satisfaction with sexual function.

Psychosocial awareness is important

One of the most important facets of dealing with urogenital cancers is the need to understand and pay attention to the psychosexual changes that result from these diseases. If you address them honestly and sensitively and can help the patient, his partner, and his family to accept and cope with his new body image and to live with any effects on his sexuality, you have achieved a prime goal in caring for patients with urogenital cancers.

APPENDICES

Oncologic emergencies

Emergency	Causes	Signs and symptoms
Infection secondary to leukopenia An invasion and multiplication of microorganisms in body tissues resulting in cellular injury or destruction; occurs mostly in skin, mucous membranes, respiratory and genitourinary tracts, and blood system	Immunity impairment due to chemotherapy, radiation therapy, malnutrition, advanced age, drugs (corticosteroids), malignancies (Hodgkin's disease, multiple myeloma), invasive procedures, hospital environment	Fever, white blood cell (WBC) count < 1,000/mm^3
Hemorrhage secondary to thrombocytopenia Bleeding due to deficiency of circulating platelets; occurs mostly in skin, mucous membranes, gastrointestinal and genitourinary tracts, and intracranial area	Chemotherapy, radiation therapy, infection, drugs, hypersplenism	Petechiae, ecchymoses, platelets < 20,000/mm^3, abnormal bleeding from any site, headache, weakness, altered mental status
Spinal cord compression Pressure on the spinal cord or nerve roots resulting in neurologic dysfunction; associated with bronchogenic, breast, prostate, and kidney cancers and multiple myelomas	Frank epidural tumor mass, venous metastases, direct lymph node extension, erosion of spinal processes with direct tumor extension, pathologic compression fracture, hemorrhage	Back pain, weakness, paresthesia, autonomic dysfunction
Superior vena cava syndrome (SVCS) Compression of the vein returning blood from peripheral circulation to right atrium of heart; associated with bronchogenic, breast, prostate, and kidney cancers and multiple myelomas	External compression from tumor mass, intravascular obstruction, tumor infiltration	Thorax and neck vein distention; dyspnea; periorbital edema; edema of face, neck, upper trunk; bleeding from nose (epistaxis); painless dysphagia; plethora
Hypercalcemia An excess of calcium in the serum (> 9 to 11 mg/100 ml); associated with carcinomas of the breast, lung, head, neck, and esophagus	Malignant cells, immobilization, parathyroid hormone production, dehydration, tumor production of prostaglandin E$_2$ or osteoclast activating factor	Lethargy, drowsiness, confusion, anorexia, nausea, vomiting, constipation, abdominal pain, polyuria and renal insufficiency, dysrhythmias (bradycardia, shortened Q-T interval)
Pleural effusion Abnormal accumulation of fluid in the pleural space; most often associated with breast, lung, and ovarian cancers and lymphoma	Direct tumor extension, lymph drainage obstruction, inflammation	Dyspnea, chest pain, fever, cough
Pericardial tamponade Accumulation of fluid in the pericardial sac causing blood flow obstruction; most often associated with lung and breast cancers, lymphoma, and leukemia	Pericardial tumor invasion, extensive infiltration, radiation pericarditis	Paradoxical pulse, hypotension, dyspnea, orthopnea, distended neck veins, tachycardia, decreased QRS voltage, pericardial friction rub
Syndrome of inappropriate antidiuretic hormone (SIADH) An excessive release of antidiuretic hormone (ADH), which upsets the fluid and electrolyte balances of the body; associated with oat cell carcinoma of the lung, Hodgkin's disease, and pancreatic cancer	Synthesis and secretion of ADH by tumor tissue, stimulation of ADH resulting from decreased blood pressure, chemotherapeutic agents, pulmonary infection, and central nervous system disorders	Hyponatremia, weight gain despite anorexia, vomiting, nausea, muscle weakness, irritability, coma
Extravasation The infiltration of intravenous fluids or medications into tissues surrounding the infusion site. Certain chemotherapeutic agents, such as vesicants, cause cellular damage. Vesicant properties are commonly associated with mechlorethamine (nitrogen mustard), vincristine (Oncovin), vinblastine (Velban), actinomycin D (dactinomycin), mithramycin, mitomycin-C, daunorubicin, doxorubicin, dacarbazine (DTIC), and streptozocin.	Vein fragility, inappropriate site or equipment, improper technique, accidental movement of needle or catheter	Pain, erythema, edema, I.V. fluid leakage, phlebitis, necrosis

Medical management	Nursing care
Blood cultures, broad-spectrum antibiotics, WBC transfusion	Thoroughly assess patient. Provide protective environment. Instruct patient, visitors, and personnel in appropriate hand-washing procedure. Provide frequent skin and wound care. Encourage regular active and passive exercises. Ensure adequate nutritional intake. Encourage expectoration and coughing.
Platelet transfusion, packing (if bleeding from a cavity), cauterization, ligation	Monitor vital signs frequently. Protect patient from injury. Avoid invasive procedures, if possible. If venipuncture is necessary, give platelet transfusion before and exert pressure on puncture site until bleeding stops. Give stool softeners.
Myelography, laminectomy, corticosteroids, chemotherapy, radiation therapy	Assess sensory and motor functions frequently. Provide surgical wound care. Monitor vital signs.
Radiation therapy, chemotherapy, corticosteroids, diuretics, anticoagulants	Monitor vital signs. Provide respiratory support. Limit patient's activities. Decrease intracranial pressure; teach patient to avoid Valsalva's maneuver and lifting and bending from the waist. Manage edema.
Isotonic saline solutions, I.V. or oral phosphate, diuretics, mithramycin; discontinue medications that decrease calcium excretion; place patient on low-calcium diet	Monitor EKGs. To promote hydration, give fluids orally or intravenously. Monitor intake and output. Encourage patient to walk and to perform range-of-motion exercises. Protect patient from injury.
Thoracentesis, thoracostomy, and sclerosis with antineoplastic agent or radioactive isotopes, systemic chemotherapy, diuretics	Monitor vital signs frequently. Assess for signs of respiratory distress. Reposition patient often. If pleurectomy is performed, provide postoperative care.
Pericardiocentesis, indwelling catheter in pericardial sac, pleuropericardial window, radiation therapy, chemotherapy, corticosteroids, colloids	Monitor vital signs and filling pressures frequently. Give oxygen therapy. As recovery may be long and difficult, provide emotional support.
I.V. saline solution; fluid restriction; discontinue drugs causing SIADH; treat underlying problem such as malignancy or pneumonia	Monitor intake and output. Weigh patient daily. Perform neurologic assessments frequently. Watch for signs of fluid and electrolyte imbalance.
Discontinue I.V.; apply ice (first 24 hours) and warm compresses (24 to 72 hours); elevate site; apply topical steroid, sterile dressing, analgesics; evaluation by plastic surgeon if extravasation is extensive	Administer vesicant cautiously. Be prepared to give emergency treatment if necessary. Never administer vesicant to determine vein patency. Slowly inject vesicant in large vein; assess I.V. site continuously.

Rare tumors

Bone tumors and soft tissue sarcomas

Tumor and cause	Clinical features	Treatment
Adamantinoma Unknown cause; most common in young adults	Malignant bone tumor involving the tibial diaphysis. Grows slowly and often metastasizes to the lungs following local recurrence or after incomplete removal of primary lesion.	Surgical removal of tumor
Giant cell tumor of the bone Unknown cause; most common between ages 20 and 40	Contains ovoid and giant cells. Characterized by pain, tenderness, and swelling; usually involves the knee. Low-grade disease recurs; high grade usually metastasizes.	Surgical removal of tumor, radiation, chemotherapy
Leiomyosarcoma Unknown cause	Malignant tumor of smooth muscle, usually retroperitoneal or uterine. Characterized by bleeding and ulceration. Retroperitoneal tumors grow rapidly. May metastasize to lymph nodes and lungs.	Surgical removal of tumor
Liposarcoma Unknown cause	Malignant lesion of adipose tissue. Characterized by a nodular tumor on the upper thigh and buttocks. Metastases to lungs and liver are common.	Surgical removal of tumor
Mesothelioma Associated with asbestos exposure	Malignant tumor of the mesothelium, mostly of the pleura. Characterized by coughing, chest pain, and digital clubbing. May be asymptomatic.	Pleuropneumonectomy, radiation, chemotherapy
Myxoma Unknown cause; commonly occurs after age 50	Usually pale gray tumors. Occur anywhere but mostly on extremities. May grow to enormous size. May infiltrate widely, but do not metastasize.	Local incision
Reticulum cell sarcoma (Non-Hodgkin's lymphoma of the bone) Possibly viral; may be familial	Lymphoid tumor containing differentiated reticulum cells. Characterized by enlarged lymph nodes, cachexia, fever, anemia, hemorrhage, and infection. May metastasize to other bones and bone marrow.	Chemotherapy, radiation

Breast cancers

Paget's disease of the nipple Unknown cause	Intraepithelial spread of underlying breast cancer. Characterized by weeping, scaliness, burning, itching, or bleeding. Often the underlying tumor can be palpated. Lesion does not respond to topical corticosteroids.	Mastectomy with axillary node dissection

Gastrointestinal cancers

Appendix (carcinoid syndrome) Most common around age 40	Neoplasm of enterochromaffin cells characterized by flushing, purple telangiectasia, GI hypermotility, diarrhea. Tumors grow slowly and rarely metastasize.	Appendectomy, chemotherapy, radiation
Extrahepatic bile ducts Associated with chronic ulcerative colitis, more common in men and after age 70	Usually adenocarcinoma characterized by pruritus, jaundice, and weight loss. Local extension to regional lymph nodes is common.	Cholestyramine resin for relief of pruritus, palliative hepaticoenterostomy (most are not surgically resectable)
Gallbladder Most common in women and after age 65	Usually adenocarcinoma. Characterized by RUQ pain, malaise, anorexia, nausea, and vomiting. Jaundice occurs later. Liver failure and biliary tract obstruction may occur.	Cholecystectomy; if metastatic, wedge excision of underlying liver tissue

Head, neck, and CNS tumors

Hypopharynx Associated with cigarette smoking and alcohol ingestion; mostly in older males	Usually squamous cell carcinomas characterized by sore throat and difficulty in swallowing. Tumors tend to remain on posterior pharyngeal wall and seldom spread laterally.	Surgery, radiation
Nasal cavity and paranasal sinuses Associated with wood dust exposure; more common in men and after age 40	Usually squamous cell carcinomas characterized by nasal discharge; obstruction; and minor, intermittent bleeding. May be asymptomatic or cause sinus aches and pains. Initially spreads to adjacent structures and perineural areas. Lymphatic metastases related to tumor extension.	Surgical removal of tumor, radiation
Nasopharynx Associated with elevated titers of Epstein-Barr virus	Usually lymphoepithelioma and transitional cell carcinomas characterized by a painless upper neck mass. Spreads to adjacent structures, causes nasal obstruction, epistaxis, and otitis media. Lymphatic metastases common.	Radiation

Head, neck, and CNS tumors (continued)

Tumor and cause	Clinical features	Treatment
Parathyroid Unknown cause	Usually adenomas or hyperplasia. Characterized by hyperparathyroidism. Tumors grow slowly; may recur after removal; may metastasize to lymph nodes, lung, and liver.	Surgical removal of tumor
Pituitary Unknown cause	Usually of epithelial origin. Erodes and expands sellar walls. Characterized by headaches. Intrasellar lesions are often small and hormonally active and rarely malignant.	Surgery, radiation, chemotherapy
Retinoblastoma Congenital, hereditary; most common primary eye tumor in children	Appears to originate in outer cell of retina. Commonly presents as strabismus. May extend locally to vitreous cavity and subretinal space. Distant metastases uncommon.	Surgical removal of eye, radiation, cryotherapy, chemotherapy

Leukemias and lymphomas

Tumor and cause	Clinical features	Treatment
Leukemic reticuloendotheliosis (hairy-cell leukemia) Associated with radiation exposure; most common in men and after age 50	Hematologic disorder of abnormal mononuclear cells with fine cytoplasmic projections. Characterized by fatigue, pancytopenia, splenomegaly. May be asymptomatic. Complete remission is unusual.	Splenectomy; radiation may be used in recurrence; usually not responsive to conventional chemotherapy
Malignant histiocytosis (histiocytic medullary reticulosis) Unknown cause; occurs at all ages; most common in men	Histiocytic lymphoma characterized by rapid onset of fever, lymphadenopathy, and hepatosplenomegaly. Highly aggressive and rapidly progressive.	Radiation, chemotherapy
Mycosis fungoides Associated with chronic exposure to industrial chemicals and drugs for skin disorders	Cutaneous malignant lymphoma. Patch stage characterized by erythematous patches (usually on trunk), pruritus. Plaque stage characterized by infiltrated, often annular plaques. Tumor stage marked by subcutaneous nodules.	Immunotherapy; total body electron radiotherapy; systemic and topical chemotherapy

Lung and intrathoracic tumors

Tumor and cause	Clinical features	Treatment
Bronchial adenoma Unknown cause	Usually carcinoid tumors of the proximal bronchi. Characterized by cough and hemoptysis. May metastasize to lymph nodes.	Lobectomy, pneumonectomy

Skin cancers

Tumor and cause	Clinical features	Treatment
Dermatofibrosarcoma protuberans Unknown cause	Benign lesions, probably histiocytic, occur anywhere on the body, mostly on the trunk. Single, cutaneous nodules grow slowly and invade adjacent tissue. Metastases are uncommon. Extensive invasion of vital organs can be fatal.	Surgical removal of lesions, radiation

Urogenital tract cancers

Tumor and cause	Clinical features	Treatment
Carcinoma of the penis Unknown cause; most common in uncircumcised males	Usually squamous cell. Characterized by phimosis, mass, or nonhealing ulcer. May metastasize by lymphatics to superficial and deep inguinal nodes.	Surgical removal of lesion, circumcision (if small tumors are limited to prepuce), partial or total penectomy
Carcinoma of the urethra (male) Most common after age 50	Tumors categorized according to anatomic region. Early lesions may invade adjacent structures and corpus cavernosum. Metastases occur by lymphatics.	Surgical removal of tumor, partial or radical penectomy with perineal urethrostomy
Choriocarcinoma Possibly nutritional and genetic; often preceded by hydatidiform mole (≈50%)	Tumor of the embryonic chorion with uterine wall invasion. May develop in pregnancy or following parturition or miscarriage. Characterized by bleeding. Grows rapidly; metastasizes via lymph or blood to vagina, lungs, and brain.	Hysterectomy; chemotherapy, especially methotrexate
Hydatidiform mole Possibly nutritional and genetic; most common in young adult women	Intrauterine mass of grapelike, chorionic villi. Characterized by disproportionate uterine growth, absence of fetal heart beat, bleeding, passage of clear vesicles, hypertension, lower abdominal pain, nausea, and vomiting. Usually noninvasive. Subsequent pregnancies are possible.	Uterine evacuation by suction curettage, curative or prophylactic chemotherapy, actinomycin D
Wilms' tumor (nephroblastoma) Associated with germinal mutation; most common in fetal stage and before age 5	Malignant neoplasm of the kidney. Can be many cell types, including epithelial, bone, cartilage. Characterized by hypertension, palpable mass, pain, hematuria.	Preoperative and postoperative radiation, nephrectomy, actinomycin D

Chemotherapeutic agents

Alkylating agents

Drug, dose, and route	Interactions	Side effects	Special considerations

busulfan
4 to 6 mg P.O. daily, up to 8 mg daily until white blood cell (WBC) count falls to 10,000 to 20,000/mm³; then, usual maintenance dose is 2 mg P.O. daily
	None significant	Neutropenia (WBC count falls after about 10 days and continues to fall 2 weeks after stopping drug), thrombocytopenia, irreversible pulmonary fibrosis (busulfan lung)	Watch for signs of infection (fever, sore throat).
			  Patient response usually begins within 1 to 2 weeks (increased appetite, sense of well-being, decreased total leukocyte count, reduction in size of spleen).
			  Warn patient that pulmonary fibrosis may be delayed for at least 4 to 6 months.
			  Persistent cough and progressive dyspnea with alveolar exudate may result from drug toxicity, not pneumonia.
			  Avoid all I.M. injections when platelets are low.

carmustine (BCNU)
100 mg/m² I.V. by slow infusion daily for 2 days; repeat q 6 weeks if platelets are above 100,000/mm³ and WBC count is above 4,000/mm³
	Cimetidine: possible increased bone marrow suppression. Avoid use if possible.	Cumulative bone marrow depression, leukopenia, thrombocytopenia, severe nausea and vomiting, intense pain at infusion site, pulmonary fibrosis	Warn patient to watch for signs of infection and bone marrow toxicity (fever, sore throat, anemia, fatigue, easy bruising, nose or gum bleeds, melena).
			  Avoid all I.M. injections when platelets are low.
			  To reduce pain on infusion, dilute drug further or slow the infusion rate.
			  Avoid contact with skin, as carmustine causes a brown stain. If drug comes into contact with skin, wash off thoroughly. Drug is unstable in plastic I.V. bags; administer only in glass containers.

chlorambucil
0.1 to 0.2 mg/kg P.O. daily for 3 to 6 weeks; then adjust for maintenance (usually 2 mg daily)
	None significant	Neutropenia (delayed up to 3 weeks and lasting 10 days after last dose), thrombocytopenia, nausea, vomiting, exfoliative dermatitis, hyperuricemia	To prevent hyperuricemia with resulting uric acid nephropathy, give allopurinol with adequate hydration. Analyze urine for stones.
			  Severe neutropenia is reversible up to cumulative dose of 6.5 mg/kg in a single course.
			  Monitor uric acid, complete blood count (CBC).
			  Avoid all I.M. injections when platelets are low.

cisplatin
20 to 70 mg/m² I.V. administered intermittently according to indication
	Aminoglycoside antibiotics: additive nephrotoxicity. Monitor renal function.	Reversible myelosuppression in 25% to 30% of patients, leukopenia, thrombocytopenia, tinnitus, hearing loss, severe nausea and vomiting, diarrhea, nephrotoxicity	Hydrate patient with normal saline solution before giving drug. Maintain urine output of 100 ml/hr for 4 consecutive hours before therapy and 24 hours after therapy. Don't use aluminum needles for reconstitution or administration of cisplatin; a black precipitate may form. Before starting cisplatin infusion, give mannitol as 12.5 g I.V. bolus. To maintain urine output during and 6 to 24 hours after cisplatin infusion, give mannitol at rate up to 1 g/hr p.r.n.
			  Renal toxicity becomes more severe with repeated doses. Renal function must return to normal before next dose can be given.
			  To prevent permanent hearing loss, tell patient to report tinnitus immediately. Assess hearing before initial dose and subsequent courses.

cyclophosphamide
40 to 50 mg/kg P.O. or I.V. in single dose or in 2 to 5 daily doses; then adjust for maintenance
	Corticosteroids, chloramphenicol: reduced activity of cyclophosphamide. Use cautiously.
	
	Succinylcholine: may cause apnea. Don't use together.
		Leukopenia, severe nausea and vomiting, cardiotoxicity (especially when combined with doxorubicin), hemorrhagic cystitis, reversible alopecia	To prevent hemorrhagic cystitis, push fluids (3 liters daily). Don't give drug at bedtime, since voiding is too infrequent to avoid cystitis. Discontinue drug if hemorrhagic cystitis occurs. Give drug by direct I.V. push into a running I.V. line or by infusion in normal saline solution or dextrose 5% in water (D₅W).
			  Warn patient that alopecia is possible, but that it's usually reversible.
			  If patient's corticosteroid therapy is discontinued, monitor for cyclophosphamide toxicity.

dacarbazine (DTIC)
2 to 4.5 mg/kg or 70 to 160 mg/m² I.V. daily for 10 days; then repeat daily q 4 weeks
	None significant	Leukopenia, thrombocytopenia, severe nausea and vomiting, flulike syndrome (fever, malaise, myalgia beginning 7 days after treatment), pain at infusion site	Give I.V. infusion in 50 to 100 ml D₅W over 30 minutes. To decrease pain at infusion site, dilute drug further or slow the infusion. Avoid infiltration.
			  Decrease dose if renal function or bone marrow is impaired. Stop drug if WBC count falls to 3,000/mm³ or platelets drop to 100,000/mm³.
			  Avoid all I.M. injections when platelets are low.

lomustine (CCNU)
130 mg/m² P.O. as single dose q 6 weeks. Reduce dose according to degree of bone marrow suppression.
	None significant	Leukopenia and thrombocytopenia, delayed up to 4 to 6 weeks; nausea, vomiting; reversible alopecia	Give drug 2 to 4 hours after meals. To avoid nausea, give antiemetic before administering.
			  Don't give more often than every 6 weeks; bone marrow toxicity is cumulative and delayed.
			  Monitor blood counts weekly.
			  Avoid all I.M. injections when platelets are low.
			  Inform patient that drug can cause alopecia, but hair will grow back.

Alkylating agents (continued)

Drug, dose, and route	Interactions	Side effects	Special considerations

mechlorethamine (nitrogen mustard)
0.4 mg/kg or 10 mg/m² I.V. as single or divided dose q 3 to 6 weeks. Give through running infusion.
	None significant	Leukopenia and thrombocytopenia, severe nausea and vomiting, metallic taste in mouth, thrombophlebitis, severe irritation if drug extravasates, reversible alopecia	If contact occurs with skin or mucous membranes, wash with copious amounts of water. Wear gloves when preparing solution.
			   Prepare solution immediately before infusion. Use within 15 minutes and discard unused solution.
			   If drug extravasates, apply cold compresses and infiltrate the area with isotonic sodium thiosulfate.

melphalan
6 mg P.O. daily for 2 to 3 weeks, then stop drug until WBC and platelet counts stop dropping. Resume with maintenance dose of 2 to 4 mg daily.
	None significant	Thrombocytopenia, leukopenia, agranulocytosis, pneumonitis, and pulmonary fibrosis	Give drug on empty stomach; absorption is decreased by food.
			   Decrease dose in renal impairment.
			   Avoid all I.M. injections when platelets are low.

pipobroman 1.5 to 2.5 mg/kg P.O. daily until WBC count drops to 10,000/mm³; then maintenance dose of 7 to 175 mg P.O. daily	None significant	Thrombocytopenia and leukopenia, delayed up to 4 weeks or longer	Monitor WBC and platelet counts until desired response or toxicity occurs (platelets less than 150,000/mm³ or WBCs less than 3,000/mm³). Avoid all I.M. injections when platelets are low.

semustine (methyl-CCNU)
150 to 200 mg/m² P.O. q 6 to 8 weeks
	None significant	Leukopenia and thrombocytopenia, delayed 4 to 6 weeks; severe nausea and vomiting	Give drug on an empty stomach; absorption is decreased by food.
			   Monitor CBC regularly for 4 weeks for delayed myelosuppression.
			   Store capsules in refrigerator.

streptozocin 500 mg/m² daily for 5 consecutive days q 6 weeks	*Other potentially nephrotoxic drugs such as aminoglycosides:* increased risk of renal toxicity. Use cautiously. *Phenytoin:* may decrease the effects of streptozocin. Monitor carefully.	Aplastic anemia, nausea, vomiting, renal toxicity (evidenced by azotemia, glycosuria, and renal tubular acidosis)	Monitor renal function before and after each course of therapy; renal toxicity is dose-related and cumulative. Inform doctor of signs of mild proteinuria. Obtain urinalysis: blood urea nitrogen (BUN), creatinine, and serum electrolyte levels and creatinine clearance before, and at least weekly during, drug administration. Continue monitoring weekly for 4 weeks after each course. Wear gloves to protect the skin when preparing the solution. Store unopened and unreconstituted vials of streptozocin in the refrigerator.
thiotepa 0.2 mg/kg I.V. daily for 5 days; then maintenance dose of 0.2 mg/kg I.V. q 1 to 3 weeks	None significant	Leukopenia, thrombocytopenia, nausea, vomiting, amenorrhea, decreased spermatogenesis	Inform female patients that drug may cause amenorrhea. Tell patients that amenorrhea and decreased spermatogenesis are usually reversible within 6 to 8 months. Give drug by any parenteral route, including direct injection into tumor.

uracil mustard
1 to 2 mg P.O. daily for 3 months; maintenance dose of 1 mg daily
	None significant	Leukopenia, thrombocytopenia, nausea, vomiting, diarrhea, epigastric distress	To reduce nausea, give drug at bedtime.
			   Don't give drug within 2 to 3 weeks after maximum bone marrow depression from past radiation or chemotherapy.
			   Avoid all I.M. injections when platelets are low.

Antimetabolites

Drug, dose, and route	Interactions	Side effects	Special considerations

azacytidine (5-azacytidine)
200 to 400 mg/m² I.V. daily for 5 to 10 days. Repeat at 2- to 3-week intervals.
	None significant	Leukopenia, thrombocytopenia, hypotension (with rapid I.V. infusion), severe nausea and vomiting, diarrhea	Monitor blood pressure before infusion and at 30-minute intervals during infusion. If systolic blood pressure falls below 90 mm Hg, stop infusion.
			   To prevent severe hypotension give drug by slow I.V. infusion.
			   To reduce nausea and vomiting, give continuous infusions. Reassure patient that tolerance to nausea and vomiting develops during extended treatment.

cytarabine (ara-C, cytosine arabinoside)
200 mg/m² daily by continuous I.V. infusion for 5 days
	None significant	Leukopenia, thrombocytopenia, megaloblastosis, nausea and vomiting, sore mouth and mouth ulcers, hyperuricemia	Monitor intake and output. Maintain high fluid intake and give allopurinol, if ordered, to avoid urate nephropathy in leukemia induction therapy.
			   Give drug by infusion, if possible. Large doses by rapid I.V. push may cause more nausea and vomiting.
			   To help prevent oral side effects, inform patient about good mouth care.

floxuridine (FUDR) 0.1 to 0.6 mg/kg daily by intraarterial infusion	None significant	Leukopenia, anemia, nausea, vomiting, enteritis, oral stomatitis, skin erythema	Check I.V. line for bleeding, blockage, displacement, or leakage. Use infusion pump. To prevent oral side effects, inform patient about good mouth care. Warn patient that therapeutic effect may be delayed 1 to 6 weeks.

Antimetabolites (continued)

Drug, dose, and route	Interactions	Side effects	Special considerations

fluorouracil (5-FU) 12.5 mg/kg I.V. daily for 3 to 5 days q 4 weeks or 15 mg/kg weekly for 6 weeks	None significant	Leukopenia, oral stomatitis (usually preceding leukopenia), nausea, vomiting, diarrhea, reversible alopecia, dermatitis	Watch for signs of toxicity, such as stomatitis or diarrhea. Use topical oral anesthetic to soothe lesions. Discontinue if diarrhea occurs.
			   In treatment of hepatic metastases, administer drug via hepatic arterial infusion.
			   Warn patient that alopecia and dermatologic side effects may occur but are usually reversible. To avoid inflammatory erythematous dermatitis, advise patient to use highly protective sun blockers.
			   Fluorouracil sometimes ordered as 5-FU. The number 5 is part of the drug name; don't confuse with dosage units.

hydroxyurea 80 mg/kg P.O. as single dose q 3 days; or 20 to 30 mg/kg P.O. daily	None significant	Leukopenia, thrombocytopenia, megaloblastosis, anorexia, nausea, vomiting, diarrhea	Monitor intake and output; keep patient hydrated.
			   Use drug cautiously in renal dysfunction. Discontinue drug if WBC count is less than 2,500/mm³ or if platelet count is less than 100,000//mm³. Avoid all I.M. injections when platelets are low.
			   If patient can't swallow capsule, tell him to empty contents into water and take immediately.

mercaptopurine (6-MP) 80 to 100 mg/m² P.O. daily as a single dose up to 5 mg/kg daily	*Allopurinol:* slowed inactivation of mercaptopurine. Decrease mercaptopurine to one-quarter to one-third normal dose	Leukopenia, thrombocytopenia, anemia, nausea, vomiting, anorexia, hepatic necrosis, jaundice	Monitor intake and output. Push fluids (3 liters daily).
			   Watch for jaundice, clay-colored stools, frothy dark urine. Discontinue drug if hepatic tenderness occurs.
			   Monitor blood count weekly; watch for precipitous fall.
			   Mercaptopurine sometimes ordered as 6-mercaptopurine or 6-MP. The number 6 is part of drug name; don't confuse with dosage units.

methotrexate 3.3 mg/m² P.O., I.M., or I.V. daily for 4 to 6 weeks until leukemia remission occurs. Higher doses prescribed when treating other neoplasms.	*Alcohol:* increased hepatotoxicity; warn patient not to drink alcoholic beverages. *Probenecid, phenylbutazone, salicylates, sulfonamides:* increased methotrexate toxicity.	Leukopenia, thrombocytopenia, oral stomatitis, diarrhea leading to hemorrhagic enteritis, nausea, vomiting, pneumonitis	To help prevent oral side effects, teach patient good mouth care. Stop drug if GI side effects are severe. Watch for rash, redness, or ulcerations in mouth and pulmonary side effects. Take temperature daily. Watch for cough, dyspnea, cyanosis; give corticosteroids to reduce pulmonary side effects. Monitor intake and output daily. Force fluids (2 to 3 liters daily).
thioguanine (6-TG) Initially, 2 mg/kg daily P.O. (usually calculated to nearest 20 mg); then increased gradually to 3 mg/kg daily	None significant	Leukopenia, thrombocytopenia (may not appear for 2 to 4 weeks), hepatotoxicity, hyperuricemia	Inform doctor if hepatotoxicity, hepatic tenderness, or jaundice occurs. Monitor serum uric acid. Avoid all I.M. injections when platelets are low. Thioguanine ordered as 6-TG. The number 6 is part of drug name; don't confuse with dosage units.

Antibiotic antineoplastic agents

Drug, dose, and route	Interactions	Side effects	Special considerations
bleomycin 10 to 20 units/m² I.V., I.M., or subcutaneous (S.C.) once or twice weekly to total of 300 to 400 units.	None significant	Oral stomatitis, prolonged anorexia, nausea, vomiting, skin erythema, hyperpigmentation and skin discoloration, acne, pulmonary fibrosis, anaphylaxis, fever, reversible alopecia	Perform pulmonary function tests to establish baseline. Stop drug if pulmonary function test shows a marked decline. Pulmonary side effects common in patients over age 70. Fatal pulmonary fibrosis occurs in 1% of patients, especially when cumulative dose exceeds 400 units. To prevent linear streaking, don't use adhesive dressings on skin. Watch for delayed allergic reactions, especially in lymphoma. Give antipyretics for bleomycin-induced fever. Administer infusions only in glass I.V. containers.
dactinomycin (actinomycin D) 500 mcg I.V. daily for 5 days; wait 2 to 4 weeks and repeat	None significant	Leukopenia, thrombocytopenia, anorexia, nausea, vomiting, diarrhea, oral stomatitis, erythema and hyperpigmentation of skin, acne, reversible alopecia	Use sterile water (without preservatives) to dilute injection. Administer drug through a running I.V. infusion. Avoid infiltration. Stop drug if stomatitis, diarrhea, leukopenia, or thrombocytopenia occurs. Warn patient that alopecia may occur but is usually reversible.
daunorubicin 60 mg/m² I.V. daily in frequency described by the particular protocol	*Heparin:* Don't use together. May form a precipitate.	Leukopenia, thrombocytopenia, dose-related cardiomyopathy, dysrhythmias and EKG changes, nausea, vomiting, cellulitis or tissue slough when extravasated, reversible alopecia	Stop drug if congestive heart failure or cardiomyopathy occurs. To prevent, limit cumulative dose to 550 mg/m²; 450 mg/m² if patient is receiving heart-encompassing radiation therapy or other cardiotoxic agent. Monitor EKG before treatment, monthly during therapy. Watch for signs of cardiac side effects, such as high resting pulse rate. Avoid extravasation; inject into tubing of freely flowing I.V. Don't give drug I.M. or S.C. Warn patient that urine may be red for 1 to 2 days and that it's a normal side effect, not hematuria. Don't confuse daunorubicin with doxorubicin (Adriamycin) since they are both a reddish color.

Antibiotic antineoplastic agents (continued)

Drug, dose, and route	Interactions	Side effects	Special considerations
doxorubicin 60 to 75 mg/m² I.V. as a single dose q 3 weeks. Maximum cumulative dose is 550 mg/m².	*Cyclophosphamide:* enhanced risk of cardiotoxicity. Use cautiously. *Streptozocin:* increased and prolonged blood levels. Dose may have to be adjusted.	Leukopenia, thrombocytopenia, dose-related cardiomyopathy, dysrhythmia and EKG changes, nausea and vomiting, esophagitis, skin hyperpigmentation, tissue slough or cellulitis when extravasated, reversible alopecia	If cumulative dose exceeds 550 mg/m² body surface area, 30% of patients develop cardiac side effects, which begin 2 weeks to 6 months after stopping. Stop drug immediately if signs of congestive heart failure occur. To prevent, limit cumulative dose to 550 mg/m²; 450 mg/m² if patient is also receiving cyclophosphamide. Monitor EKG before treatment and monthly during therapy. Watch for signs of cardiac side effects, such as high resting pulse rate. Avoid extravasation; inject into tubing of freely flowing I.V. Don't give drug I.M. or S.C. Watch for esophagitis in patients who have also received radiation therapy. Do not confuse doxorubicin with daunorubicin since they are both a reddish color.
mitomycin 2 mg/m² I.V. daily for 5 days. Stop drug for 2 days, then repeat dose for 5 more days.	None significant	Thrombocytopenia and leukopenia, which may be delayed up to 8 weeks; pain at injection site; purple coloration at nail beds; reversible alopecia	Monitor CBC and blood studies at least 7 weeks after therapy is stopped. Watch for signs of bleeding. Advise patient that alopecia may occur, but that it's usually reversible. Avoid extravasation. If I.V. infiltrates, stop immediately; use ice packs. Restart I.V.
plicamycin (mithramycin) 25 to 30 mcg/kg I.V. daily for up to 10 days	None significant	Thrombocytopenia, bleeding, severe hypocalcemia, irritation and cellulitis upon extravasation, nausea, vomiting	Monitor platelet count and prothrombin time before and during therapy. Watch for signs of bleeding, such as facial flushing. Watch for precipitous drop in calcium levels. Watch for signs of tetany, carpopedal spasm, Chvostek's sign, muscle cramps; check serum calcium levels. Avoid extravasation. If I.V. infiltrates, stop immediately; use ice packs. Restart I.V. Avoid contact with skin or mucous membranes. To reduce nausea that develops with I.V. push, infuse slowly.

Hormonal agents

Drug, dose, and route	Interactions	Side effects	Special considerations
aminoglutethimide 250 mg P.O. q.i.d. at 6-hour intervals. Maximum daily dose is 2 g/day.	None significant	Severe pancytopenia, drowsiness, nausea, anorexia, skin rash	Perform baseline hematologic studies and monitor CBC periodically. Warn patient that drug can cause drowsiness and dizziness. Advise him to avoid activities that require alertness and good pyschomotor coordination. Tell patient to report if skin rash persists more than 5 to 8 days. Reassure him that drowsiness, nausea, and loss of appetite will diminish within 2 weeks after start of aminoglutethimide therapy.
dromostanolone 100 mg by deep I.M. three times weekly	None significant	Virilism, deepened voice, facial hair growth, which may be intense after long-term treatment; hypercalcemia	Tell patient of possible virilizing effects of drug, such as skin and libido changes. Stop drug if severe hypercalcemia develops or disease accelerates. Warn patient that therapeutic effect may be delayed.
estramustine phosphate sodium 10 to 16 mg/kg P.O. daily in three or four divided doses	None significant	Myocardial infarction, cerebrovascular accident, pulmonary embolus, nausea, vomiting, breast tenderness	Weigh patient regularly as estramustine may exaggerate preexisting peripheral edema or congestive heart failure. Since estramustine is a combination of estrogen estradiol and nitrogen mustard, give drug to patients refractory to estrogen therapy alone.
megestrol acetate 40 to 320 mg P.O. daily in divided doses	None significant	Carpal tunnel syndrome, thrombophlebitis	Use cautiously in patients with history of thrombophlebitis. Therapeutic response isn't immediate.
mitotane 9 to 10 g P.O. daily in three or four divided doses	None significant	Depression, somnolence, vertigo, severe nausea, vomiting, dermatitis	Warn ambulatory patient of CNS side effects; advise him to avoid hazardous tasks requiring mental alertness or physical coordination. Reduce dosage if GI or skin side effects are severe. Obese patients may need higher dosage and may have longer-lasting side effects since drug distributes mostly to body fat. Assess and record behavioral and neurologic signs daily for baseline data.
tamoxifen 10 to 20 mg P.O. b.i.d.	None significant	Transient fall in WBC count, brief exacerbations of bone pain	Give drug to patients with positive estrogen receptors since drug acts as an antiestrogen. Tell patient that side effects are usually minor. Reassure him that acute exacerbation of bone pain during tamoxifen therapy usually indicates drug will produce good response.
testolactone 100 mg deep I.M. three times weekly; or 250 mg P.O. q.i.d.	None significant	Pain, inflammation of injection site	Shake vial vigorously before drawing up injection. Use 1½" needle and inject into upper outer quadrant of gluteal region. Rotate injection sites. Do not refrigerate. Warn patient that therapeutic response is delayed.

Vinca alkaloid and podophyllum derivative agents

Drug, dose, and route	Interactions	Side effects	Special considerations
etoposide (VP-16) 45 to 75 mg/m² I.V. daily for 3 to 5 days; repeat q 3 to 5 weeks.	None significant	Leukopenia, thrombocytopenia, hypotension from rapid I.V. infusion, reversible alopecia, anaphylaxis	To prevent severe hypotension, give drug by slow I.V. infusion (over at least 30 minutes). If patient's receiving drug over less than 2 hours, place him in recumbent position. Monitor blood pressure before infusion and at 30-minute intervals during infusion. Stop infusion and notify doctor if systolic blood pressure falls below 90 mm Hg. Be prepared for anaphylactic reaction; have diphenhydramine, hydrocortisone, epinephrine, and airway ready. Don't administer drug through a membrane-type in-line filter.
teniposide (VM-26) 50 to 100 mg/m² I.V. once or twice weekly for 4 to 6 weeks	None significant	Leukopenia, thrombocytopenia, hypotension from rapid infusion	Monitor blood pressure before infusion and at 30-minute intervals during infusion. If systolic blood pressure falls below 90 mm Hg, stop infusion and notify doctor. Be prepared for anaphylactic reaction; have diphenhydramine, hydrocortisone, epinephrine, and airway ready. To prevent hypotension, infuse over 45 to 90 minutes. Don't administer drug through a membrane-type in-line filter.
vinblastine 0.1 mg/kg or 3.7 mm/m² I.V. weekly or q 2 weeks	None significant	Leukopenia, thrombocytopenia, paresthesias, peripheral neuropathy and neuritis, nausea, vomiting, stomatitis, constipation, ileus, phlebitis	Give laxatives or stool softeners as needed. To avoid leukopenia, don't repeat dose more frequently than every 7 days. Inject directly into vein or tubing of running I.V. over 1 minute, or give D₅W or normal saline solution and infuse over 15 minutes. If extravasation occurs, stop infusion. Apply ice packs on and off every 2 hours for 24 hours. Don't confuse vinblastine with vincristine or vindesine. Vinblastine is less neurotoxic than vincristine.

vincristine
1 to 2 mg/m² I.V. weekly
	None significant	Mild leukopenia, peripheral neuropathy, loss of deep tendon reflex, parasthesias, wrist and foot drop, muscle weakness, constipation, nausea, vomiting, stomatitis, reversible alopecia	To prevent neurotoxicity, don't give drug more than once a week. Check for depression of deep tendon reflex, numbness, tingling, foot or wrist drop, difficulty in walking, ataxia, slapping gait. Assess ability to walk on heels. Support patient when walking.
			  Monitor bowel function. Give stool softener, laxative, or water before dose.
			  Don't confuse vincristine with vinblastine or the investigational agent vindesine.

vindesine 3 to 4 mg/m² I.V. q 7 to 14 days or 1.2 to 1.5 mg/m² continuous I.V. infusion daily for 5 days q 3 weeks	None significant	Leukopenia, thrombocytopenia, paresthesias, decreased deep tendon reflex, muscle weakness, constipation, phlebitis, reversible alopecia	Instruct patient to report any signs of neurotoxicity, such as numbness and tingling of extremities, jaw pain, and constipation (early sign of neurotoxicity). Assess for depression of Achilles tendon reflex, foot or wrist drop, slapping gait (late signs of neurotoxicity). Instruct patient to record his signature before each course of therapy.

Miscellaneous

Drug, dose, and route	Interactions	Side effects	Special considerations
amsacrine (m-AMSA) 30 to 120 mg/m² I.V. for 3 to 5 days	None significant	Leukopenia, convulsions, local irritation, mild phlebitis	Use glass syringes for combining the amsacrine and lactic acid. Do not administer amsacrine through membrane-type in-line filters. Inform patient that drug may turn urine orange.
Erwinia asparaginase 5,000 to 10,000 I.U./m²/day for 7 days q 3 weeks	None significant	Hypofibrinogenemia and depression of other clotting factors, lethargy, hyperglycemia, acute pancreatitis, anaphylaxis	Use Erwinia strain of asparaginase for patients with previous reactions to *Escherichia coli* asparaginase. The two forms of the drug are not cross-reactive. Administer in hospital setting with close supervision. Risk of hypersensitivity increases with repeated doses. Be prepared for anaphylaxis; have epinephrine, diphenhydramine, and I.V corticosteroids ready.
L-asparaginase 1,000 I.U./kg I.V. daily for 10 days, injected over 30 minutes or by slow I.V. push	None significant	Hypofibrinogenemia, leukopenia, severe nausea and vomiting, anorexia, azotemia, hepatotoxicity, hyperglycemia, skin rash, anaphylaxis	Administer 2-unit I.V. test dose to identify high-risk patients. Hypersensitivity may increase with repeated doses. Desensitized patient may still have allergic reactions. Give I.V. injection over 30-minute period through a running infusion of sodium chloride or D₅W injection.
procarbazine 100 to 105 mg/m² P.O. for 10 days. After bone marrow recovers, resume maintenance dose of 50 to 100 mg/day	*Alcohol:* disulfiram-like reaction	Thrombocytopenia, leukopenia, hallucinations, nausea, vomiting	Watch for signs of bleeding. Warn patient not to drink alcoholic beverages while taking this drug. Use cautiously with other monoamine oxidase (MAO) inhibitors, tricyclic antidepressants, phenothiazines, and foods with a large tyramine content.

Selected References and Acknowledgments

Selected References

Becker, Teresa M. *Cancer Chemotherapy: A Manual for Nurses.* Boston: Little, Brown & Co., 1981.

Berg, J.W. "Clinical Implications of Risk Factors for Breast Cancer," *Cancer* 53(3):589-91, February 1, 1984.

Burns, Nancy. *Nursing and Cancer.* Philadelphia: W.B. Saunders Co., 1982.

Cancer Facts and Figures. New York: American Cancer Society, 1984.

Cancer Rehabilitation: Psychosocial, Physical and Economic Interventions. Palo Alto, Calif.: Bull Publishing Co., 1982.

Carter, Frances M. *Psychosocial Nursing,* 3rd ed. New York: Macmillan Publishing Co., 1981.

Carter, Stephen K., et al. *Principles of Cancer Treatment.* New York: McGraw-Hill Book Co., 1982.

DeVita, Vincent T., Jr., and Hellman, Samuel. *Cancer: Principles and Practice of Oncology.* Philadelphia: J.B. Lippincott Co., 1982.

DiSaia, Philip J., and Creasman, William T. *Clinical Gynecologic Oncology.* St. Louis: C.V. Mosby Co., 1981.

Donovan, M. "Cancer Pain: You Can Help!" *Nursing Clinics of North America* 17(4):713-28, December 1982.

Donovan, Marilee, ed. *Cancer Care: A Guide for Patient Education,* 2nd ed. Patient Education Series. East Norwalk, Conn.: Appleton-Century-Crofts, 1981.

Drasga, R.E., et al. "The Chemotherapy of Testicular Cancer," *Ca-A Cancer Journal for Clinicians* 32(2):66-67, March/April 1982.

Friel, Mariel, and Tehan, Claire B. "Counteracting Burn-out for the Hospice Care-giver," *Cancer Nursing* 3:285-93, August 1980.

Greenwald, Edith D., and Greenwald, Edward S. *Cancer Epidemiology for Health Professionals.* New Hyde Park, N.Y.: Medical Examination Pub. Co., 1983.

Haskell, Charles M. *Cancer Treatment,* 2nd ed. Philadelphia: W.B. Saunders Co., 1984.

Henderson, I.C., and Canellos, G.P. "Cancer of the Breast: The Past Decade (Part I)," *New England Journal of Medicine* 302(1):17-30, January 3, 1980.

Henderson, I.C., and Canellos, G.P. "Cancer of the Breast: The Past Decade (Part II)," *New England Journal of Medicine* 302(2):78-90, January 10, 1980.

Holland, James F., and Frei, Emil, 3rd, eds. *Cancer Medicine,* 2nd ed. Philadelphia: Lea & Febiger, 1982.

Hutchinson, M.M., and King, A.H. "A Nursing Perspective on Bone Marrow Transplantation," *Nursing Clinics of North America* 18(3):511-22, September 1983.

Javadpour, Nasser. *Principles and Management of Urologic Cancer,* 2nd ed. Baltimore: Williams and Wilkins Co., 1983.

Johnson, Douglas, and Boileau, Michel. *Genitourinary Tumors: Fundamental Principles and Surgical Techniques.* New York: Grune & Stratton, 1982.

Lamb, M.A., and Woods, N.F. "Sexuality and the Cancer Patient," *Cancer Nursing* 4:137-44, April 1981.

McIntire, Sue N., and Cioppa, Anne L., eds. *Cancer Nursing: A Developmental Approach.* New York: John Wiley & Sons, 1984.

Margolies, Cynthia P., and McCredie, Kenneth B. *Understanding Leukemia.* New York: Scribner's, Charles, Sons, 1983.

National Cancer Institute. *A Nurse's Guide for Teaching Patients Undergoing Cancer Chemotherapy.* Washington, D.C.: U.S. Department of Health and Human Services, 1983.

National Cancer Institute. *Coping with Cancer: A Resource for the Health Professional.* Washington, D.C.: U.S. Department of Health and Human Services, September 1980.

Nunnally, C., et al. "Nutritional Needs of Cancer Patients," *Nursing Clinics of North America* 17(4):557-78, December 1982.

Rubin, Phillip, ed. *Clinical Oncology, A Multidisciplinary Approach.* American Cancer Society, 1983.

Silverberg, E. "Cancer Statistics, 1984," *Ca-A Cancer Journal for Clinicians* 34(1):7-23, January/February 1984.

Steckel, Richard J., and Kagan, Robert A., eds. *Cancer Diagnosis: New Concepts and Techniques.* New York: Grune & Stratton, 1982.

Tulley, J.P., and Wagner, B. "Breast Cancer: Helping the Mastectomy Patient Live Life Fully," *Nursing78* 8:18-25, January 1978.

Trester, A.K. "Nursing Management of Patients Receiving Cancer Chemotherapy," *Cancer Nursing* 5:201-10, June 1982.

Welch, D. "Planning Nursing Interventions for Family Members of Adult Cancer Patients," *Cancer Nursing* 4:365-70, October 1981.

Woods, M.E. "Assessment of the Adult with Cancer," *Nursing Clinics of North America* 17(4):539-56, December 1982.

Yasko, Joyce. *Care of the Client Receiving External Radiation Therapy.* Reston, Va.: Reston Publishing Co., 1982.

Acknowledgments

◆ pp. 12-13 Adapted from D.W. Allen and P. Cole, "Viruses and Human Cancer," *New England Journal of Medicine* 286(2):72 and 77, January 13, 1972.

◆ p. 19 Reproduced from *Cancer Facts and Figures,* p. 29, New York: American Cancer Society, 1983.

◆ p. 22 Reproduced with permission from *Nutrition Today,* P.O. Box 1829, Annapolis, Md. 21404, March/April 1975.

◆ p. 44 Table adapted from *Manual for Staging Cancer,* 2nd ed. Philadelphia: J.B. Lippincott Co., 1983.

◆ p. 72 Adapted from P.A. Pizzo, *Mediguide to Infectious Diseases,* vol. 2, p. 1. New York: Lawrence DellaCorte Publications, 1983.

◆ p. 84 Photo courtesy of Carl Glassman.

◆ p. 95 Table adapted from *Manual for Staging Cancer,* 2nd ed. Philadelphia: J.B. Lippincott Co., 1983.

◆ pp. 103, 119, 133, 147, 160, and 170 Tables adapted from *Manual for Staging Cancer,* 2nd ed. Philadelphia: J.B. Lippincott Co., 1983.

INDEX

i = illustration; t = table

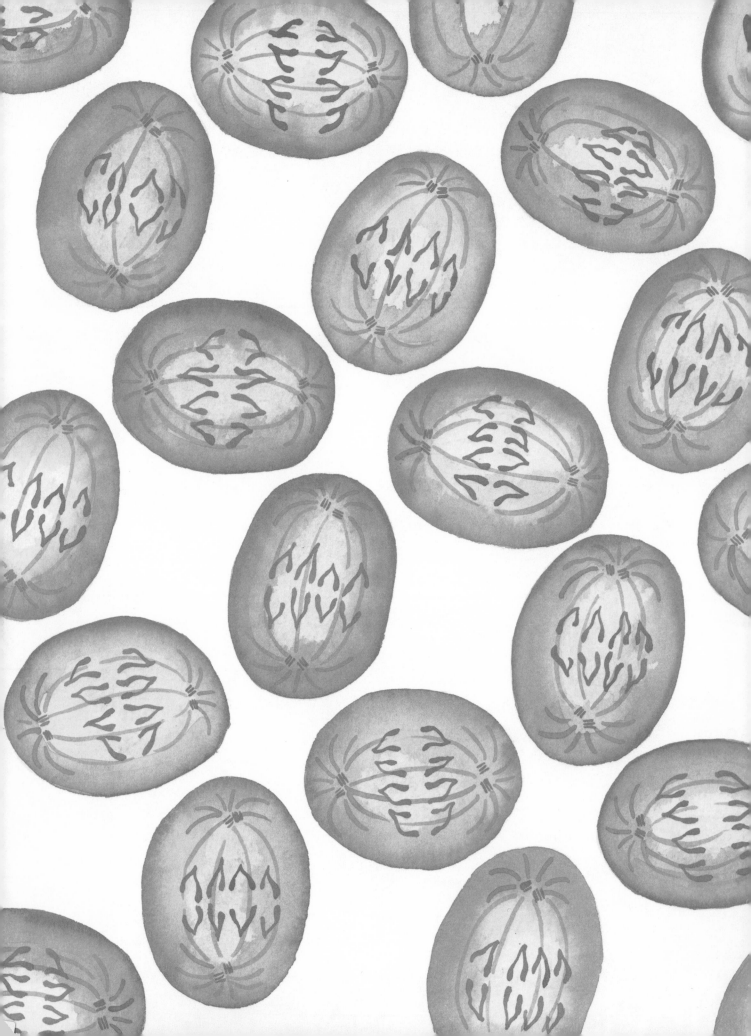